Love, Sex,
and Intimacy

Love, Sex, and Intimacy

Their Psychology, Biology, and History

Elaine Hatfield
Richard L. Rapson

University of Hawaii

HarperCollins*College*Publishers

Acquisitions Editor: Catherine Woods
Project Editor: Brigitte Pelner
Design Supervisor: Molly Heron
Cover Design: Kay Petronio
Cover Photo: James McLoughlin
Photo Researcher: Leslie Coopersmith
Production Manager/Assistant: Willie Lane/Sunaina Sehwani
Compositor: ComCom Division of Haddon Craftsmen, Inc.
Printer and Binder: R. R. Donnelley & Sons Company
Cover Printer: The Lehigh Press, Inc.

Love, Sex, and Intimacy: Their Psychology, Biology, and History
Copyright © 1993 by Elaine Hatfield and Richard L. Rapson

Library of Congress Cataloging-in-Publication Data

Hatfield, Elaine.
    Love, sex, and intimacy: their psychology, biology, and history / Elaine Hat-
field, Richard L. Rapson.
        p.   cm.
    Includes bibliographical references and index.
    ISBN 0-06-500702-6
    1. Man-woman relationships.   2. Love.   3. Sex.   4. Intimacy. (Psycholo-
gy) 5. Power (Social sciences)   I. Rapson, Richard L.   II. Title.
HQ801.H353   1993
305.3--dc20   92-34918
                                                                  CIP

93 94 95 96 9 8 7 6 5 4 3 2 1

To our friends,
Leon and Marjorie Edel

Contents in Brief

Contents

Preface

. . . I have, I know, but few and small claims upon Divine Providence, but something whispers to me—perhaps it is the wafted prayer of my little Edgar, that I shall return to my loved ones unharmed. If I do not my dear Sarah, never forget how much I love you, and when my last breath escapes me on the battle field, it will whisper your name. Forgive my many faults, and the many pains I have caused you. How thoughtless and foolish I have often times been! How gladly would I wash out with my tears every little spot upon your happiness. . . .

But, O Sarah! If the dead can come back to this earth and flit unseen around those they loved, I shall always be near you; in the gladdest days and in the darkest nights . . . always, always, and if there be a soft breeze upon your cheek, it shall be my breath, as the cool air fans your throbbing temple, it shall be my spirit passing by. Sarah do not mourn me dead: think I am gone and wait for thee, for we shall meet again.

—*Letter from Maj. Sullivan Ballou to his wife Sarah during the Civil War. One week after he wrote the letter, Sullivan Ballou was killed in the first battle of Bull Run (Quoted in Quindlen, 1990, p. A 19).*

INTRODUCTION

In Western culture, there is nothing most individuals desire more than a loving, intimate relationship that lasts for a lifetime. Yet, as a bewildered population generally recognizes, people rarely achieve such sweet, lasting attachments. Why is that so?

The mystery grows more perplexing as we realize how profoundly our society is saturated with self-help books, crammed with advice on how to make relationships work; how inundated are the airwaves with talk-show hosts, with soap operas, and with gurus of love. Our disappointments with relationships cannot be ascribed to insufficient attention to the subject; "love" is as magical a word in American culture as is "money."

We believe the problem in making love work is far more difficult than is generally recognized, that it has historical and cultural as well as psychological causes, and that understanding at the deepest and broadest levels is required if we are to make inroads on the problem. Hence in this book we attempt to pool all that we know: as researchers and teachers in the fields of psychology and history, as psychotherapists, and as human beings. We try to weave a seamless web of the latest psychological research, case studies from clinical experiences, the unknown and extraordinary conclusions of a generation of historical scholarship, cross-cultural comparisons and cultural analysis, and personal commentary in the effort to beam some light on the complicated and powerful subject of love and intimacy.

We begin the story, as most people do, with insights drawn from our own lives. Both of us were born in 1937, and there is no doubt that we have witnessed and are still in the midst of a social revolution of immense historical significance. We speak of the revolution that has changed and continues to alter the very meaning of family, that has launched unparalleled new ventures into sexuality, divorce, women's freedom and the reactions of men to the women's movement, and displaced the associations we attach to the experiences of love and intimacy. It is best for us to describe briefly as separate individuals some bits and pieces of personal experience that hint at the momentous forces reshaping all our lives.

RICHARD L. RAPSON

I am a professor of history writing about a subject traditionally associated with psychology. I am married to my coauthor, Elaine Hatfield, who is a professor of psychology. We also work together as psychotherapists. Our marriage is rich and close, but it took 45 years of life before we found each other and put behind us some relationships that were not so wonderful.

In my growing up during the 1940s and 1950s, America had reverted to some very traditional and sentimental notions about sex, love, and marriage. Sex was not openly talked about. Boys snickered and bragged about their supposed (and rarely true) exploits. They assumed that they were supposed to accumulate sexual experiences with "bad" girls and someday marry a "good" girl, that is, a virgin. The double standard was accepted as self-evident. Homosexuality was regarded as disgusting.

Our ignorance of love and sex was nearly total. For me and, I expect, for many other men, women belonged to another species altogether. In addition to the fact that discussions of sex were circumspect if not taboo, talk—even of love itself and the requirements of relationships—remained shrouded in darkest mystery. Perhaps the mystery magnified romance, but it also created rampant anxiety, unending stupidity, unrealistic expectations, warts, pimples, and a host of unfortunate marriages.

Though I received a superb intellectual education at Amherst College, my stupidity about women was not aided by the fact that Amherst was a men's college. The irony was not lost on me when, 27 years after I graduated, my *daughter* received a B.A. from the same institution. The lack of constant, informal contact with that other species (women) contributed to our easy assumption that marriage was a straightforward matter. We would each choose a good-looking woman with a good college education who would stay home and look after the husbands and the children, while the men ventured into the competitive money-earning world of work. We never thought that money would give us power over our wives; the Doctrine of the Two Spheres and the natural authority of Males simply seemed inevitable ideas.

My education into the reality of relationships began early on in my marriage (which took place in 1959, when I was barely 22). Nothing about the marriage went well, but I had no idea either why things had gone awry or what to do about it. Easy and open talk about relationships, sex, and private matters in general simply was not the norm in society even 30 years ago. If you just stuck to things with a good enough spirit, everything would eventually work out. Only crazy people went into psychotherapy, and I knew I wasn't crazy. Divorce was a no-no. You didn't burden friends or family with your problems. You just hung tough and kept to yourself. And you pursued career success.

Major social changes had begun to take place a decade later when I divorced, was granted custody of our one daughter Kim, and began to discover more about myself and women in a less restrictive nation. The "sixties" were in full flower, and questions were being asked that had rarely seen the light of day in the 1950s. Though the terms "sexual revolution" and "women's movement" require much definition, they were going on and life at its deepest levels was not the same as it had been. Life was, I might add, better.

Better, but not perfect. It was another decade before I married well. Still, in the years between 1970 and 1982 (the year when I married) or the years between the early 1960s and today when the Western world transformed (and is transforming) the meaning of family, so much was new that we did not have time to be wise. Men and women burst the bonds of tradition and tasted all kinds of new freedoms, but a deep and troubling circumstance has continued: Few people can sustain good relationships. Personally, I may have been lucky, but as a consequence of becoming a psychotherapist and of my historical scholarship, I have become powerfully aware of the difficulty people have of putting together successful and durable relationships, of the structural and psychological obstacles that stand in the way of that achievement, and how big a part accident played in my own midlife good fortune. Unsentimental humility and common sense are healthier attitudes to carry into relationships than Hollywood-induced fantasies of the ease and magic of love.

As to the connections between history and psychology, I came into my career when presidents, kings, laws, generals, battles, and dates were the common stuff of history. The change in my career and in my interests has paralleled that of society as a whole. Huge battalions of historians, men and women alike, now study not only the story of male, white power, but the tales of everyone, the ordinary as well as the powerful, women as well as men, families as well as royal dynasties, inner lives as well as external exploits. The new history is sometimes described as history from "the bottom up" instead of "the top down." In particular, I am interested in psychological history, that is, the history of love, of sexuality, and of emotions, and I have been writing books and articles on these subjects for two decades now.

One thing that history can bring to the study of love and intimacy, which I hope will be apparent in this book, is perspective. We need to know what in our psychic lives today is novel and likely to change, what seems durable and less culture-bound or temporal-bound. This perspective—this enlarged memory—may have incomparable value in helping us devise personal and social strategies for love and intimacy (and many other subjects) and is rarely included in current discussions, either in our popular self-help literature or even in more scholarly approaches to psychological issues.

At the very least, the reader of a book such as this will have knowledge of love and intimacy far beyond what I and my fellows had during our growing up and which, had we taken the data seriously, might have prevented for us all, men and women, a good deal of unnecessary hardship. When it comes to love, only in Hollywood does magic and fantasy work; the exercise of informed intelligence improves the odds in love and need not diminish the romance.

That last idea, the value of intelligence and even of science in guiding us through the treacherous and inviting channels of love, may seem self-evident to many readers these days. But when Elaine Hatfield in the 1960s decided that love, like all other subjects, could be studied empirically, she had to withstand a nation-wide avalanche of ridicule and criticism, led from the august chambers of the United States Senate itself. A dedication in a recent book on love credited her with making "the study of love a respectable scientific endeavor," but that achievement came neither painlessly nor automatically.

ELAINE HATFIELD

From 1955 to 1959 I was an undergraduate at the University of Michigan, where I studied and was delighted by Clark Hull's behavior theory. I worked with Arthur Melton and David Birch, studying learning and motivation in rats. By 1959, when I entered the Psychology Ph.D. program at Stanford, I had become interested in passionate love, in particular, and emotions in general. It seemed that learning theory didn't do a very good job of explaining these powerful experiences. I decided to conduct some research in those areas. My fellow graduate students, who were mostly hard scientists interested in constructing mathematical models of rat learning, warned me to avoid such topics. They cautioned me that I had to worry about "career management." Passionate love just wasn't a very important phenomenon and there was no hope of finding out very much about it in our lifetime. Worst of all, the whole topic just wasn't very respectable. And it wasn't "hot"; the hot topic was mathematical modeling.

Math modeling and rat runways. If we ignored the first and last thirds of the runway in rat experiments (too much variability in rat behavior there) and concentrated on the middle third of the runway (where rat behavior generally settled down) we had a real chance of making a breakthrough. Thus the conventional wisdom.

At the same time, late in the evenings after our work was done, we confided to one another about our personal problems. There, our concerns went beyond the perambulations of rodents. For most people, the rigors of graduate school were taking a toll on their romances. At one time, all the members of our group were having terrible trouble in their close relationships. Some of us couldn't find anyone to date, others were getting divorces. Things were so dismal that one night several students in the corridor lamented that things were so horrific they sometimes thought about committing suicide. One set of topics was interesting during the day; another was a source of near-obsession in our evening chats.

I was always totally unconcerned with career management, so in graduate school, although I spent some of my time on the respectable topics of the 1960s—dissonance theory and interpersonal attraction—I spent most of my time on things I wondered about. These subjects included passionate love, emotions, and the place of physical attractiveness in personal encounters.

Friends sometimes tend to assume that the highly publicized attacks on my research by Senator William Proxmire, with his "Golden Fleece Awards," are today an enjoyable memory for me. They make that assumption because the "taboo topics" I thought were fascinating have been taken up by a generation of young researchers. Today, love and emotion are the "hot" topics. But I remember those "bad, old days" with no pleasure. It was not only Proxmire and many of my colleagues who thought love should be left to the poets and to Hollywood, but public opinion polls about whether scientists should study love nearly always came out against such research. Even my mother's Catholic bishop wrote an article saying that the Catholic Church knew, and had known for centuries, everything that needed to be known about love and sex, and that we should spend our efforts getting people to adhere to Church teachings. The battle, though it had to be fought and despite the agreeable outcome, was never fun.

My personal relationships were not that much fun either, and paralleled developments in the field. When I was young, I knew little about love. In my first marriage, like most "sensible" young women, I chose a husband on the standard of what was supposed to really matter—good looks, intelligence, and a sense of humor. It did not occur to me to ask whether he was interested in putting time into the relationship, whether he was "available" for intimacy, as important criteria.

Twenty years later, in a second marriage, I am much smarter about love. The foregoing factors, particularly intelligence and humor, still matter. But I am aware of a far more complicated and interesting story. I have learned more about the extraordinary variability of humans. People enter relationships with their own physiology, temperament, family history, life experiences, preferences, and expectations—and those factors rarely coincide with those of anyone else in the world. Small wonder that couples have trouble figuring out how much time to spend together, how much time alone, how much time pursuing separate activities. And when together, will they agree on the importance of foreign films, trips to England, and classical music? It takes congruence on only a few factors to make a good date; it requires far, far more commonalities and coinciding interests even to approximate, let alone find, an appropriate marital partner.

In 25 years, the field of social psychology has become much smarter about the nature of relationships as well. In 1969, when Ellen Berscheid and I wrote the first text that considered passionate love (*Interpersonal Attraction*), we had difficulty finding much material on the topic. Today, however, there is a floodtide of information available. The 1980s saw a tremendous surge of interest in love and intimacy. In the 1980s, Steve Duck and Robin Gilmour inaugurated a series of volumes on the initiation, maintenance, and dissolution of relationships. Scientists banded together to form four international, interdisciplinary organizations designed to foster research on close relationships—the International Society for the Study of Personal Relationships, the International Network on Personal Relations, the International Society for Research on Emotions, and the International Academy of Sex Research. In 1984, Steve Duck founded the *Journal of Social and Personal Relationships*, which is devoted entirely to research on close relationships, and thousands of studies and experiments on love, sex, and intimacy have been published in various other journals. In this text, we attempt to review some of the most intriguing outcomes of this research.

OUTLINE OF THE TEXT

Psychologists are well aware that relationships develop over time. In his ABCDE model of relationship development, George Levinger (1983) traced five phases in personal relationships: (1) *A*cquaintance. (2) *B*uildup of an ongoing relationship. Couples assess the pleasures and problems of connecting with each other. (3) *C*ontinuation. Couples commit themselves to long-term relationships and continue to consolidate their lives. (4) *D*eterioration or decline of the interconnections. (5) *E*nding of the relationship, through death or separation.

Similarly, in their sweeping series entitled *Personal Relationships*, Duck and Gilmour charted, also in five steps, what was known about the initiation, maintenance, problems, repair, and termination of relationships.

In this text, we tell the story of what scientists, scholars, novelists, and wise folk have discovered about the joys and agonies that may wind their way through the various stages of a relationship—heterosexual or homosexual. In the first six chapters, we focus on the delights of love. In *Chapter 1, Beginnings,* we define passionate and companionate love. We explore what makes men and women desirable either as dates or potential mates. We track some of the effective or foolish ways of pursuing love and intimacy. In *Chapter 2, Passionate Love,* we begin by sifting through the evolutionary soil of passionate love. We wade into the treacherous waters of contradictory desires: the pleasure and the pain, the desire for closeness and separation, the longing for both security and excitement, which seem to fuel this intense emotion. In *Chapter 3, Sexuality,* we examine the nature of sex appeal. What sorts of sexual histories do modern-day men and women have? *Chapter 4, Companionate Love,* reviews the genesis of companionate love and its connection with parental behavior and tenderness. We review what reinforcement theory and equity theory have discovered about the initiation and maintenance of this gentler kind of love. In *Chapter 5, Intimacy and Commitment*, we discuss two components of intimacy. We begin by defining intimacy and inquiring why people seek it in the first place. Not everyone embarks on that search and so we explore who are the wary and why. We propose a program for couples who wish to get closer. Finally, we review what we know about commitment. In *Chapter 6, Power*, we discuss some of the bases of social power and some of its limits. Is there a battle of the sexes? If so, who is winning? We focus particularly on power in sexual relationships.

In the next three chapters we delve into the dark side of relationships. We focus on the problems that couples may confront in their relationships. In *Chapter 7, Emotional Problems*, we discuss the difficulties individuals and their families may have in dealing with depression, anxiety, or anger. In *Chapter 8, Relationship Problems*, we focus on dilemmas that couples must confront at various stages in their relationships: the early disenchantments, the conflicts, and inequities with which they must deal, and problems with alcohol or drugs that threaten marriages. In *Chapter 9, The Larger World*, we remind ourselves that couples do not love in a vacuum. First, they must deal with intimates in their personal worlds—with parents, children, stepchildren, friends, and rivals. They must face up to the demands of careers. They must handle the powerful feelings associated with jealousy. Second, couples must live in the real world. Women growing up in America, Canada, or England, for example, are faced with far different possibilities for love, sex, and intimacy than are those growing up in such repressed cultures as China, Japan, or the Arab countries. Men and women caught up in the Holocaust faced issues of life and death; they had little time to brood about problems with their in-laws, stepchildren, or disagreeable bosses. For them, such "worries" would have been a profound relief.

In the next three chapters, things brighten up. We discuss the ways in which couples can deal with relationship problems. In *Chapter 10, Dealing with Emotional Problems*, we explore a variety of techniques—cognitive, physiological, and behavioral—that couples can use to manage their emotions. We remind ourselves, however, that there is room for both sense and sensibility in the universe: It is not wise to exercise so much emotional control that one loses the valuable information that comes to us through our emotions. In *Chapter 11, Dealing with Relationship Problems and Problems in the Larger World*, we start by recognizing that couples differ in the kinds of relationships they want. Different desires lead couples to prefer different strategies for maintaining and repairing their relationships. We focus on one high-voltage problem, jealousy, in an effort to show how couples might use such techniques to help their marriages survive and flourish. In *Chapter 12, Dealing with Problems: Communication*, we focus on one of these techniques—communication. We review what psychologists and communication researchers know about effective and ineffective communication; why people lie to one another. We consider what is known about the nonverbal expression of emotion: the looks, gestures, and vocal cues that signal what we really feel about others and what they feel about us.

Finally, in the last two chapters we discuss what happens when relationships fail. In *Chapter 13, Things Go from Bad to Worse*, we discuss the stages in relationship dissolution. We track that disintegration from the point where people begin feeling vaguely uneasy about their dating relationships and marriages, sensing that something is wrong, to when they begin confiding their worries to their partners, and then as things spiral downward, to their relatives, friends, and on to the point when they decide it's over and begin the process of "grave dressing"—preparing an orderly account of its ending. In *Chapter 14, Endings,* we discuss the experience of breaking up and divorce: the whirl of emotions that lovers feel, the process of working out a divorce settlement, deciding on custody of the children, and forming new relationships. We discuss relationships that end in death, and widows' and widowers' stages of grief.

Finally, in the *Epilogue, Starting Over,* we sum up what we have learned in our study of relationships. We describe the riches and wonders that can flow from successful love affairs and we try to guess what the future holds for lovers in a world of incredibly rapid and accelerating change.

ACKNOWLEDGMENTS

We would like to thank the following reviewers, who provided helpful comments: Fred B. Bryant, Loyola University of Chicago; Judith G. Chapman, Saint Joseph's University; Dan P. McAdams, Northwestern University; Angela P. McGlynn, Mercer County Community College; Kaisa Puhakka, West Georgia College; Deborah R. Richardson, Florida Atlantic University; and Anisa Zvonkovic, Oregon State University.

We would like to thank Cynthia Clement for suggesting and tracking down many literary references. We also thank Susan Sprecher, Illinois State University, for her painstaking review. We also appreciate Phil Giammatteo, Korey Sato and Vinita Shah, who helped us find elusive references.

Elaine Hatfield
Richard L. Rapson

Love, Sex, and Intimacy

Chapter
1

Beginnings

INTRODUCTION

In modern Western civilization, most people enter love affairs with unbounded hope—believing they have found the perfect mate, imagining ever-thrilling sex, and fantasizing a happy marriage—only to see their joyous dreams turn into a nightmare of disappointment, dashed expectations, and lost faith. In the beginning, passionate love's euphoria feeds delightful conversations with friends and a joyful engagement with life. The end of love leaves people stunned; baffled about what has gone wrong. Lots of men and women have gone through this cycle many, many times.

Disappointing as the love game is for many people today, it was even worse in the years after World War II when romantics sang mindlessly about how "love and marriage, love and marriage, go together like a horse and carriage." The cultural message was clear: Find the "right" mate, marry him or her, and life's major questions will be answered in a life of Happily Ever After. We are more dubious today about that message, but it still carries tremendous power for most individuals.

We recognize this power and take it seriously. It must be noted, however, that in Western culture, love, sex, and intimacy had very different meanings in the past. In much of the non-Western world, they *still* are viewed very differently. We need perspective on our ideas and assumptions about love and intimacy. Do love and marriage really go together like a horse and carriage? Nearly every society in the world before 1700 would have assumed that such an idea was mad. Marriage-for-love represents an ultimate expression of individualism, a concept that in premodern religious, traditional, and authoritarian societies was considered, as we shall later see, dangerously sinful and traitorous. Today, some nations (such as

China, India, and the Arab countries) still consider "being in love" the worst possible reason for getting married. Individuals do not personally choose to marry other individuals; marriages are arranged by family members and go-betweens, the assumption being that the only sensible approach is for families to marry their offspring into other families.

We consider the attainment of love and intimacy to be one of life's higher goals. The idea that love and intimacy are the *sine qua non* of life is so deeply felt that we can hardly imagine it to be otherwise. But, again, in history, that is a relatively recent idea; there is no guarantee that it will be a ruling idea in the future. We shall, throughout this book, describe the ways in which others have thought about love, sex, marriage, and intimacy. This may free us to consider our own articles of faith with more freedom, flexibility, and imagination than we usually do. It may open up the question of what makes a "good" life. It may help make us more intelligent about love. When we are smarter about love, we might despair less and understand more. We might be less bewildered when the love affair that started out so magically turns into a flawed relationship between two ordinary mortals trying to get close in a culture committed to personal freedom and individualism.

Nonetheless we must begin with where we actually are: desperately desiring love. And we must start with some definitions.

Love is the word used to label the sexual excitement of the young, the habituation of the middle aged, and the mutual dependence of the old.
—*John Ciardi*

DEFINITIONS

Love is a basic emotion. It comes in a variety of forms. Most scientists distinguish between two kinds of love—*passionate love* and *companionate love*. Most of us understand the difference between the two. When Ingrid Bergman told an ardent friend that although she loved him, she was not *in* love with him, he understood the difference: He committed suicide (Leamer, 1986).

Kurt Fischer, P. R. Shaver, and P. Carnochan (1990) pointed out that love, like all other emotions, includes a number of components. They defined *emotions* as:

> organised, meaningful, generally adaptive action systems. . . . [They] are complex functional wholes including appraisals or appreciations, patterned physiological processes, action tendencies, subjective feelings, expressions, and instrumental behaviors. (pp. 84–85)

They concluded that there are five basic emotions—two positive emotions (joy and love) and three negative ones (anger, sadness, and fear) (see Figure 1.1). There are two major kinds of love: passionate love (which they labeled infatuation) and companionate love (which they labeled fondness).

Robert Sternberg (1988) proposed a more elaborate typology of the varieties of love—a triangular model of love (Figure 1.2). He argued that different kinds of love differ in how much of three different components—passion, intimacy, and the

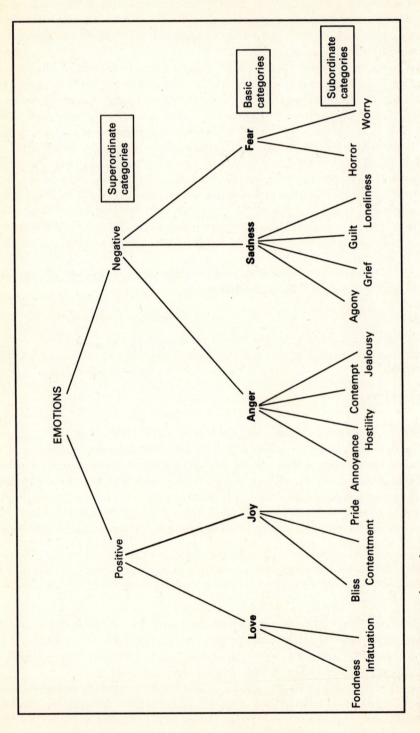

Figure 1.1 An emotion hierarchy.

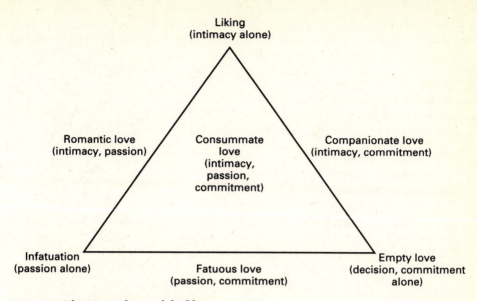

Figure 1.2 The triangular model of love.

decision/commitment to stay together—they possess. He defined passion, intimacy, and decision/commitment this way:

> *Passion* encompasses the drives that lead to romance, physical attraction, and sexual consummation;
> *Intimacy* encompasses the feelings of closeness, connectedness, and bondedness one experiences in loving relationships; and
> A *decision/commitment* encompasses, in the short term, the decision that one loves another, and in the long term, the commitment to maintain that love. (p. 32)

. Passionate love (which he labeled infatuation), for example, involves intense passionate arousal but little intimacy or commitment. Companionate love involves less passion and far more intimacy and commitment. The most complete form of love would be consummate love, which requires passion, intimacy, and commitment.

Of course, other scientists have proposed still other typologies of love (e.g., see Hendrick & Hendrick, 1989; Lee, 1973; Shaver & Hazan, 1988).

What Is Passionate Love?

Passionate love is a "hot," intense emotion, sometimes labeled obsessive love, puppy love, a crush, lovesickness, infatuation, or being-in-love. We would define the emotion of passionate love in this way:

> A state of intense longing for union with another. Passionate love is a complex functional whole including appraisals or appreciations, subjective feelings, expressions, patterned physiological processes, action tendencies, and instrumental behaviors. Reciprocated love (union with the other) is associated with fulfillment and ecstasy; unrequited love (separation) with emptiness, anxiety, or despair.

Elaine Hatfield and Susan Sprecher (1986a) designed the *Passionate Love Scale* *(PLS)* to tap the following indicants of longing for union. (The PLS is reproduced in Box 1.1.)

Cognitive Components
1. Preoccupation with the one you love.
2. Idealization of the other.
3. Desire to know and be known by the other.

Emotional Components
1. Attraction, especially sexual attraction, to the other.
2. Positive feelings when things go well.
3. Negative feelings when things go awry.
4. Longing for reciprocity. (Passionate lovers love and want to be loved in return.)
5. Desire for a complete and permanent union.
6. Physiological arousal.

Behavioral Components
1. Attempting to determine the other's feelings.
2. Studying the other person.
3. Assisting the other.
4. Maintaining physical closeness.

Are you in love with someone right now? Have you *ever* been in love? How intense are your feelings compared to those of other lovers? To find out, circle the numbers on items 1–15 in Box 1.1 that best represent your feelings for the one you love the most. Now, add up the numbers you circled. The total is your PLS score. How does it compare to the average PLS score of people your own age? Elaine Hatfield and Marilyn Easton (cited in Hatfield & Rapson, 1990b) interviewed Caucasian, Filipino, and Japanese men and women. They found that, on the average, men and women from these ethnic groups seemed to love with equal passion (see Table 1.1, p. 8). You can compare your scores with those of other students.

Box 1.1   THE PASSIONATE LOVE SCALE

Think of the person you love most passionately *right now*. (If you are not in love right now, think of the last person you loved passionately. If you have never been in love, think of the person whom you came closest to caring for in that way.) Try to tell us how you felt at the time when your feelings were the most intense.
    Possible answers range from:

(1)	(2)	(3)	(4)	(5)	(6)	(7)	(8)	(9)
Not at all true				Moderately true			Definitely true	

1. I would feel deep despair if _____ left me.
    1 2 3 4 5 6 7 8 9

2. Sometimes I feel I can't control my thoughts; they are obsessively on
_____.

1 2 3 4 5 6 7 8 9

3. I feel happy when I am doing something to make _____ happy.

1 2 3 4 5 6 7 8 9

4. I would rather be with _____ than anyone else.

1 2 3 4 5 6 7 8 9

5. I'd get jealous if I thought _____ were falling in love with someone
else.

1 2 3 4 5 6 7 8 9

6. I yearn to know all about _____.

1 2 3 4 5 6 7 8 9

7. I want _____—physically, emotionally, mentally.

1 2 3 4 5 6 7 8 9

8. I have an endless appetite for affection from _____.

1 2 3 4 5 6 7 8 9

9. For me, _____ is the perfect romantic partner.

1 2 3 4 5 6 7 8 9

10. I sense my body responding when _____ touches me.

1 2 3 4 5 6 7 8 9

11. _____ always seems to be on my mind.

1 2 3 4 5 6 7 8 9

12. I want _____ to know me—my thoughts, my fears, and my hopes.

1 2 3 4 5 6 7 8 9

13. I eagerly look for signs indicating _____'s desire for me.

1 2 3 4 5 6 7 8 9

14. I possess a powerful attraction for _____.

1 2 3 4 5 6 7 8 9

15. I get extremely depressed when things don't go right in my relationship with
_____.

1 2 3 4 5 6 7 8 9

Source: Hatfield & Sprecher, 1986a, p. 391.

Table 1.1 PASSIONATE LOVE SCALE SCORES OF
VARIOUS ETHNIC GROUPS

Group	Men	Women
Caucasians (mainland U.S.)	97.50	110.25
Caucasians (Hawaii)	100.50	105.00
Filipinos	106.50	102.90
Japanese	99.00	103.95

*Infatuation is when you think that he's as sexy as Robert Redford, as smart as
Henry Kissinger, as noble as Ralph Nader, as funny as Woody Allen and as
athletic as Jimmy Connors. Love is when you realize that he's as sexy as
Woody Allen, as smart as Jimmy Connors, as funny as Ralph Nader, as athletic
as Henry Kissinger and nothing like Robert Redford in any category—but
you'll take him anyway.*

—Judith Viorst

Passionate Love Versus Infatuation In movies, lovers never have any
trouble telling whether or not they are in love. Intense passion stalks them, shakes
them around, and, struggle as they might, overwhelms them. In real life, people are
usually not so certain about their feelings. College students at three universities
were asked what one thing they most wished they knew about romantic love
(Hatfield, & Walster, 1978). A surprisingly frequent question was: "What is the
difference between love and infatuation?" The answer to the love-versus-infatua-
tion riddle seems to be that there *is* no difference. The two do not differ in any
way—at least at the time one is experiencing them. Two sex counselors (Ellis &
Harper, 1961) who interviewed young adults about their romantic and sexual
experiences concluded that the difference between passionate love and infatuation
is merely semantic. Lovers use the term passionate love to describe loving relationships that are still in progress. They use the term infatuation to describe once-loving
relationships that have ended. It appears then that it may be possible to tell
infatuation from romantic love only in retrospect. If a relationship flowers, we
continue to believe that we are experiencing true love. If a relationship dies, we
conclude that we were merely infatuated. Of course, when our friends and parents
insist that we're just infatuated they are not really commenting on *our* feelings.
Actually they're telling us whether or not *they* approve of our relationship.

*If I have no love, I am nothing. . . . Love is patient; love is kind and envies no
one. Love is never boastful, nor conceited, nor rude; never selfish, not quick to
take offence. Love keeps no score of wrongs; does not gloat over other men's
sins, but delights in the truth. . . . Love will never come to an end.*

—I Corinthians 13

What Is Companionate Love?

By contrast, companionate love (sometimes called true love or conjugal love) is a
"warm," far less intense emotion. It combines feelings of deep attachment, commitment, and intimacy. We would define it as:

The affection and tenderness we feel for those with whom our lives are deeply entwined. Companionate love is a complex functional whole including appraisals or appreciations, subjective feelings, expressions, patterned physiological processes, action tendencies, and instrumental behaviors.

Psychologists have used a variety of scales to measure companionate love. For example, since Robert Sternberg (1988) assumed that companionate relationships possessed little passion, but a great deal of commitment and intimacy, many researchers have assessed companionate love by measuring commitment and intimacy (see Box 1.2).

Box 1.2   A COMPANIONATE LOVE SCALE

Please indicate your feelings on the following scale:

1	2	3	4	5	6	7	8	9
Not at all		Somewhat		Moderately		Quite		Extremely

Commitment
[Sternberg measured commitment by such items as these]:

1. I expect my love for _____ to last for the rest of my life.

2. I can't imagine ending my relationship with _____.

3. I am certain of my love for _____.

4. I am committed to maintaining my relationship with _____.

5. I have confidence in the stability of my relationship with _____.

Intimacy
[Sternberg assessed intimacy by such items as]:

1. I have a warm and comfortable relationship with _____.

2. I experience intimate communication with _____.

3. I have a relationship of mutual understanding with _____.

4. I receive considerable emotional support from _____.

5. I give considerable emotional support to _____.

6. I experience great happiness with _____.

A total companionate love score would be calculated by adding up respondents' scores on the commitment and intimacy subscales. The more companionately one loves another, the higher a score one would be expected to receive.

Source: Sternberg, 1986.

LOVE: HOW TO FIND IT

I can't understand why more people aren't bisexual. It would double your chances for a date on Saturday night.

—*Woody Allen*

There are times in life when people have to start from scratch in constructing their social lives: when a shy teenager yearns to begin dating; when a lonely freshman arrives at college; when a young couple breaks up or a long-married couple divorces; when a mate dies. In such circumstances, men and women face the problem of finding someone to love. People face two looming hurdles in their quest for love and intimacy: (1) to recognize what it takes to attract potential mates, dates, and friends; and (2) to devise a strategy for meeting them. Let us first consider the traits young men and women find attractive in potential dates and mates.

What Makes Someone Desirable?

What attracts men and women to one another? In part, romantic attraction is a mystery. My colleague, Ellen Berscheid (1984), reported the following example:

The author was interested to hear a man of her acquaintance exclaim that he had found, on his recent vacation to the West and after years of search, the woman with whom he wanted to spend the rest of his life. When asked what it was about this woman and/or their relationship that produced such unprecedented enthusiasm and willingness to (for the second time) contemplate the marital contract, he replied, and not so unpredictably, "We're so compatible! It's unbelievable!"

This was a striking statement because this man, having experienced a particularly unhappy and "incompatible" first marriage, had given a great deal of thought to the attributes required of the next (if there were to be a next) marital partner. The prerequisites on his lengthly list were specific and concrete: She must, first and foremost, *not* smoke. In addition, she should not drink. Further, she should be a Protestant and—desirable but not necessary—a faithful church-goer. She should be not older than 30 years of age, and preferably, never married. She should be well-educated and intelligent, and able to discuss some of the more esoteric intellectual writers of the day, as well as contemporary politics. She should—and this for him was a necessary condition—be interested in art and antiques, and if she had a particular interest in American pottery and American Indian baskets, so much the better (and if she happened to own a rare Gruby vase, she could expect a proposal of marriage on the spot). It was also desirable that she be attractive in appearance and, given his personal taste, fair of hair, eyes, and skin.

Now, given the probability that a person who embodied such a constellation of attributes actually existed somewhere on this planet, multiplied by the probability that this man would ever meet such a person, and that probability estimate multiplied in turn by the probability that such a woman would return his overtures, even a beginning student of interpersonal attraction would have to predict that this man was destined for a life of singledom. Thus, his announcement that his search had ended was greeted with incredulity.

Pursuing the matter, he was asked just *how* it was that he and this woman were so "compatible." What followed in reply was a recounting of very specific interaction episodes, including instances in which a witticism of his was understood and promptly returned, and a mention of the facts that they had played hours of gin rummy together, that they had jogged happily together, and that she had fixed sandwiches for him in preparation for his long car journey home. *That* was the sum total of his explanation! Even more disconcerting, however, was the fact that in his enthusiastic report of moments shared with the woman, it also emerged, in the most casual and incidental way, that: The woman is a chain-smoker. She drinks. She is Catholic. She is 43 years old. She has been married and divorced three times and recently terminated a three-year cohabitation relationship with a fourth man. She couldn't be less interested in antiques, in general, or pottery and Indian baskets, in particular; in fact, she heaped a pint of fresh strawberries in a $300 Indian basket he had just purchased, realizing neither its antiquity nor its value (this incident related with fond chuckles of amusement). She is largely uneducated, although she is, he said, "good looking"—with dark hair, dark eyes, and a dark complexion! But—and for him this was the joyous bottom line—with no one, *ever,* had he been so "compatible"! (pp. 144–145)

As you might guess, this affair quickly fizzled out.

Scientists may not know everything about why people are drawn to the people that they are, but they know something. Every culture has standards for courtship and marriage. Without really thinking about it, most of us dutifully follow our culture's dictates. Most of us want dates and mates who are about our own age, from the same socioeconomic class, religion, and educational level. They can't be too short or too tall. Such preliminary screenings cut out a surprising number of candidates. But most of us want more. Often we want someone who is reasonably good looking, personable, warm, and intelligent; someone whose views match our own; and perhaps even more.

Beauty is a greater recommendation than any letter of introduction.
—*Jane Austen*

Good Looks   Handsome men and beautiful women have a huge advantage in the dating market and a head start in the search for a committed relationship. Many young people work furiously hard to improve their physical appearance in the hopes of attracting desirable dates and mates. In 1990, American cosmetics firms racked up more than one and a half billion dollars in sales of beauty products (*Time,* 1991).

Most people, most of the time, *are* biased in their reactions to good-looking or unattractive people. This discovery is certainly not new. The Greek philosopher Sappho contended that "what is beautiful is good." (Actually, we will see that while it is an advantage to be good-looking to average in appearance, it is the extremely unattractive who suffer the most.) There are four steps in the stereotyping process:

1. Most people know that it is not fair to discriminate against the ugly. (They would be incensed if others discriminated against *them*). And yet . . .
2. Most people take it for granted that attractive and unattractive people are different. Generally, they assume that "what is beautiful is good; what is unattractive is bad."
3. Most people *treat* good-looking and average people better than they treat the unattractive.

4. As a consequence, a "self-fulfilling prophecy" occurs. The way people are treated shapes the kinds of people they become.

In one classic experiment, researchers (Dion, Berscheid, & Hatfield, 1972) showed college men and women yearbook photographs of men and women who varied markedly in appearance and asked them their first impressions of the students. Young adults assumed that handsome men and beautiful women possessed nearly all the virtues. They assumed that the good-looking were more sociable, outgoing, poised, and interesting; that they were warmer, more exciting, and more sexually responsive; that they had better characters, were more nurturant, kind, modest, strong, and sensitive than were their homely peers. Good-looking people were also expected to have more fulfilling lives. Students predicted the good-looking would be happier, have more successful marriages, find better jobs, and, all-in-all, live more fulfilling lives. On only one dimension were young adults suspicious of good looks; judges did not expect attractive people to make especially good parents.

Of course, social observers cannot help but recognize that good looks might have a bit of a dark side. For example, psychologists (Dermer & Thiel, 1975) asked college students to rate college women who varied greatly in attractiveness. In general, subjects did assume that attractive and average women possessed more appealing personalities and were more socially skilled than were unattractive women. In this study, however, researchers also documented some "ugly truths about beauty." Subjects expected attractive women to be more vain and egotistical, more bourgeois (i.e., materialistic, snobbish, and unsympathetic to oppressed peoples), and less committed to their marriages (more likely to have extramarital affairs and/or to request a divorce) than homely women. (Similar results have been secured by Eagley, Ashmore, Makhijani, & Kennedy, 1991.)

It is better to be beautiful than to be good. But . . . it is better to be good than to be ugly.

—Oscar Wilde

In *Mirror, Mirror: The Importance of Looks in Everyday Life*, Elaine Hatfield and Susan Sprecher (1986b) reviewed a cascade of evidence that people assume the attractive/average are very different from the unattractive. (For recent work in this area, see Buss, 1989; Buss & Barnes, 1986; Feingold, 1988, 1990; Howard, Blumstein, & Schwartz, 1987; or Snyder, Berscheid, & Glick, 1985).

What effect does such stereotyping have on men and women? Do the good-looking actually *become* more socially skilled as a consequence of their privileged position? Probably. Expectations have a way of being fulfilled. If men and women expect others to be disagreeable, they tend to treat them in ways that bring out their worst. The existence of such a self-fulfilling prophecy was demonstrated in a fascinating experiment by Mark Snyder, Elizabeth Tanke, and Ellen Berscheid (1977). Men and women at the University of Minnesota were recruited for a study on "the acquaintance process." First, men were given a Polaroid snapshot and biographical information about their partners. In fact, the snapshot was a "fake"; it depicted either a beautiful or a homely woman. Men were asked their first impressions of the women. Those who believed they had been assigned a beautiful partner expected her to be sociable, poised, humorous, and socially skilled. Those who thought they had been assigned to an unattractive one expected her to be unsociable, awkward, serious, and socially inept. Such prejudice is not surprising. We already know that good-looking people make exceptionally good first impressions.

The next set of findings, however, *was* startling. Men were asked to get acquainted with their partners via the telephone. Male expectations had a dramatic impact on the ways they talked to their partners during the telephone calls. That, in turn, created a correspondingly great impact on the response of the *women*. Men, of course, *thought* they were talking to a beautiful or homely woman; in fact, the women on the other end of the line varied greatly in appearance. (Probably most were average in looks.) Nonetheless, within the space of a telephone conversation, women became what men expected them to be. After the telephone conversations, judges listened to tapes of the women's portions of the conversations and tried to guess what the women were like just from that snippet of conversation. Women who had been talked to as if they were beautiful soon began to sound that way. They became unusually animated, confident, and socially skilled. Those who had been treated as if they were unattractive soon began acting *that* way. (They became withdrawn, lacking in confidence, and awkward.) Men's prophecies had been fulfilled.

How did this happen? When the portions of the men's conversations were analyzed, it was found that those men who thought they were talking to a beautiful woman were more sociable, sexually warm, interesting, independent, sexually permissive, bold, outgoing, humorous, and socially skilled than the men who thought they were talking to a homely woman. The men assigned to an attractive woman were also more comfortable, enjoyed themselves more, liked their partners more, took the initiative more often, and used their voices more effectively. In brief, the men who thought they were talking to a beautiful woman tried harder. Undoubtedly, this behavior caused the women to try harder too. If the stereotypes held by the men became reality within the ten minutes of a telephone conversation, one can imagine what happens when people are treated well or badly over a lifetime. In fact, researchers have found some evidence that the attractive are in fact unusually socially skilled and experienced (Curran, 1975; Kaats & Davis, 1970).

We have just seen that people are prejudiced in favor of the good-looking, treat them better, and, as a result, that the good-looking become more socially skilled. It is not surprising then that most men and women, regardless of *their own* appearance, are especially eager to date the good-looking. There is considerable evidence that this is so. In one experiment, Elaine Hatfield and her students (Hatfield, Aronson, Abrahams, & Rottman, 1966) invited freshmen at the University of Minnesota to a computer dance. Couples were promised that a computer would match them with a blind date that was just right for them. (In truth, the students were randomly matched with one another; partners' names were drawn from a fishbowl.) When the freshmen arrived to purchase their tickets for the dance, the researchers rated their social desirability—their attractiveness, intelligence, personality traits, and social skills. When freshmen signed up for the project, four ticket sellers secretly rated their attractiveness. The scientists assessed the intelligence level of the freshmen by securing transcripts of their high school grades and their scores on the *Minnesota Scholastic Aptitude Test*. They gauged their personality traits by recording their scores from a battery of tests, including the prestigious *Minnesota Multiphasic Personality Test* and the *California Personality Inventory*.

Subjects were given the names of their computer matches and were encouraged to meet at the dance. At the dance, the 400 couples talked, danced, and got to know one another. Then, during the 10:30 intermission, the experimenters swept through the building, rounding up couples from the dance floor, lavatories, fire escapes—even adjoining buildings. Researchers asked the students to tell them frankly (and in confidence) what they thought of their dates. Did they plan to ask them out again? If *they* were asked out, would they accept? Six months later the researchers contacted couples again to find out if they had, in fact, dated. Here are some of the things they found:

1. When the freshmen signed up for the dance, they were asked what kinds of dates they preferred. Everyone, regardless of what *they* looked like, preferred (in fact, insisted on) being matched with the best-looking, most charming, brightest, and most socially skilled partner possible.
2. Those whom fate matched with handsome or beautiful dates were eager to pursue the relationships. Keep in mind that some of the handsome men and beautiful women had expressed total disinterest in their dates, especially if they were unattractive; some even admitted to treating them rudely. No matter. Everyone wanted to see the good-looking computer matches again. When couples were contacted six months after the dance, participants (whether they were good-looking or homely; well treated or not) had in fact tried to date the best-looking. The prettier the woman, the more eagerly she was pursued.
3. In this study, every effort to find anything else that mattered failed. Men and women with exceptional IQs and social skills, for example, were not liked any better than those less well endowed.
4. Finally, men and women cared equally about how their dates looked.

The inordinate importance of good looks in blind-date settings has been substantiated by other investigators (see Bull & Rumsey, 1988). Appearance has particular power as the first filter when people meet. Once that first hurdle has been leaped, other qualities begin to assume ever-increasing importance. People begin to care about the personality—the intelligence, kindness, and warmth—of potential dates too. Strange to say, there even exist those odd human beings who find these latter qualities even more important than physical appearance.

What a strange delusion it is to fancy beauty is goodness!
                                        —*Leo Tolstoy*

Personality   In the midst of the Great Depression, Dale Carnegie (1936) counseled businessmen (in *How to Win Friends and Influence People*) that there were six ways to make others like you:

Rule 1: Become genuinely interested in other people.

Rule 2: Smile.

Rule 3: Remember that people's names are to them the sweetest and most important sound in any language.

Rule 4: Be a good listener. Encourage others to talk about themselves.

Rule 5: Talk in terms of the other person's interest.

Rule 6: Make the other person feel important—and do it sincerely.

Today, the evidence suggests that Carnegie was right. Men and women do prefer to date and associate with friendly, sincere people; people who are interesting and who are interested in them (Byrne, 1971; Kaplan & Anderson, 1973). Let us consider some of these important personality traits in more detail.

Intelligence and Competence   People like men and women who are socially skilled, intelligent, and competent. Some women worry that if they dazzle too brightly they might scare men off. Experiments make it clear, however, that both men and women are most attracted to potential dates who are intelligent and competent (Aronson, Willerman, & Floyd, 1966; Helmreich, Aronson, & Lefan, 1970; Solomon & Saxe, 1977). Men's preference for intelligent women seems likely to accelerate in the wake of the women's movement (Muehlenhard & Scardino, 1985).

Balthazar claimed once that he could induce love as a control-experiment by a simple action: namely telling each of two people who had never met that the other was dying to meet them, had never seen anyone so attractive and so on. This was, he claimed, infallible as a means of making them fall in love: they always did.

—Lawrence Durrell

Warmth   People like to be liked. There is overwhelming evidence that men and women respond most enthusiastically to those who like them and treat them warmly (Berscheid & Hatfield, 1978; Curtis & Miller, 1986; Folkes & Sears, 1977; Hatfield & Walster, 1978).

In one study, Debra Walsh and Jay Hewitt (1985) studied men's willingness to approach women in a singles bar. The women (college students) and the experimenter sat at an empty table in the bar from 8 to 9 P.M. each night. In the experimental condition, the women were instructed to look at one of the men, catch his eye, and smile. (The experimenter told the women who they were supposed to "give the eye."). In the control condition, the women were told just to look out on the dance floor and smile at no one in particular. Men were far more likely to come over and talk to the women who caught their eye and smiled. Sixty percent of the men approached the friendly, encouraging women; *not one* man dared to approach the women who failed to give them a friendly signal!

Solomon Asch (1946) argued that certain traits, like *warm* and *cold,* are central traits; they have a profound effect on the way people perceive and feel about others. Try this classic Asch experiment. Your best friend suggests that you go out on a blind date with one of his cousins, Jan or Terry. What are they like? Jan is warm, good-looking, intelligent, and cautious. Terry is cold, good-looking, intelligent, and cautious. Which would you date? When most people are asked their first impressions of Jan and Terry, practically everyone assumes that Jan will not only be warm, but will be happy, generous, humorous, good-natured, popular, sociable, sincere, helpful, and modest as well. They assume that Terry is not just cold but unhappy, moody, irritable, humorless, unpopular, pessimistic, and unsociable as well (Rosenberg, Nelson, & Vivekananthan, 1968). No wonder nearly everyone prefers to date Jan. In any case, people generally prefer to date those with affectionate, warm natures.

Birds of a feather flock together.
　　　　—Folk adage

Similarity   Most people are attracted, romantically, to those whose backgrounds, personalities, attitudes, and beliefs are similar to their own. Sociologists have long been interested in mate selection. In a classic paper, Alan C. Kerckhoff (1974) observed that in all societies there is a *field of eligibles;* only certain kinds of people are considered to be suitable as mates. Until recently, American society assumed that suitable dates or mates must be similar in age, race, socioeconomic status, religion, and educational level (Cargan, 1991; Kephart and Jedlicka, 1991; Skolnick, 1992).

Society also restricts young people's *field of availables.* Young people necessarily spend most of their time with people who are much like themselves: people who go to the same schools, live in the same neighborhoods, and engage in the same activities.

Kerckhoff argued that both these influences may be responsible for the strong *homogamy* that exists in mating. Like may marry like because our culture prescribes similarity between spouses on a variety of social characteristics. Like may also marry like because the field of availables is generally made up of people very similar to ourselves. Such preliminary screenings cut out a surprising number of candidates. How rigorous these initial screenings really are became all too evident to some budding computer dating companies when they began to calculate how many men and women they would have to enroll in their programs to accomplish the barest minimum of homogamous matching. These minimum requirements included matching individuals who:

- Were of the appropriate sex (homosexual clients would naturally request dates of the same sex, heterosexual clients would request dates of the opposite sex, while bisexual clients might specify dates of either sex);
- Lived in the same town;
- Were of about the same age;
- Were of the same race, socioeconomic class, religion, or educational level;
- Were roughly the same height.

To its dismay, one computer company calculated that it would need more than one million subscribers in order to match on just these basic traits. So much for shared interests, sexual compatibility, and so on. (Interestingly enough, there is no computer-match company now in business with an enrollment figure even close to one million.)

But most of us want more. Most people prefer dates and mates who are similar in personality, attitude, and a host of other traits.

In a classic study, Donn Byrne, C. R. Ervin, and J. Lamberth (1970) introduced men and women to one another. Half of the time they told couples that they were very similar in personality and attitudes; in fact, they were. Half were warned, in all honesty, that they were very different. Then the couples went out on a 30-minute blind date. Eventually, the couples wandered back to the experimental office. The psychologists asked couples how much they liked one another. They also unobtrusively recorded how close they stood to one another when turning in their questionnaires. (Were they touching one another? Standing at opposite extremes of the desk?) As predicted, the more similar couples were, the more attracted they were to one another and the closer they stood to one another. [Similar results were secured by Cappella & Palmer (1990) and Cavior, Miller, & Cohen (1975).] Recently, scientific teams have documented that people prefer to date and mate people whose personalities and attitudes are similar to their own (Broome, 1983; Byrne, Clore, & Smeaton, 1986; Smeaton, Byrne, & Murnen, 1989).

Researchers didn't stop there. They acknowledge that most people may *prefer* partners who are startlingly good-looking, intelligent, kind, and so forth. But they find that men and women are likely to *settle* for partners no better and no worse than themselves on these dimensions:

- Intelligence and education. People tend to end up with mates who are similar to themselves in intelligence and education (Hatfield et al., 1978).
- Physical attractiveness. Men and women generally end up dating and marrying those who are about as attractive as they are (Hatfield & Sprecher, 1986b).
- Mental health. People tend to marry those who are as mentally healthy or neurotic or mentally ill as themselves (Hatfield & Walster, 1978).
- Physical health. People are likely to date and marry partners with similar physical disabilities (Hatfield et al., 1978). For example, scientists (Spuhler, 1968) reviewed 42 studies of assortative mating. The studies investigated whether like-married-like, on 105 different physical characteristics—ranging from such broad characteristics as "general health" (which was assessed via nine different indicants) to such specific traits as "systolic blood pressure" and "ear lobe length"! They found that couples generally are well matched. Such homogamy seems to be especially prevalent with respect to deafness. The fact that deaf people tend to marry one another so worried Alexander Graham Bell (1884) that he felt compelled to point out the grave consequences of such homogamy in an article entitled "Upon the formation of a deaf variety of the human race."
- Other social characteristics. Men and women prefer dates and mates who share their preferences in a variety of activities (Werner & Parmelee, 1979).

People do not, of course, relentlessly seek carbon copies of themselves. Obviously men and women sometimes look for partners who are dissimilar in certain fundamental ways. For example, as Gerald Maxwell (1975) has wryly observed, most men and women prefer to marry the "opposite" sex. In traditional 1950s marriages, men and women were expected to bring different and complementary skills to their mergers. Men were expected to perform the "heavy" tasks, like mowing the lawn, shoveling the sidewalks, fixing the furnace, tinkering with the car, and taking out the garbage. Women were supposed to do the "light" work: cleaning the house, cooking, canning, shopping, and taking care of the children. These traditional sex-typed roles are changing but the principle that "opposites attract" in the division of labor may remain. Women who loathe cooking may find a man especially appealing if he is a culinary genius; men who can't tell a spark plug from a carburetor may find a woman who can very appealing. Saints may prefer sinners.

Furthermore, not everyone is interested in finding someone just like themselves to love. Recently, Eastern psychologists Arthur and Elaine Aron (1986) argued that love can best be understood in terms of a deeply felt motivation to expand the self. If men and women had sufficient self-confidence, they argued, they would be more willing to stretch themselves; to try dating people who added something new and different to their lives. There is some evidence that they may be right. In one early study, Elaine Hatfield and G. William Walster (1963) speculated that perhaps young men and women focused so single-mindedly on "similarity" not because of its intrinsic appeal (after all, it is a bit boring to date your clone) but because they were *afraid* of daring the unknown. [When people are very different from us, their social standards are unclear; we may not be quite sure how we are "supposed" to behave. Even the gentlemanly Marcel Proust (1913/1956) expressed fear that "boors and bounders," unaware of society's rules, would underrate *his* social value.] If students had more self-confidence (if they were assured they would be liked or if they were assured that it didn't matter whether they were liked), they reasoned, they might be interested in dating someone a bit more "exotic" than usual. In their experiments, the authors found clear support for this hypothesis. As predicted, students who were assured that everyone would like them were eager to associate with the dissimilar. (In fact, they vastly preferred dissimilar people to similar ones.) Students who were warned that they probably would not be liked, and who thought it was important to be liked, preferred to play it safe and talk with similar people. It appears then that the more worried we are about whether others will like us, the more anxious we are to associate with similar others. [Similar results were secured by Broome (1983).] Other researchers document that people who are psychologically secure are especially likely to associate with a wide range of people, similar and dissimilar (Goldstein & Rosenfeld, 1969).

Love is the triumph of imagination over intelligence.
                    —*H. L. Mencken*

Other Assets   What else do men and women long for? Hatfield and her students (Hatfield, Traupmann, Sprecher, Utne, & Hay, 1984) interviewed over 1000 dating couples, 100 newlyweds, and 400 elderly women, asking them to note the rewards (or lack thereof) they found to be most critical in their relationships. Their answers, some of which are shown in Table 1.2, were surprisingly similar.

Table 1.2   REWARDS IN LOVE RELATIONS

Personal rewards
  Appearance (having mates who are attractive and take care of their appearance)
  Social grace (having mates who are sociable, friendly, and relaxed in social settings)
  Intelligence (having mates who are intelligent and informed)

Emotional rewards
  Feeling liked and loved
  Feeling understood
  Feeling accepted
  Feeling appreciated
  Physical affection (being kissed and hugged)
  Sex
  Security (knowing partners are committed and there is a future together)
  Plans and goals for the future (being able to dream about your future together)

Day-to-day rewards
  Smoothly running daily routine
  Comfortable finances
  Sociability and good communication
  Decision making (having partners who take a fair share of the responsibility for making and
    carrying out decisions that affect both of you)
  Remembering special occasions

Opportunities gained and lost
  "Opportunities gained" include the things that one gets from being married: the chance to
    become a parent; the chance to be invited, as part of a "married couple," to social events;
    having someone to count on in old age
  "Opportunities foregone" include the things that one has to give up in order to be in a
    relationship: other possible mates; a career; travel; sexual freedom

What Makes Someone Undesirable?

We have reviewed what people desire in potential dates and mates. What makes people *dislike* and avoid others?

Most people have a secret fear that they will say or do something embarrassing in a social situation, and that people will react with stunned silence or snickers. Can *you* recall making any social gaffes? Who were you talking to? What did you say? How did others react? How did you try to repair the damage?

Mark Knapp, L. Stafford, and J. A. Daly (1986) asked men and women to recall their most regrettable messages; things they wish they hadn't said. Most of us can recall such *faux pas* as these:

My blind-date said that he sold office safes. I was trying to make conversation so I said "Everything valuable I keep in my drawers." People around us looked, and then started laughing. In fact, they couldn't stop laughing. I was sick with shame.

I was invited to my fiance's home for a special dinner. It was the first time I had met everyone and I was trying hard to impress them. As we sat down to eat, his father turned to me and said, "I hope you'll say grace." I was so unsettled by this request that I immediately bowed my head and said, "Now I lay me down to sleep. . . ." (p. 40)

Young people (in their twenties) suffer the most from the fear that they have made fools of themselves. Perhaps preteens are too young to care much about the impression they make. Perhaps by their thirties, forties, fifties, and beyond, people may learn to be more socially skilled, or, more likely, they may have learned to be kinder to themselves when they make inevitable mistakes. Surprisingly, most people recall making such *faux pas* not with strangers, but in their closest of relationships. People tended to cringe when recalling the following kinds of regrettable messages:

1. *Blunders* (22% of the regrettable messages). (One woman asked "How's your mother?" only to find that she had just died.)
2. *Direct attacks* (16%). (People may say "Everyone thinks you are an egomaniac," or "Your girlfriend is a slut" only to regret it later.)
3. *Group references* (14%). (People may spit out racial or ethnic slurs.)
4. *Direct criticism* (12%). (The words "You are the worst housekeeper I have ever seen" or "What kind of woman would date a married man with three little children?" may come back to haunt you.)
5. *Reveal/explain too much* (11%). (Sometimes in the excitement of the moment, people tell too much. They reveal a painful secret or violate a friend's trust. "Why did I spill my guts to her?" they moan later.)

People were asked *why* they said what they did. Their reasons were as follows.

1. *Stupid.* ("I wasn't thinking" or "It just slipped out.")
2. *Selfish.* ("I wanted him to take me to the prom and I thought I could shame him into it.")
3. *Good/innocent intention.* ("I was just trying to be nice." "I was just making small talk.")
4. *Bad intention.* ("I was jealous and was trying to get even." "I wanted to hurt him.")
5. *Humorous.* ("I was trying to be funny. Some joke.")
6. *Out of control.* ("I just got carried away." "I was drunk," "nervous," "exhausted," "under stress.")

Most of the time (77% of the time) people realize what they have said the second the words have left their mouths. They feel deeply embarrassed, hurt, filled with regret. Occasionally, they don't realize until later what they have done. Even years later, people blush when they recall their youthful mistakes. People almost always try to repair things. They apologize, deny they meant what they said ("I was just kidding"), attempt to explain, offer excuses, or try to atone for their words. (Only 7% of the time did people "do nothing," and then this was in the hope that others wouldn't notice their *faux pas*. Hope springs eternal.) Usually, people do pay for their mistakes. (Others are hurt or angry; they walk out in a huff.) Sometimes, however, they understand.

We tend to dwell on such horrors, but in fact, one or two mistakes are unlikely to shake a promising or fulfilling love relationship. In love, people generally get to make hundreds of mistakes; ideally they learn and try harder the next time. Usually, it is permanent personality and character problems that lay waste to promising relationships.

Albert Pepitone (1964) found that people disliked and rejected potential dates and friends who were arrogant, conceited, rude, or who consistently made life difficult.

What makes potential dates just plain boring? Mark Leary, P. A. Rogers, R. W. Canfield, and C. Coe (1986) tried to find out what sorts of communication styles are especially dreary. They asked students to list things "that other people do that make them seem boring to you" (p. 969). They found that eight sorts of conversational habits are especially deadly: (1) *Passivity*. (Dull people aren't really there—they seem to have no opinions of their own, they can't hold up their end of a conversation, or add anything new to a discussion.) (2) *Tediousness*. (Tiresome people have a boring communication style—they may talk veeeeeerrrrry slowly, pausing a long time before responding, ramble, include too many annoying details in their stories, or drag on and on. In a classic skit, humorists Bob and Ray pretended to interview delegates at a Slow Talkers convention. As the Slow Talkers paused interminably mid-word, members of the audience could barely refrain from rushing on ahead to finish their sentences.) (3) *Distracting* behaviors make interaction difficult. Boring people get sidetracked easily. All their talk is small talk. (4) *Low affectivity*. (Dull people rarely look others in the eye; their faces are expressionless; their voices monotonous.) (5) *Boring ingratiation*. (Tiresome people try too hard to be funny; try too hard to be nice; work too hard to impress other people.) (6) *Seriousness*. (Boring people rarely smile; they are too serious.) (7) *Self-centeredness*. (Dull people are preoccupied with themselves, with their pasts, and with their own problems. They are negative and constantly complain.) (9) *Banality*. (People who talk about trivial or superficial things, who are interested in only one topic, or who repeat the same stories and jokes again and again are boring.)

Recently, Milton Rosenbaum (1986) has argued that men and women tend to be repulsed by potential dates and mates who disagree with their cherished attitudes, beliefs, and values. People tend to assume that someone who disagrees with the ideas that seem so reasonable to *them* must be unethical, short-sighted, stupid, or maybe even a little bit crazy.

In sum: If people want to make themselves as appealing as they can, probably the best strategy is to spend some time improving their appearance . . . but not too much time. The handsome and beautiful have only a slight advantage over the average in the dating market. It is the unattractive who suffer the most. Most men and women would surely do better spending their extra time making more long-term investments—in becoming happy, interesting, personable, kind, intelligent, successful, and fulfilled—people who have a rich life of their own, buttressed with a serious career and friends.

The Importance of Proximity

Often, people's search for the ideal mate ends with the boy or girl next door—or, if they are unusually daring, with the man or woman a mile away. One sociologist (Clarke, 1952) interviewed 431 couples at the time they applied for a marriage license. He found that, at the time of their first date together, 37% of the couples were living within 8 blocks of one another and 54% lived within 16 blocks of one another. As the distance between the residences increased, the number of marriages decreased steadily. Love seemed unable to survive a very long subway ride.

Recently, *Redbook* magazine (1977) asked a scattering of celebrities how they had met their matches. Interestingly enough, almost all of these eminent men and women somehow ended up with people whom they saw on a day-to-day basis. President Jimmy Carter began by dating the girl next door and ended up marrying the woman down the street. Barbra Streisand met hairdresser Jon Peters at a party in Paris. Comedienne Joan Rivers met her husband Edgar Rosenberg when he asked her to work with him on a script.

Psychologist Leon Festinger (1951) came up with more solid evidence that people often end up dating and marrying whoever happens to be close by. He examined the development of friendships in a new apartment complex. In the complex, all the apartments, except for the end houses, were arranged around U-shaped courts. The two end houses in each court faced onto the street. Festinger and his colleagues arrived at the unsettling conclusion that, to a great extent, the architects had unknowingly shaped the social lives of their residents. The major determinant of who became friends was mere proximity—the distance between apartments. Friendships sprung up more frequently between next-door neighbors, less frequently between people whose houses were separated by another house, and so on. As the distance between houses increased, the number of friendships fell off so rapidly that it was rare to find a friendship between people who lived in houses more than four or five units apart.

Any architectural feature that forced a resident to bump into other residents now and then tended to increase his or her popularity. For example, people with apartments near the entrances and exits of the stairways tended to meet more people and make more friends than did other residents. The residents of the apartments near the mailboxes in each building also had an unusually active social life.

Any architectural feature that took a person even slightly out of the traffic mainstream had a chilling effect on his or her popularity. In order to have the street appear "lived on," ten of the apartments had been turned so that they faced the street, rather than the court. This apparently small change had a considerable effect on the lives of the people who happened to occupy these end houses. These people—who had no next-door neighbors—ended up with less than half as many friends in the complex as anyone else. Architecture had made them involuntary social isolates.

Effective Strategies for Meeting Dates and Mates

Lonely, desperate people often feel that they have to be "efficient"; they relentlessly set out to track down the right mate. They try to turn themselves into attractive "packages" so that they can attract the kind of dates they desire. Usually, *they* are interested in someone who has it all—someone who is good-looking, personable, kind, and rich. If they find a fatal flaw in prospective partners, they quickly discard them and move on to more promising candidates. They are determined not to waste their time. This strategy sounds reasonable, but the evidence suggests it does not work.

In one study, Carolyn Cutrona (1982) interviewed 354 UCLA freshmen two weeks, seven weeks, and seven months after their arrival on campus. At first, almost all the new arrivals, cut off from old romantic partners, family, and friends, were lonely. (Seventy-five percent of new students admitted they had been lonely since their arrival.) Most students were fairly resilient, however. By the end of the school year, most had made a successful social adjustment. Only a few were still chronically lonely. What were the differences between the students who were satisfied with the dates and friends they had made and those who were still miserably lonely at the end of the year? There were personality differences between the well-adjusted and lonely students. Lonely students had lower self-esteem, were more introverted, less assertive, and more sensitive to rejection; such traits slow down the process of social integration.

Well-adjusted and lonely students also tended to differ in the explanations they gave for their initial loneliness. It was disastrous if students attributed their loneliness to their own personal failings (i.e., if they assumed they were lonely because they were homely, boring, or shy) or if they assumed that they, one of the unlucky few, represented an exceptional case. If students realized that nearly everyone started in the same boat, they could more easily set out to meet friends and lovers.

What is the best way to do that?

The Direct Approach   There is no reason the lonely cannot embark on a "search and seize" mission aimed at capturing dates and mates. When University of Wisconsin students were asked whether they knew someone they would like to meet and perhaps date, 90% of the men and 80% of the women said "Yes." Men could generally think of 19 women they might be interested in; women could think of 7 men who had sparked their interest (Sprecher & McKinney, 1987). One way people can meet someone, then, is simply to select a few appealing candidates and ask them out for coffee, lunch, to join a study group, to go on a hike, or so forth. The really courageous may invite promising candidates to dinner or to a movie.

Taking the initiative may be fine advice for men, but what about women? Traditionally, women have assumed that if they are too forward, men will be scared off. The evidence doesn't seem to support that notion (Kelley & Rolker-Dolinsky, 1987; McCormick & Jesser, 1982; Muehlenhard & Miller, 1983).

But romantic passion . . . is a plant which thrives best in stony soil. Like the geranium in Erica's kitchen, the less it was watered, the better it flowered.
—Alison Lurie

Playing Hard-to-Get   According to the folklore, a woman should never "throw herself" at a man. He will flee. From Socrates to Ovid to the author of *The Kama Sutra* all the way to Bertrand Russell and even to that Sage of Sages, "Dear Abby," all agree: they say that love and passion are stimulated by excitement and challenge. *The Kama Sutra of Vatsyayana* (1963) advises women to use the following strategy to "gain over a man."

But old authors say that although the girl loves the man ever so much she should not offer herself or make the first overtures, for a girl who does this loses her dignity, and is liable to be scorned and rejected. But when the man tries to kiss her she should oppose him; when he begs to be allowed to have sexual intercourse with her she should let him touch her private parts only and with considerable difficulty; and though importuned by him, she should not yield herself up to him as if of her own accord, but should resist his attempts to have her. It is only, moreover, when she is certain that she is truly loved, and that her lover is indeed devoted to her, and will not change his mind, that she should then give herself up to him, and persuade him to marry her quickly. After losing her virginity she should tell her confidential friends about it.

Here end the efforts of a girl to gain over a man. (p. 138)

To find Wise Folk in such rare accord is refreshing. Research clearly shows that, this time, however, the sages were wrong.

The less my hope, the hotter my love.
                    —Terence

In the 1970s, Elaine Hatfield and her colleagues (Hatfield, Walster, Piliavin, & Schmidt, 1973) conducted a number of experiments designed to demonstrate that men and women prefer those who play hard-to-get. Inevitably these experiments failed.

We began our research by studying men's preferences. We began not by asking men *if* they preferred hard-to-get dates, but *why* they did so. Most men were cooperative. They explained that an easy-to-get woman spelled trouble. (She was probably desperate for a date. She was probably the kind of woman who made too many demands on a man, the kind who wanted to get serious right away. Even worse, she might have a "disease." Today, men would probably mention AIDS.) The elusive woman, on the other hand, was almost inevitably a valuable woman. The men pointed out that a woman could only afford to be choosy if she was popular—and a woman was popular for some reason. When a woman was hard-to-get, it was usually a tip-off that she was especially pretty, had a good personality, was sexy, and so on. Men also were intrigued by the challenge that the elusive woman offered. One can spend a great deal of time fantasizing about what it would be like to date her. Also, since the hard-to-get woman's desirability was well recognized, a man could gain prestige by being seen with her. In brief, nearly all men took it for granted (as we did) that men preferred hard-to-get women and they could supply abundant justification for their prejudice.

A few isolated men refused to cooperate. These dissenters noted that an elusive woman was not always more desirable than an available woman. Sometimes the hard-to-get woman was not only hard-to-get—she was impossible to get, because she was misanthropic and cold. Sometimes a woman was easy-to-get simply because she was a friendly, warm, outgoing person who boosted one's ego and ensured that dates were "no hassle." We ignored the testimony of these deviant types.

We then conducted five experiments designed to demonstrate that men valued a hard-to-get date more than an easy-to-get one. All five experiments failed. Let us consider just one of these disasters.

A flurry of advertisements appeared on campus inviting college men and women to sign up for a free computer-date-matching service. In an initial interview, men and women told the computer all about themselves. Two weeks later, the "dating bureau" asked the men to drop by to collect the names and telephone numbers of their date-matches. The dating counselor also asked them for a favor. Would they telephone their dates from the office, invite them out, and then report on their first impression of them? (Presumably, the counselor was interested in how the matches seemed to be working out.)

In fact, the dating bureau had been very busy during the two-week lull. They had contacted the women who had signed up for the computer-matching program and hired them as experimenters. They had given the women precise instructions on how they should act when their computer matches called them for a date. Half of the women were told to play hard-to-get. When a man asked them out, they were to pause . . . and think . . . and think . . . for three or four seconds before replying: "Mm (slight pause). No, I've got a date then. It seems like I signed up for that date match thing a long time ago and I've met more people since then— I'm really pretty busy all this week." When the men suggested another time, they were to accept reluctantly. Half of the women were told to act easy-to-get. They were to accept eagerly the man's offer of a coffee date.

All five experiments we conducted had the same results: Some men preferred the easy-to-get women, others the women who were hard-to-get (Hatfield et al., 1973). In a recent experiment, researchers (Wright & Contrada, 1986) found that most people prefer potential dates who are moderately selective to those who are extremely selective or extremely nonselective about whom they date.

So if you're interested in attracting someone, playing hard-to-get isn't necessarily the answer. How then should we behave? Should we admit to others that we like them or should we play hard-to-get? The best answer seems to be: Act naturally. It's impossible to predict what others will like. We have seen that, generally, most people are attracted to warm, friendly, and candid types. A few prefer those who are coolly aloof. There's nothing to be gained from *playing* at one role or another, so you might as well speak frankly and act freely. Express your admiration for those you like and your hopes for the relationship, and voice any doubts you have about either one.

Being Assertive   When men are asked how they wish women who are interested in them would act (ask them out, hint that she is interested, or wait for him to ask her out), 30% of men say they wish she would take the initiative and ask them out. Sixty-eight percent say they wish she would hint that she is interested. Only 3% say they prefer her to wait for them to ask her out. Several studies have found that even the most traditional of men are likely to accept if women ask them out. More than 95% of men said that if they were interested in dating a woman, they would gladly accept her proposal (Muehlenhard & McFall, 1981; Muehlenhard & Miller, 1983). Research documents that it is safer to take the direct approach than one might think (Kelley & Rolker-Dolinsky, 1987; Muehlenhard & McFall, 1982). People have, of course, devised time-worn ways of asking others out without risking too much. "I'm having a few friends over on Friday to cram for the exam. Would you like to come?" "We are all going to the movies. Would you like to join us?" "A friend gave me some tickets to the concert. Interested?" If the other says "No," one is protected, and can pretend he or she was merely making a friendly gesture.

Men prefer women to take some initiative. Yet, when women are asked how they would indicate their interest in a man, only 3% say they would ask him out! Sixty-three percent would *hint*. A whopping 35% of women said they would simply wait for him to ask them out. Such passivity is probably not a very good idea (Muehlenhard, Koralewski, Andrews, & Burdick, 1986). Very few men are willing to risk asking out a woman who does not even *hint* that she might be interested (Muehlenhard & Miller, 1986). Men estimated that 62% of the women they asked out for the first time had previously hinted that they would be receptive to an invitation (Muehlenhard et al., 1986).

Thus both men and women, attractive or not, can be expected to do best if they are brave enough to dare to take the initiative. They may risk their pride, but they will not damage their chances for impressing a potential date. Furthermore, they will save a lot of time (see Box 1.3). In fact, many women today are acting on such suggestions. In one study, 90% of college men said that they had been asked out and had accepted the invitation (Kelley, Pilchowicz, & Byrne, 1981).

Direct action might work best, but both men and women seem to feel most comfortable if they first hint at their interest and then watch to see how their tentative overtures are received. About two-thirds of men and women prefer this approach (Muehlenhard et al., 1986). The next question, of course, is: How does one flirt? How can men and women best hint at their romantic interest in others? Charlene Muehlenhard and her colleagues (1986) asked college women to try out various techniques. The following techniques were especially effective (see Table 1.3, p. 28). Both men and women judged women who used these techniques to be unusually attractive. They also sent the message: She was interested. (We might expect such techniques to work for men as well.)

Psychologists also give us some hints as to the best place to look for dates and mates—depending on how good-looking, personable, intelligent, and kind we are. Bernard Murstein (1970) points out that settings can be characterized by how "closed" or "open" they are. In open fields, people can approach anyone they wish. (Singles' bars, mixers, museum tours, and large social gatherings are examples of open fields.) Beautiful women and handsome men are likely to find romantic partners in open fields. In closed fields, the same people are forced to interact day after day. (Language classes, work, or hiking tours to Cornwall and Dorset are examples of closed fields.) In closed fields, people get to know one another well. People who have personality, intelligence, and kindness to offer profit from the chance to reveal their personalities to others in closed fields.

For some people, such direct approaches to meeting people work. But for most people, an indirect approach is easier and more effective.

I don't think you can look for love. All you can do is get yourself in a situation where you don't discourage something that may be rather nice.
—Popular singer Linda Ronstadt

The Indirect Approach   Many men and women are uncomfortable about asking others out. Researchers (Marwell, McKinney, Sprecher, DeLamater, & Smith, 1982) have asked college students if there is someone they would like to get to know and perhaps date. Almost all answer "Yes." What stops them? Sometimes

Box 1.3   THE TELEPHONE AS AN INSTRUMENT OF SELF-TORTURE

In *How to Make Yourself Miserable,* humorists Dan Greenburg and Marcia Jacobs (1966) described lovesick women's anguish at waiting for the telephone to ring.

Let's say you are the young lady in this case. How can you make yourself completely miserable while you wait for the young man's call, and perhaps even discourage him from asking you out once he *does* call?

Begin by assuming that if the young man *is* going to call you, it will be on the day after the party, some time after work. *But* (and this is your first anxiety) *does he know how late you work?*

He does not. Suppose he calls you shortly after 5:00 P.M. and then again at about 5:30, and he doesn't find you in either time because you work till 5:30 and don't get home till 6:00. *Will he try again at 6:00? . . . .*

That is the next step, then: *You must take off the entire afternoon and wait for his call.* Station yourself right next to the telephone and don't leave it for a second, not even to go to the bathroom. Needless to say, by the end of the evening he will not have called. . . .

Maybe he just asked you for your number so he could get away from you gracefully. Not a bad little anxiety. But here's a better one:

Maybe he has been trying to call you all night and the phone just hasn't rung because it's out of order. You must find out if this is true. Pick up the phone—and don't be disappointed when you hear the dial tone. Just because you hear a dial tone doesn't mean your phone is working. You must conduct a more conclusive test.

Call a girlfriend. When she answers say, "Don't ask me to explain, just call me right back," then hang up. Don't be dismayed when she calls you right back. At least you now know the phone is working.

This is the moment for your next anxiety: *Maybe he was trying to call you while you were checking to see if the phone was working and he got a busy signal.*

Enough anxieties for a single night. Go to bed.

Source: Greenburg & Jacobs, 1966, pp. 81–85.

men and women are thwarted by external barriers. ("I have never been alone with her." "He is going steady with someone else.") Usually, however, people admit they are paralyzed by internal barriers. ("I am too shy to approach him." "I don't think she would be interested in me." "I don't want to make a fool of myself.")

Researchers find that, shy or not, the best way to find a lover is to look for a friend. Most people are introduced to their dates, lovers, and mates by friends

Table 1.3

Verbal cues

1. She compliments him.
2. She is helpful.
3. She keeps talking rather than ending the conversation quickly.
4. If he asks her out and she has to refuse because she is busy, she adds something like, "Could we put it off until some other time?"
5. She does not talk as if she is so busy she has no time to date.
6. She asks him questions about himself.
7. If he asks for her phone number, she gives it to him.
8. If there is a short lull in the conversation, she fills in the void.
9. She mentions an activity that they could do together, such as saying there is a movie she'd like to see. She does not specifically mention their doing the activity together, but that is left as a possibility.
10. When he is talking she back-channels—that is, says a few words to show she is listening ("Umm hmm" or "Yeah").
11. She engages in small talk after, rather than before, she asks for a favor. If she talks to him and then asks for the favor, it appears her motive was to ask for the favor; if he has already agreed to do the favor, it appears her motive was to talk to him.
12. If he mentions where he will be at a future time, she says she might see him there.
13. She makes it clear she has noticed him in the past (e.g., she noticed he was absent from class).
14. If he asks a question, she gives more than the shortest possible answer.
15. She is responsive to what he says.
16. She starts a conversation with him rather than remaining silent.

Nonverbal cues

1. Eye contact: She catches his eye now and then.
2. Smiling: She smiles now and then.
3. Leaning: She leans toward him slightly.
4. Distance: She stands fairly close to him.
5. Touching: She may touch his arm or shoulder briefly now and then.
6. Catching his eye while laughing at someone else's humor. If the professor makes a joke, she might catch his eye as she laughs.
7. Attentiveness. She pays close attention to him. Her attention doesn't wander to those strolling by.
8. Using animated speech. She speaks quickly, accentuating her words with varied facial expressions and body movements.

Source: Muehlenhard et al., 1986, pp. 407, 413.

(Parks & Eggert, 1991). In one study, Gerald Marwell and his Wisconsin students (1982) tried to find out how couples actually get together. They asked a random sample of college students how they had met their last date or mate. Who, if anyone, introduced them? Where did they meet? Often, a relative, good friend, or employer brought the two together. They introduced 33% of the men and 43% of the women to their most recent dates. The rest of the time, men and women initiated the meetings themselves or they just met by "happenstance." But quite

HOW TO MEET MEN

Many women write to me and ask, "Nicole, how can I meet men?" Most of these poor women are looking in the wrong place. I ask them to remember the words of Willie Sutton. When asked why he robbed banks, he replied, "Because that's where the money is." My advice to women who want to meet men is: *Go Where the Men are!*

often even these college couples met at parties their friends were giving, when they were studying with friends, and so forth.

Where did most college couples meet? Singles usually meet at parties, social gatherings, work, or bars (Knox & Wilson, 1981; Simenauer & Carroll, 1982). For a list of the settings in which college couples met in the previous study (Marwell et al., 1982), see Table 1.4. In another study (Simenauer & Carroll, 1982) researchers interviewed 3000 men and women between the ages of 20 and 55 from 36 states. They asked: "Where do you meet most of the men/women you date?" The most common reply was "through friends." Thirty-three percent of the men and 36% of the women met their dates this way.

Why are introductions so important? Gerald Marwell and his colleagues (1982) point out:

> The friend has the right to interact with each of the two partners and he/she essentially vouches for the fact that the other person is "all right." The friend also makes it improbable that the other person will behave in a rudely rejecting manner, and may also imply with the introduction that the two partners are both "available" and appropriate for one another. (pp. 5–6)

In the research we described earlier (Cutrona, 1982), researchers found that students who assumed that the only way to end their loneliness was to find a boyfriend or a girlfriend usually failed in their attempts; they were still lonely after a year. Those who focused on finding friends were usually successful and, in consequence, were far happier at the end of the year.

In our clinical practice, when we are working with lonely clients, we usually recommend the following strategy:

1. People who long for an active social life should *not* begin by trying to find the perfect mate. If they follow that approach they are likely to make a commitment to the first promising person who comes along, invest a great deal of exclusive time in the relationship, only to find out months or years later that the person who once seemed so perfect turns out to have fatal flaws.

2. Instead, people do far better if they concentrate at first on making a few friends. They should go out of their way to say hello and to chat with the men and women they bump into at school, at work, or while participating in daily activities. They should make an effort to meet the most appealing and interesting men *and*

Table 1.4   WHERE DO MOST COLLEGE COUPLES MEET?

Meeting location	Men	Women
Party in apartment, dorm, or fraternity/sorority	28%	30%
Classes	25	16
Bar or restaurant	15	21
Dorm (but not a party)	23	7
Other public university location (cafeterias, library)	3	13
Other (sports, work)	7	13

Source: Hatfield & Sprecher, 1986b, p. 133.

women in their classes, dance groups, computer workshops, car repair sessions, or Sierra Club hikes. They needn't worry about the age, or marital status, or attractiveness of these acquaintances. What they are looking for are casual friends. They should ask those acquaintances they like best to lunches, walks, or the movies. Eventually, people are bound to settle in with a best friend or two.

3. Once people have established a network of friends, it is a short and easy step to begin to find suitable dates. People can ask their friends to introduce them to potential dates their friends think they might like. (Instead of one person searching for possible dates, now several matchmakers are involved in the project.) When in doubt about whether to date someone or not, the best strategy is to go out. Usually, it takes only a few shared interests to make a *date* interesting. Imagine that, potentially, men and women can "fit" one another on 100 traits. To make a serious love affair or marriage go, couples probably have to match on, say, 85 or 90 of those traits. (In close relationships, little differences can cause big problems.) If casual dates fit on just a trait or two they can probably still have a fine time together now and then. Some dates might share your interest in Woody Allen movies . . . and nothing else. Another might be a great dinner date and serious conversationalist; still another might be just right for spur-of-the-moment sailing trips. Another date, impossible one-to-one, may sparkle at parties. The criterion for a casual date is simply: "Would I rather be alone tonight, or with my friend for an hour or two?" The distance between what is required for an enjoyable date and what it takes to make a successful, serious relationship succeed is gargantuan.

When we suggest this strategy, men and women sometimes hesitate. Some men, for example, worry that women will think they are "cads" if they date several women at the same time; or that women will fall in love and pressure them for a commitment. Of course, if men pretend to be interested in marriage when they are not, they can expect trouble. But, we reassure men and women that if they practice "truth in advertising," if they make it clear that they plan to date several people for quite some time, most people will accept their reservations. A few will not, but at least they will know they are morally in the right if they have been clear about their intentions. Some women are hesitant to date so casually, because they are afraid to say "No" to sexual overtures. They worry that they might hurt men's feelings. They worry that men may get angry and yell at them. We remind such women that they routinely go out with their women friends; those women don't require something "extra" to make it worth their while to go out. Most men enjoy such casual friendships too. Although, of course, everyone is entitled to say "No" to sex, anytime, a few women find it easier to tell men "I never get involved this early on" if they pay their own way. Many men feel obligated to make a pass at women but a surprising number of men are relieved when women say "No," especially in this day of AIDS. Men, too, worry that their arms are too scrawny, their stomachs too big, or that they will have trouble performing. Thus it is usually fairly easy for women to slow things down so everyone can get acquainted. If all a man is interested in is sex, most women would probably not be interested in him anyway; better to find out early.

4. Once men and women have dated a variety of people, they can make a fairly sensible choice of someone who might be special. Now they can risk "seri-

ous" dating. Most experienced people, however, have been burned many times by love. They got serious with someone who was, like most Americans, expert at beginnings only to discover that by the middle of the relationship, things were not going so well. Thus they have learned to protect themselves. Even if their serious relationship is going well, they continue to cultivate men and women friends. They continue working toward stimulating careers. They insist on pursuing personally pleasurable interests, seeing old friends—whether or not their partners share those activities and friendships. With this strategy, most men and women tend to end up with lovers they really care about, a solid network of good friends, and a serious career.

Readers interested in more information about meeting dates or mates or social skills training may consult a variety of primers: See, for example, Philip Zimbardo's (1977) *Shyness* text or the book by Eileen Gambrill and Cheryl Richey (1985), *Taking Charge of Your Social Life.*

CONCLUSION

In this chapter, we have reviewed the characteristics that make people appealing dates and mates and the strategies that help them meet suitable partners. The reader may notice that the tone of this chapter, although it deals with the beginnings of love, is not superheated. No one will mistake our writing for that of Barbara Cartland or Danielle Steele.

This is no accident. Modern culture is filled with the exaggerated romanticism of pop music, of steamy romance novels, and of thousands of Hollywood movies guilty of promoting a false view of love. In so doing (in the interests of making money), they have misled the public and created wild expectations about romance that bear little relation to reality. In movies and songs, people *"fall* in love," knowing they have found their soulmate "at first sight." Their first sexual encounter sets off fireworks, earthquakes, storms—all accompanied by wild waves pounding on the shore. Happily Ever After is quickly and easily earned—no differently from fairy tales. In the Hollywood version there is no room for intelligence, experienced observation, or common sense in romance—let alone the distinction between passionate love and companionate love.

The decisions about love are no less important in one's life than those about choosing a career, handling money, or deciding where to live. Yet those latter decisions are rarely made (wisely, at least) on pure impulse and abandon; people gather knowledge and use their heads. We believe people should be as intelligent about love decisions as anything else in life, and we hope to show that considerable knowledge is available on the subject. Too many people are stupid about love, treating the phenomenon as though it were all a matter of magic and hormones. Small wonder that people continue to make unhappy decisions.

Still, there is and should be passion when it comes to love; it's a big part of the fun. In the next chapter we plunge into those wonderful but treacherous waters as we examine more passionate relationships.

Chapter
2

Passionate Love

INTRODUCTION

Passionate love is not an invention of the modern world. Expressions of passion have a long and nearly universal history. Literature and life abound in legendary lovers caught up in a sea of passion and violence. The couples are legion: Odysseus and Penelope, Orpheus and Eurydice, Maria and Tony (in *West Side Story*), Daphnis and Chloe, Dido and Aeneas, Abelard and Eloise, Dante and Beatrice, Romeo and Juliet, and, of course, Elizabeth and Richard. . . . These love affairs have assumed such a central place in Western mythology that it becomes difficult to know which are mythical, which historical. And when historical, how much is "true"?

Such a lineage suggests, when we deal with contemporary passion, that nothing much has changed; that we describe the universal and eternal when we wallow in the tales of Taylor and Burton or Edward and Mrs. Simpson. Historical research makes it clear, however, that nothing could be further from the truth. As with everything else connected with love, sex, women's place, family, child rearing, and emotions, the world has ascribed continually changing meanings and purposes to all these activities and happenstances, and that change will continue to be the norm. If so, all the more do we need perspective.

When one gazes at the stories of the great lovers of the past, it is worth noting that nothing worked out well in the end. The romances did not culminate in marriage and happy little families—let alone great sex. They were invariably unrequited, unconsummated, or ended in painful death and profound tragedy.

One major reason for this is that no society in the West before 1700 ever equated *le grand passion* with marriage or even with sex. This equation plays a large and often misleading part in the ways we think about passionate love today. In many non-Western societies, particularly in Asia, there continue to this day to be echoes of Andreas Capellanus' (1174/1941) statement in the twelfth century, in *The Art of Courtly Love:*

> Everybody knows that love can have no place between husband and wife.... For what is love but an inordinate desire to receive passionately a furtive and hidden embrace? But what embrace between husband and wife can be furtive, I ask you, since they may be said to belong to each other and may satisfy all of each other's desires without fear that anybody will object? (p. 100)

And he wasn't even talking about passionate love—just love. To make himself clear, he wrote in the same work: "We declare and we hold as firmly established that love cannot exert its powers between two people who are married to each other" (p. 106).

As late as 1540, Alessandro Piccolomini wrote peremptorily, reflecting common assumptions four centuries later, after the Renaissance, that "love is a reciprocity of soul and has a different end and obeys different laws from marriage. Hence one should not take the loved one to wife" (Hunt, 1959, p. 206). Though Piccolomini began, along with his society, to change his mind before he died, one need only to look to the great societies of Asia—China, Japan, and India (lands of the arranged marriage)—to see remnants of these attitudes alive and well (though winds of change blow worldwide these days) even as we approach the end of the twentieth century.

It is a rigid principle of Eastern life that the stability of the family and the maintenance of the social order always come before the happiness of the individual. A Chinese woman asserted: "Marriage is not a relation for personal pleasure, but a contract involving the ancestors, the descendants, and the property" (Mace & Mace, 1980, p. 134).

Yet the feeling of passionate love, the desire for union, seems wired into our brains. Cultures alarmed by these basic feelings therefore suppress them—sometimes fiercely. The response of many lovers to such suppression, well-known in Western history as well, has been suicide. Love suicides in Japan have been an institution since the end of the seventeenth century. In plays and stories, the suicide pacts were dramatized with sensational effect—the journey together to the chosen place, the leaving behind forever of familiar scenes, the agonizing mental conflicts, the last tender farewells. In Japanese thought suicide is not ignoble. It is the final vindication of what a person believes. When it is glorified by frustrated love, it becomes a sublime tragedy (Mace & Mace, 1980).

In earlier times, the actual practice of the lovesick couple was to throw themselves into the well of the parents who had refused to sanction the marriage. This was particularly true in China. In the modern era, the lovers tie themselves together and throw themselves in front of a train. Jumping off a cliff has always been a popular method. On some railroad routes, any young couples purchasing one-way tickets might be under suspicion. At one time the taking of rat poison was in fashion and drugstores were warned not to sell to young couples (Mace & Mace, 1980).

The defiance of young lovers did not always take such extreme forms. In countries where the social system was less rigid than Japan, China, or India—Burma and Thailand, for example—elopement was common, presenting parents with a *fait accompli* they could not reverse.

These tales of forbidden romance may seem ridiculous, if not tragic, to the young individualistic American and Frenchman today. However, in Western civilization, passion and sexuality have been severely restricted throughout most of human history—particularly during the Christian era. For example, for 1500 years—from the earliest days of the Roman Catholic Church to the sixteenth century Protestant Reformation and Catholic Counter-Reformation—the Church proclaimed sex (even marital sex!) to be a heinous sin, punishable by eternal damnation. Only recently has Western culture accepted and, yes, promoted the notion that passionate love can and should be transmuted into sex, marriage, and family. It is a new idea, and not an unproblematic one at that. Romeo and Juliet, Ophelia and Hamlet, Abelard and Héloïse did not make love, get married, have two children, and live happily ever after. Juliet died of poison. Romeo killed himself. Ophelia went crazy and died. Hamlet was felled by a poisoned sword-point. Peter Abelard (a "real" person) was castrated and his beloved Héloïse ended up in a nunnery. The Hollywood happy-ending outcome would have seemed absurd to our brothers and sisters of the preindustrial past. (The "happy endings" in some of Shakespeare's comedies are often seen as signs of the playwright's "modern sensibility," that of a man far ahead of his times.) The concept of romantic, marital bliss is an idea that could, quite conceivably, seem equally silly in the future. As we examine the nature of the powerful and universal emotion of passionate love, we need to recognize how changeable is its cultural and temporal meaning. Let us begin then with a *contemporary* love story.

On March 30, 1981, less than two hours before John W. Hinckley, Jr., shot President Reagan, Hinckley scrawled a final plea to the actress, Jodie Foster, with whom he had been obsessed for over two years (*The New Yorker*, 1984, pp. 46–48).

Dear Jodie.
    There is a definite possibility that I will be killed in my attempt to get Reagan. It is for this very reason I am writing you this letter now.
    As you well know by now I love you very much. Over the past seven months I've left you dozens of poems, letters and love messages in the faint hope that you could develop an interest in me. Although we talked on the phone a couple of times I never had the nerve to simply approach you and introduce myself. Besides my shyness, I honestly did not wish to bother you with my constant presence. I know the many messages left at your door and in your mailbox were a nuisance, but I felt that it was the most painless way for me to express my love for you. . . .

Jodie, I would abandon this idea of getting Reagan in a second if I could only win your heart and live out the rest of my life with you, whether it be in total obscurity or whatever.

I will admit to you that the reason I'm going ahead with this attempt now is because I just cannot wait any longer to impress you. I've got to do something now to make you understand, in no uncertain terms, that I am doing all of this for your sake! By sacrificing my freedom and possibly my life, I hope to change your mind about me. This letter is being written only an hour before I leave for the Hilton Hotel. Jodie, I'm asking to please look into your heart and at least give me the chance, with this historical deed, to gain your respect and love.

I love you forever.

John Hinckley

In F.B.I. questioning after the attempted assassination, Foster denied that she had ever spoken to or met John Hinckley.

Love is the strange bewilderment which overtakes one person on account of another person.

—*James Thurber and E. B. White*

Definitions

In Chapter 1, we defined passionate love as:

A state of intense longing for union with another. Passionate love is a complex functional whole including appraisals or appreciations, subjective feelings, expressions, patterned physiological processes, action tendencies, and instrumental behaviors. Reciprocated love (union with the other) is associated with fulfillment and ecstasy; unrequited love (separation) with emptiness, anxiety, or despair.

Other theorists have labeled this experience puppy love, a crush, fatal attraction, lovesickness, obsessive love, infatuation, or being-in-love. This chapter reviews what psychologists have learned about this fiery, but generally short-lived, emotion.

THE EVOLUTIONARY SOIL OF PASSIONATE LOVE

The Triune Brain

In the 1940s, Paul MacLean (1986) had a brilliant insight. He realized that in the course of evolution humans ended up with a mind/brain that is a "triune structure." In a sense, the brain consists of three different types of brains with different anatomical structures and chemical processes, layered one upon the other. The oldest brain is basically reptilian. The second, the neomammalian brain, is inherited from the early mammals, and the third, the late mammalian/early primate brain, from the late mammals and early primates. In their primer, Robert Ornstein and Richard Thompson (1984) provide a simple description of this layering process (see Box 2.1).

MacLean (1986) points out that the reptilian brain was primarily concerned

Box 2.1 **THE AMAZING BRAIN**

The brain is like an old ramshackle house that has been added on to over the years in a rather disorganized fashion (p. 3).

THE REPTILIAN BRAIN

The brain stem is the oldest part of the brain. It evolved more than 500 million years ago. Because it resembles the entire brain of a reptile, it is often referred to as the reptilian brain. It determines general level of alertness and warns the organism of important incoming information, as well as handling the basic bodily functions necessary for survival—breathing and heart rate (p. 4).

The cerebellum is attached to the rear of the brain stem. It automatically adjusts posture and coordinates muscular movements. Memories for simple learned responses are stored there.

THE MAMMALIAN BRAIN

The next structure on the totem pole, say the authors, is the limbic system. It evolved sometime between 200 and 300 million years ago. The limbic system is highly developed in mammals; thus this "add on" is called the mammalian brain. This brain is strongly involved in the emotional reactions—joy, love, fear, anger and sadness—that have to do with survival.

THE PRIMATE BRAIN

The largest part of the human brain is the cerebrum. It is divided into two halves, or hemispheres, each of which controls its opposite half of the body. The hemispheres are connected by a band of some 300 million nerve cell fibers called the corpus callosum. Covering each hemisphere is a one-eighth-inch thick, intricately folded layer of nerve cells called the cortex. The cortex first appeared in our ancestors about 200 million years ago, and it is what makes us uniquely human. Because of it, we are able to organize, remember, communicate, understand, appreciate, and create (p. 12).

Source: Ornstein & Thompson, 1984, pp. 3–12.

with the preservation of the self and the species. Its primitive structures were designed to guide the reptile in the processes required for obtaining food and mates (search, angry attacks, self-defense, and feeding or sexual activity). By the neomammalian brain, he continued, three new patterns of behavior had evolved. These were primarily designed to facilitate mother–child relationships. Such emotions as ecstasy, desire and affection, fear, anger, dejection, and depression all derive from activities in the limbic system. Not until the neocortex evolved in the late mammalian/primate period did symbolic or verbal information become important in shaping primate emotional experience or expression.

Love in Primates

Leonard Rosenblum (Rosenblum, 1985; Rosenblum & Plimpton, 1981) points out that even some primates (such as pigtail macaque monkeys) seem to experience a primitive form of passionate love. In some species, infant primates are prewired to cling to their mothers. Separation can be mortally dangerous. If mother and infant are separated, the infant is unlikely to find a substitute caretaker. To ensure survival, therefore, the "desire for union" is necessarily wired into primates. As long as mother and child are locked in close proximity, all goes well. Should a brief separation occur, the infant will quickly become desperate. He will begin frantically to search for his mother. If she returns, the infant will be joyous, alternately clinging to its mother and bounding about with great excitement. If his mother does not return, and his frenetic efforts to find her fail, he will eventually abandon all hope of contact, whereupon despair and probable death will follow. The experience Rosenblum describes, with its alternating lows and highs, certainly sounds much like passionate love's "desire for union." Fervent attachments seem not to be unique to humans.

Harry and Margaret Harlow (Harlow, 1973, 1975; Harlow, Harlow, & Suomi, 1971) also studied the development of love in monkeys. Early theorists had assumed that newborns become attached to their mothers and fathers because their presence is associated with feeding. (Food is, after all, the theorists reasoned, a primary reinforcer; snuggling is "merely" a secondary reinforcer.) The Harlows soon discovered that newborns care more about contact comfort than food! They tested this startling hypothesis in a classic experiment. First, they separated monkey mothers and infants. They reared infants in a cage containing two kinds of artificial "mothers." One surrogate mother possessed a "breast." (A bottle of milk was simply inserted in a cold wire mesh tube.) This wire mother provided food, but she was cold and hard. The other "mother" could not provide any food, but she was warm and soft; the monkey could cling to her. (This second wire cylinder was warmed, wrapped with foam rubber, and covered with terry cloth.) If traditional theorists were right, and infants became attached to mothers only because they happened to provide food, infants should have become most attached to the milk-providing wire "mother." But they did not. Monkeys might be willing to suck from the wire mother, but they certainly didn't want to spend their free time with her. They spent almost all their time tightly clinging to the warm, soft, cuddly mother; rubbing against her.

When monkeys were insecure or frightened, it was the terry cloth mother they ran back to for security. In one experiment, the researchers put a mechanical toy bear, which banged loudly on a drum, in the cage. The frightened infants quickly scrambled to their cloth mothers. What if *only* the wire mother was in the cage? Even then the infants would not turn to the icy mother; they simply cried and ran aimlessly around the cage; sometimes they froze in terror. Only the warm, soft, terry cloth mother could comfort them.

Harlow and his colleagues (1971) found that monkeys normally follow a predictable sequence in developing attachments. At first, newborns simply cling to anyone. Within a few weeks, however, they become deeply attached to their mothers; they wish to cling only to them. As the infants mature, however, eventually they become less interested in their mothers and more attached to their peers. They learn to play. Both their initial attachments to their mothers and these early friendships are important to their later ability to develop sexual relationships. For example, if monkeys were raised in isolation, without mothers or playmates, at first they seemed to thrive. At puberty, however, it became clear that they had serious emotional and social problems. Adult female monkeys seemed unwilling and unable to respond to males' sexual overtures. Only 4 monkeys out of 18 were able to conceive. (The others had to be artificially inseminated.) When the isolated monkeys did conceive, they were terrible mothers. Some were merely indifferent. Most were actively rejecting; they roughly pushed their newborns away. In spite of this ill-treatment, most newborns persisted in their attempts to establish a bond with their mothers. Sometimes these determined infants succeeded. They taught their mothers how to mother. In subsequent pregnancies, some of the deprived mothers became more skilled at nurturing their offspring.

Love in Children

Mary Ainsworth (1989) and John Bowlby (1969, 1973, 1980), who were well grounded in evolutionary theory, studied the process of attachment, separation, and loss in children. They found that, at certain stages in their development, infants and toddlers react to separation in the same way as did their primate ancestors. Both seemed to follow the same ancient programming.

The Theory: The Process of Attachment   Infants normally progress through four developmental phases during their first year of life (Cohen, 1976). (1) During the first few months of life, infants smile, gurgle, and snuggle into almost anyone. Anyone can provide contact comfort. (2) At about three months of age, the infants begin to notice that their mother is someone special; they respond to her with special interest. (3) At about six to nine months, infants become deeply attached to their mothers. They smile, jabber, and stretch out their arms to her; if they are separated, they protest. No one else will do. They are frightened of strangers and reject their attempts to comfort them. (4) After about 9 to 12 months, toddlers slowly begin to take an interest in a wider circle of people.

Of course, parents and infants differ in skills and temperament. Mary Ainsworth (1989; Ainsworth, Blehar, Waters, & Wall, 1978) found that mothers and children may form different kinds of attachments. Some infants are *securely attached* to their mothers. Early on, the infants cling to their mothers. As toddlers mature, they become more adventuresome. They begin to go off and explore the world. The mother remains a "safe harbor," but gradually, th infants become more independent. Other infants possess an *anxious/ambivalent* attachment to their mothers. Early on, their mothers may have been unpredictable. Sometimes they overprotected (even smothered) their infants; sometimes they ignored them. Since these infants have learned they cannot count on their mothers, they tend to be anxious and uncertain in their interactions with her. They themselves may alternately cling or ignore her. Of course, some anxious/avoidant infants were simply born with a fearful temperament. Finally, some infants develop an *avoidant* attachment with their mothers. Perhaps their mothers generally ignored them.

Perhaps the infants were simply lacking whatever it takes to form close relationships with *anyone*. In any case, such infants are unemotional and unresponsive.

Separation and Despair   Psychoanalyst John Bowlby (1969, 1973, 1980) noted the way the desire for security and the desire for freedom alternate in a small child.

> James Anderson describes watching two-year-olds whilst their mothers sit quietly on a seat in a London park. Slipping free from the mother, a two-year-old would typically move away from her in short bursts punctuated by halts. Then, after a more prolonged halt, he would return to her—usually in faster and longer bursts. Once returned, however, he would proceed again on another foray, only to return once more. It was [as] though he were tied to his mother by some invisible elastic that stretches so far and then brings him back to base. (1973, pp. 44–45)

In his research, Bowlby has found that when a child's mother is around, he's not very interested in her. He looks at her, sees that everything is all right, and sallies forth. Now and then he sneaks a quick glance to make sure she's still there or to find out whether she still approves of what he is doing, but then he is off again. Should his mother disappear for a moment, it's a different story. The child becomes very distressed and agitated. He devotes all his energy to searching for her. New adventures lose all allure. Of course, once she returns, he's off again. Should she disappear for good, he would sink into a deep despair.

Current Research   How early are children capable of falling passionately in love? The answer is: probably very early. In 1886, Sanford Bell (1902) interviewed 1,700 Indiana teachers and observed 800 children. By the end of the study, he had assembled 2,500 case reports of children who experienced intense passionate love. Bell concluded that children could experience "sex-love" as early as $3\frac{1}{2}$ years of age. From 3 to 8 years of age, the passionate longings of children could be read in word and in deed. Children in love hugged, kissed, and sat close to one another. And in time-honored fashion, they scuffled with each other as well. They shyly confessed their love to their beloved. They talked about each other with their friends. They sought each other out; grieved when they were separated; gave gifts of love; willingly sacrificed for the other; were jealous, and so forth (p. 330). Children were most likely to admit to being in love either between 4 and 8 or between 12 and 15 years of age. They were reluctant to admit to feeling "sex-love" from ages 8 to 12.

One hundred years elapsed before researchers returned to the sensitive subject of passionate love in children. Elaine Hatfield and her students (Hatfield et al., 1988) developed the *Childhood Love Scale (CLS)*, a children's version of the *Passionate Love Scale (PLS)*, which we described in Chapter 1. Each item on the PLS was translated into language so simple and so concrete that children could understand it. For example "I want _____ to know me—my thoughts, my fears, and my hopes" became "I want _____ to know me—what I am thinking, what scares me, what I am wishing for." "I possess a powerful attraction for _____" became "When _____ is around I really want to touch him (her) and be touched."

Hatfield and her students interviewed more than 200 boys and girls, who ranged in age from 4 to 18, about their romantic feelings. Their results made it clear that Bell was right—even very young children are capable of passionate love. Figure 2.1 depicts how their passions changed as they grew up. Similar to Bell's work, Hatfield and her students found that from ages 4 to 7, children reported strong passionate feelings. Boys seemed to go through a shy period from 8 to 12 years of age, when they were likely to deny they ever had such feelings. Their fervent emotions returned with full intensity during the teenage years (13 to 18).

The authors observed that it was touching to interview children in love. The kids were often very shy. They blushed and hid behind their hands. One 5-year-old girl talked about a boy she loved at the preschool she had once attended. When asked: "If I could, when I grow up I'd like to marry _____," she began to cry. "I will never see Todd again," she said woefully. Indeed, she may not, since her parents had no inkling of how deeply she felt. Subsequent research has demonstrated that anxious children who are under stress are particularly prone to fall passionately in love (Hatfield, Brinton, & Cornelius, 1989).

Passionate love becomes very powerful when children enter puberty. Perhaps this is because teenagers experience the return of old separation anxieties during the period. Perhaps they are under unusual stress as they go through the agonies of adolescence. Neurophysiologists remind us that passionate love may also be fueled by pubescent sexual and hormonal changes (Gadpaille, 1975; Money, 1980). Puberty and sexual maturity may well bring a new *depth* to passion (Rabehl, Ridge, & Berscheid, 1992).

People who are not in love themselves feel that a clever man ought to be unhappy only about such persons as are worthwhile. This is rather like being astonished that anyone should condescend to die of cholera at the bidding of so insignificant a creature as the common bacillus.

—*Marcel Proust*

LOVE IN ADULTS

Psychologists have argued that childhood experiences can shape one's passionate experiences in adulthood. Recently, Philip Shaver and Cindy Hazan (1988) proposed that romantic love should be conceived of as a form of attachment. Children's early patterns of attachment should influence their adult attachments. For example, we have observed that children are likely to become *securely attached* to their mothers if they are allowed to be both affectionate *and* independent. The authors point out that such children should mature into secure adults who are comfortable with intimacy and are able to trust and depend on those they care for. Children may become *anxious/ambivalent* if they have learned to be clingy and dependent, or fearful of being smothered and restrained, or both. Such children should become anxious/ambivalent adults who fall in love easily, who seek extreme levels of closeness and are terrified that they will be abandoned. Their love affairs are likely to be short-lived. The *avoidant* child (who has been abandoned

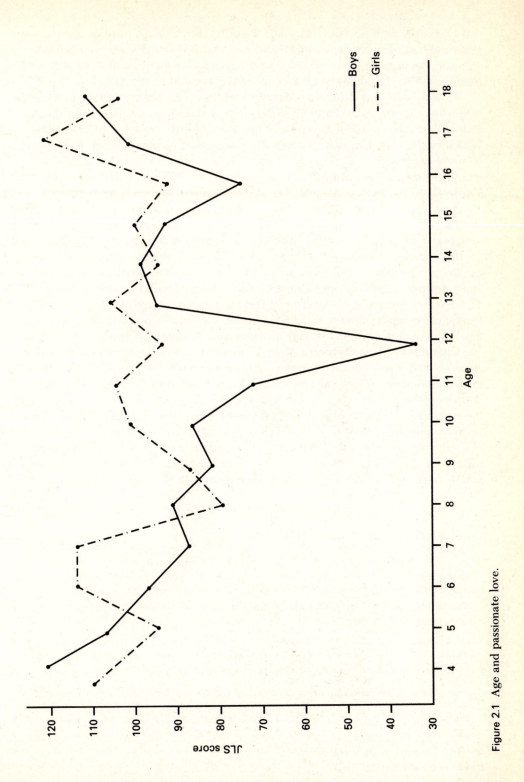

Figure 2.1 Age and passionate love.

early on) may well become an avoidant adult who is uncomfortable getting too close and has difficulty depending on others. The authors have amassed considerable support in favor of the notion that the lessons we learn as children may well be reflected in the romantic choices we make as adults.

How would you categorize yourself? Hazan and Shaver (1987) measured men's and women's attachment styles by a single self-report item (see Table 2.1). Respondents were asked to endorse one of three descriptions of themselves. Which one sounds like you? (Generally, researchers classify 62% of children as securely attached, 15% as anxious/ambivalent, and 23% as avoidant. When a wide-ranging sample of adults rated themselves, 56% rated themselves as securely attached, 19% percent as anxious/ambivalent, and 25% as avoidant.)

Kim Bartholomew (1990) proposed that people's adult attachment styles should fall into one of four patterns, depending on their self-image (positive or negative) and their image of the other person (positive or negative). (1) Men and women who have a positive self-image and a positive image of others should be capable of becoming *securely attached* to others. (2) Those with low self-esteem and a positive regard for others should be *preoccupied* with intimate relations. (3) Those who have a negative self-image and a negative image of others should be *fearful* of becoming close to others. (4) Those who have a positive self-image and a negative image of others should be *dismissing* or *detached* from others.

Carl Hindy, J. C. Schwarz, and A. Brodsky (1989) tested the notion that children who receive inconsistent love and affection will be "at risk" in their later love relationships. They gave men and women a battery of tests designed to determine the stability of their childhoods. How stormy was the marriage between their parents? Did their parents get a divorce? Then they asked them about their own romantic histories. Did they often fall passionately in love? Or did they go out of their way to avoid entanglements? How jealous were they? When their love affairs fell apart, did they sink into deep depression? They found that young men and women whose parents had been inconsistent in their love and nurturance

Table 2.1 LOVE QUIZ: ATTACHMENT STYLES

Question: Which of the following best describes your feelings?

Secure (56%): I find it relatively easy to get close to others and am comfortable depending on them and having them depend on me. I don't often worry about being abandoned or about someone getting too close to me.

Anxious/ambivalent (19%): I find that others are reluctant to get as close as I would like. I often worry that my partner doesn't really love me or won't want to stay with me. I want to merge completely with another person, and this desire sometimes scares people away.

Avoidant (25%): I am somewhat uncomfortable being close to others; I find it difficult to trust them completely, difficult to allow myself to depend on them. I am nervous when anyone gets too close, and often, love partners want me to be more intimate than I feel comfortable being.

Source: Hazan & Shaver, 1987, p. 515.

were more "addicted" to love *or* more afraid of it than was the case with those who came from more secure backgrounds.

In conclusion: Our evolutionary heritage and childhood attachments provide a rich soil for passionate love.

❖   ❖   ❖

One fifth-century Buddhist poet saw in the common water lily a symbol of transcendence. The lily's roots are bogged in the muck of the earth; yet its stalk bravely pushes up to the clear surface of the pond where it produces creamy blooms of serene beauty. This water lily provides a suitable metaphor for passionate love as well. Its roots may lie in the dependence and insecurities of childhood, but its blooms, though brief, are uncommonly beautiful. In the next two subsections we consider some of the humble roots of passionate love and some of its breathtaking flowers.

Passions usually have their roots in that which is blemished, crippled, incomplete and insecure within us.
> —*Eric Hoffer*

The Roots of Passionate Love

If passionate love is rooted in the earth of childhood attachments, it would seem that certain types of people, caught up in certain types of situations, should be especially vulnerable to the *longeurs* of passionate love. Anything that makes adults feel as helpless and dependent as they were as children, anything that makes them fear separation and loss, should increase their passionate craving to merge with the other. There is some evidence to support these speculations.

To love oneself is the beginning of a lifelong romance.
> —*Oscar Wilde*

Low Self-esteem   Theodor Reik (1949) was one of the first to propose that when self-esteem is threatened, individuals are more likely to fall prey to passionate love. Mary McCarthy (1942) in her novel *The Company She Keeps* offered an example. The heroine Margaret Sargent has been enslaved by love. In therapy, she makes an illuminating discovery:

> Now for the first time she saw her own extremity, saw that it was some failure in self-love that obligated her to snatch blindly at the love of others, hoping to love herself through them, borrowing their feelings, as the moon borrowed light. She herself was a dead planet. (p. 303)

The first actual experiment on passionate love, conducted more than 25 years ago, provided support for Reik's hypothesis. Elaine Hatfield (1965) proposed that when people's self-esteem has been bruised, they should be unusually receptive to the love and affection offered by others. To test this hypothesis, she gave Stanford University and Foothill Junior College women a battery of psychological tests—the *California Personality Inventory*, the *Minnesota Multiphasic Personality Inventory*, and the *Rorschach* test. When the women returned to secure their personality profiles, they were given bogus feedback, designed momentarily to raise, lower, or leave unchanged their self-esteem. If women had been randomly assigned to the low-esteem condition, the analysis stressed their immaturity (e.g., "Although you have adopted certain superficial appearances of maturity to enable you to adjust temporarily to life situations, your basically immature drives remain"). The analysis criticized their weak personalities, antisocial motives, lack of originality and flexibility, and limited capacity for successful leadership. Women were also told that they possessed an incapacity for openness in their dealings with other people, that their feelings of inadequacy in others' presence contributed to this lack of openness, since they undoubtedly felt it was necessary to cover up their weak points in order to gain social acceptance, and that this led them consistently to overestimate many of their own assets.

For those assigned to the high-esteem condition, the report stressed the great maturity and originality of the woman, her probable underestimation of her own attributes, and stated that she presented "one of the most favorable personality structures analyzed by the staff." She was sensitive to peers, possessed enormous personal integrity, and had a free outlook.

Women who had been assigned to the control condition were told that their tests had not yet been scored. Thus they received no feedback.

Then the experimenter left the room to retrieve the women's files. While she was out of the room, a handsome male graduate student entered the room. As he and the female subject awaited the return of the experimenter, they began to chat. The time and conversation stretched out and the graduate student eventually invited the woman to dinner and a movie the next weekend.

In later interviewing, women were asked their first impressions of the graduate student. As predicted, the women whose self-esteem had been threatened were most attracted to the potential romantic partner. The author speculated that there might be two reasons why the low-self-esteem women were so receptive to a potential romantic partner: first, women with high self-esteem (who feel they have much to offer another) may feel that they, in turn, deserve a more attractive, more personable date than do women with low self-regard; second, when women's self-regard is threatened, they probably feel an increased need for the affection and regard of others. Thus an attractive, loving, and accepting man should arouse unusual passion. [Other theorists have also found a link between low self-esteem and passionate love. See Bartholomew & Horowitz (1991) and Jacobs, Berscheid, & Hatfield (1971).]

Of course, although people with low self-esteem may long for relationships, they sometimes end up sabotaging them once they appear (see Box 2.2).

She's all he's got now, and he's all she's got. Is that love? Maybe it is.
—Clifford Irving

Dependency and Insecurity   A number of theorists have observed that people who are dependent and insecure (or who are caught up in affairs that promote such feelings) are especially vulnerable to passionate love. Ellen Berscheid and her associates (Fei & Berscheid, 1977) have argued that passionate love, dependency, and insecurity are tightly linked. When people are passionately in love,

Box 2.2   RELATIONSHIP-DESTROYING MANEUVER 1: THE GREAT LOVE TEST

Humorists Dan Greenburg and Marcia Jacobs (1966 pp. 98–99), in *How to Make Yourself Miserable,* observe that people with low self-esteem usually possess an arsenal of techniques for destroying their budding relationships. For example, they may keep questioning their lover's motivation:

> This maneuver can be used at any stage of a deep relationship, but it seems particularly well suited to the beginning stages of a romance, so we recommend it as your first major stratagem. This maneuver is, of course, based on the "reject-me formula."

Reject-me move #1:

> YOU: "Do you love me?"
> MATE: "Yes, *of course* I love you."

Reject-me move #2:

> YOU: "Do you *really* love me?"
> MATE: "Yes, I really love you."
> YOU: "You really really love me?"
> MATE: "Yes, I really really love you."
> YOU: "You're *sure* you love me—you're absolutely sure?"
> MATE: "Yes, I'm absolutely sure."
> (pause)
> YOU: "Do you know the meaning of the word love?"
> (pause)
> MATE: "I don't know."
> YOU: "Then how can you be so sure you love me?"
> (pause)
> MATE: "I don't know. Perhaps I can't."

Reject-me move #3:

> YOU: "You can't eh? I see. Well, since you can't even be sure you love me, I can't really see much point in our remaining together. Can you?"
> (pause)
> MATE: "I don't know. Perhaps not."
> (pause)
> YOU: "You've been leading up to this for a pretty long time, haven't you?"

they are painfully aware of how dependent they are on those they love; dependency naturally breeds insecurity. In an ingenious study, Ellen Berscheid, William Graziano, Thomas Monson, and Marshall Dermer (1976) found clear evidence in support of these contentions. The authors invited college men and women, who were not currently involved with anyone but who wished to be, to participate in a study of dating relationships. There was one catch, however. In order to participate, students had to agree to turn their dating lives over to the experimenter for five weeks. They were warned that some of them (those in the high exclusiveness condition) would be assigned to date one person for the entire five weeks. Others (those in the low exclusiveness condition) would date that person and a few others. Still others (those in the zero exclusiveness condition) would be assigned to date a variety of people.

Finally, some of the participants had a chance to get acquainted with one of their dates. (They had a chance to watch him or her take part in a taped discussion of "dating problems on campus.") Sometimes, of course, they knew the date was the only person they would be dating; sometimes he or she was just one of many. In the control conditions, people knew they would not be dating anyone participating in the videotaped conversation. After viewing the tape, participants were asked their first impressions of the discussants.

Students liked the discussants far more when they expected to date them later than when they did not. Furthermore, the more dependent students were on potential dates (i.e., those in the high exclusiveness group compared to those in the low and zero exclusiveness groups), the more they liked them.

An absence, the decline of a dinner invitation, an unintentional coldness, can accomplish more than all the cosmetics and beautiful dresses in the world.
                                                                    —*Marcel Proust*

Anxiety   Numerous theorists beginning with Sigmund Freud (1953) have proposed that passionate love is fueled by anxiety and fear (Carlson, & Hatfield, 1992; Hatfield, 1971a,b; Hatfield & Rapson, 1987b). This makes sense; passionate love and anxiety are closely related both neuroanatomically and chemically (Kaplan, 1979; Liebowitz, 1983).

Researchers have demonstrated that anxious individuals are especially prone to seek passionate love relationships (Peele, 1975; Solomon & Corbit, 1974). In a series of studies, Elaine Hatfield and her students (1989), for example, found that adolescents who were either momentarily or habitually anxious were especially vulnerable to passionate love. In one study, 41 boys and girls from 12 to 14 years of age, of Caucasian, Chinese, Japanese, Korean, and mixed ancestry, were asked to complete the *Child Anxiety Scale (CAS)*, which measures how anxious teenagers are generally. (The CAS includes questions such as "Are you a good or bad child?" "Are you happy or sad?") Later, these same children completed the *Juvenile Love Scale*, a child's version of the *Passionate Love Scale*, which was described in Chapter 1. Children who were habitually anxious were most likely to have experienced passionate love. In a second study, 64 adolescent boys and girls, ranging in age from 13 to 16, were given the *State–Trait Anxiety Inventory for Children*, which measures both state anxiety (how anxious children happen to feel at the moment) and trait anxiety (how anxious children generally are). Charles Spielberger and his colleagues (Spielberger, Gorsuch, & Lushene, 1970) defined anxiety as an unpleasant emotional state characterized by "feelings of tension, apprehension, and heightened autonomic nervous system responses such as sweating, heart palpitation, restlessness, and respiratory disturbance" (p. 3). Thus, in assessing state anxiety, children were asked to look at statements such as "I am tense," "I am jittery," or "I feel high-strung" and to indicate how they felt right now, at that moment. In assessing trait anxiety, children were asked to look at items like these: "I feel like crying," "I feel that difficulties are piling up so that I cannot overcome them," and "I lack self-confidence," and so indicate how they generally felt. Once again, adolescents who were either momentarily or habitually anxious were especially likely to have fallen passionately in love.

Happy people never make fantasies, only unsatisfied ones do.
                                        —Sigmund Freud

Neediness   Dorothy Parker (1944, p. 180) observed:

Symptom Recital

I do not like my state of mind:
I'm bitter, querulous, unkind.
I hate my legs, I hate my hands,
I do not yearn for lovelier lands.
I dread the dawn's recurrent light;
I hate to go to bed at night.
I snoot at simple, earnest folk.
I cannot take the gentlest joke.
I find no peace in paint or type.
My world is but a lot of tripe.
I'm disillusioned, empty-breasted.
For what I think, I'd be arrested.
I am not sick, I am not well.
My quondam dreams are shot to hell.
My soul is crushed, my spirit sore;
I do not like me any more.
I cavil, quarrel, grumble, grouse.
I ponder on the narrow house.
I shudder at the thought of men . . .
I'm due to fall in love again.

Social psychologists have found that the psychoanalysts and poets may well be right; acute deprivation does seem to set the stage for passionate love. With two colleagues (Stephan, Berscheid, & Hatfield, 1971) we tested this simple hypothesis: When we are sexually aroused, our minds wander, and pretty soon our dazzling fantasies lend sparkle to drab reality.

First, we contacted a number of college men. We identified ourselves as staff members of the Center for Student Life Studies and explained that the center was studying the dating practices of college students. We told each subject that we'd like to know how he felt about a blind date we had picked out for him. Would he participate? Most of the men said: "Sure." While the men sat around waiting to give their first impressions of their date-to-be, they whiled away the time by reading articles lying around the office. This material was carefully selected. One group of men was given fairly boring reading material, articles intended to keep them cool and calm. The second group was given *Playboy* type material, designed to make them very "hot."

Finally, the interviewer appeared with the men's files. He showed them a picture of their date (a fairly attractive blond) and told them a little about her. (She seemed to be fairly intelligent, easy to get along with, active, and moderately liberal.) What did they think of her? Well, that depended on what the men had been reading.

We proposed that the unaroused men should be fairly objective. Their fantasy life should be in "low gear" and it should be easy for them to assess the women fairly accurately. The aroused men should have a harder time of it; the luster of their daydreams should keep rubbing off on their dates-to-be. When men were feeling sexy, they should have a greater tendency to see women as sex objects. Hence they should tend to exaggerate two of their date's traits—her sexual desirability and her sexual receptivity. We found that we were right. As predicted, the more aroused the men, the more beautiful they thought their date. In addition, the more aroused, the more likely they were to assume that their dates would be sexually receptive. Unaroused men judged their date-to-be as a fairly nice girl. Aroused men suspected that she was probably "amorous," "immoral," "promiscuous," "willing," "unwholesome," and "uninhibited."

The Flowering of Passionate Love

We once saw an elderly client, a musician who had played the viola with one of the major symphonies of the world. He entered therapy because he yearned to experience passionate love just one time more before he died. He wanted to feel that rush of exultation, that yearning, the hunger for another person, a sense of complete union, one more time. Alas, there is no way to produce the dizzying ecstasy of passionate love on demand.

The previous sections, dealing with the roots of love, have painted a somewhat dismal picture. We have focused on the bruised self-esteem, the dependence, and the insecurity that make people hunger for love. In this coda, however, we want to establish a balance. The blooms of love give off a rich bouquet of perfumes.

Moments of Exultation   When love is realized, lovers may experience moments of passionate bliss, moments that are epiphanies. It was this feeling that our elderly client longed to experience yet again. Dante Alighieri first saw Beatrice in 1274 A.D., when he was nine years old and she eight. This was his reaction:

> Her dress, on that day, was of a most noble color, a subdued and goodly crimson, girdled and adorned in such sort as best suited with her very tender age. At that moment, I say most truly that the spirit of life, which hath its dwelling in the secretest chamber of the heart, began to tremble so violently that the least pulses of my body shook therewith; and in trembling it said these words: "Here is a deity stronger than I; who, coming, shall rule over me." At that moment the animate spirit, which dwelleth in the lofty chamber whither all the senses carry their perceptions, was filled with wonder. . . .
> I say that, from that time forward, Love quite governed my soul. (1964, p. 178)

Beatrice married someone else when she was 18 and died a few years later. Dante remained passionately in love with her for the rest of his long life; he dedicated all his writing to her. Several researchers have documented that when we are passionately in love we see the world through rose-colored glasses (Hendrick & Hendrick, 1988).

[In passionate love] Vanity in a merely personal sense exists no longer. The lover takes a perilous pleasure in displaying his weak points and having them, one after another, accepted and condoned. He wishes to be assured that he is not loved for this or that good quality, but for himself, or something as like himself as he can contrive to set forward.

—*Robert Louis Stevenson*

Feeling Understood and Accepted   When men and women are loved, they sometimes feel fully understood, loved, and accepted for the first time. As Laurie Colwin (1981, p. 25) observed:

> Love, in its initial stages, takes care of everything. Love transforms a difficult person into a charming eccentric; points of contention into charming divergences. It doesn't matter that popular songs are full of warnings—songs like "Danger, Heartbreak Dead Ahead" are written and sung for those who have no intention of doing anything but dancing to them. And while lovers do almost nothing but reveal themselves, who notices?

Novelist Vivian Gornick (1987) was passionately involved with Joe Durbin, a labor organizer. One day Joe's charming, endless, meaningless chatter overwhelmed her. She felt unbearably lonely and isolated:

> "Oh, stop!" I cried. "Please stop. Stop!"
> Joe's mouth closed in the middle of a sentence. His head pulled back. His eyes searched mine. "What is it, darling?" he said. He'd never heard me sound this note before.
> "Listen to me," I pleaded, "just listen to me." He nodded at me, not taking his eyes from mine. "You don't know me at all," I said. "You think I'm this hot-shot loud-mouthed liberated woman, as brash and self-confident as you, ready to walk across the world just like you, and that's not who I am at all. It's making me lonely now to make love with you, and you not know what my life is about." He nodded again.
> I told him then how I had hungered for a life like his but that I hadn't ever had it, that I'd always felt marginal, buried alive in obscurity, and that all the talk I manufactured couldn't dissolve out the isolation. I told him how sometimes I wake spontaneously in the night and I sit up in bed and I'm alone in the middle of the world. "Where *is* everybody?" I say out loud, and I have to calm myself with "Mama's in Chelsea, Marilyn's on Seventy-third Street, my brother's in Baltimore." The list, I told him, is pathetic.
> I talked and talked. On and on I went, without pause or interruption. When I stopped I felt relieved (alone now but not lonely) and, very quickly, embarrassed. He was so silent. Oh, I thought, what a fool you are to have said these things. He doesn't like any of this, not a bit of it, he doesn't even know what you're talking about. Then Joe said, "Darling, what a rich inner life you have." My eyes widened. I took in the words. I laughed with delight! That he had such a sentence in him! That he had spoken the sentence he had in him. I loved him then. For the first time I loved *him*. (pp. 170–171)

Love you? I am you.
—*Charles Williams*

Sharing a Sense of Union   In the fifth century B.C., in the *Symposium*, Plato offered a wry theory about the origins of love. Originally, he contended, humanity was divided into three kinds of people: men/men, women/women, and the androgynous—a union of the two. Human beings were round: their backs and sides formed a circle. They had one head with two faces (always looking in opposite directions), four ears, four hands, four feet, and two privy members. They could walk upright and go backward or forward, as they pleased. Or they could roll over at a great pace, turning nimbly on their four hands and four feet like tumblers.

Eventually, the gods and humanity came into conflict. To punish them for their arrogance, the gods cut the men, women, and androgynous beings into two parts, "like a Sorb-apple which is halved for pickling." Since the division, the cleft parts have wandered the earth, each searching for its lost half. In the Platonic scheme, the halves of the once-complete men became "the best of the lot." These men were valiant and manly; they embraced that which was like themselves (other men). The androgynous halves also continued to seek *their* cleft portion: the men became lovers of women while the women became "adulterous women" who lusted after men. Finally, the halves of the once-complete women continued to seek their lost selves; they yearned for lesbian attachments. Thus humanity is always longing for completion—yearning to meld with another person. This then is the nature of love according to Plato: two deficient beings made whole by union with the other.

Literature echoes the Platonic theme: in love we long to merge with our lost selves. For example, in Emily Brontë's (1847/1976) *Wuthering Heights,* Cathy pours out her heart to her nurse Nelly. She explains that she loves Heathcliff:

> It would degrade me to marry Heathcliff, now; so he shall never know how I love him; and that, not because he's handsome, Nelly, but because he's more myself than I am. Whatever our souls are made of, his and mine are the same. . . .
>
> I cannot express it; but surely you and every body have a notion that there is, or should be, an existence of yours beyond you. What were the use of my creation if I were entirely contained here? My great miseries in this world have been Heathcliff's miseries, and I watched and felt each from the beginning; my great thought in living is himself. If all else perished, and *he* remained, I should still continue to be; and, if all else remained, and he were annihilated, the Universe would turn to a mighty stranger. I should not seem a part of it. . . . Nelly, I *am* Heathcliff—he's always, always in my mind—not as pleasure, any more than I am always a pleasure to myself—but, as my own being—so, don't talk of our separation again. (pp. 100–102)

The Duke and Duchess of Windsor, in their love letters written before their marriage, referred to themselves as WE—the W standing for Wallis and the E for Edward. Sometimes *our* clients think of us as one. They often call us Dickandelaine. This is especially unsettling when only one of us is at the session: "Well, Dickandelaine, it was like this."

Feeling Secure and Safe   Lovers may feel safe and secure when they are with someone they love.

In Margaret Mitchell's *Gone With the Wind* (1936), Ashley Wilkes hears that his wife Melanie is dying and finally expresses his love for and dependence on his wife to Scarlett O'Hara.

> His eyes search her intently, hunting, hunting desperately for something he did not find. Finally he spoke and his voice was not his own.
>
> "I was wanting you," he said. "I was going to run and find you—run like a child wanting comfort—and I find a child, more frightened, running to me."
>
> "Not you—you can't be frightened," she cried. "Nothing has ever frightened you. But I—You've always been so strong—"
>
> "If I've ever been strong, it was because she was behind me," he said, his voice breaking and he looked down at the glove and smoothed the fingers. "And—and—all the strength I ever had is going with her."
>
> "Why—" she said slowly, "why, Ashley, you love her, don't you?"
>
> "She is the only dream I ever had that lived and breathed and did not die in the face of reality." (pp. 1013–1014)

Of course, Scarlett is stunned to discover that Ashley loved Melanie, who provided security and safety, more than he loved her own passionate nature.

Transcendence   When people fall in love they sometimes are able to transcend their former limitations. For example, poet Elizabeth Barrett was dominated by her selfish and jealous father; she was a recluse and an invalid. When she fell in love with Robert Browning, she was transformed into a vibrant, energetic woman. She and Robert eloped, fleeing a damp, gray England to sunny, flowering Italy. They lived there for 15 years until Elizabeth died in her husband's arms.

In summary: When passionate love is realized, it is often an idyllic experience—allowing a person to feel understood and accepted, safe, and exultant. Of course, love does not always go well. Love may be unrequited or end badly. (We discuss these realities at greater length in Chapter 14, Endings.)

Now that we have reviewed what evolutionary theorists have learned about the evolutionary underpinnings of love, let us turn to what social psychologists have learned about the nature of modern-day passionate love.

THE NATURE OF PASSIONATE LOVE

Earlier, we defined passionate love as:

> A state of intense longing for union with another. Passionate love is a complex functional whole including appraisals or appreciations, subjective feelings, expressions, patterned physiological processes, action tendencies, and instrumental behaviors. Reciprocated love (union with the other) is associated with fulfillment and ecstasy. Unrequited love (separation) with emptiness, anxiety, or despair.

Let us now review what social psychologists know about the various components of love—the subjective experiences, the central, autonomic, and somatic nervous system reactions, and the behavioral expressions of this bittersweet emotion.

The Cognitive Contribution

For centuries, writers, artists, and philosophers have bitterly disagreed over the nature of love. In recent research, Philip Shaver, Shelley Wu, and Judith Schwartz (1991) interviewed young people in America, Italy, and the People's Republic of China about their emotional experiences. In all cultures, men and women identified the same emotions as basic or prototypic emotions. These were joy/happiness, love/attraction, fear, anger/hate, and sadness/depression. They also agreed completely as to whether the various emotions should be labeled as positive experiences (such as joy) or negative ones (such as fear, anger, or sadness). They agreed completely, that is, except about one emotion—love. American and Italian subjects tended to equate love with happiness; both passionate and companionate love were assumed to be intensely positive experiences. American films, in which couples fall in love and live "happily ever after," seem to promote this benign view of love. For example, in the musical *Singin' in the Rain*, Gene Kelly fell head-over-heels in love with Debbie Reynolds. After he declares his love for her, his exuberant joy as he splashes through a downpour reminds us of the heedless delights of passion.

Chinese students, however, had a darker view of love. In Chinese there are few "happy-love" words. Love is associated with sadness. Chinese men and women associated passionate love with such ideographs (words) as infatuation, unrequited love, nostalgia, and sorrow love. Interestingly enough, the equating of love with sadness seems to be an ancient Eastern tradition. For example, in *Five Women Who Loved* (Saikaku, 1686/1956), a collection of love stories from seventeenth century Japan, almost all the love affairs ended sadly. For the heroines, impetuous passion led almost inevitably to ruin—to the suicide or the execution of the lovers. Shaver's students from the East and West never did come to an agreement as to the nature of love. Each cultural group continued to regard one another's visions of love as "unrealistic."

Despite its glories, romantic love is notorious for . . . the pain and suffering that accompany it.
                                                                —Ethel Person

In this text, we take a complex view of the nature of passionate love. We would argue that passionate love is a mixed blessing. As the definition of love indicates, passionate love sometimes *is* a joyously exciting experience, sparked by wondrous fantasies and rewarding encounters with the loved one. But that is only part of the story. Passionate love is like any other form of excitement. By its very nature, excitement involves a continuous interplay between elation and despair, thrills and terror. Think, for example, of the mixed and rushed feelings that novice skiers experience. Their hearts begin to pound as they wait to lurch onto the ski lift. Once they realize they have made it, they are elated. On the easy ride to the top, they are still a bit unnerved. Their hands shake and their knees tremble, but they slowly begin to relax. Moments later they look ahead and realize it is time to push off the lift. The landing looks icy and steep. Their rush quickly turns to panic. They can't turn back. They struggle to get their feelings under control. They jump off the lift, elated and panicky—it is hard to tell which. Then they start to ski downhill, experiencing as they go a wild jumble of powerful emotions. Eventually, they arrive at the bottom of the hill, elated, relieved. Perhaps they feel like crying. Sometimes, they are so tired they are flooded with waves of depression. Usually, they get up, ready to try again. Passionate lovers experience the same roller-coaster of feelings—euphoria, happiness, vulnerability, anxiety, panic, despair. The risks of love merely add fuel to the fire.

Sometimes men and women become entangled in love affairs where the delight is brief, and pain, uncertainty, jealousy, misery, anxiety, and despair are abundant. Recent social psychological research makes it clear that passionate love, which thrives on excitement, is linked to a variety of strong emotions—both positive and negative.

Michael Liebowitz (1983), in *The Chemistry of Love*, provided a quasi-poetical description of the mixed nature of passionate love:

> Love and romance seem to be one, if not the most powerful activator of our pleasure centers. . . . Both tend to be very exciting emotionally. Being with the person or even just thinking of him or her is highly stimulating. . . . Love is, by definition, the strongest positive feeling we can have. Other things—stimulant drugs, passionate causes, manic states—can induce powerful changes in our brains, but none so reliably, so enduringly, or so delightfully as that "right" other person. . . . If the relationship is not established or is uncertain, anxiety or other displeasure centers may be quite active as well, producing a situation of great emotional turmoil as the lover swings between hope and torment. (pp. 48–49)

We discuss some of his work on the chemistry of love later in this chapter.

Dorothy Tennov (1979) interviewed more than 500 lovers. Almost all of them took it for granted that passionate love (which Tennov labeled "limerence") is a bittersweet experience. One respondent, Philip, a 28-year-old truck driver, described his feelings this way:

> I'd be jumpy out of my head. It was like what you might call stage fright, like going up in front of an audience. My hand would be shaking when I rang the doorbell. When I called her on the phone I felt like I could hear the pulse in my temple louder than the ringing of the phone, and I'd get into such a panic listening to the ring and expecting Nelly's voice at the other end that I'd have a moment of relief if no one answered. And when she did answer, I wouldn't know what to say even if I'd gone over the whole thing in my head beforehand. And then whatever I did say never seemed to come out right. (p. 49)

Ruth described her feelings this way:

> Love is irrational. Whether you call it a mental illness or sublime spirituality, you behave in love in ways that do not represent your own true best interests, ways that deflect from the goals you've built your life around, even if the deflection is slight, even if it is easily rationalized and even when it is disguised as beauty or experienced as ecstasy.
>
> How can I say that my seemingly interminable passion for Eric, a 15-year obsession, was reasonable? Consider the 30,000 hours—I actually calculated my estimation, and that's a conservative figure—I spent going over every word he said, every gesture, every letter he wrote, when I might have been reading, or learning a foreign language, or enjoying the company of others. Instead, I was caught in a merry-go-round of

wondering how he felt, wishing he would call, anticipating our next time together, or endlessly searching in my recollections of his behavior and my convoluted reconstruction of the possible reasons for his actions for the shreds of hope on which my madness fed. (p. 105)

The obsessive love of Adele Hugo (novelist Victor Hugo's daughter) drove her to madness. In her teens she fell in love with a soldier. She followed him from posting to posting. When she was on her deathbed he finally agreed to meet this mad beauty who had tracked him so relentlessly. . . . She could not even recognize her beloved. (Somehow she thought that he was taller.) It is clear then that the term passionate love well covers any intense longing for union with another, whether one's love is reciprocated (and thus a source of fulfillment and ecstasy) or unrequited, even uncertain (and thus a source of emptiness, anxiety, or despair).

The Biological Contribution

Since antiquity, researchers have been developing methods to detect "lovesickness." Consider this report, written in the second century by Appian of Alexandria:

> At the beginning of the third century, B.C., Seleucus, one of Alexander's generals and among the ablest of his successors, married a woman named Stratonice. Antiochus, his son by a previous marriage, had the misfortune to fall in love with his new stepmother. Recognizing the illicit character of his love, and the hopelessness of its consummation, Antiochus resolves not to show his feelings. Instead, he falls sick and strives his hardest to die.
>
> We may be sure that many doctors attended the young prince, but to no avail it seems, until the celebrated Greek physician Erasistratos concludes that, in the absence of bodily disease, the boy's malady must stem from some affliction of the mind, "through which the body is often strengthened or weakened by sympathy." (Reported in Mesulam & Perry, 1972, pp. 546–547)

The physician spent several days in Antiochus' chamber, studying the comings and goings of the court. Each time a visitor came by, Erasistratos studied Antiochus' physiological reactions. Only one person produced a strong reaction in Antiochus—his new stepmother Stratonice. Each time she came to see him "lo, those tell-tale-signs of which Sappho sings were all there in him—stammering speech, fiery flashes, darkened vision, sudden sweats, irregular palpitations of the heart, and finally, as his soul was taken by storm, helplessness, stupor, and pallor" (Plutarch, first century A.D.), reported in Mesulam & Perry (1972, p. 547). On the physician's advice, Seleucus divorced his bride Stratonice so his son Antiochus could marry her; thus his son's life was saved.

Recently, psychologists have assembled information from neuroanatomical and neurophysiological investigations, ablation experiments, pharmacologic explorations, clinical investigations, and behavioral research as to the social psychophysiology of passion. These authors document that the observations of the ancients are, in part, correct. Passionate love does produce the skeletal–muscular and autonomic nervous system reactions Plutarch described. Their research also documents the contention that passionate love is indeed a complex phenomenon (Hatfield & Rapson, 1987; Kaplan, 1979; Liebowitz, 1983).

The Anatomy of Love   In Thomas Mann's *The Magic Mountain* (1924/1969), Hans Castorp described his complicated emotional reaction to Clavdia Chauchat:

> In each hour of his diminished day he had thought of her: her mouth, her cheek-bones, her eyes, whose colour, shape, and position bit into his very soul; her drooping back, the posture of her head, her cervical vertebra above the rounding of her blouse, her arms enhanced by their thin gauze covering. Possessed of these thoughts, his hours had sped on soundless feet. . . . Yes, he felt both terror and dread; he felt a vague and boundless, utterly mad and extravagant anticipation, a nameless anguish of joy which at times so oppressed the young man's heart, his actual and corporeal heart, that he would lay one hand in the neighourhood of that organ, while he carried the other to his brow and held it like a shield before his eyes, whispering: "Oh, my God!" (p. 206)

Psychiatrist Helen Singer Kaplan (1979) has explored the anatomy of passionate love and sexual desire. Cognitive factors have a profound impact on sexual desire. Thus the cortex (that part of the brain that analyzes complex perceptions and stores and retrieves memories) has extensive neural connections with the sex center.

The brain's passionate love/sex center is located within the limbic system. (The limbic system is located in the limbus or rim of the brain.) Even in primitive vertebrates, this system is the emotional control center. In humans, this archaic system remains essentially unchanged. It is here that the most powerful emotions are generated, powerfully driving behavior. Kaplan points out that the limbic system contains both activating and inhibitory centers; it is tightly tied into the pleasure and pain centers of the brain. All sexual behavior is shaped by the seeking of pleasure and the avoidance of pain. Passionate love and sexual desire, she argues, generate endorphins (chemicals that resemble morphine, causing euphoria and alleviating pain), which stimulate the pleasure centers. The result: ecstasy. Sexual desire may also stimulate the pain centers. If a person's romantic partners or sexual experiences are associated with too much pain, they will cease to evoke sexual desire.

It is not possible to disentangle the different emotions, the pride, humility, pity, and passion, which are excited by a look of happy love or an unexpected caress.

—*Robert Louis Stevenson*

The Chemistry of Love   Researchers are beginning to learn more about the chemistry of passionate love and an array of related emotions. They are also learning more about the way that various emotions, positive and negative, interact. Psychiatrist Michael Liebowitz (1983) has been the most willing to speculate about the chemistry of love. He argues that passionate love brings on a giddy feeling, comparable to an amphetamine high. It is phenylethylamine (PEA), an amphetamine-related compound, that produces the mood-lifting and energizing effects of romantic love. He observes that "love addicts" and drug addicts have a great deal in common: The craving for romance is merely the craving for a particular kind of high. The fact that most romances lose some of their intensity with time may well be due to normal biological processes. The crash that follows a breakup may be much like amphetamine withdrawal. Liebowitz also offers some speculations about the chemistry of the emotions that crisscross the consciousness of lovers as they swirl from the giddy peaks to the gloomy depths of their passions. The "highs" include euphoria, excitement, relaxation, spiritual feelings, and relief. The "lows" include anxiety, terrifying panic attacks, the pain of separation, and the fear of punishment. In *excitement,* naturally occurring brain chemicals, similar to stimulants (such as amphetamine and cocaine), produce the rush that lovers feel. In *relaxation,* chemicals related to the narcotics (such as heroin, opium, and morphine), tranquilizers, sedatives, or alcohol, and marijuana produce a mellow state and wipe out anxiety, loneliness, panic attacks, and depression. In *spiritual peak experiences,* chemicals similar to the psychedelics produce a sense of beauty, meaningfulness, and timelessness. The painful feelings of *separation anxiety, panic attacks,* or *depression* may be produced in two ways: by the production of chemicals that produce anxiety, pain, or depression; or by withdrawal from the chemicals that produce the highs. Researchers do not yet know if Liebowitz's speculations on the chemistry of passionate love are correct.

Kaplan (1979) provides some information as to the chemistry of *sexual desire.* Dopamine (a neurotransmitter) and testosterone (the major libido hormone) stimulate sexual desire. Serotonin or 5-HT (5-hydroxytryptamine) inhibits sexual desire. Kaplan observes:

> When we are in love, libido is high. Every contact is sensuous, thoughts turn to Eros, and the sexual reflexes work rapidly and well. The presence of the beloved is an aphrodisiac; the smell, sight, sound, and touch of the lover—especially when he/she is excited—are powerful stimuli to sexual desire. In physiologic terms, this may exert a direct physical effect on the neurophysiologic system in the brain which regulates sexual desire. . . . But again, there is no sexual stimulant so powerful, even love, that it cannot be inhibited by fear and pain. (p. 14)

Finally, although passionate love and the related emotions we have described may be associated with specific chemical neurotransmitters or with chemicals that increase/decrease the sensitivity of receptors in the brain, most emotions possess more similarities than differences. Chemically, intense emotions do have much in common. Kaplan reminds us that chemically, love, joy, sexual desire, and excitement, as well as anger, fear, jealousy, and hate, are all intensely arousing. They all produce an autonomic nervous system sympathetic response. This is evidenced by the symptoms associated with all these emotions—a flushed face, sweaty palms, weak knees, butterflies in the stomach, dizziness, a pounding heart, trembling hands, and accelerated breathing. The exact pattern of reaction varies from person to person (Lacey & Lacey, 1970).

Comedy and tragedy grow on the same tree. A change of lighting suffices to make one the other.

—Plato

Why Is Passionate Love So Passionate? The Cross-Magnification Process

Passionate love, as we have seen, is associated with a variety of emotions, pleasurable and painful. Elaine Hatfield (Carlson & Hatfield, 1992) goes on to argue that such emotional mixtures produce the most intense explosions of feeling.

Logically, when people are exposed to a variety of emotional stimuli, their emotions *could* interact in three different ways. First, sometimes people are able to identify the ebb and flow of their separate emotions. In such cases, they experience a series of distinct emotions, or emotional blends. (This year, Dick and I took a wonderful walking tour of the Cotswolds. We went to small towns with such names as Chipping-Camden, Folly, Plush, and Midsummer Norton. We separated in London and proceeded on to different conferences, half a world apart. In the following week, we were aware that most of the time we were still delighting in the excitement of the psychology and history meetings and our holiday. When we paused for a moment, however, we were both aware that "deep down," we felt sad and like crying. We missed each other; we were sorry that our holiday was at an end; painfully aware that we would not always be able to enjoy the minds of our aging friends and the beauty of the Cotswolds.) Second, sometimes incompatible emotions may "cancel" one another out. (For example, teenagers, who don't really know whether they should be frightened or angry in a threatening situation, sometimes report that they just feel numb.) Finally, people most often experience emotional *cross-magnification*. Passionate love, for instance, may actually be intensified by the shyness, anxiety, jealousy, or anger the other sparks in us. It is easy to identify such instances of emotional spillover in our daily lives. When we have been frenetically rushing around all day, we often end up snapping at a friend over some trifle. What would normally be slight irritation has exploded into rage; we have to remind ourselves (or *be* reminded) to "settle down." Or we trip on the threadbare carpet and catch ourselves just in time from hurtling down the stairs. We dissolve in a fit of giggles. What's so funny about almost being killed? Our sense of the absurd has been magnified by our fear and relief. Elaine Hatfield (Carlson & Hatfield, 1992) argued that in life such emotional spillover effects can have powerful consequences. Most intense emotional experiences involve such blends of emotions. This may not be pure coincidence. Perhaps emotions (especially positive emotions) have a better chance to rise to a fever pitch when several emotional units are activated. Love may be more intense than usual when it is fueled by ecstasy *and* jealousy, insecurity *and* fear of loss. The death of a mate may be especially hard to bear when combined with guilt about the way we treated the deceased. Add grief and anger at the loss to that guilt, and the darkness deepens. Mixtures of emotions most certainly can fuel passion.

Kisses made more passionate by remorse.
          —Lawrence Durrell

Evidence that Both Pleasure and Pain May Fuel Passion   Passionate love is a risky affair. Success sparks delight, failure invites despair. We get some indication of the strength of our passion by noting the intensity of our delight and despair. Trying to dissect the causes of our passionate feelings nonetheless poses difficulties. Are you high because a potential mate is ideal for you? Because the timing is right? Because it is the first day of spring? To what extent is your lover's coolness responsible for your misery? Do you feel so badly because you are lonely? Simply timid about going off on your own? Are you just generally "low"? Whatever the real reasons, there is an abundance of evidence to support the contention that, under the right conditions, a variety of intensely positive experiences, intensely negative ones, or neutral but energizing experiences can add to the passion of passion.

I believe myself that romantic love is the source of the most intense delights that life has to offer.
—Bertrand Russell

Passion and the Positive Emotions   Our definition of love stated that "reciprocated love (union with the other) is associated with fulfillment and ecstasy." No one doubts that love is such a "high," that the joys of love generally spill over and add sparkle to everything else in life. What has been of interest to psychologists is the converse of this proposition: That the adrenalin associated with a wide variety of highs can spill over and make passionate love more passionate. (Hence we see a sort of "better loving through chemistry" phenomenon.)

A number of carefully crafted studies make it clear that a variety of positive emotions—amusement (White, Fishbein, & Rutstein, 1981), erotic excitement (Istvan & Griffitt, 1978; Stephan et al., 1971), or general excitement (Zuckerman, 1979)—all can intensify passion. In one investigation, for example, Joseph Istvan, William Griffitt, and Gerdi Weidner (1983) aroused men by showing them sexy pictures. Other men viewed nonarousing, neutral fare. The two groups were then asked to evaluate the appeal of some beautiful and some unattractive women. When the women were pretty, the aroused men rated them as more attractive than the other men did. When the women were unattractive, they rated them as less attractive than the others did. Evidently, the sexual arousal of these men spilled over and intensified whatever it was they would normally have felt for the woman, for good or ill. Similarly, sexually aroused women found handsome men unusually appealing, and homely men less appealing, than usual.

And anyway, who could recount, without convincing herself of madness, the true degrees of love? Those endless discussions on that endless theme, the trembling, the waiting, the anguish when he left the room for a moment . . . the terror that each time he left my sight he would die?
—Margaret Drabble

Passion and the Negative Emotions   In defining passionate love, we also observed that "unrequited love (separation) is associated with emptiness, anxiety, or despair." The world has noted that the failure to acquire or sustain love is an extraordinarily painful experience. Quentin Crisp warned: "One should always be wary of someone who promises that their love will last longer than a weekend." Coco Chanel counseled: "Jump out the window if you are the object of passion. Flee it if you feel it. Passion goes, boredom remains." Psychologists, along with most writers, report the panic, loneliness, and eventual despair that people feel when they are separated from those they love (Peplau & Perlman, 1982).

By now, psychologists have amassed considerable evidence for the proposition that people are especially vulnerable to love when their lives are turbulent. A variety of negative experiences have been found to deepen desire. For example, Donald Dutton and Arthur Aron (1974), in a duo of studies, discovered a close link between fear and sexual attraction. In one experiment, they compared reactions of men who crossed one of two bridges in North Vancouver, Canada. The first bridge, the Capilano Canyon suspension bridge, was a 450-foot-long span that pitched, reeled, and wobbled over a precipitous drop to the rocks and shallow rapids below. The other bridge was a solid, safe cement structure. As each young man crossed one of the bridges, a good-looking college woman approached him. She explained that she was doing a class project and asked if he would fill out a questionnaire concerning his attitudes toward conservation. When the man had finished, she offered to explain her project in greater detail. She scribbled her telephone number on a scrap of paper, so he could call her if he wanted more information. Which men called? Nine of the 33 men on the suspension bridge called her; only two of the men on the solid bridge called.

This single study can be interpreted several ways. Perhaps the men who called, after making it across the precarious Capilano bridge, really were interested in ecology rather than sex. Perhaps it was not fear but relief at having survived the heights that stimulated their desire (Kendrick & Cialdini, 1977). It is always possible to find alternative explanations for any single study. But by now there is a great deal of experimental and correlational evidence for the intriguing contention that, under the right conditions, a variety of awkward and painful experiences—anxiety and fear (Brehm, Gatz, Goethals, McCrimmon, & Ward, 1978; Dienstbier, 1978; Hoon, Wincze, & Hoon, 1977; Riordon & Tedeschi, 1983), embarrassment (Byrne, Przybyla, & Infantino, 1981), the discomfort of seeing others involved in conflict (Dutton, 1979), jealousy (Clanton & Smith, 1987), loneliness (Peplau & Perlman, 1982), anger (Barclay, 1969; Driscoll, Davis, & Lipetz, 1972), horror (White et al., 1981), or even grief—can deepen passion.

I hate and I love. I feel both . . . and I am in agony.
—Quintus Valerius Catullus

Love and Hate   Writers and artists have long been aware of the shadowy boundary between love and hate. In *Of Human Bondage*, W. Somerset Maugham (1915/1953, p. 159) expressed well this curious blend of conflicting emotions:

When he lay in bed it seemed impossible that he should be in love with Mildred Rogers. Her name was grotesque. He did not think her pretty; he hated the thinness of her, only that evening he had noticed how the bones of her chest stood out in evening-dress; he went over her features one by one; he did not like her mouth, and the unhealthiness of her colour vaguely repelled him. She was common. Her phrases, so bald and few, constantly repeated, showed the emptiness of her mind; he recalled her vulgar little laugh at the jokes of the musical comedy; and he remembered the little finger carefully extended when she held her glass to her mouth; her manners like her conversation, were odiously genteel. He remembered her insolence; sometimes he had felt inclined to box her ears; and suddenly, he knew not why, perhaps it was the thought of hitting her or the recollection of her tiny, beautiful ears, he was seized by an uprush of emotion. He yearned for her. He thought of taking her in his arms, the thin, fragile body, and kissing her pale mouth: he wanted to pass his fingers down the slightly greenish cheeks. He wanted her.

Forty years ago, Theodor Reik (1949) noted that people are often fatally attracted to those who are kindest and cruelest to them. Let us consider just one example. Many years ago, one scientist (Fisher, 1955), in a study using puppies, systematically varied how he treated the young animals. He treated two groups of puppies very consistently: He always responded to some of the pups with love and kindness; he always punished some of the pups any time they dared to approach him. A third group of puppies was treated in a very inconsistent way: sometimes they were cuddled and petted; other times, for no reason at all, they were punished. The results of this study were rather surprising. As it turned out, the puppies treated inconsistently were most attracted to, and most dependent on, their trainer. This finding, and numerous others, suggests that ambivalence is a potent fuel for passion. Consistency generates little emotion; it is inconsistency to which we respond. If a person always treats us with love and respect, we may start to take him for granted. Similarly, if a person is always cold and rejecting, we eventually tend to disregard his criticisms. Again, we know what to expect. What does generate a spark of interest, however, is if our admiring friend started treating us with contempt or if our arch enemy started inundating us with kindness.

The evidence then suggests that various states of arousal can spill over and influence one another. Adrenalin makes the heart grow fonder. Although most people assume that we love the people we do *in spite* of the suffering they cause us, it may be that, in part, we love them *because* of the pain they cause. Love seems to flourish when it is nurtured by a torrent of good experiences, and a sprinkling of unsettling, irritating, and even painful ones.

Passion and Emotionally Neutral Arousal   Research indicates that passion can even be stirred by excitation transfer from such emotionally neutral but physically arousing experiences as riding an exercise bicycle (Cantor, Zillman, & Bryant, 1975) or jogging (White et al., 1981). In one experiment (White et al., 1981), some men (those in the high arousal group) were required to engage in strenuous physical exercise; they ran in place for two minutes. Other men (those in the low arousal group) ran in place for only 15 seconds. In and of itself, the exercise did not affect the men's moods; it did, however, affect their levels of arousal.

The men then watched a videotaped interview, which included a woman they expected soon to meet. Half of the time the woman was attractive; half of the time she was not. After the interview, the men were asked to give their first impression of the woman and to estimate her attractiveness and sexiness. They also indicated how attracted they felt to her and the extent to which they wanted to kiss her and to date her. The authors proposed that exertion-induced arousal would intensify the men's reactions to the women. And they found just that. If the woman was beautiful, the men who were aroused via exertion judged her to be unusually appealing. If she was homely, the men who were aroused via exertion judged her to be unusually unappealing. The effect of arousal then was to intensify a person's usual reactions to others. Arousal enhanced the appeal of the pretty woman as much as it impaired the appeal of the homely one. [See Zillman (1984) for a review of this research on excitation transfer.]

The Behavioral Contribution

People who are besotted with love sometimes devise secret little tests to see if they are loved. Judith Katz (1976) points out that people use several kinds of clues in deciding how their beloved feels about them. (1) Did he say he loved her, cook her a special dinner, or give her a present *without being prompted?* If I have to ask, most people feel, it "doesn't count." The intention to please is seen as more important than the gift. (If a secretary picked up the gift, once again it "doesn't count.") (2) Was the action appropriate and timely? If your mate asks you to dinner when you have just signed up for a diet program, that doesn't make it either. (3) Did she sacrifice herself to please you? The more she sacrificed, the more loving she is seen to be. One way people decide if they are loved is to consider the intentions of the other.

Lovers can also analyze the behavior of their beloved. There is no doubt that love leads people to act in ways that are a "tip-off" to their feelings. Some signs of love are blatant. Lovers kiss, hold hands, and embrace (Guerrero & Andersen, 1991; Lockard & Adams, 1980). But there are also more subtle signs that people are passionately in love.

Eye Contact   When people are caught up in conversation, they gaze at one another for short periods. One British scientist, Michael Argyle (1967), found that people caught up in conversation look at one another only 30 to 60% of the time. When we love someone, however, we gaze into his or her eyes far more often than that. We may try to catch their eye, even when we are across the room, just for a moment so that, with an almost imperceptible smile, we can share some secret amusement . . . or irritation (Morris, 1977; Rubin, 1970).

One's "Inclination" Toward Another   Sir Francis Galton (1884), a Victorian psychologist, became fascinated by the realization that he could ferret out his friend's most secret desires, without that other realizing it. Galton conceived of a number of schemes for invading privacy, for detecting who was secretly in love with whom. Luckily, he got distracted from putting his schemes into practice. He believed that posture provided clues; we tend to lean toward someone we like and away from someone we dislike. He observed:

> When two persons have an "inclination" to one another, they visibly incline or slope together when sitting side by side, as at a dinner table, and they then throw the stress of their weights on the near legs of their chairs. It does not require much ingenuity to arrange a pressure gauge with an index and dial to indicate changes in stress, but it is difficult to devise an arrangement that shall fulfill the three-fold condition of being effective, not attracting notice, and being applicable to ordinary furniture. I made some rude experiments, but being busy with other matters, have not carried them on, as I had hoped. (p. 184)

Contemporary researchers support Galton's postural hypothesis (Mehrabian, 1968).

The Distance One Stands from Another   Researchers find that the more we care for someone, the closer we tend to stand. Donn Byrne and his colleagues (1970) demonstrated that standing distance can serve as a useful index of romantic attraction. He introduced men and women students to each other and then sent the couples on a 30-minute "blind" coffee date. Eventually, the couples wandered back to the experimental office. As they checked in, the psychologist unobtrusively recorded how close to one another they were standing. The more the couple liked one another, the closer together they stood.

The preceding studies thus demonstrate that when people love one another they try to get close in a variety of little ways. Sometimes the desire to get close is not so subtle. In the case with which we began this chapter, John Hinckley stalked Jodie Foster to her classes, dorms, and in the streets. Jealous men and women sometimes camp outside their loved one's house or, more ominously, their rival's apartment . . . aching for a look at the other. Love leads to a desire (literally) to get close.

And vice versa. An odd corollary sometimes takes place as well. If people are forced to act *as if* they are in love—if they are induced to exchange a mutual unbroken gaze for two minutes with a stranger of the opposite sex, or to recite loving words, or to imitate loving sounds (Hatfield, Costello, Schalekamp, Denney, & Hsee, in press), or to stand close to a stranger, for example—their romantic attraction to this new person may be piqued. Let us consider two of these experiments.

Joan Kellerman, James Lewis, and James Laird (1989) investigated the link between love and feedback from expressions of love. The authors observed that "only people in love exchange those long, unbroken, close-up gazes" (p. 145). [We are reminded of the line from the Rodgers and Hammerstein (1943) musical *Oklahoma:* "Don't sigh and gaze at me . . . people will say we're in love."] To test the notion that love would follow gaze, they asked some men and women to gaze into one another's eyes continuously for two minutes; then they asked them how romantically they felt about one another. How did experimental subjects' feelings compare to the feelings of couples in the control conditions? (The authors devised three kinds of control conditions. In one, a subject gazed into the other's eyes, but the other looked away. In another, both subjects gazed at one another's hands. In yet another, subjects gazed into one another's eyes—but only in order to count how often the other was blinking!) As predicted, the mutual gaze subjects reported greater feelings of romantic love, attraction, interest, warmth, and respect for one another than did control condition subjects. In a second experiment, the authors found that passionate and romantic feelings were most powerfully stimulated if the subjects were required to gaze at one another in a romantic setting, one in which the room was dimly lit and romantic music played softly in the background.

Love ceases to be a pleasure when it ceases to be a secret.
  —*Mrs. Alphra Behn*

In a second experiment, Daniel Wegner and his colleagues (Wegner, Lane, & Dimitri, in press) explored the allure of secret liaisons. They observed:

> This experiment was designed in an attempt to capture some of what happens at the height of intrigue in a secret affair. Picture this: The couple have just brushed ankles under the table, and a look flashes between them as they both recognize instantly the precarious situation they have encountered. Others at the table do not know of their relationship—the one that is just now forming as their contact lingers—and they obviously cannot know. But the touch continues. The partners must put on a show of indifference to each other and feign interest in the above-board conversation, all the

while trying not to let their continuing covert activities seep into their minds and actions. Our prediction is that this prototypical secret liaison has the effect of producing in each partner a preoccupation with and attraction toward the other.

They tested this notion in a simple experiment. College men and women at the University of Virginia, who were strangers to one another, were invited in to play a card game. One team was told (privately) that it was their job to play the game using "natural nonverbal communication." They were to keep their feet in contact with their partner's feet for the entire game, so they could send secret signals to one another. Half of the time, in the secret condition, men and women were told that they should not let the other team know they were playing "footsie." In the nonsecret condition, everyone knew what was going on. The other team was not allowed to touch. As predicted, men and women felt more romantic attraction for one another if they had been allowed to play a secret game of "footsie." Their competitors, on the other hand, became most aroused romantically when they had been tipped off to what was going on.

Raging fires always die quickly.
—Lotte Lenya

Love: A temporary insanity curable by marriage.
—Ambrose Bierce

PASSIONATE LOVE: HOW LONG DOES IT LAST?

When individuals are dizzyingly, wildly in love, they are convinced that their passionate feelings will last forever. Yet, when we take an unflinching look at the many dismal marriages around us, it becomes clear that passion is generally fleeting (Berscheid, 1983; Hatfield & Walster, 1978.) Eric Klinger (1977) warned that "highs are always transitory. People experience deliriously happy moments that quickly fade and all attempts to hang on to them are doomed to fail" (p. 116). Richard Solomon (1980) observed that passionate love follows the same pattern as any addiction. At first, passionate love produces giddy euphoria. In time, however, it takes more and more love (or cocaine, alcohol, and so forth) to produce even a weak high. Eventually, highs become transitory. If one loses love (or if one goes "cold turkey" on a drug), one must endure the pains of withdrawal—depression, agitation, fatigue, anger, and loneliness. Marriage and family texts also warn that romantic love is temporary. Passion frequently wanes once the couple moves in together. Theodor Reik (1972) warned that the best a couple, once intensely in love, can hope for after several years of living together is a warm "afterglow."

If we'd thought of it, about the end of it . . . we'd have been aware that our love affair was too hot not to cool down.
—Cole Porter

There is indeed evidence that passionate love does erode with time. Elaine Hatfield and her colleagues (Pilleman & Hatfield, 1981) interviewed dating couples, newlyweds, and older women, who had been married an average of 33 years.

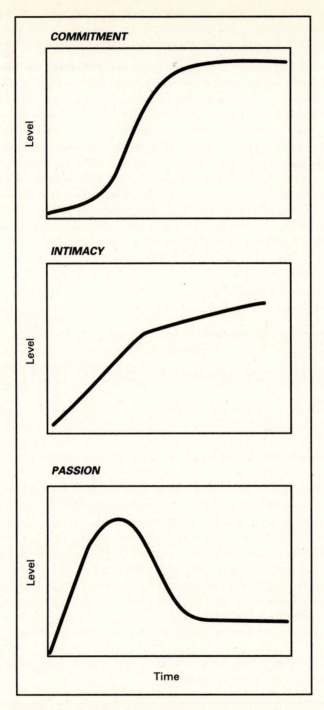

Figure 2.2 The changing ingredients of love. Aspects of love grow at different rates and vary in their ability to endure.

(The longest marriage was 59 years.) The authors predicted that passionate love would decline precipitously with time. Over time, passionate love did seem to plummet. Couples started out loving their partners intensely. Both steady daters and newlyweds expressed "a great deal of passionate love" for their mates. But after many years of marriage, women reported that they and their husbands now felt only "some" passionate love for one another.

In Chapter 1, we presented Robert Sternberg's (1988) triangular theory of love, which argued that the various forms of love involve different proportions of passion, intimacy, and commitment. Sternberg (cited in Goleman, 1985) interviewed couples married one month to 36 years. Initially, it was passion that drew men and women to one another. As the relationship matured, passion began to fade into the background. "Passion is the quickest to develop, and the quickest to fade (p. 13)," Sternberg wrote. After a while, what mattered most was companionate love—which is comprised of commitment and intimacy. It took longer for couples to feel fully committed to their marriages and to become intimate with one another, but in love, these were the things that seemed to last. Figure 2.2 illustrates the time course of the various components of love.

CONCLUSION

Love is a powerful emotion. Passionate love is stronger yet, so much so that it generates a congeries of other emotions: euphoric joy, fierce anxiety, episodes of despair alternating with exultant hope. The individual cannot sustain the intensity very long. Passionate love has, historically, been the stuff of poetry and legend. In real life, most cultures thoughout the centuries and, until recently, in the West have placed a terrifying penalty on passion, making it forbidden, sinful, and punishable in quite fearful ways. Religious and secular rulers have unambiguously disconnected passionate love from marriage and family. Despite tendencies to sentimentalize the experience, such love has had little place to go except to disaster and death. Authorities have feared its awesome force and its celebration of individual feeling over communal order.

Add to the combustible power of passionate love the igniting agency of sex, and one produces an explosion which all institutional authorities have conspired to suppress for thousands of years. By and large the authorities succeeded. But no longer: Today passionate love is *expected* to lead to sexual union, perhaps even to marriage and family. The consequences for individual and society are enormous, and we now turn to that "igniting agency"—sex—to examine some of those consequences.

Chapter
3

Sexuality

"What is love?" . . . [I end by] confessing that, in the case of romantic love, I don't really know. If forced against a brick wall to face a firing squad who would shoot if not given the correct answer, I would whisper "It's about 90 percent sexual desire as yet not sated."

—Ellen Berscheid

INTRODUCTION

Peter Abelard was the greatest philosopher of the twelfth century. Héloïse was his star pupil. When they fell in love, they defied the conventions of the time in two ways. First, they made love. Even worse, they then married. Love and sex in the twelfth century did not go with marriage. These acts enraged Héloïse's uncle. In revenge, he hired thugs who castrated Abelard. As a result, Héloïse became a nun and Abelard withdrew from the world to be a monk in the Abbey of St. Denis. Throughout their lives, they kept up a passionate correspondence. (Héloïse's letters burn with nostalgia, his are holy and world-renouncing.) In one tear-drenched letter Héloïse wrote:

> As God is my witness, I would rather be your whore than Empress of Christendom. . . . In my case, the pleasures of love which we have shared have been too sweet—they can never displease me, and can scarcely be banished from my thoughts. Wherever I turn they are always before my eyes, bringing with them awakened longings and fantasies which will not even let me sleep. Even during the celebration of the Mass, when our prayers should be purer, lewd visions of those pleasures take such a hold on my unhappy soul that my thoughts are on their wantonness instead of on prayers. I should be groaning over the sins I have committed, but I can only sigh for what I have lost. (1974, p. 133)

While few lovers today can match either the poetry or the forbidden, exalted sexuality of the two medieval martyrs, their affair strikes a distinctly modern note. Many men and women care deeply about the sexual appeal of their dates and mates. When practical friends confide that *they* plan to marry someone who is "just a friend," these modern listeners can scarcely credit it. In this chapter we ask a number of questions. What is sex appeal? How similar is the sexual behavior of men and women? How common are sexual fantasies? Are men and women equally "turned on" by pornography? Can sexual passion last?

Love is without law.
  —Barnabe Rich

Sex as Sin

Answers to these questions vary from culture to culture and from time to time. Today's Madonna and her cult would answer these questions very differently than would Christians who followed the Cult of the Madonna in the twelfth century.

Sexual desire and sexual activity are hardly modern-day inventions. People have been doing sex as long as our species has existed—else there would be no species. But love and sex need not necessarily be linked nor need sex be viewed positively (despite the fact that it is necessary if the species is to survive). The central myth of Western Christianity—the story of Adam and Eve—does not celebrate sexual desire! Its disgust with lust has played a major part in the oppression of women throughout history by defining women as vessels of temptation corrupted by sinful carnality. Men must avoid that temptation by seeking the purity of Faith in God. Women, only if chaste, could enter the Kingdom of Heaven as virgin madonnas. All other women were whores. Women are still striving today to negotiate the considerable territory between being a madonna or being a whore, a choice fostered by traditional Christianity in its horror of sexuality.

So while sex has always existed, its meanings have greatly varied with time. Historians John D'Emilio and Estelle Freedman (1988) have noted that sexuality has been associated with a wide range of human activities and values: "the procreation of children, the attainment of physical pleasure (eroticism), recreation or sport, personal intimacy, spiritual transcendence, or power over others" (p. xv). In writing their history of American sexual values, they went on:

> The dominant meaning of sexuality has changed during our history from a primary association with reproduction within families to a primary association with emotional intimacy and physical pleasure for individuals. In the colonial era, the dominant language of sexuality was reproductive, and the appropriate locus for sexual activity was in courtship or marriage. In the nineteenth century, an emergent middle class emphasized sexuality as a means to personal intimacy, at the same time that it reduced sharply its rate of reproduction. Gradually, commercial growth brought sex into the marketplace, especially for working-class women and for men of all classes. (pp. xv–xvi)

In the West, the traditional meanings attached to sexuality derived from Christianity in both its major forms—Catholicism and Protestantism. The Catholic "cult of virginity" and its praise of monasticism yielded in northern Europe and the United States to the Protestant constriction of love to "sober performance of lawful procreative tasks." Both religions, according to the eminent neo-Freudian historian Peter Gay (1986), insisted that "lust is a sin" and both "left deposits of guilt and depression" for centuries on the Western mind (p. 50).

There has been a sexual revolution underway in the West for 500 years, associated with the rise of individualism. For if we imagine that we stand alone as individuals at the core of *the* great drama (the story of our personal existences) in which we are permitted, even enjoined, to strain for personal happiness (one way to define "individualism"), that happiness will assuredly encompass sexual joy (see Box 3.1).

The sexual revolution picked up tremendous speed during the early decades of this century, spurred by rapidly changing ideas about personal freedom and advances in birth control. But utterly astonishing transformations have taken place since 1960, connected not only with the further expansion of individualism, but with its major offshoot—the latest phase of the women's movement. Historians often stress continuities between the present and past, but there is no question that we are witnessing a renewed sexual revolution of astounding proportions. Sexuality in the twentieth century has attained altogether different meanings than ever before. D'Emilio and Freedman (1988) wrote:

> By the twentieth century, when the individual had replaced the family as the primary economic unit, the tie between sexuality and reproduction weakened further. Influenced by psychology as well as by the growing power of the media, both men and women began to adopt personal happiness as a primary goal of sexual relations. (p. xvi)

Throughout this chapter, we shall see example after example of profound changes in sexual behavior and attitude in our own lifetimes. In assessing these

Box 3.1   THE FRENCH LIEUTENANT'S WOMAN

In the late nineteenth century, the English were beginning to move from the tight strictures of rigid Victorian society to the unlaced passions of the pre-Raphaelite era. Author John Fowles (1969) dramatized the anguish that accompanied this transition in his depiction of the intense affair between Charles Smithson and Sarah Woodruff in *The French Lieutenant's Woman*.

He knew why he had come: it was to see her again. Seeing her was the need; like an intolerable thirst that had to be assuaged.

He forced himself to look away. But his eyes lighted on the two naked marble nymphs above the fireplace. . . . They did not help. And Sarah made a little movement. . . .

"My dear Miss Woodruff, pray don't cry . . . I should not have come . . . I meant not to. . . ."

But she shook her head with sudden vehemence. He gave her time to recover. And it was while she made little dabbing motions with a handkerchief that he was overcome with a violent sexual desire. . . . Her defenseless weeping was perhaps the breach through which the knowledge sprang—but suddenly he comprehended why her face haunted him, why he felt this terrible need to see her again: it was to possess her, to melt into her, to burn, to burn to ashes on that body and in those eyes. To postpone such desire for a week, a month, a year, several years even, that can be done. But for eternity is when the iron bites. . . .

"I thought never to see you again."

He could not tell her how close she had come to his own truth. She looked up at him and he as quickly looked down . . . his heart raced, his hand trembled. He knew if he looked into those eyes he was lost. As if to ban them, he shut his own.

The silence was terrible then, as tense as a bridge about to break, a tower to fall; unendurable in its emotion, its truth bursting to be spoken.

Then suddenly there was a little cascade of coals from the fire . . . one or two bounced off and onto the edge of the blanket that covered Sarah's legs . . . the blanket smoldered. He snatched it away from her. . . . Both feet were bare . . . her hand reached shyly out and rested on his. He knew she was looking up at him. He could not move his hand, and suddenly he could not keep his eyes from hers. . . . How long they looked into each other's eyes he did not know. . . . Their hands acted first. By some mysterious communion, the fingers interlaced. Then Charles fell on one knee and strained her passionately to him. Their mouths met with a wild violence that shocked both; made her avert her lips. He covered her cheeks, her eyes, with kisses. His hand at last touched that hair, caressed it, felt the small head through its softness, as the thin-clad body was felt against his arms and breast. Suddenly he buried his face in her neck.

"We must not . . . we must not . . . this is madness."

But her arms came round him and pressed his head closer. He did not move. He felt borne on wings of fire, hurtling, but in such

(Continued on p. 72)

tender air, like a child at last let free from school, a prisoner in a green field, a hawk rising. He raised his head and looked at her: an almost savage fierceness. . . . He glanced at the door behind her; then stood and in two strides was at it. . . .

Each reflected the intensity in each other's eyes, the flood, the being swept before it. She seemed to half step, half fall towards him. He sprang forward and caught her in his arms and embraced her. The shawl fell. No more than a layer of flannel lay between him and her nakedness. He strained that body into his, straining his mouth upon hers, with all the hunger of a long frustration—not merely sexual, for a whole ungovernable torrent of things banned, romance, adventure, sin, madness, animality, all these coursed wildly through him. . . . He began to undress wildly, tearing off his clothes as if someone was drowning and he was on the bank. A button from his frock coat flew off and rolled into a corner, but he did not even look to see where it went. . . . Then he raised his left knee onto the narrow bed and fell on her, raining burning kisses on her mouth, her eyes, her throat. But the passive yet acquiescent body pressed beneath him, the naked feet that touched his own . . . he could not wait. Raising himself a little, he drew up her nightgown. Her legs parted. With a frantic brutality . . . he found the place and thrust. Her body flinched. . . . He conquered that instinctive constriction, and her arms flung round him as if she would bind him to her for that eternity he could not dream without her.

"Oh my dearest. My dearest. My sweetest angel . . . Sarah, . . . Sarah, . . . oh Sarah."

A few moments later he lay still. Precisely ninety seconds had passed since he had left her to look into the bedroom.

Silence.

They lay as if paralyzed by what they had done. Congealed in sin, frozen with delight. Charles—no gentle postcoital sadness for him, but an immediate and universal horror—was like a city struck out of a quiet sky by an atom bomb. All lay razed; all principle, all future, all faith, all honorable intent. Yet he survived, he lay in the sweetest possession of his life, the last man alive, infinitely isolated . . . but already the radioactivity of guilt crept, crept through his nerves and veins. . . . What a mess, what an inutterable mess!

And he held her a little closer.

Source: pp. 346–351

changes we are handicapped by their rapidity and the novelty of many of the questions we face. There is no guarantee that the movement toward increasingly greater sexual freedom will forever continue; the only linear history is the history of technology, and the AIDS epidemic has already slowed the pace of change. But the best bet is that there is unlikely to be a return to sexual "repression" or "restraint" (the term you use depends on your value system), and that means that the questions raised by today's transformations in the West are not likely to go away.

I don't know how it happened but she was in my arms. Then it was like an atomic fire searing through us. We couldn't wait to get at each other. Our clothes made a trail up the stairs to the bedroom. We fell naked on the bed, tearing at each other like raging animals. Then we exploded and fell backward on the bed, gasping for breath.

—Harold Robbins. A superheated and fanciful description of sexual attraction. Cited in Bernard Zilbergeld (1978, p. 49)

SEX APPEAL: WHAT IS IT?

Scientists and social commentators have spent an enormous amount of effort trying to discover universal standards of beauty. Greek philosophers such as Aristotle assumed that the Golden Mean was the ideal. The Golden Mean represented a perfect balance. The Romans insisted, on the other hand, that the rare and unique were most appealing. In the Renaissance, artists such as Leonardo da Vinci attempted to discover the mathematics of beauty. Charles Darwin's painstaking observations (1871) finally convinced most scientists that culture set the standard and thus it was futile to search for universals. Any lingering hopes of identifying such sweeping standards were shattered in the landmark survey by Clellan Ford and Frank Beach (1951) of more than 200 primitive societies. They too failed to find *any* universal standards of sexual allure. Table 3.1 lists some of the traits that people in various societies have considered hallmarks of women's beauty. Let us now consider some of these traits in more detail.

Many a man in love with a dimple makes the mistake of marrying the whole girl.
—Stephen Leacock

Table 3.1 SOCIETIES' PREFERENCES IN
          WOMEN'S APPEARANCE

Trait	Number of societies that admire this trait
Slim body build	5
Medium body build	5
Plump body build	13
Narrow pelvis and slim hips	1
Broad pelvis and wide hips	6
Small ankles	3
Shapely calves	5
Upright, hemispherical breasts	2
Long and pendulous breasts	2
Large breasts	9
Large clitoris	1
Elongated *labia majora*	8

The Face

Recently, sociobiologists have revived hopes that more sophisticated sociobiological theory and research techniques may finally enable scientists to pinpoint some aesthetic universals. In one promising study, Judith Langlois and Lori Roggman (1990) found evidence that the Greeks' Golden Mean may serve as the gold standard of appeal. The authors assembled photographs of the faces of people. Using state-of-the-art video and computer techniques, they generated a series of composite faces (truly average men and women). They found that composites were far more attractive than any of the individual faces. The disconcerting quirks that mar individual faces or give them distinctiveness—the oddly spaced eyes, the ears that are too large, the crooked teeth—are less appealing than the averaged face. The average of many imperfect faces results in . . . perfection. Their conclusion? "Attractive faces are only average." Other sociobiologists have embarked on testing the notion that men and women prefer faces that, in a sense, have it all—faces that combine the innocence of childhood with the ripe sexuality of the mature. Early ethologists observed that men and women often experienced a tender rush of feeling when they viewed infantile "kewpie doll" faces—a face with huge eyes, tiny noses and mouths, and adorable little chins (Eibl-Eibesfeldt, 1971). Other authors (Symons, 1979) proposed that men and women should be aroused by faces that possessed features associated with maturity, especially lush, grown-up sexuality (say, thick hair, dewy skin, and full lips) and/or mature power (say, high cheekbones or a firm jaw and chin). In a recent film, *Who Framed Roger Rabbit?* the sexy "toon" Jessica Rabbit caricatured just these traits. Most recent evidence finds that people like faces that possess both assets: say, large eyes and small noses, combined with full sensual lips and a strong jaw and chin (Cunningham, Barbee, & Pike, 1990). Whether these preferences will turn out to be universal is not yet known.

The Body

In many societies, sexual attractiveness is associated with the possession of a great body. What is the ideal shape? Nancy Wiggins and J. C. Conger (1968) tried to find out what American *men* found sexually appealing. They prepared 105 nude silhouettes. The first silhouette had a Golden Mean sort of body: She possessed average-sized breasts, buttocks, and legs. (If the Greeks and the modern scholars of composite faces were right, men should have preferred her. Alas, they did not.) The remaining silhouettes were systematically varied. The Golden Mean theory turned out to have *some* validity. Most men thought the women with medium-sized breasts, buttocks, and legs were more attractive than those with unusually small or large features. The American ideal, however, was a woman with slightly oversized breasts, medium to slightly small buttocks, and medium-sized legs.

What about women? What do they think is sexy? Paul Lavarkas (1975) tried to find out. He constructed 19 different types of men's bodies on graph paper—combining the same-size head with bigger or smaller arms, torsos, and legs. Most women were *not* attracted to the Arnold Schwarzenegger-type muscleman. They preferred instead men with a Tom Cruise, tapered V-look (medium-sized or slightly larger shoulders, waist, and hips, and thin legs). They were most "turned off" by a pear-shaped look (men with small shoulders and wide hips).

In America, then, there is considerable agreement as to what constitutes a sexually appealing body. Fortunately, there is no evidence that American preferences are universal. In most societies of the world, robust or even fat women are seen as possessing the most sex appeal. Clelland Ford and Frank Beach (1951) report:

> [Holmberg writes of the Siriono:] Besides being young, a desirable sex partner—especially a woman—should also be fat. She should have big hips, good but firm breasts, and a deposit of fat on her sexual organs. (pp. 88–89)

This makes a certain amount of sense. In many primitive societies, people are poised on the fine edge of survival. A fat wife is a status symbol. She graphically illustrates her husband's ability to provide . . . to excess.

Sexual Traits: The Fundamentals

In many societies, people are focused on the parts of the body associated with sexuality. In America, fairly large breasts are considered sexy. Other cultures have very different standards. Some people prefer small upright breasts. (The Wogeo think breasts should be firm with the nipples still facing outwards. A young girl with pendulous breasts, "like a grandmother," is pitied.) Other peoples most admire long and pendulous breasts.

In many societies, elongated *labia majora* or *minora* (vaginal lips) are considered erotically appealing. Before puberty, girls on Ponape undergo treatments designed to enlarge their clitoris and lengthen the *labia minora*. Impotent old men pull, beat, and suck the labia to lengthen them. The girls put black ants in their *vulvas* so that their stinging will cause the *labia* and *clitoris* to swell. In America, most men are not particularly focused on this area. (Another society's obsessions always seem strange while our own are, naturally, normal.) Pornographic magazines featuring "beaver shots" appeal to a minority.

In many cultures, women consider the size and shape of men's penes to be important. In the New Hebrides, men choose to exaggerate their sexual appeal. Anthropologist B. T. Somerville (1894) observed:

> The natives wrap the penis around with many yards of calico, and other materials, winding and folding them until a preposterous bundle of eighteen inches, or two feet long, and two inches or more in diameter is formed, which is then supported upwards by means of a belt, in the extremity decorated with flowering grasses, etc. The testicles are left naked. (p. 368)

Lest the obsessions of other cultures with men's genitals seem exotic, note that *Rolling Stone* magazine once devoted an entire issue to describing how magazines such as *Playgirl* and *Viva* tease, cajole, and massage the centerfold's penis to just the right stage of arousal (McCormack, 1975). Elvis Presley often used a toilet paper tube under tight pants while performing on stage to augment his penis size (Wallace, 1981).

The sweet smells of sex.
   —Psychology Today

Smell

Sexual appeal is so mysterious that some scientists have speculated that perhaps its essence lies in sexual "chemistry." In 1880, novelist Joris-Karl Huysmans celebrated armpits as a gift of nature, calling them "spice boxes" that "season and enhance the stew of love." Mammals can distinguish between 10,000 or so scents. Lower animals secrete powerful *pheromones* (biochemicals), which stimulate sexual desire and behavior. For example, butterflies exude perfumes that may smell like roses, sweetbriar, heliotrope, and other flowers; the aroma sexually attracts other butterflies (Ackerman, 1990, p. 27). Do humans secrete and respond to such pheromones? Scientists have speculated that they might. Once, when Napoleon neared the end of a campaign, he sent a famous message to Josephine: "Will be home in three weeks. Don't wash." Odor is a genetic hand-me-down; individual odors are as distinctive as fingerprints or DNA. Even among families, every member has his or her own smell. The only exception to the rule: the identical odor of identical twins. Pheromones might be produced in the armpit sweat glands, by the prepuce of the penis, and by the clitoris. Perfume company scientists try to sniff out natural pheromones so that they can duplicate their musky scent. Thus far, however, there is little evidence that humans produce such pheromones or that they are sexually excited by scent (Clegg, 1979; Griffitt & Hatfield, 1985). Madison Avenue, however, has never hesitated to sell dreams.

> Some trendy women in Manhattan are wearing a perfume called Pheromone, priced at three hundred dollars an ounce. Expensive perhaps, but what price aphrodisia? Based on findings about the sexual attractants animals give off, the perfume promises, by implication, to make a woman smell provocative and turn stalwart men into slaves of desire: love zombies. The odd thing about the claims of this perfume is that its manufacturer has not specified *which* pheromones are in it. Human pheromones have not yet been identified by researchers, whereas, say, boar pheromones have. The vision of a generation of young women walking the streets wearing boar pheromones is strange, even for Manhattan. Let me propose a naughty recipe: Turn loose a herd of sows on Park Avenue. Mix well with crowds of women wearing Pheromone eau de cologne. Dial 911 for emergency. (Ackerman, 1990, p. 28)

Most peoples are less interested in pheromones than in cleanliness and getting rid of foul and repulsive odors. Notwithstanding Napoleon, some societies use perfume to cover up "offensive" body odors. The Wogeo, for example, combat the odor of perspiration with aromatic leaves. Many peoples anoint their skin with scented oils. In many societies, men and women wear sweet-smelling flowers in their hair and on their bodies. Caypa men use sweet-scented herbs to attract women; Western Apache women wear aromatic plants to attract men.

In summary: A few sociobiologists are still engaged in the search for universals in sex appeal. However, after a painstaking search, most anthropologists have admitted defeat. Scholars have ended where they began—able to do no more than to point to the dazzling array of characteristics that various peoples in various places, at various times, have idealized.

Lois Banner, for example, has written the major history of America's changing standards of female beauty over the past two centuries. Even in so short a time, the ideals have shifted at a dizzying rate. Before the Civil War, "the frail, pale willowy woman" predominated. In the decades after 1865, "she was challenged by a buxom, hearty, and heavy model of beauty." She, in turn, had to face stiff competition from "the tall, athletic, patrician Gibson girl of the 1890s, whose vogue was superseded in the 1910s by a small, boyish model of beauty exemplified by Mary Pickford and Clara Bow." Banner then continued the merry-go-round:

> This "flapper" model of beauty was predominant throughout the 1920s. By 1930 a new, less youthful and frivolous beauty ideal came into being and remained popular through the 1950s, culminating in a renewed vogue of voluptuousness that bore resemblance to nineteenth-century types. That same decade, however, a youthful, adolescent model reappeared and continued in popularity through the 1960s, a decade that witnessed a significant rebellion, not only against the commercial culture of beauty and fashion, but also against the whole notion of a single or standard ideal of beauty based on Western European types. Black women began to be portrayed as beauties within the white community; women of distinctive characteristics such as Barbra Streisand with her Mediterranean looks, created new manners of appearance. (Banner, 1983, p. 50)

That last sentence, written about a decade ago in 1983, hinted at the erosion of the tyranny of standardized beauty. But one could argue that, at this writing, no such luck: the anorexic look and the muscular, athletic shape of iron-pumping women rank as the current *beau* ideals, exerting their awesome power on American culture to make the huge majority of women feel inadequate, embarrassed, and fat.

And yet we know the current standards of perfection will shift again in a few years, producing yet more insecurities and feverish efforts to fit the new ideals. Let us consider how people have been found to deal with such unending demands on them.

MEN'S AND WOMEN'S SEXUAL HISTORIES: THE TRADITIONAL VIEW

In the 1940s and 1950s, Alfred Kinsey and his fellows (Kinsey, Pomeroy, & Martin, 1948; Kinsey, Pomeroy, Martin, & Gebhard, 1953) shocked Americans with their profiles of national sexual habits. Kinsey found that a double standard prevailed in that era. Men were encouraged or at least allowed to be sexual; women were not. Thus it came as no surprise to discover that men and women had very different sexual histories. Most boys, for example, had begun to masturbate by the time they were 13 years old. By 18, the men were beginning to push to have sex. (Men were as interested in sex at 18 as they ever would be.) As men aged, their sexual interest began to decline. William Masters and Virginia Johnson (1966, 1970) found that by the time men were 65 years of age, 25% of them were impotent; by the time they were 75, 50% were impotent.

Women's sexual histories were very different. Women were slow to begin experimenting; at 15 (when almost all boys had already begun to masturbate), most women were quite inactive. Sometime between the ages of 16 and 20, however, they slowly shed their inhibitions. Now, women were becomingly increasingly interested in sex; they continued to be more enthusiastic about sexual activity for fully two decades. Not until their late 40s did their sexual activity begin to ebb. Kinsey and his colleagues (1953) observed that such gender differences guaranteed marital tragedy. When men were interested in sex, women weren't. By the time women were interested, men had lost it.

Theorists offered a variety of reasons as to why men and women might have such different sexual attitudes, feelings, and behaviors.

Men seek to propagate widely, whereas women seek to propagate wisely.
—Robert Hinde

Sociobiologists such as Donald Symons (1979) and Jerome Berkow (1989) pointed out that the mind evolved to solve adaptive problems. Symons argued that men and women were programmed to desire very different things. Symon's argument proceeded as follows: According to evolutionary biology, an animal's "fitness is a measure of the extent to which it succeeds in passing on its genes to the next generation" (p. 6). It is to both men's and women's evolutionary advantage to produce as many children, grandchildren, and great-grandchildren, as possible. But men and women differ in one critical respect: in order to produce a child, men need only to invest a trivial amount of energy. A single man could conceivably father an almost unlimited number of children. Since women can have far fewer children, it is to a woman's advantage to ensure that the few children she does conceive survive. Symons observed:

> The enormous sex differences in minimum parental investment and in reproductive opportunities and constraints explain why *Homo sapiens*, a species with only moderate sex differences in structure, exhibits profound sex differences in psyche. (p. 27)

What are the gender differences he insisted are wired in? According to Symons:

1. Men are genetically programmed to impregnate as many women as possible. Women have every reason to be "coy." It takes time to decide if a man is a good genetic risk—that is, is likely to be nurturant and protective.
2. For men, "sexual attractiveness" equals youth. For women, sexual attractiveness equals political and economic power.
3. Men are sexually aroused by the sight of women and women's genitals; women are not aroused by men's appearance.
4. Men desire a variety of sex partners; women do not.
5. Men are inclined to be polygamous (possessing many wives). Women are more malleable in this respect; they are equally satisfied in polygamous, monogamous, or polyandrous marriages (possessing many husbands).
6. Men are sexually jealous. Women are more malleable in this respect; they are concerned with security, not fidelity.
7. Men are intensely competitive with one another. Competition over women is the most frequent cause of violence. Women are far less competitive.

Sociobiologist Jerome Berkow (1989) has speculated that men and women should desire different things in mates. Men should prefer women who are young, who are faithful (so men will not invest resources in unrelated children), and who show intelligence, social skills, and resourcefulness (cues to the woman's maternal skills.) Women should focus on men who show the willingness and ability to invest resources in her and her children.

She's beautiful and therefore to be woo'd.
    —William Shakespeare

Since these contentions were voiced, sociobiologists have begun to test some of these notions. Let us first consider the evidence that *men* prefer the kinds of women that sociobiologists say they should. Although early sociobiologists provided an evolutionary scenario that emphasized male promiscuity and female selectivity, both men and women turn out to be extremely choosy about whom they are willing to marry (Berkow, 1989). Cross-cultural evidence is now strong that men worldwide prefer marriage partners who are younger than they are (Buss, 1989). In some cultures (but not all) men do value chastity in potential mates somewhat more than women do (Buss, 1989). Men are more likely to divorce wives who are unfaithful than vice versa (Betzig, 1989). In a study of 37 societies, sociobiologists found that in all of them men did prefer intelligent mates (Buss, 1989; Hudson & Henze, 1969).

Only God, my dear, could love you for yourself alone, and not your yellow hair.
    —William Butler Yeats

Unfortunately, researchers have been less interested in *women's* preferences in mates. There is some evidence that women in widely varying cultures value status, ambition, and industriousness (Buss, 1989; Hill, 1945) even when they have access to resources themselves (Townsend, 1989).

David Buss and his colleagues (Buss, 1988a, b; Buss & Barnes, 1986) proposed that, if the sociobiologists were right, men and women (1) should advertise very different assets when trying to attract mates and (2) should look for very different traits in mates. Buss (1988b) found that men and women did use different strategies when trying to impress potential sex partners. Men tended to brag about their status, power, strength, and achievements. Women tried to emphasize their beauty, health, and youth. Researchers (Buss & Barnes, 1986) also confirmed that men and women did look for different qualities in a mate. Everyone wanted mates who possessed intelligence and exciting personalities, mates who were kind and understanding. However, men were most attuned to signs that attested to women's reproductive fitness. (They cared a great deal about physical appearance: they valued youth, health, beauty, clear and lustrous hair, smooth skin, full lips, white teeth, and a lively gait.) Women looked for signs that men were willing and able to protect them and their offspring. (They looked for professional men with ambition, status, and money. They wanted mates who were kind and considerate, easygoing and adaptable, and who liked children.)

Sociobiology is still in its infancy. Many sociobiological predictions seem inconsistent with our knowledge of human sexual behavior. Nonetheless, behavioral genetics offer a potentially useful perspective.

It has often been pointed out that women depend lopsidedly on love for emotional fulfillment because they are barred from absorbing activity in the public domain. This is true. But it is also true that men depend lopsidedly on participation in the public domain because they are stymied by love.
—Dorothy Dinnerstein

Social learning theorists, on the other hand, insisted that most "innate" gender differences are actually learned. Men and women are very adaptable. A half century ago, Margaret Mead (1969) in *Sex and Temperament in Three Primitive Societies* discussed three cultures of New Guinea (now Papua New Guinea) and their gender role standards. She described the gentle Arapesh, a culture in which both men and women had "feminine" traits; the fierce Mundugamur, in which both genders were "masculine"; and the Tchambuli, in which the men were "feminine" and the women were "masculine." Thus, social learning theorists argued, if men and women desire different things from their sexual relationships, it is because they have been taught to do so (Griffitt & Hatfield, 1985; Howard et al., 1986; Reiss & Lee, 1988; Tavris & Offir, 1977). For example, sociologist John DeLamater (1987) pointed out that men and women of the twentieth-century Euro-American world are handed very different sexual scripts by life. In general, women are taught to take a "person-centered" orientation to sexuality. They learn that love, sex, and commitment are inextricably entwined. Men are taught to take a recreational (or "body-centered") approach toward sex. For them the goal of sex is physical gratification. There is some evidence that these social learning theorists are correct.

THE CONTEMPORARY VIEW

There are times when I am very sexual, when I'm just hungry, like a lion. But there are times when I can do without it. I don't need it. You know, it's not a necessity in my life. I swear to you, it has a lot to do with when the moon is full. The elements have a real deep effect on me and I respond to them.
—Popular singer Whitney Houston

Since Kinsey's day, generations of sex researchers have continued to interview young people. Have they ever kissed? At what age did they begin? Have they touched their lovers' breasts or genitals? Been touched? Had intercourse? Dared oral–genital sex? When we look at the pattern of these studies, it is clear that a sexual revolution has occurred. In Kinsey's era, men's and women's sexual attitudes and behavior were very different: the double standard prevailed. (Men could be forgiven, sometimes even admired, for their sexual boldness. Women could not.) In reviewing recent survey research, however, sociologist John DeLamater (1987) concluded that a single, liberal, standard now prevails: "There are few, if any, significant differences between males and females in sexual attitudes and behavior" (p. 127). Let us consider these divergent results—focusing particularly on the very few gender differences that still appear to exist.

Don't knock masturbation—it's sex with someone I love.
—Woody Allen

Masturbation

No aspect of sexual expression has escaped the condemnation of religious, medical, or scientific authorities. Theologians argued that masturbation was sinful. In the eighteenth century, physicians argued that, if not sinful, masturbation endangered the health of the masturbator. In 1758, the Swiss physician Samuel Tissot published *Onania, or a Treatise Upon the Disorders Produced by Masturbation.* This influential work claimed that masturbation was a dangerous habit capable of producing every illness known, including pimples, blisters, constipation, consumption, blindness, insomnia, headaches, genital cancer, feeblemindness, weakness, jaundice, nose pain, intestinal disorders, confusion, insanity, and a host of additional rather grotesque maladies. Taken together, theology and medical "science" acted in concert to try to persuade people that masturbation was sinful, immoral, and dangerous to mental and physical health. Such views, however, were totally ineffective in eliminating masturbation. By Kinsey's day, most boys had begun to masturbate by age 15; few 15-year-old girls had experimented with such self-pleasuring. (Most women did not begin to masturbate until they were in their 30s!) (See Figure 3.1.) Today, boys still begin to masturbate slightly earlier than do girls (see Table 3.2) but such gender differences are rapidly disappearing.

The social context in which men's and women's early experimentation takes place is still very different, however. For some boys, masturbation is a group event. Some, for example, may engage in a "circle jerk," in which a group of boys races to masturbate to climax. Girls' early sexual exploration is almost always private; only a few learn about masturbation from their friends; some are told about masturbation by their boyfriends.

Sex researchers point out that such differences might have important consequences for boys' and girls' sexual attitudes and skills. Since boys masturbate earlier, they may be more confident that they control their own sexuality, have a head start on learning what arouses them, and are more sexually skilled (Rook & Hammen, 1977). Sex therapists generally recommend that men and women who have sexual problems should learn about sex one step at a time. First, they should begin by practicing masturbating (Barbach, 1976; Zilbergeld, 1978). Once they are comfortable with the idea of self-pleasuring, aware of what arouses their sexual desire, and proficient at self-pleasuring, they can move on to the next step—coordinating sexual relations with their partners.

Sexual Fantasy While Masturbating   A woman described her sexual fantasies while masturbating as follows (Friday, 1973, pp. 16–17):

> In my fantasy I call for him to get up out of bed, I know he isn't sleeping. . . . I am about to call him again but another boy, a school friend, comes to call and I let them go off by themselves. . . . They go into the woodshed, and after a little time I creep

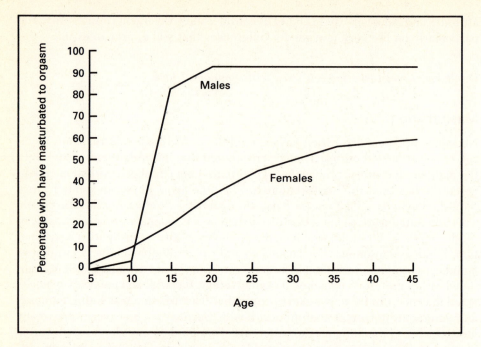

Figure 3.1 The percentage of men and women of various ages who have masturbated to orgasm.

down and peek through the planks. They are standing facing each other, their cocks out, stroking each other. I feel so bloody cross, but yet I still feel myself getting wet. I go back to the house and shriek for him to come in. I still feel like hitting him over the head. He comes in half ashamed and sneering; I myself sit down with my legs trembling. I see he has a big bulge there, he seems to be sticking it out more, then, I don't know, I open his buttons and pull his shirt up. I didn't think it was so big. I stroke him, it is hot and throbbing and he comes as quick as that, covering my hand. . . . I am shaking with sex.

People often enjoy sexual fantasies while masturbating or having sexual relations. In various studies, 88 to 99% of men and women reported that they have had sexual fantasies (Brown & Hart, 1977; Davidson & Hoffman, 1986); 80% of them fantasize while they masturbate (Hunt, 1974, p. 91). Table 3.3 lists the most

Table 3.2 PERCENTAGE OF BOYS AND GIRLS MASTURBATING BY AGE 13

	Kinsey et al. (1948, 1953)	Arafat and Cotton (1974)	Bell, Weinberg, and Hammersmith (1981)	Wyatt, Peters, and Guthrie (1988)
Men	45%	50%	63%	—
Women	15	32	32	37%

Table 3.3   COMMON MASTURBATION FANTASIES

Theme of fantasy	Percentage of men and women having a given fantasy	
	Men	Women
Having sex with someone you love	75%	80%
Having sex with strangers	47	21
Having sex with several people at the same time	33	18
Doing "taboo" things	19	28
Being forced to have sex	10	19
Forcing someone to have sex	13	3
Having homosexual relations	7	11

Source: Based on Hunt, 1974, pp. 91–93.

popular masturbation fantasies. In general, men's and women's fantasies are fairly similar. They daydream about having sexual relations with someone they love or find sexually appealing. There are a few differences in men's and women's fantasies, however. Many men are nervous about initiating sexual affairs; they fear rejection, and not without reason. Women's reluctance to have sex is part of the folklore. In *Love and Death*, Woody Allen and Diane Keaton are shown in bed on their wedding night. He timidly starts to caress her shoulder; she jerks away. "Please," she says irritably, "not here." In *Play It Again, Sam*, a luscious countess confides to Woody that she is a nymphomaniac—she is sexually insatiable. Of course, when Woody tries to kiss her, she is shocked: "What kind of a woman do you think I am?" Given their fear of rejection, it isn't very surprising that many male fantasies center around women who long for sex, beg for it, are indeed insatiable. Men also tend to imagine scenarios in which they are powerful and aggressive; swept up in impersonal and thrilling encounters.

Women's fantasies are more likely to involve romance . . . or being forced to submit (DeLora & Warren, 1977). The point of these seemingly radically different fantasies is exactly the same. Both men and women long to be loved and desired. Both also seem to want to shrug off responsibility for doing the forbidden: "It wasn't my fault; she was begging for it." "It wasn't my fault; he made me do it." It is only the way in which their desires are played out that differs.

> The sun shines for you he said the day we were lying among the rhododendrons on Howth head in the grey tweed suit and his straw hat the day I got him to propose to me yes first I gave him the bit of seedcake out of my mouth and it was leap year like now yes 16 years ago my God after that long kiss I near lost my breath yes he said I was a flower of the mountain yes. . . . and how he kissed me under the Moorish wall and I thought well as well him as another and then I asked him with my eyes to ask again yes and then he asked me would I yes to say yes my mountain flower and first I put my arms around him yes and drew him down to me so he could feel my breasts all perfume yes and his heart was going like mad and yes I said yes I will Yes.
>
> —James Joyce

Adolescent Heterosexual Behavior

Most young people in Western cultures begin to experiment sexually in early adolescence. Most boys and girls begin timidly. The boy in the movie theater may awkwardly drape his arm over the back of the chair of the girl sitting next to him. His heart pounds, partly in excitement but mainly in terror. He hopes she will think his arm just happens to be resting there. If she draws away, he can mumble an embarrassed "Sorry" and remove his arm. If she snuggles into his arm, he may more boldly hug her. Probably not. They are thrilled with very little.

With time, and practice, couples move on to more daring behavior—kissing. They learn how to kiss with their glasses or braces on, what to do with their noses. In 1979, John DeLamater and Patricia MacCorquodale interviewed more than 2000 young men and women. They found that today, men's and women's sexual histories are remarkably similar. Men and women begin to kiss, fondle, and have sexual relations at almost the same age. They also progress from kissing, to fondling, to intercourse at about the same pace. This progression usually occurs over a four-year period (see Table 3.4).

Men are somewhat more willing to experiment with recreational sex. Women are somewhat more likely to feel that they should be married, engaged, or in love before they engage in sexual relations. Nonetheless, men and women actually engage in sex for the first time at roughly the same ages (Walsh, 1989).

Men and women generally react very differently to their first sexual experiences, however. Young men often think of a sexual experience as a "rite of passage" into manhood (Carns, 1973). Most men said they felt "excited," "happy," "satisfied," and "thrilled" the first time they had sexual intercourse. For women, however, it is more risky to experiment with sex. They feel it is only "legitimate" if they are involved in a serious, meaningful relationship (Carns, 1973). Women often felt guilty, sad, disappointed, and afraid after their first sexual encounters (DeLamater, 1987; Sorensen, 1973). Unfortunately, men were usually unaware of their partners' negative reactions (Sorensen, 1973). Men were likely

Table 3.4 MEN AND WOMEN STUDENTS' SEXUAL BEHAVIORS

Behavior	Men		Women	
	Percentage engaging in behavior	Average age	Percentage engaging in behavior	Average age
Necking	97%	14.2	99	14.8
French kissing	93	15.3	95	15.8
Petting	92	15.8	93	16.6
Men fondling women's genitals	86	16.6	82	17.2
Women fondling men's genitals	82	16.8	78	17.4
Genital apposition	77	17.1	72	17.6
Intercourse	75	17.5	60	17.9
Cunnilingus	60	18.2	59	18.1
Fellatio	61	18.1	54	18.1

Source: Based on DeLamater & MacCorquodale, 1979, p. 59.

to boast to their families and friends about their sexual escapades; their families and friends were likely to approve of their behavior. Women were less likely to confide in others. It is easy to see why. Unless the couple's relationship was a deeply committed one, her family (brought up, as they were, on different and more conservative sexual mores) and even her friends generally disapproved of her behavior (Carns, 1973; DeLamater, 1987).

Nonetheless, men and women begin to experiment with the various sexual activities at roughly the same ages (again, see Table 3.4). One study of college-age individuals found that most young men had had six sexual partners and most women averaged five sexual partners over their dating histories (DeLamater & MacCorquodale, 1979). Women seemed to be more reserved than men in only one type of situation: If both were offered a chance to participate in uncertain, unconventional, or even downright bizarre sexual activities, men were more willing to take a risk than were women.

In the Forties, to get a girl you had to be a GI or a jock. In the Fifties, to get a girl you had to be Jewish. In the Sixties, to get a girl you had to be black. In the Seventies, to get a girl you've got to be a girl.

—Mort Sahl

Homosexual Behavior

Many teenagers experiment with gay, lesbian, or bisexual relations. A few find that they greatly prefer homosexual love affairs (Blumstein & Schwartz, 1983). In the 1940s and 1950s, Kinsey found that 37% of men and 13% of women had had at least one homosexual encounter in adulthood. Recent research suggests Kinsey's statistics may be a bit high. Today, the best guess is that at least 20% of men and 10% of women have homosexual relations at some time in their lives. As adults, about 7% of men and 4% of women have such experiences (Fay, Turner, Klassen, & Gagnon, 1989). How many people consider themselves to be exclusively heterosexual? Bisexual? Gay? Lesbian? Probably 80% of men and 90% of women consider themselves to be exclusively heterosexual. About 2% of men and 1% of women consider themselves to be exclusively homosexual. The remaining men and women are sexually attracted to both men and women at different times (Hyde, 1990).

Whether their sexual orientation is gay, straight, or bisexual, people confront the same emotional dilemmas in their relationships. Homosexual relationship issues differ little from heterosexual ones; they are best understood as human issues, regardless of sexual orientation. Gay men, lesbians, and heterosexuals love their mates in the same ways and display the same patterns of satisfaction and unhappiness in their relationships (Blumstein & Schwartz, 1983; Peplau & Amaro, 1982). Their sexual experiments generally follow the sequence depicted in Table 3.4.

Sex with a woman includes: touching, kissing, smiling, looking serious, embracing, talking, digital intercourse, caressing, looking, cunnilingus, undressing, remembering later, making sounds, sometimes gently biting, sometimes crying, and breathing and sighing together.
—A woman discussing lesbian sex. Hite, 1976, p. 267

I like kissing where my partner and I lie together, bodies intertwined, mouth to mouth, tongues touching, moving tongues slowly together, advancing and retreating, kissing sometimes gently, sometimes vigorously.
                                    —*A man discussing gay sex. Hite, 1981, p. 816*

Some people have difficulty imagining exactly what gay couples do in bed. Actually, they suffer from a lack of imagination, since the gays make love pretty much like many "hets." Gay men and lesbians kiss, hug, and pet; they engage in mutual masturbation and oral–genital sex (Jay & Young, 1979; McWhirter & Mattison, 1984). Gay men sometimes engage in anal intercourse (Bell & Weinberg, 1978; Blumstein & Schwartz, 1983); women sometimes practice tribadism (they rub their bodies together) (Califia, 1979). One lesbian described an especially pleasant sexual experience this way.

> We lay on top of each other kissing deeply and stroking each other. Then I started to touch her breasts—softly enveloping my hand around the roundness of her, then focusing on stimulating her nipple. I became more excited and moved my lower body on top of her. After a while I needed to suck her breasts and to gently stroke the outside of her vagina. I love to nestle my head between her breasts, whispering, "I love you," and moaning. I was kissing her chest and touching her vagina with my index finger, moving it from the lips of her vagina up to her clitoris and slowly back down to the opening of her vagina. I put some of my weight on my knees so that she too could rub my vaginal area and kiss my breasts. I felt warm, wonderful, and full, and could feel those feelings from her. We sensed that we were both very excited. I was almost dizzy. (Jay & Young, 1979, p. 401)

A gay man describes a particularly appealing sexual encounter this way:

> When I turned around to pick up his keys, he embraced me from behind, and slowly began undressing me, all the while tonguing every part of me that was freshly exposed—neck, nipples, navel, feet. It was all done so slowly and deliberately that I was getting turned on to the point where I thought I'd burst. Unable to wait, I began undressing him. He smelled faintly of musk oil and sandalwood. His silk shirt was smooth and cool, and that contrasted with the feel of old blue jeans was a knockout. We climbed into bed and Roger and I began some of the deepest soul kisses I've ever engaged in. Once again, the traveling over my body began. I'd never had my toes sucked before, and it was a different and wonderful sensation; meanwhile his fingers were going lightly up and down my spine, a feeling that's like a fuse for me. Responding, I left no area unexplored, his erect nipples, his flat stomach, till I got down to his cock. It had to be the most perfectly sculptured one I'd ever seen, long and good-sized but not too much, and shaped perfectly. I went down on him, being unable to control myself, burying myself in his groin, my hand feeling up and down that little body. Roger was moaning in French, as was I, which shocked me since I had always been quiet and reserved with my bed speech. Suddenly with a quick feat of acrobatics Roger switched positions and began sucking my cock, slowly, then quickly, alternating rhythms. I held back as long as I could and finally exploded in his mouth. . . . I was tingly all over. (Jay & Young, 1979, p. 446)

Most homosexual (and heterosexual) experiences rarely reach these heights of ecstasy, but they serve as reminders that there is much more to good sex than simultaneous orgasms—touted as late as the 1960s as the *sine qua non* of all sex.

Table 3.5   WHAT DOES AN ORGASM FEEL LIKE?

Indicate whether you think each statement was written by a man (M) or a woman (F).

M   F   1. I really think it defies description by words. Combination of waves of very pleasurable sensations and mounting of tensions culminating in a fantastic sensation and release of tension.

M   F   2. It is a very pleasurable sensation. All my tensions have really built to a peak and are suddenly released. It feels like a great upheaval; like all of the organs in the stomach area have turned over. It is extremely pleasurable.

M   F   3. A building up of tensions—like getting ready for takeoff from a launching pad, then a sudden blossoming relief that extends all over the body.

M   F   4. An orgasm is a very quick release of sexual tension which results in a kind of flash of pleasure.

M   F   5. It is a great release of tension followed by a sense of electriclike tingling which takes over all control of your senses.

M   F   6. An orgasm is a great release of tension with spasmodic reaction at the peak. This is exactly how it feels to me.

M   F   7. A building of tension, sometimes, and frustration until the climax. A tightening inside, palpitating rhythm, explosion, and warmth and peace.

1–M; 2–F; 3–F; 4–M; 5–F; 6–M; 7–F.

Source: Vance & Wagner, 1976, pp. 95–96.

The Experience of Orgasm

Lovers sometimes wonder if their partners share their delight at lovemaking, their feelings during climax. "How was it for you?" they ask. Alas, most lovers are not very good at describing their sensual feelings. Mythology provides some glib, but misleading, answers. Traditionally, it was assumed that, for men, orgasm was sudden and explosive; for women, it was supposedly more subdued. To find out, Ellen Vance and Nathaniel Wagner (1976) asked 48 young men and women to describe what an orgasm feels like. (A few of their answers are duplicated in Table 3.5.) Then they asked psychologists, medical students, and obstetricians–gynecologists to read men's and women's descriptions and to try to guess whether they were written by a man or a woman. *You* might try to see if you can guess whether a man or a woman wrote each of the following descriptions, as well. (The answers are provided at the bottom of Table 3.5.)

The authors found that not even experts were able accurately to guess whether the various descriptions were written by men or by women. It appears that both men and women share the same feelings during orgasm. [Of course, some women experience orgasm only now and then; a few never do (Griffitt & Hatfield, 1985).]

Marital Sex

In the United States, about 80 to 90% of all people marry (Gagnon, 1977). When these married couples are in their twenties, they generally have sexual relations two or three times a week. As they age, they start to have sex less frequently. Once couples are 45 and over, they have sex only about once a week on the average (see Table 3.6).

It is important, however, to remind ourselves that people are enormously variable. Some couples are extremely sexual; they would like to have sexual relations (and often do have sex) several times a day. Others just aren't interested. [When couples are in their twenties, about 5 to 10% of them have intercourse less than once a month and 8 to 12% of them never have intercourse (Hyde, 1990).] In one scene in *Annie Hall,* Woody Allen and Diane Keaton, his lover, were shown on a split screen talking to their respective psychoanalysts. "How often," the analysts asked, "do you have sex." "Almost never," complained Woody—"about three times a week." "Oh, practically all the time," lamented Diane, "at least three times a week." Researchers find that couples sometimes differ in their reports of how often they are having sexual relations. Men and women who wish they were having more sex tend to underestimate how frequently they are having sexual relations; those who wish for less sex overestimate how often they are currently having sexual relations (Masters & Johnson, 1970).

In the 1960s, commentators often talked about the "Sexual Revolution." Today, however, "revolutionaries" such as basketball star Wilt "The Stilt" Chamberlain (1991), who claimed to have sexual relations with more than 20,000 women, risk AIDS. The old joke—"nobody likes people who are too popular"— may well be true. How much sexual experience do most men and women have? Tom Smith and his colleagues (Greeley, Michael, & Smith, 1989) interviewed a national sample of 1400 adults. First, they asked respondents how many sexual partners they had *in the past year*. The breakdown appears in Table 3.7.

They also quizzed men and women about the number of sexual partners they had had since they were 18 years of age (see Table 3.8).

The preceding studies provide some information about how often couples prefer and actually do have sex. Other researchers provide information about the kinds of sexual activities men and women prefer.

Since ancient times, statues, paintings, and love manuals such as *The Kama Sutra* have illustrated a variety of positions for intercourse. In Kinsey's day, the

Table 3.6   FREQUENCY OF SEXUAL INTERCOURSE
(PER WEEK)

Kinsey (1938–1949)		Hunt (1972)	
Age	Frequency	Age	Frequency
16–25	2.45	18–24	3.25
26–35	1.95	25–34	2.55
36–45	1.40	35–44	2.00
46–55	0.85	45–54	1.00
56–60	0.50	55 and over	1.00

Source: Hunt, 1974, Table 30, p. 191.

Table 3.7   SEXUAL ACTIVITY VERSUS ABSTINENCE
              DURING THE PAST YEAR

Marital status	Average number of partners	Percent abstinent
Married	0.96	9.2%
Widowed	0.21	85.9
Divorced	1.31	25.9
Separated	2.41	20.0
Never married	1.84	24.6

Source: Greeley et al., 1989.

Table 3.8   AVERAGE NUMBER OF
              SEXUAL PARTNERS

Marital status	Average number of partners
Married	5.72
Widowed	3.01
Divorced	13.30
Separated	11.75
Never married	8.67

"missionary position" (man on top) was used by almost all married couples. Today, most couples prefer to use a variety of different sexual positions. During intercourse, the man may be on top, the woman may be on top, the man may enter the woman from the rear, or couples may have relations side to side (Griffitt & Hatfield, 1985).

One of the most dramatic changes in the past 25 years is in the acceptance of oral sex. In Kinsey's day, only 11 to 12% of couples dared to practice *fellatio* (the woman's mouth encloses the man's penis) and *cunnilingus* (the man's tongue caresses the woman's *clitoris*). By the 1980s, 90 to 93% of married couples practiced both fellatio and cunnilingus (Blumstein & Schwartz, 1983; Griffitt & Hatfield, 1985).

Fantasy During Sexual Relations   Many men and women try to enrich their marriages by spinning sexual fantasies. Some men and women get anxious during sexual relations. Some get bored. Sexual fantasies enable couples to transport themselves to more thrilling or more relaxing worlds of imagination and to add variety to their sexual encounters. Sex researchers point out that even rats respond to novelty; they respond more passionately to novel partners than to long-familiar ones. This phenomenon has been labeled, somewhat whimsically, the "Coolidge Effect," after an anecdote concerning President Calvin Coolidge. During a visit to

Table 3.9 THE TEN MOST COMMON SEXUAL FANTASIES

1. Thoughts of an imaginary lover enter my mind.
2. I imagine that I am being overpowered or forced to surrender.
3. I enjoy pretending that I am doing something wicked or forbidden.
4. I am in a different place like a car, a motel, a beach, woods, etc.
5. I relive a previous sexual experience.
6. I imagine myself delighting many men.
7. I imagine that I am observing myself or others having sex.
8. I pretend that I am another irresistibly sexy female.
9. I pretend that I struggle and resist before being aroused to surrender.
10. I daydream that I am being made love to by more than one man at a time.

Source: Hariton, 1973, p. 43.

a large chicken farm, his wife walked briskly on ahead. As the story goes: Mrs. Coolidge, observing the vigor with which one particularly prominent rooster covered hen after hen, asked the guide to make certain that the president took note of the rooster's behavior. When President Coolidge got to the hen yard, the guide pointed out the rooster and recounted his exploits. He added that Mrs. Coolidge had requested that the president be made aware of the rooster's prowess. The president reflected for a moment and replied, "Tell Mrs. Coolidge that there is more than one hen" (Blatt & Blatt, 1970).

Earlier in the chapter, we described men's and women's masturbation fantasies. But one way *couples* can also add variety and excitement to their sexual relations is to create passionate fantasies. In one study, 65% of married women said they generally fantasized while having sex with their husbands. Another 28% reported that they had occasional fantasylike thoughts during intercourse (Table 3.9). Only 7% of the women never fantasized. Women who fantasized seemed to have better sexual relationships and to have more orgasms than those who did not (Hariton, 1973). Most men and women settle on a "script" that they find exciting early on. Some couples enjoyed sharing their sexual fantasies; most wished to keep their deepest feelings secret. Some sexual fantasies that are especially common to women are given in Table 3.9.

Is sex dirty? Only if it's done right.
　　　　—Woody Allen

What Do Men and Women Want from Sex?

In 1985, Ann Landers sparked a nationwide debate by asking readers: "Would you be content to be held close and treated tenderly and forget about 'the act'?" When more than 90,000 women cast their ballots, 72% claimed to prefer affection to sex (Angier, 1985, p. 76). Humorists responded by conducting their own polls among *men.* Art Buchwald observed that, in his bachelor days, he met all 62,000 women who preferred cuddling to sex. Mike Royko (1985) asked men: "Which do you prefer: sex or bowling?" (p. B-2). Observed one respondent, Pat, of St. Louis: "I mentioned to my wife that I had to put down whether I preferred sex with her or sinking a 40-foot birdie putt. She told me the odds of either happening in the near future were about the same."

I can go to bed with either sex, but I prefer to wake up with a woman.
Women are more emotionally satisfying as companions.
—Martina Navratilova

Are men and women as different as Ann Landers suggests? The answer is "no"; but there are some slight differences in what men and women wish for in their current relations. Researchers (Brown & Auerback, 1981) interviewed 100 married couples. Most were happily married, enjoyed sex, and considered it an important aspect of their lives. When couples were asked why *they* initiated sex, woman generally said that they cared most about "love, intimacy, and holding." Men generally said they hoped for "sexual release." The authors observed: "These responses tend to support and perpetuate the cliché 'men give love to get sex, while women give sex to get love'" (p. 107). The authors sketch a composite picture of what men and women think of as the perfect sexual scenario:

> Women basically wanted to be approached in the classical romantic vein—candlelight, wine, music, and romantic settings with time standing still for love and wooing. They did not want a quick grope or a rushed sexual encounter that takes place in bed the last thing at night, but rather a slow, sensual approach with tender, loving caresses, embraces, kisses, and nonsexual body touching or massage with only occasional aggression. The women wanted to be courted, to be spoken to, and to verbally share with their partners their ideas, thoughts, and feelings about nonsexual topics. They wanted to laugh and play and to enjoy their spouses outside of bed. They sought verbal appreciation of themselves as human beings as well as sexual beings. Coitus evolved slowly out of this setting and occurred because the women felt loved and were good companions as well as being sexy. . . .
>
> The responses of the men were of two types. Approximately 40% of the men wanted a soft approach with caressing, massage, seductiveness, and one assumes tenderness. . . . The remaining 60% wanted to be approached in a verbally direct, abandoned, and aggressive manner. For a few men the aggression took the form of their being "attacked" or overwhelmed by their wives, while most of the other men desired aggression along the lines of their wives showing abandon and lack of inhibition, making it clear by their words and actions that they passionately desired their husbands. A refrain that kept repeating itself . . . "I want to feel that I am irresistible," or "I want to feel there is no sexier man in the world and that she wants me desperately." (pp. 112–113)

Men also wish that their mates would take the initiative more often, would be more eager to have sex, and would be more adventuresome (Hite, 1976). For other gender differences see Box 3.2.

Pornography

Traditionally, it was assumed that while men could be excited by pornography, women were repulsed by it. Kinsey and his co-workers (Kinsey et al., 1953) spent an entire chapter in *Sexual Behavior in the Human Female* trying to track down the neural mechanisms that would account for these "innate" differences. What

Box 3.2 WHAT MEN AND WOMEN WISH FOR IN THEIR SEXUAL RELATIONS

Hatfield and her students (1988) interviewed casually dating, steadily dating, and married couples about their sexual preferences. They asked: During sex, did they wish for more (or less) of a series of activities? Did they wish their partners to be more loving? (That is, did they desire more loving talk, more warmth, more involvement?) How eager were they to try a variety of experiences? (Did they wish their partners would surprise them by initiating sex, be more unpredictable and experimental as to when, where, and how they had sex; talk "dirty," be wilder and sexier?) Men and women were quite similar in their mutual desire for more loving, warmer, and close sexual relationships. They were very different, however, in their preference for raw excitement and diversity. Men wanted their partners to take the initiative and be more dominant. They longed for rougher treatment, dirtier talk, and wilder sex (see Table 3.10).

One surprising finding: Couples seemed to have a communication problem. Both men and women wished their partners would be braver and tell them exactly what *they* wanted sexually. These same men and women, however, were reluctant to tell *their* partners what they wanted. They kept hoping their mates would somehow be able to read their minds!

Table 3.10 WHAT MEN AND WOMEN WISH THEY HAD MORE
OF IN THEIR SEXUAL RELATIONSHIPS

Dating couples wish their partners would	
Men	Women
Be more experimental	Talk more lovingly
Initiate sex more often	Be more seductive
Try more oral–genital sex	Be warmer and more involved
Give more instructions	Give more instructions
Be warmer and more involved	Be more complimentary

Married couples wish their partners would	
Men	Women
Be more seductive	Talk more lovingly
Initiate sex more	Be more seductive
Be more experimental	Be more complimentary
Be wilder and sexier	Be more experimental
Give more instructions	Give more instructions
	Be warmer and more involved

part of the cerebrum was important? The frontal lobes? The occipital lobes? The parietal lobes? The temporal lobes? What part did the hypothalamus play? (He concluded that all these structures were important.)

In Kinsey's era, almost all pornography was written for men. Sometimes, the fabric of erotic literature was threaded through with strands of male power, sexuality, and hatred of women. No wonder women didn't like it. Consider, for example, this passage from Henry Miller's (1965) semi-autobiographical novel *Sexus*. Miller (alias Val) is faintly repelled by, and disapproving of, Ida Verlaine, the wife of his best friend. Yet Val maps out a plan to seduce, dominate, and humiliate her. "I just didn't give a fuck for her, as a person, though I often wondered what she might be like as a piece of fuck, so to speak" (p. 228).

> I would ask her to prepare the bath for me. She would pretend to demur but she would do it just the same. One day, while I was seated in the tub soaping myself, I noticed that she had forgotten the towels. "Ida," I called, "bring me some towels!" She walked into the bathroom and handed me them. She had on a silk bathrobe and a pair of silk hose. As she stooped over the tub to put the towels on the rack her bathrobe slid open. I slid to my knees and buried my head in her muff. It happened so quickly that she didn't have time to rebel, or even to pretend to rebel. In a moment I had her in the tub, stockings and all. I slipped the bathrobe off and threw it on the floor. I left the stockings on—it made her more lascivious looking, more the Cranach type. I lay back and pulled her on top of me. She was just like a bitch in heat, biting me all over, panting, gasping, wriggling like a worm on the hook. As we were drying ourselves, she bent over and began nibbling at my prick. I sat on the edge of the tub and she kneeled at my feet gobbling it. After a while I made her stand up, bend over; then I let her have it from the rear. She had a small juicy cunt, which fitted me like a glove. I bit the nape of her neck, the lobes of her ears, the sensitive spot on her shoulder, and as I pulled away, I left the mark of my teeth on her beautiful white ass. Not a word spoken. (Miller, 1965, p. 229–230)

Val powerfully dominates and degrades Ida:

> "You never wear any undies, do you? You're a slut, do you know it?"
> I pulled her dress up and made her sit that way while I finished my coffee.
> "Play with it a bit while I finish this."
> "You're filthy," she said, but she did as I told her.
> "Take your two fingers and open it up. I like the color of it. It's like coral inside. Just like your ears. You say he's got a terrific wang, Bill. I don't know how he ever gets it in there." With this I reached for a candle on the dresser at my side and I handed it to her.
> "Let's see if you can get it in all the way . . ."
> "You can make me do anything, you dirty devil."
> "You like it, don't you?" (p. 231)

Presumably, both Miller and Ida are equally "at fault" for betraying her husband and his friend. Nonetheless, Miller is smugly superior. He revels in his superiority, power, and potency:

> Her lips were chewed to a frazzle and she was full of marks, some green, some blue. I had a strange taste in my mouth, of fish glue and Chanel $976\frac{1}{2}$. My cock looked like a bruised rubber hose; it hung between my legs, extended an inch or two beyond its

normal length and swollen beyond recognition. . . . A royal bit of fucking, thought I to myself. . . . (p. 233)

Ida does not fare so well. Miller (1938/1963) recounts a "cute" story of what happened when Bill Woodruff learns about Ida's extramarital affairs:

This night, however, he (Bill Woodruff) waited up for her and when she came sailing in, chipper, perky, a little lit up and cold as usual he pulled her up short with a "where were you tonight?" She tried pulling her usual yarn, of course. "Cut that," he said. "I want you to get your things off and tumble into bed." That made her sore. She mentioned in her roundabout way that she didn't want any of that business. "You don't feel in the mood for it, I suppose," says he, and then he adds: "that's fine because now I'm going to warm you up a bit." With that he ups and ties her to the bedstead, gags her, and then goes for the razor strop. On the way to the bathroom, he grabs a bottle of mustard from the kitchen. He comes back with the razor strop and he belts the piss out of her. And after that he rubs the mustard into the raw welts. "That ought to keep you warm for tonight," he says. And so saying he makes her bend over and spread her legs apart. "Now," he says, "I'm going to pay you as usual," and taking a bill out of his pocket he crumples it and then shoves it up her quim. (p. 234)

Obviously, this erotic story has a subtext of male dominance and female submission; male sadism and female masochism, male power and female weakness. No wonder women didn't seem responsive to this sort of pornography.

In the last two decades, however, research has documented that both men and women can find erotic literature and films sexually exciting. For example, Gunter Schmidt and Volkmar Sigusch (1970) asked 250 men and women university students to watch a series of erotic slides and movies. Both the men and women found the slides and films equally arousing. In fact, women were more likely than men to follow up their viewing with sexual activity.

Is there a difference in the *kind* of pornography that men and women find sexually arousing? Kinsey and his colleagues (1953) assumed that women, if they could be "turned-on" at all, would be most aroused by stories and movies depicting loving romantic relationships; men would be most inflamed by depictions of "raw" explicit sex. Again, the evidence indicates that, contrary to Kinsey's view, both men and women are aroused by much the same kinds of things. Of course, there is some pornography so offensive or so violent that it would be hard for either men or women to find it sexually stimulating. Hence the issue of pornography divides the feminist movement.

Gunter Schmidt, Volkmar Sigusch, and Siegrid Schafer (1973) asked college men and women to read two stories, describing sexual activities of a young couples. In Story 1, love and lust were linked. The couple expressed a great deal of affection for one another. At the same time their sexual activities—flirting, petting, foreplay, and sexual intercourse in various positions—were fully described. In Story 2, love and lust were isolated. The couple expressed little affection for one another and their sexual activities were described in vulgar and graphic terms. Excerpts from the two stories follow (Schmidt et al., 1973, p. 183):

Story 1: With Affection
1. They walked for a long time in silence. Neither of them seemed to notice where. He took her into his arms. She cuddled up to him, pressed herself against his body.

Now he wrapped his arms about her tightly, so tightly that they couldn't move at all. His tongue ran tenderly across her lips . . . "I like you" he said . . . "You don't want anybody to stare into your eyes and say a lot of deep and fine things. You just love me and I love you and that's all."

2. He thrust his member into her. He felt his sperm flow into her hot vagina, he arched his back, shuddered moaning, and lay down on her breathing heavily and exhausted. Tenderly he kissed her and stroked her arms. When he slid from her slowly and softly, two glowing, sweat-covered bodies glued to each other separated. It was warm in the room, and the sweat still lay on his forehead. After they had lain there for a while in silence he asked her softly how it had been, and she answered that it was the most delightful and beautiful thing there was. Thus they lay there silently, enchanted by one another, with their hands on each other's genitals. Their limbs locked together, they gazed at one another, caressing each other with their eyes. From time to time he kissed her mouth, her throat, her breasts. . . . Both of them yielded to the pleasantness of their limpness and passivity.

3. After the orgasm which caused both of them to shudder, they lay there completely satisfied, happily exhausted. Although he knew, he asked her again how it had been. "It was good, it was so good," she whispered tenderly. That made him happy, but he said nothing, only kissed her softly, lay down next to her, and pulled her close to himself. She laid her head on his shoulder, wrapped her leg around his leg, and then she fell silent, devoid of thoughts. And he was still with her, lying there next to her in the same silence.

Story 2: Without Affection

1. They walked for a long time in silence. Then he took her into his arms, and she pressed her body against his, so that they couldn't move anymore . . . "You're pretty great," he said . . . "you don't want anybody to stare into your eyes and say a lot of deep and fine things about love. You're hot for me and I'm hot for you! That's all."

2. He shoved his cock into her. He felt his sperm spurting into her hot cunt, he arched his back, shuddered groaning, and lay down on her breathing heavily and exhausted. When he pulled it out and slid down beside her, the two glowing, sweat-covered bodies glued to each other separated. It was warm in the room, and the sweat still lay on his forehead. She lay there stretched out with her hand on his cock. . . . Both of them yielded to their limpness and passivity.

3. Exhausted and completely satisfied, they fell apart. He turned over and reached for a cigarette. That was a good fuck, he thought.

After reading one of the stories, men and women were asked to rate their own level of sexual arousal. Both men and women found Story 1 (which linked affection and sex) somewhat more arousing than Story 2 (which separated the two). Both men and women admitted to being equally aroused by both stories. Almost all of them reported experiencing physiological correlates of sexual arousal while reading the stories. Most men (90%) had at least a slight or modest erection. A few (2%) ejaculated. Most women (80%) felt genital sensations; some reported vaginal lubrication (28%). A very few (1%) had orgasms. Some researchers have done more than ask men and women about their sexual feelings. Some have actually measured men's and women's sexual excitement (see Box 3.3).

Box 3.3   PORNOGRAPHY AND SEXUAL EXCITEMENT

In a classic study, Julia Heiman (1977) did more than ask men and women how "turned on" they were. She *measured* their sexual responses. Students were asked to listen to a series of erotic audiotapes designed to provoke sexual fantasies. Some tapes were "innocent" and very romantic. Couples expressed love and tenderness for one another, but they did not engage in sex. Some tapes were unblushingly erotic. They contained powerful explicit depictions of masturbation and sexual intercourse. Some tapes were both romantic and erotic. Finally, some tapes (control tapes) were not at all sexy; they simply reproduced a typical low-key conversation.

Heiman assessed sexual response to the various tapes in three ways. First, she simply asked the men and women to describe their levels of sexual arousal. She didn't just take their word for it, however; she also measured their levels of sexual excitement. Male sexual arousal was calibrated by attaching a *plethysmograph* to the mens' penes. (This is a flexible loop that circles the penis and expands as the erection does.) Female arousal was assessed by inserting a vaginal *photoplethys-mograph* (a device about the size of a tampon, which measures vasocongestion or sexual arousal) inside the entrance to the vagina. Heiman found that the women were more sexually excited by the erotic tapes than the men! Both groups were most turned on by the erotic or the romantic–erotic tapes. Neither men nor women found the romantic or the control tapes at all exciting. Women, and perhaps men, were most aroused by "unconventional" tapes (stories in which women initiated the sexual activity and most of the attention was focused on their sexual responses).

Interestingly enough, Heiman found that although men always knew how sexually aroused they were (it is pretty hard to miss an erection), women were often unaware of how aroused (physiologically) they were. About half the time, when women said they were feeling "no sexual arousal at all," the photoplethys-mograph told a very different story—documenting that they were extremely sexually excited physiologically.

Extramarital Sex

The overwhelming number of Americans disapprove of extramarital sexual relations. In national opinion polls, 87% of Americans say that extramarital relations are "always wrong" or "almost always" wrong (Atwater, 1982). Some Americans are more permissive of extramarital activity than others, of course. Ira Reiss and his colleagues (Reiss, Anderson, & Sponaugle, 1980) have explored the background characteristics, attitudes, and experiences that shape people's extramarital sexual permissiveness. [In this research, permissiveness was measured by a single question: What is your opinion about a *married* person having sexual relations with someone *other* than the marriage partner? Is it always wrong, almost always wrong, wrong only sometimes, or not wrong at all? (Reiss, et al., 1980, p. 396).] He found that several factors were related to extramarital permissiveness:

Background Factors

Gender. Men are slightly more approving of extramarital relations than are women.

Age. Younger men and women are slightly more tolerant of extramarital sex than are older people.

Education. The better educated are slightly more tolerant.

Religiosity. Extremely religious people tend to disapprove of extramarital relations slightly more than do others.

Attitudes

Premarital sexual permissiveness. Those who approve of premarital sex are more tolerant of extramarital experimentation as well.

Gender equality. People who believe that men and women are of equal worth are slightly more permissive.

Political liberality. Conservatives disapprove of extramarital relations slightly more than do liberals.

Marital Happiness. Happily married men and women are more likely to disapprove of extramarital sex. Only 13% of happily married men and women accept the idea of extramarital sex, while 43% of unhappily married people do (Sponaugle, 1976). Only 20% of happily married wives actually engage in extramarital relations while 55% of unhappily married wives do. (Comparable figures are not available for husbands.)

People generally agree that extramarital relations are wrong. How do they behave? In the 1940s and 1950s, Kinsey found that approximately 50% of all married men and 26% of all married women had engaged in extramarital sex at some time during their lives (Kinsey et al., 1948, 1953). Other early studies came to much the same conclusion (Hunt, 1974). Studies in the 1980s confirm that here too the double standard is dying. Men and women are becoming quite similar in their willingness to experiment with extramarital sex. Almost equal numbers of men and women, about 50%, now engage in extramarital sex (Blumstein & Schwartz, 1983; Thompson, 1983). We discuss this topic in greater detail in Chapter 8, Relationship Problems.

The Divorced

Morton and Bernice Hunt (1977) interviewed 984 divorced men and women. The authors concluded that many people go through a predictable series of stages. Phase One is the stage of ego repair. In their marriages, most men and women suffer a series of devastating blows to their self-esteem. They reenter the dating world uncertain about their desirability and sexual adequacy. At first they feel extremely shy and uneasy about the idea of starting to date once again. They don't know what the rules are.

Once they begin dating, they generally discover that dating relationships are now far more open and sexual than during their teens. Women are often stunned when men they barely know casually invite them to have sexual relations. Men are equally startled when women call them, invite them out, and sometimes even hint that they might like to have sex. The authors found that in the months following a divorce, men and women often acted a bit "wild"; they engaged in a great deal of sexual experimentation. For most of them, such experiments worked. They started to feel better about themselves. As one 28-year-old automobile mechanic said:

> My ex was so cool that a blowtorch wouldn't have warmed her up. She always told me it was my fault. She said I didn't turn her on. I just didn't have it. She said it and I believed her. Well, after we split I started going out with these divorced women and doing exactly the same things. And they got turned on plenty; they liked me, they really took to me. It was terrific for my morale. I liked myself better than I ever did in my life. I don't think a person who hasn't been through this can understand what it means. (Hunt & Hunt, 1977, p. 147)

Phase Two consists of exploration of the sexuality of oneself and others. People discover how different others' sexual preferences and experiences are.

> A woman may be amazed to learn that one man can be so rough, another so tender; how hasty and self-absorbed is one, how patient, caring, and communicative another. A man might find one woman slow to respond, another astonishingly swift, one tepid and restrained, another lusty and unfettered. (p. 150)

Such experiences give men and women a clear idea about what does or does not fit their needs. Some men discover that they are delighted with passionate women; others that they like women who are a bit more restrained. Some women go for men who are excited quickly and intensely; others respond to men who are slower, who enjoy longer, more loving foreplay.

Sooner or later, people enter Phase Three: the period of reconstruction. Most people eventually tire of dating and sleeping around. They begin to hunger for a more loving, committed, deeper, sexual attachment. They are ready for a serious relationship.

All the passions are extinguished in old age.
—Voltaire

Aging

When we are young, we callowly take it for granted that sex is reserved for the young, beautiful, and healthy. The elderly should be "beyond all that." If an elderly person expressed sexual interest in someone, they were quickly dismissed as a "dirty old man" or an "old fool" (Riportella-Muller, 1989). We can recall visiting one of our grandmothers in a nursing home. Some of the elderly women had their arms tied to the arms of their hospital beds. Their crime? "They are senile; they keep trying to touch themselves," said the attending nurse in disgust. In Kinsey's day, it was assumed that marital sex not only should but did decline dramatically with age. A popular adage wryly observed:

From your wedding night until your first anniversary, put one bean in a jar every time you have sexual relations. From your first anniversary on, take one bean out of the jar every time you have sex. When you die, the jar will still be half full of beans.

In a series of early studies, researchers painted a dismal picture of the decline of sexuality with age (see Figure 3.2). As people aged, their sexual interest seemed to decline steadily.

Even today, many people assume that it is unseemly for the elderly to express an interest in sex. As we were writing this chapter, a Washington columnist lambasted Senator Ted Kennedy for spending the weekend drinking and socializing with young women. He grumbled:

People have grown tired of a man who is out of control. And they are weary of paying attention to a public person nearing 60 years of age who seems not to have the personal discipline to stay home and leave public skirt-chasing to those young enough to participate. This has nothing to do with morality and everything to do with common sense. (Quoted in Saul & Waldman, 1991, p A31)

Recent research sketches a different picture. In the Starr–Weiner Report (1981), 75% of elderly men and women said that today sex still felt as good (or even better) than when they were young. The scientists interviewed 800 men and women from senior centers from a wide variety of social, ethnic, and economic backgrounds. They concluded: "The unmistakable conclusion is that indeed older people do it . . . they like sex, want sex, feel they need sex for their physical and psychological well-being, and are frustrated when they do not have sex" (Starr,

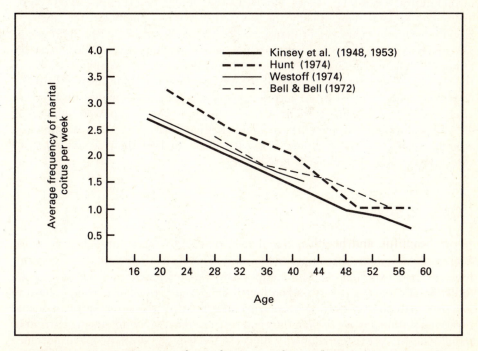

Figure 3.2 From 16 to 60 years of age: frequency of marital intercourse (per week).

1985, p. 106). While sexual interest and behavior do decline somewhat with age, substantial numbers of elderly men and women have extremely active sex lives, even in their eighties and beyond. Researchers interviewed over 200 healthy 80- to 102-year-olds; most were still sexually active. Most men (88%) and women (71%) still fantasized or daydreamed about being in an affectionate, close, and intimate relationship with the opposite sex. The authors note: "Touching and caressing without sexual intercourse was the most common activity for both men (82%) and women (64%), followed by masturbation for both men (72%) and women (40%), followed by sexual intercourse for both men (63%) and women (30%)." Interestingly enough, only 29% of the men and 14% of the women were still married (Bretschneider & McCoy, 1988, p. 125).

Some elderly couples do give up sexual relations. Usually, in this case, they do so because the husband finds it impossible to get and maintain an erection; generally, their wives are still eager to have sexual intercourse (Kinsey et al., 1948, 1953).

I caused the widow's heart to sing for joy.
        —Job, Old Testament

The Widowed

In 1985, there were 11.5 million men and 17 million women over 65 in the United States (U.S. Bureau of the Census, 1987). By the time men and women are 65, the sex ratios are extremely unbalanced. Elderly men find it surprisingly easy to attract desirable sexual partners; elderly women find it almost impossible to do so. There are several reasons why the sex ratios so favor men: On the average, women live eight years longer than men do. To make matters worse, men generally marry women three to four years younger than themselves. Thus, after 65, although 78% of men are married, only 40% of women are. While only 14% of the men have been widowed, 50% of the women have lost their husbands (Butler & Lewis, 1986). Thus it is not surprising that when men are widowed, they are almost certain to become sexually active before one year has passed, while only 43% of widows ever become active again (Beghard, 1968). If widowed men and women *do* find sexual partners, they are likely to find their sexual relations extremely satisfying (Gebhard, 1968).

CONCLUSION

In summary, recent evidence makes it clear that a sexual revolution has occurred. Men and women are becoming increasingly similar in their sexual preferences, feelings, and experiences. More important, the tendencies are largely in the direction of greater sexual freedom for all individuals. Furthermore, it is hard to imagine that non-Western cultures can long hold off the same spirit of sexual experimentation any more than they can restrain the deeper advancing current of individualism. As existential theory suggests, the ways in which people experience sex and their own sexuality are in no small part a function of their belief systems and perceptions. As those belief systems become more universally "Westernized," we can anticipate the spread throughout the world of Western modes of sexual conduct.

But the "West" is not all that uniform when it comes to sexuality. Not all feminists, for instance, are certain that the revolution has been good for their cause. Some contend that the encouragement of sexual freedom for women simply plays into the hands of men who, some feminists maintain, simply use sex to enhance their power over women. Other women's rights leaders say the issue that counts is *choice* for women, in sex as well as in everything else.

Traditionalists worry that the erosion of sexual restraint encourages selfishness at the expense of communal concern, pleasure at the expense of responsibility, sensualism at the expense of religion, tradition, and sobriety.

Sexual doubts have always resided close to the center of the great ethical and political conflicts within all cultures and throughout history. Today's sexual revolution will hardly put these debates to rest. They are sure to be argued more furiously than ever as the revolution continues along its bumpy but inexorable course.

Chapter
4

Companionate Love

INTRODUCTION

Passionate love rarely lasts. Companionate love is a heartier variety of love. Until the recent liberalizing of cultural norms about divorce and divorce laws, most marriages *did* last until "death do us part"—which in the days before the Industrial Revolution began 250 years ago was not very long. Early death ended most marriages. What does the traditional rarity of divorce say about the history of companionate love? That people loved "better" in the good old days?

    The answer seems to be no. One of the hardest, most interesting, and most

Birthday by Marc Chagall, 1915. Oil on cardboard, 31¾ × 39¼". Collection, The Museum of Modern Art, New York. Acquired through the Lillie P. Bliss Bequest.

important of historical debates centers on the when, how, and why of the tender emotions. Historians know that marriage for love did not begin in the West before the eighteenth century, and even then it was practiced only among a minority of the population in a minority of countries. Outside the West, marriage for love has still not established itself as the norm even today, but change in that direction is proceeding quite rapidly.

But what about marriages that had been made between families for economic and social purposes and that were not initiated for reasons of personal love? Did love eventually develop and grow between husband and wife, knowing as they did that divorce was not an available option for them? Because most humans before the eighteenth-century Enlightenment neither read nor wrote, it is not easy for historians to find sufficient evidence to answer this question. It is the opinion of Lawrence Stone (1977) in his pathbreaking *The Family, Sex, and Marriage: England 1500–1800* that companionate love and intimacy were very scarce commodities before the modern age. In describing the family pattern of the late medieval period and the sixteenth century (roughly 1400 to 1600) in England, Stone emphasized the importance of the extended family and the community in raising children (as distinct from the nuclear family) and went on to note the absence of many features of family life that we today tend to take for granted.

> There was no sense of domestic privacy, and interpersonal relations within the conjugal unit, both between husbands and wives and between parents and children were

necessarily fairly remote, partly because of the ever-present probability of imminent death, partly because of cultural patterns which dictated the arranged marriage, the subordination of women, the neglect and early fostering out of children and the custom of harsh parental discipline. Child-rearing practices, especially swaddling, the lack of a single mothering figure, and the crushing of the supposedly sinful will by brute force at an early age, tended to create special psychological characteristics in adults. (Stone, 1977, pp. 408–409)

At this point Stone indulged in some fascinating speculation in which he attempted to connect his report of distant and raw family relations—a family system featured by "psychological distance, deference" and a lack of privacy (p. 409)—to a general emotional profile of sixteenth century England. English adults, he thought, tended to display "suspicion towards others, proneness to violence, and an incapacity to develop strong emotional ties to any one individual" (p. 409).

Stone's challenging explorations have generated lively debates among historians and many other scholars. Can one properly connect so directly the emotions generated by family practices to the overall history of society? Were those emotions as crude, ugly, and remote as he characterized them? Some historians suggest that a strong and warm emotional bond might biologically have been inevitable between mother and infant when the mother fed her baby at her breasts. They and others propose a modestly brighter scenario about pre-Industrial intimacy in general (Gadlin, 1977; Ladurie, 1979; Taylor, 1989). The questions are intriguing, but whatever the eventual answers (should any emerge), Stone has, in fact, made a most persuasive case for likely and suggestive linkages between family life and emotional outcomes of that life with the overall history of nations and empires.

That the very ideas of emotional warmth, intimacy, and kindness to others may be quite new goals in human history has been given further weight by the great art historian Kenneth Clark (1969). In Lord Clark's depiction of the signal achievement of the nineteenth century—a moment ago in historical time—he singled out an idea often assumed to have been around forever: that feeling of responsibility to other people, which we call "humanitarianism." Clark (1969) described it in his TV series, *Civilisation*, as "the greatest achievement of the nineteenth century," and went on to indicate how new a notion it was.

> We are so much accustomed to the humanitarian outlook that we forget how little it counted in earlier ages of civilisation. Ask any decent person in England or America what he thinks matters most in human conduct: five to one his answer will be "kindness." It's not a word that would have crossed the lips of any of the earlier heroes of this series. If you had asked St. Francis what mattered in life, he would, we know, have answered "chastity, obedience and poverty"; if you had asked Dante or Michelangelo they might have answered "disdain of baseness and injustice"; if you had asked Goethe, he would have said "to live in the whole and the beautiful." But kindness, never. Our ancestors didn't use the word, and they did not greatly value the quality. (p. 329)

The development of kindness in human life was inhibited by the ghastly conditions under which most humans labored before the coming of the Industrial Revolution—conditions that led to early death, nearly constant misery, and a dark view of earthly existence. It is small wonder that promises of the afterlife seemed so appealing to the poor people who lived like the peasants of early modern France portrayed in Robert Darnton's (1984) *The Great Cat Massacre*. Noting that family size was kept down by the ubiquity of death, that of the mother and those of her babies during childbirth and infancy, Darnton offered this general picture of rural life in the seventeenth and early eighteenth centuries:

> Stillborn children, called *chrissons*, were sometimes buried casually, in anonymous collective graves. Infants were sometimes smothered by their parents in bed—a rather common accident, judging by episcopal edicts forbidding parents to sleep with children who had not reached their first birthdays. Whole families crowded into one or two beds and surrounded themselves with livestock in order to keep warm. So children became participant observers of their parents' sexual activities. No one thought of them as innocent creatures or of childhood itself as a distinct phase of life, clearly distinguishable from adolescence, youth, and adulthood by special styles of dress and behavior. Children labored alongside their parents almost as soon as they could walk, and they joined the adult labor force as farm hands, servants, and apprentices as soon as they reached their teens.
>
> The peasants of early modern France inhabited a world of step-mothers and orphans, of inexorable, unending toil, and of brutal emotions, both raw and repressed. The human condition has changed so much since then that we can hardly imagine the way it appeared to people whose lives really were nasty, brutish, and short. (pp. 27–29)

Darnton and Stone may have a somewhat bleaker view of the crudity of emotional life as the norm for the pre-modern past than some other historians. Yet it is quite clear that there exists precious little evidence of companionate love as a social standard before 1700—historically again, only yesterday. Even though there was a tender aspect in much of history's great literature from Sappho's lesbian poetry in the Roman era to Jesus preaching for kindness on the Mount to Japanese court poetry of the early Middle Ages to the early medieval Cult of the Madonna to the love-longings of the late medieval troubadors to the sublimities of Shakespeare, the hard historical truth is that, insofar as they are thought to address the real lives experienced by the vast majorities, these have been marginal voices. The brevity and difficulty of pre-Industrial life rendered irrelevant for most humans the tender sensibilities. Intimacy was an indulgence affordable by few. Intimacy, like kindness, is a relatively new idea in history.

Why then its development in the past 250 years? There are two leading general paradigms to explain this phenomenon: first, that humans are biologically wired to be intimate, second, that intimacy is primarily a social construction, a product of time-bound human-made definitions of what is good and desirable.

In this chapter we address the debate as psychologists see it today. But if the historical perspective is useful, the newness of companionate love and intimacy as norms gives—in this particular context—somewhat greater weight to the "social constructionist" view. If intimacy comes naturally, how could it have been so successfully repressed by political and religious authorities and by patriarchy for so long?

That must remain an unanswered question; but more certain is that if the modern age has validated kindness and if the great accompanying modern tendency has been the advance of individualism, it is not farfetched to imagine that expressions of companionate love and the willingness to stay in a relationship have something to do with the personal rewards realized by the individual in the relationship. Expressions of self-interest and behavior based on it no longer result inevitably in incarceration, torture, death, and damnation. With the liberalization of divorce laws and attitudes, if the personal rewards in a relationship are outweighed by negative experiences, individuals simply leave that relationship and consciously seek out a better one.

Love is friendship embellished by pleasure; it is the perfection of friendship. It is the supreme sentiment that focuses all our behavior, that employs all our faculties, that satisfies all our desires, that combines all our pleasures. It is the masterpiece of our being.

—*Destutt de Tracy*

DEFINITIONS

In Chapter 1, we defined companionate love as:

> The affection and tenderness we feel for those with whom our lives are deeply entwined. Companionate love is a complex functional whole including appraisals or appreciations, subjective feelings, expressions, patterned physiological processes, action tendencies, and instrumental behaviors.

Sometimes companionate love is called tender love, marital love, or true love. What does it mean when we say companionate lovers' lives are "deeply entwined"? Earlier, we saw that Robert Sternberg (1988), in his "triangular model of love," assumed that unlike passionate love, a "hot" emotion, companionate relationships were "warmer"; they possessed little passion but a great deal of commitment and intimacy. C. S. Lewis (1960, pp. 55–57) described it this way:

> Its object must be familiar . . . the use of "old" or *vieux* as a term of affection is significant. . . . This taking for granted, which is an outrage in erotic love, is here right and proper . . . it fits the comfortable, quiet nature of the feeling. There is . . . a peculiar charm . . . about those moments when Appreciative love lies, as it were, curled up asleep, and the mere ease and ordinariness of the relationship (free as solitude, yet neither is alone) wraps us round. No need to talk. No need to make love. No needs at all except perhaps to stir the fire.

Recently, Harold Kelley and his colleagues (1983) observed that in close, companionate, relationships, couples' thoughts, emotions, actions, and lives are profoundly linked. They observed: "The close relationship is one of strong, frequent and diverse interdependence that lasts over a considerable period of time" (p. 8).

Ellen Berscheid (1983) points out that in a marriage, the couple's plans, behaviors, or organized action sequences ("intrachain and interchain sequences") may be more or less tightly linked. For example, imagine that every Sunday John and Susan invite their best friends to brunch. John's and Susan's actions could be fairly independent. (Their action sequences could be independent.) He might take full responsibility for the Sunday brunch on the first and third Sundays of the month—inviting people, cooking the meal, and cleaning up. She might take full responsibility on the second and fourth Sundays of the month.

On the other hand, John's and Susan's lives could be tightly meshed. (Their action sequences might be almost completely interdependent.) If they are a compatible couple, their interactions would be facilitative. They might decide who they'd like to see together; make a shopping list together. When they shop for brunch, she might read through the grocery list item-by-item. He might run from aisle to aisle, tossing the items in their cart. And they might cook breakfast and clean up together. If John and Susan are a strife-torn couple, their connections would be disruptive. As Susan reads through the grocery list, John might sigh in irritation, shifting from foot to foot in boredom. Then pushed beyond endurance by her need for an extra bottle of Worcestershire sauce, he might begin to berate her for her extravagance. This cheery conversation may soon degenerate into claims and counterclaims against their respective families. They might begin fighting about the right way to serve orange juice or prepare eggs Benedict as they fix the breakfast. Now they're on a roll, as they continue their squabbling right on through brunch, enlisting guests on one side or the other in their battle.

Berscheid points out that whether intimates love, hate, or are indifferent to their mates, they are nonetheless likely to be intensely "emotionally invested" in them. When relationships end, through breakup or death, people's lives are often severely disrupted. When individuals lose their mates, they lose, in part, the ability to run off their well-oiled action sequences. Now Susan may keep losing her place in the grocery list. She can't find anything on the shelves. It was John who knew where everything was. He has no one to share "that look" with when their friends begin to argue about whether or not George Bush should have invaded Iraq. There are no hidden understandings. In our definition of companionate love, then, two things are required: (1) Couples must love or like one another, and (2) their lives must be deeply entwined.

Now that we have defined companionate love, let us turn to a discussion of its possible origins.

Love between men and women . . . is a hunger that mere possession can never quench.

—Joyce Carol Oates

THE EVOLUTIONARY SOIL OF COMPANIONATE LOVE

Theorists who try to explain the origins of any emotion such as love generally take an evolutionary approach. Robert Plutchik (1980), for one, argued that at every phylogenetic level (from the lowest single-celled organisms, to reptiles, to mammals, up to the highest primates) organisms face the same problems. If they are to survive and reproduce they must find food, avoid being killed, and reproduce. Emotional "packages" are inherited, adaptive, patterns of emotional experience, physiological reaction, and behavior. You will recall that, in Chapter 1, emotions were defined as:

organised, meaningful, generally adaptive action systems. . . . [They are] complex functional wholes including appraisals or appreciations, patterned physiological processes, action tendencies, subjective feelings, expressions, and instrumental behaviors. (Fischer et al., 1990, pp. 84–85)

Presumably, the reason such emotional patterns developed in the first place, were shaped and reshaped over the millennia, and continue to survive is because they were once adaptive. These adaptive reactions include *protection* responses (flight, avoidance, hiding, and playing dead), *destruction* responses (clawing, biting, and hitting), and, most important for our interests here, *reproduction* responses (courting, copulating, and egg laying). Many theorists believe that companionate love is built on the ancient circuitry evolved to ensure that mammals and primates mate, reproduce, and care for the young. Recently, neuroscientists and anthropologists have begun to learn more about companionate love. They have begun to study the subjective feelings, expressions, patterned physiological processes, and action tendencies associated with this form of love's ancient heritage.

The Chemistry of Companionate Love

Neuroscientists know very little about the biological bases of companionate love and tenderness. Researchers have just begun to speculate. Recently, neuroscientists identified a hormone, *oxytocin*, which seems to promote close, intimate bonds. Oxytocin is a tiny, powerful peptide secreted by the almond-sized pituitary gland at the base of the brain. The brain has receptor areas for this hormone in the *ventral medial nucleus,* the *amygdala,* and the *hypothalamus*—areas that are involved in joyous (Caldwell, Jirikowski, Greer, & Pedersen, 1989), affectionate, sexual, and reproductive behavior (Carlson & Hatfield, 1992; Griffitt & Hatfield, 1985; Pedersen, Caldwell, Jirikowski, & Insel, 1991). Zoologist Sue Carter (Angier, 1991) observes: "It [oxytocin] facilitates tactile contact between animals, and that's an early step in the development of social attachment" (p. B8).

In studies of rats, rabbits, sheep, and other animals, researchers have discovered that oxytocin acts on the regions of the brain involved in affectionate and sexual behavior. Oxytocin is the spark that makes animals (primed by sex hormones such as estrogen and testosterone) seek out sexual and reproductive partners. It also intensifies the pleasure of sexual arousal and climax (Carter, 1991). Psychiatrist Frank L. Moore (Angier, 1991) found that in the moments preceding orgasm, men's and women's blood contains three to five times their normal levels of oxytocin.

Oxytocin also promotes more intense bonds between parents and children; it increases eagerness to nurture the young. Mother rats given extra oxytocin tend to pick up and nuzzle their pups more frequently than they normally would. Father rats given oxytocin are more likely to build a nest for the pups and to guard them more fiercely than usual. (When father rats are injected with a drug that blocks the activity of oxytocin, they not only become less nurturant, but they sometimes eat their offspring!)

Finally, oxytocin appears to increase contact between same-sexed pairs as well. Researchers at the National Institutes of Mental Health in Maryland noted that if the brains of field mice are responsive to oxytocin, the mice tend to crave the companionship of other mice. If these same mice are given extra oxytocin, they tend to become exceptionally eager for physical contact, "striving to get so close that they are practically crawling beneath one another's fur" (Angier, 1991, p. B8).

The Looks, Sounds, and Postures of Companionate Love

Love's ancient beginnings can be read today in the look, gaze, and sounds of companionate love.

Love is . . . a tender look which becomes a habit.
—Peter Ustinov

The Look of Love   Emotions researchers have found that the universal emotions—joy, love, sadness, fear, and anger—are associated with certain characteristic facial expressions (Ekman, 1982). In recent research, scientists have tried to pinpoint the facial expressions associated with joy and love (Box 4.1).

Scientists (Ekman, Friesen, & O'Sullivan, 1988) have discovered that when people are experiencing joy, they display a characteristic face in which they smile brightly and crinkle up their eyes. When men and women are experiencing companionate love their faces are just a bit different (Hatfield et al., 1991). They take on the expression mothers often display when they are happily, tenderly gazing at their young infants. They gaze downward (at the child). Their faces soften, and a slight, tender smile plays about their lips. [Bloch, Orthous, & Santibanez (1987) secured much the same results.]

Love must be fostered with soft words.
—Ovid

The Sounds of Love   French psychophysiologist Susana Bloch and her colleagues (1987) argued that not just joy but also passionate love ("eroticism") and companionate love ("tenderness") are associated with different breathing patterns and sounds. Mothers often coo or croon softly with their mouths held near the infant's head. They speculated that such tender maternal sounds become the forerunners of the breathing patterns and sounds associated with love. She studied the basic emotions of joy, love/eroticism, love/tenderness, fear, anger, and sadness and discovered that the breathing patterns associated with eroticism and tenderness were somewhat different:

> In *eroticism*, the principal feature of sexual activation is an even breathing pattern which increases in frequency and amplitude depending on the intensity of the emotional engagement; inspiration occurs through a relaxed open mouth. The face muscles are relaxed, and the eyes are closed or semi-closed. In the female version of the erotic pattern, the head is tilted backwards, and the neck is exposed. (p. 6)

On the other hand, in *tenderness*, the emotion in which we are most interested:

> The breathing pattern is of low frequency with an even and regular rhythm; the mouth is semi-closed, the relaxed lips forming a slight smile. Facial and antigravitational muscles are very relaxed, eyes are open and relaxed, and the head is slightly tilted to

Box 4.1 THE LOOK OF LOVE

In one experiment, Elaine Hatfield and her students (Hatfield, Costello, Schale-kamp Denney, & Hsee, 1991) asked men and women to read scripts depicting the five universal emotions—joy, love, sadness, anger, and fear. They assumed their reading was done in private. Actually, however, it was secretly filmed on video-tape. (At the end of the experiment, the experimenters secured the subjects' permission to view their videos.) If students had been assigned to read a script in which they expressed joy and happiness, the script went like this:

> Today is the happiest day of my life. It's my twentieth birthday. Some buddies of mine decided to throw a surprise birthday party for me. They rounded up a bunch of my friends, snuck into my apartment, decorated it, and waited for me to come in from work. When I walked in the door, there they were! I couldn't believe it. There was screaming and shouting and I could hardly stop laughing. I can't imagine I'll ever have a day like that again.

If they had been assigned to read a script in which they declared their love and delight in another, the script went like this:

> Well, let me tell you. Now that I'm in love, I think about John (Susan) constantly. I can twist any conversation around in my mind so that it's really about him (her). I imagine what he (she) would say to me and how I might tell him (her) things I have never told anyone else before. When I see him (her), POW!, my heart takes a leap, my cheeks flush, and I can't help smiling. At night before I go to bed, I think of how adorable he (she) is and how much I love him (her).

The authors found that there was indeed a characteristic look of love. People who read the loving script not only came to feel more loving than those who read any of the other scripts, but judges rated their faces as looking "more loving" than the faces of men and women who had read any of the other scripts. The subjects' faces seemed softer, more tender and relaxed.

the side. The postural attitude is one of approach. Vocalization includes a humming type lullaby sound. (p. 6)

The Postures of Love   Desmond Morris (1971, p. 12) observed:

> These, then, are our first real experiences of life—floating in a warm fluid, curling inside a total embrace, swaying to the undulations of the moving body and hearing the beat of the pulsing heart. Our prolonged exposure to these sensations in the absence of other, competing stimuli leaves a lasting impression on our brains, an impression that spells security, comfort and passivity.

After birth, mothers instinctively try to re-create the security of the womb. Mothers kiss, caress, fondle, and embrace their infants; they cradle them in their arms. In the womb, neonates hear the steady drumbeat of the mothers' heart—beating at 72 beats per minute. After birth, mothers instinctively hold their babies with their heads pressed against their left breasts, closest to the maternal heart. (Toy companies have taken advantage of this discovery by marketing stuffed animals that beat in time to the mother's heart.) When their infants fret, mothers unconsciously rock them at a rate of between 60 and 70 rocks per minute, the rate that is most calming to infants. Morris points out: "It appears as if this rhythm, whether heard or felt, is the vital comforter, reminding the baby vividly of the lost paradise of the womb" (p. 14). Of course, in adulthood, these same kisses, tender caresses, and embraces continue to provide security for men and women—unconscious of their early origins.

Other Indicators of Love   Finally, anthropologist Irenaus Eibl-Eibesfeldt (1971), in *Love and Hate*, observed that primate mothers and infants reveal their close bonds in certain characteristic ways. Human mothers and their infants express their feelings for one another in much the same ways. And, in adulthood, men and women in all cultures cannot help but show their companionate love in the same ways they did as infants. For instance, newborn infants rhythmically rotate their heads from side to side as they root for their mothers' nipple. You might observe yourself, sometime, as you playfully nuzzle someone you love. Perhaps you will find yourself using motions and gestures and rhythms from the distant past: holding his or her head in your hands or rubbing your lips against his or her cheek with a sideways movement of your head. Eibl-Eibesfeldt graphically illustrates the kissing, mutual feeding, and embracing that bond people together. We see then that people telegraph their feelings of companionate love for one another in their looks, sounds, and postures.

We cannot tell the precise moment when friendship is formed. As in filling a vessel drop by drop, there is at last a drop which makes it run over; so in a series of kindnesses there is at last one which makes the heart run over.
—*James Boswell*

COMPANIONATE LOVE AND REINFORCEMENT THEORY

Many psychologists cite *reinforcement theory* principles to explain why people are attracted to some people and repelled by others (Berscheid & Hatfield, 1969; Thibaut & Kelley, 1959).

If you would marry wisely, marry your equal.
        —*Ovid*

Sociologists observe that Americans tend to choose marital partners who are very similar to themselves in age, race, religion, and educational attainments (Scanzoni and Scanzoni, 1988).

Love begins with love.
—*Jean de La Bruyère*

According to reinforcement theory we come to care for those who provide us with important rewards and dislike those who punish us. The human mind is like a giant computer. It swiftly tallies up how pleasurable or painful a lifetime of fleeting encounters with a person has proved to be, sums and "spits out" an emotional reaction. A very handy tally indeed. If, for example, we receive a letter from a former girlfriend (we immediately recognize her flowing handwriting and the violet ink on the envelope) and our heart sinks, we would be wise to heed that bodily warning. Regardless of how we think we "should" feel about her, our emotions tell us how in fact we *do* feel. We can be fairly sure that, on balance, our past encounters with her have not gone well and that we are doomed to more bad stuff if we keep up an active correspondence.

At first glance, our reaction to this "law of attraction" might be, "So what? We figured that out long ago!" Reinforcement theory, however, leads to some conclusions that are not so obvious. Researchers have found that people also come to like and love people who are merely *associated* with pleasure and to dislike those who are merely *associated* with pain. For example, when you are sitting on the beach, gazing at a sunset, you might feel a rush of affection for the date seated next to you who just happens to be sharing your experience. Conversely, if you have a splitting headache and are under pressure to finish a project, you may explode in anger when your sweetheart interrupts you to read you choice bits from *The New York Times*.

Social psychologists have amassed considerable evidence for their contention that we all practice love or hate, by association. In one experiment, James May and Phyllis Hamilton (1980) showed women photographs of college men and asked them to rate the appearance, interpersonal attraction, intelligence, and morality of the men. Sometimes women rated the men while pleasant light-rock music was playing. Sometimes, the room was silent and at other times unpleasant, dissonant avant-garde classical music was playing. Women were most attracted to the men if they assessed them while the light rock was playing. The men fared poorest when the dissonant music pierced the ears.

Other researchers have documented that men and women are more positive about one another when they meet in pleasant surroundings (in rooms with soft lighting, elegant draperies, beautiful paintings and sculpture, and plush, comfortable chairs) than when they meet in ugly rooms (rooms that have harsh lighting, torn window shades, drab walls, and are shabby, dirty, and littered with cigarette butts) (Maslow & Mintz, 1956). Men and women also like others better when they meet in cool, temperature-controlled rooms than when they meet in hot, damp, sticky rooms (Griffith, 1970). In reinforcement theory, then, we like people who reward us and we dislike those who punish us. We also like (or dislike) people who are merely associated with reward (or punishment).

What rewards seem to matter most in companionate love relationships? Donn Byrne and Sarah Murnen (1988) argued that if couples wish to maintain a loving relationship, they must be careful to keep communicating their positive feelings to one another. In new affairs, this is easy. Couples can't help themselves; they unconsciously express their intense feelings for one another in a thousand little ways—by physical closeness, eye contact, expressing sexual interest, uttering kind words, holding hands, giving presents, and generally expressing their affection. The authors observe: "Very often, a given act—a thoughtful phone call informing a partner you will be late, a sexual interaction, or a birthday gift—is more important for the message of love it sends than for its intrinsic value" (p. 301).

Unfortunately, as couples settle into a routine, kind words are often replaced by harsh evaluations, thoughtful courtesies by neglect. For some reason, married couples frequently treat one another worse than they would treat total strangers. Some couples stop looking at each other, stop touching, stop talking kindly. Byrne and Murnen observed: "We also seem to feel free in a close, loving relationship to criticize, nag, and complain. . . . Compounding the problem is the fact that negative words and deeds from someone we like is unexpected and more upsetting than such responses from someone we dislike" (p. 302).

John Gottman and his colleagues (Gottman, Notarius, Gonso, & Markman, 1976) contrasted the behavior of married couples who were reasonably happy with those who were distressed. They found that happy couples generally had positive exchanges. They smiled, nodded, and made eye contact. They spoke to each other in soft, tender, happy voices. They leaned forward to catch one another's words. Distressed couples had evolved corrosive patterns of interacting. They tried to bludgeon one another into agreements by complaints and punishment. They sneered, cried, and frowned at one another. Their voices were tense, cold, impatient, whining. They made rude gestures, pointed, jabbed, and threw up their hands in disgust; or they simply ignored one another. As soon as one partner resorted to these tactics, the other began to respond in the same way, leading to an escalation of reciprocal aversiveness. Gary Birchler, Robert Weiss, and John Vincent (1975) observed married couples chatting or discussing fairly serious issues with one another and then with strangers. They found that both happily married *and* distressed married couples were less positive toward their mates than they were toward complete strangers! Even the happily married couples gave their mates (compared with the strangers) 30% fewer rewards (smiles, touches, or agreements) and 80% more punishments (criticisms, ignoring them, or disagreements)!

Byrne and his colleagues contend that companionate love and liking are the most important rewards/costs involved in a relationship. In Chapter 1 (Box 1.1) we listed a number of other personal, emotional, and day-to-day rewards, along with the opportunities gained and lost that seem to be critically important in love relationships. As an old song goes: "You've got to ac-cen-tu-ate the positive/ E-li-mi-nate the negative/Latch on to the affirmative/Don't mess with Mr. In-Between."

Love and you shall be loved. All love is mathematically just, as much as the two sides of an algebraic equation.
                                                            —*Ralph Waldo Emerson*

COMPANIONATE LOVE AND EQUITY THEORY

Couples care both about how rewarding their relationships are *and* with how fair they seem to be.

Marry her, Charlie. Just because she's a thief and a hitter doesn't mean she isn't a good woman in all other departments.
                    —*Anjelica Huston to Jack Nicholson in the movie* Prizzi's Honor

The Communal Perspective

A few theorists would disagree with the assertion that lovers care about fairness. They argue that companionate relationships are special relationships. For example, Margaret Clark and Judson Mills (Clark & Reis, 1988) have argued that people have very different ideas as to the nature of appropriate behavior in *communal* relationships (such as love relationships, family relationships, or close friendships) as opposed to *exchange* relationships (such as encounters with strangers or business associates). In communal relationships, people feel responsible for one another's well-being (Williamson & Clark, 1989b). They wish to benefit others, to show their love and affection, or simply to help them. They expect nothing in return. In exchange relationships, on the other hand, acquaintances do not feel particularly responsible for one another. They care very much about "what's in it for me?"

In a series of experiments, college men, who were naturally eager to meet suitable women, were introduced to a beautiful, single woman. In the communal condition, she too was said to be potentially available for a romance. (She had just arrived in town and was eager to meet men.) In the exchange relationship condition, she was, alas, married. (She had presumably been in town for a long time and was not eager to meet anyone new.) The authors found that men treated the beautiful, single woman very differently than the married woman. In the communal condition, men were unusually alert to the beautiful woman's needs. They were delighted to help her, especially if she was sad and needy (Clark, Mills, & Powell, 1986). They were disappointed, in fact, if she insisted on paying them back in kind immediately (Clark & Mills, 1979). They did not keep track of who contributed what to joint tasks; they preferred to think of their projects as a joint effort (Clark, 1984). Even if the men ended up providing all the help, they did not feel exploited (Clark & Waddell, 1985). In the exchange condition (when the woman was married), on the other hand, men were concerned with the short-term equity of the relationship; that is, they liked the married woman most if she kept track of who contributed what to the various tasks they both performed (Clark, 1984) and if she paid them back for their help (Clark & Mills, 1979). In fact, they felt exploited when their help was not reciprocated (Clark & Waddell, 1985).

Clark and her colleagues (Clark, Ovellette, Powell, & Milberg, 1987) argued that men and women might differ in whether they prefer communal or exchange rules to operate in their companionate love relationships. Men may be more exchange oriented. They may get upset and feel unjustly treated if people are ungrateful for their contributions and if no effort is made to repay their benefits. Women may be more communally oriented. They may be particularly upset and feel unjustly treated if others do not welcome their help (or even seem to resent it!) or if their needs are not met. Love relationships, the authors argue, probably go best if both couples are high in communal orientation. Obviously, couples do worst if they are mismatched.

The Equity Perspective

Most theorists, however, take the equity perspective. They assume that couples must be careful to ensure that their partners feel loved, rewarded, and fairly treated. Otherwise, love relationships will suffer and possibly dissolve. Zick Rubin (1973, pp. 82–83) clearly stated this point:

> Exchange theory postulates that human relationships are based first and foremost on self-interest. . . . Such characterizations contrast sharply with what many of us would like to think of friendship and love, that they are intimate relationships characterized at least as much by the joy of giving as by the desire to receive. But although we might prefer to believe otherwise, we must face up to the fact that our attitudes toward other people *are* determined to a large extent by our assessments of the rewards they hold for us.

Gerald Patterson (1971, p. 26) added:

> There is an odd kind of equity which holds when people interact with each other. In effect, we get what we give, both in amount and in kind. Each of us seems to have his own bookkeeping system for love, and for pain. Over time, the books are balanced.

Persons generally believe that if their partners loved them they would *wish* to treat them fairly; but it doesn't always work that way. If men and women get too much or too little from their relationships for too long a time it leads to serious trouble. Let us begin by reviewing equity theory (Hatfield et al., 1978, 1984) and then proceed to discuss some research findings.

The Theory   Equity theory is a simple theory; it consists of four propositions:

> Proposition I: People will try to maximize their outcomes (their rewards minus costs).
> Proposition II: Groups can maximize collective reward by evolving accepted systems for equitably apportioning resources among members. Thus, they will evolve such systems of equity and will attempt to induce members to adhere to them. They will reward people who treat others equitably and punish those who do not.
> Proposition III: When people participate in inequitable relationships, they will become distressed. The more inequitable the relationship, the more distress they will feel.
> Proposition IV: People who discover that they are in inequitable relationships will attempt to eliminate their distress by restoring equity. The greater the inequity, the harder they will try to restore equity. (Hatfield et al., 1984, pp. 1–2)

Essentially, then, the equity argument goes as follows: People may be motivated by self-interest, but they soon learn that the best way to survive is by following social rules . . . or at least to appear to be doing so. Thus men and women all-in-all will feel most comfortable when they are getting roughly what they deserve from their relationships—no more and certainly no less. If men and women exploit their mates, or allow themselves to be exploited, they will experience distress. If you think about the affairs of some of your friends, you can probably come up with some examples of people who are always willing to give too much . . . or who are emotionally stingy and willing to give too little in relationships . . . and how these unbalanced affairs have worked out. Here are some of ours.

One of our clients was very paternal; he was always attracted to "wounded birds"; beautiful young girls who were so troubled, so uneducated, that they couldn't make it on their own. He tried to anticipate all their needs and showered them with expensive presents. Anytime trouble threatened, he tried harder and gave yet more. Inevitably, his relationships fell apart. His young girlfriends were grateful; they felt they *should* love him (and were ashamed that they couldn't). But they just didn't. "Where was his self-respect? Why was he so desperate?" They felt smothered. They couldn't bear to touch him. They had to flee.

Another of our clients was appallingly narcissistic. He was good-looking and had a sort of raffish charm, but he wasn't willing to make *any* compromises. "You compromise once," he said, "and you set a precedent; there's no end to it." In singles bars, women swarmed around him. However, once they started spending time with him, they soon became irritated. At first they could convince themselves that it was "just this once" that they would be stuck in the kitchen preparing a "spontaneous" dinner for ten while he watched the Super Bowl with his friends. Only this once would he ask her to research and type his term papers while he took a nap. But as the days turned into weeks and the "just-this-onces" became routine, the rationalizations turned to seething rage. They felt "ripped off." Eventually they left the kitchen, the typewriter, and the relationship.

Researchers have devised a simple scale for measuring how equitable men and women believe their relationships are. Technically, an equitable relationship is said to exist if both partners are doing equally well in the marital give-and-take:

$$\frac{(O_A - I_A)}{(|I_A|)^{k_A}} = \frac{(O_B - I_B)}{(|I_B|)^{k_B}} \tag{4.1}$$

In the preceding formula, I indicates what persons A and B are investing or putting *into* their relationship; O indicates what they are getting *out* of it. This formula then says that in a fair relationship, the more men and women put into a relationship, the more they should get out of it. Relationships are patently unfair if person A does all the giving and person B does all the taking. Researchers, such as Elaine Hatfield and her colleagues (Hatfield et al., 1984, p. 1), measured how equitable couples perceive their relationships to be by asking each of them:

> Considering what you put into your (dating relationship) (marriage), compared to what you get out of it . . . and what your partner puts in compared to what (s)he gets out of it, how does your (dating relationship) (marriage) "stack up"?

> +3:   I am getting a much better deal than my partner.
> +2:   I am getting a somewhat better deal.
> +1:   I am getting a slightly better deal.
>   0:   We are both getting an equally good, or bad, deal.
> −1:   My partner is getting a slightly better deal.
> −2:   My partner is getting a somewhat better deal.
> −3:   My partner is getting a much better deal than I am.

On the basis of their answers, persons were classified as overbenefited (receiving more than they deserve), equitably treated, or underbenefited (receiving less than they deserve).

How do couples, caught up in unbalanced relationships, generally handle their feelings of distress? Men and women have been found to reduce distress via three techniques:

1. Restoration of *actual equity*. One way individuals can restore equity to an

unjust relationship is by voluntarily setting things right . . . or at least urging their partners to do so. There is a great deal of evidence that couples do often make considerable effort to balance things out. The husband who has been irritable because of stress at work may try to make amends by taking the family on a holiday when the pressure lets up.

2. Restoration of *psychological equity*. Unfortunately, couples in inequitable relationships can reduce distress in a second way. They can distort reality and convince themselves (and perhaps others as well) that things are perfectly fair just as they are. A variety of studies document the imaginative techniques that men and women use to justify injustice. Some studies find, for example, that harm doers rationalize the harm they inflict on others by denying they are responsible for the victim's suffering ("I was just following orders"), by insisting that the victim deserved to suffer, or by minimizing the extent to which the victim suffered from their actions (Brock & Buss, 1962; Glass, 1964; Sykes & Matza, 1957). There is even some sparse experimental evidence that under the right circumstances, victims will justify their own exploitation (Austin & Hatfield, 1974; Leventhal & Bergman, 1969).

One of the first experiments to demonstrate that men and women routinely justify the pain they inflict on others was conducted by Keith Davis and Edward Jones (1960). The authors recruited college students to take part in an experiment on "first-impression" formation. The students were told their main task was to form a first impression of a fellow student in an adjoining room. First, the experimenter interviewed the man while the students listened. (Actually, the interviewee was an actor who answered all the questions in a friendly way; he seemed slightly nervous and eager to create a good yet honest impression of himself.) When the interview was over, the experimenter asked students to give their first impressions of the interviewee. Then the experimenter said that there was a second part to the experiment: He was interested in finding out how the man would respond to flattery or insults. He showed students two scripts. The complimentary evaluation contained statements like:

> You sound like one of the most interesting persons that I have met since I came to Chapel Hill. I would really like to get to know you much better. (p. 404)

The harsh evaluation said:

> As I understand it, my job is to tell you in all honesty what my first impression of you is. So here goes: I hope that what I say won't cause any hard feelings, but I'll have to say right away that my overall impression was not too favorable. To put it simply, I wouldn't go out of my way to get to know you. . . . Your general interests and so on just strike me as those of a pretty shallow person. To be more specific: Frankly, I just wouldn't know how much I could trust you as a friend after hearing your answers to those moral questions. (p. 405)

Would the student read the harsh evaluation to the fellow student (in reality, the actor), pretending that he agreed with those views? Almost all students agreed to cooperate. After the students had delivered the insulting evaluation, the experimenter asked them to rate the man's likability, warmth, conceit, intelligence, and adjustment. The authors found that students generally salved their consciences by convincing themselves that their fellow student (actor) deserved what he got. After they had delivered the sharp critique, students tended to put a bad face on the other student's likability, warmth, modesty, intelligence, and adjustment. Researchers have often found that people justify the harm that they do. The paradox exists, then, that people come to love those they treat with kindness and to despise those they abuse. One implication of the paradox is that relationships should go best when they are balanced, when both people love one another, sacrifice for one another, and are loved in return. Often, people, desperate to make their relationships go, forget this principle. They assume that the more they love others and sacrifice on their behalf, the more solid their dating relationship or marriage will be. They are wrong. Love and kindness do strengthen a relationship . . . up to a point. However, men and women have to be able to set limits. If loving people become aware that their mates are acting like "spoiled brats," they must have the strength to complain, withdraw, or draw the line. Otherwise, the relationship becomes a dangerously inequitable one. Similarly, if men and women know deep down that they are taking advantage of their partners, they should be warned that they may be playing a dangerous game. Sometimes, people win all the battles only to lose the war. Their partners give in and give in, until finally they have had enough: They get fed up and leave.

3. Finally, if couples are unable to restore equity to their intimate relationships, there is a third way they can try to set things right. They can *leave the relationship.* This does not always mean divorce. A person will sometimes "opt out" by abandoning their partners emotionally. New mothers, less attracted to their husbands than to their newborns, may insist that their infants sleep between them. This is a most effective strategy for keeping the couple apart. Or couples may spend all their leisure time "drinking with the boys" or "shopping with the girls," ensuring that they will rarely spend time alone together as a twosome. Both partners may risk their hearts in extramarital affairs. Or, finally, they may simply leave altogether. [See Sprecher & Schwartz (1992) for a review of the popularity of these alternative strategies.]

The Research   Now that we have described equity theory, let us review the research that exists in this area. In a number of studies, equity considerations have been found to be extremely important in determining who gets into relationships in the first place, how those relationships go, and how likely they are to endure. Specifically, researchers find that:

Dating couples who feel that their relationships are equitable are most likely to progress to even more intimate relationships.   When pop-psychological counselors give advice, they often act as if everyone is entitled to "the best." People are eager to take such "advice." We once asked one of our clients, who felt all the good men were taken, what she was looking for in a mate. She quickly produced a list of qualities she thought were most important in a husband:

Responsible

Neat and tidy

Personally and professionally self-confident

Organized—personally and professionally

Sexually adventurous (variety)—not inhibited

Good sense of humor—laughs easily; tells jokes; any humor fine

Loves to travel

Healthy

Physically fit—not obsessive with exercise routine

Loves to eat—follows my food preferences

Successful in business, rich

Articulate

Adventurous and outdoorsy

Loves horses

Tasteful dresser, wears no "plastic" fabrics

Monogamous

Has lotsa $ (financially independent; makes it himself or from retirement)

Understands "private time"

Is a "controlled" spender

$ generous

Good taste/taste good

Likes to hike

Likes motorcycles

Is imaginative with gifts

Sends flowers

Thoughtful

Good w/my family

Good, warm (♡)

Likes nature

Well connected

Good personal hygiene

Has a "crazy" side of personality

Generous with my family (time, $, whatever)

Does not want children

Likes spur of the moment activities

Must like oral sex (either way)

Patience—in general and with me

Willing to help with housework

Likes to cook (so so)

Polite

Has good credit

Honest

Penis not too big

Supportive

Faithful

Loves to go out to eat

Loves to eat in general

Avant-garde dresser

Compatible astro sign (preference)

Nonsmoker

Smooth, soft skin

5′8″–6′

Flexible/adaptable

Caucasian—close to a must

OK to be a little overweight

Able to defend himself (me too) faced with violence

Smells good naturally

Not argumentative

Able to share (feelings)

Keeps his word (trustworthy)

Sensitive to my moods

Educated

Good companion

Good communicator (listener/talker)

Romantic

Sex a few times a week (3×)

Appreciative (of me too)

Self-motivated

Physically strong

This list was presented without a trace of irony! Many people, sad to say, think very much along these lines (though in perhaps less exaggerated form) and are convinced that they are entitled to and can "have it all." And, you may ask, why not?

To equity theorists, such expectations are wildly impractical. Of course everyone longs for perfection. Unfortunately, it simply does not exist. While in fairy tales the perfect man might be able to attract the perfect woman, and vice versa, in real life, imperfect humans with run-of-the-mill flaws like all of us had better resign themselves to the fact that they will have to settle for other humans no better and no worse than themselves.

One dimension of equitability in mergers centers on "looks." There is considerable evidence that couples are more likely to pair up if they are comparable in physical attractiveness. Irwin Silverman (1971) observed couples in several natural settings—in movie theater lines, in singles bars, and at assorted social events. A team of researchers rated the daters' looks. Most couples were found to be remarkably similar on the attractiveness dimension. A beautiful woman was most likely to be standing with a handsome man. A homely man was most likely to be spotted buying a drink for a homely woman. Furthermore, similarity did seem to "breed content." The more alike the couple was in physical appeal, the more delighted they seemed to be with each other, if intimate touching was any indication of their feelings. Sixty percent of the couples comparable in attractiveness were engaged in some type of fondling, while only 22% of mismatched couples were touching.

In a later study, Valerie Folkes (1982) secured similar results. Individuals were invited to join a video-dating service. They could come in, check out a selection of videotapes, read background information about the occupations, attitudes, interests, and backgrounds of the prospective dates. Then they could invite anyone they found appealing for a date. Of course, anyone they contacted had the option of checking *them* out before they accepted or rejected the date. Which couples ended up dating? The more similar men and women were in appearance, the more likely they were to date one or more times. Gregory White (1980) found that first-time or casual daters were only somewhat matched in attractiveness. Serious daters, engaged couples, and married couples were far more comparable.

Physical appearance is hardly the only issue in mate selection. Couples can be well or ill-matched in a variety of ways. For example, Olympic skier Ivana Trump (and model Marla Maples. . . . and model Rowanne Brewer) chose "the Donald," who was not equally good-looking but was unusually bright, charming, and (at the time!) very rich. Recently, a columnist speculated that Ted Turner and Jane Fonda, who have clashing political passions, must have fallen in love because few other equitable relationships were available!

After two failed marriages apiece, Ted and Jane have found each other, and become the embodiment of the new power couple. Their kids are grown, they have known much wedded unhappiness, any official coupling will cost them a fortune in lawyers' fees, and still they believe in marriage. Even more unusual is that they are the same age. In Hollywood, where youthful beauty is everything, the idea that a powerful, famous 52-year-old man would choose a woman his own age (Fonda, 53, is actually 11 months older) is downright incredible. Of course, Jane Fonda does possess one of the most fit bodies in town.

"I think that from her point of view he's one of the most interesting, fascinating, globally thinking people she's ever encountered. From his point of view, she's serious and smart and beautiful and passionate, and that's a very powerful energy when it comes together," says a Fonda friend.

"I think what intrigues everyone about them is that they're equals," says one Fonda associate. "Given who they are, the probability of them each being with an equal is unlikely." (Hall, 1991, p. 20)

The evidence supports the contention that people do engage in such complicated balancing and counterbalancing when selecting mates (Hatfield & Sprecher, 1986b).

After I have looked around the world for a mate,
then I might fall back on you.
When I am convinced that there is no better fate,
then I might decide if you will do.
  —*Romantic song from the Jerome Kern and*
      Oscar Hammerstein musical Showboat

A proposal of marriage in our society tends to be a way in which a man sums up his social attributes and suggests to a woman that hers are not so much better as to preclude a merger or partnership in these matters.
                                    —*Erving Goffman*

In one study, 537 dating college men and women were interviewed (Hatfield et al., 1978). The researchers found that couples in equitable relationships were most likely to become sexually involved and to fall in love. Couples in inequitable relationships tended to stop before "going all the way." Couples who were sexually intimate were asked why they had made love. Couples in equitable affairs were most likely to say that *both* of them wanted to have sexual intercourse. Couples in inequitable relationships were less likely to claim that sex had been a mutual decision; many felt pressured into having sexual relations in order to keep the relationship alive. It is not surprising then that couples in equitable relationships have more satisfying sexual lives (Traupmann & Hatfield, 1981).

Leslie Baxter (1986) asked undergraduates who had decided to break up with a dating partner in the past 12 months to write an essay on "Why we broke up." She found that about 12% of them mentioned the lack of equity as a precipitating factor. Women were most likely to mention inequity as the reason they wanted out.

Other studies document that judiciously matched couples expect their relations to evolve into more permanent ones. [For some recent research on this topic, see Berg & McQuinn (1986); Cate, Lloyd, & Long (1988); Matthews & Clark (1991); Michaels, Acock, & Edwards (1986); or Van Ypern & Buunk (1990).]

A poor man who marries a wealthy woman gets a ruler and not a wife.
—Anaxandrides

Equitable Relationships Are Comfortable Relationships   Researchers have interviewed dating couples, newlyweds, couples married for various lengths of time, and the long married. In all these circumstances they find that equitable relationships are the most comfortable at every stage.

In part, lovers sometimes wish to demonstrate their love by sacrificing for their beloved. The popular arts and culture contributed to the myth that self-surrender is the very essence of love. In Charles Dickens's (1859/1962) *A Tale of Two Cities,* Charles Darnay and Sidney Carton are virtually indistinguishable; both are besotted with Lucie Manette. But Lucie loves Darnay. Thus Sidney Carton sacrifices his life for Lucie's happiness. (He takes Darnay's place and is sentenced to death by the guillotine.) Schoolchildren throughout the world thrill to Carton's ringing declaration, "It is a far, far better thing that I do, than I have ever done; it is a far, far better rest that I go to than I have ever known" (p. 358).

Mutual love is especially poignant. To love and to be loved is a heady combination. The lovers, for example, in O. Henry's (1906/1942) short story *The Gift of the Magi,* a poor couple, are doubly appealing; each sells his most precious possession in order to buy a Christmas gift for the other. Della crops off her long brown hair so she can sell it to buy a platinum fob chain for Jim's gold watch. Jim, meanwhile, has sold his antique watch (his only inheritance from his father and grandfather before him), in order to buy Della a set of tortoise shell combs to wear in her beautiful hair. The double sacrifice is doubly rewarding: They have exchanged gifts of the heart.

But there are limits. If lovers give too much and receive nothing in return (not even gratitude), they eventually begin to feel uneasy. Does the other really love *them*? If so, why doesn't he seem to appreciate their sacrifices? The selfish person usually begins to have his doubts too. What kind of a woman would allow herself to be made a doormat? Doesn't she have any pride? There is considerable evidence that inequity is distressing for couples of all ages and at all stages of a relationship. Men and women who receive far more than they deserve have been found to feel slightly uneasy (they often feel loved *and* slightly guilty and distressed). Not surprisingly, those who receive less than they deserve feel far more upset (more angry, distressed, and depressed). It appears that one never gets used to injustice. [See Sprecher (1986) and Sprecher & Schwartz (1992) for a review of this research.]

Equitable Relationships Are Especially Stable   Couples are most committed to their relationships and less willing to end them when they feel equitably treated [see Sprecher (1992) for a review of this research]. Equitably treated men and women are reluctant to risk their marriages by getting sexually and emotionally involved with someone else. Elaine Hatfield, Jane Traupmann, and G. William Walster (1979) found that in equitable relationships, both partners are motivated to be generally faithful. Inequitable relationships are more fragile. The under-benefited, who feel they are not getting their just deserts in their marriages, are more likely to explore fleeting or even permanent love affairs. The tendency for the underbenefited to have more extramarital affairs sooner in the relationship is depicted in Figure 4.1. [Similar results were secured by Prins, Buunk, & Van Ypern (1991).]

Researchers disagree as to how *important* equity is in determining whether or not couples remain together, separate, or divorce [see Sprecher & Schwartz (1992) for a review of this research].

In many ways I haven't changed a bit. I am still the same self-absorbed guy I was when I married Ava [Ava Gardner]. I like to do what I want, when I want, where I want, without much thought for the wants of others. The people around me fare best when they do not challenge me.
—Film star Mickey Rooney

Gender Differences in Willingness to Sacrifice   Equity researchers who have studied couples' implicit marriage contracts (their unspoken assumptions as to what constitutes a balanced give-and-take) have attempted to determine how fair men and women perceive their marriages to be. Researchers have generally found that regardless of whether couples are newlyweds, married for several years, or

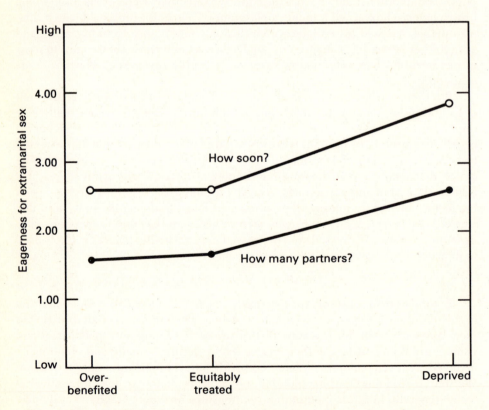

Figure 4.1 The relationship between equity and eagerness for extramarital sex.

long married, both men and women agree that men are getting the "best deal." Both genders concur that, in general, men contribute less to a marriage than women do and get more out of it (Buunk & Van Yperen, 1989; Hatfield et al., 1984; Sprecher, 1988; Van Ypern & Buunk, 1990, 1991).

I have always thought that every woman should marry, and no man.
—Benjamin Disraeli

Jesse Bernard (1973) provided additional support for the notion that women sacrifice more for love than men do. In her review of the voluminous literature contrasting "his marriage versus her marriage," she observed a strange paradox. Women are more eager to marry than men; yet women are the losers in marriage. She noted, for example, that "being married is about twice as advantageous to men as to women in terms of continued survival" (p. 27). As compared to single men, married men experience far better mental health, greater happiness, increased earning power, better health after middle age, and, to top it off, they live longer. The opposite is true for married as compared to single women. For example, all symptoms of psychological distress among married women show up more frequently than expected: nervous breakdowns, anxiety, inertia, insomnia, trembling or perspiring hands, nightmares, fainting, headaches, dizziness, and heart palpitations. They show up much less frequently than expected among unmarried women. These data then suggest that, like it or not, women sacrifice the most for love. Perhaps, for women, marriage should carry a warning label: "This relationship may be hazardous to your health."

Individual Differences in Concern with Equity   Of course people differ in how much they care about justice and fairness. Most people are exquisitely attuned to the delicate balances of relationships. However, a few people are narcissistic and selfish; the feelings of others mean nothing to them. A few "people who love too much" have learned to neglect their own feelings and interests and focus overmuch on those they love. Researchers have speculated that some people may care more about equity and fairness than do others (Clark et al., 1987; Murstein, Cerreto, & MacDonald, 1977; Murstein, Wadlin, & Bond, 1987). In a revision and extension of an earlier scale (Murstein et al., 1977), Susan Sprecher (1992) developed an *Exchange Orientation Scale* to show how concerned men and women would be if they were overbenefited (the OEO scale) or underbenefited (the UEO scale). Typical items from these scales appear in Box 4.2.

Sprecher found that the scales were useful in distinguishing exchange orientation. The higher people scored on the OEO scale, the more upset they were when they received far more than they deserved and the more likely they were to try to set things right. The higher they scored on the UEO scale, the more upset they became when they were cheated and the more determined they were to try to get what they deserved.

Differences in Casual Versus Intimate Relationships   Finally, equity researchers point out that intimate and casual relationships differ in certain ways

Box 4.2   THE EXCHANGE ORIENTATION SCALE

Please indicate your answers on the following scale:

   1 = strongly disagree (definitely not)

   2 = mildly disagree (probably not)

   3 = undecided (not sure)

   4 = mildly agree (I believe so)

   5 = strongly agree (definitely yes)

The Overbenefiting Exchange Orientation (OEO) Scale

1. I usually do not forget if I owe someone a favor.

2. When I exchange gifts with a significant other on an important occasion (Christmas, anniversary), I feel badly (guilty) if I have spent significantly less money on him/her than he/she has on me.

3. If my partner does dishes three times a week, then I expect to do them three times a week also (or something equivalent).

4. It bothers me if people I like do more for me than I do for them.

The Underbenefiting Exchange Orientation (UEO) Scale

1. I usually do not forget if someone owes me a favor.

2. When I exchange gifts with a significant other on an important occasion (Christmas, anniversary), I feel badly (cheated) if I have spent significantly more money on him/her than he/she has on me.

3. If I do dishes three times a week then I expect my partner to do them three times a week also (or something equivalent).

4. It bothers me if people I like do less for me than I do for them.

Source: Sprecher, 1992; adapted from earlier work by Murstein, Cerreto, & MacDonald, 1977; and Murstein, Wadlin, & Bond, 1987; p. 60.

that affect how the partners calculate equity and how eager they are to restore equity in the short versus the long run.

   1. *Intensity of loving/liking.* Couples who companionately love one another care far more about one another than do casual acquaintances. In part, then, lovers' joys and sufferings are necessarily entwined.

   2. *Length of relationship.* Intimate relationships are expected to endure and generally do endure over a long period of time; casual relationships are usually short term. This fact should have two important consequences for the way equity/inequity principles operate in intimate versus casual relationships.

*The reason that husbands and wives do not understand each other
is because they belong to different sexes.*
> —Dorothy Dix

(a) *Perception of inequity.* It should be easier to calculate equity in casual relationships than in intimate ones. Over a short span it is easy to assess who owes whom what. Strangers in a bar need only remember who bought the last drink to determine who should pick up the tab for the next round. In intimate relationships it is far more difficult to calculate equity. We have all heard fights that escalate interminably: She: "I asked him to come over because I was jealous and desperate, but he just abandoned me." He: "Well, the last time I came over when we'd both been drinking, we got into a fight and you called the police. I can't trust you." She: "Well, I haven't learned to trust you yet. You hit me. I can never forgive you for that." Soon our brains blow a fuse as we try to record their complicated calculus of grievances. How far back in a relationship is it fair to go in making such calculations? In short-term relationships, participants can usually distinguish with some ease what is equitable and what is not. Participants in intimate relationships often have a far harder time defining equity/inequity.

Keep thy eyes wide open before marriage, and half shut afterwards.
> —Benjamin Franklin

(b) *Tolerance of perceived inequity.* Participants in casual versus intimate relationships may differ in their insistence that perceived inequities be redressed immediately. Casuals may be fully aware that unless existing imbalances are redressed soon, they will probably never be redressed at all. Intimates, committed to long-range interaction, should be more tolerant of momentary imbalances, since they know they will have ample time in the future to set things right.

The movie *Paper Moon* provides a comic illustration of this point. Nine-year-old Addie has convinced herself that Mose (a traveling con man) is her father. As long as they have a father/child relationship, she allows him to spend her money freely on himself. The moment she realizes that their "partnership" is about to end, however, her feelings change precipitously. She suddenly begins to insist loudly, "I want my $200!"

3. *Value of resources exchanged.* A variety of exchange theorists have observed that as a relationship grows in intimacy, the potency of the rewards and punishments a pair can give one another increases.

A friend's frown is better than a foe's smile.
> —James Howell

(a) *Value of rewards.* Many theorists have observed that intimates' rewards are especially potent. The same reward—"I love you. You are a wonderful wife"—is far more potent when it comes from a loved one than from a casual acquaintance.

In addition, companionate lovers possess a bigger storehouse of rewards than do casuals. Generally, people are more willing to invest their resources in intimate relationships than in casual ones. Thus intimates usually provide their partners with more and more valuable rewards (time, effort, intimate information, money) than do casuals.

Those have most power to hurt us, that we love. We lay our sleeping lives within their arms.

—*Francis Beaumont*

(b) *Value of punishments.* Intimates' rewards may be unusually potent, but so are the punishments they can inflict on each other. For example, if a stranger at a party loudly announces that I am a selfish bore, I lose little; I can dismiss his words as those of a creep who doesn't really know what kind of a person I am. But if my husband were to tell me the same thing, I would be crushed—he knows me, and still thinks that! Intimates command one unique and potentially potent punishment: They can threaten to end the relationship. People feel that love relationships should be long-term relationships. Husbands and wives should remain married "until death do us part." Thus if an intimate is willing to suffer himself, he has the power to deliver a devastating blow to his partner. He has the power to expose his partner to public humiliation; to make it clear to everyone that his mate is a "defective" person. The intimate who is willing to "cut off his nose to spite his face" can punish his partner in more practical ways. People take their relationships for granted; they come to depend on them. When a person precipitously terminates an intimate relationship, he abandons his partner to a lonely and painful unknown.

Marriage is something we make from available materials. In this sense it's improvised, it's almost offhand. Maybe this is why we know so little about it. It's too inspired and quicksilver a thing to be clearly understood. Two people make a blur.

—*Don DeLillo*

4. *Variety of resources exchanged.* As a relationship grows in intensity, the variety of rewards and punishments a pair can give one another increases. Recent theoretical and empirical work by Uriel Foa (1971) provides a useful framework for discussing this point. He has argued that the resources of interpersonal exchange fall into six classes—love, status, information, money, goods, and services. Theoretically, all resources can be classified according to their "particularism" and "concreteness" (Foa & Foa, 1974). The dimension particularism refers to the extent to which the resource's value is influenced by the person who delivers it. Since money is valuable regardless of its source, it is classed as nonparticularistic. Since love's value depends very much on who is doing the loving, it is classed as "particularistic." The dimension concreteness refers to the resource's characteristic form of expression. Since money, goods, and services involve the exchange of tangibles—things you can see, smell, and touch—they are classed as concrete. Since love, status, and information are usually conveyed verbally, they are classed as symbolic.

We suspect that casual versus intimate relationships may differ markedly in both the variety and types of resources participants commonly exchange. In casual exchanges, participants generally exchange only a few types of resources.

In addition, since casual relationships are such short-term relationships, we suspect that casuals probably feel lucky if they can manage to negotiate an exchange of resources whose value is commonly understood. Casuals simply aren't "in business" long enough to work out any very complicated or troublesome exchanges. Thus we suspect that casuals' exchanges are generally focused primarily on nonparticularistic and concrete resources (i.e., money, goods, services, and information).

We suspect that in intimate exchanges, however, participants generally exchange resources from all six classes. Like casuals, intimates can exchange nonparticularistic and concrete resources. But, in addition, they can, and do, go to the trouble of negotiating more complicated exchanges. They can work out exchanges of symbolic and particularistic resources (love, status, services, and information). (It may even be that intimates are primarily concerned with such exchanges.)

If casuals usually exchange concrete and nonparticularistic resources, while intimates exchange not only these but a variety of other resources, whose value depends on each person's idiosyncratic evaluation of both the giver and the reward, this fact provides a second reason why it is easier in casual than in intimate affairs to calculate equity. Casuals are exchanging resources of set value; thus it is fairly easy to calculate equity. Intimates exchange these set-value commodities, plus a potpourri of ambiguous value commodities. It is no wonder then that intimates may find the calculation of equity/inequity a mind-boggling task.

5. *Interchangeability of resources.* We venture into far shakier territory with our next characteristic of intimacy. We would speculate that, within a particular exchange, casuals tend to be limited to exchanging resources from the same class. Intimates, on the other hand, have far more freedom to exchange resources from entirely different classes. Casual relationships usually exist in a single context, where like is exchanged for like. If I lend my notes to the classmate I see three times a week, I expect to be repaid in kind the next time I miss a lecture. If I am invited to my neighbor's parties with great regularity, I know full well that unless I reciprocate and invite her to mine, I will be considered antisocial, unappreciative, and will very likely be dropped from her guest list. But inviting her to my parties is all I need do, unless I want the relationship to progress to deeper levels, perhaps to intimacy. (In that case, I would attempt to exchange with her some of the resources characterized above as typical of intimates: affection, status, disclosures of personal information.)

In contrast, intimate relationships exist in a variety of contexts. Participants have at their disposal the whole range of interpersonal resources and freely exchange one type for another. Thus the wife whose husband has been working two jobs to help pay her graduate school fees can pay him back in a number of ways: She can defer to his conclusion that he is entitled to go golfing on Sunday (status), make him a special dinner (services), or tell him how much she loves him and appreciates his generosity (love). Her husband may well prefer these gifts to direct monetary repayment. Intimates spend considerable time negotiating the values and exchangeability of various behaviors; negotiating the "terms" of their relationship.

Once again, our comparison of the variety of resources involved in casual versus intimate relationships leads us to the conclusion that it is easier for everyone to calculate equity in casual relationships than in intimate ones. We have just concluded that participants in casual relationships trade "in kind." Intimates may trade vastly different resources. It is easy enough to know that a round of beer on Monday night equals a round on Tuesday. It is far more difficult to decide if dinner at an expensive restaurant on Monday balances out three nights of neglect due to a heavy work load.

Therefore shall a man leave his father and his mother, and shall cleave unto his wife: and they shall be one flesh.

—*Old Testament*

6. *The unit of analysis: From "you" and "me" to "we."* We've seen how many of the unique characteristics of intimate relationships make assessments of equity, from outside as well as inside the relationship, a formidable task. Another characteristic of intimate relationships, which may add complexity, is that intimates, through identification with and empathy for their partners, come to define themselves as a unit; as one couple. They see themselves not merely as individuals interacting with others, but also as part of a partnership, interacting with other individuals, partnerships, and groups. This characteristic may have a dramatic impact on intimates' perceptions of what is and is not equitable.

Just what do we mean when we say intimates see themselves as a "unit"? Perhaps the simplest way of describing this wholeness is by saying the unit is a "we." Examples of this "we-ness" are the joy and pride a parent feels at the success and happiness of his child ("That's my boy!"); the distress a wife experiences when her husband has been denied a hoped-for opportunity; the intense pleasure a lover feels while working to make his beloved happy. Now, certainly in the examples above, the "identifiers" are directly affected by what happens to their partners. The parents may be supported in their old age by a successful son, the wife's household allowance as well as the husband's suffers when he is denied his hoped-for promotion, the lover may receive affection for his labors. But the intimates' identification with their partners may cause them to experience genuine, "firsthand" emotions aside from these returns. Intimates' outcomes often become hopelessly intertwined.

CONCLUSION

In sum, we see that people care about both how rewarding their relationships are and how fair they seem to be.

In the great debate over whether companionate love and intimacy are instinctive and "hard-wired" into humankind or whether they are better explained by less sentimental "programming" models, which suggest that people must be taught to behave in fair and loving ways, we wish we could be romantic and opt for biology and instinct. But though the evidence is not complete, and though psychologists, historians, philosophers, theologians, poets, and scientists continue to struggle with the issue, it looks to us that companionate love and intimacy are primarily social constructions. They are relatively new in human history and not inevitable partners of our future destiny. And they are derived significantly from personal calculations of reward and punishment, allowed expression as long as individualism continues to be the cultural standard—a standard that might seem universal and eternal to white, middle-class North Americans and Europeans but that in actuality is accepted even today by only a minority (though a rapidly growing minority) of the whole human family.

Researchers (Sternberg, 1988) have pointed out that companionate love is comprised of two components—commitment and intimacy. Let us now consider these two components of love in greater detail.

Chapter
5

Intimacy and Commitment

INTIMACY

Introduction

In the United States and much of the Western world, the word "intimacy" has taken on a cachet not unlike "motherhood" and "apple pie." The achievement of intimacy in one's life is a worthy goal. People want intimacy; they celebrate it; they honor it; they envy others who seem to have it. It seems to express a noble achievement in human evolution.

The glorification of intimacy is not senseless. The ability of individuals to be close to others, to disclose themselves and to be open to the revelations of others, requires human capacities of a very high order and speaks well of our aspirations. Yet it is important to remember that the attainment of intimacy was rarely even a *desideratum* in the West before the Renaissance 500 years ago and hardly existed as a reality before 1800. Even today, few achieve intimacy, despite its honored reputation. And many in the West, particularly men, still fail to take it seriously enough to learn about it or develop techniques to aid in gaining a measure of it. Indeed, for many men, "intimacy" only means "sex." Anything else seems high-falutin', exotic, or even "a woman's thing."

Outside the West, the weak hold of intimacy as a life goal is yet more striking. Many Arab men and women, Japanese and Chinese, South Asians, and Africans reading the first paragraph of this chapter might find it totally incomprehensible. In poor societies, that constitutes no surprise; intimacy means little when there is insufficient food. But in wealthy Japan, intimacy was never a goal nor is it yet today; a complex set of rituals defines human relationships in the service of stability and the avoidance of shame.

So when we talk about the rich rewards of intimacy in this chapter, we are describing something quite new in human history and quite culture-bound. Tender feelings and the capacity to get close to other humans elevate our species far beyond the norms of practically the entire planetary past: violence, raw and repressed emotions, primitive hatreds and vendettas, submission to authority (worship of the "alpha-male"), short and brutal lives.

Fragile flower though it is, intimacy's seeds are spreading. If the grandest historical movement of the past five centuries has been the advance of individualism, its manifestations have been manifold. In political life democracy and protected human rights are expressions of valuing and dignifying the individual. In economic life, materialism is its offspring. In intellectual life, creativity and freedom of expression are children of individualism. And in psychological and philosophical arenas, the very notion of personal happiness as a goal in life represents the fullest flowering of this extraordinary modern idea.

Unfettered individualism, however, can lead to loneliness and narcissism. Intimacy works as a counterpoise to such isolation. One cannot get close to another human without self-awareness and the capacity derived from the awareness—to feel empathy with and care for that other person. But intimacy is not only the offspring of individualism; it ameliorates the dangers of individualism's isolating powers.

Does our praise of intimacy suggest a certain cultural insensitivity, since the high value placed on intimacy is so Western? (So is rampant materialism!) That is a difficult question, making it deceptive to hide behind the mask of objectivity. The very existence, after all, of the discipline of psychology, the study of the psyche—of the self—reveals a bias in the direction of individualism and intimacy. Right now, the question of cultural relativism may be moot. For better or for worse, we believe that individualism continues to spread and that we are witnessing its slow, uneven conquest of the world. As that happens, we expect that the desire for intimacy will become increasingly a universal rather than a Western phenomenon, and that the better we understand it, the better will be our chances for attaining this profoundly rewarding state.

DEFINITIONS

The word intimacy is derived from *intimus,* the Latin term for "inner" or "inmost." It may be defined as "a process in which one person expresses important self-relevant feelings and information to another, and as a result of the other's response comes to feel known, validated, and cared for" (Clark & Reis, 1988, p. 628).

Recently, Daniel Perlman and Beverley Fehr (1987) reviewed the way most theorists have used this term. They found that almost all of them assumed that intimate relationships involved affection and warmth, self-disclosure, and closeness and interdependence.

What do most people mean by "intimacy"? Vicki Helgeson, Phillip Shaver, and Margaret Dyer (1987) asked college men and women to tell them about times when they felt most intimate with (or most distant from) someone they cared about. Presumably, as people recalled these intensely intimate moments, their unspoken implicit definitions of intimacy would come spilling out. For most people, intimate relations were associated with feelings of affection and warmth, with happiness and contentment, talking about personal things, and sharing pleasurable activities. And what sorts of things put an impenetrable wall between couples? Distant relationships were associated with anger, resentment, and sadness as well as criticism, insensitivity, and inattention.

Men and women seemed to mean something slightly different by intimacy. Women tended to focus primarily on love and affection and the expression of warm feelings when reliving their most intimate moments. They rarely mentioned sex. For men, a key feature of intimacy was sex and physical closeness.

Assessing Intimacy

Mark Schaefer and David Olson (1981) developed the most popular intimacy measure, the *Personal Assessment of Intimacy in Relationships* (PAIR). They have identified five types of intimacy:

1. *Emotional intimacy*—experiencing a closeness of feelings;
2. *Social intimacy*—the experience of having common friends, similarities in social networks, and so forth;
3. *Intellectual intimacy*—the experience of sharing ideas;
4. *Sexual intimacy*—the experience of sharing general affection and/or sexual activity;
5. *Recreational intimacy*—shared experiences of interests in hobbies, mutual participation in a sporting event. (pp. 8–9)

The PAIR defines and assesses how much intimacy couples expect and actually realize in their close relationships. (You might try to find out how intimate *your* love affair is by answering the sample questions that appear in Box 5.1.)

Other researchers (Guerney, 1977; Miller & Lefcourt, 1982; Tesch, 1985; Waring, 1984) have developed still other scales for assessing intimacy.

The Components of Intimacy

The threads of intimacy—affection, trust, emotional expressiveness, communication, and sex—are so entwined that it is almost impossible to tease them apart.

Love and Affection   Men and women generally feel more love and affection for their intimates than for anyone else; such mutual affection is probably the first condition of intimacy. When people know they are loved and liked, they naturally become more willing to risk exposing their ideas and feelings (Berscheid, 1985; Gottman, 1979). That is not as easy as it sounds, for people are often more timid than one might think. Even a hint of rejection seems to inhibit self-disclosure (Taylor, Altman, & Sorrentino, 1969). People rarely confide in others who are uncaring or disinterested (Reis & Shaver, 1988). And some cultures actually discourage self-disclosure.

If you talk about yourself, he'll think you're boring. If you talk about others, he'll think you're a gossip. If you talk about him, he'll think you're a brilliant conversationalist.

—Linda Sunshine

Personal Validation   At various times in our lives, most of us feel that we don't quite fit in. The wail of the adolescent is "Nobody understands me!" One of the most transforming things about a love relationship is that, finally, someone loves, understands, and approves of you. One of our middle-aged clients instantly fell in love with her husband when he was delighted by her most embarrassing

Box 5.1   THE PAIR INVENTORY

INSTRUCTIONS: This inventory is used to measure different kinds of intimacy in your relationship. Indicate how intimate your relationship is on the following five point scale.

0	1	2	3	4
Strongly disagree	Somewhat disagree	Neutral	Somewhat agree	Strongly agree

I. Emotional Intimacy

   *1. I often feel distant from my partner.

   2. My partner can really understand my hurts and joys.

   3. My partner listens to me when I need someone to talk to.

   4. I can state my feelings without him/her getting defensive.

II. Social Intimacy

   1. Having time together with friends is an important part of our shared activities.

   2. We enjoy spending time with other couples.

   *3. We usually "keep to ourselves."

   *4. We have very few friends in common.

III. Sexual Intimacy

   1. I am satisfied with our sex life.

   *2. I "hold back" my sexual interest because my partner makes me feel uncomfortable.

   *3. I feel our sexual activity is just routine.

   *4. My partner seems disinterested in sex.

IV. Intellectual Intimacy

   *1. I feel "put-down" in a serious conversation with my partner.

   *2. I feel it is useless to discuss some things with my partner.

   3. We have an endless number of things to talk about.

   *4. My partner frequently tries to change my ideas.

V. Recreational Intimacy

   1. We enjoy the out-of-doors together.

   2. We enjoy the same recreational activities.

3. I think that we share some of the same interests.

4. We like playing together.

*These items are scored in the reverse direction; they tap a *lack* of intimacy.

To calculate your PAIR score, simply add up your rating on each of the individual items. The higher your score, the more intimate your relationship is. (Remember to reverse the scoring on items preceded by an asterisk. These items indicate a lack of intimacy, of course.)

Source: Instructions—Olson & Schaefer, 1981 (PAIR item booklet); items—Schaefer & Olson, 1981, pp. 53–54.

flaw—her inability to explain herself. She was bright enough, but when she tried to make a point, her ideas spun out in a hopeless tangle. She would breathlessly present her main point, hurriedly anticipate any and all objections, and rush on to a muddled defense. Usually people looked at her blankly and then went on. When she was dating the man who became her husband, however, he immediately grasped what she was trying to say. To the assembled group, he said: "What a brilliant idea!" He proceeded to explain slowly what she had been trying to say to everyone else. This time, her ideas sparked excited conversation. His explanation for her problem was equally kind-spirited. He took it for granted that she was just so brilliant that she could grasp the big picture instantly. She simply had to learn to slow down enough so that mere mortals could work their way through what she was trying to say. No wonder she loved him. Everyone, not just our client, finds such validation extremely liberating (Derlega, Winstead, Wong, & Greenspan, 1987; Gottman, 1979).

Trust   People seldom risk exposing their dreams or fears to people unless they know it is safe to do so. Sometimes, all it takes is one bad experience to make intimates withdraw. Another of our clients, a military officer, once told his wife that he had been molested as a child. Soon after, in a fight, she used that secret knowledge to hurt and humiliate him. It didn't matter to him that moments later she was appalled at what she had said and apologized. She didn't get a second chance.

Self-disclosure   In his classic book, *The Transparent Self*, Sidney Jourard (1964) presented *The Self-Disclosure Questionnaire*, designed to assess the extent to which individuals reveal their attitudes, feelings, and experiences to others. (See Box 5.2 for a sampling of his questions. You might see how self-disclosing *you* tend to be.) Jourard contended that when men and women are able to reveal their inner feelings and experiences to others, relationships bloom. Caring and trust may be the soil in which self-disclosure thrives, but self-disclosure, in turn, nourishes love, liking, caring, trust, and understanding.

A whirl of research followed in the wake of Jourard's book. Psychologists

Box 5.2 **THE SELF-DISCLOSURE QUESTIONNAIRE**

Read through each item and indicate on the following scale the extent to which you have talked about that item to *the person to whom you are closest.*

0 Have told the other person nothing about this aspect of me. Or: Have lied or misrepresented myself to the other person so that he has a false picture of me.

1 Have talked in general terms about this item. The other person has only a general idea about this aspect of me.

2 Have talked in full and complete detail about this item to the other person. He knows me fully in this respect and could describe me accurately.

Attitudes and Opinions
1. What I think and feel about religion.

2. My views on the present government.

3. My personal views on sexual morality.

4. My personal standards of beauty and attractiveness in women.

5. The things that I regard as desirable for a man to be.

Tastes and Interests
1. My favorite foods, the ways I like food prepared, and my food dislikes.

2. My likes and dislikes in music.

3. The kind of party or social gathering that I like best, and the kind that I wouldn't enjoy.

Work (or Studies)
1. What I find to be the most boring and unenjoyable aspects of my work.

2. What I enjoy most and get the most satisfaction from in my present work.

3. What I feel are *my* shortcomings and handicaps that prevent me from getting further ahead in my work.

4. What I feel are my special strong points and qualifications for my work.

5. How I really feel about the people that I work for, or work with.

Money
1. How much money I make at my work, or get as an allowance.

2. Whether or not I owe money; if so, *how much.*

Personality
1. The aspects of my personality that I dislike.

2. The facts of my present sex life—including knowledge of how I get sexual gratification; any problems that I might have; with whom I have relations, if anybody.

3. Whether or not I feel that I am attractive to the opposite sex.

4. Things in the past or present that I feel ashamed and guilty about.

5. The kinds of things that make me just furious.

6. What it takes to get me feeling real depressed or blue.

7. What it takes to get me real worried, anxious, and afraid.

8. What it takes to hurt my feelings deeply.

9. The kinds of things that make me especially proud of myself, elated, full of self-esteem or self-respect.

Body

1. My feelings about the appearance of my face—things I don't like, and things that I might like about my face.

2. How I wish I looked.

3. My past record of illness and treatment.

4. Whether or not I now make a special effort to keep fit, healthy, and attractive.

5. My present physical measurements.

The higher the score, the more intimate a person is with those who are close.

Source: Jourard & Lasakow, 1958, p. 92.

Irwin Altman and Dalmas Taylor (1973) reviewed a series of studies on the "social penetration process." They made two major discoveries. (1) Intimacy takes time. As couples began to get better acquainted, they began to disclose more. At first, they began to increase the *breadth* of the topics they touched on in conversation. Later, as they came to feel even closer to one another, they increased the *depth* of their revelations. There seemed to be no such thing as "instant intimacy." (2) Acquaintances tended to match one another in how intimate their disclosures were. In some relationships, both participants were willing to reveal a great deal about themselves. In others, both confined themselves to small talk.

Recently, researchers have observed that intimates confide two very different kinds of information—feelings and facts—to one another. Teru Morton (1978) distinguished between *evaluative self-disclosure* (in which people reveal their deepest personal feelings) and *descriptive self-disclosure* (in which people simply recite the facts of their lives). When men and women first meet, they are generally fairly wary. While they are eager to make a good first impression—to attract appealing potential dates and gracefully to get rid of unappealing ones—they have no time to worry about intimacy (Miell & Duck, 1986; Miller & Read, 1987). People tend to "freeze out" undesirable potential dates by refusing to self-disclose (Davis, Dewitt, & Charney, 1986). The date might try to get a conversation going, but if the other isn't interested, his bored and unresponsive "Uh-huh" soon puts a dismal end to things. If he is interested, however, he is likely to be animated, responsive, and far more forthcoming (Berg & McQuinn, 1986). On a first encounter, however, acquaintances usually reveal only the bare facts of their lives; they talk little about their feelings. ("Where are you from?" "Stamford, Connecticut." "Where are you from?" "Detroit." "Do you know Mary Brown?") New acquaintances are careful not to reveal too much too soon; and not to reveal much more than their partners do (Morton, 1978; Won-Doornick, 1979).

Daters tend to warm up fairly quickly, however. After six weeks or so, people are already confiding in one another at about as high a level as they ever will (Hays, 1985). It is in long-term love relationships that intimates can be *most* relaxed and trusting. Once couples know each other well, the recital of mere facts counts for little; it is the communication of feelings that is critical to dating and marital satisfaction (Fitzpatrick, 1987, 1988). In long-term relationships, moment-to-moment reciprocity becomes unimportant. Things can wait.

When relationships are about to end, however, the pattern of self-disclosure changes. Now, words can be used to wound. Altman and Taylor (1973) assumed that as relationships began to dissolve, couples would begin to confide in one another less and less. Recent studies make it clear that this is not the case. In terminal relationships, couples often begin to spew out the ugly accusations that they have kept hidden. They begin to spill out years of hatred, anger, and exaggerated grievances. Couples may begin to talk through the night, trying to figure out what went wrong and if there is any chance to set things right (Baxter, 1987; Tolstedt & Stokes, 1984).

There is no disguise which can for long conceal love where it exists or simulate it where it does not.

—Duc de La Rochefoucauld

Nonverbal Communication   Intimates feel comfortable in close physical proximity. They sneak little looks at their mates to convey shared understandings, gaze at one another (Argyle & Dean, 1965; Rubin, 1970), touch, stand close (Allgeier & Byrne, 1973), and even lean on one another (Galton, 1884; Hatfield, Roberts, & Schmidt, 1980). Of course, people can reveal how alienated and distant they feel from one another via the flip side of these same techniques. If a woman feels that a man she has just met is moving too fast and she is starting to feel cornered, she can reduce intimacy in several ways—by averting her gaze, shrinking back, shifting her body orientation, or simply by changing the subject and steering clear of intimate topics. We all know how enemies behave when they want to sever all contact. They glare, clench their jaws, sigh in disgust, or walk on ahead. Once a teenage boy visited us in Hawaii. For some reason, he became furious at his girlfriend when she mentioned that he had better bring some shoes so they could go right from the beach to dinner. He glared at her, his jaw thrust out, his body became rigid. He spit his words out through clenched teeth: "Fine. I'm not going to the beach. I'll just get dressed up right now, if that's what you want." The sight and sounds of distance.

THEORIES AND PERSPECTIVES ON INTIMACY

Recently, Daniel Perlman and Beverley Fehr (1987) observed that theorists had taken a trio of approaches to intimacy.

Life-Span Developmental Models

Developmental theorists have observed that young people must learn how to be intimate. Erik Erikson (1982) pointed out that "anything that grows has a ground plan, and that out of this ground plan parts arise, each part having its special time of ascendancy" (p. 92). Infants, children, adolescents, and adults face a continuing series of developmental tasks (see Table 5.1). If loved and nurtured, infants develop a basic trust in the universe. They develop the ability to hope. In early, middle, and late childhood, children learn to be autonomous, to take initiative, and to be industrious. They develop a will of their own, a sense of purpose, and a belief in their own competence.

The next two stages are those in which we are primarily interested. In adolescence, teenagers must develop some sense of their own identity. They may carefully observe movie, TV, and sports stars in an attempt to find their bearings. Only when adolescents have formed a relatively stable, independent identity are they able to master their next "crisis"—to learn how to become intimate with someone, to learn how to love. Mature relationships, according to Erikson, involve an ability to balance intimacy and independence.

Most Americans are wonderful at beginnings. At first, lovers can be swept along in a slaphappy haze; they love; they are sure that love will last forever. Then they bump rudely into reality; they hit the middle of a relationship. Often, at that point, things fall apart. Sometimes heartsick lovers, exhausted from their repeated romantic failures, berate themselves. "What's wrong with me?" "What did I do wrong?" They fail even to ask two possibly more relevant questions: "Is there anything wrong with *him* or *her*?" "Has he or she ever been intimate with anyone else?" Erikson's model makes it clear that not everyone successfully navigates the shoals of psychosocial development. Many people have not yet learned how to be

Table 5.1   MAJOR STAGES IN PSYCHOSOCIAL DEVELOPMENT OVER THE LIFE SPAN

Stages	Psychosocial crisis	Basic strengths/weaknesses
1. Infancy	Basic trust versus basic mistrust	Hope/withdrawal
2. Early childhood	Autonomy versus shame and doubt	Will/compulsion
3. Play age	Initiative versus guilt	Purpose/inhibition
4. School age	Industry versus inferiority	Competence/inertia
5. Adolescence	Identity versus identity confusion	Fidelity/repudiation
6. Young adulthood	Intimacy versus isolation	Love/exclusivity
7. Adulthood	Generativity versus stagnation	Care/rejectivity
8. Old age	Integrity versus despair	Wisdom/disdain

intimate/independent. They are incapable of being deeply intimate with *anyone*. When faced with the seductions of intimacy, they run.

Researchers provide some evidence in support of Erikson's theorizing. In one study Jacob Orlofsky and Sheila Ginsburg (1981) interviewed young people about their dating and marital experiences. They found that men and women, and their relationships, fell into five different categories. Couples in relationships that involved closeness, caring, mutuality, respect, and open communication could be classified as either *preintimate* or *intimate*, depending on whether the couple was poised on the brink of a love affair or firmly committed to one another. Many men and women were involved in flawed relationships—relationships that were either superficial or constricting. Relationships were classified as *stereotyped* if they were conventional and superficial or as *pseudointimate* if they possessed neither closeness nor depth. *Isolates* avoided all social relationships. Stephanie Tesch and Susan Whitbourne (1982) found, as Erikson might have foreseen, that men and women who had established solid identities were most capable of the higher levels of intimacy. [Bellew-Smith and Korn (1986) secured similar results.]

Perlman and Fehr remind us that other researchers have taken a different approach to intimacy.

Motivational Approaches

Psychiatrists and psychologists have pointed out that people are *motivated* to be intimate (Maslow, 1968; Sullivan, 1947). One of the most modern advocates of that position is Don McAdams (1992). Intimacy reflects an "individual's preference or readiness for experiences of closeness, warmth, and communication" (McAdams, 1982, p. 134). McAdams and his colleagues (McAdams, 1992) found that people who were high in intimacy motivation were different from their peers. They were more loving and affectionate, warmer, and more egalitarian and less self-centered and dominant. They spent more time thinking about people and relationships, more time talking and writing to others; they were more tactful and less outspoken. They stood closer to others. Not surprisingly, others liked them too.

Equilibrium Models

Researchers point out that people prefer an optimal level of intimacy. Too much or too little intimacy makes everyone uncomfortable. Miles Patterson (1976) proposed that when people get close to us, we become physiologically aroused. If we feel positive about this arousal we will get closer to them. If it is "too much" we will back off. Michael Argyle and Janet Dean (1965) tested such an equilibrium model. We literally back up when someone gets too close too fast. We move forward when they seem to be slipping away. In one study, for example, they found that people unconsciously signal "come closer" by making eye contact, smiling, moving closer, or starting to talk about very intimate things. If an acquaintance begins to get too close, however, people unconsciously signal that she should "back up" by looking away, looking stonefaced, moving away, or changing the subject to a less intimate topic. Such intricate ballets ensure that equilibrium is continually maintained. To test their model, the scientists asked subjects to

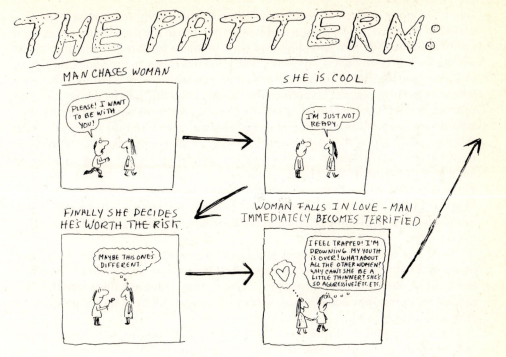

stand "as close as is comfortable to see well" and slowly to approach either a life-sized photograph of a person or the same person (in the flesh) whose eyes were either open or shut. (Presumably, it is most intimate to stare at someone who is staring back.) As predicted, subjects stood 11 inches closer to the photograph than to a living person and $8\frac{1}{2}$ inches closer to a person whose eyes were shut than one whose eyes were open. The authors also studied the flip side of the equilibrium process. Students were seated either 10, 6, or 2 feet from one another. As they talked, one student (an experimental confederate) gazed into the other's eyes for three minutes during the conversation. As soon as the confederate began to stare, most subjects immediately reduced eye contact. They looked away or down—anywhere but right at him. The closer they were, the more they averted their eyes. Perhaps you have seen the same sort of intimacy regulation operating in elevators. When people are forced to stand much too close to strangers, they tend to look nervously up at the ceiling or down at the floor, anywhere, avoiding one another's eyes.

Two features of the Argyle–Dean model are worth noting. First, they view intimacy from a dialectical perspective. They see people as constantly adjusting the level of their intimate encounters. Second, they point out that once the intimacy equilibrium has been disturbed, any of several different techniques can be used to set things right.

Harry Reis and Phillip Shaver (1988) pointed out that people differ markedly in how much intimacy they desire. (Of course, many non-Westerners come from cultures that traditionally do not value intimacy to begin with. However, even Americans and Europeans differ in how much they value intimacy.) We know couples who wish to be together most of the time. They tell one another little jokes, talk in silly voices, bump into each other. We have other married friends, in Germany, who cherish their time alone. Recently, they bought a duplex. His half is a stark artist's studio; hers is a cozy apartment crammed with knick-knacks. A wall with a locked door separates them so that they can be together when they want and separate when they don't. For years, they would try living together in the conventional way. They would fight. (She wanted him to pay his income taxes; she worried that his cavalier attitude would land them in jail. He wanted her to quit inviting over hordes of friends late at night.) They would separate. They would get lonely, get together and things would go wonderfully. Then they would start to fight. After going through this cycle again and again, they finally got it. Their current unconventional arrangement has worked wonderfully now for two decades.

Attaining the "right degree" of intimacy often requires a delicate balancing act. In any relationship, lovers' yearning to be close pushes them toward more profound encounters. Their fears of intimacy pluck them back from the depths of intimacy. But even in splendid relationships, enough can be enough. People crave closeness some of the time, but they also need time to be alone (sometimes just to stare at the walls and allow the brain to fire randomly). They need to work and to be with their own friends and acquaintances. Theorists have learned more about how couples subtly negotiate a compromise between how much intimacy *they* want and how much intimacy their *partners* feel comfortable with.

Let us now consider some of the factors that propel people toward intimate relationships, the factors that draw them back from the brink of intimacy and the ways in which people settle on the level of closeness that works best for them.

WHY PEOPLE SEEK INTIMACY

It seems a bit odd to ask *why* people wish for intimacy. When scientists ask men and women what they most desire in life, they generally mention a close intimate relationship (Astin, 1985; Berscheid & Peplau, 1983). In a classic monograph, Robert Weiss (1973) pointed out that people can feel sad and lonely for two very different reasons. Some lonely people are experiencing *emotional loneliness;* they hunger for one special intimate. Others are experiencing *social loneliness;* they merely lack friends and casual acquaintances. Of the two, it is emotional loneliness that is the more painful. Contentment is better predicted by the existence of intimacy (i.e., lack of loneliness) than popularity, the frequency of contact with friends, or the amount of time spent with acquaintances (Cutrona, 1982; Wheeler, Reis, & Nezlak, 1983). Theorists contend that intimacy has three major beneficial effects.

Its Intrinsic Appeal

Jonathan Freedman (1978) found that if people were happily in love, over 90% of them were also "very happy in general." If they were generally unhappy, most thought that love was the one thing that they needed to be happy. So people long for intimacy in and of itself. Intimacy also has some side benefits (Rook & Pietromonaco, 1987).

Its Links to Psychological Well-Being

Dan McAdams and George Vaillant (1982) interviewed single and married men when they were 30 years old and then again when they were 47. Those men who valued intimacy when they were 30 had the happiest and stablest marriages two decades later. A number of studies document that intimacy and psychological health seem to go hand-in-hand (McAdams, 1992). In early adulthood, intimate relationships foster creativity, productivity, and emotional integration (Erikson, 1959). Intimacy has been shown to be associated with happiness, contentment, and a sense of well-being (Loevinger, 1976; Reis, 1987). Happy (intimate) marriages provide real social support (Gove, Hughes, & Style, 1983). Intimacy problems are closely linked to many mental health disorders (Fisher & Stricker, 1982).

Its Links to Physical Well-Being

A number of medical researchers have confirmed that intimacy and physical well-being are connected. Intimate relationships apparently buffer the impact of stress (Jemmott & Magloire, 1988; Miller & Lefcourt, 1982). If persons have a chance to disclose emotionally upsetting material to someone who seems to care, they exhibit improved mental and physical health in follow-up physical examinations (Pennebaker, 1990; Pennebaker & Beale, 1986).

Most of our knowledge about the ties between intimate relationships and physical health comes from studies of the impact of a husband's or wife's death on the survivor's mental and physical health. Investigators find that bereavement increases the likelihood of a host of mental and physical problems (Stroebe & Stroebe, 1987; Traupmann-Pillemer & Hatfield, 1981). Bereavement (1) increases vulnerability to mental illness; (2) produces a variety of physical symptoms, including migraines, other headaches, facial pain, rashes, indigestion, peptic ulcers, weight gain or loss, heart palpitations, chest pain, asthma, infections, and fatigue; (3) aggravates existing illnesses; (4) causes physical illness; (5) predisposes a person to engage in risky behaviors—such as smoking, drinking, and drug use; and (6) increases the likelihood of death.

Murray Parkes (1964) found that of 4486 widowers 55 years or older, 213 died within six months after the death of their mates. This was 40% above the expected statistical rate. After six months, the rates gradually fell back to normal. The stress of bereavement may elevate the risk of death in several ways. It may lead to depression, and the depressed may then neglect their own health (Satariano & Syme, 1981); or in extreme cases, depression may lead to drug abuse and/or suicide (Schuckit, 1977; Sendbuehler & Goldstein, 1977). The stress may also lead to dysfunctions in neuroendocrine balance and, in turn, a reduction in immunity to disease (Timiras, 1972). For example, the bereaved are at risk for coronary heart disease and cirrhosis of the liver (Jacobs & Ostfeld, 1977).

Of course, a "close" relationship filled with hatred and strife can be worse than no relationship at all for couples' mental and physical health (Barbee, Gulley, & Cunningham, 1990; Rook & Pietromonaco, 1987).

I have spread my dreams under your feet;
Tread softly because you tread on my dreams.
                    —*William Butler Yeats*

INTIMACY: WHY NOT?

Given all the advantages of intimate relationships, why would people ever be reluctant to become intimate with others? As discussed previously, in earlier eras marriages were more distant (Gadlin, 1977) and in some other cultures they still are (Dion & Dion, 1988). Hatfield (1984) points out that there could be several valid reasons why, even today in the Western world, men and women are hesitant to get too deeply involved with others.

Fear of Angry Attacks

One reason people are reluctant to reveal themselves to others is the fear that the other person will get angry and attack them for daring to tell the hard truth. A client, Sara, was a Mexican-American army wife. Her parents had divorced when she was three. Her father was granted custody, and thereafter abused her both sexually and physically. Sara was justifiably proud of the fact that she had learned to be a "perfect lady" in even the most impossible of circumstances. Her voice was always calm, her emotions in control. She took pride in not ever needing anyone for anything. Her only problem was that she did not have a single friend in whom to confide. At long last, she decided to trust one of her sisters. She painfully revealed that her marriage was falling apart and that she was contemplating filing for divorce. Her sister became enraged and denounced her. What kind of Catholic was she! She had had a sick relationship with their father and now she was destroying her husband's and child's life. Similarly, a powerful businessman we interviewed observed that were he to reveal that he was worried about getting old, worried that he was not as smart as his computer-age competition, he could expect his competitors to seize on his revelations with glee and exploit the weaknesses. Sometimes it *is* dangerous to trust.

Fear of One's Own Destructive Impulses

Many of our clients keep a tight lid on their emotions. They fear that if they ever got in touch with what they are feeling, they would begin to cry . . . or kill. One of our Korean clients was a short but powerfully built man, a Tai Chi expert. He possessed traditional macho values. As he sat in our office he often explained that men had to be icy cool. He refused even to allude to the things that were bothering him. Yet it was obvious to us that he was anything but cool. As he explained "analytically" how he felt about things, his eyes blazed, his jaw clenched, he smashed his fist into the palm of his other hand. He had to stay cool at all times he insisted . . . otherwise he would kill. He was undoubtedly wrong. We have found in therapy that as people learn to be ever more aware of what they are feeling, they find that their emotions are not so powerful, not nearly so overpowering or threatening as they had assumed. They discover the possibility of expressing feelings in a controlled, constructive, and liberating way. Yet the fear is real.

Never let them see you sweat.
  —Axiom for business people

Fear of Exposure

In deeply intimate relationships we disclose far more about ourselves than in casual encounters. As a consequence, intimates share profound information about one another's histories, values, strengths, weaknesses, idiosyncracies, hopes, and fears. One reason then that all of us are afraid of intimacy is that those we care most about are bound to discover all that is "wrong" with us—to discover that we possess taboo thoughts and feelings and have done things of which we are deeply ashamed. Worse yet, we know that when this affair is over, there is a possibility that a vindictive date or mate may confide the innermost details of our lives to subsequent dates, mates, and business associates. In the movie *Manhattan* (Allen, 1982), Ike Davis's (Woody Allen's) worst nightmares become reality when he discovers that his ex-wife Jill has written a best-selling autobiography of their married life. He confronts her with "Everybody who knows us is going to know everything. You're going to put all the details in the book, right?" She does. After publication, his current lover (Diane Keaton) reads exerpts from the book aloud in his presence:

FRIEND: "Is it true, did you make love with Jill and another woman?"

WOODY: "She wanted to. I didn't want to be a bad sport."

KEATON: "He was given to fits of rage, Jewish liberal paranoia, male chauvinism, self-righteous misanthropy, and nihilistic moods of despair. He had complaints about life, but never any solutions. He longed to be an artist, but balked at the necessary sacrifices. In his most private moments, he spoke of his fears of death, which he elevated to tragic heights, when in fact it was mere narcissism." (pp. 258–259)

We have all met angry individuals who collar us at parties to tell us their stories, their bitter tales of how hideously they were treated by someone we barely know. As we recall our own relationships that have ended badly, leaving behind a disappointed or enraged suitor, we might think that "there but for the grace of God go I."

If you never want to see a man again, say, "I love you, I want to marry you. I want to have children." . . . *they leave skid marks.*

—Rita Rudner

Fear of Abandonment

A fourth reason people fear exposure is because they are wary that if others get to know them too well, they will be abandoned. One of our friends was a beautiful Swede. She seemed to be self-confident, bright, and charming. At one time, three appealing men were in love with her. Her problem? In promising affairs, each time she tried to be herself and admit how massively insecure she felt at times, the men quickly lost interest. They wanted to be in love with a star, a fantasy of perfection, not a mere mortal. In her autobiography, film star Rita Hayworth claimed that her five marriages floundered for exactly that reason: "Men go to bed with Gilda, but wake up with me" (Leaming, 1989, p. 122). Disillusioned, they all left.

Many people are frightened to admit that they are in love. In *Strangers and Brothers* (C. P. Snow, 1960/1981), the world-weary Lady Boscastle talks to the story's narrator, Lewis, about her niece Joan, who is about to reveal her feelings to her boyfriend and thereby "make a hash of it."

As for her niece, Lady Boscastle had a pitying affection.

She speculated on what was happening that night. "There's thunder in the air," she said. She looked at me.

"I know nothing," I said.

"Of course, he's breaking away," said Lady Boscastle. "That jumps to the eye. And it's making her more infatuated every minute. No doubt she feels obliged to put all her cards on the table. Poor Joan, she would do that. She's rather unoblique."

Lady Boscastle went on:

"And he feels insanely irritable, naturally. It's very odd, my dear Lewis, how being loved brings out the worst in comparatively amiable people. One sees these worthy creatures lying at one's feet and protesting their supreme devotion. And it's a great strain to treat them with even moderate civility. I doubt whether anyone is nice enough to receive absolutely defenceless love."

"Love affairs," said Lady Boscastle, "are not intriguing unless both of you have a second string. Never go lovemaking, my dear boy, unless you have someone to fall back upon in case of accidents." (p. 157)

A second reason then that people are reluctant to risk intimacy, to admit how needy they are, is that they are terrified that those they love will flee at the news and abandon them.

Beware of men who cry. It's true that men who cry are sensitive to and in touch with feelings, but the only feelings they tend to be sensitive to and in touch with are their own.

—Nora Ephron

Fear of Loss of Control

Another hazard of closeness involves the fear that one might lose control. Men may be particularly afraid of intimacy and the loss of power that might follow (Hatfield, 1982b). Bryan, a pilot with a faltering eastern airline company, and his wife Betty came to see us for marital therapy. They wanted to work on their "communication problems." She knew he loved her "deep down," but he just couldn't seem to express it. He turned out to be communicating perfectly well. He had things exactly as he wanted them in the marriage and he wanted to keep it that way. He liked her to be at home, warmly welcoming, when he arrived. The problem? She never knew when, or if, he would arrive. (He had to fly when the opportunity presented itself.) When he was home he was "crabby and rude"; he bossed everyone around. (He was under "a great deal of stress"; "the company was on the rocks," he countered.) She was bored and lonely. (She should "just be patient until all this blew over.") He didn't want his wife running around at night with a bunch of women on the prowl. How could she take a job? He wanted to go hunting with her if he ever got any free time. (She hoped he didn't get enough time for that. She hated standing wet and cold in duck blinds, for hours at a time.) She kept trying to get him to talk; he kept refusing. He wasn't stupid. He knew that if they ever started talking, things would have to change . . . and he didn't want that.

Traditionally, men are supposed to be in command—of themselves, of other people, and of the situation. The ideal man carefully controls his thoughts. He presents himself as logical, objective, and unemotional. He hides his feelings, or if he does express them he carefully collapses the complex array of human emotions into a single powerful emotion: anger. Many "real men" hold in their feelings for a long time until that volcanic eruption of fury ruptures all possibilities of communication.

The ideal woman, in contrast, is supposed to be expressive and warm. She excels at expressing a rainbow of "feminine" feelings—love, anxiety, joy, and depression. (She may be less in touch with anger.) She is responsive to other people and the environment. Inge Broverman and her colleagues (Broverman,

Vogel, Broverman, Clarkson, & Rosenkrantz, 1972) asked psychiatrists, psychologists, and people in general what men and women *should* be like; and what they are *really* like. The answer from both sexes: Men should be (and, they believed, in fact are) in control and instrumental. Women should be (and in fact are) expressive and nurturant. According to some theorists, this suggests marked gender differences in three areas. Men more than women have the desire to be "in control," the desire to dominate their partners, and the desire to "achieve" in love and sexual relations. If such gender differences exist, it is not surprising that women feel more comfortable with intimacy than do men. Unfortunately, although a great deal has been theorized about these topics, there is almost no research documenting that such gender differences do in fact exist (Hatfield, 1982b). If they do exist, the question lingers as to whether they are biologically or culturally based. The advance of the women's movement is already producing millions of women who would be skeptical that such gender differences should or do exist today.

Fear of Having to Take Care of Others

Many people rightly fear that if they get too close to others they will have to take care of them. Some women who have been forced to care for an ailing husband for 20 years resolve that they will never get married again after their mates' deaths. They are tired of sacrificing themselves for spouses, children, and friends (Hobfoll & Stokes, 1988). Many young men hesitate to get too close to women. They think of women as weak and needy and worry that if they ever let their guard down, they will be stuck taking care of someone who will have every right to make terrible claims on their time, energy, and money. They do not realize that they have the right to expect women to be equals; the right to say "No."

Dolores, I live in fear. My love for you is so overpowering, I'm afraid that I will disappear.
          —*Paul Simon's (1977) lyrics from the song "Slip-Slidin' Away"*

Fear of Losing One's Individuality or of Being Engulfed

One of the most primitive fears of intimacy is the feeling that if people acknowledge that they love another they will be engulfed. Vivian Gornick (1987) in *Fierce Attachments* felt overwhelmed by her powerful, intrusive, and controlling mama:

> My skin crawled with her. She was everywhere, all over me, inside and out. Her influence clung, membrane-like, to my nostrils, my eyelids, my open mouth. I drew her into me with every breath I took. I drowsed in her etherizing atmosphere, could not escape the rich and claustrophobic character of her presence, her being, her suffocating suffering femaleness. (pp. 79–80)

A few people worry that they will literally disappear as they lose themselves in the other (Diamond & Shapiro, 1981). More commonly, individuals worry that if they love someone, they will become responsible for never hurting the other; thus to avoid causing their partner pain, they will have to surrender themselves to the whims of the partner. Better to stay away.

Lovers who fear that those they love will try to change them have legitimate concern. One of the hardest things for people to learn is that others are *not* like themselves. Thus, even with good intentions, individuals will indeed often try to control the one they love the best. Filmmaker Alfred Hitchcock, for example, inevitably fell in love with the cool unattainable women he chose to star in his pictures—Ingrid Bergman, Grace Kelly, Kim Novak, Eva Marie Saint, and Tippi Hedren—and just as inevitably set out to remake them. He didn't just want to direct them on the set. He wanted to control their every move, onscreen and off. When, for instance, he chose Tippi Hedren to star in *The Birds*, he began with gentle persuasion. He reminded her that he had rescued her from obscurity; he could make her a major Hollywood star. She should be grateful for his advice. He wouldn't hear that she didn't want to be a star. He had chosen her, he was training her, and that was that. On the set, he meticulously directed every shot. He told her how to move her eyes and how to hold her head. Then he began to try to control her behavior offscreen. He began to tell her what to wear after work, what she should eat, which friends she could see. He drew up lists of who was "good enough" for her company. He hired crew members to keep a check on her when she left the set. Whom did she visit? Where did she go? How did she spend her free time? He became furious if she didn't ask his permission to visit friends in the evenings and on weekends. Tippi Hedren despised his attentions. She became more and more anxious. After that experience she left films, never again to return (Spoto, 1983, pp. 481–482).

Leslie Baxter and William Wilmot (1985) interviewed men and women about their platonic friendships, potential romantic relationships, and established romantic relationships. What sorts of topics were taboo, off-limits, in these affairs? The authors found that women felt more topics were taboo than did men. Men and women were most hesitant to talk about the state of their relationship (see Table 5.2a). They worried that by saying too much they might frighten their dates or hurt them and destroy what they had. One woman said:

> For me right now, there's no way I'll get married, but sometimes I think he's more serious. . . . It's a sore subject and it makes me feel on the defensive. (pp. 259–260)

Table 5.2a   WHAT TOPICS ARE TABOO?

Taboo topic	Relationship type		
	Platonic friendship	Potential romance	Established romantic relationship
State of the relationship	50%	88%	59%
Extrarelationship activity	42	24	30
Relationship norms	33	24	23
Prior relationships	17	12	32
Conflict inducing	17	12	26
Negatively valenced self-disclosure	17	12	19
Other	0	1	1

Source: Baxter & Wilmot, 1985, p. 259.

Table 5.2b   WHY ARE THE VARIOUS
TOPICS TABOO?

---

1. The state of the relationship
   - 41%   Relationship destruction
   - 19%   Individual vulnerability
   - 17%   Effectiveness of the tacit mode
   - 14%   Futility of talk
   - 10%   Closeness cueing
2. Extrarelationship activity
   - 63%   Negative relational implications
   - 15%   Right to privacy
   - 11%   Negative network implications
3. Relationship norms
   - 55%   Negative relational implications
   - 32%   Embarrassment
4. Prior relationships
   - 50%   Relationship threat
   - 27%   Irrelevance of the past
   - 14%   Impression management
5. Conflict-inducing topics
6. Negative self-disclosure

Source: Baxter & Wilmot, 1985, p. 260.

Other people simply felt that a person risked too much, became too vulnerable by raising such issues:

> The relationship itself [is a taboo]. I just never talk about those kinds of things. Never. Big mistake. Actually the only time I talk about those kinds of things is when I'm really drunk . . . 'cause then I don't care [what I find out]. It's a big mistake to talk about it because you leave yourself very vulnerable, which I don't like to be—your feelings can get hurt. (p. 261)

Others felt that words were a poor substitute for what is "just understood," that it was useless to talk ("What will be will be), or that it was too early to raise such issues:

> The only thing we can't talk about is how much we really like each other; not in a romantic way or anything but just caring and liking. A serious talk about it would imply something that neither of us wants. So we just joke around about it. (p. 262)

People provided additional reasons why they didn't talk much about rival relationships either. Many knew their dates or mates would simply get angry or jealous if they knew what was going on:

> I spent the summer in Guatemala and met this guy there. I write to him regularly, but I wouldn't tell this to my boyfriend because I don't want to hurt him. He's the all or nothing sort of person. It is all him or nothing. I don't want to make waves. (p. 262)

Others felt that they had a right to privacy; or that if they told their romantic partners everything that they would be betraying confidences or getting someone else in trouble. For other reasons why men and women felt certain topics were taboo, see Table 5.2b.

Other theorists have detailed a host of other practical problems that emerge when we are intimate with others (Pollak & Gilligan, 1982; Rook & Pietromonaco, 1987).

MEASURING FEAR OF INTIMACY

Many people, then, with good reason, are acutely aware of the risks associated with intimacy. How much do *you* fear intimacy? Constance Pilkington and Deborah Richardson (1988) developed a scale to measure *Perceptions of Risk in Intimacy*. Some sample items appear in Box 5.3.

Box 5.3 **SOCIAL INTERACTION INVENTORY**

Using the scale below, indicate the extent to which you agree with each statement by writing the appropriate number in the blank beside each item.

1 = Very strong disagreement

2 = Moderate disagreement

3 = Slight disagreement

4 = Slight agreement

5 = Moderate agreement

6 = Very strong agreement

1. _____ It is dangerous to get really close to people.

2. _____ I prefer that people keep their distance from me.

3. _____ I'm afraid to get really close to someone because I might get hurt.

4. _____ I find it difficult to trust other people.

5. _____ I avoid intimacy.

6. _____ Being close to other people makes me feel afraid.

7. _____ I'm hesitant to share personal information about myself.

8. _____ Being close to people is a risky business.

The higher the score, the more people perceive intimacy to be a risk rather than a pleasure.

Source: Pilkington & Richardson, 1988, p. 505.

The authors found that people who exaggerate the dangers of intimacy pay a cost. They have neither a romantic partner nor very many close friends; they distance themselves from others. They are less sociable, assertive, and trusting than others.

INDIVIDUAL DIFFERENCES IN INTIMACY

Of course, people differ both in how *interested* they are in intimate relationships and even more in how *capable* they are of maintaining them. They differ markedly in the "preference or readiness for experiences of closeness, warmth, and communication" (McAdams, 1982, p. 134). Dan McAdams (1980, 1992) found that sorority and fraternity members who were high in intimacy motivation were warmer, more loving and sincere, and less dominant, outspoken, and self-centered than their peers. Not everyone has what it takes to maintain an intimate relationship. Cindy Hazan and Phillip Shaver (1987) have argued that if there are problems in the infant–caregiver attachment, adults may well have serious intimacy problems in later life. There is some evidence for this contention. Researchers have found that young men and women who have problems getting close to others or who are too dependent find it difficult to establish deeply intimate relationships (Levitz-Jones & Orlofsky, 1985).

Are There Gender Differences in Intimacy?

Researchers have observed that there is a gap between men and women in their ideas of what constitutes intimacy. Ted Huston interviewed 130 married couples at the University of Texas (Goleman, 1986). He found that for the wives, intimacy meant talking things over. The husbands, by and large, were more interested in action. They thought that if they did things (took out the garbage, for instance) and if they engaged in some joint activities, that should be enough. Huston found that during courtship men were willing to spend a great deal of time in intimate conversation. But after marriage, as time went on, they reduced the time for close marital conversation while devoting increasingly greater time to work or hanging around with their own friends. Huston observed: "Men put on a big show of interest when they are courting, but after the marriage their actual level of

interest in the partner often does not seem as great as you would think, judging from the courtship. The intimacy of courtship is instrumental for the men, a way to capture the woman's interest. But that sort of intimacy is not natural for many men" (p. Y19). Women complain about men's "emotional stinginess" (Christensen & Heavey, 1990 Fishman, 1978; Roberts & Krokoff, 1990). Huston suggested a compromise: Couples should try to engage in the sort of intimate conversation that springs spontaneously from shared interests. This requires, of course, that couples share some interests—that they read books, or watch films, or plan trips to Europe together, and so forth.

Carol Gilligan (1982) pointed out that men are taught to take pride in being independent while women take pride in being close and nurturant (see also Goleman, 1986; Pollak & Gilligan, 1982). Erik Erikson (1959) contended that as men mature, they find it easy to achieve an independent identity; they experience more difficulty in learning to be intimate with those they love. Women have an easy time learning to be close to others; they have more trouble learning how to be independent (Hodgson & Fischer, 1979; White, Speisman, Jackson, Bartis, & Costos, 1986). Family therapists such as Augustus Napier (1977) are acutely aware of what happens in any relationship when one person is desperate for intimacy, willing to do whatever it takes to make the relationship work, and terrified of rejection and abandonment . . . while the other fears being suffocated and stifled. He observed that couples' efforts to get as close as *they* would like often spark a vicious cycle. Wives (seeking more closeness) clasp their husbands tightly, "smothering" them. Husbands (seeking more distance) retreat, which causes their wives to panic, inducing further "clasping." In therapy, one way to short-circuit this problem is to focus on the people who are craving more closeness. People who crave intimacy surely have a right to expect *some* of their needs to be fulfilled by their mates. But they may have to have some of their intimacy needs satisfied by friends, children, work, and activities. People who are easily overwhelmed by too much intimacy may be able to learn to be a little more loving and attentive, but usually things will go best if they learn to recognize when they are starting to feel overwhelmed, and let their mates know they temporarily need more distance; often their mates can learn to give them a little breathing room—confident that they'll soon be back together.

There is considerable evidence that men are less comfortable with intimacy than women. Researchers have found the following:

1. *In casual encounters,* women disclose far more to others than do men (Cozby, 1973; Jourard, 1971). In our culture (at least since the beginning of the nineteenth century), women have traditionally been encouraged to show feelings. Men have been taught to hide their emotions and to avoid displays of weakness (Pleck & Sawyer, 1974; Rubin, Hill, Peplau, & Dunke-Schetter, 1980). Kate Millett (1970) observes that "women express, men repress." In a study of college students, Mayta Caldwell and Anne Peplau (1982) found that women's friendships were more deeply intimate than were men's. (Androgynous men's friendships were far more intimate than were those of traditional men.) Women place great emphasis on talking and emotional sharing in their relationships. Men tend to emphasize shared activities; they generally limit their conversations to sports, muscles, money, and sex.

2. *In their deeply intimate relationships,* however, men and women differ little, if at all, in how much they are willing to reveal to one another. Rubin and his colleagues (1980), for example, asked dating couples via the *Jourard Self-Disclosure Questionnaire* how much they had revealed to their steady dates. Did they talk about their current relationships? Previous affairs? Their feelings about their parents and friends? Their self-concepts and life views? Their attitudes and interests? Their day-to-day activities? Overall, men and women did not differ in how much they were willing to confide to their partners. They did differ, however, in the kinds of things they shared. Men found it easy to talk about politics; women found it easy to talk about people. Men found it easy to talk about their strengths; women found it easy to talk about their own fears and weaknesses. Interestingly enough, traditional men and women were most likely to limit themselves to stereotyped patterns of communication. More modern men and women were more relaxed about discussing all sorts of intimate matters—politics, friends, their strengths, and their weaknesses.

In her biography of her father John Cheever, Susan Cheever (1984) contrasted her mother's and her father's ways of being:

> My father was drawn to strength. My mother is drawn to need and the sweetness of the needy. An injured animal, a waif, a person in trouble—all elicit overwhelming concern from her. . . . My warmest memories of my mother are from times when I was sick, or in pain, or in some kind of trouble.
>
> My father, by the way, would have nothing to do with discussions like this. He never spoke about feelings or allowed himself to speculate on the inner mechanics of the family. "I love you all equally," he would say, or "I adore your mother." People remember my father's candor. "Although his manner was reticent, there was nothing John would not say about himself," Saul Bellow recalled in his eulogy at my father's funeral. In a way, that was true. He would tell you exactly what he had done to this or that mistress in a room at the St. Regis or in a motel in Iowa, and he would tell you that *The New Yorker* had paid him less than $1,000 for a story, and he would tell you that he took two Valiums and drank a pint of gin every day before noon. That was different, though. He did not like to talk about how these things felt; he did not like to talk about human emotions. He did talk, often eloquently, about human behavior. Are they really the same? I don't think so. (pp. 76–77)

Recently, Deborah Tannen (1990), a linguist, in *You Just Don't Understand,* has detailed some communication problems that men's and women's different orientations cause (see Box 5.4).

Some authors have observed that currently neither men nor women may be getting exactly the amount of intimacy they would like. Women tend to desire more intimacy than they are getting; men may prefer more privacy and distance ("Just leave me alone!"). Couples tend to negotiate a pattern of self-disclosure that is bearable to both (Derlega & Chaiken, 1975). Unfortunately, in the words of *My Fair Lady,* this may ensure that "neither really gets what *either* really wants at all."

3. *Women receive more disclosures than do men.* This is not surprising in view of the fact that the amount of information people reveal to others has an enormous impact on the amount of information they receive in return (Altman, 1973; Hill, Rubin, & Peplau, 1979). In any case, both men and women seem to feel

Box 5.4   MEN AND WOMEN IN CONVERSATION

According to Tannen, many men are socialized to think of themselves as part of a hierarchical social order; they are either one-up or one-down. Conversations are negotiations in which they try to achieve and maintain the upper hand (if they can) or at least protect themselves from others' attempts to put them down. Life is a struggle to preserve independence. Many women, on the other hand, see themselves within a network of connections. Conversations are negotiations for closeness in which people try to reach consensus and to give and get support. They try to protect themselves from others' attempts to push them away. Life then is a struggle to preserve intimacy and avoid isolation. These themes show up, she argues, when we eavesdrop on men's and women's conversations:

Example 1: "Put down that paper and talk to me."
In public, men dominate conversations. They lecture. They speak more and at greater length. They interrupt. Yet many women complain that, at home, men suddenly become silent. They bury their heads in their newspapers; lose themselves in their favorite television programs. How is it that men are such impressive public speakers and often such poor conversationalists in private? Tannen suggests an answer:

> For everyone, home is a place to be offstage. But the comfort of home can have opposite and incompatible meanings for women and men. For many men, the comfort of home means freedom from having to prove themselves and impress through verbal display. At last, they are in a situation where talk is not required. They are free to remain silent. But for women, home is a place where they are free to talk, and where they feel the greatest need for talk, with those they are closest to. For them, the comfort of home means the freedom to talk without worrying how their talk will be judged. (p. 86)

Example 2: Talking at Cross Purposes

> Eve had a lump removed from her breast. Shortly after the operation, talking to her sister, she said that she found it upsetting to have been cut into, and that looking at the stitches was distressing because they left a seam that had changed the contour of her breast. Her sister said, "I know. When I had my operation I felt the same way." Eve made the same observation to her friend Karen, who said, "I know. It's like your body has been violated." But when she told her husband, Mark, how she felt, he said, "You can have plastic surgery to cover up the scar and restore the shape of your breast."
>   Eve had been comforted by her sister and her friend, but she was not comforted by Mark's comment. Quite the contrary, it upset her more. Not only didn't she hear what she wanted, that he understood her feelings, but, far worse, she felt he was asking her to undergo more surgery just when she was telling him how much this operation had upset her. "I'm not having any more surgery!" she protested. "I'm sorry you don't like the way it looks." Mark was hurt and puzzled. "I don't care," he protested. "It doesn't bother me at all." She asked,

"Then why are you telling me to have plastic surgery?" He answered,
"Because you were saying you were upset by the way it looked." . . .

Eve wanted the gift of understanding, but Mark gave her the gift
of advice. He was taking the role of problem solver, whereas she
simply wanted confirmation for her feelings. (pp. 49–50)

[A side note: In therapy, it often comes as a big relief to men when Dick tells
them that when women cry, or recount problems, all they're hoping for is that their
boyfriends and husbands will listen and be sympathetic. Many men assume that
they are expected somehow magically to "fix things." When they can't, or when
she's not interested in their "solution," they feel helpless and react with anger.]

Tannen suggests several techniques by which men and women can open
lines of communication. First, men and women benefit simply by understanding
that different people may have very different ways of communicating. It helps just
to realize that people communicate differently, not because they are stupid,
wrongheaded, or mean, but just because they are different. It helps even more if
men and women develop more flexible conversational skills. Men can learn to be
more interested in others, to become better listeners; to learn to get close without
seeing it as a threat to their freedom. Women can learn to become more "selfish";
to be less obsessed with being liked and nurturing others; to become more independent; more comfortable with competition and conflict. They can learn to
become better at getting the things they want.

most comfortable confiding in women. Modern tradition dictates that women
should be the "intimacy experts."

What happens if, stimulated by the growing independence of women, this
situation changes? Such social changes have already begun (Rubin et al., 1980).
The prognosis is mixed. Young women usually say that they would be delighted
if the men they love could be more intimate. We are a bit skeptical that it will be
this easy. Change is always difficult. More than one man has complained that
when he finally dared to reveal his weaker aspects to a woman, he soon discovered
that she was shocked by his lack of "manliness." Family therapists such as Napier
(1977) have warned us that the struggle to find individuality and closeness is a
problem for everyone. As long as men were fleeing from intimacy, women could
safely pursue them. Now that men are turning around to face them, women may
well find themselves taking flight. In any case, the confrontation is likely to be
exciting, surprising, and profoundly significant. The women's movement brings
change as far-reaching for men as for women.

A PRESCRIPTION FOR INTIMACY

Most humans appear to flourish in a warm intimate relationship. Yet intimacy is
risky. What then is the solution? How can one secure the benefits of closeness
while not being engulfed by its dangers? Social psychological research and clinical
experience furnish some hints.

According to theorists, one of the most primitive tasks people face is to learn how to maintain their own identity and integrity while yet engaging in deeply intimate relationships with others (Erikson, 1982). Intimacy and independence are not opposite personality traits but interlocking skills. This is not a self-evident point since our movies, television, and pop songs have repeatedly linked *dependency* with intimacy. What higher love, they insist, than "I *need* you! I can't live without you"? Desperate, needy, clingy love has been the *ne plus ultra* of love—as portrayed in popular culture.

But the clingy, desperate person, when faced with the need to criticize a partner, may demur out of fear that the partner will get angry and leave. The needy person cannot risk such intimacy because she (or he) fears she can't "make it" without the other. So she stuffs her emotions and discards intimacy. The persons who know they can survive on their own, who are independent, can more easily risk saying the hard things that need to be said simply *because* they are not dependent. Hollywood notwithstanding, intimacy goes with independence, not dependence. This crucial point is not generally acknowledged, and we shall have much more to say about it later in this book. In therapy, we often try to help couples develop the confidence that they are separate people, with separate ideas and feelings, who can sometimes come profoundly close to one another: two separate individuals who are part of a couple.

Intimacy is called forth in only a handful of our social encounters. Most of the time one has to be at least tactful. With 99% of the human race we can only practice ritual courtesy. When a stranger asks "How are you?" we are not required to tell the total truth! In a few situations we must learn to be downright manipulative in order to survive; not everyone has our best interests in mind. But on those rare, special occasions when real intimacy is possible, men and women can recognize its promise, seize the opportunities, and take a chance.

Despite good reasons for fearing it, humans appear to blossom with intimacy. So we are back to the question: What advice can social psychologists give as to how to secure the benefits of deep commitment without being engulfed by its dangers?

Developing Intimacy Skills

Don't compromise yourself. You are all you've got.
                    —Janis Joplin

Encouraging People to Accept Themselves as They Are   We are greatly tempted to dwell in the Kingdom of the Absolutes. Religion has not been alone in often casting people as either saints or sinners. Men have traditionally defined women as either madonnas or whores. We wish ourselves to be perfect; we often can't settle for less. Yet saintliness/evil do not describe the most interesting of human conditions. Real life is lived in the rich, fertile territories between these two extremes. Real humans inevitably exhibit some real strengths. But we carry within ourselves, simultaneously, "forbidden" impulses, quirky attributes, profound terrors, and irksome shortcomings that practically define what it means to be human and that make us what we are. The real challenge to living a rich and valuable life is not just to tolerate this complexity within oneself, but to relish it and work with it within oneself and with others.

A first step in learning to be independent/intimate is to come to accept the fact that we are entitled to be what we are—to have the ideas we have, the feelings we feel, and to do as well as we can based on the full truth of who we are. Honest self-recognition is not all there is to life, but it is not a bad place to start.

In therapy, we try to move people from the notion that one should come into the world perfect and continue that way unto death. We prefer the realization that wisdom often grows in small steps. We *cannot* be anything we wish to be just by willing it. The Religion of Positive Thinking, most pronounced in America, goes much too far and often results, because of the untruthfulness of its basic premise, in depression. We can change behaviors and ideas, however, by proceeding one step at a time. That way change is manageable and possible (Watson & Tharp, 1990). Accomplish Behavior One and move on to Two. Perfection lies beyond our reach (thank goodness!); but improvements do lie within our grasp.

A good man doesn't just happen. They have to be created by us women. A guy is a lump like a doughnut. So, first you gotta get rid of all the stuff his mom did to him. And then you gotta get rid of all that macho crap that they pick up from beer commercials. And then there's my personal favorite, the male ego.
—*Roseanne Arnold*

Encouraging People to Recognize Their Intimates for What They Are

People may be hard on themselves, but they are generally even harder on their partners. Most people have the idea that everyone is entitled to a perfect partner, or at least one a little bit better than the one available (Hatfield & Rapson, 1990b). If people are going to have an intimate relationship, they have to learn to enjoy others as *they* are, without engaging in secret strategies to fix them up.

It is extraordinarily difficult to accept that friends and loved ones are entitled to be who they are. From the individual vantage point, it seems obvious that everything would be far better if our mates became the people we wanted them to be, if they realized our plans and fantasies for them. "Why don't they? Why are they so stubborn? If they really loved me, they'd change." It would take so little for them to change their entire character structure!

If we can come to the realization that our lover or friend is the person who exists right now—not the person we wished for in our dreams, not the person he "could" be, but what he is—once that realization occurs, the possibilities for intimacy are greatly enhanced. Behavior can change, but basic personalities rarely do.

Encouraging People to Express Themselves

Next, intimates have to learn to be more comfortable about expressing their ideas and feelings. This is harder than one might think. Intimate relations are usually our most important relationships. When passions are so intense, consequences so momentous, people are often hesitant to speak the truth. From moment to moment, they are tempted to present a consistent picture. If they are in love, they are hesitant to admit to their nagging doubts. What if they hurt the person they love? What if their revelations destroy their marriage? And on the far extreme, when they are angry, they don't speak with complexity about their love, self-doubts, or hurt; they want to lash out against the other.

To be intimate, people have to push toward a more honest, graceful, complete, and patient communication, to understand that a person's ideas and feelings are necessarily complex, with many nuances, shadings, and inconsistencies. In love, there is time to clear things up. In love, many mistakes and false starts are allowed. In true love, no single attempt at truth-telling can be fatal.

One interesting thing that people often discover is that their affection increases when they begin to admit their irritations. People are often surprised to discover that sometimes, just when they think they have fallen out of love, or that they are "bored" with the other, things change when they begin to express their anger and ambivalence; they often feel their love come back in a rush. In *The Family Crucible*, Augustus Napier and Carl Whitaker (1978) described just such a phenomenon:

> What followed was a classic confrontation. If John's affair was a kind of reawakening, so now was this marital encounter, though of a very different sort. Eleanor was enraged, hurt, confused, and racked with a sense of failure. John was guilty, also confused, but not apologetic. The two partners fought and cried, talked and searched for an entire night. The next evening, more exhausting encounters. Feelings that had been hidden for years emerged; doubts and accusations that they had never expected to admit articulated.
>
> Eleanor had to find out everything, and the more she discovered, the more insatiable her curiosity became. The more she heard, the guiltier her husband became and the angrier she grew, until he finally cried for a halt. It was his cry for mercy that finally led to a temporary reconciliation of the couple. They cried together for the first time either of them could remember.
>
> For a while they were elated; they had achieved a breakthrough in their silent and dreary marriage. They felt alive together for the first time in years. Somewhat mysteriously, they found themselves going to bed together in the midst of a great tangle of emotions—continuing anger, and hurt, and guilt, and this new quality: abandon. The lovemaking was, they were to admit to each other, "the best it had ever been." How could they have moved through hatred into caring so quickly? (p. 153)

Teaching People to Deal with Their Intimates' Reactions   To say that you should communicate your ideas and feelings, *must* communicate if you are to have an intimate affair, does not mean your partner is going to like it. You can expect that when you try to express your deepest feelings, it will sometimes hurt. Your lovers and friends may tell you frankly how deeply you have pained them, and that may make you feel extremely guilty. Or they may react with intense anger.

Intimates have to learn to stop responding in automatic fashion to such emotional outbursts from the other—to quit backing up, apologizing for what they have said, measuring their words. They have to learn to stay calm, remind themselves that they are entitled to say what they think, feel what they feel, listen to what their partners think and feel, and keep on trying. We often learn from pain . . . and so might our partners who may not be beyond using guilt and anger to shut us up.

When we realize we are entitled to try to speak truthfully—a realization that may require bravery—only then is there a chance for an intimate meeting.

What a woman says to her lover should be written in wind and running water.
—Catullus

COMMITMENT

Definitions

In Chapter 1, Robert Sternberg (1986, p. 6) pointed out that "decision/commit-ment refers, in the short-term, to the decision that one loves a certain other, and in the long-term, to one's commitment to maintain that love."

Marriage and family researchers sometimes use the Broderick Commitment Scale (Table 5.3) to assess dating couples' commitment to their relationships and husbands' and wives' commitment to their marriages.

Table 5.3   BRODERICK COMMITMENT SCALE

Commitment can be viewed as the degree to which an individual is willing to stand by another even though that may mean putting aside one's own needs and desires for the sake of the other; it can mean a time of accepting the other person in spite of his/her faults or problems that may make one's own life more difficult; it can mean thinking less about the immediate advantages and disadvantages of the relationship and working to make the relationship last in the long run.

Given this description, select a number from the scale below to indicate how "committed" you are to your marriage.

100	Extremely committed
75	Very
	Choose a number from the scale on the left that corresponds to your commitment to your marriage and write it here: _____
50	Moderately
25	Slightly
0	Not at all committed

Source: Beach, Sandeen, & O'Leary, 1990, p. 101.

Theoretical Background

It is not always easy for people to know how committed they are to others. Pam Houston (1992), in *Cowboys Are My Weakness,* is a shrewd observer. She admits that she often thinks she wants commitment, only to run when she gets it. She realizes she is attracted to the unattainable.

> It was the old southern woman next door, the hunter's widow, who convinced me I should stay with him each time I'd get mad enough to leave. She said if I didn't have to fight for him I'd never know if he was mine. She said the wild ones were the only ones worth having and that I had to let him do whatever it took to keep him wild. She said I wouldn't love him if he ever gave in, and the harder I looked at my life, the more I saw a series of men—wild in their own way—who thought because I said I wanted security and commitment, I did. Sometimes it seems this simple: I tamed them and made them dull as fence posts and left each one for someone wilder than the last. Jack is the wildest so far, and the hardest, and even though I've been proposed to sixteen times, five times by men I've never made love to, I want him all to myself and at home more than I've ever wanted anything. (pp. 25–26)

All she wants is what she can't have. Naturally she's heartbroken when she can't have it. The cowboys, hunters, and trackers in her life are equally ambivalent.

> The hunter will talk about spring in Hawaii, summer in Alaska. The man who says he was always better at math will form the sentences so carefully it will be impossible to tell if you are included in these plans. When he asks you if you would like to open a small guest ranch way out in the country, understand that this is a rhetorical question. Label these conversations future perfect, but don't expect the present to catch up with them. Spring is an inconceivable distance from the December days that just keep getting shorter and gray.
>
> He'll ask you if you've ever shot anything, if you'd like to, if you ever thought about teaching your dog to retrieve. Your dog will like him too much, will drop the stick at his feet every time, will roll over and let the hunter scratch his belly.
>
> One day he'll leave you sleeping to go split wood or get the mail and his phone will ring again. You'll sit very still while a woman who calls herself something like Janie Coyote leaves a message on his machine: She's leaving work, she'll say, and the last thing she wanted to hear was the sound of his beautiful voice. . . .
>
> A week before Christmas you'll rent *It's a Wonderful Life* and watch it together, curled on your couch, faces touching. Then you'll bring up the word "monogamy." He'll tell you how badly he was hurt by your predecessor. He'll tell you he couldn't be happier spending every night with you. He'll say there's just a few questions he doesn't have the answers for. He'll say he's just scared and confused. Of course this isn't exactly what he means. Tell him you understand. Tell him you are scared too. Tell him to take all the time he needs. . . .
>
> Your best male friend will say, "Didn't you know what would happen when you said the word 'commitment'?"
>
> But that isn't the word you said.
>
> He'll say, "commitment, monogamy, it all means just one thing." (pp. 14–16)

Of course, the hunter knows all along that he is spending Christmas with Janie Coyote. And, he knows all along that, eventually, he plans to come back.

> He will say whatever he needs to win. He'll say it's just an old friend. He'll say the visit was all the friend's idea. He'll say the night away from you has given him time

to think about how much you mean to him. Realize that nothing short of sleeping alone will ever make him realize how much you mean to him. He'll say that if you can just be a little patient some good will come out of this for the two of you after all. He still won't use a gender-specific pronoun. (p. 18)

Couples may commit themselves to stay in a relationship for either of two reasons, because they want to or because they have to. In their classic text, John Thibaut and Harold Kelley (1959) pointed out that loving or liking someone is very different from being committed to them. A college beauty may like a fellow a lot and delight in his company . . . but not enough to marry him. The battered wife may hate her brutal husband and be totally miserable . . . but not enough to leave. She may fear that she and the children would suffer from loneliness, hunger, and poverty if she abandoned the relationship.

Thibaut and Kelley argued that we can predict how much men and women will love and like their mates and how satisfied they will be with their dating relationships and marriages, if we know two things: (1) how profitable those relationships are and (2) how profitable men and women *expected* them to be (i.e., their *Comparison Levels (CLs)*. How attracted men and women are to their mates and how satisfied they are with their relationships depends on whether the profits they receive are above or below their CLs:

> If the outcomes in a given relationship surpass the CL, that relationship is regarded as a satisfactory one. And, to the degree the outcomes are supra-CL, the person may be said to be attracted to the relationship. If the outcomes endured are infra-CL, the person is dissatisfied and unhappy with the relationship. (p. 81)

I never knew what real happiness was until I got married. And by then it was too late.
> —*Groucho Marx*

Thibaut and Kelley argue that how *commited* people are (whether or not they will choose to remain in the relationship) will depend on their *Comparison Level for Alternatives* (or *CLalt*). A person's CLalt is defined as:

> the lowest level of outcomes a member will accept in the light of available opportunities. . . . The height of the CLalt will depend mainly on the quality of the best of the member's available alternatives, that is, the reward—cost positions experienced or believed to exist in the most satisfactory of the other available relationships. (pp. 21–22)

How committed people are to their relationships will depend on whether the outcomes they receive are above or below their CLalts. People may abandon a fairly affectionate and satisfactory relationship simply because a better one comes along. Similarly, they may stick with appalling mates and relationships (where their outcomes are far below the CL) simply because they have so little self-confidence, feel so unattractive, or are so hemmed in that they fear that nothing better will be available (the outcomes they get from a dismal relationship are at least above their CLalts).

Researchers have begun to elaborate on how the commitment process works. George Levinger (1979) proposed that three kinds of forces influence cohesiveness: attractiveness of the relationship, the attractiveness of alternative attractions, and any existing barriers against leaving the relationship.

In the past, researchers who were interested in commitment tended to be interested in the factors that caused dating couples to commit themselves to marriage. In the 1980s, however, there were two demographic trends that changed researchers' focus. First, at one time, few couples lived together before marriage. Now, by their early thirties, almost half of the population has lived with someone, sometime (Bumpass & Sweet, 1989). Second, couples are now marrying later than ever before. In 1988, the average age of marriage for men was 25.9 years; for women 23.6 years (U.S. Bureau of the Census, 1988). As a consequence of these changes, mate selection researchers have become interested in how premarital relationships (heterosexual or homosexual) are established, maintained, or dissolved. Here, we review the factors that determine whether casual relationships turn into more serious ones—whether the couples eventually end up marrying or living together or not. Generally, researchers ask respondents to think back and try to reconstruct their relationships from memory. You might try it yourself. Get a piece of graph paper. On the far left of the horizontal axis, print "we met"; on the far right, print "where we are today." On the vertical axis, print "100%" at the top and "0%" at the bottom. Try to recall how committed you were to one another as your relationship progressed. When you spot a sudden upturn or downturn on the graph, explain *why* you became more or less committed to one another at that time. Researchers who have done this find that couples give very different reasons for making a commitment to another; their graphs of the commitment process look very different. A few couples leap into an affair or marriage; most slowly tiptoe in the marital waters (Baxter & Bullis, 1986; Lloyd & Cate, 1985; Surra, 1990). Catherine Surra (1990) found that the reasons couples decide to marry, the shape of their commitments (fast or slow; smooth or up-and-down), are reflected in their later married lives. Some couples (about 5%), for example, decide to get married because it seems like the thing to do (it is "time" to do so). Here, Mavis Gallant (1957) describes how Jean decided to marry Tom Price.

> At twenty-four I was ready to love anyone. I had never left home. I had not been sent to boarding school, like Isobel and Frank, and when I was ready for college, and in robust health, my mother decided I was delicate and would never stand the strain.
>
> It was Isobel who brought Tom Price to the family. She invited him for a weekend at the lake. . . . My mother instantly saw in Tom a man who would do for either daughter. . . . I decided to love him with a determination I had never shown about anything else. (pp. 101–105)

Bette Midler gives this account of her marriage:

> "When I met him, I was thirty-eight years old," says Midler. "I wasn't getting any younger. What else is there? Are men really that different after you've met *so* many men? After you've known *so* many? How different can they be? I married the best person who wanted to marry me." (*Vanity Fair*, 1991, p. 260)

Sometimes these relationships work out, sometimes not.

Other couples' (about 30%) commitments are more turbulent. Sometimes, couples feel pushed into marriage for external reasons. Everyone expects them to get married; all their friends are getting married. Sudden events (parents' illnesses, job firings, and so forth) propel them into marriage. In such cases, couples may rush into a commitment; then, stunned at what they have done, they draw back only to get involved yet again. Such early on-again, off-again relationships tend to be equally rocky later on.

Most couples (65%) get committed to one another in a slow, orderly way. (They spend time together, get to know one another, and confide in one another. They discover they are compatible.) Not surprisingly, such "practical" relationships tend to be happier and to last longer than the others (Surra, 1990).

We discuss the factors that keep people committed to faltering love relationships at length in Chapter 13, Things Go from Bad to Worse.

CONCLUSION

The desirability and attainment of intimacy and commitment are new goals in human history and, as the twentieth century ends, still confined to segments of Western civilization. They are fragile, require highly developed human skills, and are far from being universal. They are goals not yet celebrated by all humanity and are subjects of some debate. Yet there is little question in our minds that the search for and occasional achievement of intimacy and commitment in personal relationships tell a far happier and rewarding tale than that phenomenon which in fact has in the past and still today continues to shape most relationships and which is the subject of the next chapter. That less appealing phenomenon of which we speak is . . . power.

Chapter
6

Power

Where love reigns, there is no will to power; and where the will to power is paramount, love is lacking. The one is but the shadow of the other.

—Carl Gustav Jung

INTRODUCTION

Love is sometimes a battleground. Men and women attempt to seduce, persuade, or even force their loved ones to do what they want. Such power struggles often denote the death of love and intimacy. Men have possessed most of the direct power for most of recorded history. And though the powerless do have their ways of exerting influence, the struggle has been largely one-sided, rendering love and intimacy irrelevant to the huge majority of relationships. In profound ways, times indeed are changing; in many others, however, *plus ça change, plus c'est la même chose.*

To understand power is to comprehend the essence of the human condition.
—Bertrand Russell

DEFINITIONS

Power has been defined as "the ability to influence another person's attitudes or behavior" (McCormick & Jesser, 1982, p. 65). How to assess such power? Sometimes, scientists simply ask people: "Who wins most of the arguments—you or your husband? Who is the boss in your family—your mom or your dad?" Sometimes, researchers ask couples who has the most power in a number of representative situations. In their classic work on power, for example, sociologists Robert Blood and Donald Wolfe (1960, p. 20) asked:

> In every family somebody has to decide such things as where the family will live and so on. Many couples talk such things over first, but the *final* decision often has to be made by the husband or the wife. For instance, who usually makes the final decision about . . . ?

People were then asked about eight kinds of decisions—"what sort of career to pursue; what kind of car to get; where to go on their next vacation, and so forth." Other scientists insist that it is best to ascribe power by observing couples in action. Typically, they have asked couples to debate some controversial issue like "where should we spend our vacation?" They then observed the progress of the argument and recorded whose initial preference prevailed in the end (Olson & Rabunsky, 1972).

Some researchers have employed extremely subtle techniques. In *Body Politics,* Nancy Henley (1977) pointed out that people automatically telegraph their status and power in almost every move they make. Table 6.1 lists a number of behaviors that she identified as signaling dominance or submission.

Henley contended that in any social encounter, the powerful make the rules. They take up a great deal of space. They are loud; they decide which topics are interesting and which are not. They interrupt others. They may pat others condescendingly on the head or arm. When they are angry, they yell. The powerless reply with cheerful words, lowered heads, averted eyes. They try to shrink into as tiny a space as possible, to become invisible. Some examples include the following:

When John Kennedy's nomination for president became a certainty:

> Kennedy loped into the cottage with his light, dancing step, as young and lithe as springtime, and called a greeting to those who stood in his way. . . . The others in the room surged forward on impulse to join him. Then they halted. A distance of perhaps 30 feet separated them from him, but it was impassable. . . . They could come by invitation only, for this might be a President of the United States. (White, 1961, p. 171)

Table 6.1   BEHAVIORS ASSOCIATED WITH DOMINANCE AND SUBMISSION

Dominance	Submission
Crowd into another's space	Yield, move away
Keep others waiting	Wait
Interrupt	Stop talking
Stare	Lower eyes, avert gaze, blink
Touch	"Cuddle" to the touch
Frown, look stern	Smile
Point	Obey, stop action (or stop talk); move in pointed direction

Source: Henley, 1977, p. 187.

Novelist Marge Piercy (in the voice of Wanda, an organizer of a theater group) taught actors how to move like men and women.

> Wanda made them aware of how they moved, how they rested, how they occupied space. She demonstrated how men sat and how women sat on the subway, on benches. Men expanded into available space. They sprawled, or they sat with spread legs. They put their arms on the arms of chairs. They crossed their legs by putting a foot on the other knee. They dominated space expansively.
>
> Women condensed. Women crossed their legs by putting one leg over the other and alongside. Women kept their elbows to their sides, taking up as little space as possible. They behaved as if it were their duty not to rub against, not to touch, not to bump a man. If contact occurred, the woman shrank back. If a woman bumped a man, he might choose to interpret it as a come-on. (1973, p. 438)

At the time of the Watergate scandals, reporters commented on the startling disrespect shown President Nixon by his aides:

> Haldeman and Ehrlichman treat the President barely as an equal; they do not say "sir"; they interrupt him, contradict him, bully him as he vacillates." (TBR, 1974, p. 23)

> Haldeman sounds as if he has more important things to do than talk to the President of the United States. His answers are monosyllabic, and there are long pauses where Nixon runs out of gas and Haldeman says nothing. Finally Nixon hangs up. (Totenberg, 1975, pp. 38–43)

Researchers have documented that the powerful do signal their status in a variety of subtle ways. Sociologists Peter Kollock, Philip Blumstein, and Pepper Schwartz (1985) listened in on conversations between the powerful and powerless, but added to the mix the variable of gender. They examined couples who were living together. They asked the couples to discuss a variety of controversial topics. They tape recorded and then carefully analyzed the conversations. In polite conversation, people normally are supposed to take turns. They are expected to emit appropriately timed, conversation-encouraging "uh-huhs" at appropriate points to indicate that they are fascinated with the other's words of wisdom. When their partners enthusiastically recount a story, they are not expected to respond with a stony silence or a bored grunt. Conversations between the powerful and the powerless and/or between men and women are not always so polite. Kollock and his colleagues (in their research with couples) observed many of the same differences that other communication researchers have reported:

According to the mythology, women love to talk. Research makes clear, alas, that this is an "old wives' tale" (as told by men). Men have been found to talk far more in almost all social settings than women (Argyle, Lalljee, & Cook, 1968; Bernard, 1972).

Men dominate conversations. Men not only speak more, but when their partners try to sneak in a word or two, they are likely to interrupt. Men make 96% of the interruptions, women 4% (Zimmerman & West, 1975)!

Men tend to make "minimal responses" to their partners' conversational points; women do not. (By a minimal response we mean such simple one- or two-word unethusiastic grunts as "yeah," "uh hum," or "umm," timed so as to discourage more discourse.) Speakers often quit talking when they receive such a disparaging response (Fishman, 1978).

Men and women play different roles in conversation. Men play a dominant role, controlling the interaction, and frequently violating the rules of polite turn taking. Women are more submissive, seeking permission to speak, and taking more responsibility for supporting other speakers.

Kollock and his colleagues (1985) wanted to know more, however. Was it power or gender that promotes different conversational privileges and responsibilities? The authors tried to find out by contrasting the behavior of homosexual couples (similar in gender; differing or not differing in power) versus heterosexual couples (differing in gender and power). They concluded that, in the end, it is power differences, not gender, that probably account for traditional male/female differences in conversational style.

THE BASES OF SOCIAL POWER

In a valuable paper, John French and Bertram Raven (1959) observed that individuals can use five different types of power to get their way: reward power, coercive power, legitimate power, referent power, and expert power (see Table 6.2).

More recently, Raven and his colleagues have discovered some additional techniques that people use to influence one another. Some people possess *informational power*. This is power based on the persuasiveness of a logical argument. ("Honey, we will save $12,000 if we refinance now; interest rates are supposed to rise at the end of the year.") People can also use *environmental manipulation*. If an exhausted mother gets sick and tired of yelling at her children to keep their dirty feet off her white sofa, she might give up and cover it with plastic. Or, the mother might *invoke the power of a third party*. She may warn her children that your father is going to hear about *this* when he gets home (Frost & Stahelski, 1988; Raven, 1988a; Raven, Centers, & Rodrigues, 1975).

Other researchers, of course, have proposed other classifications of the types of resources that influence marital power. Constantine Safilios-Rothschild (1976) identified love and affection, expressions of understanding and support, compan-

Table 6.2   TYPES OF SOCIAL POWER

Type of power	Definitions and examples
Reward power	Power based on the perception that the other has the ability to reward them.
	"If you'll just be patient, when tax season is over, I'll take you to Tuscany."
Coercive power	Power based on the perception that the other has the ability to punish them.
	"If you don't shut up, I'll knock you across the room."
Legitimate power	Power based on the perception that the other has a legitimate right to tell them what to do. (In many contemporary societies, money equals power. One does not have to be a Marxist to recognize how financial control can be seen to convey not only "legitimate" power, but reward and coercive power as well. Social norms, however, sometimes *also* dictate that if people are too young, too sick, or too old to help themselves, they have the right to demand help from others.)
	"As long as I earn the money, I call the shots."
	"Mommmy, pleasssssse. Help me buckle up my snow-boots!"
Referent power	Power based on the identification with, and desire to be like, their "ideal."
	"All the guys work out at Bryan's gym; don't you want to buy a membership too?"
Expert power	Power based on the perception that the other has some special knowledge or expertness.
	"I'll be happy to telephone them for you, honey; I know how much you hate conflict."

Source: Based on French & Raven, 1959.

ionship, sex, socioeconomic resources, and services as the resources that "count." She (like other sociologists) has observed that, when we are in love, we surrender much of our power:

> *The Principle of Least Interest:* That person is able to dictate the conditions of association whose interest in the continuation of the affair is least. (Waller & Hill, 1951, p. 191)

> *The Law of Personal Exploitation:* In any sentimental relation the one who cares less can exploit the one who cares more. (Ross, 1921, p. 136)

In a classic study, Robert Blood and Donald Wolfe (1960) proposed a *resource theory* of power. They argued that socioeconomic resources are most important in love relationships. The person who "brings home the bacon" generally gets to call the shots.

Finally, Hyman Rodman (1972) tried to integrate all these theories in a *normative theory* of power. He argued that cultural norms determine how marital power is allocated. The most traditional, primitive cultures are *patriarchal*. Here, husbands possess all the power. As cultures evolve into *modified patriarchies* (cultures such as Greece), the upper classes begin to develop more egalitarian beliefs; the lower classes are still stuck in patriarchy. In such societies, socioeconomic status and power will actually be negatively related! (The rich will be more egalitarian than the poor.) In a third evolutionary stage, *transitional egalitarianism* (in cultures such as the United States and Western Europe), society no longer dictates who should have the most power. In such societies, socioeconomic resources will determine who can wield the most power. Finally, in the most advanced, egalitarian societies (such as Sweden and Denmark) social norms endorse the equal sharing of power. Here, power will no longer be affected by the possession of socioeconomic resources.

THE LIMITS TO POWER

Power plays don't always work. Unrequited lovers may plead with their beloveds just to give them a chance, but the plea will go unheeded. A wife, armed with a battery of statistics, and worried about her husband's cough, may beg him to stop smoking, but he will continue to puff away. The Iraqis may torture Kuwaiti resistance leaders, but some of the Kuwaitis will nonetheless refuse to divulge their military secrets. There are many reasons why power plays fail. At other times a process such as psychological reactance may make pressure counterproductive.

Psychological Reactance

Pressure can backfire. The put-upon person may so resent being told what to do that he or she will insist on doing just the opposite. (Most of us can probably remember times in our childhood when we were so stubborn that we could be beaten to a pulp and yet we would still defiantly refuse to give in.) Jack Brehm (1966) identified this phenomenon as *psychological reactance*. Americans have a deep-seated desire to maintain their personal freedom of action. Anytime their freedom is threatened, they take immediate steps to try to assert it. They may stubbornly refuse to comply with a request . . . or even insist on doing just the opposite to "show" the other person. We are all too familiar with the toddler (entering the "terrible twos") who thrusts out her jaw and hisses "I won't" every time she is asked to do anything. When her parents (resorting to reverse psychology) shrug their shoulders and say, "All right, then, don't," she may then insist on doing what she was asked to do in the first place. Adults defend their freedom with equal vigor, and sometimes with equal stupidity!

Power . . . is the measure of manhood.
            —*J. G. Holland*

"I'm getting tired of you throwing your weight around."

THE BATTLE OF THE SEXES

Theorists generally assume that men have the most power in love relationships. There are a variety of reasons why this is so. Sociobiologists and sociologists point out that men have a physical advantage: they are generally bigger, stronger, and more aggressive than women (Komarovsky, 1967). Historians point out that men have a historical advantage; the patriarchal tradition took it for granted that husbands should dominate wives. Their power was buttressed by religious and legal structures (Gray-Little & Burks, 1983; Lerner, 1986). Economists point out that men have a socioeconomic advantage; they possess higher status and earn more money (Blood & Wolfe, 1960; D'Andrade, 1966; Scanzoni, 1979). Sociologists point out that men may possess a great demographic advantage once they hit their mid-thirties (see Box 6.1).

Theorists offer a number of reasons why—even though the conventional wisdom asserts that a relationship that involves the give-and-take of equals is most desirable—men in fact wield more power in love relationships than women. What do the data say? In general, research indicates that men generally do have more power in relationships. In addition, men and women seem to use slightly different techniques when trying to get their way. Men use the techniques of the powerful, women the manipulative strategies of the powerless.

Men Possess the Most Power

Anne Peplau (1979) asked dating partners to think about a series of potential conflicts and to guess how they would resolve them. A typical situation:

Box 6.1   TOO MANY WOMEN

It's easy to take it for granted that for every man there is a woman. Yet the sweep of history often produces a very differential impact on men and on women. In ancient Greece, the Spartans (determined to breed warriors) exposed their sickly infant sons on a sacred rock to die. Not surprisingly Sparta had too few men. In China, a long sad history has resulted in centuries of female infanticide. With so many baby girls murdered, women have been at a premium. In World War I, millions of men were slaughtered. The European colonies, Siberia, and the American West were settled by men; so women were scarce. In a fascinating series of studies, Marcia Guttentag and Paul Secord (1983) examined the effect of high or low male/female sex ratios on love relationships. They demonstrated that scarce commodities are always valuable. The fewer the men there are, the more valuable they will be, and the more power they will have to "call the shots" in love relationships (see Illustration on page 175).

What are sex ratios in America? Early on, women have, despite other social inequities, many advantages. When men and women are in their teens and early twenties, it is men who suffer from the marriage squeeze (there are slightly more eligible men than women). After 25, however, there are increasing numbers of women (Kennedy, 1989; Sprecher, 1991). Men of almost all ages are interested in competing for younger women; they are in great demand. As men and women age, however, the ratio of men to women and the subsequent balance of power begin to change dramatically. Older men continue to be interested in younger women. They also begin to die.

In therapy, when we see men 35 years old (and older), who have been tossed back into the dating market, we can be reassuring to them. They may have had trouble getting dates in high school, but they are going to be in demand now. Many women who wouldn't have given them a second look in high school will suddenly be available. The news for 35-year-old women (and older) is not so encouraging; there are too few men. In 1986, *Newsweek* magazine released some startling statistics. For young people, men and women were in equal supply. After that, men were in increasingly short supply. If college-educated women were still single at 30, they had only a 20% chance of ever marrying. By the time they reached 35, they had only a 5% chance. Forty-year-olds, *Newsweek* cautioned, had only a 2.6% chance of marrying. They were "more likely to be killed by a terrorist than to get married!" (p. 55). Demographers working for the Census Bureau quickly pointed out that this conclusion was somewhat exaggerated (Faludi, 1991). Nonetheless, the authors were right in their recognition that after 35 there are "too few men."

Such gender differentials have a profound effect on the power balances in love relationships. Most people have at least a hazy sense of what is available out there. Unbalanced sex ratios are likely to affect the choices and compromises made by men and women.

You and _____ are trying to decide how you as a couple will spend the weekend. You really want the two of you to go out with some of your friends, but _____ wants just as strongly for the two of you to go out with some of [his/her] friends. Obviously you can't go out with both sets of friends at once. Who do you as a couple decide to go out with?

The women generally believed that *they* would be the ones to give in, while their boyfriends were certain that the conflict could be resolved either way. [Similar results were secured by Safilios-Rothschild (1969).] Women seemed well aware that they generally gave in; the men may have been more oblivious—thinking everyone was satisfied with the status quo.

Since the pioneering study of Blood and Wolfe (1960) almost all researchers have found that husbands wield more power than their wives (Huston, 1983; Szinovacz, 1987). There is evidence, as a result of social change, that patriarchy, along with the male monopoly on power, may be eroding. Historians expect such erosion to continue, though not without lurches (Rapson, 1980). The data to support that prediction are many: women continue to become educated in ever greater numbers; they achieve higher-status jobs; they make more money. As a result, they continue to gain increasing power in their love relationships (Maret & Finlay, 1984). In fact, even today, a few researchers are beginning to fail to find any gender differences in power (Huston, 1983; Olson, 1972). Since male domination has been one of the most consistent and significant tendencies of human history, the social revolution through which we are living (of which the women's movement looms large) counts as extraordinarily important and will likely affect all our lives in profound ways.

Be reasonable; do it my way.
        —Anonymous

Men and Women Use Different Power Strategies

Returning to the present, we see that both men and women try to influence other people, but there is some evidence that they go about it in slightly different ways (Winter, 1988).

Judith Howard and her colleagues (1986) have argued that powerful people should use somewhat different strategies than the weak to get what they want. Consider the following six kinds of influence strategies:

Bullying includes making threats, insulting others, ridiculing them, becoming violent.

Autocracy includes insisting, claiming greater knowledge, and asserting authority.

Manipulation includes dropping hints, flattering, behaving seductively, and reminding people of all you've done for them.

Supplication includes pleading, crying, acting ill, and acting helpless.

Bargaining includes reasoning, offering to compromise, and offering a trade-off.

Disengagement tactics include sulking, trying to make one's partner feel guilty, and leaving the scene.

The first two, bullying and autocracy, seem most appropriate for people who possess real power. The next two strategies, manipulation and supplication, are clearly tactics to which only the weak must resort. The final two tactics, bargaining and disengagement, could be used by both the powerful and the powerless.

Never go to bed mad. Stay up and fight.
        —Phyllis Diller

Are there gender differences in the use of such power tactics?

Toni Falbo and Anne Peplau (1980) asked 200 college students to write an essay on "How I get my way" in their romantic and sexual relationships. The power strategies mentioned are reported in Table 6.3. The researchers then classified the power tactics: Were their attempts to influence direct or indirect? (Did they ask straight out for what they wanted or did they hint?) Were their tactics unilateral or bilateral? (Did students take matters in their own hands or did they try to engineer a compromise?) Consider this man's description:

> This depends on who I am trying to get it from or with. With my parents, I tell them I want something, then play it cool and eventually get it. With friends, I will fight verbally although not physically for it. With girlfriends, I simply turn the other way, walk off, or whatever the situation demands. (Falbo & Peplau, 1980, p. 618)

With friends, this man utilizes a direct and interactive strategy for getting his way. With his girlfriend he relies on indirect and unilateral power plays. Researchers

Table 6.3 STUDENTS' POWER STRATEGIES

Type of strategy	Example
Asking	I ask him to do what I want.
Bargaining	We usually negotiate something agreeable to both of us. We compromise.
Laissez-faire	We do our own thing. I just do it by myself.
Negative affect	I pout or threaten to cry if I don't get my way.
Persistence	I repeatedly remind him of what I want until he gives in.
Persuasion	I try to persuade him my way is right.
Positive affect	I smile a lot. I am especially affectionate.
Reasoning	I reason with her. I argue my point logically.
Stating importance	I tell him how important it is to me.
Suggesting	I drop hints. I make suggestions.
Talking	We talk about it. We discuss our differences and needs.
Telling	I tell her what I want. I state my needs.
Withdrawal	I clam up. I become silent.

Source: Falbo & Peplau, 1980, p. 621.

generally find that powerful people can afford to rely on direct, bilateral tactics (they simply demand what they want and expect their partners to cooperate). The weak are forced to use indirect, unilateral tactics; they avoid confrontation; they hint, plead, pout, or manipulate. If such indirect tactics fail, they give up and withdraw (Howard et al., 1986; Johnson, 1978). In this study, men were confident that they had the power. They were bargaining from strength, while their girl-friends were bargaining from a position of weakness. Thus it is not surprising that the men generally used the tactics of the powerful: they used direct and bilateral power tactics. Women generally relied on the power tactics of the weak: they used indirect and unilateral strategies. If one has little power, such indirect strategies make a great deal of sense. Such "weak" strategies, however, may take a psychological toll. If women habitually present themselves as worthless and incompetent, it could erode their self-esteem and strengthen existing power inequities (Raven et al., 1975).

We'll lead an ideal life if you'll just avoid doing one thing: don't think.
—Ronald Reagan to then wife Jane Wyman

Kenneth Gruber and Jacquelyn White (1986) provide some additional insight into why men are so effective in getting their way in love. Men and women both believe in gender stereotypes. When the authors asked how women and men generally behave, the students (male and female) were convinced that men generally use such "masculine" tactics as logical persuasion, reason, yelling, or physical force and that women generally employ such typically "feminine" tactics as pleading, begging, praying, flattering, or compromising. When they asked men and women how *they* tried to get their way, however, they found that the stereotypes were off. As predicted, men used masculine power tactics more often than did women. However, both men and women used feminine power tactics equally often. Women seem to be constrained by social norms—using only those power tactics that are seen as socially acceptable for women. Men seem to be free to exercise whatever stratagems they think will work.

An Ideal: Egalitarian Relationships

In romantic novels, passion and sacrifice and enslavement form a heady brew. In Somerset Maugham's novel *Of Human Bondage*, Philip Carey falls in love with Mildred, a cheap, vulgar, rather stupid waitress. Despite his saintly generosity and the fact that he ruins himself for her, she betrays and humiliates him time and time again. She leaves him for another . . . and another—men as cheap and vulgar as herself.

Charles Swann, in Marcel Proust's (1956) *Swann in Love*, is obsessed and enslaved by his love for Odette, a prostitute. He marries her, sacrificing everything for her. Once married, he wakens from his dreams of love, cold-eyed and cold-hearted. "To think that I have wasted years of my life, that I have longed for death, that the greatest love that I have ever known has been for a woman who did not please me, was not my style!" (Proust, 1956, p. 549).

In *Tender Is the Night* by F. Scott Fitzgerald (1962), psychiatrist Dick Diver is ultimately destroyed by his relationship with Nicole, one of his patients. These may be love stories, but in the hands of fine novelists like Maugham, Proust, and Fitzgerald (unlike more popular "romance writers"), there is a clear-eyed recognition that such relationships simply do not work.

Naïve lovers assume that if they sacrifice all to "save" a wounded bird, the little bird will at least be grateful, but the wounded rarely are—simply because they *are* wounded. Usually the Mildreds and Odettes and Nicoles of the world feel trapped. Because they are aware of their own worthlessness, they not only find it hard to admire (or even respect) such worms, they actually despise such desperate, self-abnegating lovers as Carey, Swann, and Diver. Or in the rare circumstances in which the bruised get healed, they demand something other than the rescuer–rescued love affair.

In *real* life, egalitarian relationships, happy day, seem to work the best. We once saw a traditional newlywed couple in therapy. The man was funny, smart, and very "macho." He had vague connections to the Mafia. The wife was a tiny, beautiful doll. She wanted very much to be what she thought of as an upper-class wife. Her street-smart origins sometimes butted against her "lady-of-the-manor" performance. Once, when we said: "Of course marriage involves a give-and-take," the husband erupted. "I don't want a 50–50 relationship—I want 90–10. If I could have it, I would want 100–0. I run all the risks and make all the money. I want all the power." His wife glowed with pride at his machismo.

Things change, however. We began to see them again three years later. By now, the husband was somewhat subdued; he had grown to love his wife, to enjoy what she did for him, and to cherish their new daughter. His wife had become disenchanted, with him and with the idea of marriage itself. He turned out not to be at all what she had thought. He wasn't nearly so brave or confident as he had pretended. He had far less money than he had claimed. She had lost interest, become bored. She had gone back to school. And she wanted out.

The vast majority of young couples say they want an egalitarian relationship (Peplau, 1983). They admit that their parents' marriages were unbalanced. (Only 18% of them were reared in egalitarian households.) Yet, when they are asked who should have the most control in relationships, 95% of the women and 87% of the men said that both should have an *"exactly* equal say." Love does not always work out that way; patriarchy lingers. Nonetheless, the new ideal still represents something for which to strive. The evidence makes it clear that love relationships that are egalitarian are the happiest and produce the most satisfaction (Gray-Little & Burks, 1983) and are associated with the most trust, commitment, and concern for the other (Grauerholz, 1987).

Bernadette Gray-Little and Nancy Burks (1983) reviewed 21 studies exploring male and female power in marriage. Couples came from different countries—Mexico, Yugoslavia, Sweden, France, England, Greece, Austria, and America. Power was assessed in a variety of ways ranging from asking couples to say who possessed the most power all the way to rigorously observing them in action. The result was clear: Egalitarian couples had the happiest marriages and were most satisfied with them. Couples in either husband- or wife-dominant marriages were far less happy. (Of the two, "traditional" husband-dominant marriages tended to be happier than wife-dominant marriages.)

An asymmetrical relationship has hidden costs. Morton Deutsch (1975) showed that affectional bonds are eroded by discrepancies in power. Both the powerful and the powerless may feel guilty, embarrassed, and angry (Emerson, 1962; Hatfield et al., 1978) at such inequitable balances. When people know they can be heard by their partners, they are willing to be logical and fair in their arguments. When they know, on the other hand, that their needs will be ignored, they often resort to desperate measures. They may pout, cry, or make scenes (Falbo & Peplau, 1980). If all else fails, they may walk out.

When marriages break up, women often report the problems as long in the making, while men perceive the breakup as abrupt and unexpected (Hagestad & Smyer, 1982). Researchers (Helgeson et al., 1987) suggest a reason for this. When in arguments their anger leads their partners to comply, men may view themselves as victorious and in control. The female partners, however, feeling hurt and frustrated, may not really be patiently compliant; they may be accumulating and keeping track of injuries over an extended period of time. When their feelings finally lead them to abandon a relationship, it comes as a surprise to their repeatedly "victorious" male partners. What price victory? (For an alternative view, see Box 6.2.)

Probably both men and women are right when they complain that their partners suffer from a "little failure to communicate." Both men and women may be hesitant to reveal painful truths to those they once cared for. Both may try to soften their blows. And, in turn, when the blows rain down, both men and women may flinch before the painful facts that threaten to send them reeling.

Sex: the thing that takes up the least amount of time, and causes the most amount of trouble.
                                                                                    —*John Barrymore*

Box 6.2 **THE OTHER SIDE OF THE STORY**

Men need not take such conclusions lying down. Some men complain that the problem is with *women*. They argue that women refuse to admit what they are thinking and feeling until things have spun out of control:

> She will fool you at the end, one way or another. As far as you know, the relationship is fine, give or take a few fresh wounds, a few deeper sores, festering but curable. But all the time she is planning to leave you, and you don't even know it. . . .
>
> Reasons will be given, of course. . . . She may be brutal: "I just don't love you any more." But that doesn't help. It isn't a real reason, it merely provokes a further "why?"—a question she is either not prepared or not able to answer. Equally, she may try to let you down gently: "It's only because I love you that I have to leave you. I'm leaving you for your own good." That doesn't help either. . . . It leaves the same "why?" hanging in the air. . . .
>
> The cruel reality is that when a relationship ends, truth is the first casualty. An earthquake has erupted in your life, and is explained by a cliché. The answers are never quite adequate. . . . There is something monstrous in coating savage reality in the blandest prose, but the woman has her reasons. She may genuinely not know why. . . . At the other end of the conscious spectrum is the woman who knows exactly why she is leaving, but cannot reveal the truth. . . .
>
> When a couple splits up, the force-fields are never equal. One is leaving, the other is being left, and often without knowing why. The pain of abandonment is sharpened by uncertainty. We have all seen the dying of the light, the deadened eyes and wailing voice pleading for understanding: "Why did she have to leave me?" The human mind copes badly with uncertainty, but men go to their deaths not knowing why one of the most traumatic events in their life happened.
>
> A part of us condones the deception. We are not sure that we want to know the real reason. It may be unacceptable. It may hurt more than the convenient fiction. At our deepest, often unconscious, levels we fear it has something to do with sex, and few of us relish being told we are no good in bed.
>
> But even when the reasons—or at least the triggers—are trivial, we probably don't want to know.

Source: Graham, 1991, pp. 100–101.

POWER IN SEXUAL RELATIONSHIPS

Young men and women use a variety of power tactics in flirting and in persuading others to date them, cuddle, have sexual relations (or refrain from doing so), to engage in the sexual practices they like, and in negotiating how committed and intimate their relationships will become.

In traditional societies, parents had a great deal of power in scripting sexual and marital scenarios. Until recently, cultural convention dictated that men and women should follow a double standard. Men were supposed to push for sexual favors; women were supposed virtuously to resist. An apocryphral story said that on her wedding night, Queen Victoria's mother counseled her on how to endure the unpleasantness of sexual relations: "Lie back and think of England." Today, however, as patriarchy weakens, the young generally have the power to decide how far they will go.

Increasingly, both men and women are trying to write their sexual scripts so that they get what they want out of love.

> In his History class, Richard Rapson shows a film series entitled *In Search of the Sixties*. In one segment, *The Seeds of the Sixties,* students are reminded of what it was like to date in the 1950s. The depiction is depressing. The typical scenario goes like this. Joe must make the first move. He picks up the telephone and begins to dial. He begins to perspire and cringe with anxiety; he hangs up before completing the call. After gathering his courage, he calls again. Is Julie free for a movie next week? She takes a moment to "look at her engagement book" so that Joe will realize that she is popular; he just can't take her for granted. "Yes," she'd love to.
>
> On Saturday, Joe shows up right on time. He is carefully dressed in a sports jacket and slacks. Julie isn't ready yet; she does not want to seem "too eager." While he waits, Joe chats uneasily with Julie's Mom and Dad. They skeptically look him over. Julie finally appears, beautifully dressed. Her parents caution her to be home early. She proffers a token "Oh, Dad!" and the ordeal is over.
>
> After the movie, Joe drives to a lookout over the city, presumably so that they can look at the lights. He timidly hangs his arm over Julie's shoulder. When she doesn't resist, he tentatively tries to kiss her. She pretends to look at her watch. "It's time to go home" she realizes. He drives her home and after giving him a perfunctory kiss and a "thank you for a lovely evening," she rushes into the house. The evening has ended with both Joe and Julie in a state of total sexual confusion.

The 1950s seem like ancient history. A new script has been written, with change catalyzed during the 1960s. How do power considerations operate in the 1990s? How do men and women persuade dates and mates to do what they want in the sexual realm? More confusingly, "What do men and women want?"

Flirtation: The Power to Be Noticed

Timothy Perper and Susan Fox (1980) spent 300 hours observing couples in singles bars. They made a surprising discovery. It was women who generally made the first move, even though men often actually made the verbal overtures and thought they controlled the action. Unless, however, a woman glanced at a man once or preferably twice or stood close to him, he usually did not have the courage to approach her and make that verbal overture.

The researchers found that neither men nor women alone could determine whether the initial flirtation would result in the couple leaving the bar together. In Figure 6.1 Perper and Fox provide a "flow chart" of the steps that take couples from the first time their eyes meet until they leave the bar together. It is clear that at each step, both men and women must signal their eagerness to continue

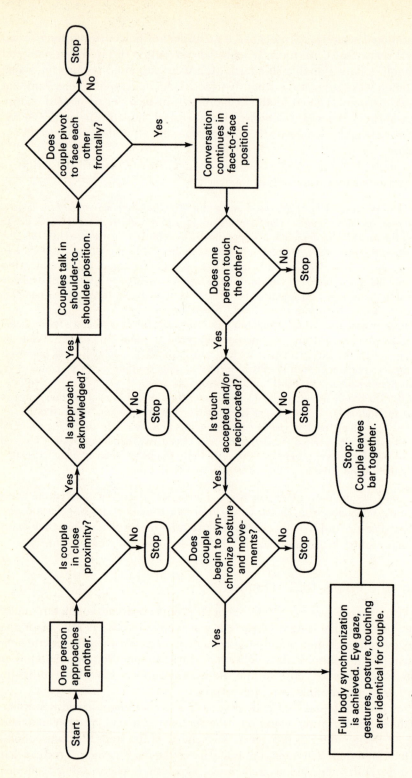

Figure 6.1 Flirtation in bars.

interacting if that interaction is to continue. Either person has the power to break things off at any time. All the signals sent by women and by men tend to be quite subtle.

> [A woman] commonly touches the man before he touches her. Her touch is made, typically with the palm of the hand flat, and not with the fingertips, in a light, fleeting and pressing gesture. . . . She might brush against him with her hip or back, she may lean on him briefly, or she might brush against him while she turns to look at something. An alternative is for the woman to remove an otherwise nonexistent piece of lint from the man's jacket (men's jackets in bars collect such lint very readily). (Perper & Fox, 1980, p. 18)

Naomi McCormick and Clinton Jesser (1982) point out that it is not an accident that signals are so subtle and that touch is so important. Touching is safe. If someone rejects your move, you can pretend that the whole thing was just a misunderstanding. You were only being friendly; the touching was accidental. This saves everyone's face.

The Power to Ask for a Date

In the recent past, the man always was assigned the task of directly asking for the first date. A woman could make herself attractive, but she was not supposed to telephone to ask him out. Women were expected to wait patiently by the telephone, afraid of missing The Call. Times may be changing and telephone answering machines short-circuit some misery, but old conventions die hard. Today, men wish that things would change and that women would ask them out sometimes (Hite, 1981). Women, though, remain resistant. (Probably they are no more eager to face rejection than men are.) It is still men who ask women out on the first date. It is still men who pay for things on the first date (Allgeier, 1981; Green & Sandos, 1983). After the first hurdle has been surmounted, however, both men and women feel freer about taking the next set of initiatives.

The Power to Initiate a Sexual Encounter

Historically, a double standard has existed. Sex for recreation has never been sanctioned by religion and never was generally approved before the twentieth century—and then never openly. Yet men were implicitly permitted, if not encouraged, to get sex whenever and wherever they could. Women were supposed to "save themselves" for marriage, and even after marriage only procreation was a generally accepted purpose of sexual congress for women. According to myth: "Good girls don't say Yes; real men don't say No." In light of this double standard, it is not surprising that both men and women agreed that men should initiate sex and that single women should resist sexual advances until married. After wedlock, a woman should passively acquiesce to her husband's desires (Ehrmann, 1959; Long-Laws, 1979; Peplau, Rubin, & Hill, 1977; Reiss, 1967).

These traditions are being battered these days in every corner of the world, but even in the West they are not yet dead. Contemporary college students naturally explicitly reject the double standard (Hopkins, 1977). When they are asked to guess how men and women usually behave in dating relationships, they nonetheless believe that the "battle of the sexes" still rages. They assume that men use a wide array of power techniques to seduce women into having sex and that women use all their wiles to resist (LaPlante, McCormick, & Brannigan, 1980).

When men and women are asked how *they* try to shape their sexual encounters, however, a more complex picture emerges. Naomi McCormick (1979) asked college students to imagine that they were alone with an attractive date whom they had known for a few weeks. They had "necked" but they had not yet had sexual intercourse. How would they persuade their date to have sexual intercourse? Both men and women said they would employ *indirect* strategies of seduction. One man, for instance, wrote: "First of all, I would put on some soft music and offer some wine, then I would start kissing gently and caressing her body, then I would give her a massage with oil" (p. 199). The use of body language (sitting closer, touching) and setting the stage (putting on music, dimming the lights) are common. One woman described her indirect seduction techniques this way:

> I would start caressing his body and start kissing his chest, maybe stomach. I would try to be very sexy, doing this especially with lots of eye contact, probably a few sighs here and there to let him know I feel sexually stimulated. This would probably be all I would do aside from wearing something slinky and bare. I could not get myself to perhaps start unbuckling his pants. (McCormick & Jesser, 1982, p. 82)

College students were also asked how they would *avoid* having sex with a "turned on" date. Here, both men and women preferred the direct approach (McCormick, 1979). The favorite tactic of both men and women was to emphasize that it was too early to have sex. Others proposed using logic or information, such as saying "I'm not in the mood for sex" or "I'm worried about pregnancy." A few individuals suggested using body language (moving further away) or changing the topic. A few would invoke moral principles. In theory, then, men and women agree on the most effective ways to seduce another or to reject another's attempts at seduction.

What do men and women do when faced with the same situations in real life? Here, men and woman admit to a tendency toward following conventional gender role norms. In actual dating, it is generally men who are the sexual initiators who try to seduce their partners and women who set limits and avoid sex (LaPlante et al., 1980; McCormick, 1977).

Recently, F. Scott Christopher and Michela Frandsen (1990) asked 366 men and women which power tactics they had used on their most recent date either to have sex or to avoid it. They found that college students generally used the kinds of influence strategies given in Table 6.4 to get their way sexually.

First, they explored whether men and women reported using different influence techniques. They found only one difference: Men relied on pressure and manipulation to get their way more than did women. Next they explored whether

Table 6.4 SEXUAL INFLUENCE TACTICS SCALE

1. **Emotional and physical closeness**

   Told partner how much I loved him or her.
   Put myself physically closer to my partner.
   Did something special for my partner.
   Talked about our relationship and what it means to me.
   Acted seductively.
   Communicated what I wanted with my hands.
   Flattered my partner.
   Dropped hints about what I wanted.

2. **Logic and reason**

   Used reason.
   Claimed to be knowledgable about how sexual we should be.
   Asserted my authority.
   Used logic.
   Compromised with my partner.
   Suggested limiting our sexual interaction.

3. **Pressure and manipulation**

   Pressured my partner.
   Ignored my partner's actions.
   Used persuasion.
   Used alcohol and/or drugs to more easily influence my partner.
   Manipulated my partner's mood.
   Was persistent.
   Made excuses.
   I talked fast and told white lies.
   Threatened to break off the relationship.

4. **Antisocial acts**

   Overt antisocial acts
   Used physical force.
   Verbally or physically threatened my partner.
   Insulted my partner.
   Ridiculed my partner.

   Covert antisocial acts
   Sulked.
   Acted helpless.
   Made my partner feel guilty.
   Reminded partner of past favors.
   Pleaded.
   Acted ill.
   Got angry with my partner.

Source: Based on Christopher & Frandsen, 1990, pp. 95–96.

(1) couples who were already involved sexually used different tactics than did those who were not, and (2) whether those who were pressing for sex used different tactics than did people who were trying to slow things down. They found that when couples were eager for sex, both of them relied on physical and emotional closeness. When both wanted to wait, they both invoked logic and reason to slow things down. When only one person wanted sex, however, they employed rougher tactics. They relied primarily on pressure and manipulation and, if all else failed, they were sometimes willing to resort to antisocial acts. People who were resisting premature involvement tended to invoke reason and logic.

How well do men and women do in setting sexual limits? Russell Clark and Elaine Hatfield (1989) tried to find out with a simple experiment. College men and women, who varied from slightly unattractive to moderately attractive in appearance, agreed to serve as experimenters. They strolled across the quadrangle at Florida State University. As soon as they encountered attractive men and women of the opposite sex, they approached them and said: "I have been noticing you around campus and I find you to be very attractive." Then they asked them one of three questions: (1) "Would you go out with me tonight?" (2) "Would you come over to my apartment tonight?" or (3) "Would you go to bed with me tonight?" To the authors' surprise, they found it was surprisingly easy for men and women to get a date even with a complete stranger. As you can see from Table 6.5, more than half the men and women agreed to go out on a date! Another surprise in this day of AIDS was the fact that men were generally willing to have sexual relations with practically any woman who asked. Men readily accepted sexual invitations (75% agreed to go to bed with the women). Women were totally unwilling to go to bed with a stranger (0% agreed to do so). In general, men were intrigued by the sexual invitation. They made comments such as, "Why do we have to wait until tonight?" Often the men who said "no" were apologetic. They said "I'm married" or "I'm going with someone." In contrast, the women were stunned and angry at such invitations: "You've got to be kidding" or "What's wrong with you, creep, leave me alone."

In spite of the AIDS crisis, similar results have been found in later studies (Clark, 1990).

We live during a historical moment of sexual novelty and experimentation; rules that existed for decades, centuries, and sometimes millennia are being challenged. Today, men wish women would take the sexual initiative (Hatfield, Sprecher, Pillemer, Greenberger, & Wexler, 1988; Hite, 1981). Ironically, women sometimes hold back out of fear that their assertiveness will be seen as unfemi-

Table 6.5   PERCENTAGE OF COMPLIANCE WITH EACH TYPE OF REQUEST

Sex of person making request	Type of request		
	Date	Apartment	Bed
Man/woman's response	56%	6%	0%
Woman/man's response	50%	69%	75%

nine. Men, however, desire more assertive sexual partners. For example, many older men agree that "it's exciting when a woman takes the sexual initiative" (Tavris, 1978, p. 113). In fact, college men view women who initiate sex more positively than women do (Allgeier, 1981). It is perhaps not surprising then that women are getting more comfortable about hinting and even directly expressing their eagerness to have sex (Jesser, 1978). Men are also becoming more comfortable about refusing to have sex when they are not interested. Nothing can be assumed about the sexual ballet in an age of more openly expressed homosexuality and, on the sinister side, in an age of AIDS.

Giving Clear/Ambiguous Messages

Sometimes in sexual encounters there is sexual miscommunication. Men and women are not always completely honest with each other. Researchers (Sprecher, Hatfield, Potapova, Levitskaya, & Cortese, 1992) asked men and women in the United States, the Soviet Union, and Japan if they had ever engaged in token resistance to sex (i.e., said "no" when they really wanted to have sex) or token acceptance of sex (i.e., "yes" when they really didn't want to have sex). They asked:

> Has the following situation ever happened to you? You were with a person who wanted to engage in sexual intercourse and you wanted to also, but for some reason you indicated that you didn't want to, although *you had every intention to and were willing to engage in sexual intercourse.* In other words, you indicated "no" and you meant "yes."
>
> Possible answers were "never" or "once or more." Has the following situation ever happened to you? You were with a person who wanted to engage in sexual intercourse and you did not want to, but for some reason you indicated that you did want to. In other words, you indicated "yes" and you meant "no." (pp. 9–10)

As is evident from Table 6.6, both men and women admitted they were sometimes afraid to admit their real feelings. Almost half of them (49% of men and 43% of women) acknowledged that at some time in their lives they had said "no" when they actually meant "yes."

Why did young people pretend to be less interested in sex than they were? Earlier researchers (Muehlenhard & Hollabaugh, 1988) asked men and women

Table 6.6 TOKEN RESISTANCE AND TOKEN ACCEPTANCE OF SEX FOR MEN AND WOMEN IN THREE COUNTRIES

	United States		*Soviet Union*		*Japan*	
	Men	Women	Men	Women	Men	Women
Token resistance (saying no; meaning yes)	50%	38%	47%	64%	45%	37%
Token acceptance (saying yes; meaning no)	28%	41%	37%	28%	18%	14%

why they had pretended sexual disinterest. Some said they denied their feelings because they possessed strong moral convictions, which prohibited sexual expression. Others worried that their partners would think less of them if they admitted their passionate desires. A few were worried that their partners would lose interest in them once they had sex. Sometimes, they knew the timing was wrong: Their parents were home; they didn't have any birth control. So they said "no," even though they were secretly hoping to be overruled.

Sprecher and her colleagues (1992) also found that both men and women admitted that they had been pressured into saying "yes" when they really meant "no." (Thirty percent of men *and* women had said "yes" while meaning "no" at least once.)

Previous researchers have found that there are a number of reasons why men and women have sex when they don't want to. They don't want to hurt their partners' feelings, they were drunk, they were afraid their peers would think less of them if they said no; they were forced to have sex (Muehlenhard & Cook, 1988).

Power During a Sexual Encounter: Who's on Top?

Women, if they were "good," were not, in the past, sexual beings; they therefore were expected to be relatively passive during sexual relations (Ford & Beach, 1951; Rubin, 1976). A few decades ago, couples almost always had sexual relations in the "missionary position," in which the woman lies on her back while the man is on top of her (Kinsey, Pomeroy, & Martin, 1948). Today, the "missionary position" is still the most common coital position in America (Allgeier, 1981; Blumstein & Schwartz, 1983). Perhaps this is because it fits the stereotype in our society that the men should be active while the women should remain passive during sexual intercourse. Research in 1978 shed some light on the matter. Unmarried college students were asked to give their opinions of couples who were having sexual intercourse in various positions. Interestingly enough, women were more conservative than men in their disapproval of the woman who is on top. Women, not men, had a real distaste for the couple in the woman-above position. They rated the woman as "dirtier, less respectable, less moral, less good, less desirable as a wife, and less desirable as a mother when she was on top than when she was beneath the man during intercourse" (Allgeier & Fogel, 1978). Women also claimed that the man-above position offers greater "emotional satisfaction" than the woman-above position (Allgeier, 1981).

A 1976 study of unmarried students found that once couples had begun to have frequent sexual relations, the man had more to say than the woman about the frequency and type of sexual activity (Peplau, Rubin, & Hill, 1976). If a dating couple decided to abstain from coitus, it was the woman's veto that was the major restraining influence (Peplau et al., 1977).

It appears then that it was not male but female attitudes that were the greater barriers to egalitarian sexual behavior. Women were more attached to the gender role norms that prescribed female sexual submissiveness than were men (Allgeier & Fogel, 1978; Jesser, 1978). Time will tell if this, too, changes.

Rape

The contemporary view of rape sees it as an act of violence expressing power, aggression, conquest, degradation, anger, hatred, and contempt.
                                    —*Lynda Holstrom and Ann Burgess*

In 1991, on Good Friday in Palm Beach, Florida, William Kennedy Smith (Ted Kennedy's nephew) met a woman in a bar and invited her to his beach home late at night. He claimed she agreed to have sex and then repented. She says she was raped and beaten. In the flurry of publicity that followed, a furious debate about the nature of "date rape" exploded. Eventually, Smith was found not guilty.

    When most people think about rape, they think of horrifying events—attacks by sinister strangers lurking with ice picks in the shadows, a gang of wild boys throwing a jogger to the ground in Central Park and raping and almost killing her, a psychopath preying on college women alone in their apartments. Yet such rapes, involving strangers, account for only one out of five rapes. Most women are raped by men they know and like. The nice fellow in their English class comes over to study, their brother's best friend brings them a bottle of celebratory champagne; their date takes them for a moonlit walk on a deserted beach; their boss asks them to stay late to get out a report; they go for a drink later. In all cases, the evening ends with sex/rape. Men and women may torture themselves with questions. Should I have guessed what he had in mind? Protested more vigorously? Fought harder? Was I really listening to what she said or was I carried away by what I wanted? Will she press charges? Will I go to jail? Most thoughtful people take the position that if a man or woman says "no" to sex, they should be taken at their word. In love relationships, there is time to wait; time to clear up ambiguities. Most Americans seem to agree with that truism. Recently, *Time*/CNN polled Americans about their attitudes toward women who engaged in a variety of activities. Was a woman to blame for a rape if she initially agreed to have sex and then changed her mind? "No," most Americans agreed; even then her opinion should be respected (Gibbs, 1991). Most Americans would probably also agree that regardless of how a woman dresses, whether the couple has been out drinking, regardless of whether they have been kissing on a deserted beach at 3 A.M., lying on his or her bed in his or her apartment, regardless of how late it is, a woman (or a man) is still entitled to say no; and that the sexual activity must stop there. Is it rape if a man uses emotional pressure to get a woman to have sex? (Thirty-three percent of men and 39% of women say yes.) Is it rape if a man has sex with a woman who has passed out after drinking too much? (Seventy-seven percent of men and 88% of women say yes.) (Gibbs, 1991). Other issues are harder: Is it rape if the man tells the woman he loves her and then admits after they have had sex that he lied to get her to have sex? If *both* the man and the woman are drunk? If they both enthusiastically agree to have sex in the evening but wake up in the morning, horrified at what they have done? Such questions spark intense debate. Usually, however, couples know full well when persuasion has shaded over into intimidation, when intimidation has turned into force.

    Mary McCarthy (1954), in *A Charmed Life*, described a sexual encounter between Martha and her ex-husband Miles. They met, by chance, at a party and

Box 6.3   A CHARMED LIFE

Up to that moment, he had not been sure whether he wanted to dally with her or not. But now the old Adam in him sat up and took notice. They were alone, hubby was gone—why not. He stood by the fireplace, pretending to examine a picture. She sat down on the sofa opposite him. There was one of those pregnant silences. He tossed off his highball, wiped his lips, took a quick look at his watch, and started across the room for her.

She had struggled at first, quite violently, when he flung himself on top of her on the sofa. But he had her pinioned beneath him with the whole weight of his body. She could only twist her head away from him, half-burying it in one of the sofa pillows while he firmly deposited kisses on her neck and hair. Her resistance might have deterred him if he had not been drinking, but the liquor narrowed his purpose. He was much stronger than she was, besides being in good condition, and he did not let her little cries of protest irritate him as they once might have done. The slight impatience he felt with her was only for the time she was wasting. She wanted it, obviously, or she would not have asked him in. The angry squirming of her body, the twisting and turning of her head, filled him with amused tolerance and quickened his excitement as he crushed his member against her reluctant pelvis. He had no intention of raping her, and it injured him a little to feel how she pressed her thighs, which she had managed to cross, tightly together to protect the inner sanctum, when all he wanted, for the moment, was to hold her in his arms.

Her hair slipped from its pins, and he seized the long tress eagerly in his hands, pressing his mouth into it and inhaling deeply. From the sofa pillow came a muffled cry of disgust; when she turned her head, finally, to mutter "Stop," he planted kisses on her cheek and ear. Breathing in the fragrance of her hair, nuzzling in her neck, he grew almost worshipful and ceased to hold her securely. Seeing this, she at once scrambled over onto her stomach and lay taut, as if waiting. Encouraged, he sought the zipper on the side of her dress—women's clothes always bamboozled him—but she took advantage of his preoccupation to struggle up to a sitting position and began to push him away, with her small hands against his chest. She was wearing a high-necked black dress of thin wool; he could see her small, full breasts, like ripe pears, straining against the material, and he bent down to taste them through the wool. But she would not permit this; her hands sprang up, blocking his approach, as he bore her down again. He kissed her white neck and the hollow of her throat, but whenever he tried to reach her mouth, she turned her head away sharply.

He began to get the idea. The thing was to respect her scruples. She did not seem to mind if he kissed her arms and shoulders; it was her breasts and mouth she was protecting, out of some peculiar pedantry. And yet she was not really frightened. She did not scream or try to hit him or scratch him, as she might have, and he, on his side, did not try to raise her skirt. The struggle was taking place in almost complete silence, as if they were afraid of being overheard. There was only the sound of their breathing and an occasional muffled "Stop" from Martha. They made him think of a pair of wrestlers, heaving and gasping, while taking care to obey the rules. A string of beads she was wearing broke and clattered to the floor. "Sorry," he muttered as he dove for her left breast.

He heard Martha laugh faintly as she pushed his head away from her tit. The humor of it was beginning to dawn on her, evidently. She was too ironic a girl not to see that one screw, more or less, could not make much difference, when she had already laid it on the line for him about five hundred times. His hunger for her now, when he was so well fixed up at home, was a compliment, which she ought to accept lightly. This was the trouble with intelligent women; there was always an *esprit de serieux* lingering around the premises. They lacked a sense of proportion. But she was commencing to see it from his angle; her struggles were becoming more perfunctory. "You want it, say you want it," he mumbled in her ear. He was getting exasperated, foreseeing that he would be nervous during the act itself if she did not stop procrastinating.

She shook her disheveled head and wrenched away from him, but just then he found her back zipper. He tugged, and the steel moved on its tracks; the back of her dress fell open. He could feel her stiffen, as he moved his hand, carefully, under her slip, up and down her spine and over her smooth shoulder blades. He bent down to kiss her there, and she did not try to stop him; her back, apparently, was not covered by the ground rules. She lay almost torpid, and he ventured to try to pull her dress off the shoulders in front. "Don't," she cried sharply, as the material started to tear. She sat up in indignation, and his hand slipped in and held her breast cupped. "Take it off," he urged, speaking of her dress in a thick whisper. "I can't," she whispered back, as his other hand stole in and grasped her other breast. They began to argue in whispers. She mentioned Helen, the Coes, New Leeds, but not—and this was curious—her husband. "Please don't," she begged, with tears in her eyes, while he squeezed her nipples between his fingertips; they were hard before he touched them; her breath was coming quickly. She had caught his lower lip between her teeth, and there was a drawn look on her face, which meant that she was ready for it. "Stop, Miles, I beg you," she moaned, with a terrified air of throwing herself on his mercy. "It won't make any difference," he promised hoarsely. She shook her head, but as they were arguing, she let him slip her dress off her shoulders. He freed her breasts from her underslip and stared at them hungrily. Martha's eyes closed and she took a deep breath, like a doomed person. "All right," she said.

Glancing at her wrist watch, she got up and took her dress off and put it on a chair while he hastily undressed himself and turned off the lights. But to have allowed this interval was a mistake. Women were funny that way—give them time to think and the heat goes off, downstairs; he had often observed it. Now he found, once he had got well started, with her arms and legs where he wanted them, that she was no longer responding. She had a lot of will power and she had probably figured out, while she was undressing, that she would not "really" be unfaithful to Sinnott if she did not come to climax. Or else she had begun feeling remorseful. She was nice enough about it; she went through all the motions, trying to give him a good time. But he could not really rouse her, and it took the heart out of him. He regretted the whole business before he was halfway through. He detected that she was trying to hurry him, which made him stubborn, though he was colder than a witch's tit and anxious to get home. Her movements subsided; her limbs became inert. It occurred to him, with a start, that she was actually very drunk, though she had not showed it especially. Compunction smote him; he ought not to have done this, he said to himself tenderly. Tenderness inflamed his member. Clasping her fragile body brusquely to him, he thrust himself into her with short, quick strokes. A gasp of pain came from her, and it was over.

Source: McCarthy, 1954, pp. 199–203.

he offered to give her a ride home. She invited him in for a drink (see Box 6.3). Would you consider this seduction or rape? Why?

Last year, columnist Ellen Goodman (1991) offered her thoughts on date rape.

Two people leave the scene of a sexual encounter, one remembering pleasure, the other pain.

In the most often cited 1985 study of 6,000 college students, University of Arizona Professor Mary Koss found that over 25% of college women had experienced a completed or attempted rape since their 14th birthday. Four out of five of these encounters were with men they knew. But among college men, only 8% admitted to behavior that fit these definitions.

It isn't that the same 8% of the men are assaulting 25% of the women. Nor are they necessarily lying. The kernel of that research suggests, rather, that many men simply don't believe they have used force. Not really. Nor do they believe that the women have resisted. Not really.

In alleging date rape, Koss says, "The women reported that they had said 'no' forcefully and repeatedly. The men held out the possibility that 'no' meant 'yes.'

"The women considered the amount of force as moderately severe. The men, though they noticed a degree of resistance, believed it could be consistent with seduction. They believed women enjoyed being roughed up to a certain extent."

How is it possible that there is such a perceptual gap about "consent" for sex? It is, in part, the Gone-With-the-Wind fantasy: Scarlett O'Hara carried to bed kicking and screaming, only to wake up humming and singing. It is the bodice-ripping, Gothic novel, rock-and-rape cultural message. It is the ancient script of the mating game—he persists, she resists—that passes for "normal" sexual relationships. . . .

When date rape reaches the courtroom as it rarely does, says Koss, picking her words carefully, "The only way to convince a jury that his force went beyond the 'normal' male assertiveness in pursuing his sexual agenda, and that her resistance went beyond the 'normal' female reticence in the interest of protecting her purity or inexperience, is if she sustained a lot of injury."

Without such an injury, without a witness, we have only the two and opposing views of a man and a woman. Without a legal recourse, the hope lies on "crime-prevention" and that means closing the gap in sexual perceptions. (p. A22)

Researchers have begun to interview rapists, attempted rapists, and men who say they would rape women if they were assured they would not be caught, to find out what makes them tick. Surprisingly high percentages of men fall in these categories. For example, in a sample of American and Canadian college men (Briere & Malamuth, 1983), about 30% of men admitted they might be likely to rape if they could be assured that no one would ever know and they would not be punished. About 30% more said they would be likely to use force to coerce women into other sexual acts. (For example, such men might be willing to tell women that they would kill or beat them if they didn't cooperate; they might twist their arms or hold them down, to force reluctant women to kiss or pet.) About 40% of men said that they would be totally unwilling either to rape women or use force, whether they could be caught or not.

Researchers paint a consistent picture of such violent men. First, rapists, attempted rapists, and men who admit to a propensity to rape possess an ideology that makes it easy for them to justify violent behavior. Such men endorse "traditional" gender role stereotypes. They think of men and women as very different "species." Men are supposed to take what they want. They believe dating relationships are adversarial; it is necessary to be aggressive; that women secretly desire to be victimized; they deserve what they get. Rape-prone men accept rape myths. They endorse such items as: "It would do some women good to be raped." "A man's got to show a woman who's boss right from the start or he'll end up henpecked." "Being roughed up is sexually stimulating to most women." " 'Nice' women don't get raped." "Most charges of rape are unfounded," and "If a woman is going to be raped, she might as well relax and enjoy it." Such men have a callous attitude toward rape (Malamuth, 1984). "The victim is viewed, at best, as not acting responsibly in avoiding a potential rape situation, and at worse, provoking or actually desiring sexually aggressive actions" (Koss & Leonard, 1984, p. 223). Rape-prone men often suffer from character disorders: they are narcissistic and insensitive to others' feelings. They have little capacity for warmth, trust, compassion, or empathy (Groth & Birnbaum, 1979). They are not deterred by even the most forceful "No!" They are exquisitely aware of what *they* want; but they are oblivious to the woman's feelings. In *all* situations, sexual or not, they push relentlessly to get what they want (Calhoun, 1991).

Social scientists have also begun to study the victims of sexual coercion and violence. For example, Mary Koss and her colleagues (Koss, Dinero, Seibel, & Cox, 1988) surveyed more than 6000 college women. They found that 15% of the women had been sexually assaulted. [It is estimated that 26% of women are raped at some time in their lives (Russell & Howell, 1983).] To their surprise, the researchers found that more than half the assaults (53%) were "date rapes," perpetrated by steady or casual dates; only 11% of the assaults were committed by strangers (see Box 6.3). Fewer than 2% of the date rapes were reported to the police. Other researchers have found that 10% of married (or once-married) women reported that their husbands used threats and/or force to make them have sex. Many of the women had experienced repeated attacks. Fifty percent of them had been assaulted 20 or more times (Finkelhor & Yllo, 1985).

On rare occasions, men are raped. Various medical centers report that from 0 to 10% of the sexual assault victims they treat are men. Most of these men were assaulted by other men (Forman, 1982). Nonetheless, women sometimes pressure men into having sexual intercourse. Survey researchers found that 16% of college men reported that women pressured them into having sexual relations against their will. Most (52%) were pressured into submitting. (The men were afraid that they would be ridiculed or would look unmasculine if they refused.) Some of the men (38%), however, were simply physically forced to have sex (Struckman-Johnson, 1988).

Some lesbian and gay relationships involve sexual violence and coercion. Surveys find that 31% of lesbians and 12% of gay men were forced to have sex by their partners (Waterman, Dawson, & Bologna, 1989).

In his classic study, Menachem Amir (1971) found that all rapists use threats: They rely on intimidation, threats, and brandish knives or guns. Most rapists go even further; 85% of rapes involved physical force and violence. The attackers were rough; they pushed and held the victims (30% of the time), slapped them, and brutally beat them (pummeling them with their fists and kicking them) (22% of the time). The rapists choked many women into submission (12% of the time).

Victimized women were often forced to perform degrading and humiliating acts (84% of the time).

Lynda Holstrom and Ann Burgess (1980) studied 115 children, adolescents, and women who had been raped. Ninety-six percent of the children and women were forced to yield to vaginal intercourse; 5% to anal intercourse. Women were sometimes required to perform fellatio (22%) or cunnilingus (5%). They were made to dance in the nude, lick the rapist's anus, or to engage in homosexual activities while the rapist(s) watched. Some women reported that the rapists urinated on them, inserted objects into their vaginas, bit or burned their breasts, or ejaculated on them. It is not surprising then that women who have been raped often bear the psychological and physical scars of the attack all of their lives (Muehlenhard, Goggins, Jones, & Satterfield, 1991). Such accounts make it horribly clear that rape has more to do with power, anger and aggression, and contempt for women than with sexuality.

CONCLUSION

The accumulation of data jumps out at us with a battering consistency. Power has played and continues to constitute an enormous part of the human story of relationships (misnamed "love") and of sex. And in that long, sad story of power, men have had nearly all of it; women have had little.

Some scholars believe that *all* issues boil down to the question of power. Who has it? How has it been employed? They see power everywhere—in political and economic life, of course, but also in religion, literature, families, class, and increasingly in sex, marriage, and all relationships. Many feminists, among these scholars, contend that the ubiquitous power issue has been that of gender, and that all history has been pervaded by male power over women.

Whether or not they are right in all respects, the evidence of the prevalence and uses of power (particularly male power) in sex and relationships is overwhelming. It ranges from the horrors of violent rape and the insidious cultural conventions surrounding sex to the passive acceptance of centuries of customs and laws that have placed marital and familial power in the hands of men. Many women no doubt believed in these conventions as much as the men; many others probably felt—correctly—that they had no choice.

And now the power balance is changing, with the promise of more change ahead as women increasingly amass the modern key to power—money. In the last chapter we contended that *intimacy* was a new and fragile idea. In this chapter we have tried to demonstrate that *power* is an old idea, powerfully buttressed by religion, law, and centuries of custom. People often wonder whether or not the world is progressing. But we have suggested that a large element of the social revolution of our times is that intimacy and equality in relationships are forging a mighty challenge to the entrenched authority of power and inequality in relationships. If that is so, and if the challenge is maintained and developed, that would surely seem to be an instance of significant advance in the story of humankind.

Chapter
7

Emotional Problems

Drowning Girl by Roy Lichtenstein, 1963. Oil and synthetic polymer paint on canvas. 60¼ × 36¼″. Collection, The Museum of Modern Art, New York. Philip Johnson Fund

INTRODUCTION

Not everyone agrees that the uneven efforts toward enlarging the sphere of equality in relationships represents an advance for humanity. Traditionalists point at the modern problems that seem new to the realms of love, sex, and intimacy: divorces, broken families, the AIDS epidemic, and general permissiveness. They see in these and other developments a breakdown of order, the disintegration of that self-denial sought by religion and law, and an erosion of responsibility. While not sure of what or whom to blame, they believe that the authoritarian, hierarchical, patriarchal, and regulated world of the past was a better place than ours today.

We believe that all social transformation brings on new social problems for the bane and benefit of the world. We believe that some of the problems mentioned by the critics of modernity, individualism, and gender equality are not new and much of the past's "order" was often synonymous with repression. And we believe the miseries produced by the exercise of male power to gain absolute control over the realms of love and sex were greater than the unsettled state in which we find relationships today.

Nevertheless, "unsettled" does describe the state of love and sex in our times. We all find a host of problems afflicting love lives, and we propose to begin a systematic and utilitarian discussion of them with this chapter. We have tried to set the scene in the first six chapters by looking at the deep structures—psychological, biological, and historical—that undergird love relationships. Now we take a somewhat more specific and practical look at what it takes to make, break, and remake relationships.

We begin, in Chapters 7 to 9, by outlining the actual problems faced by couples. In the chapters that follow, we propose ways, based on research, psychotherapy, and general knowledge, for dealing with them. We divide the problems into three categories, though we are fully aware of the arbitrariness of such a division and the ways in which problems overlap. First, some issues are functions primarily of the *personal* and *individual* emotional difficulties experienced by one or both members of the couple. Second, there are issues that are functions primarily of *relational* dilemmas, and third come those that are functions primarily of the *external world* impinging on home and hearth.

On this latter point, we have in mind the utter havoc that can be visited on couples by war, death, poverty, immigration, persecution, and a flood of other horrors that, in fact, describe the reality for hundreds of millions of human beings and that can even invade the fragile sanctuaries of the middle classes throughout the world. This havoc has been the normal condition for most of our species for most of our history. It is well that we remind ourselves that the breakdown of our love affairs—which we often regard as deeply tragic—may be fairly trivial in the light of the disasters that can and do weigh so heavily on the lives of the majority of humankind.

Nonetheless, the fact remains that we *do* deeply care about our relationships, and we must take this caring seriously. We do tend, perhaps inevitably, to view our own individual lives as the universe's central drama. So let us begin by turning to the individual and personal issues that so powerfully can complicate any relationship. When many couples enter therapy, they often misidentify their problems. Many will say to us: "We have a communication problem." They assume that a few mastered communication tricks will lead to major improvements in their relationships.

Would that things were so easy. On a very few occasions, a handful of such hints can help. But almost always the reality turns out to be harder and more complex. The dream is this: If my partner understands the needs I am trying to communicate, love is all you need. Love will be sufficiently strong that my needs, now understood, will be granted. But shining a light on one person's needs often highlights how different are those of the partner. Soon we are dealing with two different personalities *truly* at odds over how to raise their children, how to deal with their parents and in-laws, how to create a mutually satisfying sexual life, how to handle money or deal with two different sets of friends or two different sets of interests, values, hopes, and fears.

An even harder dilemma occurs when one, or both, of the partners has a serious personal, individual problem: alcoholism, drug addiction, poor health, or any of a set of emotional problems. In those cases, we frequently have to work on those latter emotional problems (we refer addicts, alcoholics, and the physically ill to the proper specialists) before we have a ghost of a chance of making any inroads on the love issues. If, for instance, one of the duo (or family) suffers from depression, or experiences lots of off-the-wall anxiety, or continually goes into rages, those problems must be addressed before much headway can be made on "communication problems."

Luckily, in most areas of individual emotional problems—specifically depression, anxiety, and anger—fine research has been done. In this chapter, we attempt to describe some of the recent ground-breaking research on emotional disorders that threaten love relationships. When such problems exist, they must be addressed before relational or social problems can be tackled. So, on to anxiety, anger, and depression—beginning with depression. A note: We use the word "marriage" as a shorthand for all arrangements, homosexual as well as heterosexual, in which individuals live together and feel committed to one another in ways recognizable as wedlock—even if paperless.

Depression is a howling tempest in the brain.
          —William Styron

DEPRESSION

Depression is an age-old problem. The Old Testament recounted Job's and Saul's depressions. Today, in the United States, 10 to 14 million people suffer from depression (Gallagher, 1986). When couples come in for marital counseling, one of the duo—more than 50% of the time—is depressed (Beach, Jouriles, & O'Leary, 1985; Weissman, 1987). Similarly, half of depressed women suffer marital problems (Rounsaville, Weissman, Prusoff, & Herceg-Baron, 1979a, b).

Two-thirds of depressed Americans are beset by *unipolar* depression. (They possess low self-esteem, experience debilitating sadness, and have difficulty performing even the simplest of tasks.) In his memoir, *Darkness Visible,* novelist William Styron (1990) portrayed the feelings associated with a deep unipolar depression:

> The loss of self-esteem is a celebrated symptom, and my own sense of self had all but disappeared, along with any self-reliance. This loss can quickly degenerate into dependence, and from dependence into infantile dread. One dreads the loss of all things, all people close and dear. There is an acute fear of abandonment. Being alone in the house, even for a moment, caused me exquisite panic and trepidation. (pp. 56–57)
>
>   In depression this faith in deliverance, in ultimate restoration, is absent. The pain

is unrelenting, and what makes the condition intolerable is the foreknowledge that no remedy will come—not in a day, an hour, a month, or a minute. If there is mild relief, one knows that it is only temporary; more pain will follow. It is hopelessness even more than pain that crushes the soul. So the decision-making of daily life involves not, as in normal affairs, shifting from one annoying situation to another less annoying—or from discomfort to relative comfort, or from boredom to activity—but moving from pain to pain. . . .

That December evening, for example, I could have remained in bed as usual during those worst hours, or agreed to the dinner party my wife had arranged downstairs. But the very idea of a decision was academic. Either course was torture, and I chose the dinner not out of any particular merit but through indifference to what I knew would be indistinguishable ordeals of fogbound horror. At dinner I was barely able to speak, but the quartet of guests, who were all good friends, were aware of my condition and politely ignored my catatonic muteness. Then, after dinner, sitting in the living room, I experienced a curious inner convulsion that I can describe only as despair beyond despair. It came out of the cold night; I did not think such anguish possible. (pp. 62–63)

The rest suffer from *bipolar* depression. In this form of depression, manic periods (in which people feel joyous, powerful, and feverishly excited) alternate with periods of black, devastating misery. Novelist Virginia Woolf (1953), who was probably a manic–depressive, recorded those feelings in her diary shortly before she committed suicide:

Lord how I suffer! What a terrific capacity I possess for feeling with intensity—now, since we came back, I'm screwed up into a ball; can't get into step; can't make things dance; feel awfully detached; see young; feel old; no that's not quite it: wonder how a year or so perhaps is to be endured. Think, yet people do live; can't imagine what goes on behind faces. All is surface hard; myself only an organ that takes blows, one after another; the horror of the hard raddled faces in the flower show yesterday: the inane pointlessness of all this existence: hatred of my own brainlessness and indecision; the old treadmill feeling, of going on and on and on, for no reason: Lytton's death; Carrington's; a longing to speak to him; all that cut away, gone . . . Rodmell spoilt; all England spoilt. . . .

A saying of Leonard's [her husband] comes into my head in this season of complete inanity and boredom. "Things have gone wrong somehow." (p. 171)

(We consider a third kind of depression, anxious depression, in the next section.)

He was down so often that he had a dozen words for it: cafard, the megrims, depresh, the blues, low again.
    —Susan Cheever, describing the depression of her father, John Cheever

Diagnosing Depression

It is easy to diagnose depression. Clinicians have developed a number of scales to do so. Table 7.1 is a list of the symptoms of depression according to the National Institute of Mental Health (1992).

Depression is a contagious disease.
    —Anonymous

Table 7.1   SYMPTOMS OF DEPRESSION

Not everyone who is depressed experiences every symptom. Some people experience a few
  symptoms, some many. Also, severity of symptoms varies with individuals.

Persistent sad, anxious, or "empty" mood
Feelings of hopelessness, pessimism
Feelings of guilt, worthlessness, helplessness
Loss of interest or pleasure in hobbies and activities that you once enjoyed, including sex
Insomnia, early-morning awakening, or oversleeping
Appetite and/or weight loss or overeating and weight gain
Decreased energy, fatigue, being "slowed down"
Thoughts of death or suicide, suicide attempts
Restlessness, irritability
Difficulty concentrating, remembering, making decisions
Persistent physical symptoms that do not respond to treatment, such as headaches, digestive
  disorders, and chronic pain

(The higher the score, the more depressed the person is assumed to be.)

Source: National Institute of Mental Health, 1992, p. 2.

There are other ways, of course, to diagnose depression. Therapists (as well
as husbands, wives, friends, and family members) can generally tell when others
are depressed by observing how *they* feel when they are in the company of the
unhappy. Depression, like other emotions, seems to be contagious. [See Hatfield,
Cacioppo, and Rapson (1992) and Hatfield et al. (in press) for a discussion of this
process.] Depressives may try to put a bright face on things, but they signal their
despair in a hundred little ways—by the anguished expressions that flicker across
their faces, in their hopeless, endless recitals of boring facts, in their morose voices,
or dejected postures. Therapists and others may not be able to say how they know
something is wrong, but they do. It is depressing to live with a depressed person.
Researchers find that if college students are assigned to live with a mildly depressed roommate, they get increasingly depressed themselves as time passes
(Howes, Hokanson, & Lowenstein, 1985).

Never eat at a place called Mom's. Never play cards with a man named Doc.
And never lie down with a woman who's got more troubles than you.
                                                                    —Nelson Algren

What Causes Depression?

Depression may be caused by biological factors or precipitated by life events. Both
factors usually contribute to the disease. Let us consider a sampling of the most
popular theories of the etiology of depression.

There is no vulture like despair.
    —George Granville

Genetic Models of Depression Theorists have long observed that certain people are genetically predisposed to depression. Sir Richard Burton (1621/1927), in *The Anatomy of Melancholy*, noted that the "inbred cause of melancholy is our temperature, in whole or part, which we receive from our parents" (p. 184). Today, medical researchers have found that he is right (Kendler, Heath, Martin, & Eaves, 1987; Nurnberger & Gershorn, 1982). Medical sociologist Janice Egeland and her colleagues (1987) studied the Old Order Amish of Lancaster County, Pennsylvania. In such an ultraconservative religious group, people who are manic–depressives stand out. The Amish explanation for their peculiar behavior, *"Siss im blut"*—"it is in the blood"—seems to have some validity. The sociologists chose to study the Amish for a variety of reasons. The Amish have a tradition of marital fidelity. Thirty Amish pioneers came to America during the early eighteenth century; all 12,000 of their descendants are still living in the Lancaster community. Best of all, the community keeps unusually detailed handwritten genetic records. To track the genetic transmission of depression, the authors examined records and conducted psychiatric interviews with family members who were still living. They also obtained blood samples from each of them. They found that the major depressive disorders are biologically transmitted; they even identified the chromosome on which this defect is located. If parents have this genetic anomaly, they have a 50–50 chance of passing it on to their children. If their children inherit this anomaly, they have a 63% chance of developing depression.

Biological Models of Depression Thoughts, feelings, and behavior affect our body chemistry. They, in turn, can be radically altered by minute chemical changes in the brain. Researchers believe that in depression the neurotransmitters norepinephrine and serotonin (and possibly dopamine) are in short supply. [Neurotransmitters are chemicals that help speed messages (over the neurons) from one part of the brain to another.] Such shortages have profound effects (Beach et al., 1990).

The mass of men lead lives of quiet desperation.
  —Henry David Thoreau

Cognitive–Behavioral Models of Depression Some theorists have argued that the way depressives think undergirds the disorder. Aaron Beck (1967) contended that depressives have problems in the way they have learned to view themselves, their world, and their futures. They see themselves as deficient and unworthy, the world as frustrating and unfulfilling, and their futures as hopeless. For example, we once treated a depressed woman who struck the people around her as lively and happy. The world saw the feisty, articulate, witty attorney dealing confidently with her career and friends; they did not see her at home. She was trying single-handedly (though married) to keep house, raise her 18-month-old son, and conduct a full-time corporate law practice. Her husband, an advertising executive, was a high-strung man, who got extremely angry at any disturbance to his daily routine. At the slightest irritation he would lash out at his wife. One day their toddler got sick while our client was defending one of her clients in court and hence could not be reached. He accused her of being an unnatural, unfeeling mother. Yet, when the bills began to pile up, he criticized her for not investing more in her career. He accused her of being a "free-loader" who couldn't pull her weight. Surprisingly, this woman, who was so quick and brazen in court, was a pushover at home. She responded to each of his attacks by docilely accepting his criticism and berating herself for being so stupid. She continually resolved to do better next time. And she sank into the pits of depression.

Cognitive–behavioral therapists try to replace clients' self-defeating ideas with more constructive ways of thinking. First, patients are told to monitor carefully and record their automatic, negative thoughts. (A running critique is typical: "You are a terrible mother. You should be spending more time with your child." Or, "You are a terrible lawyer. You should be spending more time at work." "Selfish, selfish.") No matter which way our attorney-client turned, she saw herself as selfish and a failure.

Therapists can then try to help clients to quit playing and replaying old tapes and to think about things a bit more reasonably and realistically. In the case of this client, she had adopted thought patterns that made failure inevitable and had developed a strategy of short-term appeasement that actually rewarded her husband for attacking her. When her husband attacked her, she inevitably responded by apologizing, criticizing herself, and attempting to appease him. We insisted that they sit down when things were going well and forge an agreement as to just how much time they would each spend on household tasks, child care, and work, and to revise the definitions of "success" and "failure." If her husband started to rant and rave, that was a signal for her to offer some reminders to herself, when the inevitable disasters struck. "Slow down. He is just angry. You are doing exactly what the two of you agreed. Hooray for staying so calm. Shame on him for yelling at you." Essentially, she had learned to replace self-critical thoughts with self-nurturing ones. In time, when faced with her calm but unrelenting reaction, her husband learned that when he felt extremely anxious, he'd better go jog. He was not going to get away with attacking her and redefining reality. In time, she learned to appraise with coolness a situation before responding to anyone's criticism . . . and to hire a full-time housekeeper! Part of Beck's cognitive–behavioral therapy, then, is simply teaching people how the world works.

There are two tragedies in life. One is not to get your heart's desire. The other is to get it.

—*George Bernard Shaw*

Behavioral Models of Depression Other theorists argue that moods depend on the amount of social reward or punishment they receive (Lewinsohn, 1986; Staats & Heiby, 1985). For instance, Peter Lewinsohn and his colleagues (Lewinsohn, Hoberman, Terri, & Hautzinger, 1985) observed that the depressed often have relatively pleasureless lives. There are a variety of reasons why this is so. Some depressives lack social skills. Family and friends may "reward" their self-pity and suffering; others are generally less kind. The depressed are often buffeted by painful life events. For example, Peter Lewinsohn and Joseph Talkington (1979) developed the *Unpleasant Events Schedule,* which asks how often a series of disasters (accidents, school failures, sexual rejections, financial losses, and the like) have happened in the past 30 days. As you might expect, the depressed have unusually miserable lives. It is not surprising that they finally give up. To turn things around, Lewinsohn teaches clients a package of skills—including daily planning, time management, and relaxation techniques. He also prods them into seeking pleasant experiences and figuring how to sweeten or avoid negative ones. Such techniques are extremely effective in reducing depression (Heiby, 1979).

In marriage they legitimized despair.
  —*Lawrence Durrell*

Interpersonal Models of Depression   The *Marital Discord Model of Depression* proposes that happy, stable, love relationships protect couples from depression, while unhappy relationships increase their risk of suffering a major depressive episode (Beach, Arias, & O'Leary, 1987). If couples are unhappily married, their risk of falling prey to depression increases 25 times the normal rates of depression (Weissman, 1987). Of course, once men and women are depressed, their marital problems increase (Beach et al., 1990).

Steven Beach and his colleagues (1990) have identified some of the main ways in which happy or unhappy marriages protect couples or leave them vulnerable to depression (see Figure 7.1). As you can see, in a happy marriage couples provide love, sex, and intimacy as well as practical assistance for one another. This increases their resistance to depression. In unhappy marriages, on the other hand, constant criticism, angry exchanges, physical violence, and the disruption of lives increase vulnerability to depression.

Other therapists have proposed yet other theories of depression (Abramson,

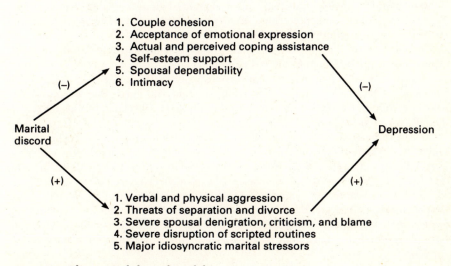

Figure 7.1 The marital discord model.

Seligman, & Teasdale, 1986; Freud, 1917/1959). Luckily, psychiatrists and psychologists are very effective in treating depression, regardless of whether it has a genetic, biological, or interpersonal basis. Therapists may use either psychotherapy, drugs, or both. Both psychotherapy and drugs seem to be equally effective; both succeed with 60 to 80% of depressed patients (Rosenfeld, 1985).

The mean reds are horrible. You're afraid and you sweat like hell, but you don't know what you're afraid of. Except something bad is going to happen, only you don't know what it is.

> —*Truman Capote:* Breakfast at Tiffany's

ANXIETY

When people are anxious, sometimes they become obsessed. They brood over what might happen, what could happen. Here, a man suffering from an anxiety disorder (an obsessive compulsive disorder) made vivid his thoughts and behavior:

I'm driving down the highway doing 55 MPH. I'm on my way to take a final exam. My seat belt is buckled and I'm vigilantly following all the rules of the road. No one is on the highway—not a living soul. . . .

While in reality no one is on the road, I'm intruded with the heinous thought that I might have hit someone . . . a human being! God knows where such a fantasy comes from.

I think about this for a second and then say to myself, "That's ridiculous. I didn't hit anybody." Nonetheless, a gnawing anxiety is born. . . .

I reason, "Well, if I hit someone while driving, I would have *felt* it." This brief trip into reality helps the pain dissipate . . . but only for a second. Why? Because the gnawing anxiety that I really did commit the illusionary accident is growing larger—so is the pain.

The pain is a terrible guilt that I have committed an unthinkable, negligent act. At one level, I know this is ridiculous, but there's a terrible pain in my stomach telling me something quite different.

Again, I try putting to rest this insane thought and that ugly feeling of guilt. "Come on," I think to myself, "this is *really* insane!"

But the awful feeling persists. The anxious pain says to me *"You Really Did Hit Someone."* The attack is now in full control. Reality no longer has meaning. My sensory system is distorted. I have to get rid of the pain. Checking out this fantasy is the only way I know how.

I start ruminating, "Maybe I did hit someone and didn't realize it . . . Oh my God! I might have killed somebody! I have to go back and check." Checking is the only way to calm the anxiety. It brings me closer to truth somehow. I can't live with the thought that I actually may have killed someone—I have to check it out.

Now I'm sweating . . . literally. I pray this outrageous act of negligence never happened. My fantasies run wild. I desperately hope the jury will be merciful. I'm particularly concerned about whether my parents will be understanding. After all, I'm now a criminal. I must control the anxiety. I am checking it out. Did it really happen? . . .

I've driven five miles farther down the road since the attack's onset. I turn the car around and head back to the scene of the mythical mishap. I return to the spot on the road where I "think" it "might" have occurred. Naturally, nothing is there. No police car and no bloodied body. Relieved, I turn around again to get to my exam on time.

Feeling better, I drive for about twenty seconds and then the lingering thoughts and pain start gnawing away again. Only this time they're even more intense. I think, "Maybe I should have pulled *off* the road and checked the side brush where the injured body was thrown and now lies? Maybe I didn't go *far enough* back on the road and the accident occurred a mile further back." (Rapoport, 1989, pp. 21–23)

He checks again, but of course that doesn't end it. He quickly realizes that he didn't get out of the car and look on the side of the road. He checks again. Perhaps he didn't look thoroughly enough. He checks. Then he worries that perhaps the police already came by and cleared the body off the side of the road . . . and so on and on and on.

Few people, of course, experience such unrelenting anxiety. Few have such debilitating obsessions or compulsions. Yet most of us can recognize in our own anxious thoughts a pale reflection of his ruminations. Not surprisingly, such anxiety, especially when it is shared, often drives those we love crazy.

The little habits people possess to deal with *their* anxiety—drumming on the table, scratching their heads, cracking their knuckles, jiggling the keys in their pocket, eventually drive those they love wild.

Some people try to control their own "twitchy" anxiety by controlling others. They criticize the way we make ice cubes. They snatch pancake flippers out of our hands to instruct us angrily on just the right action to produce the right kind of flip. They point out the fact that the glasses aren't quite in an even line in the cupboard. Not surprisingly, their families for some strange reason seem to resent their busybody ways. Novelist Philip Roth (1991), in *Patrimony*, recounted how his 86-year-old father attempted to deal with his own anxiety and fears (about an impending life-threatening operating) by supervising every move of his girlfriend, the ever patient Lil.

Lil was apparently using the manual opener screwed to the wall beside the sink, because I heard my father telling her, "Hold the can from the bottom. You're not holding it from the bottom."

"I know how to open a can of soup," she said.

"But you're not holding it right."

"Herman, let me be. I *am* holding it right."

"Why can't you just do what I ask you when I ask you? It *isn't* right. Hold it from the *bottom.*"

And from the other room I [Philip Roth] had all I could do not to shout, "You're on the brink of a catastrophe, you idiot—let her open the can any fucking way she wants!" though I was also telling myself, "Of course. How to open a soup can. What else is there to think about? What else is there that matters? This is what's kept him going for eighty-six years and what, if anything, is going to get him through now. Hold it from the bottom, Lil—he knows what he's saying."

Admittedly, he went overboard about how she was heating up—or failing to heat up—the soup. After setting our three places at the table, he returned to the kitchenette and stood next to her over the saucepan. She kept insisting the soup wasn't hot yet and he kept insisting it had to be—it didn't take all day to heat up a can of vegetable soup. This exchange was repeated four times, until his patience—if that is the word—ran out and he pulled the pot off the burner and, leaving Lil empty-handed at the stove, came into the dining room and poured the soup into the bowls and onto the place mats and over the table. Maybe because of his bad eyes, he didn't see the extent of the mess he'd made.

   The soup was cold. Nobody said so. He probably didn't even notice. (pp. 117–118)

   Roth's father was not without an answer to his son's insistence that he should "back off." In the following letter, his father maintained that if you love people, when they do something wrong, family members should just "hock" them and hock them and hock them until they come to their senses. (Roth defines hock as "a Yiddishism that in this context means to badger, to bludgeon, to hammer with warnings and edicts and pleas—in short, to drill a hole in somebody's head with words" (Roth, 1991, p. 80). His father's letter is given in Box 7.1.

   We see the suffering undergone by anxious people. Those who are loved (and "hocked") by those anxious folk suffer at least as much.

Diagnosing Anxiety

Anxiety is quite prevalent. Approximately 10 million Americans (4% of the population) develop an anxiety disorder at some time in their lives (Kidman, 1989). Anxiety is also easy to diagnose. Once again, let us turn to Virginia Woolf's (1953) *A Writer's Diary,* in which she detailed a panic attack.

   Wednesday, August 17th. Shall I then describe how I fainted again? That is, the galloping hooves got wild in my head last Thursday night as I sat on the terrace with L. How cool it is after the heat! We were watching the downs draw back into fine darkness after they had burnt like solid emerald all day. . . . Then my heart leapt: and stopped: and leapt again: and I tasted that queer bitterness at the back of my throat; and the pulse leapt into my head and beat and beat, more savagely, more quickly. I am going to faint, I said, and slipped off my chair and lay on the grass. Oh no, I was not unconscious. I was alive: but possessed with this struggling team in my head: galloping, pounding. I thought, something will burst in my brain if this goes on. Slowly it muffled itself up and staggered, with what infinite difficulty and alarm, now truly fainting and seeing the garden painfully lengthened and distorted, back, back, back— how long it seemed—could I drag myself?—to the house: and gained my room and fell on my bed. Then pain, as of childbirth; and then that too slowly faded; and I lay presiding, like a flickering light, like a most solicitous mother, over the shattered splintered fragments of my body. (p. 185)

   Today, the most frequently used measure of anxiety is the *State–Trait Anxiety Inventory* (Spielberger et al., 1970) The STAI distinguishes between state anxiety (how people happen to feel at the moment) and trait anxiety (how they usually feel). We are all anxious and frightened sometime or other. Most people can take such momentary blips of anxiety in stride. It is trait anxiety that wreaks the most

Box 7.1   A LETTER FROM "ONE WHO CARES" ENOUGH TO "HOCK"

Dear Sandy [Philip Roth's brother].

I think there are two type's of (among people) Philosophies. People who care, and those that dont, People who *do* and people who Procrastinate and never *do* or *help*.

I came home from the office and did not feel well, you and Phil were very young. Mother made dinner. I did not sit down to eat, instead I went into the liveing room. Within the hour Dr. Weiss was in the house, mother called him. This was the scenario, he asked me what was wrong. I told him, I had a pain over my heart, after examination, he told me he could not detect anything wrong with me. He then asked me what I did in excess. I told him the only thing I could think of I smoke a lot, He said how about cutting it down to three instead of 24 a day. I said why not none and within the week my pain disappeared I cut out smokeing completely. *Mother cared, Dr. Weiss advised, I listened,* There are many advisers in this world, also people who *care* and *do*, and people who listen. In many instances lives are safed, and there are also overindulgers, those who smoke to much and drink to much, take drugs, and also are impulsive eaters. In each case all these conditions can cause sickness and sometimes even worse.

You wanted a house. I went at once and got you the money to buy it. Why? because I cared. Phil needed an operation for Hernia, I took him to the Dr. and he was operated on. Same with mother after she suffered for 27 years./ Why because I cared and I am a doer. Did her parentss care, I guess so, but I felt the pain of both and did, *I did not procrastinate*. I tell Jon and *hock him*. I use all kinds of Cliches, 'Like,' a fool and his money are soon parted) (A Penny saved is a penny earned) (someday there will be an old man dependent on you." and when he asked who, I tell him its you." etc I don't tell him once, I keep telling or Hocking, why, because he forgets, like a compulsive drinker, or drug taker, etc. Why do I continue, hocking? I realize its a pain in the ass, but if its people I *care for* I will try to cure, even if they object or wont diceplin disaplin themselves I including myselve. I have many battles with my conscience, but I fight my wronge thoughts. *I care*, for people in *my way*.

Please excuse the spelling and writing. I was never a good writer but now its worse, I don't *see so good*
The Hocker, Misnomer
it should be the carer
Love
  Dad.
I will always continue to
Hock and Care. Thats me
to people I care
      for

Source: Roth, 1991, p. 80.

havoc on relationships. The trait anxiety measure has 16 items, which look something like this (Carlson & Hatfield, 1992, pp. 233–234):

A TYPICAL MEASURE OF TRAIT ANXIETY

Directions: A number of statements which people have used to describe themselves are given below. Read each statement and then circle the appropriate number to the right of the statement to indicate how you *generally* feel.

Key

1 = Almost never
2 = Sometimes
3 = Often
4 = Almost always

1. I feel like crying.	1	2	3	4
*2. I feel rested.	1	2	3	4
*3. I am "calm, cool, and collected."	1	2	3	4
4. I feel that difficulties are piling up so that I cannot overcome them.	1	2	3	4
5. I lack self-confidence.	1	2	3	4

---

*Scored in reverse direction. (A high score signals high anxiety.)

People can usually guess when others are anxious. Anxiety simply shoots out. For example, when mob boss Frank Costello was forced to testify before the Kefauver Senate crime committee, he tried to look cool, but his hands tapped out his anxiety (Gould, 1951, p. 1):

> As he [Costello] sparred with Rudolph Halley, the committee's counsel, the movement of his fingers told their own emotional story. When the questions got rough, Costello crumpled a handkerchief in his hands. Or he rubbed his palms together. Or he interlaced his fingers. Or he grasped a half filled glass of water. Or he beat a silent tattoo on the table top. Or he rolled a little ball of paper between his thumb and index finger. Or he stroked the side piece of his glasses lying on the table. His was video's first ballet of the hands.

Researchers find that conversations between men and women are more frequently punctuated by quick, jerky, nervous gestures than are conversations between two men or two women (Sechrest, 1965). The anxious jiggle their legs and scratch their heads (Sechrest & Flores, 1971).

What Causes Anxiety?

Anxiety (like depression) may be triggered by genetic or biological factors or by anxiety-producing life events.

Genetic and Biological Models of Anxiety   People can inherit a tendency to be anxious. Researchers have found, for example, that even if identical twins are reared apart, they are more similar in how much anxiety they experience day-to-day than are fraternal twins, who are less similar genetically (Loehlin, 1989; Smith, 1991; Tellegen, Dykken, Bouchard, Wilcox, Segal, & Rich, 1988).

Cognitive Models of Anxiety   Cognitive-learning theorists such as Aaron Beck and his colleagues (Beck, Emery, & Greenburg, 1985) and Donald Meichenbaum (1977) have speculated that expectations play a critical role in the development of anxiety. The anxious, for instance, overestimate the dangers of life (Beck et al., 1985) ("Watch out, someone will push you onto the subway tracks if you stand too close to the edge.") They exaggerate the severity of feared events ("If I make a fool of myself at this party, my life will be ruined"). They underestimate their own coping abilities and the willingness of others to assist them. Clinicians who take a cognitive–behavioral approach try to instill a more realistic view of the world in patients.

When you arrive at a fork in the road, take it.
                                   —Yogi Berra

Behavioral Models of Anxiety   Many couples are anxious because they have allowed their lives to spin out of control. They are trying to cope with too many major stressors and minor hassles.

Major Stressors   Major life events, from infancy to death, place pressures on our minds and bodies. They force couples to make significant changes in their lives. Psychiatrists Thomas Holmes and Richard Rahe (1967) developed the *Social Readjustment Rating Scale* (SRRS) (see Table 7.2). How stressed are you? Look through the SRRS and check off the events that you have been forced to confront within the past year. (To calculate a final score, simply add up the points associated with those events. A score of 300 indicates that life has placed you under "high stress." Some critics have wondered if this scale needs to be updated. One might argue, for example, it is less upsetting to divorce than to go to jail! For some, marriage is a jail sentence; divorce the release from confinement.)

Life's "Hassles"   Our lives are shaped not only by big dramatic events. The little day-to-day happenings forge, sustain, and trouble us and the irritating hassles frequently drive us nuts. For this reason, Richard Lazarus and his colleagues (Kanner, Coyne, Schaeffer, & Lazarus, 1981) developed two scales—the uplifts scale and the hassles scale. Daily *uplifts* are positive emotional experiences: the joy of love, relief at hearing good news, the pleasure of a night's rest, and so forth. *Hassles* are the irritating, frustrating, and distressing events that blight our days (Kanner et al., 1981). The hassles scale asks people if they have encountered any of 117 possible annoyances recently. Some items from this scale are reproduced in Table 7.3.

Table 7.2 THE SOCIAL READJUSTMENT RATING SCALE

Rank	Life event	Score
1	Death of spouse	100
2	Divorce	73
3	Marital separation	65
4	Jail term	63
5	Death of close family member	63
6	Personal injury or illness	53
7	Marriage	50
8	Fired at work	47
9	Marital reconciliation	45
10	Retirement	45
11	Change in health of family member	44
12	Pregnancy	40
13	Sex difficulties	39
14	Gain of a new family member	39
15	Business readjustment	39
16	Change in financial state	38
17	Death of close friend	37
18	Change to different line of work	36
19	Change in number of arguments with spouse	35
20	Mortgage over $10,000	31
21	Foreclosure of mortgage or loan	30
22	Change in responsibilities at work	29
23	Son or daughter leaving home	29
24	Trouble with in-laws	29
25	Outstanding personal achievement	28
26	Wife begin or stop work	26
27	Begin or end school	26
28	Change in living conditions	25
29	Revision of personal habits	24
30	Trouble with boss	23
31	Change in work hours or conditions	20
32	Change in residence	20
33	Change in schools	20
34	Change in recreation	19
35	Change in church activities	19
36	Change in social activities	18
37	Mortgage or loan less than $10,000	17
38	Change in sleeping habits	16
39	Change in number of family get-togethers	15
40	Change in eating habits	15
41	Vacation	13
42	Christmas	12
43	Minor violations of the law	11

Source: Holmes & Rahe, 1967, p. 216.

Table 7.3   THE HASSLES SCALE

Directions: Hassles are irritants that can range from minor annoyances to fairly major pressures, problems, or difficulties. They can occur few or many times.

   Listed are a number of ways in which a person can feel hassled. First, circle the hassles that have happened to you *in the past month.* Then look at the numbers on the right of the item you circled. Indicate by circling a 1, 2, or 3 how SEVERE each of the *circled* hassles has been for you in the past month. If a hassle did not occur in the last month do NOT circle it.

Severity

1 = Somewhat severe
2 = Moderately severe
3 = Extremely severe

1.	Misplacing or losing things	1 2 3
2.	Inconsiderate smokers	1 2 3
3.	Concerns about owing money	1 2 3
4.	Too many responsibilities	1 2 3
5.	Problems getting along with fellow workers	1 2 3
6.	Laid off or out of work	1 2 3
7.	Having to wait	1 2 3
8.	Inability to express yourself	1 2 3
9.	Too many meetings	1 2 3

The higher the score, the greater the hassle.

Source: Kanner et al., 1981, pp. 24–30.

Dealing with Anxiety, Stressors, and Hassles   Individuals can use a variety of techniques to tame anxiety. Often the anxious become calm and cool (and less anxious) if they become aware of the rhythm that suits them best . . . and redesign their lives to fit their temperaments. Some people thrive on excitement. (In fact, they may get depressed if things are too tame.) But many people get shell-shocked if they try to take on too much. They can spend some time with people, working, confronting the hurly-burly of life, but soon they have had enough. When they reach that point, they do best if they can go home, read, work on their computers, bathe, or simply stare at the ceiling. They may also practice meditation or relaxation techniques or exercise.

   Couples have a special problem, of course, if they are mismatched. If one of them is trapped at home all day, bored, longing for a bit of excitement while the other comes home after a long, overwhelming day, longing for a little peace and tranquility, they are bound to clash. It helps some if the couple merely understands the nature of the problem. It helps even more if they resolve to devise a permanent solution to the problem, brainstorming some way to ensure that both of them have a balanced life that fits *each* of their temperaments.

ANGER AND VIOLENCE

Defining Anger

Joel Davitz (1969) asked men and women to describe what they felt like when they were angry. Their reactions are shown in Table 7.4. (The percentage of people checking each statement is indicated in parentheses.)

When we want to read of the deeds that are done for love, whither do we turn: To the murder column.
> —*George Bernard Shaw*

It is easy to spot the telltale symptoms of anger. In the following, the fiction writer Margaret Drabble (1972) vividly evoked the long slow buildup of anger that is released suddenly and explosively.

> It was after midnight before the Houghtons and the Simpsons left. Having resented their presence during most of the evening, he found himself dreading their departure, knowing that he would have trouble he was allowed to go to bed. And so he did, for Julie, once the door had closed upon them, turned upon him with an anger that had four and a half hours to gather and thicken, and which had been not at all assuaged by her original hostilities when he had first entered. He had seen the storm signs during dinner, hung as clearly as a black cone by a bad sea: the violent way she had slopped his chicken onto his plate, the over-forceful way with which she had put that same plate down on the table before him, the way she had pulled her chair sharply to one side when he crossed behind her to get the corkscrew, the noises she made in her throat—sighings, clickings, dismissals—whenever he opened his own mouth. She had not looked at him once during the meal, nor addressed one remark to him indirectly; she had been biding her time: and now she let him have it, all of it, trembling with rage as she denounced his cruelty, his rudeness, his inadequacies as husband and father, his dullness as companion and host and guest. She went back over the whole of their past, raking up ten-year-old offences, divining in their pattern a deliberate plot of destruc-

---

Table 7.4 WHAT ANGER FEELS LIKE

My blood pressure goes up (72%)

My pulse quickens (56%)

I feel that I'll burst or explode; as if there is too much inside to be held in (48%)

My fists are clenched (52%)

There is a narrowing of my senses, my attention becomes riveted on one thing (52%)

There is an impulse to strike out, to pound, or smash, or kick, or bite; to do something that will hurt (50%)

I want to strike out, explode, but I hold back, control myself (46%)

I want to say something nasty, something that will hurt someone (42%)

I'm easily irritated, ready to snap (64%)

My teeth are clenched (52%)

My whole body is tense (60%)

I seem to be caught up and overwhelmed by the feeling (64%)

I keep thinking about what happened over and over again (44%)

Source: Davitz, 1969, pp. 35–36.

tion, ending up, as so often, yelling at him, her face discoloured with emotion, her hair damp and oddly flying from her face in strange directions. (p. 173)

The Buss–Durkee Inventory, named after its developers, Arnold Buss and Ann Durkee (Buss, 1961), nicely measures hostile/aggressive behaviors. Buss argued that men and women can express angry feelings in a variety of ways.

1. *Resentment:* jealousy and hatred of others. A feeling of anger at the world over real or fancied mistreatment.
2. *Irritability:* a readiness to explode at the slightest provocation. This includes quick temper, grouchiness, exasperation, and rudeness.
3. *Suspicion:* attributing ones' own hostility to others. This varies from merely being wary of people to being convinced that others are trying to humiliate and harm one.
4. *Negativism:* oppositional behavior, usually directed against authority. This involves a refusal to cooperate that may vary from passive noncompliance to open rebellion against rules or conventions.
5. *Verbal aggression:* negative affect expressed in both the style and content of speech. Style includes arguing, shouting, and screaming; content includes threats, curses, and being overcritical.
6. *Indirect aggression:* both roundabout and undirected aggression. Roundabout aggression includes malicious gossip or practical jokes. Undirected aggression is expressed against no one in particular and includes temper tantrums and slamming doors.
7. *Assault:* physical violence against others. This includes getting into fights.

You might be interested to see how you would score on some items from the Buss–Durkee Inventory (see Box 7.2). Respondents are given one point for each true answer. The higher the score, the more hostile/aggressive they are assumed to be.

The Roots of Anger

Social scientists know a great deal about the nature of anger. They know who is most likely to make us angry, what enrages us, how we react when we're furious (with violence or with restraint), and why we act that way.

Sometimes I wish I could fall in love. Then at least you know who your opponent is.
—Peter Ustinov

Marriage is the triumph of habit over hate.
—Oscar Levant

Who Incites Anger?   Most people get angry anywhere from several times a day to several times a week (Averill, 1982). James Averill (1983) asked people to describe the last time they had gotten angry or had someone get angry at them. Averill made an unexpected discovery. In most people's minds, anger and hatred are virtually synonymous. Yet he found that it was the people we love and like who were most likely to enrage us. Loved ones spark 29% of angry episodes, someone well-known and liked 24%, and acquaintances 25%. Only rarely does someone we

---

Box 7.2   THE BUSS–DURKEE INVENTORY

Directions: Please answer the following questions about yourself by marking either *True* or *False* on the sheet.

Resentment

T   F   1. Other people always seem to get the breaks.

T   F   2. Although I don't show it, I am sometimes eaten up with jealousy.

Irritability

T   F   1. Sometimes people bother me just by being around.

T   F   2. I often feel like a powder keg ready to explode.

Suspicion

T   F   1. I tend to be on my guard with people who are somewhat more friendly than I expected.

Negativism

T   F   1. When someone is bossy, I do the opposite of what he asks.

Verbal

T   F   1. If somebody annoys me, I am apt to tell him what I think of him.

Indirect

T   F   1. I sometimes spread gossip about people I don't like.

T   F   2. When I am mad, I sometimes slam doors.

Assault

T   F   1. Whoever insults me or my family is asking for a fight.

T   F   2. I have known people who pushed me so far that we came to blows.

Source: Buss, 1961, pp. 171–173.

---

dislike (8%) or a stranger (13%) ignite strong angry feelings. It appears then that those whom we love are most capable of provoking us.

What Causes Anger?   People who behave in socially unacceptable ways—who are ugly and ill-kempt (Hatfield & Sprecher, 1986b), arrogant and insulting (Pepitone, 1964), phony and manipulative (Jones, 1964), of low character (Hatfield et al., 1978), who are shiftless, or boring, or who dare to disagree with us (Byrne, 1971)—arouse our wrath. People who were involved in angry interchanges were asked what had sparked the trouble (Averill, 1983). It is clear that anger is an accusation. The angry eagerly cast blame. Their mates naturally decline to accept it. It is not that they fail to *understand* the accusations. They know full well why the other was angry; they simply deny any wrongdoing (i.e., "I had every right to do what I did," or "It couldn't be helped").

Once anger is unleashed, what effect does it produce?

Expressions of Anger   Angry people theoretically could express their feelings in a multitude of ways. They could mock, sulk, demand explanations, or stomp off in a huff. How do they in fact *usually* express their anger? In the study we described earlier, scientists (Averill, 1983) asked men and women to recall the last time they felt anger and to indicate their reaction. What did they *wish* they could have done? What did they actually do? With wishes, we note the desire to pour out wrath, to say something sharp. Persons are less likely actually to desire to *do* something, say, "to punch the jerk out." (To a lesser extent, people wish to set things right—to calm things down and talk them over.)

When looking at the ways angry people actually do respond, things generally are fairly civilized. People usually respond softly, they do try to calm the situation and to talk things over. On those few occasions when they lash out, they do so with their tongues; they are verbally aggressive. Rarely are they physically aggressive. In brief, how people feel like acting and how they actually do act are two different things. Generally, they coolly select the best way to express their hot feelings. In Averill's findings, as in much social scientific research, we are led again to wonder what happens when cultural, class, and historical variables are factored in. How much anger-expression, for example, is "socially constructed," how much biological and universal? Do some cultures encourage the expression of anger (Latin American? or Italian?) more than others (Japanese? or Canadian?)? While stereotypes can mislead, just to ask the question suggests the case to be made for the significant contributions of culture.

Why do the angry respond as they do? Theorists have focused on two very different possibilities when trying to come up with an answer. Some theorists focus on the "hard wiring"—a universal factor. They point to evolutionary factors that predispose species to react aggressively or submissively. Others focus on the "programming"—a culturally specific, class-specific, or temporal-specific factor. They point out that people can be taught to be patient or violent.

The "Hard Wiring" of Aggression

Theorists argue that the potential to react aggressively is "wired" into men and women.

The Sociobiological Perspective   Early sociobiologists such as Edward O. Wilson (1975) and ethologists such as the Nobel Prize winner Konrad Lorenz (1965) or Nikolas Tinbergen (1951) assumed that patterns of aggression were wired into all species. When appropriate stimuli were presented, aggressive patterns could be triggered. Ethologists assumed that innate aggressive tendencies had been transferred virtually intact to humans (Dart, 1953). Luckily, they thought, species also possessed instinctive mechanisms to check aggression. Animals rarely kill members of their own species; mechanisms have evolved that generally inhibit intraspecies aggression (Konner, 1982; Lorenz, 1965). Baboons, for example, usually bare their teeth. They shriek loudly and assume threatening postures before they fight. Generally, such threats are enough to frighten weaker baboons, who then back off. If there is a fight, baboons have a way of signaling "Uncle." When baboons are losing a fight, they often turn and present their rear ends to the other baboon. The victor responds by breaking off the fight and mounting the loser (Washburn & DeVore, 1962). The species best equipped for hunting and killing possess the strongest inhibitory mechanisms. Primitive humans were a fairly puny species with small teeth and brittle claws. Thus they had no need for a powerful instinctive mechanism to inhibit aggression. In modern times, the development of lethal weapons—knives, guns, bombs, and missiles—means that the human capacity to commit violent acts far outstrips its inhibitions. The evolutionary balance has been destroyed and threatens the survival of marriages, families, and even our species (and most other species, as well).

Today, sociobiologists such as Melvin Konner (1982) in *The Tangled Wing* have learned more about the "biological constraints on the human spirit."

The Anatomy of Anger

The Look of Anger   It is easy to recognize the face of anger. Carroll Izard (1977) provides a meticulous description of the facial expressions associated with rage. In anger, the muscles of the brow move inward and downward, creating a frown. There is a foreboding appearance about the eyes; the eyes themselves are fixed in a hard stare directed at the target. The nostrils dilate and the wings of the nose flare out. The lips are opened and drawn back in a rectangle-like shape; the teeth are clenched. Often the face is flushed. The look is unmistakable, especially in children. When our daughter Kim was a child, she used to practice her "famous dirty look," instinctively reproducing the very stare that Izard describes. She was hoping that it would be lethal enough so that both her parents would wither away and die. They did not, so Kim has become a clinical psychologist, fully prepared to employ subtler techniques.

Leon Bing (1991), in *Do or Die*, interviewed members of Los Angeles gangs, the Crips and the Bloods. Here is one interview with Faro, a homeless 17-year-old who crippled a mother and her baby in a wanton drive-by shooting:

> "See them two dudes?" Faro's voice, unaccountably, has dropped to a whisper . . .
> "I'm gonna look crazy at 'em. You watch what they do." He turns away from
> me. . . . The driver, sensing that someone is looking at him, glances over at my car. His
> eyes connect with Faro's, widen for an instant. Then he breaks the contact, looks
> down, looks away. And there is no mistaking what I saw there in his eyes: It was fear.
> Whatever he saw in Faro's face, he wasn't about to mess with it.
>
> Faro giggles and turns back toward me. He looks the same as he did before to me:
> a skinny, slightly goofy-looking kid. . . . I ask Faro to "look crazy" for me. He simply
> narrows his eyes. That's all. He narrows his eyes, and he looks straight at me and
> everything about his face shifts and changes, as if by some trick of time-lapse photogra-
> phy. It becomes a nightmare face, and it is a scary thing to see. It tells you that if you
> return his stare, if you challenge this kid, you'd better be ready to stand your ground.
> His look tells you that he doesn't care about anything, not your life and not his. (*The
> New York Times Book Review*, 1991, p. 7)

The Nazis too recognized the look of seething resentment.

> The Nazis officially recognized and tortured the silent nonconformists among their prisoners. The stubbornness they purported to read on their prisoners' silent faces was called "physiognomical insubordination." Prisoners in their strategy of non-cooperation were not allowed silent protest; they had to look stupidly meek and innocent, otherwise the aggressor feared the silent reproach of his victim. (Meerloo, 1964, pp. 21–22)

Similarly, 1960s revolutionary Jerry Rubin (1970) wrote of his arrest "for smiling" in the United States.

The Neuroanatomy and Neurophysiology of Anger   What happens beneath the surface of anger? Scientists point out that humans, rational as they try to be, cannot overcome their neural heritage (Moyer, 1968). In the brains of all animals, specific neural systems exist, which trigger anger, hostility, and aggression.

Neurochemical changes, hormonal changes, and a variety of pharmaceutical agents can ignite anger and hostility (Brain, 1980). Animal breeders have known for centuries that a raging bull can be converted into a gentle steer by castration, which reduces testosterone levels in the bloodstream. Some psychologists have argued that testosterone may be equally important in sparking male aggression (Dabbs, 1990). Psychologists (Persky, Smith, & Basu, 1971) studied men who ranged in age from 17 to 66. They found that the younger men produced twice as much testosterone as the older men. The more testosterone they produced, the more hostile and aggressive they were. Men may not be alone in showing a relationship between angry feelings and hormonal levels. A few women find that the week before menstruation (when estrogen and progesterone levels fall sharply), they feel irritable, hostile, and are easily provoked (Hopson & Rosenfeld, 1984).

The Visceral Determinants of Anger   When people are angry, they show a strong autonomic nervous system (ANS) reaction. Both branches of the ANS—the sympathetic system (the branch that speeds you up, preparing you for action) and the parasympathetic system (the branch that prepares you to calm down and "mellow out") may be engaged. When people are angry, they show evidence of sympathetic activity: Their hearts pound, their breathing becomes hot and jagged, and they begin to sweat (Arnold, 1950; Ax, 1953; Ekman, Levenson, & Friesen, 1983).

It is clear then that anger is shaped in part by genetics and biology. Let us now turn to the contribution that social learning makes to the experience and expression of anger.

When angry, count four; when very angry, swear.
> —*Mark Twain*

The Programming: Social Learning Theory

Albert Bandura (1983) noted that society can train people to be aggressive or peaceful. They often learn how to be aggressive (or gentle) simply by observing the behavior of those around them and imitating it (Bandura & Walters, 1959).

People hit and abuse other family members because they can.
                                                    —*R. J. Gelles*

Learning to Be Aggressive   We witness aggressive acts on TV, in the movies, and at home. From our families we learn, from thousands of observations, how intimates deal with each other. And within families, the old adage holds true: Violence breeds violence. Some social scientists have gone so far as to describe the family as the "cradle of violence" (Steinmetz & Straus, 1973; Straus, Gelles, & Steinmetz, 1980). And within the family, violence is commonplace.

If I'd rather my man would hit me,
than for him to jump up and quit me,
It ain't nobody's business if I do.
I swear I won't call no copper,
if I'm beat up by my papa;
Ain't nobody's business if I do.
   —*Blues singer Billie Holiday, 1949*

I am woman, hear me roar.
   —*Australian feminist,*
      Helen Reddy, 1972

Dating and Marital Violence   On September 17, 1991, Hawaii's entry, Carolyn Sapp, was named Miss America. The next day, Hawaii's newspapers exploded with the news that the year before, when she had tried to break up with her boyfriend, Nuu Faaola, a former professional football player, he had tried to throw her out of a moving car. She complained to the police that Faaola

> physically beat, kicked, punched, threatened to kill me, tore my clothes, choked me, took a knife to me and held it to my neck and skin, and emotionally threatened me. . . . tried pushing me out of a car driving high speeds on the H-I, then strangled me with the seat belt until I couldn't breathe. (Glauberman, 1991, p. A-4)

Folksinger Joan Baez is a Quaker and a pacifist. She has devoted her life to promoting world peace. Yet her early love relationships were not always very peaceful. In her autobiography, she wrote:

> Michael and I hung out in the living room, drawing, talking, making love, and fighting. . . . One night Michael and I had been to the movies. The last scene had left Joanne Woodward standing on a street corner yelling at her husband, who was driving away with his lovely young mistress. On the way home I had a nausea attack. . . . Michael was telling me that I was like Joanne Woodward, and I had thought I was like the lovely young mistress.
>   Suddenly, very suddenly, the nausea vanished and I found myself flexing my toes around the upright lamp we'd bought at the flea market, and in dreamlike slow motion, lifting it with my leg and hurling it across the room. It landed directly on Michael's head. His mouth froze open over the avocado and banana sandwich and the whole scene vanished into darkness.
>   I got up feeling like Godzilla and headed toward the living room. The first thing to catch my eye was the wine bottle with a candle in it and a year's supply of wax

dripping down in multicolored lumps. I grabbed it by the neck and threw it against the wall with all my might and was rewarded by the sound and sight of shattering glass and wax chips in flight. But I was already on my way to the kitchen. First the coffee pot went, but it was metal and suffered only a small dent while spewing the cup or two of stale coffee and the grounds into splotches against the wall. I headed for the plates in the cupboard. Michael stepped up behind me, saying, "You stupid . . . Are you crazy, or what?" and grabbed my arms at the elbows. Empowered with the strength of rage, I turned myself around, and in a quiet and determined frenzy, grabbed his hair and pulled, kicking furiously at his ankles. He hopped up and down to get out of the way of my feet, squeezing my wrists to unlock the grip I had on his curly locks, and cursing and hissing in shock and anger. I finally gave up and collapsed in tears. (1990, pp. 80–81)

Abuse begins early in many love relationships. Couples may slap, shove, grab, bite, kick, or hit one another with their fists. They threaten one another with knives or guns and beat one another (Marshall & Rose, 1987). Twenty-two to 40% of dating couples and 38% of engaged couples report that they have had physically violent confrontations with their partners (Cate, Henton, Koval, Christopher, & Lloyd 1982; Gryl, Stith, & Bird, 1991). More than half the time (68%), *both* partners are abusive (Cate et al., 1982). As casual dating relationships begin to get serious, the likelihood that things will build to an explosion increases (Cate et al., 1982). Usually because men and women feel they have no other alternative, couples generally decide to stay in these abusive relationships (O'Leary, Arias, Rosenbaum, & Barling, 1986).

Frances Gryl and her colleagues (1991) asked 280 first-year college students, who were in a serious dating relationship, how violent those relationships were. Their replies are given in Table 7.5. As you can see from the table, in this study men and women were equally likely to inflict and sustain violence. Almost 30% of the women and 23% of the men admitted that they had been violent. Almost 28% of the women and 39% of the men reported that they had sustained violence.

Table 7.5   VIOLENCE INFLICTED AND SUSTAINED IN CURRENT DATING RELATIONSHIP

Type of violence	Expressed violence		Sustained violence	
	Women % ever	Men % ever	Women % ever	Men % ever
Pushed, shoved, or grabbed	19.9	11.3	19.9	18.5
Wrestled or pinned down	5.1	9.7	9.0	3.2
Threw an object at	7.1	4.0	3.8	15.3
Clawed, scratched, or bit	5.1	.0	1.3	12.1
Slapped	17.9	8.9	7.7	21.8
Punched with fist	4.5	3.2	1.9	8.1
Hit with object	1.9	.0	2.6	5.6
Kicked	3.2	2.4	1.9	7.3
Attempted to strangle	0.6	1.6	0.6	0.8
Used lethal weapon (knife, gun, etc.)	1.3	0.8	0.6	0.9

Source: Gryl et al., 1991, p. 254.

Most studies find that men (because of their greater strength and violence) are more likely to injure seriously their dating partners—emotionally, sexually, and physically (Makepeace, 1986; Marshall & Rose, 1987).

Men and women generally *say* they disapprove of violence. Yet further probing makes it clear that couples involved in violent encounters are more "forgiving" of violence than they should be. Many couples seem to make love *and* war. When researchers (Henton, Cate, Koval, Lloyd, & Christopher, 1983) asked couples who had experienced violence what meanings they associated with violence (love, hate, anger, confusion, fear, sadness, or other), many of them (29%) associated *love* with violence! Most linked anger (73%) or confusion (49%) with violence. Only a very few (8%) thought hate generated violence! For some couples, then, love does not have the power to inspire them to treat one another lovingly; rather, love is what keeps them together in spite of violence! When Frances Gryl and her colleagues (1991) asked couples how their relationships had been affected by the eruption of violence, only 15% of them indicated that violence made things worse. Eighty-five percent of them believed that their relationships had either stayed the same or improved as a result of the violence.

A study of more than 2,000 American married couples (Straus et al., 1980) found that more than 25% of them had engaged in some form of violence during their married life (see Table 7.6). Suzanne Steinmetz (1978) estimated that 3,300,000 American wives and 250,000 American husbands have been beaten severely by their mates. Men, far more than women, engaged in serious physical abuse. Women usually limited their attacks to making accusations, slapping, or hurling inanimate objects. Husbands tended to beat their wives or use a knife or a gun.

Modeling suggests ways people *might* behave. Whether or not they *do* act that way when it comes to violence depends on whether they expect physical abuse to be rewarded, ignored, or punished. There is ample evidence that aggression "pays off." Men and women were asked to think of the last time they had

Table 7.6   PERCENT OF COUPLES ENGAGING IN VIOLENT ACTS

Type of violence	Percentage	
	in 1975	Ever
Threw something at spouse	6.7	16.7
Pushed, grabbed, shoved spouse	13.0	23.5
Slapped spouse	7.4	17.9
Kicked, bit, or hit with fist	5.2	9.2
Hit or tried to hit with something	4.0	9.5
Beat up spouse	1.5	5.3
Threatened with a knife or gun	1.0	4.4
Used a knife or gun	0.5	3.7
Any of the above	16.0	27.8

Source: Data from Straus et al., 1980.

been angry (not necessarily violent) at someone and then to recall what were the consequences of their anger expression (Averill, 1983). By the time most people got worked up enough to express their feelings, anger had been effective. The chances were three to one that the outburst would get them what they wanted. The "wrongdoers" were likely to gain new respect for the angry person, to admit that they were wrong, and/or to try to make things up to him or her. In the short run, then, violence may work. In the long run it is a dangerous or even lethal strategy.

Child Abuse   Children too are often victims of verbal, sexual, and physical abuse. Child developmentalists have long counseled parents that the most effective way to "shape up children" is to lavish praise on them when they behave properly and either reason with them, ignore them, assign them a "time out" in their rooms, withdraw their privileges, and so forth when they don't behave properly. Physical punishment is rarely effective.

Yet a recent survey of university students revealed that during their final year of high school, more than half of them had either been threatened with or experienced physical punishment. Vivian Gornick (1987) told of her college years, in which she was locked into combat with her mother.

> I was seventeen, she was fifty. I had not yet come into my own as a qualifying belligerent but I was a respectable contender and she, naturally, was at the top of her game. The lines were drawn, and we did not fail one another. Each of us rose repeatedly to the bait the other one tossed out. Our storms shook the apartment: paint blistered on the wall, linoleum cracked on the floor, glass shivered in the window frame. We barely kept our hands off one another, and more than once we approached disaster. (p. 109)

Serious abuse is extremely common. In 1986, there were more than 2.1 million reported cases of child sexual and physical abuse (shaking of children or beating them). Box 7.3 describes some of the warning signs that children may be being abused. In 1986, more than 5000 children died from such battering.

The consequences of such parental abuse extend far beyond the immediate incident. Parents who were abused as children are six times more likely to abuse their own children (Straus et al., 1980) and to favor violence as a means of achieving personal and political ends (Owens & Straus, 1975). Violent teenagers tend to come from homes where discipline takes the form of harsh physical punishment (Straus et al., 1980).

Parents are not the only models for their children. Children watch in fascination as their classmates sarcastically challenge their teachers . . . or reason things out, patiently construct a compelling argument . . . or build pipe bombs. Television and movies are powerful models of how couples or parents and children "ought" to behave. The statistics on TV viewing are staggering. Most people spend about $4\frac{1}{2}$ to 7 hours each day watching television—over 1000 hours a year (Nielsen Television, 1981). There is a very heavy dose of aggression in the TV diet. Eight out of ten programs contain violence (Gerbner, Gross, Segnorielli, & Morgan, 1980). Saturday morning children's programs, such as the *Roadrun-*

Box 7.3 CHILD ABUSE: HOW TO HELP

The signs of child abuse are often subtle. Recognizing and reporting evidence of violence can help make a difference.

What to Look For
Unexplained bruises, welts, burns, broken bones

Children who are consistently unkempt and hungry

Torn, bloody underwear or genital irritation (may signify sexual abuse)

Inappropriate dress (summer clothing in winter)

Prolonged listlessness

Abrupt changes in behavior

Children who are desperate to please

Sudden drops in school grades

Suicide attempts

What to Do
Most state child-welfare agencies have hot line numbers (anonymity guaranteed)

National referral service: 1-800-4ACHILD

In emergencies, call the police

Source: *Newsweek*, Dec. 12, 1988, p. 61.

---

ner series, average 18 violent acts per hour. Prime-time shows, such as *Miami Vice*, average five violent acts per hour. By age 16, the average child will have witnessed more than 13,000 TV killings (Waters & Malamud, 1975). What effects do relentless onslaughts of TV violence have? The evidence seems clear. Media violence makes people callous about violence (Thomas, 1982), increases their aggressiveness (Freedman, 1984), and shapes viewers' assumptions about the real world. Heavy viewers (who watch TV 4 hours a day or more) have exaggerated estimates of how much violence there is in the world (Gerbner et al., 1980). They are also more likely to tolerate aggression in others (Drabman & Thomas, 1974). Children who succeed in intimidating other children naturally become even more aggressive (Patterson, Littman, & Brecker, 1967). In all these cases, fierceness seems to pay.

The United States, more than other nations, seems to be experiencing an epidemic of violence, which includes the numbness toward it and resignation in the face of it. This is tragic because we can also learn calmer, more reasonable, ways of behaving.

In 1900, Andrew Carnegie forecast that in the twentieth century, "To kill a man will be considered as disgusting as we in this day consider it disgusting to eat one."

—David Myers

Learning to Be Nonaggressive   Most of us want to be able to choose from a number of options the most appropriate ways to respond when we get angry. Couples sometimes want to keep their angry feelings in check while they work things out. Parents and teachers want to be able to teach children to respond gracefully to frustration. The same principles that cause people to respond angrily can be used to lead them to react in calmer, cooler, and more collected ways (Bandura, 1983).

Producing Calm Children   Psychologists Gerald Patterson (1971) and Robert Johnson (1973) have maintained that social learning theory, which highlights the importance of observational learning and reinforcement, is a powerful guide to teaching children to respond cooperatively rather than aggressively. Consider, for example, a typical fight between 5-year-olds in nursery school, depicted in one of Patterson's films. John, muttering to himself, calls Peter a "rat sticker." Peter is enraged. He hurls a rubber ball at John and knocks him down. John begins to howl in pain. Students crowd around, excited. The teacher races over. "Quit that! Peter, you apologize to John," she threatens. Peter is not about to apologize. His tight little red face is screwed up in defiance. "My uncle can beat you up," he counters. Soon fellow students, aroused by the hubbub, are dancing around, shouting out aggressive taunts "Oh yeah! Well my mother can beat up your uncle." "Dork," another exclaims. They engage in mock violence. "Bang, bang. You're dead," they crow.

Social learning theorists point out that when we slow down the action in such encounters, it is obvious that observational learning and reinforcement/punishment are crucial to the action. Passive bystanders see the fight and add such action to their repertoire. They watch the teacher grant her attention (a priceless commodity to children) to the two boys locked in combat. They see aggression pay off in other ways too. They see Peter's sneer of power as John falls. They note John's delight when the teacher yells at Peter, publicly humiliating him. They see aggression breeding aggression. Social learning theorists point out that the way to turn things around, to shape peaceful instead of aggressive behavior, is to arrange things so that children observe peaceful behavior and observe such behavior being rewarded. For example, in this setting, teachers might, first, model alternate nonaggressive interactions. The teacher could show Peter and John how to cooperate on a project, how to negotiate. Second, the teacher could pay attention to the team as they work together. She could praise children and touch them affectionately when they behave appropriately. Third, the teacher could ignore minor instances of aggression, depriving the aggressive act the reward of attention. Finally, if the aggression is too blatant or too serious to ignore, she can ensure that brief aversive consequences follow. She can impose a "time out," insisting that the child sit in a separate room for 10 minutes, deprived of toys, friends, and the excitement of combat. Now, nursery school students observe a peaceful encounter; they add that to their repertoire. They observe cooperation and negotiation leading to reward.

Interviewer: *You've been married to Jessica Tandy for so many years. Have you ever thought of divorce?*
Hume Cronyn: *Divorce . . . no. Murder . . . Often.*

Producing Calm Adults   The United States, as the most dangerous of the developed countries, represents a frightening case because it is also the world's most powerful nation. Have you ever wondered what your chances are of getting murdered during your lifetime? In 1986, the FBI released some statistics that revealed that the chance of an American citizen getting murdered in his or her lifetime is 1 in 153 (Shearer, 1986)! The statistics also vary depending on sex, race, and age (see Table 7.7). Given these statistics, it is not surprising that Americans are eager to find ways to reduce aggression.

When we compare these statistics with those of other nations, the differences are startling, particularly the horrific figures for nonwhite males. The homicide rate among young men in the United States is 4 to 73 times the rate in other industrialized nations (see Table 7.8).

In this century, leaders such as Mahatma Gandhi and Martin Luther King, Jr., have been powerful advocates and models of nonviolence. Laboratory studies document that such models are critically important. Restraint is as contagious as belligerence (Baron, 1977). Modeling teaches us how we might behave.

The manner in which nations, couples, and families actually behave in a situation depends on what is rewarded. People are very adaptable. They can learn many ways of dealing with anger. They can learn to smile, calm things down, talk at length about their feelings, set limits. If all else fails, they can even learn to explode on demand (Tavris, 1989).

For example, couples become less aggressive when their aggressive behavior is ignored and their nonaggressive behavior is rewarded (Hamlin, Buckholdt, Bushell, Ellis, & Ferritor, 1969). Punishment is not so effective in reducing aggression, because with punishment comes a modeling of aggression.

In real life, some natural checks—such as guilt, empathy, and fear of retaliation—exist that nudge angry couples to consider gentler reactions and to avoid cruel, hurtful ones. Again, the consequences matter.

Table 7.7 PROBABILITY OF MURDER

Total U.S. population	1 out of 153
Men	1 out of 100
Women	1 out of 325
Total white population	1 out of 240
Men	1 out of 164
Women	1 out of 450
Total nonwhite population	1 out of 47
Men	1 out of 28
Women	1 out of 117

Table 7.8   YOUNG MEN AT RISK

Killings per 100,000 men 15 through
24 years old for 1986 or 1987.

0.3	Austria
0.5	Japan
1.0	W. Germany
1.0	Denmark
1.0	Portugal
1.2	England
1.2	Poland
1.3	Ireland
1.4	Greece
1.4	France
1.4	Switzerland
1.4	Netherlands
1.7	Belgium
2.3	Sweden
2.5	Australia
2.9	Canada
3.0	Finland
3.3	Norway
3.7	Israel
4.4	New Zealand
5.0	Scotland
21.9	United States

Source: Journal of the American Medical Association. Quoted in The New York Times, June 27, 1990.

Guilt. Angry men and women tend to respond in ways that their families and friends deem appropriate (Blanchard & Blanchard, 1982). In Hawaii, for example, the Japanese disapprove of aggressive men and women (especially women). Thus it is not surprising to discover that even when angered, Japanese women display little aggression. Women of Chinese, Caucasian, or Hawaiian descent come from cultures in which assertiveness is more acceptable. When angered, they feel less guilty and freer to express their feelings. (See Hatfield, Schmitz, Parpart, & Weaver, 1986, for similar results.)

Empathy. The attributions we make as to *why* people act the way they do influence our feelings about and reactions to them. Experiments (Feshbach & Feshbach, 1981) confirmed that empathy tends to check aggression. When trained to recognize the feelings of others, to assume their perspective, and to share their emotions, behavior becomes significantly less aggressive.

Fear. It is hard to say just what effect threatening one's husband that "I'll tear you from limb from limb if you hit our daughter one more time" is supposed to have. On the one hand, the enraged wife is modeling the very action she is trying to prevent. (It is hard to teach "Do as I say, not as I do.") On the other hand, she is making clear the unprofitability of child abuse. Surely the most telling strategy is calmly but forcefully to convey the message that reason will be tolerated, while brutality will not. To make such calm threats, however, one must have a safety net—family, friends, and a career that allow one to be self-sustaining.

According to social learning theory, then, whether we act calmly or aggressively when angered depends on the consequences we anticipate.

Maybe we need the catharsis of bloodletting and decapitation like the ancient Romans needed it, as ritual but not real like the Roman circus.
—Martin Scorsese

I don't understand where emotions go if you deny them. Do they wither or moulder or gather strength underground?
—Marge Piercy

Catharsis

Sigmund Freud proposed a "pressure-cooker" model of anger and aggression. When angry pressures build, people have to release them one way or another.

People have a choice. They can discharge their angry feelings in small, sizzling displays, or they can hold them in until eventually there is a large eruption. Freud's early model had a profound impact on psychotherapy. Some therapists have argued that angry men and women need to "blow off steam" now and then. Otherwise there will be a marital explosion. Freud's perspective dominated therapeutic practice during the first half of this century, and in the 1960s it took an extreme (and fashionable) form which might have made even Freud wince. Couples were encouraged to imagine they were ripping a piece out of their mates' bodies. In "encounter groups" they were encouraged to smack their sweethearts with foam baseball bats, to "primal scream," and to beat on pillows in the expectation that angry feelings so powerfully expressed would spend themselves. Does catharsis work? Alas, not really. The evidence suggests that things are more complex than Freud or the later Californians had hoped (Tavris, 1989). Angry couples have a double problem. They first have to deal with their own emotions. Then they must address the problems they are facing. When couples are enraged and feel dangerously out of control, at first it may seem helpful to cry and pound on pillows until exhaustion sets in. In that sense, there is some merit to the claim that "violent emotional expressions" may have some benefits.

But the rub comes when we ask "What next?" While sometimes an expression of anger helps clear the air, the direct expression of anger can be self-indulgent. Anger begets more anger and aggression, commencing a cycle of rage difficult to contain. More important than whether couples express anger or withhold it in a single instance is whether they use their anger to change the things that upset them in the first place. Let us review some of the research that leads to these conclusions.

Jack Hokanson and his Florida State University colleagues (Hokanson, 1970) conducted a brilliant series of studies, furnishing insight into the cathartic process. In an early study, Hokanson and Burgess (1962b) set out to discover (1) what effect frustration has on physiological arousal and (2) what effect it has when one has a chance to get even. To find out, they required college students to perform several extremely difficult intellectual tasks. Half the time (in the control conditions), the researchers were civil and helpful. But the rest of the time (in the anger conditions), they set out to enrage the students. The experimenters were critical; they repeatedly interrupted and harassed students at critical moments. As you might expect, when the subjects encountered repeated frustration, they showed a strong physiological reaction; their hearts raced and their systolic blood pressure shot up.

In the next step, researchers set out to determine the consequences of allowing students to retaliate against others. Some students were given a chance to aggress verbally against the irritating experimenter. Others were given a chance to aggress physically against him. Still others had no chance to retaliate. (Some of them could at least conjure up aggressive fantasies if they wished, but others were not permitted even to do that.) This early study *seemed* to find that under the right conditions, retaliation did seem to produce catharsis. When frustrated subjects were able verbally or physically to attack their frustrator, their blood pressure and heart rate returned to normal with surprising rapidity. When they were not allowed to retaliate, their blood pressure and heart rate remained high.

Anybody can become angry—that is easy; but to be angry with the right person, and to the right degree, and at the right time, and for the right purpose, and in the right way—that is not within everybody's power and is not easy.

—Aristotle

Subsequent research, however, has made it clear that a catharsis effect operates only under very limited conditions:

1. People must be angry and aroused at the time they are given an opportunity to retaliate (Bramel, Taub, & Blum, 1968; Doob, 1970).
2. They must have the chance to retaliate against the person who "caused" their problem. And if that person had behaved in arbitrary, malevolent, obnoxious, and aggressive ways, so much the better (Konecni, 1984). It does not help much to attack a surrogate for the evil-doer (Hokanson, Burgess, & Cohen, 1963). Although many believe that indulging in vengeful daydreams, punching walls, or kicking the cat ventilates feelings, research indicates that just letting off steam does little good in the long run (Konecni, 1984).
3. The victim must get what he deserves, no more and no less. Going overboard may leave a residue of guilt, while pulling punches may allow the initial resentment to remain (Hatfield et al., 1978, 1984).
4. The target must be nonintimidating to avoid anxiety afterward (Hokanson & Burgess, 1962a).

These conditions do not occur all that often, and very rarely do they appear in combination. But there are still more difficulties for the catharsis hypothesis than simply that it has limitations. Other research warns that when people express their angry aggressive feelings, they often get themselves so worked up that things may become worse than they were before.

An array of laboratory experiments and correlational studies have come to the same conclusion: Anger expressed is often anger/aggression increased. [See Ebbessen, Duncan, and Konecni (1975) for a sampling of such studies.] In short, feuds like those of the Hatfields (the good guys!) and the McCoys have their own momentum. A wiseguy remark results in a slap to the face. Justification follows justification. Soon no one is speaking. In the old Laurel and Hardy silent comedy routines, a tiny irritation inevitably escalated into a pie-throwing melee, houses were razed, and city blocks collapsed. It appears that sometimes life has more in common with a Laurel and Hardy routine than we might like to believe.

Gender Differences in Catharsis   The most devastating blow to Freud's catharsis formulation, however, was yet to come. After conducting a number of studies, Hokanson (1970) observed that individuals seemed to have quite different reactions when they were forced to deal with an impossible person. He began to suspect that perhaps people could be taught to respond to provocation in a wide variety of ways. If the techniques they tried worked, they would feel "catharticlike relief." "What works" for men, however, differed from what worked for women, and usually for cultural reasons. When men feel anger, they are "expected" to express it. This can work (Hokanson & Burgess, 1962b). Women are "supposed" to react quite differently. They are expected to smile, try patiently to figure out what went wrong, and calm things down. *This* is "what works" (Hokanson & Edelman, 1969). In short, there may be no universal "catharsis response." The power of cultural programming (and expectation) again raises its giant head.

In subsequent research, Hokanson and his colleagues found that while, traditionally, men benefit from expressing their angry feelings, women do not. Scientists (Hokanson & Edelman, 1969; Hokanson, Willers, & Koropsak, 1968) found that men and women responded quite differently to aggression. When men and women were shocked, both of them became extremely aroused. Their heart rates soared and their blood pressure rose. Men and women responded quite differently to provocation, however. The men responded angrily; they gave their antagonist "a taste of his (or her) own medicine." The chance to be aggressive apparently was a relief to the men, a kind of Clint Eastwood "make my day" syndrome. Their heart rates dropped and their blood pressures fell. When they tried to ignore aggression or to "turn the other cheek," catharsis did not occur. Women responded more calmly when they were provoked, even though they were equally upset. They tried being extra friendly to their attackers. And generosity was a relief to women. Their heart rates dropped and their blood pressures fell. If they tried to ignore aggression or retaliate, catharsis (in the sense of lowering of arousal) did not occur! Perhaps it is not surprising that when men and women respond to provocation as they have in the past, whether it is to be extra friendly or to counterattack, they experience relief.

Sex roles are, of course, learned, and what is learned can be unlearned. In a series of experiments, Hokanson and his colleagues (Hokanson et al., 1968) found that men and women could be taught new ways to behave . . . sometimes in a matter of minutes. For example, if men were rewarded every time they responded to shock with friendliness and women were rewarded every time they showed a little aggressive spunk, it took only a few minutes before both sexes began to adopt very different strategies. The men quickly learned the value of generosity and the women quickly learned that aggressiveness pays. Under these conditions, the traditional gender differences were reversed. Women showed catharsis-like reduction in heart rates and blood pressures when they responded aggressively and had a slow vascular recovery when they were friendly. The opposite was true for the men: Catharsis now followed friendliness, not belligerence.

In a final study, the scientists (Hokanson & Stone, 1969) showed that people could learn to do almost anything, even "masochistically" shocking themselves if it paid off, and that such responses would reduce their arousal levels. Social psychological research then casts doubts on the Freudian "pressure-cooker" model of anger/aggression. It documents that people can learn a variety of techniques for dealing with angry feelings. They probably do best if they learn several ways of coping with their own feelings and with life's problems. Angry people ought to be able to explain their ideas and feelings to their partners and try to understand their mates' points of view (Feshbach, 1956), act sweetly or angrily as the occasion demands, make practical changes so that the cause of irritation is eliminated (Straus et al., 1980), or recognize when things are hopeless and abandon the relationship (Hatfield, 1984).

CONCLUSION

The research into the nature, causes, and consequences of anger, depression, and anxiety is still in its infancy, but enough has been learned to suggest consequences for couples in relationships. It is often impossible to make headway in a troubled relationship when one or both of the partners suffer from depression or high anxiety or cannot cope constructively with anger. Just as therapists often must focus on these problems in one member of a marriage before they can hope to make progress relationally, so one partner in any couple should not underestimate the difficulties ahead if their partner suffers from one of these afflictions. And the problem may be impossible for them if their partner refuses to seek help. That refusal has an especially tragic side to it, since valuable remedies do exist for the disorders described in this chapter.

Chapter 8

Relationship Problems

By all means marry; if you get a good wife, you'll be happy. If you get a bad one, you'll become a philosopher.

—Socrates

INTRODUCTION

The modern world highly esteems individualism: personal freedom, personal expression, personal growth, personal fulfillment. It also celebrates relationships between two loving and committed people; many historians of ideas indeed see individualism and intimacy as two sides of the same modernist coin. Sadly, in the realm of quotidian life, it is hard for many people to put these two values together, either theoretically or practically. Being a free individual does not easily comport with the commitment, fidelity, bargaining, and compromises that successful relationships generally seem to require. The two *desiderata* pull in two different directions.

One expression of individualism can be seen in the high expectations we have concerning our relationships. If we expected little, we would accept marriage for better or for worse, as is, with resignation. But we expect a lot, and the thwarting of those dreams produces a great deal of suffering. So there exists a terrible and hard contradiction between the demands of individualism and those of relationships, which won't go away and which inevitably present all of us with a tremendous obstacle in making love affairs work.

In this chapter, we focus on some of the relational dilemmas modern-day couples commonly face; problems that lead couples to be so acutely disappointed in their love lives. We look at the rhythms of love, at existing gender role inequities, and at the nature of conflict itself; we look at problems with mates who use alcohol or drugs. Later in the book, we propose some ameliorative strategies, though a few will be mentioned in this chapter as well.

THE STAGES OF LOVE

Family therapist Myron Weiner (1980) wrote that most dating relationships/ marriages go through five predictable stages.

Love is what happens to a man and woman who don't know each other.
                                                    —*Somerset Maugham*

1. *Stage one: Early courtship—the moment before falling in love.* When couples first meet, they strive to make a good impression. They exchange carefully edited versions of their life histories. They size up one another. (We discussed this stage in some detail in Chapter 1, Beginnings.)

Falling in love with love/ is falling for make-believe.
                                                    —*Richard Rodgers*

2. *Stage two: Passionate love.* Sometimes, couples fall in love. Lovers idealize one another; they "fuse" with one another, emotionally and physically. In this honeymoon period, lovers assume that the other will fulfill all their needs. (We discussed this stage in some detail in Chapter 2, Passionate Love, and Chapter 3, Sexuality.) In Leonard Bernstein's musical version of *Candide* (Bernstein, 1976), Candide and Cunegonde share their dreams for marriage. Candide dreams of buying a modest little farm in Westphalia. There, they will tend cows and chickens, go on Sunday picnics, walk their faithful dogs; have scores of children. Cunegonde's dreams are "identical" to his. She, however, wants to dress in ropes of pearls, live in mansions in Paris and Rome, grow as rich as Midas, entertain lavishly. They conclude in harmony: "It's very rare/ How we agree./ Oh, happy pair!/ How we agree./ I love marriage (Candide);/ So do I (Cunegonde)."/ Even in this "best of all possible worlds," our two heroes shall inevitably wake up to discover "how the other has changed."

Love is an ideal thing, marriage is a real thing; a confusion of the real with the ideal never goes unpunished.
                                                    —*Johann von Goethe*

3. *Stage three: Unmasking.* Lovers cannot stay on their best behavior forever. Soon, they begin to notice one another's imperfections.

A woman thinks as she goes down the aisle "Aisle, altar, hymn."
— *Old English saying*

4. *Stage four: Changing the other.* The disappointed lovers attempt to force their beloveds to become what they think they should be. Sometimes change is possible; usually it is not.

We were happily married for eight months. Unfortunately, we were married for four and a half years.
— *Pro golfer Nick Faldo, when asked about his ex-wife*

5. *Stage five: Resolution.* Illusion is recognized as illusion. Couples may come to understand their companions better and thus be able to accept their irritating habits. A personal example. When first married, when on walks together we were perplexed by the other's habits. Elaine tends to focus on things one at a time with laserlike attention. When her concentration gets interrupted she experiences an almost physical shock. Dick likes to play with several ideas at a time. His mind darts around. Early in our marriage, Elaine would be engrossed in thought and Dick would jar her with a series of fascinating and difficult questions: "Do you think the European Community will be able to switch to a single monetary system?" Just as she began to think out her answer to that, another, equally hard and related question had crossed his mind: "Where would you like to go in Europe next year? Small towns or big cities?" Followed by his lament that the United States has so little knowledge of or interest in the past. When we learned how differently, and consistently, our respective minds worked, it was easy for Dick to learn to stroll in silence or for Elaine to learn to give more playful answers or half-answers to his questions. Our minds work as they always did, but the different rhythms, fully understood, please and amuse us rather than irritate us; it has been easy to compromise.

The resolution stage is a critical period for relationships. It determines whether couples will feel loved and understood, or whether they will be locked into an endless power struggle, a stalemate, or end up feeling abandoned and unloved. Such a resolution is the hallmark of a truly adult love relationship: It is based not on idealization but love for the other as he or she really is. (Techniques for achieving such resolutions are discussed in Chapters 10 to 12.) Unfortunately, other forms of "resolution" exist: Things may go from bad to worse; marriages can end. (We discuss these processes in Chapters 13 and 14.) In this chapter we begin by focusing on *stage three—Unmasking*, when the trouble begins.

UNMASKING AND DISENCHANTMENT

In Gabriel García Márquez's (1985) *Love in the Time of Cholera*, Florentino Ariza happens to glance at 13-year-old Fermina Daza and instantly falls in love:

[He sees Fermina walk by] in her blue-striped uniform, stockings that reached to her knees, masculine laced oxfords, and a single thick braid with a bow at the end, which hung down her back to her waist. She walked with natural haughtiness, her head high, her eyes unmoving, her step rapid, her nose pointing straight ahead, her bag of books held against her chest with crossed arms, her doe's gait making her seem immune to gravity. (p. 56)

After Florentino Ariza saw her for the first time, his mother knew before he told her because he lost his voice and his appetite and spent the entire night tossing and turning in his bed. But when he began to wait for an answer to his first letter, his anguish was complicated by diarrhea and green vomit, he became disoriented and suffered from sudden fainting spells, and his mother was terrified because his condition did not resemble the turmoil of love so much as the devastation of cholera. (p. 61)

Florentino conveyed his love to Fermina in letters, packets of letters, bundles of letters. Her imagination caught fire too. For two years, they corresponded secretly, overcoming all obstacles just to catch a glimpse of one another.

It was the year they fell into devastating love. Neither one could do anything except think about the other, dream about the other, and wait for letters with the same impatience they felt when they answered them. Never in that delirious spring, or in the following year, did they have the opportunity to speak to each other. (p. 68)

Then, one day, when Fermina was 18, Ariza finally got the chance to speak to her. He spied her in the market. He moved behind her and uttered one line:

"This is not the place for a crowned goddess."
She turned her head and saw, a hand's breath from her eyes, those other glacial eyes, that livid face, those lips petrified with fear, just as she had seen them in the crowd at Midnight Mass the first time he was so close to her, but now, instead of the commotion of love, she felt the abyss of disenchantment. In an instant the magnitude of her own mistake was revealed to her, and she asked herself, appalled, how she could have nurtured such a chimera in her heart for so long and with so much ferocity. She just managed to think: My God, poor man! Florentino Ariza smiled, tried to say something, tried to follow her, but she eased him from her life with a wave of her hand.
"No, please," she said to him. "Forget it."
That afternoon, while her father was taking his siesta, she sent Gala Placidia with a two-line letter: "Today, when I saw you, I realized that what is between us is nothing more than an illusion." (p. 102)

The magic was gone. He was unmasked; she was disenchanted. They did not meet again for half a century; when they did finally meet, once again they fell in love—this time, however, with the precious, aging reality of one another.

The unpleasant, acrid smell of burned poetry.
            —P. G. Wodehouse

Family therapists point out that given the passionate illusions of lovers, disillusion is practically inevitable. For example, passionate lovers, particularly the young, sometimes idealize the traits they themselves do not possess. The shy, timid, woman may go wild for the rough, macho biker. She envisions him bravely fighting her fights for her. (She does not realize that he is more likely to fight *with* her.) The well-behaved, earnest scholar may fall in love with the sexy "bad girl." (He does not realize that she may embarrass him at faculty parties; drive him crazy by flirting with his friends.) Family therapists such as David Olson and Mark

---

Box 8.1   REVERSE REASONING

She married him because he knew how to get what he wanted.
She divorced him because he was too controlling.

He married her because she was so tiny and delicate.
He divorced her because she was weak and clinging.

She married him because he was rich.
She divorced him because all he ever did was work.

He married her because she was beautiful.
He divorced her because she was obsessed with her appearance.

She married him because he was so sociable.
She divorced him because he was never home.

He married her because she was such a good listener.
He divorced her because she had nothing much to say.

Source: Based on Olson & Schaefer (1977). Permission granted, 1992.

Schaefer (1977) observe that the very things most men and women find so exotically attractive in the beginning often become irritating incompatibilities when you have to live with them. (See Box 8.1.) In any case, once the "honeymoon is over" most couples are disappointed.

In addition to the inevitable disenchantments of marriage, couples often must confront more serious problems—role strain, conflicts over a variety of issues, and/or problems with drugs or alcohol.

Do you think your mother and I should have liv'd comfortably so long together, if ever we had been married?

—*John Gay*

ROLE STRAIN: FROM THE DOCTRINE OF THE TWO SPHERES TO THE SECOND SHIFT

Historians point out that we are caught up in the midst of a social revolution (Degler, 1980; Rapson, 1988). Until a few years ago, social marriage custom proclaimed the "Doctrine of the Two Spheres." Husbands and wives were consigned very different social roles. The sphere of the husband was the world outside the home. He was expected to be engaged in politics and work. The sphere of the wife was the home. It was her job to nurture her husband, maintain the home, and take care of the children. English television star Jean Alexander (1989) described her family: she thought she was describing an unusual family. A historian would recognize it as the standard family of 50 years ago:

My father worked for a firm of electrical engineers which specialized in shipyard contracts, so he was away from home a lot, sometimes for a month at a time, either at Southampton, Belfast, Barrow or Glasgow. His wages during my early years were not more than £3 a week and he was not paid for holidays. We missed him very much when he was away and his return was always a joyous occasion, not least because there was always some small present for Ken and me. He was not a very demonstrative person. His words were few but carefully chosen and exactly right for the occasion, and because of his direct and uncomplicated nature he got on with everybody. He was very self-contained, never got into a flap, and if he said, "That's it!" that *was* it. His word was law, and our love for him was tinged with a little awe; there was always a slight distance between him and his children. But what was so good was the feeling of stability, and the knowledge that when he was around the world would never go wrong.

Because dad was away so much the bringing up of Ken and me devolved on our mother. She moulded and directed us, gave us loving hugs and sometimes slaps that hurt. It was she we argued with, cajoled and ran to in times of childish crisis. And if we misbehaved she had only to say, "I'll tell your father" and all wickedness would stop. We knew that he would never lay a finger on us but we did not want him to know that we had been naughty.

As far as we were concerned, dad never did anything wrong. He was the upright one, the head of the family; he brought home the money and kept us all going. (pp. 13–14)

Today, families have changed radically. In *The Second Shift,* sociologist Arlie Hochschild (1989) points out that in 1950, only 30% of American women worked outside the home; by 1986, 55% were working—most full time. In 1950 almost no women with infants worked; today half of new mothers do. Today, it is assumed that both men and women will be lovers, parents, and have careers. But there is one big difference between men's and women's lives. When couples come home in the evening, the men's workday is generally over; they can relax. Women, alas, go on to a "second shift." They often spend their evenings shopping, running errands, preparing dinner, doing the laundry, ironing, straightening up the house, and taking care of the children. According to some statistics, 82% of women still do all or most of the housework (Atkinson & Huston, 1984). Employed wives spend 26 hours a week on housework; their husbands spend 36 minutes (Cruver, 1986)! Not surprisingly, most women feel unfairly treated in their marriages.

In a recent article, Louise Silverstein (1991, p. 1029) observed:

We know that problems in providing adequate, affordable child care are major factors that cause families stress. Kamerman (1980b) documented the stress that working parents experience in a society that is unresponsive to the needs of families. She reported that, in the absence of a government-sponsored family policy, families are forced to "package". . . . child care. These "packages" involve multiple kinds of arrangements such as those with school, spouse, relative's home, and teenage baby-sitter. The presence of two or more children substantially increases the likelihood of an individual family requiring multiple types of arrangements. In the 200 families studied, 28% used four to six types of child care per week. The stress involved in keeping a system of multiple-care arrangements going falls primarily on women.

Today, women's awareness and resentment of such inequities are the primary causes of marital conflict. Women become angry and resentful; they lose interest in sex and begin to complain about their husbands. Husbands have a choice; they can distance themselves from their wives and families and rationalize the status quo or begin to do their share. If at all possible, the couple may do best if they also sacrifice in order to hire housekeepers, gardeners, and child-care experts (Hochschild, 1989). Of course, it would be best if society attempted to provide a comprehensive solution to these problems, rather than force couples to work out their own individual, piecemeal solutions (Silverstein, 1991).

Philip Blumstein and Pepper Schwartz (1983) interviewed 4314 married and cohabiting couples, 969 gay couples, and 788 lesbian couples. The found that the gay and lesbian couples were far more likely to share household work equally than were heterosexual couples.

In Chapter 4 we observed that men and women are happiest when they feel equitably treated. How fair do men and women perceive their "marriage contracts" to be? Not surprisingly, regardless of whether couples are newlyweds, married 20 or 30 years, or long marrieds, both men and women agree that the men get the "best deal." Both agree that, in general, men contribute less to a marriage than women do and that they get more out of it (Hatfield et al., 1984). See Box 8.2.

As the nuclear family goes critical, so to speak, the roles associated with it begin to shiver and crack—with excruciating personal impact.
—Alvin Toffler

Sometimes clinicians talk about the circle of sacrifice. One person makes a sacrifice for another. A wife knows her husband has a heavy docket of court cases. So to spell him for a week, she does everything around the house. She does the dishes, watches the children. Naturally she has certain inchoate expectations. She probably assumes that he will appreciate her sacrifices and that when his load lightens he will return the favor. If he takes her for granted, and one week stretches into two or three, she may well become angry and resentful. She may brood; she may call her friends, complain, and ask their advice. They, in turn, may contribute to her confusion. One may consider her husband's selfishness shocking—"just like a man!" Another may point out how lucky she is to even have a husband. "If I could find someone to love, I'd be willing to do everything; nothing is worse than being alone." Sooner or later, anger cools into guilt. She feels terrible; she'd like to make amends for her vicious thoughts. And how can she do that? By sacrificing more. The circle is complete.

Clinicians note that in the best relationships, that circle is short-circuited; it never closes. People, they argue, should only make sacrifices if they feel comfortable about them. A wife must mention her expectations to her husband. If her husband is unwilling to do his share, she should refuse to sacrifice further. She must do something: hire household help, baby-sitters; get a gardener; eat out; let the mess build up. If relationships are to flourish, individuals have to know when to set limits.

Of course, it is difficult for men and women to fashion a nontraditional, modern, equitable relationship. Both men and women may find themselves demanding a transformation and then, perversely, sabotaging real change when it occurs. Men have a variety of tricks for resisting change. The Nobel Prize-winning chemist may not quite be able to get the hang of how one goes about mixing

Box 8.2 EQUITY THROUGH THE LIFE SPAN

Jane Traupmann and Elaine Hatfield (1983) interviewed 400 women living in Madison, Wisconsin. The women ranged in age from 50 to 92. Women were asked how equitable their marriages had been when they first began dating, when they were newly wed, and when they were in their thirties, forties, fifties, sixties, seventies, and eighties. Possible answers ranged from +3 (if the woman thought she was getting a far better deal than her husband), to 0 (if she thought they were both getting an equally good or bad deal), to −3 (if she felt her husband received a far better deal).

    In previous studies (Hatfield, Greenberger, Pillemer & Lambert 1982; Pillemer, Peterson, Utne, & Hatfield, 1981), researchers had found that when couples were first dating or married, both men and women felt they were getting more from their relationship than they had a right to expect (see Figure 8.1). Once the honeymoon was over, however, while young men continued to feel they were unduly blessed, young women, for the first time, started to feel ill-used. The reports of mature women mirrored these findings. They too remembered the halcyon days of courtship and marriage. They too felt they had gathered up more than they deserved . . . at first. After the honeymoon period, however, the women began to feel that they were sacrificing more and getting fewer rewards than were their husbands. It was not until they were in their eighties that women began to feel fairly treated once again! [Similar results were secured by Davidson (1984); Michaels, Edwards, and Acock (1984); and Sprecher, Metts, and Hatfield (1990).]

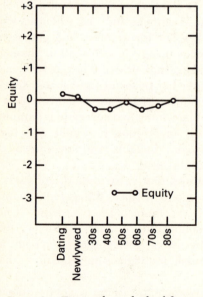

Figure 8.1 Equity through the life span.

HELP

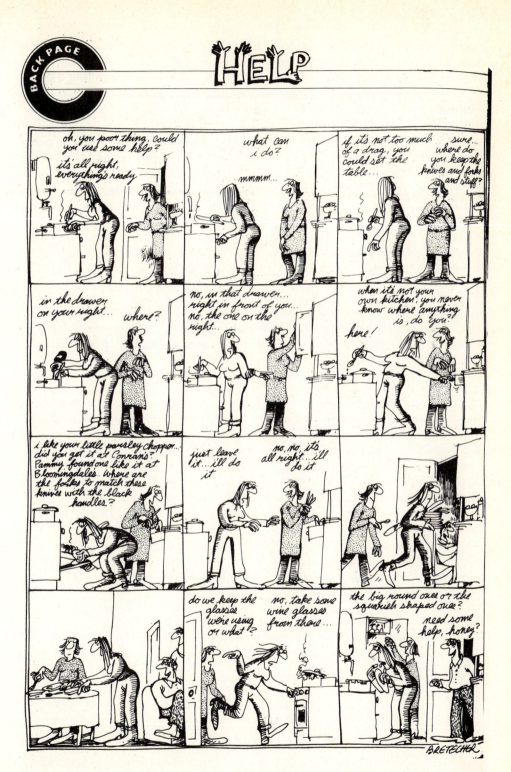

together all those complicated ingredients, the flour, sugar, and milk, to make a cake. Engineers may not quite be able to master turning the washer on and off. They look dully at the "On" button and mumble "How do you turn that washer on again? I always forget." They "accidentally" mix pink and white clothes. Husbands may "forget" to wash the pans; the ants notice their lapse. Women often get so irritated at—"Where does this go? And this?" "Sure I'll bring in the groceries. Just give me five minutes. . . . Whoops, I forgot. Did the ice-cream melt? Sorry"—that they give up. "Get out of my kitchen! I'd rather do it myself!" they scream. (Needless to say this is not a clever response. He is more than happy to go.) Women, on the other hand, are equally good at sabotaging change. Some delight in taking the moral high ground. They complain that he does not help. But when he tries, nothing is ever good enough. She insists he do it *her* way: "How can you put the forks tine down in the washer. Don't you know they have to be tine-up?" "Everyone knows cups have to be hung on little hooks." She gloats at his every failure. Not surprisingly, the men refuse to help. Change is always difficult.

My dad didn't do anything around the house . . . and he was proud of it. He'd say "That's just the way it is. You better get used to it." My brother-in-law doesn't do anything either, but at least he feels guilty about it. At least we're making some progress.

—A man in Richard Rapson's class

It remains likely that as our society gets more and more used to women working in careers outside the home, we will move closer to the egalitarian ideal. Just as women can be expected to move into more prestigious and higher-paying jobs, so men can be expected to take on more and more of the responsibilities of housework and child care. If men refuse the new bargain (and even if they accept it), society will have to evolve social arrangements for professional housekeepers, paid maternal and paternal work leaves, high-quality preschools, national baby-sitting services, and a variety of creative solutions to this emerging problem, which simply will not go away (Atkinson & Huston, 1984). The models of likely solutions may be found in France, The Netherlands, and the Scandinavian countries. Specific comparisons will be made in the next chapter between France's farsighted programs to help families and the disconcertingly retrograde state of American family policies.

We had more fun fighting than most people have making love.
—Elizabeth Taylor commenting on her marriage to Richard Burton

CONFLICT

When couples are casually dating, it is easy to avoid conflict. Once dating grows serious and activities require coordination, conflicts begin to arise (Braiker & Kelley, 1979). Scientists have studied the sparks that keep such conflicts smoldering or cause them to explode. In particular, what explanations (or attributions) do couples make for existing differences? What is the emotional tone of their exchanges? How do they behave in conflict situations?

Attribution Theory: How Couples Explain Their Differences

Attribution theory analyzes the way people go about making judgments about themselves and others. Attribution theorists share several assumptions (Jones, Kanouse, Kelley, Nisbett, Valines, & Weiner, 1971, p. xi):

I. The individual attempts to assign a cause for important instances of his behavior and that of others; when necessary, he seeks information that enables him to do so.

II. His assignment of causes is determined in a systematic manner.

III. The particular cause that he attributes for a given event has important consequences for his subsequent feelings and behavior.

Fritz Heider (1980), the first attribution theorist, was interested in "naive psychology"—the cause and effect analyses of behavior made by the "man in the street." He, and later attribution theorists such as Bernard Weiner (1986), maintained that men and women tend to refer to certain standard dimensions when making causal attributions: (1) Where is the *locus* of action; that is, who (or what) is responsible for what happened? (2) Did the person do what he or she did *intentionally or unintentionally?* (3) Who was in *control* of events, the person or someone else? (4) How *stable* are such occurrences? Is this a once in a lifetime event or is it likely to recur again and again? (5) How *specific or global* is the action? Is this event an exception to the rule or typical? For instance, when a wife discovers that her husband has "forgotten" to pick the children up from nursery school, she can attribute his behavior to very different causes. He is, to be sure, responsible for the event. But she may code his forgetfulness as accidental or "accidental on purpose." It may be stable ("he is always selfish and thoughtless") or unstable ("it was an accident"). She may define the problem as a global one ("he is irresponsible about everything") or a specific one ("he forgot this one time; it will never happen again"). The attributions that couples make obviously affect their feelings for one another.

Researchers (Ovris, Kelley, & Butler, 1976) studied attribution conflicts of young couples. They were surprised at how couples often see things in very different ways. When couples were happy with the status quo, they were unlikely to bother trying to understand why things were going so well. When unhappy, however, they willingly spent a great deal of time figuring out who was in the wrong and why. Unfortunately, such ruminations were almost inevitably self-serving. Couples were eager to believe their own justifications and excuses; they rarely admitted even to themselves that they were selfish, neurotic, stupid, or mean. They were more than willing to see their partners in a negative light, however. When people replay old grievances over and over again in their minds, they usually come up with the same old answer: "I am right and you are wrong." As a consequence, attributional disagreements are usually unresolvable (Snyder, Higgins, & Stucky, 1983).

Thomas Bradbury and Frank Fincham (1990) reviewed 23 attribution studies.

They found that the way married couples interpret one another's behavior depends on how happy they are. Happy duos make *relationship-enhancing* attributions. If their husbands ask them out to dinner, happily married wives give the husbands full credit for their generosity. (Their behavior is attributed to internal, stable, and global causes.) They explain away their husbands' flaws. (Here, they make external, unstable, and specific attributions.) Distressed couples do just the opposite; they can find an unflattering explanation for almost anything. They make *distress-maintaining* attributions. If their husbands do something wonderful for them, unhappily married wives explain it away. (They attribute good behavior to external, unstable, and specific causes.) The carefully chosen bouquet of woodland flowers is scorned; he just picked it up on the highway to buy a little peace; it's a poor excuse for a present. Distressed couples exaggerate their partner's flaws. (They attribute them to internal, stable, and global causes.) If his wife leaves her soggy towel on the bed, he assumes the moral high ground. That is just one more bit of damning evidence; she is selfish, unconcerned with anyone else's feelings, and she'll never change.

Happy and distressed couples don't just differ in the way they think about events; they differ in the way they feel about them as well.

It is very difficult to maintain a relationship based solely on mistrust.
                                                                  —Pierce Brosnan

Emotional Conflict: Exchanges That Spiral from Bad to Worse

Sometimes couples get locked into stereotyped gender roles. She tries to communicate. He is inexpressive and nonresponsive. She becomes more and more emotional, trying futilely to push him into conversation. He gets overwhelmed and withdraws. Eventually, if sufficiently provoked, he may explode in anger. Generally, however, he just withdraws (Levenson & Gottman, 1985; Notarius & Johnson, 1982). Each partner insists that the other must change.

Columnist Ellen Goodman (in Notarius & Johnson, 1982, p. 483) described a typical encounter:

> The couple were seated at the window table eating their dinners. She was looking at him. He was looking at his plate.
> "What are you thinking about?" she asked finally, engaging him with a half-smile, cocking her head flirtatiously, her fork poised in the air.
> He returned her smile for a minute and said, "Oh nothing," and went back to his dinner. His wife, with a glimmer of disappointment, a hint of hurt, pierced a heart of lettuce and joined him in a somewhat silent meal.

The emotional exchanges between couples who are happy or who are miserable differ immensely. Happy couples are positive; distressed couples are negative in their interactions. Happy couples know how to de-escalate conflicts. John Gottman (in Goleman, 1984, p. 20) observes:

> When tensions are low, it typically is the husband who plays the role of managing negative feelings. The wife will say something negative, and he'll respond in a positive way, keeping things from escalating. These husbands have a marvelously gentle way of deflecting their wives' negative feelings.
> But when things flare up, it's the wife who takes the crucial role in managing

things. Husbands don't seem as flexible as wives when feelings are intense; for example, men in both happy and unhappy marriages tend to respond to anger with anger. In happy marriages, though, the wives are able to switch to a de-escalating response during intense conflicts. Men are poorer at making up when things have gotten to this point.

Troubled duos, on the other hand, quickly get locked into negative tit-for-tat exchanges; their conflicts quickly spiral out of control (Gottman, 1979; Pike & Sillars, 1985). They are engaged in a duel. One glare begets another; one disgusted expression provokes another. Exchanges become stereotyped. We all know couples like this and can predict the dismal sequence. He will shout. She will take on an air of injured martyrdom, and do exactly what he demanded. His Pyrrhic victory, routed by her superior tactics, causes his heart to sink and leads to the inevitable apologies (Baucom & Adams, 1987).

Novelist David Lodge (1980) depicts one such conflict:

While they were clearing up after the dinner party, Michael and Miriam had a row. She accused him of provoking an embarrassing scene between Angela and Dennis. Nonsense, he said, it was all in fun. We were all a bit merry, except you. That's another thing, said Miriam, you pour out far too much wine, you only think a party's going well if everybody's half-seas over, it's not necessary. I hate dinner parties, anyway, she said, scraping plates angrily into the garbage can, you always tell me to cook too much, and then look at the waste. Yes, said Michael sarcastically, you could feed a whole street in Calcutta for a week on our leftovers. Well, it's true, said Miriam, and while we're on the subject, I want to covenant a tenth of our income to CAFOD [a Christian charity]. You're insane, said Michael, that's over five hundred pounds a year. If the developed countries are going to help the Third World, said Miriam, they've got to accept a drop in their standard of living. We could do without the car, for instance. I'll give up my car if everyone else will give up theirs, said Michael, but I'm damned if I will otherwise. Is that what you call Christian leadership? said Miriam. It's what I call common sense, said Michael, what use is my five hundred pounds to the Third World, most of it would disappear into the pockets of bureaucrats and middlemen anyway. All right, pay me a proper wage for keeping house, and I'll make my own arrangements, said Miriam. Don't be ridiculous, said Michael. It's not ridiculous, said Miriam, white with anger now. Anyway, I'm fed up with housekeeping, I'll get a job of my own. . . .

Michael snatched up the garbage pail and took it outside to the back garden, where he relieved his feelings by banging the dustbin lids. When he returned to the kitchen with a fully worked out account of why he couldn't reorganize his teaching schedule, Miriam had gone to bed, leaving him the rest of the washing-up. Moodily he made himself a cup of instant coffee. The mild lechery which he had been fuelling throughout the evening with wine and sexy talk had evaporated, and he knew exactly what an unfriendly posture Miriam would have adopted in bed upstairs—her face turned towards the wall, her shoulders hunched, her nightdress pulled down and locked between her ankles. These rows, which had become more frequent of late, frightened him, not so much because of the aggression they released in Miriam but because they made him wonder whether they should ever have married each other. . . . Miriam seemed like an utter stranger. (pp. 200–201)

Such conflicts can be remarkably stable. For example, writers George Sand and Alfred de Musset had an incendiary love affair, alternating between adoring love letters and furious scenes. Their biographer Andre Maurois (1953) noted that "man is so made that he turns from what he can have, and pursues what he cannot" (p. 189). He reported:

> Can those who revel in suffering ever wholly renounce an opportunity for renewing it? . . . Musset became once more a prisoner within a hellish treadmill. He was the victim of a masochistic need to know the worst. There was jealousy, there were upbraidings, terrible scenes, followed by remorse, pleas for forgiveness, exquisite tenderness, or, if he met with opposition, illness. And so the vicious circle travelled round and round. . . . But they were both afflicted by that worst of follies—a craving for the Absolute. From breach to breach, from reconciliation to reconciliation, their dying passion twitched and gibbered in the nervous spasm of approaching dissolution. They were like two men fighting to the death, both drenched with blood and sweat, clinging together, raining blows on one another, beyond the power of the onlookers to separate. (pp. 189–191)

We see that happy and unhappy couples communicate emotionally in very different ways. Some couples seem unable to step away from even the most brutalizing of conflicts. They must stay, flailing away, until they "win."

Conflict Behavior

Donald Peterson (1983) provided an overview of conflict behavior (see Figure 8.2), which offers some insight into what sorts of events precipitate conflict, how couples typically deal with it, and how various conflicts are generally resolved. Conflict is defined as "an interpersonal process that occurs whenever the actions of one person interfere with the actions of another" (p. 356).

Beginnings   Warring couples can manage to fight over almost anything. They fight over their personal dispositions (he is messy; she is compulsive), over marital norms (what is "right" or "wrong"; he doesn't spend enough time with the children; she doesn't keep the house clean enough), or over a thousand and one specific issues (she left her nylons dripping in the tub; he borrowed her razor) (Braiker & Kelley, 1979). One of our friends is a musician. His wife loves to sing to herself as she washes the dishes. Unfortunately, she generally knows only the first two lines of most popular songs. Last week as she mindlessly hummed the first two lines of "Jingle Bell, Jingle Bell, Jingle Bell Rock" over and over again, a bit off-key, as she washed the dishes, he could stand it no longer. He tried to teach her the third and fourth lines. "Just try" he encouraged her. She was understandably irritated. "Leave me alone; if you want to sing, sing your own songs" she hissed between clenched teeth. Some common sources of conflict are listed in Table 8.1 on page 246.

According to Peterson (1979), four kinds of initiating events spark conflict: criticism, illegitimate demands, rebuffs, and cumulative annoyances.

1. Criticism. Things may start out well. The couple may be working together or taking a holiday, when all of a sudden one person insults or criticizes another. The mother may be bundling her four children into snowsuits, when her husband asks impatiently: "What's keeping you?" The ill-timed criticism sparks an explosion.

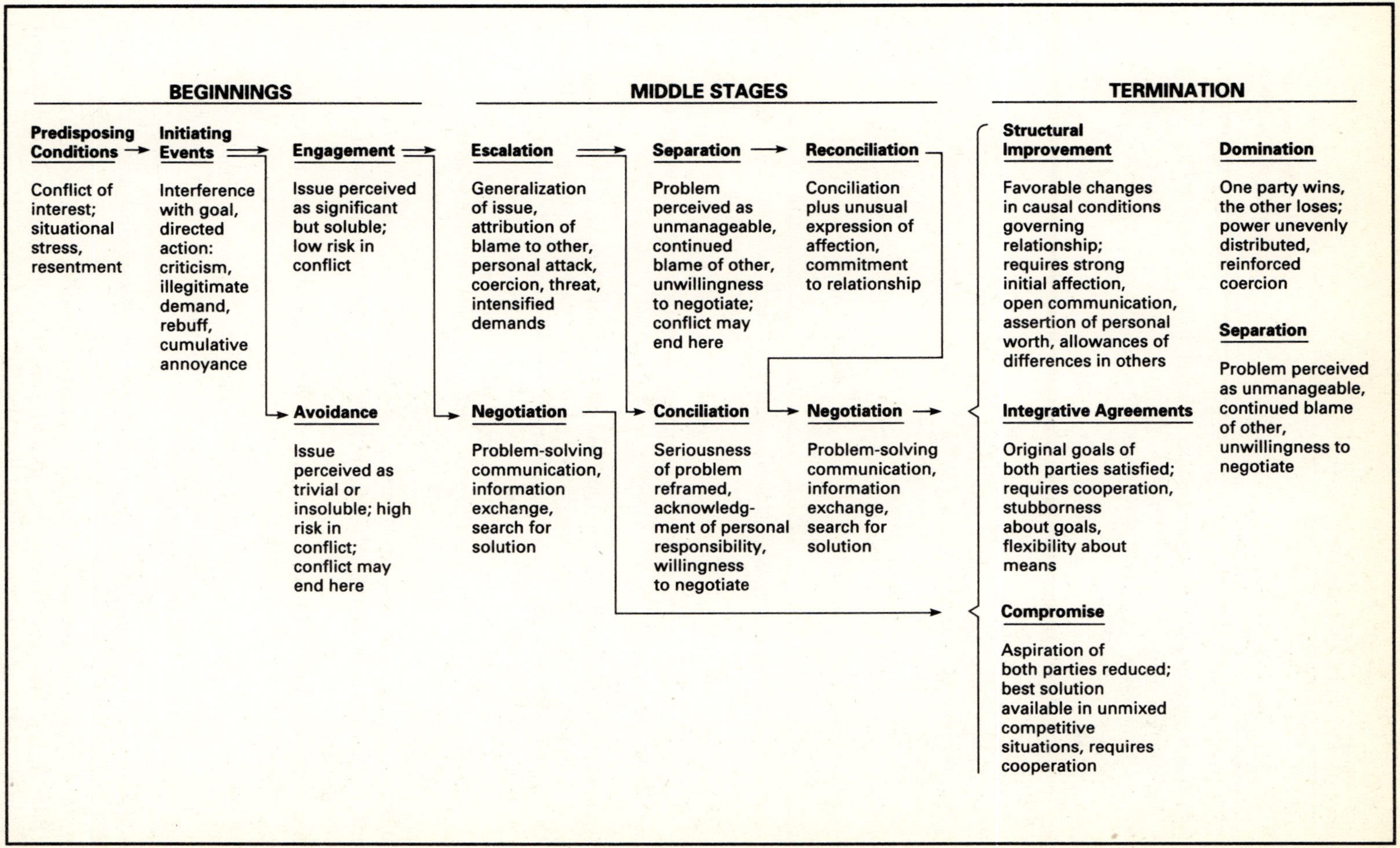

BEGINNINGS

Predisposing Conditions
Conflict of interest; situational stress, resentment

→

Initiating Events
Interference with goal, directed action: criticism, illegitimate demand, rebuff, cumulative annoyance

⇉

Engagement
Issue perceived as significant but soluble; low risk in conflict

Avoidance
Issue perceived as trivial or insoluble; high risk in conflict; conflict may end here

⇉

MIDDLE STAGES

Escalation
Generalization of issue, attribution of blame to other, personal attack, coercion, threat, intensified demands

Negotiation
Problem-solving communication, information exchange, search for solution

⇉

Separation →
Problem perceived as unmanageable, continued blame of other, unwillingness to negotiate; conflict may end here

Conciliation
Seriousness of problem reframed, acknowledgment of personal responsibility, willingness to negotiate

Reconciliation
Conciliation plus unusual expression of affection, commitment to relationship

Negotiation ↑
Problem-solving communication, information exchange, search for solution

TERMINATION

Structural Improvement
Favorable changes in causal conditions governing relationship; requires strong initial affection, open communication, assertion of personal worth, allowances of differences in others

Integrative Agreements
Original goals of both parties satisfied; requires cooperation, stubbornness about goals, flexibility about means

Compromise
Aspiration of both parties reduced; best solution available in unmixed competitive situations, requires cooperation

Domination
One party wins, the other loses; power unevenly distributed, reinforced coercion

Separation
Problem perceived as unmanageable, continued blame of other, unwillingness to negotiate

Figure 8.2 The possible courses of conflict.

Table 8.1   SOURCES OF CONFLICT

Problem	Percentage of couples reporting this problem
1. Division and fulfillment of responsibility.	13.0%
2. Failure to give appreciation, understanding, affection.	12.5
3. Carelessness, sloppiness, impulsivity.	11.7
4. Conflicting preferences about leisure time, where and how to live, and so forth.	9.9
5. Inadequate and poor communication.	7.6
6. Influence attempts, nagging, making decisions.	7.4
7. Independence, external involvements.	6.9
8. Attitudes and behavior toward parents.	5.6
9. Interference with partner's study, work, and so forth.	4.6
10. Aggressive behavior and temper.	4.3
11. Inappropriate behavior in social situations.	4.3
12. Excessive worry, compulsivity, moodiness.	4.1
13. Dependence, possessiveness.	3.1
14. Attitudes and behavior toward friends.	2.6
15. Passivity, lack of confidence, lack of ambition.	2.2

Source: Kelley, Cunningham, & Stambul, 1973; cited in Kelley, 1979, p. 19.

2. **Illegitimate demands.** When people feel unfairly treated, serious conflicts may arise. An example:

> I asked Jim if he would do the dishes—to get them out of the way—while I fixed the handle of the teapot so we could have some tea. Negative vibrations from Jim who immediately suggested we do the dishes together, implying that I should wash. I asked if he would like to wash them and he said, "Well, I would if it were just the dinner dishes, but there's all that other stuff in the sink." I had been cooking all afternoon for a camping trip and Jim didn't like the way I left pans and things around. General manifestations of disgust from both participants at this point. (Peterson, 1983, p. 371)

Injustice is hard for people to understand. Often they keep replaying the interaction again and again, trying to figure out how their mates could have treated them so unfairly.

3. **Rebuff.** When a person's appeals for love, attention, or help are rebuffed, serious conflict is likely to erupt.

> I came home from work and went to sit on Bert's lap. I kissed him and began to tell him something that had happened to me during the day. Bert said it was time for the news. End of encounter. (Peterson, 1983, p. 371)

A person who experiences such rebuffs feels humiliated and angry and often withdraws.

4. **Cumulative annoyance.** A first act may be unnoticed. A second and even a third or fourth repetition may be ignored. But then some threshold is exceeded. "That does it!" says the respondent and the fight is on.

Once an initiating event has occurred, the interaction takes a decisive turn. The couple may either engage in conflict or avoid it. Generally, powerful people are more likely to join in battle; the powerless are more likely to try to avoid trouble. If things get bad enough, however, even a powerless person may be driven to "stand up and fight."

Engaging in Overt Conflict   People can address difficult issues in graceful or appalling ways. Partners who love one another and are eager to stay married, who are confident that things can be resolved, and who possess communication skills are likely to try to figure out what the problem is and to devise a plan to set things right. In such cases, conflict can make relationships more rewarding and stable (Braiker & Kelley, 1979) (see Figure 8.2).

Sometimes, however, couples are no longer sure if they are in love; no longer sure they want to stay together. They assume things are hopeless. Sometimes, they lack communication skills. Here, conflict may well whirl out of control (Lloyd & Cate, 1985; O'Brien, 1972).

Avoiding Conflict   Often people choose to avoid conflict. Many happily married couples simply ignore small day-to-day irritations (Rausch, Barry, Hertel, & Swain, 1974). Couples may also avoid conflict for less appealing reasons. Some men or women are bullies. A wife may know she can get her way simply by laying down the law and refusing to discuss things. Her husband may be afraid to "push it." He may know he can get his way by nagging, nagging, and nagging (Roloff & Cloven, 1990). Sometimes couples avoid conflict because they know that it is hopeless. They have been through the same discussion again and again; it never goes anywhere and they are simply tired of the fight. Such marriages may seethe with hidden conflict. Some older couples settle for empty relationships. In these melancholy marriages, former lovers now just don't care enough even to fight (O'Brien, 1972).

Middle Stages   Peterson (1983) points out that once conflict has been engaged, it can take either of two main turns—toward direct negotiation and resolution or toward escalation and intensification of conflict (again, see Figure 8.2).

Direct Negotiation   Couples can settle their disagreements by bargaining. Both state their positions in a straightforward way. Pertinent information is accurately expressed and received without distortion. Intimates feel confident that their partners care about them. They try to figure out a solution that feels right to both of them.

Escalation   Some conflicts quickly spiral out of control. Couples insult, threaten, lie, and try to force the other to see things their way (Deutsch, 1980). Not surprisingly, conflicts quickly escalate.

In therapy, we have observed that perfectly sensible people, who so hate conflict that they will do anything to avoid it, sometimes end up in the most conflict-filled relationships. Their lovers, children, and friends quickly discover that threats work and so they begin to use them more and more often. The wife may try mild criticism and intimidation, in order to push her husband to do what she wants. He refuses. Her attacks increase in ferocity. Stunned, he gives in "to avoid trouble." It doesn't occur to him that he has actually taught her that insults and blackmail work; that she has become more likely, not less likely, to use them again.

I don't know a dream that's not been shattered or driven to its knees.
—Paul Simon

Termination   One way or another, all conflicts end. Peterson (1983) considers five kinds of endings—separation, domination, compromise, integrative agreement, and structural improvement (again, see Figure 8.2). Let us consider each of these in some detail.

"I knew our marriage was shot to hell when we started watching TV in different rooms," he said. "If her sound was up loud enough, I could hear her change channels in there. When she went to the same channel I was watching, I switched channels myself. I couldn't bear watching the same stuff she was watching. I believe this is called estrangement."

—Don DeLillo

Separation   If people fail to make progress in a dispute, they may choose temporarily to withdraw. This gives them a chance to "cool off" and try to come up with some creative solutions to the problem. Sometimes, of course, separation short-circuits a real solution to the problem. The wife may stomp out, spewing out insults as she goes. The husband may refuse to discuss an issue, knowing that they will continue to do things his way, whether his wife likes it or not. If the conditions that led to the quarrel are not changed, the quarrels are likely to continue.

Domination/Submission   Some conflicts end in conquest. The most powerful person gets his or her way; the other gives way. Sadly, such bullies do not realize that although their strategy may work in the short run, it is unlikely to work in the long run. Tyrants who are willing to do whatever it takes to get their way may think they have "won." They will probably discover that they have won the battle, but lost the war.

Scientists find that after a divorce, husbands and wives give different accounts as to how long the problems were accumulating. Men generally have the most power in love relationships. All along the way, they may have used threats and coercion to get their way. They think they have won the day. Thus they are amazed when their wives "suddenly" leave them. They thought things were going fine, just fine. (They were . . . for them.) The wife had been complaining for years about her unhappiness; the husband just refused to listen (Bee, 1959).

Martyrs can be equally shortsighted. They may think they are gaining a moral victory or being a "model wife." Most people probably find their behavior a bit irritating. As an example, President Franklin Roosevelt was good-looking, flirtatious, lively, and gregarious; he loved high-spirited parties. He wanted to stay on and on, into the night. For his shy, gawky wife, Eleanor, such parties were a nightmare; she hated them. One night she slipped out and left for home early in the evening. Historian Geoffrey Ward (1989) told this story:

At her front door, Eleanor discovered that she had forgotten her keys. The children's nurse must have been asleep upstairs. So were the children. There may have been other servants as well.

She did not ring the bell.

Instead, she sat down on the doormat in the vestibule and waited, brooding. She was still sitting there, grim and sleepless, when Franklin and the Robbinses arrived not long before dawn, "all flushed with wine and good cheer," according to Alice Longworth.

Franklin was astonished.

Why on earth hadn't she rung the bell or gone next door and asked to use the telephone, he asked, unlocking the door.

She had not done that, she said, because "I've always understood one should try and be considerate of other people."

Then why hadn't she hailed a taxi and driven back to the club for his key?

"I knew you were all having such a *glorious* time," she said, "and I didn't want to *spoil the fun.*"

At this point in retelling this story, Alice liked to add, "So noble, so noble." Mrs. Robbins, the eyewitness from whom she heard it, was more blunt: *she* would not have blamed Franklin then, she said, "if he had slapped her hard."

In the Oyster Bay branch of the family, Joseph Alsop remembered, the sort of patient martyrdom Eleanor displayed was known as the "I am not angry, only a little sick at heart" ploy. (p. 451)

Compromise   Theorists conceive of compromise as a process in which two individuals both give up a little bit so that the other can get some of their needs met. (Or, as Professor Higgins wryly observes in *My Fair Lady*, so "*nei*ther gets what *ei*ther really wants at all.") For example, a Hawaii couple we know was fighting over the division of household tasks. Both were working all day. They picked up the children, made dinner, cleaned up, and fell into bed totally exhausted. They were arguing about who should do the gardening. This tiny issue assumed gargantuan proportions since neither had any more to give. A compromise might involve something like each getting up an hour earlier on Sundays to garden before going to church.

Integrative Agreements   Best by far are integrative agreements. Sometimes lovers are determined that their "little sweetheart" will get what he or she wants. They are certain that "where there's a will there's a way." Usually, such couples can envision a creative way for both of them to get almost the essence of what they want. In the preceding example, the couple would surely end up with a better marriage and happier children if they moved to a smaller apartment and cut back on daily expenses so that they could afford to hire a part-time housekeeper and gardener.

The keys to attaining integrative agreements, according to Pruitt and Carnevale (1982), involve a mutually cooperative orientation, confidence that they are both determined to work out a solution that pleases them both, and "flexible rigidity" in regard to the means and ends of conflict resolution. Couples have to be flexible about the means for attaining their goals but stubborn about their basic goals. If either of them sacrifices too much, both of them will eventually be sorry.

Structural Improvement   In close relationships, affection deepens with time as the partners come really to know one another. Sometimes, after severe conflict, people step back and try to see the big picture. For example, in the previous example, the Hawaii couple came to realize they they were sacrificing their marriage and their children to try to stay in expensive Hawaii. They realized that if they moved to Oregon they could have a normal marriage and family life and buy a home . . . all on a 40-hour work week. All they had to sacrifice was good weather. In this case, they chose to make that particular structural change.

PROBLEMS WITH MATES WHO USE ALCOHOL OR DRUGS

Alcohol has been used throughout history for celebration and to promote relaxation. It has also been one of the chief causes of marital problems. There exists a desperately sad and long history of alcoholic husbands and their long-suffering wives. Today, many alcoholic wives have begun to add to the family's problems. Here, Susan Cheever (1984) describes her father's decline into alcoholism:

> It became clearer and clearer that my father was the worst kind of alcoholic. He seemed intent on destroying himself. I suppose he had always been an alcoholic. . . . My father's focus on liquor was so intense that he judged people primarily by how much they drank and by the strength of the drinks they served him. When he came back from a visit to F. Scott Fitzgerald's daughter in Georgetown, I remember him explaining how much he liked her—especially because of the robustness of the drinks she served, which seemed, the way he told it, to reflect an excellence of character. For him, hospitality meant offering each guest in his house a drink the moment they stepped through the door and then mixing whatever they asked for in proportions that would have knocked out an elephant. He was proud of the fact that he had made his father's first martini cocktail—and that the old gent had said it was "strong enough to draw a boat." Friends and interviewers often left my father's house in a happy daze, convinced that they had been unusually witty and charming.
>
> In the 1960s two things changed almost simultaneously. My father began to need more liquor to make him feel satisfactorily high, and his body began to tolerate it less. . . .
>
> As the months went by in the last years of the 1960s and the first years of the 1970s, the inevitable first drink of the day came sooner and sooner. Eventually it blended with the last drink of the evening, or the drink at midnight or three in the morning so he could get back to sleep. There was always an excuse. (pp. 161–163)

At low doses, alcohol depresses central nervous system functioning and removes inhibitions. As inhibitions crumble, drinkers may become happier and more relaxed, more sentimental or even maudlin, or more furious. These effects are more pronounced when blood alcohol is rising than when it is falling. Thus people are tempted to keep on drinking once they begin. Soon they reach the point (0.01 to 0.10% blood alcohol) at which alcohol begins to cause depression, sedation, and impairment of cognitive functioning and motor activity. While people who drink just a little now and then may derive some pleasure and relaxation, alcoholics drink far too much. Johns Hopkins University Hospital in Baltimore, Maryland, uses test questions such as those in Box 8.3 to determine whether and when a person is an alcoholic.

When people begin to drink heavily, the costs—to themselves, to their lovers and families, and to society—skyrocket. Recently, authors such as Claudia Black (1982, *It Will Never Happen to Me!*) and Robin Norwood (1985, *Women Who Love Too Much*) and groups like Al-Anon (which treat the families of alcoholics) have begun to observe the personality changes that occur in those families—in husbands, wives, and children—as they try futilely to accommodate themselves to the relentless demands of alcoholics. Meanwhile, the alcoholics inevitably deny that anything is wrong with them.

According to Norwood (1985) (who bases her conclusions on her clinical experience, the folklore of Alcoholics Anonymous and Al-Anon, as well as a bit of research) children of alcoholics (especially if they are women) tend to develop some typical characteristics for dealing with those they love:

1. Typically, you come from a dysfunctional home in which your emotional needs were not met.
2. Having received little real nurturing yourself, you try to fill this unmet need vicariously by becoming a care-giver, especially to men who appear, in some way, needy.
3. Because you were never able to change your parent(s) into the warm, loving caretaker(s) you longed for, you respond deeply to the familiar type of emotionally unavailable man whom you can again try to change, through your love.
4. Terrified of abandonment, you will do anything to keep a relationship from dissolving.
5. Almost nothing is too much trouble, takes too much time, or is too expensive if it will "help" the man with whom you are involved.
6. Accustomed to lack of love in personal relationships, you are willing to wait, hope, and try harder to please.
7. You are willing to take far more than 50 percent of the responsibility, guilt, and blame in any relationship.
8. Your self-esteem is critically low, and deep inside you do not believe you deserve to be happy. Rather, you believe you must earn the right to enjoy life.
9. You have a desperate need to control your men and your relationships, having experienced little security in childhood. You mask your efforts to control people and situations as "being helpful."
10. In a relationship, you are much more in touch with your dream of how it could be than with the reality of your situation.
11. You are addicted to men and to emotional pain.
12. You may be predisposed emotionally and often biochemically to becoming addicted to drugs, alcohol, and/or certain foods, particularly sugary ones.
13. Being drawn to people with problems that need fixing, or by being enmeshed in situations that are chaotic, uncertain, and emotionally painful, you avoid focusing on your responsibility to yourself.
14. You may have a tendency toward episodes of depression, which you try to forestall through the excitement provided by an unstable relationship.
15. You are not attracted to men who are kind, stable, reliable, and interested in you. You find such "nice" men boring. (pp. 10–11)

Box 8.3 SYMPTOMS OF ALCOHOLISM

ARE YOU AN ALCOHOLIC?

To answer this question ask yourself the following questions and answer them as honestly as you can.

	Yes	No
1. Do you lose time from work due to drinking?	____	____
2. Is drinking making your home life unhappy?	____	____
3. Do you drink because you are shy with other people?	____	____
4. Is drinking affecting your reputation?	____	____
5. Have you ever felt remorse after drinking?	____	____
6. Have you ever gotten into financial difficulties as a result of drinking?	____	____
7. Do you turn to lower companions and an inferior environment when drinking?	____	____
8. Does your drinking make you careless of your family's welfare?	____	____
9. Has your ambition decreased since drinking?	____	____
10. Do you crave a drink at a definite time daily?	____	____
11. Do you want a drink the next morning?	____	____
12. Does drinking cause you to have difficulty sleeping?	____	____
13. Has your efficiency decreased since drinking?	____	____
14. Is drinking jeopardizing your job or business?	____	____
15. Do you drink to escape from worries or trouble?	____	____
16. Do you drink alone?	____	____
17. Have you ever had a complete loss of memory as a result of drinking?	____	____
18. Has your physician ever treated you for drinking?	____	____
19. Do you drink to build up your self-confidence?	____	____
20. Have you ever been to a hospital or institution on account of drinking?	____	____

If you have answered Yes to any one of the questions, there is a definite warning that *you may be alcoholic.*

If you have answered Yes to any two, *the chances are that you are an alcoholic.*

If you answered Yes to three or more, *you are definitely an alcoholic.*

The above test questions are used by Johns Hopkins University Hospital, Baltimore, Maryland, in deciding whether or not a patient is an alcoholic. Reprinted by permission of Johns Hopkins University.

[For evidence in support of some of these contentions, see Coleman (1987), Finnegan and McNally (1989), Potter-Efron and Potter-Efron (1989), Smalley and Coleman (1987), and Wright and Wright (1990).]

Here, John Steinbeck IV (1990), whose parents were alcoholics, described the alcoholic haze in which he allowed his own marriage and family to disintegrate:

One night a group of us met at my one-room apartment in the Village. . . . We planned to call a comrade. . . . I decided to tape the call for everyone's entertainment.

All things considered, it should have been a loving night of grace and gratitude that we were all reasonably whole and well. The problem was that I wasn't. Not long after everyone's arrival, I began to celebrate our special togetherness with a half gallon of cheap Scotch. Things turned inappropriate, then became downright ugly. . . .

The phone call was a disaster of filthy, rambling interjection by me. Afterward, for some strange reason, I put a fresh cassette in the slot. The ensuing two hours of madness went on tape and were waiting for me like a mugger the next morning when I woke up from a blackout abruptly at dawn. I gazed at the infernal machine with what had become an increasingly familiar sense of disease.

Timidly, putting in the earplug, I began to listen to myself and my world go insane. I heard my friends excuse themselves to Chrystal and leave under the hostile fire and unprovoked ground assault of my surging abuse. I heard my child begin to cry and go mute when I yelled at her to shut up. I heard myself storm out of the apartment toward a neighborhood bar, only to come right back, screaming at the top of my lungs from the street for the keys that I had forgotten. I heard the scuffle on the stairs with the landlord, who was protesting about the hour and the constant yelling in my apartment. I heard myself curse and threaten his life as I nearly pushed him over the banister. I heard my friend's valuable lease torn to pieces. I heard my family shift around in their silent fear of my increasing violence. But most of all, I heard my mother, and then, turning off the tape, I heard my own tears.

That cold morning I was dreadfully and irrefutably awakened to the family disease of alcoholism. (p. 57)

It took Steinbeck 18 years to manage to give up alcohol.

Alcohol is likely to cause problems then for the alcoholics themselves, for their families and co-dependents, for their friends and co-workers, and for society as a whole. For example, an alcoholic's life expectancy is shortened by 10 to 12 years (DeLuca, 1980). Alcoholic mothers are likely to give birth to children with a variety of birth defects. Fifty-five percent of automobile accidents and 50% of all homicides involve alcohol abuse (Kinney & Leaton, 1982). America spends at least $13 billion per year attempting to deal with alcohol-related diseases (Mayer, 1983).

Drugs such as cocaine and heroin (and even marijuana) can present similar problems—some, of course, even more awful than the havoc wrought by alcohol abuse. Usually the only way to deal with such problems is to get the addict and the family into a treatment program (Alcoholics Anonymous, Adult Children of Alcoholics, Narcotics Anonymous, medical chemical dependency treatment programs, or individual therapy) or, failing that, to run away from the relationship—as fast as possible.

CONCLUSION

When the duet of love begins to hit wrong notes, turning harmony into dissonance, the causes are not always easy to sort out. The distinction between problems that are primarily the property of one individual (discussed in the previous chapter), those that are inherent in the nature of relationships themselves (this chapter), and those that are catalyzed from without (next chapter) is not always clear. Among those latter catalysts are children, in-laws, money and career issues, extramarital affairs, and the sometimes all-controlling political and socioeconomic imperatives that come from the society in which we live. There are many factors that can lay waste to a relationship. Perhaps we should be less surprised at the number of love affairs that are waylaid than by the fact that a good number manage to survive and prosper.

Chapter 9

The Larger World

INTRODUCTION

Love does not exist in a vacuum. Relationships are affected by networks of family, friends, career, and workmates (Huston & Burgess, 1979) and—perhaps most important of all, but frequently ignored by psychological researchers—conditions in the world-at-large in which the lovers must play out their lives.

When couples with troubled marriages try to decide whether to work on their relationships or to divorce, we sometimes suggest they try an experiment. They should try to enrich their lives by getting more involved in the outside world. They are sometimes better able to deal with their marriages and give to them with greater esprit when they are buoyed by the delight of supportive friendships and rewarding careers and are engaged in outside activities. The satisfaction of the world beyond the hearth may, alas, only highlight the barrenness of their marriages. When that happens, their fuller involvement with life then makes it possible to ease out of the marriage without unbearable pain because supports have been established. Often the best strategy for either saving a relationship or ending it, paradoxically, is the same: engagement with life outside the home.

In this chapter, we discuss the ways that outside relationships—with family, children, friends, and workmates—affect the primary love relationship. We also look beyond those relationships to the larger forces that shape the way we all live.

THE PERSONAL WORLD

Home is the place where, when you have to go there,
They have to take you in.
                                                            —*Robert Frost*

Family

Parents In some parts of the world, parents have complete control over their children's lives: Parents simply go ahead and arrange the marriages they like. The children's futures may be settled at birth. In America, parental pressure is usually more subtle. If parents are close to their children or have power over them, their approval of their childrens' choices in dates and mates may mean a great deal. Parents may warn their children that it will "kill" their mother or father or grandmother or grandfather if they ever bring home a _____ guy (fill in the racial or ethnic group of your choice). Parents may urge their children to marry a "nice" Jewish, or Catholic, or Mormon boy. They counsel: "It is as easy to fall in love with a rich man/woman as a poor one" (Prather, 1990). Parents often choose to live in a good neighborhood and send their children to a good college, in the hopes that their children will associate with the right kind of mates (Rubin, 1973). The "shotgun wedding" in which a father forces a young man to marry his pregnant daughter is the ultimate in parental coercion. Some teenagers marry wildly unsuitable mates just to get out of the house. Such forced marriages, too, are in a sense due to parental pressure.

Of course, equally often parents try to *extinguish* passionate affairs. They warn their children that it is too early to marry. They should finish their education, embark on a career, save some money, perhaps retire first. (This reminds us of the couple who waited until they were 90+ to divorce. Asked why they waited so long they said: "We wanted to wait until our children died first.") Fathers may try to put a stop to homosexual love affairs. Mothers may sniff at their son's choice in a woman. Both may issue dire warnings about character. Parents' efforts to put a stop to a blazing love affair don't always work, however. Sometimes, especially if the generations are locked in combat, parental meddling merely adds fuel to the fire. Richard Driscoll and his colleagues (1972) observed a fascinating paradox. Parents interfere in passionate relationships in the hope of destroying them. But sometimes such meddling simply intensifies the couple's feelings. In Roman mythology, the tale of Pyramus and Thisbe is built on the intensification of love by parental opposition: "They longed to marry, but their parents forbade it. Love, however, cannot be forbidden. The more the flame is covered up, the hotter it burns" (Hamilton, 1942, p. 101).

Shakespeare wrote of Pyramus and Thisbe in *A Midsummer Night's Dream*. But his most famous love story tells of those two teenagers Romeo and Juliet. Their brief but intense love affair took place against the background of total opposition from their two feuding families, the Montagues and the Capulets. The difficulties, rages, separations, and deaths that the family conflict created magnified Romeo's and Juliet's longing for one another. During the 1870s, the Hatfield– McCoy feud (these Hatfields were Elaine Hatfield's forebears) ignited over a love affair between Johnse Hatfield and Rose Anne McCoy. Family anger at the romance led to a bitter trial over a razorback hog, the stabbing of Ellison Hatfield, and the vengeful shooting of the three McCoy boys who had murdered him. The feud actually went on for 20 years and involved the governors of Kentucky and West Virginia in its last phases. Hatfields were kidnapped in West Virginia and jailed in Kentucky—a states' rights mix-up that went to the U.S. Supreme Court. In the 1900s, the feud finally ended when "Devil Anse" Hatfield was baptized and the feud guns were stacked (Jones, 1948). Denis de Rougemont (1940), in his historical analysis of romantic love, emphasized the persistent association of obstacles or grave difficulties with intense passion. An affair consummated without major difficulty seemed to lack zest.

We have underscored the difference between romantic or passionate love and conjugal (companionate) love. Romantic love thrives on the fires of challenge and uncertainty. Conjugal love, on the other hand, flowers from the seeds of trust and genuine understanding. Driscoll's group also observed this distinction and proposed that parental opposition would deepen romantic love while having a negative effect on companionate love. They invited 49 dating couples and 91 married couples to participate in a project. During an initial interview, all the couples filled out three scales:

1. *Assessment of parental interference.* This scale asked couples to estimate the extent to which their parents meddled and caused problems in their relationships. Couples were asked whether or not they had ever complained to their mates that their parents tried to make them look bad, did not accept the couple, interfered, were a bad influence, or hurt the relationships.
2. *Assessment of passionate and companionate love.* Couples assessed both how passionately and how companionately they loved one another.

The authors found that parental interference did indeed tend to intensify couples' passionate feelings for one another; young lovers loved more passionately when they were besieged by difficult, interfering parents than when they were not.

The researchers also investigated whether *increasing* parental interference would provoke increased passion. Six to 10 months after the interview, the authors invited the couples back for a second interview. They asked them whether their parents had continued to interfere or had become resigned to their relationships, and how the couples felt about one another now. As parents began to interfere more in a relationship, yet again the couples appeared to fall more deeply in love. If the parents had become resigned to the relationships and had begun to interfere less, the couples began to care less intensely about one another. Parental interference took a toll, however, on the companionate love married couples felt.

Generally, however, parents and children care deeply about one another; they are not locked in a battle. In such cases, parents and kin do seem to have a great influence on children's choices. Love seems to go better if parents are fond of their children's romantic partners and if the partners like the parents too. Diane Felmlee and her colleagues (Felmlee, Sprecher, & Bassin, 1990) interviewed 598 young men and women, early in the college year (when relationships were just beginning). They asked men and women if their own and their dates' families approved of their affairs. The more the families approved of the relationships, the more likely they were to survive. The authors also asked men and women how much they liked their dates' families. Again, the more the dating couples liked their lovers' parents, the more likely the relationships were to survive.

Once some couples marry, parents generally have less impact on their children's lives. On the average, most adults spend only about 18 minutes a day with their parents and close kin (Milardo, Johnson, & Huston, 1983). However, there are exceptions. Some couples are just a tiny tile in a huge mosaic of complicated family relations. They may have to deal with powerful, rich, and demanding parents. They may be overwhelmed by obligations to attend family dinners, celebrations, and religious and ethnic functions with their huge extended families. They may be expected to care for elderly parents, troubled brothers and sisters, or hordes of small children. In such cases, a couple's happiness will depend not just on one another but on their relatives as well. They have married not just a lover but a whole family.

An example: President Franklin Roosevelt's mother Sara had an iron will (Ward, 1989). Her domination blighted Franklin's teenage years and made Franklin's and Eleanor's early married life a misery.

> From his earliest days, Franklin's proximity to his mother, his unconscious adoption of many of her mannerisms and turns of phrase, even the physical resemblance to her that was already marked during his boyhood and grew steadily until her death—all had made some of those he met dismiss him as a "mama's boy."
>
> The Oyster Bay Roosevelts, Alice Longworth remembered, privately called the youthful Franklin "Miss Nancy" "because he pranced around and fluttered." . . . They had thought his tennis pathetic, his overeagerness to impress embarrassing, his table manners altogether too good, above all, his acquiescence in the wishes of his mother, that "domineering tartar," too demeaning. . . . [At Harvard] his classmates routinely teased him about his good looks: A *Crimson* poster billed him as "Rosey Roosevelt, the Lillie of the Valley." Even as adults, he and Livy Davis, whose comparable looks

ensured that he would suffer the same sort of kidding, sometimes ruefully addressed one another with cloying nicknames coined in college: "Sweetness," "Cunning Little Thing," "Dearest," "Old Lady," "Pretty Face." (pp. 550–551)

When Franklin and Eleanor married, the strong-willed Sara simply took over the control of their house and the rearing of their children. Eleanor rarely dared offer an opinion. But in the evenings she often sobbed in an uncontrolled hopeless way over her dismal life.

Families have a powerful impact on us not because they somehow magically mark us for all time, but because as we grow up we practice the skills we need to get on with our families. We may well become experts at those coping skills. In some families, children learn never to say a bad word about anyone; in others that "if you have something nasty to say, come over here and sit right by me." In some families, "children are seen but not heard." In others, the children better learn to fight for their rights or they will be trampled underfoot. When people marry, make friends, or begin to associate with co-workers, they soon learn that they have to develop a broader repertoire of skills if they are to survive.

Love as a relationship between men and women was ruined by the desire to make sure of the legitimacy of children.

—*Bertrand Russell*

No. Children are the great gamble. From the moment they are born, our helplessness increases. Instead of being ours to mould and shape after our best knowledge and endeavour, they are themselves. From their birth they are the centre of our lives, and the dangerous edge of existence.

—*Josephine Hart*

Children   Children are a mixed blessing. In patriarchal, agricultural societies, children were assumed to be God's gift. Children were needed to help at home, in the fields, and to support parents in their old age. Today, too, men and women can provide a number of reasons for having children. Children give life meaning and provide a link with the future. Children are a source of love, joy, companionship, excitement, and fun. Most people feel that when they become parents, they are finally adults. They are proud to have produced and reared a child; proud of their children's achievements ("My son, the doctor"). They feel important, altruistic; they have enormous power over their childrens' lives. Children bring couples closer together (Hoffman & Manis, 1982; Veroff, Douvan, & Kulka, 1981). Parents who have just had a new baby *are* more likely to stay together than they normally would be; the birth of a child *does* delay divorce. Only 12% of couples with young children divorce during the first five years of marriage; 50% of couples without children do (Rankin & Maneker, 1985).

Yet the truth is more complicated than this. Surveys consistently find that couples with children feel less adequate, worry more, are less happy and satisfied in their marriages, and have more marital problems than do childless couples (Belsky, 1990; Belsky & Rovine, 1990). Children shatter intimate moments. They make it difficult to have an exciting sex life (Blumstein & Schwartz, 1983). They are a source of stress and strain. Children make everything difficult. Things that were once simple, like going out to dinner, become almost impossible. ("I'll give the baby-sitter a call—maybe she's stuck in traffic." "If she can't come, do you think you could give your sister a call?" "Could you get Jon's diaper bag, honey? No, no, he likes that *blue* blanket." "Susan, don't! Mama's on the phone. Get down from there. Aiiiea!") Children cause conflict and discord (Belsky, 1990; Belsky & Rovine, 1990). They are expensive. Regardless of a couple's race, creed, educational level, occupation, or income, on the average, parents are less happily married than are the childless. Figure 9.1 summarizes the results of a number of studies of marital satisfaction at different points in the family cycle. It is obvious that marital happiness plummets when the first child is born and remains low as long as there are children at home. Once teenagers leave home (to go to college, marry, or work), marital happiness rises sharply. Couples will never be as happy as they were in the beginning, before their children were born, but they will be happier than before (Rollins & Cannon, 1974).

We have provided a general overview of the impact of parenthood on marital happiness. To make some sense of the statistics, let us take a whirlwind tour of the joys and problems parents can anticipate at various stages in their children's lives.

When couples discover they are expecting a child, most are delighted. Of course, most young couples have some reservations as well. Many are stunned when they discover they really are going to be parents. "How could a little person like me be a mother or a father?" they wonder.

During pregnancy, men's *and* women's attitudes begin to change in ways that may surprise them. They might start out thinking that having a child is not going to change them, but change is inevitable. Most expectant couples find themselves becoming far more traditional than before (MacDermid, Huston, & McHale, 1990). They begin to get interested in their own grandparents and parents. What were they like when they were young? How did their parents raise *them*? They begin to spend more time with their folks. Wives begin to withdraw from the workplace. Husbands realize with a shock that now they will be the primary breadwinner. Men and women become less egalitarian (Cowan et al., 1985; Cowan & Cowan, 1989).

Pregnant women long for husbands who will be strong, protective, and sensitive. (Take two traits from the Charles Bronson column; one from the Alan Alda column.) Nearly all women worry about the pain of childbirth. They worry that their newborns will have some horrible birth defect or die. Half of pregnant women are nauseated and ill during the first three months of pregnancy. They may be exhausted during the final trimester.

Fathers-to-be often feel ill at ease too. Jerrold Shapiro (1987) interviewed 227 expectant fathers. Expectant fathers experienced four kinds of fears—performance fears, security fears, relationship fears, and existential fears. Most worried that at the time of birth they would not be able to come through for their wives: They felt too young to be fathers, too young to be responsible for supporting a family. What would happen to their marriage now; what if their wife liked the baby more than them? They suddenly began to worry about their own mortality. What if they died? Who would take care of the family then?

Once the infant is born, many new mothers fall wildly in love with their new babies. A. S. Byatt (1985, pp. 100–101) described such feelings:

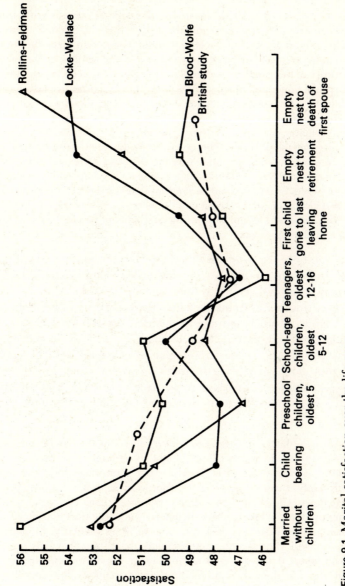

Figure 9.1 Marital satisfaction over the life span.

She had not expected ecstasy. She noted that he was both much more solid, and, in the feebleness of his fluttering movements of lip and cheek muscle, the dangerous lolling of his uncontrolled head, more fragile, than she had expected. His flesh was dark and mottled, and creamy wax and threads of blood clung here and there. Pasted to his pointed head, its overlapping cap of bone already springing apart under the elastic scalp, was a mat of thick black hair. He had a square brow, Daniel's brow, tiny nostrils, and a creased, emphatically large mouth. A clenched fist, smaller than a walnut, brushed a finely curled ear. He bore little, but not no, relation to the furious thing that had breached her. As she looked he frowned, increasing his look of Daniel, and then, as though aware of her gaze, opened ink-blue eyes and stared at her, through her, past her. She put out a finger and touched the fist; he obeyed a primitive instinct and curled the tiny fingers round her own, where they clutched, loosened, tightened again. "There," she said to him, and he looked, and the light poured through the window, brighter and brighter, and his eyes saw it, and hers, and she was aware of bliss, a word she didn't like, but the only one. There was her body, quiet, used, resting; there was her mind, free, clear, shining; there was the boy and his eyes, seeing what? And ecstasy. Things would hurt when this light dimmed. The boy would change. But now in the sun she recognized him, and recognized that she did not know, and had never seen him, and loved him, in the bright new air with a simplicity she had never expected to know. "You," she said to him, skin for the first time on skin in the outside air, which was warm and shining, "you."

Many new mothers are swept off their feet; they are fascinated with the sight, sound, and feel of their infants. They think every yawn is adorable. They are obsessed. Sometimes they become so fiercely protective that they begin to think of the two of them (mother and child) against the world. The father feels excluded, and rightly so. He is. Mothers assume he couldn't possibly understand how *they* feel. He couldn't possibly parent. Yet, at times, even these mothers feel overwhelmed by responsibility, exhausted, longing to be young and free again. A few mothers find they don't like being mothers. They find they can't bear to tear themselves away from their friends or work. Ann Beattie (1989) depicted some of the wonderful joys and terrible fears that were experienced by Jody, the mother of an infant:

There are so many books published to advise you about the child's upbringing. . . .
The message is always to change doubt to certainty and proceed. Sit by the sandbox with newfound strength. Embrace the squirming child and urge him to behave differently. Insist on eye contact when you speak. Do not let others turn the child upside down. Check the baby-sitter's references. Lock the cabinet that contains the cleaning products below the sink. Regular visits to the doctor. Two security blankets, so one can be washed. Check toe room in shoes regularly, by depressing the leather underneath your thumb. Comb tangled hair from the ends up. Speak out against environmental hazards. Look out for danger, but do not communicate your fear to the child. Do everything right, all the time, and the child will prosper. It's as simple as that, except for fate, luck, heredity, chance, the astrological sign under which the child was born, his order of birth, his first encounter with evil, the girl who jilts him in spite of his excellent qualities, the war that is being fought when he is a young man, the drugs he may try once or too many times, the friends he makes, how he scores on tests, how well he endures kidding about his shortcomings, how ambitious he becomes, how far he falls behind, circumstantial evidence, ironic perspective, danger when it is least expected, difficulty in triumphing over circumstance, people with hidden agendas, and animals with rabies. (p. 52)

Fathers may also have surprisingly intense reactions to their newborns. Some fathers also fall passionately in love with their newborns (Greenberg, 1986). Many do not. Here, Beattie (1989, pp. 130–131) described an "old-fashioned" father's reaction to his wife and infant son:

> He could still remember quite distinctly the fatigue that came from living with a woman who was always exhausted, which was a quite separate issue from your own exhaustion. It was numbing, like trudging through wet sand. It seemed that you had married a ghost, a wife who would never again have color in her face, and whose skin had strangely paled to match the baby's translucence. Will had screamed for the first six months of his life: first colic, then one allergic reaction after another when Jody had to stop nursing because her nipples were so badly cracked. Jody had made him get up half the time, in the middle of the night, to soothe Will, and he had cooed and cajoled with words that meant nothing to Will, rocked him, walked the floor. Other times he had stared in disbelief down his son's pink throat. He still dreamed about Will's gaping mouth, his wet, marble eyes, the pulse beating in his throat, his face turning purple. Many dawns Wayne had considered stuffing a diaper into his mouth, plugging the entrance to the cave of noise, or pinching him, holding him upside down, pushing a pillow into his face. He had never hurt him.

In Box 9.1, a middle-aged father contrasts the old-fashioned versus modern views of what fatherhood involves. With experience, he has opted to become a modern, involved, and enthusiastic father.

Many couples fight about child rearing, with serious consequences for their marriages and families. Couples who disagreed on child-rearing attitudes and values when their children were preschoolers were more likely to be divorced a decade later (Block, Block, & Morrison, 1981).

And some people have several children because they know there are going to be failures. They figure that if they have a dozen, maybe one or two will work out.

—*Bill Cosby*

For many parents, adolescents are a particular trial. Teenagers are supposed to begin to separate from their parents, and the "divorce" hurts—both of them. One of our graduate students, deemed beautiful and charming by her fellows, was a source of shame to her teenage children. When she waited for them outside their high school, they asked her nervously if she would be willing to duck down under the dashboard so that no one would recognize her. At movies, would she mind sitting on the other side of the theater? They could compare notes later. She, remembering her own childhood, found this amusing. Some parents, however, are devastated. Of course they felt that way about *their* parents, but how could that little child, who admired them so much at two, feel that way about them now?

And the disenchantment cuts both ways. In *The War Between the Tates*, Alison Lurie (1974) describes her feelings toward her adolescent children:

> They were a happy family once, she thinks. Jeffrey and Matilda were beautiful, healthy babies; charming toddlers; intelligent, lively, affectionate children. There are photograph albums and folders of drawings and stories and report cards to prove it. Then last year, when Jeffrey turned fourteen and Matilda twelve, they had begun to change; to grow rude, coarse, selfish, insolent, nasty, brutish, and tall. It was as if she were keeping a boarding house in a bad dream, and the children she had loved were

Box 9.1 FATHERHOOD: THE SECOND ROUND

His first round of fatherhood, a quarter-century ago, was done the old-fashioned way—as a benevolent bystander. He and his new bride were children. In their 20's. With not the slightest idea of how to nurture a child or share a household.

A father, as they understood it, put bread on the table, played with his child after work and went along on family outings, leaving the hard and dirty chores to the mother. The day his baby was due, he dropped his wife at the hospital and was shooed off to work by the doctor. Later, he got a call. It was a boy, healthy, 7 pounds 5 ounces.

Neither he nor his wife found anything odd in his detachment. Family lore held that he had changed only a single diaper. Whenever asked to pitch in, he loved to reply, "Bring the man-child to me when he is 21."

Looking back, his years of fatherhood seemed largely a void, broken by a few sporadic memories. Belly-tickling. Hide-and-seek in the apartment. A temper tantrum at the shoe store. Embarrassed retreats from restaurants.

Father's Day, in his experience, was the very opposite of Mother's Day—less homage for a job well done than mandatory annual torture. Like that hectic outing at the zoo, where his son squirmed into the bear enclosure, or the sweltering picnic at the lake, engulfed by mobs and rotting fish.

Just a few weeks ago, while on vacation together, he asked his son, now 27, what he recalled of his Daddy. It was pathetically little. The father felt he had known his son least as a child—and loved him most as a young man.

His second stab at fathering is being done the new-fashioned way—tuning in, not out. His second wife, with a career of her own, was not about to let him sit on the sidelines. Not with twin daughters.

They arrived 10 weeks early, so tiny only a doll's clothes would fit them. And as they struggled for breath and life in the intensive-care nursery, he came every day to root them on, cradle them in the crook of an arm, or deliver a vial of breast milk. Daily, their bonds grew stronger.

Later, when they came home, he fell easily into the role of chief attendant. Older, wiser and looser now, he became a champion diaper changer. In the mornings, he ruled over breakfast, pleased that his toaster waffles and instant hot cereal became the standard of excellence.

He is still no Mr. Mom. Too much childish prattle bores him, and a full day of girl-tending can be disabling. But he is involved, and having fun. As his daughters approach their fourth birthday, he is enraptured by their beauty, their brilliance, their individuality.

Though twins, they are not identical. One is gregarious, empathetic, cautious. The other a loner, moody, reckless. He basks unashamedly in their adoration. In the evenings, tired from work and commute, he will often ignore his keys and reach for the doorbell, setting off squeals of delight and a pell-mell rush to admit him.

For weeks now the girls have been preparing his Father's Day cards, and picking shirts of his favorite color. But there will be no special trip to the zoo or the lake; it's not necessary. For in this new and better age, Father's Day is not an annual event. It occurs daily.

Source: *The New York Times*, June 16, 1991, p. E16.

turning into awful lodgers—lodgers who paid no rent, whose leases could not be terminated. They were awful at home and abroad; in company and alone; in the morning, the afternoon, and the evening. (p. 3)

Erica contemplates her children, whom she once thought were the most beautiful beings on earth. Jeffrey's streaked blond hair hangs tangled and unwashed over his eyes in front and his collar in back; he hunches awkwardly above the table, cramming fried egg into his mouth and chewing noisily. Matilda, who is wearing a peevish expression and an orange tie-dyed jersey which looks as if it had been spat on, is stripping the crusts off her toast with her fingers. Chomp, crunch, scratch. (p. 2)

Though equally awful, the children are awful in somewhat different ways. Jeffrey is sullen, restless, and intermittently violent. Matilda is sulky, lazy, and intermittently dishonest. Jeffrey is obsessed with inventions and space; Matilda with clothes and pop music. Matilda is extravagant and wasteful; Jeffrey miserly and ungenerous. Jeffrey is still doing all right in school, while his sister's grades are hopeless; on the other hand, Matilda is generally much cleaner than Jeffrey.

Erica knows and remembers that Jeffrey and Matilda had once loved her. They had loved Brian. Now they quite evidently do not like either of their parents. They also do not like each other: they fight constantly, and pick on each other for their respective failings.

The worst part of it all is that the children are her fault. (p. 4)

Parents worry about their children. One father spoke touchingly about his longing to protect his 20-year-old daughter who was "drawn to the flame." Sure she was right, she would not even listen to the mildest of his suggestions. He was rightly worried that her late night escapades would end with his sweetheart being raped or murdered. Yet he had to step back; to submit to the inevitable; let her fly. Problems between parents and teenagers can take a toll on even the happiest of marriages (Steinberg, 1987).

People once thought that when teenagers left home for good, when the "nest" was "empty," it produced serious problems. Studies consistently show, however, that marital happiness and satisfaction improve markedly when the last children leave home (Radloff, 1975).

If parent–child relationships go well, parents and children can become fast friends once again when children are adults—especially when children become parents themselves. Parents can calm themselves when teenagers fight and flee; families are in business for a long time.

Some parents reap enormous benefits from their adult children. They now have distinctive personalities and exciting lives of their own. Parents become grandparents and have all of the benefits and few of the costs of children. They have a link to the future. Children, especially daughters, often care for their aging parents. Of course, the responsibilities of parenthood never really end. Sometimes, parents must deal with adult children who have problems all of their lives. Parents don't always like their childrens' personalities (see illustration).

Parents must sometimes reconcile themselves to adult children who have chosen to fulfill not the parents' dreams but their own; children who marry someone they can't stand; children who have miserable marriages; children who drink or take drugs; children who neglect or abuse their own children; and so forth. There are no guarantees. These problems too can take a toll on a marriage, especially when parents disagree about how to handle such problems.

I HATED THE WAY I TURNED OUT..

SO EVERYTHING MY MOTHER DID WITH ME I HAVE TRIED TO DO THE OPPOSITE WITH MY JENNIFER.

MOTHER WAS POSSESSIVE. I ENCOURAGED INDEPENDENCE.

MOTHER WAS MANIPULATIVE. I HAVE BEEN DIRECT.

MOTHER WAS SECRETIVE. I HAVE BEEN OPEN.

MOTHER WAS EVASIVE. I HAVE BEEN DECISIVE.

NOW MY WORK IS DONE. JENNIFER IS GROWN.

THE EXACT IMAGE OF MOTHER.

Stepchildren   Demographers estimated that by 1990, most couples who married for a second time had to "blend" their families. By 1990, 25 to 33% of all children had lived in blended families sometime during their childhood (Santrock, Sitterle, & Warshak, 1988). Sometimes, these blends go easily from the start. In Anne Tyler's (1989) "The Artificial Family," Toby, a new stepfather, describes his delight in Samantha:

> The daughter was five years old. Her name was Samantha, and it suited her: she was an old-fashioned child with two thick braids and a solemn face. When she and her mother stood side by side, barefoot, wearing their long dresses, they might have been about to climb into a covered wagon. They presented a solid front. Their eyes were a flat, matching blue. "Well!" Toby would say, after he and Samantha knew each other better. "Shall we all *three* go somewhere? Shall we take a picnic lunch? Visit the zoo?" . . .
>
> Toby's study became the center of the apartment, and every evening while he read Mary sat with him and sewed and Samantha played with cut-outs at their feet. Mary's pottery began lining the mantel and bookshelves. She pounded in nails all over the kitchen and hung up her saucepans. Samantha's formal bedtime ritual changed to roughhousing, and she and Toby pounded through the rooms and pelted each other with sofa cushions and ended up in a tangle on the hallway carpet. . . .
>
> How could he refuse anything to Samantha? With him, she was never disobedient. She shrieked with him over pointless riddles, she asked him unanswerable questions on their walks home from the lab, she punched at him ineffectually, her thumbs tucked inside her fists, when he called her Sam. (pp. 140–143)

For most couples in these second marriages, however, the greatest stumbling block is figuring out how to deal with their stepchildren (Duberman, 1975). The transition is a difficult one for everyone.

Most biological parents are fiercely protective of their own children. The idea that some "stranger" would try to be mother or father to their children, try to tell their children what to do, might even spank their children, fills them with rage. How dare they!

Children in blended families find themselves caught in a web of conflicting loyalties too (Boszormenyi-Nagy & Spark, 1973). Both biological and stepparents want the children to appreciate *their* position. To be loyal to biological parents means to despise the stepparents. Parents question their children carefully. You don't call her mom do you? You don't call *him* dad?

Stepparents face an uphill battle. Dr. Benjamin Spock, child-care expert, was humbled by the difficulties of stepparenting, after marrying a woman with a 10-year-old daughter. "Being a stepfather was the most painful experience in my life, and it was obviously even more painful for my stepdaughter," he said (Nordheimer, 1990, p. C8). They may have to deal with stepchildren who are arrogant, surly, and rude. They are uncertain as to what role they ought to play. Their former mates and biological children may be jealous of any love, affection, time, or money they parcel out to their stepfamilies; their new families may resent the love, time, and money they lavish on their "real" children (Santrock et al., 1988).

They have to negotiate with new husbands and wives who assume *they* should have the final say-so about their own children . . . and who, at the same time, insist the stepparents love their stepchildren as their own.

Many therapists have found from bitter experience that only certain types of relationships seem feasible in blended families. Sometimes, when all is said and done, the biological parents really insist on being in complete control of their children. In such cases, the stepparents' only alternative is to back up and opt out of parenting. This can work . . . but it has one inevitable side effect. It means the stepparents and children will never be emotionally close. They will not learn to share one another's styles and interests.

Sometimes, parents do want the stepparents and children to blend into a real family. Many mothers, for example, welcome a stepfather, who steps in to control a wild son. In such cases, biological parents have to bite their tongues and back up. They have to be silent when stepparents argue with and discipline their children; when they don't seem to love the stepchildren as much as they "should." This is hard, but there is a side benefit. The parents know that, in the end, stepparents and children will probably be close. They will find it easy to interact; they will share one another's interests. In any case, most therapists caution new stepparents to go slowly (Visher & Visher, 1979). Stepparents too advise "move slowly," "be patient," and "it takes time." At first, stepparents may take the role of a somewhat distant, slightly wary friend. As parents and children get acquainted with one another, and become friends, stepparents can begin to act as authoritative, warm, intimate fathers and mothers. If children are younger than 9 years old when their parents remarry, eventually stepparents and children are likely to form a warm, intense attachment. If teenagers are older than this (say between 9 and 15 years of age) it is less likely that they will form a tight bond (Hetherington, Cox, & Cox, 1982). Usually, it takes two years before such "blended families" really do blend easily together (Santrock et al., 1988).

Only choose in a marriage a woman whom you would choose as a friend if she were a man.

—Joseph Joubert

Friends

Couples vary enormously in how much time they spend with their friends and whether their friendships complement or compete with their love affairs. In early courtship, most young couples still spend a considerable amount of time with their friends. As lovers get more intensely involved with one another, however, their friendships usually begin to wane. Casually dating couples spend about three hours a day with close friends; engaged couples spend only about one hour per day with close friends. Sociologists call this phenomenon "dyadic withdrawal" (Milardo et al., 1983; Surra, 1990). Not surprisingly, friends often complain that the minute people get involved in a serious love affair, they abandon their old friends. The besotted couple simply has no time for anyone else. Some couples lose all interest in others until their affair begins to unravel or ends; then they regain their earlier interest in their old chums.

Generally, lovers' friends do have a great influence on whether or not lovers end up together. Researchers (Sprecher & Felmlee, 1991) find that if a person's friends support a love affair, the affair is likely to go better—couples love one another more, are more committed, more satisfied with their love affair, and are more likely to stay together—at least for a year or two. Love seemed to go better if the romantic couple liked one another's friends and possessed mutual friends, as well (Parks & Eggert, 1991; Surra, 1990).

Usually, a marriage is enriched by outside friendships. People who have more friends and who spend more time with their friends tend to be happier (Larson, 1978). Friendships are especially important for young people and the elderly. In her groundbreaking study of friendships, Lillian Rubin (1986), in *Just Friends,* found that men and women differ in their patterns of friendships:

> The results of my own research are unequivocal: At every life stage between twenty-five and fifty-five, women have more friendships, as distinct from collegial relationships or work mates, than men, and the differences in the content and quality of their friendships are marked and unmistakable.
>
> Other research shows that these differences persist right up through old age. . . .
>
> Generally, women's friendships with each other rest on shared intimacies, self-revelation, nurturance and emotional support. . . . In contrast, men's relationships are marked by shared activities. (pp. 60–61)

Of course, couples can carry a good thing too far. In therapy, we often see men and women in despair because their mates spend all their time away from home. One husband played basketball on Tuesday and Thursday and drank and gambled with "the boys" on the weekend. When his wife asked if there were any interests they could share, he puzzled and then speculated that if she would learn mathematics perhaps she could help him with his paperwork.

Too many couples expect a love affair to fulfill all their needs. When lovers fall short, as they inevitably do, friends can take the pressure off. If a husband works late, the bored wife can ask a chum to a movie. If a wife is beautiful but easily bored, the disappointed husband can invite a friend to talk about high fashion, Kant, or hiking in the Alps. In Lillian Rubin's (1986) study of friendships, one woman explained that she longed for some sort of reciprocal sharing of herself and her experiences. Her husband wanted her to come and sit by him, "nice and quiet."

> With a sigh of resignation, the same woman explained: My being on the phone at night makes problems, I know it does. Larry just hates it. Most of the time he keeps quiet, but sometimes there's a big blowup about it. Then we have one of those stupid fights where we both holler dumb things at each other.
>
> Even though I usually only say it when I get mad like that, I really think I wouldn't talk on the phone so much when he's around if he'd talk to me. But he doesn't; he's content just to sit quietly, maybe reading or watching TV or something. If I try to talk to him, you know, to find out what's going on with him, he doesn't really say much. Even if I tell him something about the kids or some problem I've been thinking about, he'll listen, but it doesn't turn into a conversation the way it does with a woman friend. So after a while, I begin to feel kind of lonely, and I go make a call, or someone calls me and I'm glad for the chance to talk. (pp. 140–141)

Having friends, said many men and women, allowed them to focus on the things their mates could provide, rather than on those they couldn't. It took the pressure off.

Rivals: Extramarital Sex

I think a man can have two, maybe three affairs while he is married. But three is the absolute maximum. After that, you are cheating.

—Yves Montand

Political and religious figures are often brought down by the discovery of their sexual affairs. (This is far more true, interestingly enough, in the relatively puritanical United States than in countries such as France.) In 1987 U.S. Senator Gary Hart was on the threshold of winning the Democratic party nomination for president of the United States. When accused of being a "womanizer," he challenged the press to prove their charges. Thirteen weeks later, after press photographs documenting his overnight tryst with Donna Rice, a 29-year-old beauty, were splashed across the nation's front pages, he was out of the running. An array of prominent politicians have had their political careers destroyed by such sex scandals. Among these are congressmen Wilbur Mills (with Fannie Fox) and Wayne Hayes (with Elizabeth Ray). U.S. Senator Edward Kennedy's presidential hopes were probably permanently dashed by the infamous 1969 "Chappaquiddick scandal," in which Mary Jo Kopechne was drowned when she and Kennedy accidentally drove off a bridge after a late-night party. Jim Bakker, top-grossing TV evangelist, came to ruin (if not damnation) with his extramarital affair. A year later, Jimmy Swaggart, the rival evangelist who had been accused of blowing the whistle on Bakker, was himself defrocked for sexual misconduct. Prostitutes in New Orleans revealed that he visited them each week to watch pornographic acts.

Americans disapprove of extramarital sex (Reiss et al., 1980; Weis & Slosnerick, 1981). In national surveys, 87% said that extramarital relations were "always wrong" or "almost always wrong" (Atwater, 1982). Two of the Ten Commandments proscribe such behavior: "Thou shalt not commit adultery" and "Thou shalt not covet thy neighbor's wife." In many American states, extramarital sex is a criminal offense. For example, in Minnesota, adultery is a crime punishable by a fine of up to $3000 and/or up to a year in jail (*St. Paul Pioneer Press Dispatch,* 1987). Yet 50% of men and 30% of women admit they have engaged in such relations (Sponaugle, 1989).

In *How Far Can You Go?* David Lodge (1980) showed how easily, and how thrillingly, men and women can slip into an extramarital affair.

> "Pity we don't have a bit of mistletoe in here," he [the married Dennis] said, attempting a light-hearted tone that came out as a strangled croak.
>
> She [his secretary, Lynn] looked up quickly. "I'll remember to get some next year, then," she said. . . .
>
> His hand closed over hers and pulled her gently forward over the desk. "I can't wait that long," he said, "to wish you a happy Christmas."
>
> What followed took Dennis completely by surprise. He had had in mind a single, wistful kiss, a tender but decorous embrace that would convey his appreciation of Lynn and his affection for her, but at the same time confirm their mutual awareness of the circumstances that made any deeper relationship impossible. Lynn, however, clung to him as if she would never be pried loose, she flattened herself against him like a climber marooned on a cliff-face, she shuddered in his arms and sighed and moaned and ran her fingers through his hair and thrust her tongue between his teeth as if she wanted to climb inside his mouth and wriggle down his throat. Dennis's feeble lust was soon swamped by this demonstration. He was appalled by the intensity of the passion he had aroused, and daunted by the task of seeming equal to it. At last Lynn peeled her lips from his, sighed and nestled against his shoulder. Dennis, stroking her back as if comforting a child, stared past her head at the dusk gathering over the company car-park. What now, he thought, what now? What does one do next? What does one say? There was nothing he could say, he realized, after trying out a few phrases in his head, that wouldn't sound either coldly dismissive or recklessly committing. It seemed to Dennis that a stark choice already stared him in the face between being a cowardly prig or an unfaithful husband; that, incredible as it seemed, one kiss had tumbled him irretrievably into a maelstrom of tragic passion and insoluble moral dilemmas.
>
> "Shall I take you home?" (pp. 204–205)

I'm always true to you darling
In my fashion.
Yes I'm always true to you, darlin'
In my way.
> —*Cole Porter*

Psychiatrist Frank Pittman (1989) contended that there are several different kinds of infidelity—accidental infidelity, philandering, romantic affairs, and marital arrangements.

1. *Accidental infidelities* ("It just happened") are those unplanned acts that "just happen," leaving everyone disoriented. Men might be vulnerable to a sexual encounter for several reasons. They may be sexually innocent and remain curious about what they are missing. Even those who have had vast experience may think it wasn't enough or was the wrong kind. People who missed out on such things earlier may drive themselves crazy until they can experience a threesome, an orgy, a professional, a giant, a dwarf, something homosexual, something animal, vegetable, or mineral—whatever they might have missed. Some men and women were

unpopular as teenagers. Now as adults they can't believe that what they once longed for has become theirs for the asking.

Ado Annie in *Oklahoma!* bemoaned the fact that she just "cain't say no." Some men and women have had no practice in gracefully refusing a sexual invitation. Women may worry that they might crush a man's delicate ego. Men are afraid "the Good Ole' boys" will think him a "wimp" if he declines. Thus they accept invitations they don't really want. Sometimes, people are drunk or have taken drugs. Or maybe they have just had a bad (or good) day. Or else they are horny. In any case, they just slide into an affair, without really thinking about it. Later, they may be sorry.

Joyce Carol Oates (1989) portrayed such an affair. Antonia is attending a writer's conference. She and her husband have been arguing, long distance. The Russian speeches are interminable and incomprehensible. She is simply exhausted and overwrought. Her heart goes out, momentarily, to Vassily Zurov, a member of the Soviet delegation:

> In Antonia's room, she said, far too rapidly, to Vassily: "I'm not here to practice diplomacy, I'm a cultural critic, I think of myself as an amateur even at that, I don't have the stamina, the nerves, for this sort of thing—"
>
> "I came here to talk about literature, I didn't come to hear debates about politics, it's very upsetting to me, to all of us, I mean the American delegation—I mean—"
>
> Vassily seized her hands, staring urgently at her.
>
> "You are not leaving?"
>
> He kissed her hands, stooping over. She stared at the top of his head, at the thinning hair at the crown, feeling a sensation of . . . it must have been a wave of . . . something like love, or at least strong affection, emotion. He was so romantic, so passionate, he was an anachronism in her own world, she did love him, suddenly and absurdly. She could not understand his words—he was speaking now in Russian, excitedly—but there was no mistaking the earnest, almost anguished look in his eyes. She felt a sensation of vertigo, exactly as if she were standing at a great height with nothing to protect her from falling.
>
> In an impulsive gesture she was to remember long afterward she reached out to hold him, to bring his head against her breasts. He was crouched over, one knee on the edge of her bed, gripping her tightly, murmuring something she could not understand. She felt him trembling; to her amazement she realized that he was crying. "You're so sweet," she murmured, hardly knowing what she said, wanting only to comfort him, "you're so kind, so tender, I love you, I wish I could help you, you don't know anyone here, you must be homesick, the strain of these past few days has been terrible, I wish we could go away somewhere and rest, and hide. I wish there were just the two of us, I've never met a man so kind, so tender. . . ." He held her close, desperately; she could feel his hot anxious breath against her breasts; he seemed to be trying to burrow into her, to hide his face in her. "I know you've suffered," she said softly, stroking his hair, stroking the back of his warm neck, "you can't be happily married, I know your life has been hard, they've tried to break you, I wish I could help you, I wish we could be alone together without all these other. . . ."
>
> They would be lovers, Antonia thought wildly. Perhaps she would return with him to Moscow. Perhaps she would have a baby; it wasn't too late, she was only thirty-six. It wasn't too late. . . .
>
> "You're so far from home," she murmured, confused. "We're all . . . we're all homesick. . . ."

He straightened to kiss her, and at that moment the telephone rang, and it was over. He jumped away from her, and she away from him, as the phone rang loudly, jarringly, and it was over.

Disheveled, flush-faced, Vassily backed out of her room like a frightened guilty child, muttering words of apology she could not understand. (pp. 97–99)

I've got those "God-why-don't-you-love-me-oh-you-do I'll-see-you-later" Blues!
—"Buddy's Blues" from Stephen Sondheim's Follies

2. *Philandering.* The "Battle of the Sexes" is "the habitual sexual activity that seems natural to the philanderer and is motivated more by fear of and lust for the 'opposite sex' than by any forces within the marriage or the immediate sexual relationship" (Pittman, 1989, p. 133). Pittman argues that philanderers are obsessed with gender. Some are frightened of women; they avoid committing themselves to anyone. Some hate women; they use seduction to humiliate them. Some think of women as a different species; they believe in a double standard. They depersonalize women, thinking of them as interchangeable.

If it seems wrong enough, then it must be right. Such is the nature of romance.
—Frank Pittman

3. *Romantic affairs* (temporary insanity) are "those crazy in-love states that cloud people's minds and make them forget their marriage and family" (Pittman, 1989, p. 133). Pittman wrote that:

> The ideal shared romance would be the one that is most intense, the one that receives no support from anyone, that exposes the lovers to mortal danger, and that ends in the death of both, preferably at the moment of consummation. . . .
>
> In almost all of the great romantic operas, such as those of Verdi, the ill-fated lovers try to get together over the opposition of their parents and political forces. They come together and then they die for their love. The idea of the plot is to find the lovers who are most mismatched, who are absolutely ill-suited for each other, lovers whose mating could guarantee disaster. Accordingly, Don Carlo lusts after his stepmother, King Gustav lusts after his best friend's wife, the court jester's daughter lusts after the married duke. The prude's son chooses a prostitute, Joan of Arc is in love with the dauphin. The Ethiopian slave girl wants the princess's boyfriend who has just been made commander of the Egyptian forces to invade Ethiopia, where her father is the king. The idea is that the love is unquestionably doomed from the beginning, and everybody knows it—even the lovers. They fully expect to die from their love. And they do. . . .
>
> One of the standard rules of romance is that love cannot be socially sanctioned. Romance, at all costs, must not be comfortable. It must not be functional. It must be in conflict with the world, so that the lovers have to choose between living in the fantasy world of being in love or in the real world of going around setting priorities and balancing realities. The romance must require sacrifice, and it can start with the sacrifice of all of one's other relationships and priorities. To do this, it must be illicit. (pp. 185–186)
>
> Romantics don't tolerate real people very well. (p. 189)

In *Gone With the Wind*, Scarlett O'Hara, who could have had Rhett Butler, threw herself at Ashley Wilkes—the one man who didn't want her. She pined away for Ashley, who was too pure and noble to betray his wife Melanie. It wasn't until Melanie died and bequeathed Ashley to Scarlett that she realized she didn't want him. Suddenly, she preferred her husband, the dashing Rhett Butler. Alas, now he no longer "gave a damn" about her. Poor Scarlett, all she wanted was what she couldn't have.

4. *Marital arrangements* are "efforts to maintain a distance that is required by one of the partners. They range from sexual supplements to flamboyant revenge affairs that keep stormy marriages in a state of intense passion and jealousy. The sex goes outside the marriage, but the emotion is still directed in" (Pittman, 1989, p. 133). Unhappily married couples may stay together for a variety of perfectly good reasons. They may decide to stay together "for the sake of the children," to protect the couple's family, careers, or finances.

Pittman discusses several common types of marital arrangements. We have known some married couples who live in different countries! Some people are in a permanent process of "getting a divorce." Their state of prolonged separation protects them from having to get seriously involved with anyone else. Some are just "shopping around" to see if they can find more suitable mates. Some are "psychiatric nurses"—taking care of schizophrenics who are frighteningly fragile, manic–depressives who undergo wild mood swings, or depressives who are so shell-shocked by life that they seem to require constant padding and insulation. Such marriages may be extremely stable. The nurse-spouse has signed on for this job and will stick with it. The nurse-spouse may need support too, however, and so may keep an affair going.

Laurie Colwin (1981) depicted this classic arrangement. Greenway falls in love with Alden Robinson.

> From Alden, I was learning how to give life some shape, how real work was performed in the world, how to harness energy to a project. I cleared my desk. I began to pay my bills on time. . . .
>
> From me, Alden was learning how to float, how to relish life without such strict rules for it. Our best selves, I thought, were on display. The variance of our natures seemed like art—light and shadow. . . . He was a pet from another country whose life was not, like mine, a relief map full of valleys, hills, and moraines, but was a hard, straight road that got you to an appointed city. Alden was pleased with my relief map. It was full of turns he had never taken. I was entranced by his straight road. We had absolutely nothing in common. (p. 146)

Suddenly, it is over. He is returning to his wife, Eleanor. She too was an economist. They have common memories, shared ideas and goals. She thought it was a serious love affair. Now she realizes she was only a brief, liberating diversion. She realizes she has been used.

> I was not prepared for the aftermath of this affair. The distress I felt seemed uncontainable. At the shop I found myself in the bathroom in tears, running the faucets so that Pete would not hear me weeping. . . . I was beset by devils I had not known existed: grief, rage, longing and pure desire. (pp. 148–149)

Romantic partners can be found to provide whatever is lacking—sex, excitement, sanity, chaos—from the marriage. Some couples may embark on an extramarital affair as an act of revenge. Other couples may be engaged in a power struggle. Having an affair gives them ammunition to use against one another. Such arrangements may work well for the couple. They often work less well for outsiders, who find out too late that the couple was the main attraction; they were only a sideshow. In Carol Clewlow's (1989) *A Woman's Guide to Adultery*, Monica's and Paul's marriage seems perpetually on the brink of divorce; both fall headlong into passionate, wonderful affairs. But eventually the lovers are abandoned. Finally, one lover recognizes what has been going on.

> "I see it all now, Monica," he says. "How could I have been so stupid?"
>
> "I've been used, haven't I, Monica? You used me as he used his lovers. All of us, them and me, keeping your tawdry little marriage together. What is it we gave you, Monica, him and you? It's life blood, isn't it, Monica? That's what we gave you. You're a couple of vampires sucking the life blood from your lovers to pump back into your dead little marriage."
>
> "I see it all, Monica," he repeats, his eyes boring into hers. "I thought I was something special but I was just part of a system. Can you believe it? There I was worrying seriously about the morality of breaking up your marriage when all the time I was just helping to keep it together."
>
> "You fall in love with someone who is married and you think it's your story, hers and yours, you think it's your plot and your narrative and you think you're in charge. But then suddenly there's a twist in the plot and you find out that it was never your story at all. That it was someone else's story, her story and *his* story, their story together, the story that started long before you arrived on the scene, the story that will finish long after you've gone, the story in which you were just a chapter.
>
> "It's funny, Monica," he says, . . . "I thought I was the hero, the leading man, but I wasn't, was I? I was just a character, a character like all the rest, not even a lesser character, but one of those minor characters who appear once or twice to nudge the plot along, one of those characters so unimportant they don't even warrant a name."
>
> "What am I to you, Monica?" he asks, a bitter smile beginning to draw back the corners of his mouth.
>
> "I'm a spear-carrier, aren't I? A bit-part player. A walk-on part." (pp. 204–205)

Adultery's a good subject for jokes because it's a sad business.
     —*Carol Clewlow*

How Likely Is Adultery to Lead to Trouble?   Scientists are not certain. Certainly when couples discover their mates are wildly in love with someone else they may be bruised. In commenting on the 50-year marriage of Harold Nicolson and Vita Sackville West, their son Nigel Nicolson (1973, p. ix) observed:

> It is the story of two people who married for love and whose love deepened with every passing year, although each was constantly and by mutual consent unfaithful to the other. Both loved people of their own sex, but not exclusively. Their marriage not only survived infidelity, sexual incompatibility and long absences, but it became stronger and finer as a result. Each came to give the other full liberty without inquiry or reproach. Honour was rooted in dishonour. Their marriage succeeded because each found permanent and undiluted happiness only in the company of the other. If their marriage is seen as a harbour, their love affairs were mere ports of call. It was to the harbour that each returned.

When the bohemian couple was apart, they suffered terribly. In a letter to Vita, Harold told of his loneliness:

When I closed your bedroom door at Rasht, I stood for a moment on the landing with a giddy agony, which made the whole house swing and wobble. With a great effort I stopped myself bursting into your room again—where I should have found your dear head bowed in tears, and your green pyjamas still wet from them. I went down the stairs into the garden and looked back at your window. I longed to call, "Vita, Vita, I can't bear it!"

I found your fur cap in my cupboard. I flung myself on the bed in an agony of suffering such as I have never known. I walked up and down in the dark saying, "Vita, Vita, Vita, Vita, Vita!" with the tears splashing on the dark floor. I felt that this is not to be borne. One can't be as unhappy as this. (Nicolson, 1973, p. 227)

Kinsey and his colleagues (1948, 1953), however, concluded that adultery can be fairly harmless in a marriage—if the spouse doesn't find out. How often do husbands and wives find out about their mates' extramarital affairs? Unfortunately, in collecting data for *Sexual Behavior in the Human Male*, Kinsey didn't bother to ask men whether or not their wives had discovered their infidelities or how they felt about them. By the time he got around to writing *Sexual Behavior in the Human Female*, though, Kinsey realized that these were important questions and asked them. About half of the women who had had affairs reported that their husbands had no inkling of them. About 9% of the women worried that their husbands might know and 40% were certain that they did know.

How did their husbands react to these affairs? Kinsey found that when the man didn't know about the affair, it rarely precipitated trouble in a marriage. (If the tree falls in the forest and no one sees or hears it, did it fall?) When he did know, there was "no" difficulty or "minor" difficulty 58% of the time. Only 42% of the time was there "serious" trouble. Kinsey's conclusion: 71% of the time, extramarital relationships cause no marital trouble at all—either because the partners don't find out or because they don't care deeply when they do (Table 9.1).

Psychologist John Gagnon (1977) wryly responded:

> In the Kinsey research there is a table, rather amusing because it is so self-serving. When people were asked, "Did *your* extramarital intercourse figure in your divorce?" they answered one way. When they were asked, "Did your *spouse's* extramarital intercourse have any effect on your divorce?" they answered another. When *they* had the sex, they said it had very little effect on their divorce. . . . But when they knew their spouse was having extramarital sex, it was viewed as a very important factor, especially by men. (p. 219)

When scientists asked couples seeking a divorce what caused their breakup, many cited infidelity as the problem (Blumstein & Schwartz, 1983; Buunk & Bringle, 1987) (see Box 9.2).

The commonest thing is delightful if only one hides it.
—Oscar Wilde

Recently, Daniel Wegner and his colleagues (in press) proposed that the secrecy of extramarital affairs may add to their thrill. When men and women are involved in secret affairs, the mental strategies and deceptive practices they must adopt to maintain the secret naturally drive a wedge between them and their mates and cause the two secret lovers to become obsessed with each other. After all, it is only to one another that they can speak mindlessly; tell all. Secrecy adds an extra thrill—which may vary from a shiver of delight to a rush of terror, depending what is being risked—to each encounter. Secrets make it harder to get over covert extramarital affairs once they end. To test these hypotheses, the authors asked men and women to list "hot flames" and "cold flames"—early crushes or extramarital affairs that they still agonized over (hot flames) or rarely

Table 9.1   EFFECT OF EXTRAMARITAL SEX ON DIVORCE

Question	Major effect	Moderate effect	Minor effect	No effect at all
Did *your* extramarital sex have any importance in causing your divorce?				
Women	14%	15%	10%	61%
Men	18	9	12	61
Did your *spouse's* extramarital sex have any importance in causing your divorce?				
Women	27%	49%	24%	0%
Men	51	32	17	0

Reprinted by permission from John H. Gagnon, *Human Sexualities* (Glenview, IL: Scott, Foresman, 1977), p. 220. Copyright © 1977 by Scott, Foresman, & Company.

Box 9.2 TESS OF THE D'URBERVILLES

Thomas Hardy (1891), in his classic tale of *Tess of the D'Urbervilles*, painfully highlighted the existence of a brutal double standard in the nineteenth century.

"Do you remember what we said to each other this morning about telling our faults?" he asked abruptly, finding that she still remained immovable. "We spoke lightly, perhaps, and you may well have done so. But for me it was no light promise. I want to make a confession to you, love."

This, from him, so unexpectedly apposite, had the effect upon her of a providential interposition.

"You have to confess something?" she said quickly and even with gladness and relief.

"You did not expect it? Ah—you thought too highly of me. Now listen. Put your head there, because I want you to forgive me and not to be indignant with me for not telling you before, as perhaps I ought to have done."

How strange it was! He seemed to be her double. She did not speak, and Clare went on: "I did not mention it because I was afraid of endangering my chance of you darling, the great prize of my life . . . Well, I would not risk it . . . But I must, now I see you sitting there so solemnly. I wonder if you will forgive me?"

"Oh yes! I am sure that—"

"Well, I hope so . . ." He then told her of that time of his life . . . when, tossed about by doubts and difficulties in London, like a cork on the waves, he plunged into eight-and-forty hours' dissipation with a stranger . . . "Do you forgive me?"

She pressed his hand tightly for an answer.

"Then we will dismiss it at once and forever!" . . .

"Oh, Angel—I am almost glad—because now *you* can forgive *me!* I have not made my confession. I have a confession, too—remember, I said so."

"Ah, to be sure! Now then for it, wicked little one."

"Perhaps, although you smile, it is as serious as yours or more so."

"It can hardly be more serious, dearest."

"It cannot—oh no, it cannot!" She jumped up youthfully at the hope. "No, it cannot be more serious, certainly," she cried, "because 'tis just the same!" . . . and pressing her forehead against his temple, she entered on her story of her acquaintance with Alex d'Urberville and its results, murmuring the words without flinching, and with her eyelids drooping down. . . .

After stirring the embers he rose to his feet; all the force of her disclosure had imparted itself now. His face had withered . . . "Tess!"

"Yes, dearest."

"Am I to believe this? From your manner I am to take it as true. Oh, you cannot be out of your mind! You ought to be! Yet you are not . . . My wife, my Tess. . . ."

"I am not out of my mind," she said. . . . "In the name of our love, forgive me!" she whispered with a dry mouth. "I have forgiven you for the same!"

And as he did not answer, she said again, "Forgive me as you are forgiven! *I* forgive *you*, Angel."

"You—yes, you do."

"But you do not forgive me?"

"O, Tess, forgiveness does not apply to the case! You were one person; now you are another." . . .

"I thought, Angel, that you loved me—me, my very self!" . . . .

"I repeat, the woman I have been loving is not you. . . ."

She perceived in his words the realization of her own apprehensive foreboding in former times. He looked upon her as a species of impostor, a guilty woman in the guise of an innocent one. . . . The horrible sense of his view of her so deadened her that she staggered. . . .

"Sit down, sit down," he said gently. "You are ill, and it is natural that you should be."

Source: pp. 291–299

---

thought about (cold flames). They asked respondents if they still loved the other, how often they still thought about them, and whether or not anyone knew about the affair. They found that if early crushes or affairs had been kept secret, men and women were more likely still to care for their partners, think more about their affairs, and to be more actively involved in trying to get over them and to get on with their lives. If they had been able to "talk these crushes or affairs to death," to deal with them openly, their passion was more likely to have spent itself; they were less likely still to think about these burnt-out affairs.

Jealousy

No matter how perfect—or practically perfect—a wife may be, she always has to watch out for the Other Woman. The Other Woman, according to my definition, is anyone able to charm my husband, amuse my husband, attract my husband, or occupy his wholehearted interest for more than 30 seconds straight.

—Judith Viorst

Simone de Beauvoir (1967), in *The Woman Destroyed*, wrote about a jealous wife's collapsing world. It is a painful chronicle. The woman is in her fifties. If you asked her if she loved her husband, she would say, "Of course," but the passion in their relationship has long ago flickered out. They now simply take one another for granted. She spends her days comfortably—visiting with her children, shopping, helping friends. When her husband, Maurice, admits that he is having an affair, everything changes. The wife is alternately calm and frantic. She wants to hurt and punish him. She disdains him and she loves him more than ever.

And I went to have a talk with Isabelle [a friend]. . . . She advised me to be patient. What gives this sort of affair its piquancy is its newness; time works against Noellie; the glamour she may have in Maurice's eyes will fade. But if I want our love to emerge from this trial unhurt I must play neither the victim nor the shrew. "Be understanding, be cheerful. Above all be friendly," she said to me. . . . Patience is not my outstanding virtue. But I certainly must do my best. (pp. 136–137)

Moments later, her fantasies and discoveries plunge her into despair. She minutely calculates how much time Maurice spends with her compared with her rival Noellie. She calls Maurice's office to check on him and camps outside Noellie's apartment in the hopes of seeing them together, hoping she can gauge the intensity of Maurice's love for Noellie by his gaze, by how they walk together. She both avoids information and seeks it desperately.

I am afraid of sleeping on the nights that Maurice spends with Noellie. That empty bed next to mine, these flat, cold sheets. . . . I take sleeping pills, but in vain, for I dream. Often in my dreams I faint with distress. I no longer know anything. The whole of my past life has collapsed behind me, as the land does in those earthquakes where the ground consumes and destroys itself—is swallowed up behind you as you flee. There is no going back. I am so destroyed by the morning that if the daily woman did not come at ten o'clock I should stay in bed every day until past noon, as I do on Sundays. Why doesn't he love me anymore? The question is why did he love me in the first place? One never asks oneself. (pp. 193–195)

De Beauvoir's chronicle details the chaotic jumble of emotions that jealousy creates. What do social scientists know about these painful feelings?

He that is not jealous, is not in love.
         —*St. Augustine*

For love is as strong as death, jealousy is cruel as the grave.
         —*Song of Solomon*

The Experience of Jealousy   What is jealousy? Robert Bringle and Bram Buunk (1986, p. 226) defined it as "the aversive emotional response to a partner's real, imagined, or potential attraction for a third person." Sometimes, people are jealous without reason. Leo Tolstoy (1889/1985, p. 25) portrayed such feelings:

I lost all control over my imagination: it began to paint for me, in the most lurid fashion, a rapid sequence of pictures which inflamed my jealousy. . . . They were all of the same thing; of what was happening there, in my absence, of her being unfaithful to me. I was consumed with rage, indignation and a kind of strange drunken enjoyment of my own hurt pride as I contemplated these pictures. . . . I couldn't tear myself away from them, I couldn't erase them from my mind and I couldn't stop myself dreaming them up. But that wasn't all: the more I contemplated these imaginary pictures, the more I believed they were real.

Sometimes, of course, people have every reason to be jealous. Their mates *are* in love with someone else; they *are* having an affair; they *are* planning to leave.

Jealousy seems to involve a blend of anger, a desire for revenge, sadness, fear, hurt, and disgust (Sharpsteen, 1991). Susan Pfeiffer and Paul Wong (1989) developed the *Multidimensional Jealousy Scale* to measure the thoughts, emotions, and actions associated with jealousy. A sampling of questions from the MJS is in Box 9.3.

There is more self-love than love in jealousy.
  —*François, Duc de La Rochefoucauld*

The Causes of Jealousy

Threats to Self-esteem   Sigmund Freud (1922) considered normal jealousy to be a complex emotion consisting of self-criticism, a narcissistic wound, grief over the potential or actual loss of the beloved, anger at the rival, and impulses to compete. Margaret Mead (1931) contended that the more shaky one's self-esteem, the more easily one would fall prey to the pangs of jealousy. When men and women have low self-esteem, they wonder "Why would anyone stay with *me*?" Mead observed: "Jealousy is not a barometer by which the depth of love can be read. It merely records the degree of the lover's insecurity. . . . It is a negative miserable state of feeling having its origin in a sense of insecurity and inferiority" (p. 92). A variety of researchers have found that people with low self-esteem are especially vulnerable to jealousy (Bringle & Buunk, 1986; White & Mullen, 1989).

Jealousy is the experience of being left out, rejected, dispensed with, or betrayed.
  —*L. James Grold*

Dependence and Insecurity   Ellen Berscheid and Jack Fei (1977) pointed out that the more people need someone, the more insecure they are, and the more their relationship is threatened, the more susceptible they will be to jealousy. Bram Buunk (1982) found that the more emotionally dependent men and women were on their relationships, the more jealous they knew they would be if their partners were interested in someone else.

Lovers may be dependent on their current relationships for several kinds of rewards—self-esteem, emotional closeness, sexual intimacy, money, or for the thousand and one practical benefits that come from dating and marriage (Buunk & Bringle, 1987). When relationships are threatened, people suddenly realize what they have to lose.

Robert Bringle and Bram Buunk (1986) interviewed 218 Dutch men and women whose partners had recently had an extramarital relationship. What caused them the most suffering? (1) *Loss of self-esteem*. What was wrong with them?, they wondered. Was she smarter than they were? Better looking? Was something wrong with their relationship? (2) *Loss of specialness*. People felt they had lost the special place they once held in their lover's affections. (3) *Loss of intimacy*. Things they had once shared were now exposed to outsiders. (4) *Feeling excluded*. (5) *Feeling unjustly treated*. Interestingly enough, if one has been "faithful" oneself, a partner's extramarital affair was especially galling; it seemed inequitable. (6) *Uncertainty*. Would they or would they not lose their partners?

Bringle and Buunk (1986) found that most men and women feel comfortable if their mates have intimate conversations and lunches with close friends of the

Box 9.3   MULTIDIMENSIONAL JEALOUSY SCALE

COGNITIVE

How often do you have the following thoughts about X? (Indicate your answers on the following scale: 1 = never to 7 = all the time.)

1. I am worried that some member of the opposite sex may be chasing after X.

2. I suspect that X may be attracted to someone else.

3. I suspect that X may be physically intimate with another member of the opposite sex behind my back.

EMOTIONAL

How would you emotionally react to the following situations? (Indicate your answers on the following scale: 1 = very pleased to 7 = very upset.)

1. X comments to you on how great looking a particular member of the opposite sex is.

2. A member of the opposite sex is trying to get close to X all the time.

3. X is flirting with someone of the opposite sex.

4. X hugs and kisses someone of the opposite sex.

5. X works very closely with a member of the opposite sex (in school or office).

BEHAVIORAL

How often do you engage in the following behaviors? (Indicate your answers on the following scale: 1 = never to 7 = all the time.)

1. I look through X's drawers, handbag, or pockets.

2. I call X unexpectedly, just to see if he or she is there.

3. I say something nasty about someone of the opposite sex if X shows an interest in that person.

4. I question X about his or her whereabouts.

5. I join in whenever I see X talking to a member of the opposite sex.

The higher your score, the more jealous you are.

Source: Pfeiffer & Wong, 1989, p. 187.

opposite sex; such friendly encounters are not threatening. What is threatening is if their partners have an erotic interest in someone else—if they flirt, pet, or have sexual relations with others. It is especially threatening if the Othellos imagine that their rivals are sexually more skilled or attractive than they are.

Jealousy: that dragon which slays love under the pretense of keeping it alive.
—Havelock Ellis

Coping with Jealousy Peter Salovey and Judith Rodin (1985) surveyed 25,000 people. How had they reacted when they were jealous? These jealous lovers described behavior that is familiar to all of us. Lovers became obsessed with painful images of their beloved in the arms of their rivals. They sought out confirmation of their worst fears. They looked through their partner's personal belongings for unfamiliar names and telephone numbers. They telephoned their mates unexpectedly just to see if they were where they had said they would be. They listened in on their telephone conversations, and followed them. They gave their mates the third degree about previous or present romantic relationships. Researchers noted:

> Checking . . . is an almost universal behavior among jealous people. Checking their lovers' accounts of their movements; checking that they are where they say they are and with whom they say; cross-checking, rechecking; checking the mail, checkbook stubs, and credit card returns for payments to restaurants, motels, or florists—life for jealous individuals is an unending task. Nothing is irrelevant. A clue or even final confirmation may be waiting in the next mail delivery, in a husband's coat pocket, in a wife's purse. (White & Mullen, 1989, p. 183)

At the same time, many jealous lovers seek constant reassurance that what they fear isn't so. ("Say it isn't so Joe.") They beg for repeated declarations of love. They need to be kissed, cuddled, held. The same lovers who are so suspicious and wily when they are searching for confirmation that their mates are having an affair are the same lovers who then believe the most fantastic of excuses when they discover that their mates are, after all, having an affair. ("I was so tired, I just fell asleep; we didn't sleep together the week we were together in Paris.") Gregory White and Paul Mullen (1989) determined that people try to cope with their jealous feelings, the threats to their self-esteem, and their fears of loss in a variety of ways: Sometimes, lovers refuse to see what they don't want to see; they deny there is a problem. ("They're just good friends. Very good friends.")

Some jealous lovers focus on *themselves*. "What's wrong with me?" "What did I do wrong?" they ask. Once they spot "the problem," they set out to try to make themselves more appealing. They begin to wear more make-up; they buy a new wardrobe. They start to work out more at the gym. They devour pop psychology books; they see therapists. They embark on campaigns to improve their affairs or marriages. They invite their mates to candlelit dinners, give them jewelry or new cars, or they try to nag less.

Other lovers focus on eliminating *the rival*. They may drop not so subtle hints about her appalling character ("Do you think she has AIDS? No? How about herpes?"). They point out that if their mates leave They Will Pay. They try to make their mates feel guilty. ("I've given you the best years of my life.") They demand that their mates make a choice. ("It's him or me.") They track their mates to their new apartments and make scenes. They beat up their rivals. [In other cultures, at other times, men took an even more direct and extreme approach. In medieval times, while they were off at the Crusades, British and European nobility locked their wives up in chastity belts. Other cultures have utilized infibulation (stitching together the labia majora), vaginal plugs, and clitoridectomy (a form of female castration, designed to eliminate sexual pleasure) to keep women in check (Daly, Wilson, & Weghorst, 1982).]

Some people give up. They recognize that the relationship is over and try to get on with their lives. They call up old lovers; they begin dating. They seek consolation. They try to spend more time with their family and friends. They buy a pet. They bury themselves in work.

Sometimes lovers take revenge on their mates. (See Box 9.4.)

What about the "other man" or the "other woman" in a romantic triangle? How jealous are they? Researchers (Bringle & Boebinger, 1990) interviewed college students who were dating someone or seeing someone who they knew was seriously involved or married to someone else. They found that men and women

---

Box 9.4 **TAKE THAT!**

Humorist Tony Rivers (1991, p. 86) reviews some of the ways women might take revenge on their feckless lovers:

> Accepting that it is no longer possible to behave in the grand manner of a heroine of Greek myth—ship burning, castrating, poisoning—but wishing to keep up the old traditions and motivated by identical passions, the modern woman must be inventive and have an intuitive understanding of symbolism. (At its simplest she can't stab him but she can mutilate his suits.) The substitute revenges that women have taken have become the stuff of modern urban legend.
>
> The basic scenario is always the same. The woman is rejected and ejected but still has access to the flat of her ex-lover who conveniently is away for a week or two. She does one (or several) of the following. She rings the Sydney speaking clock and leaves the phone off the hook (economic warfare). She saturates the carpet with water and plants mustard seeds (despoils territory). She cuts the crotches and armpits out of all his suits (castration). She removes the ends of the wooden curtain rods and packs the cavities with prawns in order that the resultant smell will cause him to destroy his own flat in a futile search for its source (sets self-destruction in motion). She spikes his food with laxatives (poisoning and humiliation). She places skin irritant in the contraceptive cap of her replacement (incapacitates her rival). She takes a key and runs envy stripes down the side of the car. She cakes his car in a fast-setting flour and water mixture. Alternatively, she has his beloved car resprayed two-tone cerise and lime green (forms of emasculation once removed).

who were involved in illicit affairs generally were *not* jealous of their lovers' mates. It was not that these men and women were incapable of jealousy. They had experienced jealousy in other dating relationships. Here, however, they were not. Evidently they protected themselves from pain by holding back. They did not allow themselves to love too much; stopped short of making a unilateral commitment; did not expect to have their needs fulfilled by someone who was married to another.

What's wrong with revenge? It's the best way to get even.
                                                                    —*Anonymous*

I've got eyes with which to give you dirty looks
I've got words for you that don't come from children's books
There's this trick with a knife I'm learning to do
And everything I've got belongs to you.
                                                                    —*Eartha Kitt ballad*

Vengeance   Of course, some people react more violently. In the seventeenth century, Robert Burton (1621/1927) wrote in *The Anatomy of Melancholy* that "those which are jealous proceed from suspicion to hatred; from hatred to frenzie; from frenzie to injurie, murder and despair" (p. 428). The king of the Plateau tribes of Zimbabwe executed men caught with any of his wives. The wives were grossly mutilated (Gouldsbury & Sheane, 1911). In earlier times, Apache husbands also killed their rivals and mutilated their wives (by cutting off the end of their noses); presumably that made them less appealing the next time (Goodwin, 1942)!

In America, family peace centers report that about two-thirds of the wives who are forced to seek shelter do so because their husbands' excessive and unwarranted jealousy has led them repeatedly to assault the women (Gayford, 1979). Most violent women admit that jealousy motivated their violence (Stets & Pirog-Good, 1987). Emile Zola (1890/1948) mentioned such a case. Roubaud, a stationmaster, discovers that his young bride Severine had a lover when she was 16. At first, she denies his accusations. But he batters her into a confession:

He threw her across the bed and beat her blindly with both his fists. In three years, he had not even flicked her with his finger, and now he was beating her, blindly, drunkenly, in a brute rage, with his heavy truckman's fists. . . .
"Confess you slept with him!"
"No! No!"
He picked her up, held her in his arms, to keep her from falling face down on the covers to hide. He forced her to look at him. . . .
"Confess that you slept with him!"
She did not dare say no any more, and she did not answer.
"Confess that you slept with him, by God, or I'll cut your heart out!"
She read clearly in his eyes that he would kill her.
As she fell, she had seen the knife, lying open on the table; she could still see the glint of the blade, she thought he put out his hand. She felt cowardly all at once, ready to abandon herself and everything else, eager to end it.
"Well, yes! Yes, it's true. Let me go away."
It was terrible, then. This confession he demanded so violently had struck him full

in the face, an impossible, monstrous thing. . . . He took her head and beat it against a table-leg. She struggled, and he dragged her across the room by the hair, bumping against the chairs. Every time she made an effort to rise, he knocked her back on the floor with his fist. He panted between clenched teeth, in a savage, imbecilic madness. The table, pushed back, narrowly missed upsetting the stove. There was hair and blood on a corner of the sideboard. (pp. 25–27)

Of course, that didn't end it. Roubaud, like most jealous lovers, wanted more, far more; he cross-examined her; demanded specific, explicit details. And he wants the story repeated again and again.

He tortured her with questions, with his inextinguishable need to know. . . .

Why struggle? Her very being fled from her. He would have taken out her heart with his heavy workman's hands. The cross-examination continued, and she told everything, in such a depth of shame and fear that her whispered words were scarcely audible. And he, gnawed by his terrible jealousy, whipped himself to a mad rage with the suffering caused by the pictures he himself evoked. He never knew enough, he forced her to return to details, check up each fact again. His ear to the miserable woman's ear, he tortured himself with this confession, extracted by the continual threat of his fist, ready to strike again if she should stop. (pp. 27–28)

Jealous people kill others. Othello smothered Desdemona in a fit of jealous rage. Glenn Close tried to murder her beloved in *Fatal Attraction*. Up to 20% of all murders involve a jealous lover. In Western cultures, men are far more likely to beat or murder their girlfriends and wives than their rivals. Bullies often attack "women and children first" (White & Mullen, 1989).

In many countries, the courts have been sympathetic to such "crimes of passion." Traditionally, it was considered to be a man's right to defend his "honor." For example, in São Paulo (Brazil's most populous city), in 1980–1981, 722 men claimed "defense of honor" for murdering their wives. Brazilian women adopted the slogan "Lovers don't kill," and campaigned against allowing such a defense in murder trials. In 1991, a landmark case came before the Brazilian Supreme Court.

In the coffee-processing town of Apucarana in Parana State, Joao Lopes became enraged in August 1988 when his wife, Teresa, announced that she was leaving him. Mr. Lopes searched the town for two days until he caught up with his wife and her lover, Jose Gaspar Felix, at a hotel.

Bursting into the hotel room, Mr. Lopes knifed his rival to death on the spot, then caught up with his fleeing wife in the street and killed her with two knife blows.

At the first trial, a jury of nine men accepted the argument that Mr. Lopes had killed to defend his honor. An appeals court upheld the verdict. (Brooke, 1991, p. B9)

The Supreme Court, however, ruled that men can no longer kill their wives and win acquittal on the grounds of "legitimate defense of honor." The Court ruled:

Homicide cannot be seen as a normal and legitimate way of reacting to adultery. Because in this kind of crime what is defended is not honor, but vanity, exaggerated self-importance and the pride of the lord who sees a woman as his personal property. (Brooke, 1991, p. B9)

Today, in America, jealousy is a frequent cause of homicide. The eighteenth-century English jurist William Blackstone commented that killing in a situation where a man or woman is caught in the act "is of the lowest degree of manslaughter; . . . for there could not be a greater provocation" (quoted in Smith & Hogan, 1983, p. 288). Until 1972, under Article 1220 of the Texas Penal Code, a man could murder his wife and her lover if he found them in a "compromising position" and get away with it as "justifiable homicide." Women did not have equal shooting rights (Ivins, 1991, p. 169). Today, if a man or woman intentionally kills his or her mate, the lover, or both, the crime is considered not murder but involuntary manslaughter (La Fave & Scott, 1972).

Consider this recent case: Elizabeth Anne Broderick eased into her former husband's bedroom and shot him and his new wife, Linda Broderick, to death. Daniel T. Broderick III was a medical-malpractice lawyer who earned one million dollars a year. After Dan and Elizabeth Broderick had been married for a few years, a poisonous domestic dispute began. Ms. Broderick discovered her husband was having an affair with Linda. Elizabeth demonstrated her disapproval by burning her husband's custom-made clothing in the backyard. She wrecked his bedroom, shattered windows, and spray-painted the inside of their house. The warfare escalated when he filed for divorce. He won custody of their three children; he began to pay her up to $16,000 a month in alimony. She claimed she could not live on that and requested $25,000. When Daniel and Linda Broderick bought a home, Elizabeth rammed her car through the front door.

As a result of these activities, she went to jail three times and was committed for three days to a mental hospital. Daniel sold their home without permission. Finally, enraged, she killed him. Her first murder trial ended after four days of deliberation when jurors could not agree on the extent of her guilt. In February 1992 in a second trial she was sentenced to the maximum term—32 years to life in prison—for the murders (*The New York Times*, September 20, 1991, p. A17; *The Los Angeles Times*, 1992, p. A1).

Can Jealousy Be Controlled?   The answer to this question usually depends on whom you ask. The traditionalists take it for granted that marriage should be permanent and exclusive. Thus they have a certain vested interest in believing that jealousy is a natural, universal emotion, "bred in the bone." They generally begin their spirited defense of jealousy by pointing out that even animals are jealous. They cite the "jealous" courtship battles of stags, antelopes, wild pigs, goats, seals, kangaroos, howler monkeys, and so on (see Bohm, 1967).

The "new humanists" see things differently. Radical reformers such as Marguerite and Willard Beecher (1971) or Nena and George O'Neill (1972) believe that our personal lives would be more satisfying, and our professional lives more creative, if we felt free to love all humankind—or at least a larger subset of it. Thus they naturally prefer to believe that society has the power to arouse or to temper jealousy as it chooses, that it is a "social construction."

In most societies, men are allowed to have more than one partner. For example, Clellan Ford and Frank Beach (1951) reported that in 84% of the 185 societies they studied, men were allowed to have more than one wife. Only 1% of the societies permitted women to have more than one husband. Most societies also look more tolerantly on premarital and extramarital sex than does our own. Alfred Kinsey and his colleagues (1953) noted that most societies permit men to have extramarital relations if they are reasonably circumspect about it—if they are careful not to neglect their families, outrage their relatives, or cause a scandal. Extramarital activity is much less frequently permitted for women. Nonetheless, women are allowed to engage in such activities with certain people or on certain special occasions (at weddings, during planting season, and so forth). For example, Ford and Beach report that when Chuckee men (in Siberia) travel to distant communities, they often engage in sexual liaisons with the wives of their hosts. The visitors reciprocate in kind when their hosts visit *their* communities.

The new humanists point out that, traditionally, American society has strongly fostered marital permanence, exclusivity—and jealousy. Yet in spite of the fact that their culture tells men and women they *should* be jealous of their mates, many Americans are not. For example, Kinsey and his associates (1953), after claiming that extramarital relations often engender no "serious difficulty," argued that with a little effort we could train ourselves to be far less jealous. People are far more jealous when they are newlyweds than at any other time. The longer couples are married, the less jealous they are.

Recent research suggests that the truth probably lies somewhere between these two extremes. Almost everyone experiences jealousy at some time or other. Nonetheless, society can shape the nature and intensity of our jealous reactions, how they are felt, and how they are expressed.

Every move you make
Every step you take
I'll be watching you
Oh, can't you see
You belong to me.
        —Sung by Sting

Gender Differences in the Experience/Expression of Jealousy   Recently, Clanton and Smith (1987) reviewed the existing clinical research on jealousy and found that the following differences seem to exist in the way American men and women respond when they are jealous:

> Men are more apt to *deny* jealous feelings; women are more apt to *acknowledge* them. Men are more likely than women to express jealous feelings through rage and even violence, but such outbursts are often followed by despondency. Jealous men are more apt to focus on the outside *sexual* activity of the partner and they often demand a recital of the intimate details; jealous women are more likely to focus on the *emotional* involvement between her partner and the third party. Men are more likely to *externalize* the cause of the jealousy, more likely to blame the partner, or the third party, or "circumstances." Women often *internalize* the cause of jealousy; they blame themselves. Similarly, a jealous man is more likely to display *competitive* behavior toward the third party while a jealous woman is more likely to display *possessive* behavior. She clings to her partner rather than confronting the third party.
>   In general, we may say that male and female experiences and expressions of jealousy reflect male and female role expectations. (p. 11)

California psychologist Jeff Bryson (1977) found that most jealous people respond in one of two ways. (1) Some people try to protect their own egos. For example, they berate their partners, beat them up, or try to get even. (2) Some people try to improve their floundering relationship. They try to make themselves more attractive, talk things out, and learn something from the experience. He concluded that men and women seem to respond quite differently to jealous provocation. In general, jealous men concentrate on shoring up their sagging self-esteem. Jealous women are more likely to do something to strengthen the relationship. Bryson speculated that perhaps these male/female differences are due to the fact that most societies are patriarchal. It is acceptable for men to initiate relationships. Thus when men are threatened, they can easily go elsewhere. Women may not have the same freedom. Thus they devote their energies to keeping the relationship from floundering.

Communication researchers (LePoire & Strzyewski, in press) conducted an experiment to test these hypotheses. When couples (who were romantically involved with one another) reported for the experiment, the experimenter introduced them to a young experimental "assistant," a handsome man or a beautiful woman. During the experiment, the assistants began to flirt with and flatter one of the subjects. They moved their chairs closer to the subject, gazed into the others' eyes, and touched them. They asked for their telephone numbers and to meet them later for a drink. Confederates completely ignored their "rivals." How did the young couple react in such a situation? (Hidden video cameras recorded their reactions.) Both men and women began to "cling" to their mates when the assistant began flirting with their partners. (Jealous subjects' "immediacy" was assessed by measuring closeness, eye gaze, body lean, and body orientation.) Jealous men and women tried to ignore their rivals, when they began to "come on" to their partners. (Again, immediacy was assessed as before.) Jealous women kept smiling; jealous men scowled. (Facial pleasantness was tapped by assessing overall facial pleasantness, smiling frequency, and nodding frequency.)

Thus far, we have considered how couples' happiness can be altered by families, friends, and rivals. But a career is important too.

One can live magnificently in this world if one knows how to work and how to love.

—*Leo Tolstoy*

You couldn't pay me to work there. I only do it for the money.
                                  —*Advertising executive*

Career

In the nineteenth century, men were the breadwinners and women were home-makers. Today fewer than 7% of families fit that pattern. Both men *and* women now work. In the 1990s, 75% of women with school-age children will be in the labor force (Silverstein, 1991).

In general, a happy marriage has a greater impact on overall happiness than does anything else—work included. Nonetheless, sometimes when we see couples in troubled marriages, it does no good to focus exclusively on improving their marriages. Love affairs go best when couples are equals.

Some women enjoy staying home, tending the house, baking, and gardening.

Most do not. In the 1950s we knew many women who felt they "should" enjoy being full-time homemakers, but they did not. They considered housework boring; they found caring for children unfulfilling and exhausting.

Sometimes we see women who have no power in their marriages. For example, we once saw Karen, a military wife who had only a fifth-grade education and four young children. Her husband, a major, treated her shabbily. We saw them both but we could make no progress. Her husband liked things just as they were. He had no reason to change. His "barefoot and pregnant" wife felt stuck; she had no power to force change. She knew she couldn't survive on her own.

In such cases, the woman's only alternative is to start by getting an education, finding a career, and/or establishing a network of friends. In the case we just described, Karen began by studying for and passing a General Equivalency Exam, which earned her the equivalent of a high school education. Then she enrolled in the University of Hawaii, using money from the National Student Loan Program to pay her tuition. Eventually, she got a degree in accounting and began to work part time. Only then did the marital balance begin to change. Now for the first time, the husband looked at his wife, more confident now, better dressed, with money of her own, and began to realize she might well walk out. For the first time he became interested in seeing if the marriage could be improved.

We might wonder to what extent the kinds of careers people enter affect the way they deal with love relationships. In the 1980s we could glimpse some wry speculations on bumper stickers:

Newscasters do it nightly.

Bankers do it with interest. Penalties for early withdrawal.

Divers do it deeper.

Lawyers always want to get into your briefs.

Firemen are always in heat.

Social psychologists are experimental.

Sociologists do it in groups.

Be that as it may, we know that marital happiness and career satisfaction are linked (Hazan & Shaver, 1990). It is hard to have a happy marriage if the rest of your life is a disaster. Most couples do best if they have a happy marriage and children *and* a fulfilling career *and* a few good friends. Men and women who have fulfilling careers have a number of advantages. They have something interesting to tell their mates at the end of the day. When one or another of them is absorbed in a project, his or her mate has something delightful to occupy his or her time. Couples with reasonably paying careers can afford to hire the backup help that makes life easy—housekeepers, gardeners, or nannies. Most young parents find a little goes a long way in child rearing. When young parents are ill or overwhelmed, most need the help of family, friends, or household help. A reasonable income makes such luxuries possible.

When one is stuck in an unfulfilling job or unemployed, it takes a toll (Benin & Nienstedt, 1985). When men and women lose their jobs, they may lose their identities, status, and social contacts along with their incomes. No wonder the unemployed sometimes become depressed, their mental health sometimes deteriorates, and they may become physically ill or even suicidal (Argyle, 1987). Women who work outside the home are emotionally and physically healthier than are women who are full-time homemakers (Barnett & Baruch, 1987). Unemployed men sometimes take their frustrations out on their wives. Eight percent of unemployed men (compared to 4% of employed men) admit pushing, shoving, and throwing things at their wives during arguments and their wives push and shove back. Wives were physically violent in 14% of marriages when their husbands were unemployed (as compared to 4% when they were employed) (Straus & Gelles, 1986; Straus et al., 1980).

Of course, here too things can be carried too far. Some men and women are such "workaholics" that they have no time, interest, or energy for their loved ones; all their passion is spent on work (Small & Riley, 1990). In *The Power Broker*, historian Robert Caro (1975) reported that when the young idealistic Robert Moses first met Mary Sims, he had unlimited time for her.

> "He was," a friend said, "very, very much in love."
>
> His devotion was complete. Taking Mary along on his walks around the city, he poured out to her his ideas—and his frustration at the indifference with which they were received by the Bureau [of Municipal Research]. At the Bureau, they would meet in the library, among the books, and they would sit and talk for hours. He introduced her to his friends. (p. 69)

Once Moses became secretary of state [for New York City], he began to devote the same passion exclusively to his career.

> Moses had always possessed tremendous energy and the ability to discipline it. Now he disciplined it as never before, concentrated it, focused it on his work with a ferocious single-mindedness.
>
> Sloughing off distractions, he set his life into a hard mold. . . .
>
> The amenities of life dropped out of his. He and Mary had enjoyed playing bridge with friends; now they no longer played. Sundays with his family all but disappeared. He did not golf; he did not attend sporting events, he was not interested in the diversions called "hobbies" that other executives considered important because they considered it important that they relax; he was not interested in relaxing. Since he left to Mary the paying of bills and the selection of his clothes, even the hiring of barbers to come to his office and cut his hair, his resources of energy were freed for the pursuit of his purposes. His life became an orgy of work.
>
> Even so, there was never enough time; minutes were precious to him. To make sure that he had as many of them as possible, he tried to make use of all those that most other men waste.
>
> He had always worked in his car while traveling; now he turned the big Packard limousine into an office. With Howland sitting beside him on the rear seat, three other engineers swiveled around on the jump seats and another two crammed in beside the chauffeur, he held staff meetings in the limousine—while another limousine trailed behind so that when Moses was finished with his men, he could drop them off and they could be driven back to Belmont Lake while he continued on to his destination. The door pockets in the Packard were crammed with yellow legal note pads and sharp-pointed pencils, and he spent his hours alone in the car writing letters and memos that his secretary could type up later. (p. 266)

In the end, Moses built an empire; he personally conceived and pushed through public parkways, parks, beaches, bridges, and buildings costing more than 27 billion dollars. As you might guess, the marriage suffered hugely. He and Mary rarely saw one another. In the end, he died a bitter man—feeling unloved and unappreciated.

The research suggests that marriages are especially likely to suffer when men and women work such long hours that there is never any time to catch up on keeping their marriages alive, on household tasks, and child rearing. If husbands and wives work all week *and* all weekend, if they are always stressed, if family plans are always canceled because of crises at work, things soon begin to fall apart (Barling, 1990). Interestingly enough, sometimes it takes couples quite a long time to recognize that one of them is a workaholic. Once, for example, we saw a successful stockbroker. She insisted that she longed to spend weekends with her husband and children. Once she had established a list of clients, she would have time for them. "Things will get better, I promise." She and her husband were truly surprised when the emergencies seemed to continue year after year. First she had to put in extra hours because the market was climbing. It was the chance of a lifetime. Then she had to work late because the recession had hit unexpectedly. People may think they don't like working so much, but if they continue to do so year after year, one must question their self-knowledge. Husbands and wives do best if they assume that the status quo is likely to continue forever. Lonely husbands and wives probably do best if they take immediate steps to find family, friends, and careers to fill the void in their lives. Any workaholics might think through their "temporary" choices to make sure they realize what they are sacrificing for the single-minded pursuit of money and success. Many dads work long hours "for their wives and families." Now and then their wives and family counter "Hey, don't do it for us! We'd rather have you home and live in a smaller house, have a smaller car." Rarely do the husbands listen. At retirement, Dad finally gets some time at home. Now he is ready for them. They, of course, can't be bothered. He is a stranger.

In a world of destruction one must hold fast to whatever fragments of love are left, for sometimes a mosaic can be more beautiful than an unbroken pattern.
—Dawn Powell

THE WORLD-AT-LARGE

We illustrated earlier how the issues of love, sex, and intimacy which so obsess us in the West today barely troubled our forebears in history—West or East—before 1700. They had other rather more pressing concerns, such as trying to avoid starvation, disease, the elements, repression, murder, torture, damnation, and—in general—early, terrible, and painful deaths. Our troubles with relationships, our often-suicidal agonies with love affairs that disappoint, must be considered, in historical perspective, a marvelous luxury. The nostalgics, disgusted by today's "selfishness" (which is what they call our hunger for personal fulfillment), wistfully gaze back into the past as a lost, sweet time of communal togetherness. They forget the suffering and harsh repression of previous eras. There were no "good old days" for 95% of the human race. Most people in most societies suffered for most ages of history under fear, tyranny, and suppression of earthly joy and choice. The common lot was nearly constant material deprivation and the imminence at all times of death.

Holocausts

We are not, unfortunately, limited to the years before the beginnings of the material advances of the modern era (historians tend to locate the birth of the Industrial Revolution in mid-eighteenth-century England) to discover the ways in which tyrannies, religious paranoias, general repression, and group hatreds have blighted the lives of most people and made the longings for love resemble an impossibly distant dream. In our own time, in all corners of the world (including some glittering, advanced, and sophisticated symbols of Western "civilization"), we have seen one horrifying instance after another of the ways in which the nightmarish conditions of the external world can render meaningless and even frivolous all that has been discussed in these pages. Consider the testimony of Hermann Friedrich Graebe, sworn on November 10, 1945 at Wiesbaden, Germany (quoted in Arendt, 1962, pp. 1071–1073):

On 5 October 1942, when I visited the building office at Dubno, my foreman Hubert Moennikes of 21 Aussenmuehlenweg, Hamburg-Haarburg, told me that in the vicinity of the site, Jews from Dubno had been shot in three large pits, each about 30 meters long and 3 meters deep. About 1500 persons had been killed daily. All of the 5000 Jews who had still been living in Dubno before the pogrom were to be liquidated. As the shootings had taken place in his presence he was still much upset.

Thereupon I drove to the site, accompanied by Moennikes and saw near it great mounds of earth, about 30 meters long and 2 meters high. Several trucks stood in front of the mounds. Armed Ukrainian militia drove the people off the trucks under the supervision of an SS-man. The militia men acted as guards on the trucks and drove them to and from the pit. All these people had the regulation yellow patches on the front and back of their clothes, and thus could be recognized as Jews.

Moennikes and I went directly to the pits. Nobody bothered us. Now I heard rifle shots in quick succession, from behind one of the earth mounds. The people who had got off the trucks—men, women, and children of all ages—had to undress upon the order of an SS-man, who carried a riding or dog whip. They had to put down their clothes in fixed places, sorted according to shoes, top clothing and underclothing. Without screaming or weeping, these people undressed, stood around in family groups, kissed each other, said farewells and waited for a sign from another SS-man, who stood near the pit, also with a whip in his hand. During the 15 minutes that I stood near the pit I heard no complaint or plea for mercy. I watched a family of about 8 persons, a man and woman, both about 50 with their children of about 1, 8 and 10, and two grown-up daughters of about 20 to 24. An old woman with snow-white hair was holding the one-year old child in her arms and singing to it, and tickling it. The child was cooing with delight. The couple were looking on with tears in their eyes. The father was holding the hand of a boy about 10 years old and speaking to him softly; the boy was fighting his tears. The father pointed toward the sky, stroked his head, and seemed to explain something to him. At that moment the SS-man at the pit shouted something to his comrade. The latter counted off about 20 persons and instructed them to go behind the earth mound. Among them was the family, which I have mentioned. I well remember a girl, slim and with black hair, who, as she passed close to me, pointed to herself and said, "23." I walked around the mound, and found myself confronted by a tremendous grave. People were closely wedged together and lying on top of each other so that only their heads were visible. Nearly all had blood running over their shoulders from their heads. Some of the people shot were still moving. Some were lifting their arms and turning their heads to show that they were still alive. The pit was already $\frac{2}{3}$ full. I estimated that it already contained about 1000 people. I looked for the man who did the shooting. He was an SS-man, who sat at the edge of the narrow end of the pit, his feet dangling into the pit. He had a tommy gun on his knees and was smoking a cigarette. The people, completely naked, went down some steps which were cut in the clay wall of the pit and clambered over the heads of the people lying there, to the place to which the SS-man directed them. They lay down in front of the dead or injured people; some caressed those who were still alive and spoke to them in a low voice. Then I heard a series of shots. I looked into the pit and saw that the bodies were twitching or the heads lying already motionless on top of the bodies that lay before them. Blood was running from their necks. I was surprised that I was not ordered away, but I saw that there were two or three postmen in uniform nearby. The next batch was approaching already. They went down into the pit lined themselves up against the previous victims and were shot. . . .

On the morning of the next day, when I again visited the site, I saw about 30 naked people lying near the pit—about 30 to 50 meters away from it. Some of them were still alive; they looked straight in front of them with a fixed stare and seemed to notice neither the chilliness of the morning nor the workers of my firm who stood around. A girl of about 20 spoke to me and asked me to give her clothes, and help her escape. At that moment we heard a fast car approach and I noticed that it was an SS-detail. I moved away to my site. Ten minutes later we heard shots from the vicinity of the pit. The Jews still alive had been ordered to throw the corpses into the pit—then they had themselves to lie down in this to be shot in the neck.

I make the above statement at Wiesbaden, Germany, on 10th November 1945. I swear before God that this is the absolute truth.

Hermann Friedrich Graebe

The Holocaust, the systematic murder of six million Jews by Nazi Germany, has come to stand as the central symbol for the multiple horrors of this, the twentieth century. This has been so because the perpetrator could never be dismissed as a "backward" country. How could it have happened anywhere, let alone in a nation so central to the highest and most splendid creative achievements of Western civilization? In the sublime realm of music, for instance, Germany and Austria gave us the two giants of the early eighteenth century, Johann Sebastian Bach and Georg Frideric Handel. From these societies emerged the twin wonders of the late eighteenth century—Franz Josef Haydn and Wolfgang Amadeus Mozart. (Is anyone in the world so universally loved today as Mozart? Even reverence for Jesus cannot make a claim of universality equal to Mozart's.) The transition to nineteenth-century Romanticism was shaped by Ludwig van Beethoven and Franz Schubert, to be followed later in the century by such geniuses as Felix Mendelssohn, Robert Schumann, Richard Wagner, Johannes Brahms, Gustav Mahler, and a host of others. In philosophy, Germany gave the world in the nineteenth century, among others, Goethe, Heine, Schiller, Schopenhauer, Hegel, Marx, Nietzsche, and Freud. In the nightmare of Hitler's Germany, where does one begin to talk about guidelines for a successful Jewish family life (such as that of the family of eight witnessed by Graebe) or for their having rewarding sex and delightful relationships? To ask such questions borders on obscenity.

Sad to say, Germany has not been alone in producing horrific events in our century on such a scale as to render all other issues but survival and the avoidance of torture and pain irrelevant. Untold millions were murdered during the years of Stalin's rule in Russia. Millions more were obliterated during the tyrannies in China of both the right-wing Chiang Kai-shek and the Communist Mao Tse-tung. And the century has witnessed the unrelenting cruelty and bloodshed of two world wars, Korea, Vietnam, the Iran of both the Shah and the Ayotollah, Saddam Hussein's Iraq, apartheid-ridden South Africa, the "disappeared" in Pinochet's Chile, Protestants and Catholics still killing each other in Northern Ireland, tribal slaughter in Biafra, starvation and cynicism in Ethiopia, terrorism everywhere, and on and on and on. For billions of people in this century, life has been shaped by these circumstances, rendering many "personal issues" trivial.

Outside the West

The awesome impact of culture or the larger world on love, sex, and intimacy, on women and on family life can be illustrated further by examples from today's headlines. Here are some culled from *The New York Times* in the summer months of 1991, suggesting that everyone can come up with a multitude of one's own illustrations at any time and from any source.

Beginning with one final instance of the horrific and then proceeding to more mundane and even hopeful cases, we note a story that appeared in *The New York Times* on July 29, 1991. It told of a group of young teenage Kenyan boys at St. Kizito's School rampaging wild through an adjacent girls' dormitory to rape 71 teenage schoolgirls and kill 19 other girls. "This tragedy has underscored the abominable male chauvinism that dominates Kenyan social life," wrote Hilary Ng'Weno, editor in chief of *The Weekly Review*, the nation's most widely read magazine. "The lot of our women and girls is lamentable. We treat them as second-class beings, good only for sexual gratification or burdensome chores. We bring up our boys to have little or no respect for girls." The deputy principal of the school "told President Daniel arap Moi when he visited the destroyed dormitory: 'The boys never meant any harm against the girls. They just wanted to rape' " (Perlez, 1991, p. A4).

There are signs around the world that these assumptions of the worthlessness of women, and the absolute rights of men to have their way over them, may not be immutable doctrines. The changes of modernism sweeping around the world are making their way into some of the sanctuaries of the most deeply entrenched male-dominated societies. A headline in *The New York Times* of April 17, 1991, read: "Divorce Rate Soars as Chinese Decide Love Is Part of Marriage" (Wu-Dunn, 1991, p. A4). Does this mean that marriage for love is making its way to China two centuries after its arrival in Europe and North America?

Two months later, on July 19, 1991, *The New York Times* ran a front-page story about changes in China uncovered in a huge new study of sexual behavior. The study "suggests that many young Chinese are enjoying their own sexual revolution." The study profiles "a society that remains fundamentally prudish, yet one that is becoming more free-wheeling at the youthful and intellectual fringes" (Kristof, 1991, p. A1). "Free-wheeling" Chinese-style hardly means what it does in the West. But the changes in sexual behavior are telling nonetheless.

> "Free-wheeling" in a Chinese context may mean little more than removing one's clothes. . . . Foreplay is often rudimentary or nonexistent, the survey found, perhaps because many couples keep as much clothing on as possible. Among peasants, 34 percent engaged in less than one minute of foreplay. . . . Partly because of the hasty and purposeful manner with which sex is apparently conducted, more than a third of women reported pain during intercourse. The survey did not ask about female orgasm, for fear that many respondents would not understand the concept, but only a third of urban women and a quarter of rural women said they "very often" felt pleasure during intercourse. (Kristof, 1991, pp. A1, A7)

Clothed sex, perfunctory foreplay, minimal pleasure for women: examples of how deeply cultural norms can affect the most intimate details of our private lives. But this story also indicates that cultural norms can be altered, and when they do, rapid and unsettling transformations likely can occur. Take the headline, "School Teaches Japanese Men Art of Flirting," which quotes Satoshi Noguchi, founder of the Marriage School: "In Japan the men nowadays . . . do not know how to enjoy themselves. . . . I have to teach them how to enjoy life" (Warner, 1991, p. F3).

Back Home: Some Priorities in America and in France

Thin SWM, 50, Lawyer seeks female companion who is very thin. She can be gay or straight and from anywhere. Do you like to dine out and travel? Are you someone who doesn't have to be entertained and do you easily meet people? Write RB, P.O. Box 90009, Honolulu, HI 96835. Give wgt.
                                                            —*Classified advertisement*

American readers should not be under the illusion that they, unlike Kenyans, Chinese, or Japanese, operate as free individuals unfettered by the sometimes crazy demands of their culture or the larger world. The American fetish for female thinness, to take one particularly vivid instance of cultural lunacy, illustrates painfully how a weird social norm can wreak havoc on the confidence, sense of priorities, and happiness of an entire gender. Janet Maslin's review of the film *The Famine Within,* a "documentary about American women's collective obsession with body weight" makes some telling points. Some anecdotes from the film:

Chris Alt, the heavier sister of Carol Alt, the successful model, describes seeing a photograph of the singer Karen Carpenter in the last stages of starvation and thinking "she was very lucky." Ms. Alt recalls having "wondered how I could get that skinny without dying." Another woman remembers dieting frantically as a teenager because she had a chance to meet Elvis Presley in Las Vegas and indeed being complimented by Elvis on her good looks. That accomplished, she ballooned back up to 200 pounds (Maslin, 1991, p. B3).

The film's director, Katherine Gilday, commented that "it's a critical brain drain that we have" (p. B3), considering the amount of feminine energy and intelligence devoted to weight loss. The film cites surveys that indicate "that the majority of American women are more unhappy about weight than ever before, that they are happier about losing weight than about career advancement or success in love, and that they fear being fat more than they fear death" (p. B3).

Other notes: (1) In 1954, the average Miss America contestant was 5 foot 8 inches and weighed 132 pounds; (2) by 1980, the height of the beauties remained the same, but the average weight had dropped to 117 pounds; (3) the average North American woman is about 5 feet 4 inches tall and weighs 144 pounds, dramatizing how "radically different" is the physical ideal celebrated by the national media from the national reality; and (4) "Eighty percent of fourth-grade girls have already been on their first diets" (Maslin, 1991, p. B3).

The larger world weighs heavily on the way we think, feel, and behave about sex, love, life, and ourselves as persons. Usually the weight is a burden that mightily limits freedom, confidence, joy, and choices. But culture can also enrich choices, support family life, and improve the chances for healthy relationships. In this vein we wish briefly to mention some of the policies consciously developed in France to nurture their children and improve the chances for marriages to work. These policies have echoes in many other European societies but have failed thus far to make a dent in the United States.

1. Maternal leaves with pay begin 6 weeks before birth and continue for 10 weeks after delivery. Business leaders in France support this policy. "By contrast," wrote Fred Hechinger, education editor of *The New York Times*, "American business interests lobbied so successfully against legislation that would have provided 10 weeks of *unpaid* maternity leaves that President Bush vetoed it" (Hechinger, 1990, p. B8).

2. French parents may take off two years without pay after a child's birth, knowing that their jobs remain protected. In contrast to the 6 weeks that a mother in the United States is lucky to get (without pay), mothers in Norway, Austria, Portugal, The Netherlands, Sweden, Denmark, the United Kingdom, Finland, Italy, Belgium, Ireland, Spain, Israel, Greece, and Canada receive leaves of 12 to 24 weeks with full or partial pay. Unpaid leaves for longer periods can be taken with a guarantee that mothers can return to their jobs (Lande, Scarr, & Gunzenhauser, 1989).

3. Prenatal and postnatal health care, immunization, and high-quality low-cost day care for children under 3 are anchored in French national policy.

4. Preschool for 3- to 5-year-olds is free, and 98% of the children attend it, "more than three times the American percentage" (p. B8).

5. French preschool teachers possess the equivalent of the Master's degree in early childhood and elementary education. Pediatric nurses direct child-care centers, while staff members have taken four years of courses related directly to child care and education.

6. France offers free college tuition plus a stipend to students of preschool education if the student pledges to work five years after graduation in the field.

Hechinger (1990, p. B8) concluded:

A look at child care in industrial societies suggests that under regulated capitalism, as in France, or in social democracies, as in Scandinavia, children's welfare is protected because it is viewed as crucial to the children's and the nations' futures.

By contrast, leaving child care exposed to the uncertainties of a largely un-regulated free market, as in the United States and Britain, has created conditions that [are] crazy. The practice leaves many children with inadequate care and permanently damaged, a costly liability to society.

CONCLUSION

The larger world, for better and for worse, plays a huge and insufficiently studied or understood role at the most intimate level of our personal lives. We in the industrialized countries today are lucky to have the luxury of contemplating choices in our personal lives, which most humans have never had. When we think back to the Graebe Memorandum, which tells only one horror story among millions about the Holocaust, it may provide some salutary perspectives for us. This book exists only because people care so deeply about love, sex, and intimacy—and it is right to care; these are very important matters. But when we contemplate the image of, let us say, the American teenager who commits suicide over an ended love affair, a useful cautionary note may be in order. We can feel sad for the friends and families of the teenager who has died over lost love. But when we contemplate the miseries that most humans have had to suffer for most of human history (and still do), our obsession with relationships and beauty and immediate gratification can look not only frivolous but sometimes remarkably stupid. There are more things to justify the gift of life than happy-ever-after romances.

Chapter
10

Dealing with Emotional Problems

INTRODUCTION

The twentieth century entered its final decade on the wings of promising historical transformations. The Cold War, which had threatened the entire planet with nuclear annihilation, had ended. The repressions of right- and left-wing tyrannies in the Soviet Union, all over Eastern Europe, in South Africa, and in many nations of Latin America were giving way to embryonic democracies. The economic powerhouse of Japan was entering the world after long centuries of geographic and cultural isolation; even China gave signs of trying to join the community of nations. And the cultures of Western Europe, which had furnished most of the genius of the past five centuries and most of the trouble in this century, were overcoming ancient divisions as they entered into the European Community—in perhaps the most far-reaching and important of all these developments.

The United States was struggling internally, ripped apart by unresolved racial hatreds, by crime, drugs, tribalism, a failing legal and political system, by economic unproductivity, and educational disaster. Yet in America, as in Europe and the rest of the developed world, there finally existed enough stability, prosperity, and the possibility of peace so that most of its citizens possessed the luxury to focus on their personal loves—particularly the issues of love, sex, and intimacy.

Relationships did not stand up well under the delights of individualism, but the celebration of individualism has, paradoxically enough, also permitted us to figure out how to do better in our love lives. We have, in these pages, joined this enterprise, devoting the last three chapters to trying to develop an understanding of the problems that lacerate relationships. Let us now describe the research designed to help us overcome some of these problems.

DEALING WITH PROBLEMS: THE LAZARUS MODEL

We begin by outlining Richard Lazarus's (1991) general model of how people cope with problems. Lazarus pointed out that couples go through a series of steps in deciding how to respond to potential marital and relationship problems. They appraise the situation, try to cope with it, and then reappraise the situation to see how well their efforts have worked.

Primary Appraisal

First, let us look at appraisal. Imagine you spot your boyfriend in a restaurant with another woman. How you feel about spotting him will depend on how you appraise the situation. If you assume she is a platonic friend or a co-worker of his, you might be delighted to see them. Other attributions might make you more uneasy. Was he trying to make you jealous? Well, that might be good news or bad. Or is it a cause for real concern? If you assume that he is besotted with his lunch date—if you start to imagine his hand tenderly brushing her long, tangled hair, if you allow your worst imaginings to take you down that path—you might end up extremely upset.

Researchers have found that men and women sometimes differ in how they appraise situations. Kim Rapson (1990) asked men and women which of 29 stressful events they had experienced in the past 12 months. Some items described relationship problems:

Broke up with a dating partner.

Realized that a relationship would not work.

Had a serious fight/argument with a dating partner.

Others described achievement problems:

Failed a course.

Was not hired for a job.

Lost a job.

Earned considerably less money than I expected, needed, or assumed I was qualified for.

Men and women were asked to indicate how important and how stressful were each of the problems they had encountered. She found that women appraised relationship problems as being far more important, distressing, and stressful than did men. Both men and women found achievement, educational, or work failures equally upsetting.

Coping

Once people have assessed the situation, they have to decide what to do about it. Lazarus (1991) argued that people may use two very different strategies in coping with problems. First, they can focus on controlling their own emotions. (They resolve to worry about problems "tomorrow," convince themselves that things will change "somehow," or shrug off their troubles: "There's no use crying over spilt milk.") Or, second, they can try to deal with the problem itself.

If people decide to focus on emotional control rather than direct problem solving, again they have two choices. They can try to manage their emotions in two different ways. In *intrapsychic palliation* people use a variety of cognitive strategies to avoid painful confrontations with reality. They often employ the kinds of defense mechanisms Sigmund Freud described (see Table 10.1).

Living is easy with eyes closed
Misunderstanding all you see.
            —Beatles' song

Such defensive techniques can help people survive. Sometimes, however, the rigid use of palliative techniques can be dangerous. Individuals who repress their emotions or toughen themselves to feeling may lose a sense of their own humanity. They may come to disdain those who have chosen to deal with reality in a more clear-eyed way. They may fail to take the precautions they need to stay alive. It can be like the frog that is placed in a beaker of water that is gradually heated. Instead of jumping out, it will adapt to the new conditions and continue on and on to adapt to the uncomfortable heat. Finally, it can adapt no longer; it is dead. Some people seem to behave like that.

Who invented the human heart, I wonder? Tell me, and then show me the
place where he was hanged.

            —Lawrence Durrell

By contrast, in *somatic palliation*, people try to modify their physiological reactions to emotional events. They may meditate, jog, drink, or take drugs. For example, the businessman who is involved in make-or-break negotiations may pop tranquilizers, drink, sneak off to the movies in the middle of the day to try to forget his troubles for awhile, try to work out his frustration in a frenzied game of squash, or try to knock himself out at night with sleeping pills. He can attempt a thousand and one other techniques designed to quiet his panicky arousal. Such coping techniques may or may not work, depending on the circumstances.

Table 10.1   DEFENSE MECHANISMS

According to Freud, the conscious mind employs a variety of defense mechanisms to shield itself from painful unconscious information. How does this work? Essentially, the conscious mind clamps down a lid when it spots threatening ideas and feelings trying to escape from the dark regions of the unconscious. In Freud's conception, the conscious mind simultaneously knows and does not know what is in the unconscious. Since Freud's time, theorists such as his daughter Anna Freud (1966) have identified literally dozens of defense mechanisms and have confirmed human readiness to engage in self-serving self-deceptions.

Controlling	Attempting to ward off anxiety by keeping a tight rein on people and events
Compensation	Attempting to cover up weakness in one area by going overboard in another area (of greater strength)
Denial	Refusing to see what one does not wish to see
Displacement	Instead of expressing pent-up feelings directly, people pick a safe target; for example, the man who is angry at his boss may shout at his cat
Fantasy	Daydreaming; satisfying frustrated desires in imagination
Identification	Identifying with a powerful person or institution in order to boost one's self-esteem
Isolation	Splitting off affect from content; or keeping incompatible attitudes in logic-tight compartments
Projection	Attributing one's own unacceptable desires to others
Rationalization	Providing "rational" reasons for attitudes, emotions, or behavior that in fact have darker motivations.
Reaction formation	Keeping down dangerous impulses by endorsing opposing attitudes and behavior
Regression	Retreating to an earlier stage of development to avoid the anxieties of adulthood
Repression	Preventing painful thoughts from entering consciousness—the most basic of the defense mechanisms

Source: Carlson & Hatfield, 1992, pp. 33–34.

Generally, however, people try to shape their lives. They choose to engage in another form of coping—*direct action*. They can choose, plan, postpone, avoid, escape, or demolish (Lazarus, 1977). To some extent, they can even select their environments. People who hate confrontation can choose friends who are sweet, agreeable, and very timid. People who can't bear boredom can choose friends who are eccentric, fiery, flamboyant, troublesome, and just a bit mad.

Coping Resources   Lazarus and Susan Folkman (1984) observed that if we are to cope with stressful situations, it helps to possess several resources: a positive attitude, problem-solving skills, social skills, social support, health and energy, and material resources. Let us consider some of these assets.

1. *Problem-solving skills.* When figuring out how to attack a problem, we must make a quick calculation of our problem-solving abilities.

Problem-solving skills include the ability to search for information, analyze situations for the purpose of identifying the problem in order to generate alternative courses of action, weigh alternative courses of action, weigh alternatives with respect to desired or anticipated outcomes, and select and implement an appropriate plan of action. (p. 162)

How good couples are at solving practical problems will depend on the intellectual abilities of the individuals, their self-control, and their past experience (Rosenbaum, 1980).

2. *Social skills.* Traditionally, IQ tests have assessed language and mathematical ability. Recently, psychometricians have begun to recognize the importance of social skills in enabling people to deal with loved ones, friends, acquaintances, and the world. (We all know brilliant people who are so arrogant, obnoxious, irritating, or insensitive that their intelligence does them little good. Others end up muttering "I'll be darned if I'll cooperate with that jerk.") "Social skills refer to the ability to communicate and behave with others in ways that are socially appropriate and effective" (Lazarus & Folkman, 1984, p. 163). Ronald Riggio (1986) developed the *Social Skills Inventory* to assess whether or not students possess seven basic social skills. They are asked to look at 105 statements and to indicate, on a 9-point scale, how true those statements are. Possible answers range from -4: "Not at all true of me," to $+4$: "Very true of me." Table 10.2 contains some sample items.

Riggio found that women scored higher than men on the expressivity and sensitivity scales. Men scored slightly higher on the control and manipulation scales. Social skills allow people to shape social situations, cooperate with others, and solve problems. People's social competence cannot help but influence how comfortable they feel in romantic social settings and how adeptly they deal with social difficulties.

3. *Social support.* In recent years, individuals have begun to recognize how much of a "safety net" other people provide (Barbee et al., 1990; Duck, 1991; Hobfoll, 1990). Recently divorced men and women joke how "I'm building up my support network" as they go about the process of making new friends and rebuilding their lives. People can receive all sorts of support from others—emotional, informational, and practical. If you are ill with the flu, a friend can drop by to cheer you up, bring you some orange juice and a hot meal, and telephone your office to say you won't be able to come in to work. Those who have no one to help may find themselves walking shakily to the store on icy sidewalks or trying to negotiate with some frustrating bureaucrat when they have a fever of 103 degrees.

When social support networks are weak, even mild stressors begin to take a toll; severe stressors may prove to be overwhelming (Cohen & Syme, 1985; Nerem, Levesque, & Cornhill, 1980). In old age, as family members and friends die, colleagues forget to call, and social support systems are lost, the elderly become more vulnerable to disease and death (Schwarzer & Leppin, 1991). On the other hand, after a divorce or death of a spouse, after unemployment or retirement or an illness, if people make new friends, join volunteer groups, go back to work part time, and generally bulwark their social support networks, their problems begin to diminish (Pilisuk, 1982; Schwarzer & Leppin, 1991).

Table 10.2   SOCIAL SKILLS INVENTORY

Emotional expressivity
[the ability to communicate attitudes, emotions, and information about one's own status]

When I get depressed, I tend to bring down those around me.
I have been told that I have "expressive" eyes.
Quite often I tend to be the "life of the party."

Emotional sensitivity
[the ability to decode others' attitudes, beliefs, emotions, and cues as to their status-dominance]

It is nearly impossible for people to hide their true feelings from me.
At parties I can instantly tell when someone is interested in me.
People often tell me that I am a sensitive and understanding person.

Emotional control
[the ability to control and regulate emotional communications and nonverbal displays]

I am able to conceal my true feelings from just about anyone.
I am very good at maintaining a calm exterior, even when upset.
When I am really not enjoying myself at some social function, I can still make myself look as if I am having a good time.

Social expressivity
[the ability to engage others in social interaction; skill in speaking]

At parties I enjoy speaking to a great number of different people.
When in discussions, I find myself doing a large share of the talking.
I usually take the initiative and introduce myself to strangers.

Social sensitivity
[the ability to receive and understand verbal messages; knowledge of the norms governing appropriate social behavior]

Sometimes I think that I take things that other people say to me too personally.
I often worry that people will misinterpret something that I have said to them.
While growing up, my parents were always stressing the importance of good manners.

Social control
[skill in self-presentation]

I find it very easy to play different roles at different times.
When in a group of friends, I am often spokesperson for the group.
I can fit in with all types of people, young and old, rich and poor.

Social manipulation
[a belief that in certain social situations it is necessary to manipulate others, to shape social encounters]

I am not always able to tell the truth.
If I really have to, I can "use" other people to get what I want.
Sometimes I feel that the social rules that govern other people don't really apply to me.

Note: The higher the score, the more socially skilled the person would be said to be.

Source: Riggio, 1986, p. 652.

Friendship in bohemia meant money borrowed, recriminations, complaints, tears, theft, and deceit.

—*Mavis Gallant*

Of course, the same family and friends that provide social support for us expect us to return the favor, if necessary. Some researchers point out that a reasonably small, intimate group of family and friends is actually likely to be most supportive. If one has too many family obligations or if one's friends are less emotionally stable, affluent, competent, or healthy than oneself, a support network may actually drain one's coping resources (Belle, Burr, & Cooney, 1987; Coyne & Bolger, 1990).

4. *Material resources.* Money may not be able to buy happiness, but it can help to avoid a host of stressors. Recently, a bright graduate student at the University of Hawaii reviewed his problem. If he could deliver some graphics he had drawn, he'd get paid. But he couldn't deliver them because his car was uninsured. (It is illegal to drive in Hawaii without insurance.) He couldn't get insurance, because he was too poor to buy the tires he needed to pass the safety inspection. And on through the cycle. Without money, everything becomes a maddening trial. Every decision, large or small, can end up as a fight: "We can't afford to do that!"

Money can be used to buy housekeeping and gardening services (saving time, energy, and avoiding frustration for dual-career families), to secure the best medical treatment, to hire legal assistance, to have fun, to foster romance, and to modify the physical environment in a wide range of stress-reducing ways. Money may be used to buy a house in the safest neighborhood, near the best schools, and allow one to avoid the stress of overcrowded conditions, crime, and helplessness (Selye, 1978).

All these strategies may come to naught in trying to save a foundering relationship. When nothing works, when couples are unable either to reconcile themselves to the status quo or to solve their problems, they have one more problem-solving option: they can decide to end the relationship (Folkman & Lazarus, 1980).

Reappraisal

Finally (after having appraised a situation and having tried to cope with it), couples can see how well or badly their coping strategies have worked. In such a continuing process, they "fine-tune" their relationships.

Now that we have reviewed the Lazarus model, let us consider some of the ways that couples might deal with the two kinds of marital problems we have discussed—the emotional and the interpersonal.

DEALING WITH EMOTIONAL PROBLEMS

French philosopher René Descartes (1694/1967) made a sharp distinction between mind and body. Reason was enshrined, emotion despised. Mankind possessed reason, opening the way for control of the bestial side of our nature. In Descartes' view (and in the view of the powerful Roman Catholic church of that time), people should and could exercise emotional control, and thereby distinguish themselves from the rest of the animal kingdom. Descartes probably would have considered as his offspring the fictional detective Sherlock Holmes. From the Victorian era to today, Holmes has been revered for his "rational" approach to life. In the selection below, we see that even in love the great Sherlock could not be seduced into feeling.

> To Sherlock Holmes she is always *the* woman. . . . It was not that he felt any emotion akin to love for Irene Adler. All emotions, and that one particularly, were abhorrent to his cold, precise but admirably balanced mind. He was, I take it, the most perfect reasoning and observing machine that the world has seen; but as a lover, he would have placed himself in a false position. He never spoke of the softer passions, save with a gibe and a sneer. They were admirable things for the observer—excellent for drawing the veil from men's motives and actions. But for the trained reasoner to admit such intrusions into his own delicate and finely adjusted temperament was to introduce a distracting factor which might throw a doubt upon all his mental results. Grit in a sensitive instrument, or a crack in one of his own high-power lenses, would not be more disturbing than a strong emotion in a nature such as his. And yet there was but one woman to him, and that woman was the late Irene Adler, of dubious and questionable memory. (Sir Arthur Conan Doyle, 1891/1974, p. 161)

Today, self-help books, cassette tapes, and popular magazines are filled with advice on how to control mood. On a more elevated level, Fay Weldon (1974), in her novel *Female Friends*, supplied a compendium of the way women deal with terror and resentment:

> Marjorie, Grace and me. How do we recover from the spasms of terror and resentment which assail us, in our marriages and in our lives? . . . When we cry and sob and slam doors and know we have been cheated, and are betrayed, are exploited and misunderstood, and that our lives are ruined, and we are helpless. When we walk alone in the night planning murder, suicide, adultery, revenge—and go home to bed and rise red-eyed in the morning, to continue as before. . . .
>
> Marjorie recovers her spirits by getting ill. She frightens herself with palpitations, slipped discs, stomach cramp. Snaps out of anxiety and depression and into hypochondria. . . . Life continues.
>
> Grace takes direct action. She throws out the offending lover, has hysterics, attempts to strangle, breaks up her home, makes obscene phone calls, issues another writ, calms down. . . . Life continues.
>
> I, Chloe, move in another tradition. . . . Mine is the mainstream, I suspect, of female action and reaction—in which neglected wives apply for jobs as home helps, divorcees go out cleaning, rejected mothers start playgroups, unhappy daughters leave home and take jobs abroad as au pairs.
>
> Rub and scrub distress away, hands in soap suds, scooping out the sink-waste, wiping infants' noses, the neck bowed beneath the yoke of unnecessary domestic drudgery, pain in the back already starting, unwilling joints seizing up with arthritis. Life continues. (pp. 143–144)

Oscar Hijuelos (1989) recounted the story of Cesar and Nestor Castillo, the Mambo Kings. Here, the author told of how they attempted to deal with the depression they felt when love affairs, marriages, or work went wrong.

Cubans then (and Cubans now) didn't know about psychological problems. Cubans who felt bad went to their friends, ate and drank and went out dancing. Most of the time they wouldn't think about their problems. A psychological problem was part of someone's character. Cesar was *un macho grande*; Nestor, *un infeliz*. People who hurt bad enough and wanted cures expected these cures to come immediately. Cesar was quite friendly with some *santeras*, really nice ladies who had come from Oriente Province and settled on 110th Street and Manhattan Avenue. And whenever Cesar felt bad about anything, if he felt depressed about the fact that he still had to work in a meat-packing plant to maintain his flamboyant life-style, or when he felt guilty about his daughter down in Cuba, he would go see his friends for a little magical rehauling. These *santeras* liked to listen to the radio all day, loved to have children and company around them. If he felt bad, he would just go in there and drop a few dollars into a basket, lie on his stomach on a straw mat on the floor, ring a magic bell (which symbolized his goodness, Caridad, or charity) and pay homage to the goddess Mayari, for whom these women were intermediaries. And pssssst! his problems would lift away. Or they would lay hands on him. Or he would just go over to 113th and Lenox, to a *botanica*, and get himself a "cleaning"—the saint pouring magic herbs over him—guaranteed to do the trick. Going to confession at the Catholic church did the same job: a heartfelt opening of the heart and an admission of sins; then the cleansing of the soul. (And no death-bed confession either, no admission to heaven because of last rites. These Cubans died as they lived, and a man who would not confess his sins at age twenty-five was not going to do so at seventy.)

Nestor went with Cesar and was cleaned, paid obeisance, and felt better for a few days. Then the feeling came back to him and he was unable to move. (pp. 114–115)

Variable responses to life's twisty ways. Do some ways work better than others? Let us review what psychologists now know about emotional control. Imagine that you are upset at the way your life has been going. You are eager to calm things down, so that you can begin to figure out how to solve your problems, or at least learn to live with them. What is the best way to deal with your emotions?

All this buttoning and unbuttoning.
  —*Eighteenth-century suicide note*

The Cognitive Control of Emotion

One way people try to deal with their feelings is to focus on trying to think "positively" . . . or "rationally" or whatever. For aid in that endeavor, they can modify their thoughts, beliefs, attitudes, ways of looking at their problems, and all the myriad of cognitions that accompany emotional states. The overwrought may try to calm themselves down enough so that they can instigate effective action. They may puzzle through alternative actions and clarify the reasons for their feelings. Or, if the situation is hopeless, they may concentrate on reconciling themselves to the irreconcilable. Today, cognitive approaches to controlling emotion are becoming extremely popular.

Everyone can master a grief but he that has it.
              —*Shakespeare*

American pop psychology would have us believe that "thinking makes it so." True devotees of positive thinking vastly exaggerate the possibilities of feeling what you want to feel, being whatever you want to be. Best-sellers include such self-help paperbacks as *Getting Control, Taking Charge of Your Emotional Life, Do It!*, or *Love Power in a World Without Limits*. They all emphasize the power of positive thinking, believing, or visualization in securing an emotionally controlled (and hence "better") life. Realistic constraints are waved away with a dismissive gesture. In some measure, then, the innocent American tradition of believing in "mind over matter" combined with good old American optimism has furnished the soil that has nourished a complex blossom: cognitive psychology. Clinicians have developed several cognitively based therapies that teach people to use mental techniques to shape emotion and behavior. Let us now review some of them. They may not be so magically all-powerful as the New Age mythology or the new cognitive control advocates contend, but they are effective in varying degrees.

Cognitive Therapies   Since the early 1900s, intellectuals have been aware of psychodynamic principles, defense mechanisms, and the fact that people employ a variety of unconscious strategies to shield themselves from pain and anxiety. More recently, cognitive theorists have begun to explore the conscious cognitive techniques available to mask or alter feelings. Several cognitive therapy programs are especially popular. These include Aaron Beck's (1976) cognitive therapy (for depression and anxiety) and Donald Meichenbaum's (1977, 1985) stress innoculation training.

Beck's Cognitive Therapy   Cognitive therapy is based on the simple premise that people's thoughts and self-statements are important in molding their behavior. If we analyze the cognitions of people with emotional problems to ascertain how they perceive and interpret the world, their feelings and behavior now make a great deal of sense. Aaron Beck (1976) observed: "The role of anticipations in influencing feelings and action is far more dominant than is generally recognized" (pp. 40–41). A given culture or family may teach children rules, which they internalize (something like "Never hurt anyone" and "Stand up for yourself") and which simply do not work. Such nonfunctional rules may produce emotional disorders. Beck continued: "When rules are discordant with reality or are applied excessively or arbitrarily, they are likely to produce psychological or interpersonal problems" (p. 52).

The meanings that people assign to the events determine how they will respond emotionally. This premise "forms the core of the cognitive model of emotions and emotional disorders" (Beck, 1976, p. 52). Among these disorders:

1. Beck said that depression is initiated by the experience of real or perceived loss. In especially severe cases, the depressed assume that their problems are their own fault but there is nothing they can do to change things. In such instances, nothing is left to the depressed, if they are desperate enough, but to commit suicide.
2. Anxiety is initiated by real or perceived threats to maintaining control (or

by actual loss of control). The anxious may become paralyzed by fear; they stay alert to the smallest danger, obsessively worrying about what might be. They overgeneralize, terrorized by a host of mythical dragons. Their bodies may remain in a permanent state of physiological readiness to the detriment of their health or they may simply fail to function.

3. Cognitive distortions produce both the sorts of hysterical reactions Freud discussed (such as when a neurotic person becomes paralyzed) and psychosomatic disorders. For example, the person who continually catastrophizes may put an unbearable strain on the body machinery. Eventually, the cognitions may produce a problem with no organic basis or even eventuate in a real physical breakdown.

Beck's (1976) cognitive therapy aims at "correcting faulty conceptions and self-signals" that underlie psychological distress (p. 214). Therapists go through a series of steps in cognitive therapy. The first step is to persuade clients that the therapist is trustworthy and credible. This takes a bit of time; they have to get to know one another. Then the therapist can point out that "a perception of reality is not the same as reality itself. . . . [and that the client's] interpretations of his sensory input are dependent on inherently fallible cognitive processes" (pp. 233–234). As therapists get to know their clients, they learn just what sorts of self-defeating ideas the clients have. This can be accomplished with some ease, since certain standard self-defeating ideas are associated with various emotional problems. For example, the depressed tend to blame themselves for things that go wrong and to see themselves, others, and the world in bleak ways. Clients are encouraged to adopt a new, more realistic view of reality. Then they can begin to deal with their problems in more practical ways. In short, Beck, like most other cognitive therapists, believes that cognitive reorganization leads the way toward producing behavior change.

Meichenbaum's Stress Inoculation Training Donald Meichenbaum's (1977) approach to cognitive therapy—termed cognitive-behavior modification—emphasizes the client's thinking or "inner dialogue," and its relationship to a person's emotional activities as well as other activities. Meichenbaum suggested that "how one responds to stress in large part is influenced by how one appraises the stressor, or to what he attributes the arousal he feels, and how he assesses his ability to cope" (p. 202).

These processes of appraisal, attribution, and assessment are a function of the person's self-statements: "[O]ne function of internal dialogue in changing affect, thought, and behavior is to influence the client's attentional and appraisal processes" (Meichenbaum, 1977, pp. 206–207). For example, through cognitive therapy, clients can learn to change their labeling of emotional arousal:

Sweaty palms, increased heart and respiratory rates, muscular tension, now became "allies," cues to use the coping techniques for which they had been trained. . . . This shift in cognitions in itself may mediate a shift in autonomic functioning. The present theory postulates that it is not the physiological arousal *per se* that is debilitating but rather what the client says to himself about that arousal that determines his eventual reaction. (pp. 207–208)

Meichenbaum tries to "inoculate" people against stress. The immunization procedure consists of three graded phases—the educational phase, the rehearsal phase, and the application phase. In the first, educational phase, clients are given a logical framework that enables them to (1) interpret their emotional response to stress and (2) develop a general plan for dealing with problems. For example, they might be warned that their first response to stress may well be panic, but that is only a first response. A sensible person can proceed to deal with problems with an orderly sequence of responses: preparation, confrontation, coping, and, eventually, self-reinforcement for coping.

In the rehearsal phase, clients are taught a variety of coping strategies. They practice taking direct action, learning how to reshape difficult situations, or else how to escape from them. They are taught cognitive coping techniques. For example, they are told to become alert when they start making negative self-statements (e.g., "You moron, what are you doing?"). They should use such statements as a cue for making positive self-statements that can facilitate coping. (For example, "Relax, you're in control. Take a slow, deep breath"; "Relax"; "You can develop a plan to deal with the problem, you'll see"; or "It worked; you did it!")

In the third (and critical) application training phase, clients are exposed to stressors in the clinic. They are expected to deal with them by utilizing the techniques they have just practiced. If they fail, the therapist can model appropriate coping strategies. Luckily, the techniques that clients practice in the clinic do seem to generalize to real-life situations. "It was quite common for clients in the stress-inoculation group to report spontaneously that they had successfully applied their new coping skills in other stressful situations. . . . The change in attitude seemed to encourage clients to initiate confrontations with real-life problems" (Meichenbaum, 1977, p. 159).

Wine maketh glad the heart of man.
—Old Testament

The Biological Control of Emotion

In this section, we focus on some psychoactive drugs that have been found to be useful for reducing painful emotions to manageable proportions. When people take over-the-counter drugs, prescription drugs, or "street" drugs, they are attempting to control certain central nervous system (CNS) processes and certain autonomic nervous system (ANS) responses, and thereby gain control over their emotions.

Antidepressants   When people are merely sad, mildly depressed, or are briefly depressed for reasons that would make *anyone* melancholy, antidepressants are not recommended. (This would include people who are sad because their social life is nil, their dating relationship is disintegrating, they are lonely after a divorce, or there has been a death in the family.) If these people feel they need therapy, psychotherapy is the treatment of choice. Even when patients are suffering from moderate to severe depression, some studies have shown that psychotherapy is as effective as drug therapy (Murphy, Simons, Wetzel, & Lustman, 1984). However, when depression is unusually severe or persists, and its cause is unclear, antidepressant drug therapy (or drug therapy supplemented with psychotherapy) is indicated. Today, psychiatrists and psychologists can use three different kinds of drugs to treat the various forms of depression: the tricyclics (and a related compound, Prozac) are used to treat unipolar depression. The MAOIs (monoamine oxidase inhibitors) are used to treat anxious-depression. Lithium is used to smooth out bipolar mood swings.

Anti-anxiety Drugs   Sometimes people suffer from intense anxiety. They can feel their hearts pound, they gasp for breath, and their stomachs churn. Under such conditions, psychiatrists or physicians sometimes prescribe drugs to help the high-strung take the edge off their anxiety. The most frequently used anti-anxiety drugs are the major tranquilizers, the minor tranquilizers, barbiturates, beta blockers, and the antidepressants. Of course, all drugs have side effects and so psychiatrists do not prescribe them unless they are necessary.

The only cure for grief is action.
        —G. H. Lewes

The Behavioral Control of Emotion

People can try to control their emotions in yet another way—by controlling their emotional behavior. Pop artist Andy Warhol tried to control his fears by avoiding intimate relationships and keeping himself so busy he didn't care.

> Maybe it's time to do away with the oft-repeated point about Warhol's lack of feeling. "If you want to know all about Andy Warhol," said Andy, "just look at the surface of my paintings and films and me, and there I am. There's nothing behind it." There may be nothing behind the surfaces, but there's a lot contained in the surfaces themselves. In these pictures there's a powerful tension between the feeling implicit in the images and Andy Warhol's attempt to keep his emotions under control. "I still care about people but it would be so much easier not to care," he said. "It's too hard to care. . . . I don't want to get involved in other people's lives. . . . I don't want to get too close. . . . I don't like to touch things . . . that's why my work is so distant from myself."
> Viva, one of the "superstars" Warhol created in his movies, recalled that if she tried to touch him "he would actually shrink away. Shrink. I mean shrink backwards and whine. . . . We were all always touching Andy just to watch him turn red and shrink. Like the proverbial shrinking violet." Warhol . . . made another, more social point: "During the '60s, I think, people forgot what emotions were supposed to be. And I don't think they've ever remembered. I think that once you see emotions from a certain angle, you can never think of them as real again. That's what more or less has happened to me. . . . I want to be a machine," said Warhol. (Kroll, 1987, pp. 65–66)

Clinical psychologists who call themselves behavior therapists focus on behavior and emphasize overt behavioral change. Their approaches are based on learning principles: on classical (or Pavlovian) conditioning, operant (or instrumental) conditioning, observational learning, or "modeling." In this section, we examine some methods of emotion control that rely on classical and operant learning principles.

Fear makes men ready to believe the worst.
    —*Quintus Curtius Rufus*

Therapies Emphasizing Classical Conditioning Principles   More than 60 years ago Mary Cover Jones (an associate of the arch-behaviorist John Watson) reported the case history of Peter, a boy who was terrified of animals and a great deal more. Peter exhibited signs of fear in response to an assortment of cues including a laboratory rat, a rabbit, fur rugs, cotton, and feathers. Jones and Watson tried to help Peter overcome his fears:

> We determined then to use another type of procedure—that of *direct uncondition-ing.* We did not have control over his meals, but we secured permission to give him his mid-afternoon lunch consisting of crackers and a glass of milk. We seated him at a small table in a high chair. The lunch was served in a room about 40 feet long. Just as he began to eat his lunch, the rabbit was displayed in a wire cage of wide mesh. We displayed it on the first day *just far enough away not to disturb his eating.* This point was then marked. The next day the rabbit was brought closer and closer until disturbance was first barely noticed. This place was marked. The third and succeed-ing days the same routine was maintained. Finally, the rabbit could be placed upon the table—then in Peter's lap. Next tolerance changed to positive reaction. Finally he would eat with one hand and play with the rabbit with the other. . . . [Moreover] *fear responses to cotton, the fur coat, and feathers were entirely gone.* (Watson, 1924/1930, p. 174)

Today, the techniques used by these early behaviorists have been refined both conceptually and procedurally. They are referred to as *systematic desensitization* (Wolpe, 1973/1982). The principal methods in this process are training in relaxa-tion and gradual exposure to stimuli that more and more closely resemble those that evoke fear or anxiety.

Imagine you are uneasy in social situations. First, a therapist would make a determination of the *hierarchy* of things that make you uneasy—which possibili-ties are most frightening, which are somewhat unsettling, and which are no problem at all. Next, the therapist would provide brief training in relaxation. You would be seated in a comfortable chair with your eyes closed. Then you would be asked to relax the muscle groups, one after the other (e.g., facial muscles, arms, chest, . . . right down to your toes) until you report feeling very much at ease. Next, you would be asked to think about a slightly fearful scene (say, a mere 1 on your fear "hierarchy"). For instance, you might be asked to imagine that you are telephoning a friend to ask if he is planning to go to Studebaker's, a singles bar, this next weekend. If you feel comfortable thinking about chatting with your friend, you proceed to the next step. You are asked to imagine that you and he are going to Studebaker's together. You get in the car and begin driving there. If you begin to feel slightly anxious (say, +3) you alert the therapist who tells you to stop imagining the scene. She then returns you to the relaxation exercises. In short, gradually and usually across weeks of therapy sessions, the imagined scenes bring you closer and closer to calling a friend, arranging to go to Studebaker's together, watching the action for awhile, smiling at a single woman, walking up to her, asking her to dance—all accompanied by techniques designed to prevent the recurrence of anxiety.

As a supplement to the imaginal processes in the clinic, your therapist might then encourage actual exposure to some of the feared events—a process called *in vivo* (real-life) desensitization. You might take a trip to Studebaker's during the day, have a drink there, walk around the dance floor.

Methods That Emphasize Operant Behavior   Early on, learning theorists who wished to apply behavior modification principles to real-life situations had to concoct some simple ways to reward clients for good behavior and to punish them for behaving badly. They soon devised the "token economy" system. In this method, the therapist targeted behaviors that he or she wanted to increase (via positive reinforcement) or eliminate (via extinction procedures). If a behavior was to be encouraged, a "token" (say, a poker chip or a point) was given as a rein-forcer. These chips or points could be collected and exchanged later for more significant reinforcers. In a mental hospital, for example, patients can earn points for "proper" behavior and exchange them for such privileges as the opportunity to watch television on the ward (Ayllon & Azrin, 1968). In families, husbands and wives can often trade in chips for dinner out at any restaurant they choose, a shopping spree, or a trip to the country. Children can use them to buy a book, a Ninja-turtle video, or to get out of eating their brussels sprouts. (As George Bush said: "I'm the President of the United States, and I'm not going to eat any more broccoli" (*The New York Times*, 1990, p. A14).

People can also use a self-modification program to keep their own fears, anxieties, and other emotional responses in check. David Watson and Roland Tharp (1990) proposed a series of steps to increase self-control. You might be able to use some of these techniques yourself.

> Successful self-modification always contains certain essential elements: self-knowl-edge, planning, information gathering, and modification of plans in the light of new information. There is a definite sequence in deliberate self-modification. Most self-change programs involve these steps:
>
> 1. Select a goal and specify the behaviors you need to change in order to reach the goal. These behaviors are called *target behaviors.*
> 2. Make observations about the target behaviors. You may keep a kind of diary describing those behaviors or count how often you engage in them. Try to discover the events that stimulate your acts and the things that reward them.
> 3. Work out a plan for change, applying basic psychological knowledge. Your plan might call for changing a pattern of thought that leads to unwanted behavior. You might gradually replace an unwanted behavior with a desirable one. You might reward yourself for a desired action. . . .
> 4. Readjust your plans as you learn more about yourself. As you practice analyzing your behavior, you will be able to make more sophisticated and effective plans for change.
> 5. Take steps to ensure that you will maintain the goals you make. (pp. 13–14)

Relaxation, Meditation, and Exercise Newsman Robert MacNeil (1989) graphically depicted his mother's attempts to cope with her loneliness, fear, and distress while her husband was away during World War II.

> We did not go to the beaches only in nice weather. We went when we went. We enjoyed the beaches as often on grey, cloudy days with a fresh wind blowing as on days when the sand reflected a dazzling sun with no wind. More typically, there was wind and a strong lungful of breathtaking freshness tasting of iodine and seaweed clean enough to eat.
>
> From my mother came the idea that going down to the sea repaired the spirit. That is where she walked when she was sad or worried or lonely for my father. If she had been crying, she came back composed; if she had left angry with us, she returned in good humor. So we naturally believed that there was a cleansing, purifying effect to be had; that letting the fresh wind blow through your mind and spirits as well as your hair and clothing purged black thoughts; that contemplating the ceaseless motion of the waves calmed a raging spirit. (p. 75)

Increasingly, researchers have begun to recognize the importance of behavioral relaxation techniques in reducing stress. People may be trained by psychotherapists, meditation instructors, or Zen masters. They may be self-taught or have devoured some of the "pop" psychology literature. In any case, the methods they will use to relax, if effective, will rely on behavioral principles.

Relaxation Techniques: Benson's Relaxation Response Method Researchers have found that some standard relaxation techniques can be extremely effective in reducing anxiety and stress. Herbert Benson's (1975) book, *The Relaxation Response,* recommended the following procedure. You might want to try it yourself when you feel anxious and tense.

1. Sit quietly in a comfortable position.
2. Close your eyes.
3. Deeply relax all your muscles, beginning at your feet and progressing up to your face. Keep them relaxed.
4. Breathe through your nose. Become aware of your breathing. As you breathe out, say the word, "ONE," silently to yourself. For example, breathe IN . . . OUT, "ONE"; IN . . . OUT, "ONE"; etc. Breathe easily and naturally.
5. Continue for 10 to 20 minutes. You may open your eyes to check the time, but do not use an alarm. When you finish, sit quietly for several minutes, at first with your eyes closed and later with your eyes opened. Do not stand up for a few minutes.
6. Do not worry about whether you are successful in achieving a deep level of relaxation. Maintain a passive attitude and permit relaxation to occur at its own pace. When distracting thoughts occur, try to ignore them by not dwelling upon them and return to repeating "ONE." With practice, the response should come with little effort. Practice the technique once or twice daily. (pp. 162–163)

Exercise Finally, an increasingly popular way to control sadness, fear, or anger is by exercising. The Greeks were the first to note the benefits of a sound mind in a sound body. Today, health psychologists have documented the profoundly beneficial effects that regular exercise has on self-esteem, psychological well-being, cognitive functioning, mood, and physiological functioning (Emery &

Blumenthal, 1990; Goldwater & Collis, 1985; Plante & Rodin, 1990). Exercising has become an increasingly popular way to begin or end a stressful day. After running, people's moods improve: they become less anxious, angry, and depressed than before (Markoff, Ryan, & Young, 1982). Thus exercise is another excellent behavioral method for emotion control.

Combining Techniques in Therapy   Most marital therapists are eclectic: They use any and all of the techniques we have discussed to implement change. For example, Steven Beach and his colleagues (1990) provided a step-by-step plan of marital therapy for depression. In the 15-week plan, almost all the techniques we have described play a part. There are three phases in their treatment program (see Figure 10.1). First, therapists focus on identifying things the couple used to enjoy doing together and they urge them to engage in such activities once again. They also identify and eliminate extreme stressors within the relationship. This should boost couples' morale and allow them to confront the second stage of therapy: the restructuring of the marital relationship.

STAGE I		STAGE II		STAGE III
Rapidly eliminate major stressors and enhance couple cohesion, caring, and companionship	$\longrightarrow$	Restructure communication and interaction to build stable, functional relationship	$\longrightarrow$	Enhance maintenance, focus on relapse prevention

Figure 10.1 Marital therapy: a flowchart.

The second phase of therapy focuses on the way couples communicate, interact day-to-day, and solve any problems that arise. If this stage of therapy is a success, not only does their current relationship improve, but they are left better able to handle difficulties that may arise in the future.

Finally, the third phase of therapy is designed to prepare the couple to terminate therapy. They are taught to identify hints of impending trouble and to avoid high-risk situations.

Fear not. Suffer in silence. Quit whining. Be cool.
        —Traditional advice

SHOULD YOU TRY TO CONTROL YOUR EMOTIONS?

We have now reviewed a myriad of cognitive, biological, and behavioral methods that people can use to keep their feelings reined in. Is it wise to focus so single-mindedly on emotional control? We would argue that, in many instances, perhaps the best way to "deal with" emotions is to experience them fully; to be quite aware of what we are feeling and why; to decide how much of our inner life we are willing to share with others; and to take the time to explore in depth how we want to handle our feelings and the events that have provoked them.

Some people have such a firm lock on their feelings that they are unaware of feeling anything at all (Hochschild, 1983). Consider this example of a couple we once saw in marital counseling. They were charming, intelligent, and sweet. They had lived together, apparently blissfully, for 12 years. She was now 39 and thought it was time to marry and have children. He didn't want to marry, but he didn't know why. As we talked to them about this potentially emotionally laden topic we found it easy to understand her. We all spoke "the same language." But it was extraordinarily difficult to understand him. He seemed to lack even a language for expressing feelings. He hadn't the faintest idea why he didn't want to get married. Did he feel pinned down? Frightened at the responsibility? Bored with her? Irritated? He couldn't say. He seemed unable to quite grasp what we wanted from him. It was as if we three were speaking French, while he only understood Romanian. In the course of therapy as he learned to be more aware of his thoughts and emotions, he could finally begin to talk about his hopes and fears about the relationship.

Men, in particular, seem especially prone to this problem, acculturated as they are to control feelings (except anger) rather than to express them easily and openly. Men also frequently get uncomfortable when their partners cry, having been taught since they were young boys to be "problem-solvers." They often believe they are supposed to "do" something about the tears, to stop them, to explain how unnecessary they are, to offer solutions designed to sweep away the causes for the tears. When these strategies fail, men will often get angry or frustrated or withdraw from the scene. In fact, all men usually need to "do" is to relax about emotional expression, listen to their partners, and perhaps give a little hug. Therapy often addresses the value of emotional expression and teaches men and women to relax, attend to, and enjoy openness about feelings rather than always trying to stuff them. We look more closely at this phenomenon later in this chapter.

Out of the marriage of reason with emotion there issues clarity with passion. Reason without emotion would be impotent, emotion without reason would be blind. The combination of emotion and reason guarantees man's high degree of freedom.

—*Silvan Tomkins*

Reasons for Sense *and* Sensibility

Such cases of marital difficulty are sharp reminders that an emotional vocabulary and emotional awareness serve some critically important functions.

Information   Most people get a great deal of information by "checking out" their feelings. "Would you like Mexican food tonight?" asks the husband. Semi-consciously, we might find out by visualizing biting into a forkful of chicken enchiladas. If we feel a warm glow, we say "sounds great." If not, we respond, "Not tonight." People who have little or no access to their interior landscapes, their "private events," are seriously handicapped in figuring out what they like and don't like (Hochschild, 1983). Clients who have no habit of feeling their preferences are reduced to such absurd practices as observing their behavior, as if from a distance, when deciding what they want to do: "Let's see, do I like Suzy? Well, I don't know. I guess I like Suzy. I've dated Suzy more than anyone else. But really, I guess either Suzy or Fran is OK. What do you think?"

People gain information about more than *themselves* when they explore their inner lives. They can also gain a great deal of information about the personalities, characters, and emotions of *others* by "checking out" their own reactions. For example, one of Elaine Hatfield's colleagues at the University of Hawaii is a world-famous scholar and scientist; he is arrogant, hard driving, and successful. Their encounters are never boring. Yet, although close friends and political allies, every time she talked with him, she came away from the conversation feeling that she had said something stupid and had bored him. She felt awkward, uncomfortable, and ill at ease. After each encounter, she resolved to try harder next time. One day, in the midst of a particularly painful conversation, she realized what was going on. She had been blinded by focusing overmuch on what she was doing wrong. She had come up with attributions that dealt entirely with her own contribution to the continuing fiasco. She had been oblivious to what was going on with him! As she stepped back and analytically began to assess what he was saying and feeling, she realized that he was acutely anxious. She observed that he might be a big bear of a man, dominant and forceful, but he was always ill at ease in conversation. Brief expressions of anxiety crossed his face, his voice rose, he "twitched," transferring his weight nervously from foot to foot. She was picking up his anxiety with a kind of built-in radar. That discovery enabled her, once she had coded it correctly by reading her own feelings, to try to put *him* at ease the next time they talked.

We can learn a great deal about other people by attending to *our own* often-unexpected emotions in their presence. Are they depressed? (do I begin to get sleepy and sluggish?), anxious? (do I feel suddenly panicky?), passively aggressive? (I know I should like her, but my heart sinks at her approach; she brings out the worst in me), and so forth. If one is trying to figure out other people, intellect plus emotion equals a potent concoction. That sum allows one to do far better detective work than does the operation of naked intellect alone. Theodor Reik (1948) described this process:

> The torch that psychoanalysis puts into the hands of the investigator lights up the darkest corners and throws a beam down the deepest shafts. The "instincts," which indicate, point out, hint at and allude, warn and convey, are sometimes more intelligent than our conscious "intelligence." . . . The psychoanalyst has to learn how one mind speaks to another beyond words and in silence. He must learn to listen "with the third ear." The task of the analyst is to observe and record in his memory thousands of little signs and to remain aware of their delicate effects upon him. . . . The student often analyzes the material without considering that it is so much richer, subtler, finer than what can be caught in the net of conscious observation. The small fish that escapes through the mesh is often the most precious. (pp. viii, 144–145)

We discuss the process of emotional contagion in greater detail in Chapter 12, Dealing With Problems: Communication.

Dealing with Others   There is a second reason why people must learn to become comfortable with emotion. People cannot live alone or with a tight little emotionally controlled group like themselves. They must enter the real world and deal effectively with a wide variety of people, some of whom are tight and constrained, others who scream and threaten to "get them," and still others who weep and tell them how badly they have behaved. When people have learned to deal with their own emotions by keeping a tight lid on them, they often have difficulty dealing with more expressive people.

One place, as we have noted, where this problem shows up most poignantly is in intimate encounters. There is abundant anecdotal evidence that men and women differ in how comfortable they are in dealing with emotionally "hot" topics. May Sarton (1982), in her novel *Anger*, highlighted some of these failures to communicate emotionally. At first, Anna and her mother discuss Ned's inability to engage in intimate conversation:

> "Well," Ernesta said in her practical voice, "that is no news. All men wince at a woman's tears. It's in the genes." And she added, "My husband simply cleared out and left the house when I cried. They take it as an assault, an unfair weapon, and act accordingly."
>
> "Why is it unfair to be upset? Why is it feeling, almost *any* feeling, if expressed is an assault? That's what I can't understand. Ned won't even talk about it quietly after we have a fight. He says things like 'We have had one scene already!' " (pp. 114–115)
>
> Anna tries, but fails, to explain her feelings to Ned:
>
> "I think you were conditioned never to allow yourself anger. Was it considered a crime in your mother's house?"
>
> "Yes, it was."
>
> "Why?"
>
> "We were brought up to believe that the surfaces must be kept pleasant."
>
> "And if they were, then everything was presumed to be all right? So your brother

tried to commit suicide and you bury your feelings so deep you can't behave like a human being!"

"It's a matter of ethos, Anna, can't you see?"

"Oh yes, I see all right," Anna said bitterly. "But you married someone with quite a different ethos."

"Unbuttoned ego, my mother calls it."

"I think it's much healthier to let anger out than to bury it so deep you don't even know it is there."

"It may be better for oneself but it's hard on other people."

"Oh Ned, do you think it's easy on me when you freeze up against me? Can't you see that that is just as punishing as you feel I am when I attack you? And it's worse, maybe, because you refuse to have it out. You refuse to talk. And every time you do that and bury your own anger, we get further apart." (p. 89)

Recently, Shere Hite (1987), in *Women and Love,* interviewed 4500 women about the men in their lives. This sample was admittedly haphazard. Hite found that the vast majority of women were disillusioned with men and marriage. They complained that men did not talk or listen, would not do enough of the emotional work in the relationship, expected to be the stars in the relationship, while the women were satellites, revolving around them. Worse yet, men showed little interest in changing. As a result, women were distancing themselves—pouring their energies into affairs, children, or work. Some were filing for divorce. (Of course, if men had been interviewed, some of them would surely have been just as bitter.)

There is some evidence that men and women do tend to deal with emotional issues somewhat differently (Brehm, 1992). Men generally have the most power. They can often afford to act with the quiet confidence that, in the end, things will go their way. Women often have to develop a wide variety of techniques for gaining influence (Snodgrass, 1985). Harold Kelley and his colleagues (Kelley, Cunningham, Grisham, Lefebvre, Sink, & Yablon, 1978) argued that men are conflict-avoidant. They find it upsetting to deal with emotional problems. Women are conflict-confronting. They are frustrated by the avoidance and ask that the problem and the feelings associated with it be confronted. A woman in Hite's study expressed just such a frustration: "I would like for us to be able to say what is on our minds. . . . My clue that something is bothering him is when he grinds his teeth when he sleeps" (Hite, 1987, p. 6).

Men and women possess somewhat different strengths in trying to sort out the threads in an emotionally tangled web. Typically, women are more comfortable with emotional conversation and expression than are men. They appear to be especially adept at sending and receiving nonverbal messages (Hall, 1978). Perhaps this is because they are trained to be more socially sensitive, perhaps because they spend more time dealing with the intense passions of children, or perhaps because love relationships matter more to them. Women are better able to paint a clearer picture of their emotional ideas and feelings and listen patiently to others (Miller, Berg, & Archer, 1983). They may also be better at dealing with people in distress. Men tend to condemn people who are upset, ignore their feelings, or try to distract them in some way. Women are more likely to acknowledge the feelings of others and try to deal with their emotional problems (Burleson, 1982).

Men, however, may have other special talents for dealing with emotion. In an extensive study of communication in marriage, researchers found that husbands were most eager to restore harmony and resolve conflict. They showed more concern for their wives' feelings. They reassured, sought forgiveness, and attempted to compromise more than did women. Wives tended to appeal to fairness or guilt, or to be cold and rejecting. The researchers observed that "women, as a low power group, may learn a diplomacy of psychological pressure to influence male partners' behavior" (Raush et al., 1974, p. 153). Husbands may be calmer and more problem-oriented when discussing conflict-ridden topics (Gottman, 1979).

Emotions May "Transform" Us   There is another reason why people need to be alive to their emotions. Ironically, it is those very people who know full well what they feel, and who have learned to be comfortable dealing with their own and others' emotions, who have the potential to reveal or manage their feelings in the most appropriate way. There are many reasons why this is so. If people are fully aware of their feelings, they can recognize those dangerous "warning signs" and do something to calm themselves down before they erupt. The unaware can only "stuff it" until they explode. If people feel comfortable dealing with emotion, they can be generous and set limits. When people possess the ability to say "No," they can gracefully sidestep situations that are irritating, provoking, and emotionally charged.

CONCLUSION

In this chapter, we have observed that in different circumstances, people may choose to deal with their emotions in a variety of different ways. At times it is critically important to be able to control feelings—especially their overt expression. Perhaps there are even times when it is best not to know what you feel. In this chapter, we have reviewed a variety of cognitive, physiological, and behavioral techniques that allow people to control their emotional thoughts, feelings, and behaviors.

Sometimes, however, people want fully to experience their emotions. Generally, they want to experience the conscious play of their emotions; to attempt to understand the causes and consequences of their feelings. They are usually less enthusiastic about fully experiencing the debilitating physiological consequences of extreme emotion or engaging in antisocial, out-of-control emotional behavior. Yet sometimes it is simply a pleasure to be able to relax, feel wildly elated or silly, or even—in retrospect—to have plumbed the depths of anxiety, anger, or despair. To be an emotional person means to be part of the rich intensity that is life. To be without feeling is to be dead to the possibilities of experience. More eloquently, William James (1890/1961), the pioneering philosopher–psychologist remarked: [As with love] so with fear, with indignation, jealousy, ambition, worship. If they are there, life changes."

Chapter
11

Dealing with Relationship Problems and Problems in the Larger World

INTRODUCTION: RELATIONSHIP PROBLEMS

Though many believe that a relationship is a relationship is a relationship—as though it just happened magically and you either make it work or fail to make it work, the reality is far more complex and interesting. There exists a multitude of types of couples, and each duo can and indeed must write their own music and compose their own harmonic forms. Every couple possesses the opportunity and faces the necessity to negotiate any of a number of types of relationships. Thus put, relationship making is, in reality, a sophisticated and creative art form.

TYPES OF RELATIONSHIPS

Sociologists and family therapists have proposed a variety of typologies to describe the most common relationship forms (Cuber & Harroff, 1965). They find that couples in different types of relationships confront different types of problems and try to deal with them in different ways. Family therapist Mary Anne Fitzpatrick (1988), for example, found that most couples settle into one of three types of marriages: traditional, separate, or independent. Couples in these marriages want very different things from marriage. They make different assumptions about the roles husbands and wives should play, they deal differently with marital conflicts, and communicate with one another in quite disparate ways.

The *traditionals* accept "conventional" notions of what marriage should be. These conventions derive from the nineteenth-century model of the Doctrine of the Two Spheres. Society has provided them with a clear set of guidelines (see Box 11.1 for a sampling of some traditional notions). Marriage furnishes them with a committed, stable relationship and they have strong ties to their communities. Couples accept traditional gender roles. Husbands see themselves as analytical, assertive, and dominant in marriage. Wives see themselves as warm, expressive, and nurturing. Most traditional marriages are reasonably happy. The spouses are fairly stoic and do not expect too much from marriage. Couples are fairly good at predicting one another's moods and feelings. They claim they can discuss anything with one another, but in fact they generally only tell one another about their positive feelings. They are polite, smile, physically lean toward one another in conversation, and finish each other's sentences. They rarely engage in power struggles. When they do, they tend to exchange orders rather than negotiating. They tend to avoid confronting disagreements. This strategy, surprisingly, seems to work because, given the ritualized nature of their shared view of matrimony, they have very few conflicts.

The *separates* start out expecting to have a traditional marriage, but somehow their marriages fail. They are still married, but they go their separate ways. They stay married out of convenience rather than a real desire to be in one another's company. They spend little time together. They feel they cannot express their deepest feelings toward one another. They open up neither to each other nor to outsiders. They are extremely careful in their conversations with one another. They go to great lengths to avoid conflicts. Sometimes they confront one another in a type of verbal guerrilla warfare. One spouse takes a verbal potshot at the other; the attacked partner ignores it. Later the other takes a turn. At the first sign of conflict, they withdraw and go their separate ways.

The *independents* are more typical of modern-day marriages. They have nonconventional ideas about marriage and family life. They choose not to rely on stereotyped conceptions of marriage. They choose to design a relationship that fits them. They are venturing where few couples have gone before, settling on new rules and roles for marriage. They believe in an egalitarian marriage (see Box 11.1 for a sampling of such items). Love and marriage should lead to a pleasurable, companionate marriage. Both think of themselves as androgynous—possessing both masculine and feminine personality traits. Such couples try to balance inti-

Box 11.1 **GENDER ATTITUDES**

Traditional Attitudes

1. A man can make long-range plans for his life but a woman has to take things as they come.

2. It is more important for a wife to help her husband's career than to have a career herself.

3. It is much better for everyone involved if the man is the achiever outside the home and the woman takes care of the home and family.

4. A preschool child is likely to suffer if his mother works.

5. Women who do not want at least one child are being selfish.

Egalitarian Attitudes

1. A working mother can establish just as warm and secure a relationship with her children as a mother who does not work.

2. Parents should encourage just as much independence in their daughters as in their sons.

3. Men should share the housework, such as doing dishes, cleaning, and so forth, with women.

4. Men and women should be paid the same money if they do the same work.

5. Women should be considered as seriously as men for jobs as executives or politicians or even president.

Source: Mason, Czajka, & Arber, 1976. Reprinted by permission.

---

macy and independence, togetherness and privacy. Independents are passionately involved with one another. They do share their innermost thoughts, feelings, and anxieties, including their negative as well as positive feelings. They love one another more intensely and are happier in their marriages than are other couples *and* they engage in more spirited conflicts than do the other types.

Fitzpatrick classified 20% of American couples as traditionals, 17% as separates, and 22% as independents, while 41% are mixed types. The wife, for example, might be a traditional, but the husband a separate, going his own way.

What strategies do the various types of couples use to resolve conflict? Fitzpatrick believed that couples can attempt to resolve conflict in four different ways:

I left the room with silent dignity, but caught my foot in the mat.
            —George and Weedon Grossmith

1. *Conflict avoidance.* Some couples work hard to avoid conflict. They may use several tricks to sidestep "hot" issues. They may speak abstractly (avoiding getting into personal issues), change the subject when "hot" topics are raised, give evasive

answers, deny that any problems exist, make jokes, or—if all else fails—refuse to engage in conversation. (Conflict avoidance isn't all bad. It is reasonable to take a "time out," to cool off before discussing explosive issues. And, if couples have talked and talked an issue to death, and no resolution is in sight, sometimes it is best just to agree to disagree. But, usually, too much avoidance means that problems just simmer until the live volcano erupts—often with destructive consequences.)

2. *Accommodation or yielding.* People give in to please their mates. They value the relationship more than they value getting their own way. Too much yielding, however, may cause problems. There is an old joke: "Marriage requires give-and-take. She gave and I took." If one person does all the giving, trouble is inevitable. Givers soon come to feel bad about themselves, to resent their sacrifices, to think about getting out. Takers too get stuck. They remain self-centered adolescents—never maturing into generous grown-ups. They come to take their mates for granted or, even worse, to vaguely despise them for their weakness.

Although man and woman unite they nevertheless represent irreconcilable opposites which, when activated, degenerate into deadly hostility. This primordial pair of opposites symbolizes every conceivable pair of opposites that may occur; hot and cold, light and dark, north and south, dry and damp, good and bad, conscious and unconscious.

—Carl Gustav Jung

3. *Competition or contending.* People try to impose their solutions on others in a variety of ways. They criticize others, rejecting them and their opinions outright. They threaten and demand that their partners change, pepper them with hostile questions, make nasty jokes or sarcastic remarks, or attribute thoughts, feelings, and intentions to their mates. These attackers also deny that they have any responsibility for the problem.

4. *Problem solving and cooperation.* Some couples try to find solutions that satisfy both sides. They try to analyze the problem, ask one another about their feelings, seek a variety of possible solutions, and strive to agree on a mutually acceptable solution. Each person tries to achieve his or her aims without sacrificing too much themselves.

Couples differ in how they prefer to deal with conflict. Traditionals try to avoid conflict (especially over "trivial" issues). They tend to sweep minor problems under the rug, rather than dealing directly with them. If problems loom large, however, traditionals are cooperative and conciliatory. Since traditionals agree about almost everything, it is usually fairly easy for them to solve problems.

Separates also tend to avoid discussing hard issues. They often express hostility toward one another, but if their partners challenge them, they immediately withdraw. They slip away from conflict. Such conflict avoidance is fairly easy since separates are already emotionally divorced.

Independents tend to dig right in to conflict situations. They spend time negotiating marital rules and roles. In such individually crafted marriages, a certain amount of conflict, stress, and tension is inevitable. So they try hard to deal with problems as they arise. Independents won't allow their partners to opt out of the relationship by passively yielding to them; they certainly won't yield themselves. They insist on coming up with doubly satisfying solutions to problems. This makes sense, since independents are passionately involved in their relationships *and* insistent on preserving their own individuality and autonomy.

We see then that different types of couples may choose to cope with conflict in very different ways. In the next section, we expand the range. We shall, in the interest of enlarging our repertoire of problem-solving tools, consider the vast array of techniques available to men and women, regardless of typologies, for coping with conflict.

The only time love is an easy game/ Is when two other people are playing it.
—Paul Simon

STRATEGIES FOR DEALING WITH PROBLEMS

Kathryn Dindia and Leslie Baxter (1987) took the notion that "marriage takes work" literally. They investigated the strategies used by partners to maintain and repair their damaged relationships. The authors interviewed 50 married couples. They asked them two questions:

1. We are trying to determine what spouses do when they are trying to maintain their relationship in a healthy state. This usually happens when one or both spouses think that the relationship is good the way it is and he and/or she wants to prevent the relationship from going downhill. What do you do, or have you done in the past, when you are trying to keep your relationship from going downhill?
2. We are trying to determine what spouses do when they are trying to repair their relationship. This usually happens when one or both spouses think that the relationship is not as good as it used to be, that the relationship has gone downhill, and he and/or she wants to restore the relationship to its previously healthy state. What do you do, or have you done in the past, when you are trying to bring your relationship back to what it was in the past?

They found that men and women had a rich array of strategies available to maintain and repair their marriages. In general, couples employed similar tactics to keep things going well and to try to fix things when their marriages had begun to deteriorate. The tactics they claimed to use (in order of popularity) are given in Table 11.1.

Some scientists have tried to condense the 11 techniques listed for dealing with conflict into a few categories. In a series of studies, Caryl Rusbult (1987) classified attempts to deal with marital dissatisfactions into four categories (see Figure 11.1, p. 327). She began by pointing out that different people respond to conflict in very different ways (see Figure 11.1, the box marked "Individual Factors"). Individuals who differ in self-esteem, age, education, income, and marital status may typically choose to deal with relationship problems in diverse

Table 11.1 STRATEGIES OF MAINTENANCE AND REPAIR

Strategy	Maintenance	Repair
1. *Prosocial strategies* (e.g., be polite, cheerful, warm, and friendly; refrain from criticizing the other; give in, sacrifice, or compromise)	77%	51%
2. *Togetherness* (e.g., try to spend more time together)	63	26
3. *Ceremonies* (e.g., celebrate, kiss and make up, go out to dinner, give a present)	58	39
4. *Communication strategies* (e.g., call at noon to enquire how things are going, try to share feelings and be more open and honest)	53	30
5. *Metacommunication* (e.g., try to talk about the problem and make suggestions for improvement; check on progress; decide to take a "time out")	21	47
6. *Seeking outside help* (e.g., talk to family and friends, a minister, a therapist; pray)	19	10
7. *Antirituals/spontaneity* (e.g., bring home a surprise)	12	1
8. *Seeking/allowing autonomy* (e.g., give the other some space)	7	5
9. *Avoid metacommunication* (e.g., avoid a potentially volatile issue by keeping quiet and "letting it pass")	6	3
10. *Antisocial strategies* (e.g., be rude, threaten the partner; give him or her the "silent treatment"; fight; move out)	1	5
11. *Changing external environment* (e.g., arrange romantic candlelight dinner)	1	1

Source: Dindia & Baxter, 1987, pp. 152–153.

ways. Spouses also differ in how committed they are to their relationships, and thus how they respond to marital problems (see Figure 11.1, the box marked "Investment Factors"). Rusbult observed that the more satisfied couples are, the more time and effort they have invested in their marriages, and the fewer alternatives they see to staying in their present marriages, the harder they will work to keep their relationships going. (Similar results were secured by Rusbult, Verette, Whitney, Slovik, & Lipkus, 1991.)

Alice: "Would you tell me, please, which way I ought to go from here?" "That depends a good deal on where you want to get to," said the Cat.
                                                    —*Lewis Carroll in* Alice in Wonderland

Finally, Rusbult (1987) wrote that people can respond to trouble in four very different ways (again, see Figure 11.1, "Responses to Dissatisfaction"):

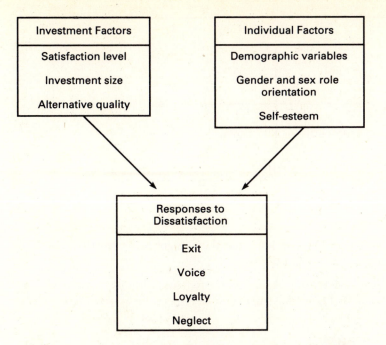

Figure 11.1 Possible reactions to dissatisfaction in close relationships.

1. *Voice*—discussing problems, compromising, seeking help from a therapist or member of the clergy, suggesting solutions to problems, asking the partner what is bothering him or her, and trying to change oneself or one's partner. (p. 213)

Voice is an attempt to salvage something of value that is in danger of being damaged.

2. *Loyalty*—waiting and hoping that things will improve, "giving things some time," praying for improvement, supporting the partner in the face of criticism, and continuing to have faith in the relationship and the partner. (p. 213)

Loyalty is a conservative response, one that serves primarily to maintain the status quo (i.e., "Why mess with a good thing?").

3. *Neglect*—ignoring the partner or spending less time together, refusing to discuss problems, treating the partner badly emotionally or physically, criticizing the partner for things unrelated to the real problem, "just letting things fall apart," chronically complaining without offering solutions to problems, *perhaps* developing extrarelationship sexual involvements. (p. 213)

Neglect is basically an ineffectual response, one likely to occur when the individual doesn't really know what to do or isn't motivated to do much of anything about a troubled relationship.

4. *Exit*—formally separating, moving out of a joint residence, deciding to "just be friends," thinking or talking about leaving one's partner, threatening to end the relationship, actively destroying the relationship, or getting a divorce. (p. 213)

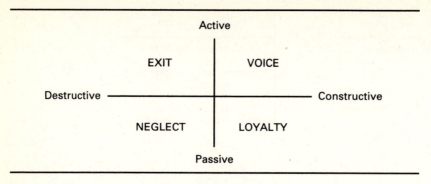

Figure 11.2 A typology of basic coping strategies.

People exit when they believe that what they've got is not worth saving and that they have little to lose by getting out.

These four reactions to trouble differ on two dimensions: how active or passive the reaction is and how constructive or destructive it is (see Figure 11.2).

We boil at different degrees.
—Ralph Waldo Emerson

GENDER AND SEX ROLE ORIENTATION DIFFERENCES IN COPING WITH CONFLICT

Caryl Rusbult and her colleagues (Rusbult, Zembrodt, & Iwaniszek, 1986) interviewed men and women, who varied in sex role orientation, and who were currently involved in gay, lesbian, or heterosexual dating or marital relationships. How did people react when they encountered periodic problems in their love relationships? Men and women did not really differ in how they responded. What was important was men's and women's sex role orientation. Most sex role theorists characterize psychological masculinity as an individualistic orientation; one associated with power and dominance, problem solving, and a concern with work success. Psychological feminity is characterized as a communal orientation; one associated with warmth and intimacy, communication, and a concern with interpersonal relations (Bem, Martyna, & Watson, 1976; Wiggins & Holzmuller, 1981). The *Interpersonal Disposition Inventory* (Berzins, Welling, & Wetter, 1978) was used to assess gender role orientation. People with a masculine orientation would be expected to endorse such items as "If I have a problem, I like to work it out alone," "I seek out positions of authority," "When I am with someone else I do most of the decision making." Those with a feminine orientation endorse such items as "I like to be with people who assume a protective attitude toward me," "People like to tell me their troubles because they know I will do everything I can to help them," "When I see a baby I often want to hold him or her," "To love and be loved is of the greatest importance to me." As predicted, men and women who had a masculine orientation were not willing to invest very much in keeping their love affairs going. When trouble struck, they tended to respond destructively—by passively allowing things to deteriorate *(neglect)* or by threatening to end it *(exiting)*. Those with a feminine sex role orientation, on the other hand, reacted constructively to problems: They either actively attempted to solve them *(voice)* or, if that was impossible, remained quietly loyal to the relationship, waiting for things to improve *(loyalty)*. It seems that biological gender is less important than psychological masculinity/femininity in shaping how people try to deal with relationship problems.

PERSONALITY DIFFERENCES IN COPING WITH CONFLICT

Psychologists have defined personality as "a distinctive and stable pattern of behavior, thoughts, motives and emotions that characterizes an individual" (Wade & Tavris, 1990, p. 386). Theorists have proposed a variety of schemes for classifying people. Sigmund Freud, for example, proposed a taxonomy based on the fact that people must pass through a series of developmental stages (the oral, anal, phallic, latency, and genital stages) on their way to adulthood. If people got fixated at one or another stage, he reasoned, it should have a powerful impact on their personalities. He thus classified people as having "oral," "anal," "phallic" personalities and so forth. The intellectual heirs of Sigmund Freud are such stage theorists as Carl Gustav Jung, Alfred Adler, Karen Horney, and Erik Erikson. Other theorists have proposed taxonomies that focus on other traits. In ancient Greece, physicians from the time of Hippocrates (ca. 460–357 B.C.) to Galen (A.D. 130–201) believed that people's temperaments depended on which of four bodily fluids or "humors" were dominant:

Types	Humors
Choleric (angry)	Yellow bile
Phlegmatic (slow and lethargic)	Phlegm
Melancholic (sad and brooding)	Black bile
Sanguine (joyful and good-natured)	Blood

Today, *trait* theorists such as Gordon Allport, Raymond Cattell, and Hans Eysenck have proposed a variety of taxonomies for categorizing people according to the traits they possess. Psychologists who have conducted "meta-analyses" of existing personality studies have concluded that people's personalities can best be described by the "Big Five"—five basic traits that seem most important in classifying personality (Digman, 1990).

1. *Extraversion/introversion.* Extraverts direct their attention outward. They are not very introspective; instead, they focus on other people and the

environment. Introverts focus inward; they tend to think their own thoughts and to shrink from social contacts.

2. *Friendliness/hostility.* Some people are altruistic, nurturant, caring, and emotionally supportive. Others are more hostile, indifferent to others, self-centered, spiteful, and jealous.

3. *Conscientiousness.*

4. *Neuroticism/emotional stability.*

5. *Intellect (or openness).*

The "Big Five" factors turn up in studies of Chinese, Japanese, Filipino, Hawaiian, and Australian adults (Digman & Inouye, 1986; Noller, Law, & Comrey, 1987). Longitudinal studies with men and women, who ranged from 21 to 96 years of age, made it clear that these traits are remarkably stable. Scientists can still detect the faint shadows of the 3-year-old rebel in the 96-year-old nonconformist (Costa & McCrae, 1988). We might expect men and women whose basic personalities are very different to handle dating and marital conflict in different ways (Frost & Wilmot, 1978).

Ralph Kilmann and Kenneth Thomas (1975), using a Jungian classification scheme, tried to classify individual styles of dealing with conflict (see Figure 11.3). In *Psychological Types,* Carl Gustav Jung (1938) pointed out that people perceive and process information about the world in very different ways. As a consequence, people possess very different personalities and characters.

1. *Perceiving information.* Theoretically, people can perceive the world around them in two different ways—by sensation or intuition. People who rely on *sensation* trust the evidence of their five senses. "Seeing is believing." Those who rely on *intuition* are much more likely to rely on unconscious data, on their hunches.

2. *Judging information.* Theoretically, people can make judgments in two different ways: by thinking or feeling. People can think about facts—naming, categorizing, organizing, analyzing, and synthesizing them—or they can feel about them—judging how good or bad, pleasant or unpleasant, acceptable or unacceptable things are. In thinking, people form concepts, manipulate ideas, try to assess the truth of various ideas, solve problems, and understand things. Thinking involves the analytical, logical, sequential processing of information (Jung, 1938). By contrast, feeling tells one whether something is agreeable or disagreeable, "what a thing is worth to you" (Jung, 1968, p. 1).

3. *Acting.* Finally, Jung (1953) observed that people differ markedly in attitude. Some are shy and introverted, while others are outgoing and extraverted. *Introverts* possess a "subjective attitude." They focus their psychic energy inward. They think their own thoughts, sometimes trying to catch inner rhythms they can barely sense. They are "hesitant, reflective and retiring." Others sometimes see them as aloof, antisocial, and reserved and preoccupied. They seek answers from themselves. *Extraverts* possess an "objective attitude." They focus their psychic energy outward and are interested in people and things. They are "outgoing, candid, and accommodating." They seek information from objective reality.

Interestingly enough, although most people tend to deal with the world in repetitive, stereotyped ways corresponding to their personality types, that is not the ideal in Jung's view. If people are too extraverted (or introverted) or too obsessed with thinking (to the exclusion of feeling), they cut themselves off from the possibilities of human experience. For the psyche, the ideal is equilibrium.

Kilmann and Thomas (1975) tried to build on Jung's model. People can deal with conflict by assertiveness (attempting to satisfy their own concerns) or cooperation (attempting to satisfy the other person's concerns) (see Figure 11.3). Those who possess a competitive style, for example, generally pursue their own interests, assertively. They are more than willing to sacrifice others. Those who possess an accommodating style will sacrifice themselves in order to please their partners. In all of the other styles—collaboration, compromise, and avoiding—couples try to compromise. For the authors, a perfect compromise (a compromising style) would generally be the ideal.

The authors found that people with different personality styles [as measured by the *Myers–Briggs Type Indicator* (Myers, 1962)] differ in how they try to deal with conflict. They found that how people *perceived* information (whether they relied on sensation or intuition) had no effect on how they dealt with conflict. How people made judgments (thinking versus feelings) and how they acted on them (as introverts or extraverts) did seem to matter. The more thinking (and the less feeling) people were, the more self-interested their strategies for dealing with conflict were. Furthermore, the more introverted (and the less extraverted) people were, the less likely they were to try to cooperate with others in finding a solution to conflict.

Other researchers document that people with different personality types generally do deal with conflict in characteristic ways. When watching the Ayatollah

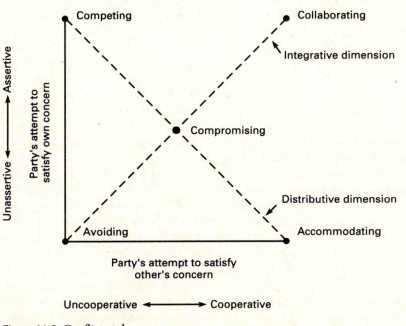

Figure 11.3 Conflict styles.

Khomeini, Muammar el-Qaddafy, Idi Amin, Manuel Noriega, or Saddam Hussein furiously present their own positions on television and vilify the opposition as "tools of Satan," we as therapists are glad we don't have to try to deal with Their Eminences and their hapless wives (or concubines) in counseling! But would they in fact be so difficult to deal with?

Robert Sternberg and Lawrence Soriano (1984) wondered whether people *are* consistent and uniformly yielding/unyielding in their attempts to cope with conflict. Do they confront their families in the same way as they face their political adversaries? Perhaps they are not so one-dimensional. Consider, for instance, Alec Guinness's masterful presentation of the spymaster George Smiley in John le Carré's *Tinker, Tailor, Soldier, Spy.* As the head of Control, Smiley was powerful, cold, and ruthless. But the minute Smiley began to talk to his patrician wife, he somehow shrank into a little old man, nervously fingering his glasses.

So the authors' question is a legitimate one. Do people tend to have a consistent style for dealing with intimate problems, organizational problems at work, and international relations? To find out, the researchers asked men and women to consider a number of conflicts and recommend the strategies they would use to solve them. Personal problems were such things as: (1) what a married couple should do about the wife's elderly mother who is too old and too ill to live by herself; (2) what a wife should do about a husband whose extremely busy schedule keeps him away from her and the children for large blocks of time; and (3) what a man should do about an ex-wife who is preventing him from seeing his children as often as he believes the court order permits him. Organizational conflicts dealt with such conundrums as what a leading wire news service should do about a competing service that is taking away its customers. The international conflicts addressed such issues as what one nation should do about another that is drilling for shared oil supplies at a rate that is depriving the first nation of its rightful share of the profits.

Subjects were asked to indicate how they would try to solve such problems. They could choose one of seven different types of tactics: *physical action* (such solutions as "Mr. Martin could physically bar the mother-in-law from entering the house against his wishes," or "Egypt could take action to destroy Sudan's dams and factories along the border"); *economic action* ("Bob could start withholding alimony payments from Ann to force her to start letting him see the children regularly again"); *wait and see* ("Kathy could decide to take no action at this time and wait to see what Tom will do"); *accept the situation* ("Mr. Martin could just accept the mother-in-law's moving into the house and try to make the best of a difficult situation"); *step-down* ("Bob might try being nicer to both Ann and the children by sending them letters and gifts to prove he cares and to persuade Ann to change her position"); *third-party intervention* ("Kathy might try to find some counseling for the couple to work out an agreement that is satisfying to both"); or *undermine esteem* ("Bob might try criticizing Ann before family and mutual friends to get Ann to reconsider her stand").

The researchers found that intellectual abilities and personalities affected the kinds of solutions favored by their subjects. (For example, the intelligent were more inclined to favor "wait and see" approaches; the less intelligent preferred strong, immediate, physical action to solve problems). [This reminds us of the famous lament that William Butler Yeats uttered in the period between the two world wars: "The best lack all conviction, while the worst are full of passionate intensity" (in Jeffares, 1984, p. 246).] People did tend to find the same sorts of solutions appealing in settling personal, organizational, and international conflicts. The same kind of person who was eager to take physical action in the personal example ("Mr. Martin could physically bar the mother-in-law from entering the house against his wishes") recommended physical action in the international realm ("Egypt could take action to destroy Sudan's dams and factories along the border"). The same kind of person who wanted to wait and see in the personal realm recommended exercising the same caution in international conflicts.

This research does indeed confirm the instinct we all have that working with Saddam Hussein in therapy on his marital problems would not be a pleasant enterprise.

We see then that couples of goodwill can use an armenteria of techniques for dealing with relationship problems. Let us now see how therapists and couples might try to deal with a sample relationship problem—jealousy.

MANAGING JEALOUSY

Jealousy is a common problem. Researchers (White & Devine, in press) surveyed 60 clinical psychologists, social workers, and psychotherapists who were members of the American Association of Marriage and Family Therapy. How many of their clients had serious problems with jealousy? Jealousy was the reason 10% of the couples entered therapy in the first place. Twenty-two percent of clients admitted that jealousy was a major problem; 30% of couples admitted that it was a minor problem. Young couples had the most trouble dealing with jealous feelings. Fifty-nine percent of clients under 30 were judged to have a major problem with jealousy compared with 39% for those in the 30 to 45 age group, 21% for those 46 to 60, and only 13% for those over 60.

It is not love that is blind, but jealousy.
—Lawrence Durrell

Therapists were asked what they thought led men and women to be so jealous. The most important causes of jealousy were chronic feelings of low self-esteem and being excessively dependent on the partner. Next in importance were feelings of inadequacy, excessive need for attention, and worries about sexual fidelity. Finally, couples who felt they were more involved in the relationship than their partners were, and who knew that they were investing more in their inequitable relationship than were their partners, were more jealous. Women who had little power in their marriages were especially vulnerable to jealousy. (Perhaps because men generally had more power in their marriages, there was no evidence that a lack of power made men vulnerable to jealousy.)

How do therapists generally attempt to deal with clients' jealousy? Gregory White and Therese Helbick (1988) reviewed the clinical literature and reported that clinicians generally had seven goals in treating jealousy:

1. To challenge couples' irrational beliefs and assumptions.
2. To improve couples' communication skills.

3. To facilitate negotiations and agreements as to what is acceptable and unacceptable with others.
4. To help the jealous increase their self-esteem.
5. To resolve any personal or relationship issues that may have provoked the problem in the first place.
6. To help couples understand what the rivalry means to each of them.
7. To develop couples' coping skills. (p. 262)

White and Helbick (1988) developed a two-day jealousy workshop for couples. In these workshops, they set five basic goals:

1. Educating each couple about the causes and consequences of jealousy.
2. Training the partners in communication and negotiation skills.
3. Helping the couple to identify and assess the utility of their current coping strategies.
4. Designing new coping strategies.
5. Promoting discussion of the possibility of seeking relationship counseling. (p. 261)

Let us slowly walk through a therapy program or a weekend workshop that attempts to train people to deal with jealousy. Perhaps you can adapt some of these techniques in your own lives.

Jealousy is always born with love, but does not always die with it.
—François, Duc de La Rochefoucauld

The Assessment Interview

Therapists' first step is to do some detective work. They try to figure out exactly why this man or that woman is so jealous. Men's and women's life histories usually provide some clues. Often therapists ask clients questions like the following:

1. A cultural and family history. What does their culture say about jealousy? Is it good or bad? What are their standards for marital behavior? Were they brought up with the idea of a single or a double standard? Were their parents jealous?

2. Relationship history. Did they date much? Have they been married before? Have they had a good deal of sexual experience? How did these relationships go? Were they ever jealous before? When? (Pathological reactions may have their roots in previous experiences of desertion and betrayal. Partners may be unaware that they are paying the price of the jealous person's past losses.)

How did the couple meet? What once attracted them to one another? How were their marriages going before the jealousy erupted? What does each of them get from the relationship? How intimate is their marriage? Who had the most power in the relationship? How fair and equitable is it? Do they have friends? Fulfilling careers?

3. A history of the present jealousy. How does the person experience jealousy? The jealous are often hurt and frightened, humiliated, shattered. Sometimes they are angry. They may be in a state of shock. Despairing. (Their partners may be chagrined, angry, defiant . . . or totally matter-of-fact.) Some jealous people get perverse pleasure out of occupying the moral highground; they enjoy making their partners Pay for What They Have Done. Some insist all they want to know is the

truth; the truth, of course, is never enough. Some will forgive everything, even grovel, if only their partners will come back.

When did they first become suspicious? Did they spy on their partners? Did their partners admit to having affairs? Do they have evidence that they did? Are their mates generally liars? Have they had affairs before? Are the affairs over?

Have they tried to deal with their jealousy before? How did these attempts work out? Did they dampen jealous feelings or backfire? Is either of them violent?

When people are jealous, they often threaten one another. Gregory White and Paul Mullen (1989) have suggested that therapists should also ask the jealous whether they have done the following:

1. Destroyed the partner's property or broken and smashed objects during an argument.
2. Pushed, shoved, or shaken the partner in anger.
3. Struck the partner, and if so, whether with open hand or fist.
4. Thrown objects at the partner with the intention of hurting him or her.
5. Attempted to throttle the partner, or put hands around his or her throat in anger.
6. Attacked the partner with a clublike object, a knife, or a gun.
7. Taken any other action that could have injured or harmed the partner (e.g., poisoning, driving at the partner, pushing him or her in front of traffic, etc.). (p. 259)

Surprises often occur in such questioning. Husbands and wives may be ashamed to admit what they have done; their mates may want to protect them. A question, however, may provide an unexpected answer.

> One middle-aged lady appeared amazed at the inquiries about threats and violence, dismissing them with detached humor, until the interviewer asked whether she had ever done anything else aimed to hurt or harm her husband. After a brief pause, she quietly confessed to having attempted to poison him some weeks previously. (p. 259)

Do couples drink? Take drugs? (Jealousy sparks violent feelings. When people are drunk it is easy to translate such impulses into action.)

The questions continue: What will it take to make things right? Is it enough if the partners are sorry? Can they ever trust them again? Is it all over?

The Clinical Treatment of Jealousy

The next step is to try to do something about jealousy. The jealous have several options: They can work on reducing their own jealousy; they can pretend they are not jealous (perhaps secretly trying to control their partners by sarcasm, complaints, and/or veiled threats); they can try to persuade their mates to stop doing the things that make them jealous; or they can get out of the relationship (Clanton & Smith, 1987).

In attempting to help couples work through issues of jealousy, therapists may attack the problem on any of three levels—the personal, the relational, or the situational (or on all three.)

Focusing on Personal Issues   Often, the spotlight is beamed on the jealous themselves. They are responsible for perceiving things clearly, interpreting them accurately, and managing their feelings. Sometimes, the jealous parties' cultural and family backgrounds predispose them to be jealous. They were programmed to assume that if you love someone, you are naturally jealous and possessive. Most people know this is not so. One clinician, Ronald Mazur (1987), made the observations on jealousy and possessiveness given in Box 11.2.

In Chapter 9, we found that both low self-esteem and excessive fear about losing relationships predispose men and women to be unreasonably jealous. Thus one of the first things clinicians set out to do is to help the jealous to build their own self-esteem and to make themselves less desperately needy on this one relationship for all their life satisfactions. Many people think the way to build self-esteem is to give yourself inspirational messages: "I am wonderful." They

---

Box 11.2 **BEYOND JEALOUSY AND POSSESSIVENESS**

Possessiveness is culturally sanctioned but nevertheless a dehumanizing process. The possessive person does not know the inherent value or even the identity of the person possessed. The possessor is also possessed by private versions of reality—a reality requiring order, reassurance, and respect from without, and a sense of power and control. This allows for predictability, homage, and manipulation, but negates the qualities of spontaneity, authentic self-esteem, and mutuality of relationship. By perceiving the other merely as an extension of one's own life—even when romantically intended—that other person is deprived of dignity, individuality, and freedom to be and become with integrity. Possessiveness can, of course, be symbiotic in the sense that both spouses build their lives around it and feed off each other. This is so much the case that possessive marriage has superseded religion as the "opiate of the masses"; it is a stupefied security without joy, enthusiasm, or adventure.

The double-standard reinforces the sanctions for possessiveness in accordance with the best interests of males. When the male is possessive-jealous, the female is supposed to feel proud and grateful. When the female is possessive-jealous the male flaunts it as a sign of his desirability and attractiveness as long as the female doesn't push too hard. But when the female becomes too demanding she is demeaned as being nothing but a castrating bitch.

Possessive-jealousy is perhaps the most raging and wrathful form of jealousy, leading to acts of cruel vengeance and even murder. "You belong to me and if you cross me I'll get even with you. If I can't have you nobody is going to have you." That sentiment sounds as if it comes from one of those unbelievably trite movies. Yet, the sentiments of possessive people *are* unfortunately trite, and potentially destructive.

Is it possible to be monogamously committed to someone without possessiveness? We pose the question because many couples seem to confuse commitment with belonging to. Possessiveness is commitment without trust. Conversely, commitment with trust celebrates the autonomy of the other; rejoices in the uniqueness of the other; is aware of the privacy needs of the other. There need be no contradiction between mutual commitment and the mutual allowance for emotional space. (p. 183)

write notebooks full of affirmations—"I think I can . . . I think I can . . . I know I can." (It reminds us a little bit of the *Little Engine that Could* from our nursery school days.) That doesn't work very well. Such messages may work for a few hours or a few days; eventually, however, people slip right back to where they were before. Now they have failed yet again. What works far better is to raise self-esteem by helping men and women to develop a solid base of real achievement. Our clients began to think better of themselves when they went back to school, or got a job, or made some friends. Of course, at first they are frightened to try. It would be so much easier if their mates were just there to hold their hands. But by going in slow steps—having them walk on campus one day, drop into the admissions office the next, showing them how to fill out a college admission application the next—almost all are able to make steady progress. If some people are stuck, either because they are too anxious or too depressed to go, we have had great success with prescribing anti-anxiety or anti-depressant medication. If they have no money, we can usually point them to a work-study program or a student loan program. Similarly, the jealous can reduce their terror of being left alone by slowly building up a safety net: initiating contacts with relatives, making some best friends, finding some new acquaintances, getting part-time jobs.

The same things that work to make the marriage stronger are the same things that make it easier for the jealous to survive if they are abandoned or to leave if the marriage proves impossible.

Jealousy is a sign that something is wrong, not necessarily rotten, in the organism of love.

—Theodor Reik

Focusing on the Relationship   Sometimes therapists choose to focus on the couple and their relationship.

In some cases, the couple agrees that there is no reason for jealousy. They both love one another; the relationship is a fine one; there is no rival. For example, one couple we saw was happily married. She was a violinist; she had played with a major orchestra. He was a physicist. She was extremely jealous. When she was in her twenties, she had lived with a divinity student for three years. One day she came home to find a note tacked to the door. He had loaded up all their possessions in a moving van and moved out. He had run away with her best friend. Eventually, her two friends married.

What precipitated the jealous explosion in her current marriage? One day, in passing, her husband mentioned that as a boy he had experimented sexually with a playmate. She found this revelation so shocking that she lost all trust in him. Was he a latent homosexual? Would she be left again—this time for another man? In this case, it was clear that her jealousy was irrational. She had nothing to fear. This time around, the couple could design the solution. Her husband began to make a special effort to court her. He reassured her that he was crazy about her. They had little picnic dinners, took a holiday to the Grand Canyon. She was touched by his dedication. They had a great deal of fun on this second honeymoon. Her jealousy diminished and soon disappeared.

Sometimes, couples can deal with jealousy by hammering out an agreement as to what is acceptable and what is not. Surprisingly, few couples that we see have ever explicitly agreed on sexual "rules." They *think* they have unspoken understandings, but no one knows for sure. Spelling things out helps. Once they put their expectations into words, almost all our clients end up with the same standards. Both of them are allowed to have friends of the opposite sex. They can certainly see these friends for lunch. Most can understand that a little flirting is part of almost every male–female relationship; they agree that flirting must not be serious, however. Many dual-career couples even feel comfortable if their mates take friends of the same or opposite sex to dinner or the movies when they are out of town. Most feel comfortable allowing a friendly hug hello or goodbye. Hardly any feel comfortable with mates who neck, pet, or have sexual relationships with anyone else.

(This is not strictly true in all cases. Some couples are so guilty, but so eager to divorce, that they wish their mates would find someone else and leave them; then they would be free. But for these couples jealousy is not the problem. The problem is how to make an exit.)

Sometimes, however, jealousy is realistic. It is an early warning system that something has gone wrong, very wrong, in the marriage. The couple may be bored. Their relationship may be quite superficial; neither loves nor feels deeply loved and understood. One of them may feel excluded from all the good times. ("You never take *me* anywhere. How come you have time to drink; go out with the boys? How come your work always come first?") Sometimes their mates *are* having an affair. Here, more serious work is required. Here, the couple may be starting off with less goodwill. They cannot trust one another. How can you make agreements when you don't trust your partner to keep them? They have real problems. Worse yet, at least one of them may have a "better alternative" lurking in the wings.

When someone is passionately in love, as we saw in Chapter 2, they may not be thinking clearly. We have seen clients who know they should give up a passionate liaison: they know it can only end in disaster. They know an affair would be dangerous to them, their families, and their careers. And yet. . . . Sometimes they get no further than our waiting room before their resolution falters and they telephone their new lover . . . just to explain why things have to end. Maybe over dinner. Maybe a weekend somewhere.

Sometimes, however, couples are willing to commit themselves to sorting out their problems, to putting the rival on hold, or even terminating the alternative relationship. Then the couple can begin to work on their own relationship. Sometimes, when things are going well in the marriage, the temptation to have extramarital affairs withers away.

Trying to Alter the Situation   As we saw in Chapter 10, the couple does not exist in isolation. Sometimes women are stuck at home, with howling children and dirty dishes. Their husbands may spend their afternoons drinking and socializing with clients. When they do come home they are too tired to do much more than sit, stupefied, in front of the television. Some women are jealous because they never see their husbands. Their husbands spend all their spare time with "the boys": They go to singles' bars on Saturday night, trying to pick up women, and spend the other nights drinking or playing basketball with the boys. That cultural disparity—she is at home waiting, he is out in the world—dooms her to being a jealous woman; him to feeling pressured. Often, if the jealous are to quit being jealous, if the marriage relationship is to improve, a structural change must occur. Couples may have to think through what they really want out of life. If it is evident to everyone that the marriage is eroding year by year and nothing is being done, couples will have to change their lives drastically: In the previous examples, he may have to search for a job that allows him to have more time at home with the family and more leisure time *or* she will have to accept an "empty" marriage and begin to fashion a life without him—dinners and movies with friends; holidays with family and friends; go back to school, begin to build her own career. They must make a choice. Unless a major structural change occurs they will end up with a dead marriage. Sometimes, if couples are unwilling to settle for the status quo or to change, they may decide to end their marriages.

We see then how some of the techniques we described for dealing with relationship problems can be applied to a real-life problem, jealousy.

PROBLEMS IN THE LARGER WORLD

Eventually, most couples face major problems. Couples may lose their jobs when there is a recession. Their homes may be destroyed by fires, tornados, or floods. When America declared war on Iraq, husbands and wives were sent off to war; their children sometimes had to be sent to relatives and sitters. Sociologists have long been interested in the factors that determine how couples and families adapt to such crises.

In 1949, Reuben Hill, in *Families Under Stress*, proposed a classic analysis of the factors that determine how well couples cope with such problems. Presumably, before the crisis hit, couples had simply gone along, experiencing the usual ups and downs. The family was in a state of equilibrium. Then disaster struck and the equilibrium was shattered. At that moment, the family swept into action, struggling to set things right. Usually they succeeded. Hill (1965) called his paradigm the *ABCX* model of family crisis. He argued that three factors—A, B, and C—would determine how severe the crisis, X, would be. A represents the crisis-precipitating event. Consider, for example, the military men and women who were sent off to the Persian Gulf War in 1991. Military families were disrupted. They had to deal with loneliness and separation. They had to work out new living arrangements, child-care plans; their incomes fell sharply; and so forth. B represents the family's crisis-meeting resources. Researchers have identified both individual and family system resources that they believe are important. Individual resources include such things as members' self-esteem (Bandura, 1982), socioeconomic status (Lefcourt, Martin, & Saleh, 1984), knowledge and skills, and so forth. Family system resources include a shared awareness of the existence of a problem, consensus on a solution, and agreement on action (Montgomery, 1982); cohesion, adaptability, communication (Olson, McCubbin, Barnes, Larsen, Muxen, & Wilson, 1983), and social support (Pilisuk & Parks, 1983; Silver & Wortman, 1980) are critically important too. C represents the family's definition of the event. If the family perceives the event to be one it can handle, they may take it in stride. If the family panics, the crisis will be especially severe. X represents the crisis.

Hill pointed out that intrafamily events (such as mental breakdown, alcoholism, nonsupport, or infidelity) may well tear the family apart. External events (political and religious persecutions, war, floods, tornadoes, hurricanes, and other "acts of God"), on the other hand, usually bring the family closer together.

For 30 years, researchers have used this *ABCX* model to predict how well couples and families would cope with stress (McCubbin et al., 1980).

In a recent study, Yoav LaVee and his colleagues (1985) suggested "a Double ABCX" model of family stress and adaptation. Sociologists have pointed out that families have both histories and futures. Some families are already beset with a pileup of problems when disaster strikes. Naturally, such troubled families will have unusual difficulty in dealing with yet one more source of stress (McCubbin & Patterson, 1982). Essentially, then, LaVee, McCubbin, and Patterson (1985) simply tested the notion that *family history (ABCX)* and the *ABC* factors that Ruben Hill identified determine how effectively families cope with family stress. They interviewed 1227 American Army families who had been relocated to Germany. For most couples and families, relocation is a hardship. Couples and their children must leave their families, close friends, and acquaintances. Before the move, they have to rush to get passports and immunizations. They must sell homes and cars. Once there, they must quickly find a new house, furnish it, and buy a car. Children have to be enrolled in schools. They must all begin to accommodate to a foreign culture, learn new social customs and languages, deal with a different currency, get used to new traffic laws and transportation systems, and so forth.

In their interviews, the researchers found that couples who already had their hands full when the move was announced—those who had just gotten married, had children, were already in financial trouble, or who had family members or friends who had just died—found the move far more stressful than did others. Their families were especially likely to suffer severe emotional, relational, and health problems after the move.

Researchers also found strong support for the *ABCX* model. Both family system resources and social support helped the family deal with the crisis, but in different ways. The family with strong social support perceived the move to be less stressful than did others. Families with strong system resources adapted to the move far better than did most families.

CONCLUSION

These multiple efforts to discover tactics for solving relationship problems and problems in the larger world really boil down, in our experience, to one large proposition. The conventional wisdom on love, particularly in the United States, too often consigns love to the realm of fairy-tale romance. When Cinderella and Prince Charming find each other, bliss shall follow for all eternity. Find your one true love and two souls shall melt into one.

Our large proposition is, simply put, that one plus one does not equal one; it equals two. The most common affliction we have found among couples who enter therapy is that they refuse to believe that their partners are not, deep down, the same as they are. When the husband talks while making love and remains silent while watching television, the wife is certain that he does not love her. If he did, he would know that *everyone* stays quiet during sex while chattering during television programs. The husband believes his wife is crazy when she jumps into the ocean impetuously, when the *world* knows one should enter the sea slowly and carefully.

The two members of a duo enter their love affair with two different biologies, two different bodies, two different family histories, two different sets of life experiences, two different strings of preferences, tastes, and values. The key to successful problem solving in relationships derives in all cases from recognition, acknowledgment, and appreciation of those differences. Everything follows from that assumption; without it, even among two believers in "tradition," all solutions will fail.

That consciousness of difference—that $1 + 1$ equals 2, not 1—may seem obvious. But we have seen too many people who *truly* believe that "love conquers all," that if one is loved or if one loves, all problems will be solved. That strikes us as faith in magic and we propose the use of intelligence as well as affection in trying to resolve the different hopes, preferences, and perceptions that two human beings inevitably must bring into any one relationship.

Thus we return to the notion that making love work is a creative act—even a creative art. It requires affection, intelligence, ingenuity, imagination, experience, and knowledge in different measures. As the power of tradition and clarity about the "rules" of love erode, we are forced to develop inner resources for crafting our own relationships. Not everyone possesses those inner resources, but too many people simply refuse to believe that they ought to develop them. The decline of clear rules for relationships strikes many as extremely distressing news. There surely is distress abroad, but we believe that the call for each couple to use their wits to create wonderful relationships represents less decline than the opening of rich opportunities for love affairs that really fit the uniqueness of the two participating individuals.

Chapter
12

Dealing with Problems
Communication

Emotional Experience and Facial, Vocal, and Postural
    Feedback
      Evidence That Emotional Contagion Exists
Conclusion

INTRODUCTION

Love flowers most bounteously when couples can talk to one another affectionately, comfortably, and effectively. When communication falters, it is usually not
long before a relationship begins to wilt (Cahn, 1990). But communication does not
always come easily.

We heard recently in therapy a startling, but not atypical, example of miscommunication. Joe and Clare, who have been dating, had a marvelous Fourth of July
weekend. They picnicked, went swimming, and made love. On Sunday night,
before he left for his own apartment to prepare for a tough week back at work,
he murmured to Clare: "This has been such a perfect holiday. I wish it didn't have
to end."

After he left, Clare returned to her place, feeling extremely nervous. She
"realized" that Joe was saying goodbye for good. He was expressing bittersweet
sorrow that their *relationship* was at an end. She then proceeded to become upset
and to engage in desperate behavior—calling him in the middle of the night,
sobbing, hysterically marshalling her "evidence" that he doesn't know how to
love, attributing his inability to get close to his disastrous relationships with his
parents, and on and on. In the end, she produced what she had most feared.
Having endured too many of such scenes, he now, in fact, wanted out.

Communication requires more skills than one might realize. You would think
it would be relatively easy to "say what you mean and mean what you say." Yet
it is not. Now and then, as an experiment, we have recorded a typical, low-key
conversation between a couple in therapy. When we try to slow it down, and ask
exactly why they said certain things as they did, *exactly* what they meant, the
exposition is always illuminating. We and the spouses are always dumbfounded.
We all had thought we understood the conversation perfectly. Now the four of us
find we were all listening to very different conversations. In analyzing verbal
exchanges, we must, of course, pay close attention to content. But we must also
attend to a variety of nonverbal cues to decipher the simplest of conversations. As
linguistic philosophers and absurdist dramatists constantly remind us, nothing is
as it seems—especially words.

DEFINITIONS

*The husband who wants a happy marriage should learn to keep his mouth shut
and his checkbook open.*

                                            —Groucho Marx

Many scientists have suggested definitions of communication that are laughably
abstract. For example, in their classic work *Communication, Conflict and Mar-*

riage, Harold Raush and his colleagues (1974) provided this definition of communication:

> Now we can be more precise in our definition of what communication is. We can say that information flows from system A to system B when a selection in system A (event X) reduces the degree of uncertainty about—that is, to some extent selects or constrains—what happens in system B. Cherry notes: "The information conveyed by signals is always relative; it depends upon the difference in the receiver's doubt before and after their receipt" (1966, p. 182). We may think of information gained as a ratio between *a posteriori* probabilities—Y, knowing X—and *a priori* probabilities—Y, not knowing X (Cherry, 1966, pp. 62–66). (p. 20)

So much for clear communication! Here, such definitions will not do. Some psychologists have defined communication more simply (and communicably) as "transmitting, or transmitting and receiving, information, signals, or messages by means of gestures, words, or other symbols, from one organism to another" (English & English, 1958, p. 99).

Let us review what communication researchers and clinicians know about the process of communication.

CONVERSATIONS

Conversational Styles

Robert Norton (1979) pointed out that men and women differ markedly in the ways they establish contact with others. Some people are *active* communicators. (They are dominant, dramatic, animated, contentious, open, and make a lasting impression.) Others are more *passive*. (They are friendly, attentive, and relaxed.) (See Box 12.1 for a description of these various styles.)

Of these types, who claim to be the best communicators? When Norton asked college students how good they were at communicating with those they cared for, he found that those who were dominant/contentious, impression-leaving, open, and relaxed thought they were excellent communicators. He also noted that others generally agreed with these assessments. In a study of social magnetism, the author compared four types of communicators: Dominant/Open, Dominant/Not Open, Not Dominant/Relaxed, and Not Dominant/Not Relaxed. He found that people were most attracted to Dominant/Open communicators and least attracted to Not Dominant/Not Relaxed communicators.

Good Versus Bad Communication

A good argument settles an issue without unsettling a relationship. A bad argument rarely settles any issue.

—*Barbara Montgomery*

Researchers find that happy couples and distressed couples communicate in very different ways. Jordan and Margaret Paul (1983) in *Do I Have to Give Up Me to Be Loved by You?* wrote that in marriage, conflicts are inevitable (see

Box 12.1 **ASSESSING COMMUNICATOR STYLE**

The Communicator Style Measure (CSM) begins by asking individuals how they usually communicate.

> You have impressions of yourself as a communicator. The following questions are not designed to look at *what* is communicated; rather they explore the way you communicate. Please give us your first impression as to whether or not the following items describe you. Indicate your answer on the following scale:

YES! = strong agreement with the statement

yes = agreement with the statement

? = neither agreement nor disagreement with the statement

no = disagreement with the statement

NO! = strong disagreement with the statement

1. Dominant Style
Dominant communicators control conversations; they come on forcefully. They speak loudly and at length. On the CSM, they would be expected to say "YES!" to items such as these:

1. In most social situations I generally speak very frequently.

2. In most social situations I tend to come on strong.

3. I have a tendency to dominate informal conversations with other people.

4. I try to take charge of things when I am with people.

2. Dramatic Style
Dramatic communicators exaggerate, sprinkle their conversation with jokes, anecdotes, tell tall tales, and use flamboyant language. On the CSM they agree with such items as:

1. I *very frequently* verbally exaggerate to emphasize a point.

2. Often I physically and vocally act out what I want to communicate.

3. *Regularly* I tell jokes, anecdotes, and stories when I communicate.

4. I dramatize a lot.

3. Contentious Style
Contentious people are argumentative. They tend to say "YES!" to such items as:

1. Once I get wound up in a heated discussion I have a hard time stopping myself.

2. Very often I insist that other people document or present some kind of proof for what they are arguing.

3. In arguments I insist upon very precise definitions.

4. When I disagree with somebody I am very quick to challenge him or her.

4. Animated Style

Animated communicators convey ideas and emotions through their lively facial expressions, voices, gestures, and postures.

1. I actively use facial expression when I communicate.

2. I am *very expressive* nonverbally in social situations.

3. I tend constantly to gesture when I communicate.

4. People generally know my emotional state, even if I do not say anything.

5. Impression-Leaving Style

Some people make a lasting impression.

1. *What* I say usually leaves an impression on people.

2. The *way* I say something usually leaves an impression on people.

6. Relaxed Style

Relaxed people are very calm and serene. They are not tense.

1. As a rule, I am very calm and collected when I talk.

2. Under pressure I come across as a relaxed speaker.

3. The rhythm or flow of my speech is [not] affected by my nervousness.

7. Attentive Style

Attentive people listen carefully to people and empathize with them.

1. I am an *extremely* attentive communicator.

2. I can always repeat back to a person *exactly* what was said.

3. I always show that I am very empathetic with people.

8. Open Style

Open communicators are conversational, expansive, affable, convivial, gregarious, unreserved, unsecretive, frank, outspoken, extraverted, and obviously approachable. They readily reveal personal things about themselves.

1. I readily reveal personal things about myself.

2. I am an *extremely* open communicator.

3. As a rule, I *openly* express my feelings or emotions.

9. Friendly Style

People have a friendly style if they readily express their admiration and affection for others.

1. Most of the time I tend to be *very* encouraging to people.

2. I habitually acknowledge verbally others' contributions.

A number of Yes! answers indicate that a person often communicates in a given style. These styles tend to be reflected in clusters of traits. For example, a person could be friendly, open, and relaxed in style.

cathy®   **by Cathy Guisewite**

Figure 12.1). What critically matters is how people deal with them. When faced with conflict, do lovers try to learn something about themselves and their partners or do they try to protect themselves?

1. *The intent to learn.* Some couples respond to conflict by trying to learn about one another. The authors observed:

> What do we mean by an intent to learn? It is the willingness to be vulnerable and open, to feel our feelings directly rather than through the filter of our protections, and to discover why each of us is feeling and behaving as we do. We engage in a process of exploration to discover the answer to such questions as:
>
> What important reasons does my partner have for behaving this way?
> What part do I play in this problem?
> How is my partner's behavior affecting me? (threatening? irritating?)
> Why does it affect me that way? What personal issues does it stir up?
> Why is it so important to get my way, or to be right?
> What fears, values, expectations, and beliefs lie behind my feeling threatened or irritated?
> How does my anger, irritation, or indifference affect my partner?
> How does my partner respond?
> What are the consequences? (p. 9)

2. *The intent to protect.* Some couples try to defend themselves against the threat, real or imaginary, of emotional pain.

> People protecting themselves run the gamut from the most timid to the most aggressive. A man who threatens his opponent with towering rages, a woman who dissolves in self-pitying tears, or the debater who uses calm rational logic to carry a point are all being equally self-protective. None of them wants to learn. *Any response to a conflict other than openness to learning is protective.*
>
> All protective behavior in a conflict falls into one of three categories: (1) Compliance—giving ourselves up to avoid a conflict by denying our own feelings or needs and going along with what the other wants because we fear rejection. (2) Control—trying to change the other's mind or behavior by making him or her feel guilty or afraid. Disapproval (in the form of anger, criticism, tears, threats, lectures) tells the other: "You are wrong" and "I won't love you until you do things my way." (3) Indifference—ignoring the conflict, withdrawing into separate preoccupations (TV, work,

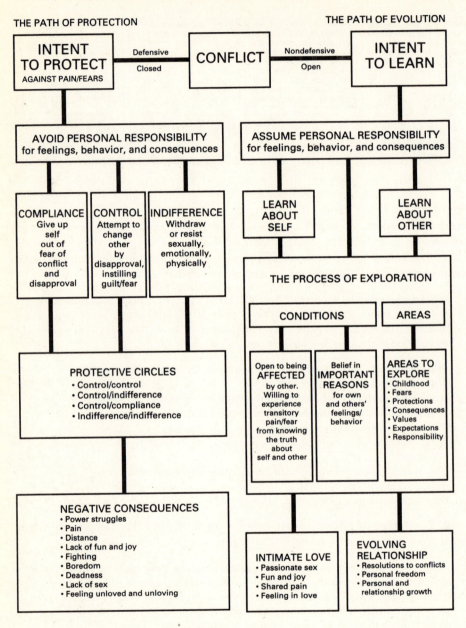

THE PATHS THROUGH CONFLICT

THE PATH OF PROTECTION

INTENT TO PROTECT AGAINST PAIN/FEARS

Defensive
Closed

CONFLICT

Nondefensive
Open

THE PATH OF EVOLUTION

INTENT TO LEARN

AVOID PERSONAL RESPONSIBILITY for feelings, behavior, and consequences

ASSUME PERSONAL RESPONSIBILITY for feelings, behavior, and consequences

COMPLIANCE Give up self out of fear of conflict and disapproval

CONTROL Attempt to change other by disapproval, instilling guilt/fear

INDIFFERENCE Withdraw or resist sexually, emotionally, physically

LEARN ABOUT SELF

LEARN ABOUT OTHER

THE PROCESS OF EXPLORATION

CONDITIONS

AREAS

PROTECTIVE CIRCLES
• Control/control
• Control/indifference
• Control/compliance
• Indifference/indifference

Open to being **AFFECTED** by other. Willing to experience transitory pain/fear from knowing the truth about self and other

Belief in **IMPORTANT REASONS** for own and others' feelings/ behavior

AREAS TO EXPLORE
• Childhood
• Fears
• Protections
• Consequences
• Values
• Expectations
• Responsibility

NEGATIVE CONSEQUENCES
• Power struggles
• Pain
• Distance
• Lack of fun and joy
• Fighting
• Boredom
• Deadness
• Lack of sex
• Feeling unloved and unloving

INTIMATE LOVE
• Passionate sex
• Fun and joy
• Shared pain
• Feeling in love

EVOLVING RELATIONSHIP
• Resolutions to conflicts
• Personal freedom
• Personal and relationship growth

Figure 12.1 The paths through conflict.

drugs, sports). This implies "I'm not affected by you, and you can't hurt or control me." (pp. 7–8)

In the next two sections, we focus on what social scientists have learned about ways that foster communication and openness versus defensive, noncommunicative interactions.

How to Communicate   Happy spouses explain themselves to one another far better than do unhappy ones.

Happy couples are comfortable revealing their thoughts and feelings. They try to explain *exactly* how they feel about things. They don't exaggerate or minimize their feelings. (They may admit: "Yes, I know I am often crabby. But I don't think I was feeling crabby just then.") They do not expect their partners to read their minds (Gottman et al., 1976). Of course, couples needn't communicate everything they think. Sometimes there are things it is too painful to admit, even to oneself. Sometimes our partners would be devastated if we told all the truth ("I wish you were better-looking; you're really too fat"). We don't have to disclose our fantasies. There are times for biting our tongues or being discreet or withholding total revelations. Lovers know, nonetheless, that they can say almost anything if they say it with love and at the right time (Duck, 1988).

Happy partners are good listeners. They ask their mates about *their* intentions, thoughts, or feelings ("Does it bother you when I'm out with my friends?"). Distressed couples generally blithely assume they know what their mates feel, but they are often dead wrong (Noller, 1987).

In one experiment, Patricia Noller (1987) tried to find out how effective happy couples and distressed couples were in communicating with one another. How good were they at sending the messages they wished to send? How good were they at reading their mates' messages? To find out, she gave the husbands or wives a script and asked them to do their best to let their mates know what they felt. (In the example below, the husband was given the script.) The catch? They could utter only one line: "Do you know what a trip like that costs?"

Husband's Script (He Must Send the Message)

> *Situation:* Your wife tells you about the wonderful vacation that one of her friends just took with her husband. She says that she wishes you and she could also take a trip to the same place.
>
> *Your Intention:* You feel that a trip to that place is unappealing and would hardly be worthwhile.
>
> *Your Statement:* Do you know what a trip like that costs?

Wife's Decoding Card

> *Situation:* You told your husband about the wonderful trip that one of your friends just took with her husband. You said that you wished you and he could also take a trip to the same place.

His Statement: Do you know what a trip like that costs?

His Intention:

(a) He feels that a trip to that place is unappealing and would hardly be worthwhile.
(b) He is pleased that you would want to go with him on such a trip and he would like to make serious enquiries about it.
(c) He is interested in finding out if you know the approximate cost of their trip before committing himself one way or the other (p. 154).

Sometimes the husbands were supposed to make it clear that they were dead set against taking a trip. Sometimes they were to indicate that they were eager to take a trip. At other times, they were supposed to make it clear that they didn't have any particular feelings about the trip, one way or another. Their wives were to listen to their statement ("Do you know what a trip like that costs?") and to try to guess what their intentions were.

Objective judges also viewed the marital interaction. They too were supposed to decide what the spouses were trying to say. This procedure gave the experimenters a chance to classify senders as "good" or "bad" at sending messages, depending on whether or not judges could guess the messages. Noller found that happy and unhappy couples differed markedly in their communication skills.

1. Those in happy marriages were skilled at sending the messages they wanted. They were able—partly by facial expression (their smiles, furrowed brows, or gestures), but mostly by their tone of voice—to make it clear how they felt about the idea of a trip. Even in the shakiest of marriages, however, women were quite good at conveying their feelings. It was their husbands who had a communication problem. They were extremely inexpressive. When they attempted to send messages of encouragement, not even the objective judges could figure out what they were trying to say. The husbands did a slightly better job at signaling their disapproval.

Other studies (Noller, 1982) have demonstrated that unhappy wives get particularly upset about the lack of positive communications from their husbands; the wives longed for more affection, appreciation, and attention. It seems here that even when the men do try to send positive messages, they have trouble getting them across. Perhaps such men do intend to be rewarding, but just don't know how. Or perhaps even their most positive messages are contaminated by "leakage" from the anger and hostility they actually feel for their wives.

2. In successful marriages both men and women were very good at guessing how the other felt about the various issues, simply by attending to tone of voice. In faltering marriages, women were good at such detective work, too. (If anything, they tended to judge their husbands' messages to be more positive than they actually were.) Again, however, the troubled husbands seemed to have a problem understanding their mates. They were confident that they knew what their wives were feeling, but they were wrong. They tended to interpret even the most positive messages as critical.

3. Happy couples validate the opinions of their spouses. They see things in the best positive light ("I can see why you would be upset").

4. Happy couples "accentuate the positive and eliminate the negative" in their nonverbal behavior. They smile and gaze at one another; their voices are warm, tender, and caring. They sound joyful and laugh when speaking with one another. They touch each other in a supportive way. Unhappy couples frown, smirk, look daggers at one another, or display disgust. Their voices are cold, hard, and sarcastic; their messages are angry, blaming, hurt, depressed, or accusing. They make rude gestures, throw up their hands in disgust, or simply ignore one another (Gottman et al., 1976).

5. Happy couples keep on target. They focus on negotiating agreements and solving problems.

John Gottman and his colleagues (1976) in *A Couple's Guide to Communication* urged couples to schedule a family meeting once a week for a "gripe time" in order to raise issues that have bothered them during the week. They offered some clear guidelines as to how such meetings should be conducted.

First, couples must state their complaints as precisely as possible. Family members should try to understand exactly what is the other person's complaint. (They might double-check to make sure they understand by summarizing and paraphrasing what they think their mate is saying.) Together, they should try to turn *nebulous* gripes (such as "You're never affectionate") into *specific* descriptions of the problems (such as "You never touch me, hug me, or kiss me unless you want sex"). Once a clear understanding of the exact problem has been established, one can come up with a positive suggestion for solving the problem far more easily ("I wish we could snuggle for 15 minutes or so while we watch TV"). When mates exchange gripes, they may have to help one another formulate their vague complaints in specific terms. Box 12.2, in the left-hand column, lists 16 vague gripes. See if you can rewrite each of these into a very specific complaint. Try to state specifically what it is your mate does (or does not do) that drives you up the wall. Give an example of the last time it happened. (If this is not possible, say "I'll point it out the next time it happens, OK?").

The duo must now draw up an agenda. First, they list all their specific problems. Then they pick out one or two major problems on which to focus. Next, they should try to figure out the specific kinds of changes that would improve things. All easier said than done.

Many individuals have no trouble engaging in character assassination and complaining. The trouble starts with constructive action; lots of gripers find it painfully daunting, even impossible, to think of *anything* positive their mates could do to set things right. We remember being at a restaurant with some other couples. One wife kept criticizing her husband for choosing the wrong wine, picking a terrible main course, and so on. The waiter, irritated, said: "Why don't you choose then?" She was witty enough to recognize what was going on and said brightly, "Oh no, my job isn't to make the decisions. He makes the decisions. I criticize."

Obviously, if one cannot turn general gripes into specific complaints or if one fails to articulate what specifically the partner could do to set things right, even the best-intentioned mate will find it impossible to "improve." (If you want to practice figuring out how to reframe particular grievances into constructive recommendations for specific change, you might practice the exercises depicted in Box 12.3.)

Box 12.2   TURNING NEBULOUS GRIPES INTO SPECIFIC COMPLAINTS

A Typical Vague Gripe   A Specific Complaint

1. You're never affectionate.
2. You're selfish.
3. You're inconsiderate.
4. You're a slob.
5. You're narrow-minded.
6. You're lazy.
7. You're not very nice.
8. You're a weak person.
9. You're immature.
10. You're irresponsible.
11. You're too jealous.
12. You're insensitive.
13. You never listen to me.
14. You don't respect me.
15. You don't love me.
16. You don't care about me.

(How are you doing? Here are a few examples of the specific complaints others have formulated.)

Specific Complaints

1. You don't touch me, kiss me, or hug me except when you want sex.
2. When you get up from watching TV to get a beer, you don't ask me whether you can get me something too.
3. You invite people over for dinner without first finding out what my plans are.
4. You often don't wear a shirt to dinner.
5. You make fun of my opinions about music.
6. You still haven't fixed the dining room table the way you said you would.
7. You rarely pay me a compliment.
8. You still haven't returned that expensive watch that broke because you say you can't face the clerk.

Source: Based on Gottman et al., 1976, pp. 77–78.

Box 12.3 STATING SPECIFIC COMPLAINTS, FORMULATING SOLUTIONS

Take some time now to practice turning some specific complaints into positive suggestions for change.

Specific Complaints

1. You rarely pay me a compliment.

2. You write checks without figuring out the balance.

3. You don't touch me, kiss me, or hug me except when you want sex.

4. You invite people over for dinner without first finding out what my plans are.

5. At a party, you get mad if I'm talking to someone else.

6. You don't ask for my opinion on major decisions.

7. You don't help me prepare any meals.

8. You broke the table; you said you'd fix it, and you haven't.

9. At breakfast you bury your head in the newspaper.

10. You never throw out your beer cans.

11. When you drive to school, you often park illegally and get a ticket, which we can't afford to pay.

12. You never bring the rent over to the land-lord.

13. Often, when I try to study, you decide to vacuum and I can't concentrate.

14. You haven't cleaned the playroom in three months.

15. On Friday, you didn't say anything about the dinner I spent three hours preparing.

Proposed Solutions

(Example: I will pay you at least one compliment a day.)

Source: Gottman et al., 1976, pp. 78–79.

Some lovers even prepare a contract. The contract indicates small changes husbands and wives will try to make in their behavior ("I will take her to the movies every Wednesday night") and the reward they will receive for carrying out the contract ("I will get two hours on Sunday to work alone in my darkroom"). Such contracts enable us to see whether or not things are improving.

Good communication is, of course, what works for the couple.

How *Not* to Communicate Some people have such poor communication skills that they have difficulty getting in a relationship in the first place. Lonely people are generally poor conversationalists (Jones, Cavert, Snider, & Bruce, 1985). Lonely people may be shy: They avoid eye contact and do not smile very often. Sometimes, lonely people are narcissistic. They are unable to put themselves in another person's place (Leary et al., 1986). Researchers have found that the most boring people are those who make others feel that they are not valued. The speaker is unconcerned with the thoughts or feelings of the listener. He cares little about social relationships. People feel kept at a distance and excluded (Burgoon & Koper, 1984). Sometimes people are lonely because they are just not really interested in people. It is not surprising that other people aren't very interested in *them*. Usually, however, people's poor conversational habits show up only once they enter into a relationship.

In *The War Between the Tates*, Alison Lurie (1974) recreated, blow-by-blow, a fight between Brian, a political science professor, and his wife Erica, who is trying to decide whether or not she wants to begin working again now that their children are grown. It provides a fine example of how *not* to interact:

> "I was thinking some more about that research job," she said. "I ought to let Mr. Barclay know by Monday if I'm going to take it; it's only right."
>
> "I thought we'd decided you wouldn't," said Brian glancing at his wife briefly and frowning with impatience. "I thought we decided that two days ago."
>
> "Mm, but you know, I was thinking about it again." Erica smiled charmingly.
>
> "Oh, really." Brian looked up; his frown and her smile collided in mid-air; both exploded.
>
> "Yes." Erica kept her voice even and clear. "It occurred to me that I could easily manage it if I got someone to come in two or three afternoons a week. Someone who could be here when Matilda and Jeffrey get home; and maybe she could do some of the cleaning and laundry too. A sort of housekeeper. Do you think that's a good idea?"
>
> "No, not very," Brian replied. This was the wrong answer. He should have said, as he often did, that of course she could have help if she wanted it; whereupon she would have said, as she always did, that she wasn't sure she wanted to have any other woman taking care of her house and family.
>
> "You know I don't like to have strangers in the house," Brian added.
>
> "I know." Erica frowned; now he was saying her lines.
>
> "Anyhow, we can't afford it."
>
> This too was her line. Erica began to feel that she had decided against the job for Brian's reasons not her own. After all, her first impulse had been towards it. If she were to back out now she would have wasted a lot of time and effort for nothing, except possibly to prove her own cowardice. Privately, she had thought of the job as a test: in a week she would be forty, and she had never earned money for anything except writing stories for children and drawing pictures and baby-sitting. . . .
>
> "I don't want strangers taking care of The Children," Brian announced, his tone

capitalising the noun like an honorific or divine title—which it was . . . "The sort of person you're likely to find is going to, at the best, neglect The Children." Brian's voice was beginning to get tight, as if a heavy rubber band of the sort which propels toy fighter planes were being wound up in his throat. Erica knew that if the topic of conversation didn't change soon he would take off. But she could not bring herself to change it.

"I don't see why—"

"I've explained to you why." Another twist of the rubber band. "I don't want you to take on an exhausting job, and I don't want you to hire anybody. I wouldn't be comfortable if I knew we were both away from home, and there was someone here who might hurt Matilda or Jeffrey, or burn down the house." Brian's voice was dangerously tight now, knotted.

"No, of course not. Neither would I." Erica beat off the implications of her husband's remark. "I think you're being a little ridiculous," she added, laughing. "I imagine I could manage not to hire a psychotic housekeeper."

"I'd rather be ridiculous than have to worry about The Children," Brian hissed. The plane had taken off; he was, in effect, whirring about the room now, his face pale and hard, his eyes glaring.

Erica cowered and flung up her arms. "Of course, if you feel that strongly about it," she bleated.

"I feel extremely strongly about it." The plane buzzed overhead once more, then cut its engines and returned to base. "You know that." Brian grinned at Erica—the conspiratorial, condescending grin of a moral victor.

"Yes." She smiled weakly and falsely back. (pp. 62–64)

Brian may have "won" this skirmish, but Erica's failure to have more spunk and Brian's focus on dominating rather than trying to find a creative solution that would please them both moved them one inevitable step closer to a divorce.

What is the anatomy of communication breakdown? What are the elements of fiasco in conversations of the Brian/Erica sort? After performing a dissection, we shall then try to improve on conversational calumnies by reviewing what researchers have learned about the most effective ways for people to communicate with one another.

John Gottman and his colleagues (1976) have identified several conversational habits that seem to be a prescription for disaster.

Hidden Agendas   Sometimes couples are afraid to say what is on their minds. They disguise their complaints. For example, Deborah Tannen (1986) reproduced two conversations. They seem confusing, but actually both deal with intimacy and responsiveness. Both illustrate the feeling that your mate is not really interested in you, not actively engaged with you.

Conversation #1: (Here, we might guess, the wife is longing for more closeness and more conversation.)

w: You never talk to me.
h: What's on your mind?
w: It's not what's on *my* mind; it's that I never know what's on *your* mind.
h: What do you want to know?
w: Everything!
h: That's crazy!
w: Here we go again. . . .

Conversation #2: (Here, we might guess, the husband is longing for more independence and quiet time to collect his thoughts.)

H: You talk too much!
W: About what?
H: About everything.
W: One of us has to talk!
H: You talk but you never say anything.
W: That's crazy.
H: You're damned right!
W: What do you mean?
H: You make a lot of noise, but that makes it impossible for us to have a real talk. (p. 95)

The couple would, of course, do a lot better if they could state with greater clarity their desires for more closeness or for more time out.

Mind Reading   Married couples often assume that they know what their mates are thinking and feeling without bothering to ask. Here are some typical conversations:

PEGGY: When does Christmas vacation begin?
MICHAEL: Don't worry, I can wear my brown suit.

WENDY: Can you pick a bottle of wine up at the grocery store?
ROB: The Harmons will be bringing their children.

Sometimes married couples *can* read one another's minds. The seeming *non sequiturs* make perfect sense to them! (Michael may have been right in guessing that Peggy was wondering if there was time to get his black suit to the cleaners and back after his big winter business trip. Rob may have been right in guessing that Wendy wouldn't serve wine to the heavy drinking Harmons if there were children to be driven home.) But often, mind readers are infuriating because they make us ask the same questions again and again while they engage in a sort of 20 questions. Often, Peggy is planning her time and wants to know just what she says she wants to know: when Christmas vacation begins. Often, Wendy wants Rob to pick up a bottle of wine, Harmons or no. Mind readers are especially infuriating when they impugn our best intentions by ascribing to us the most malignant of motives. They enrage us when they assume that we don't know what we think or feel . . . that they know best.

Not Listening   Couples don't listen to one another.

Cross-complaining   Some people respond to any complaints with a list of their own grievances. (She: *"I'm* late! You're not so considerate yourself you know. Who invited his mother here without telling me?" He: "Oh yeah! Well who keeps me up half the night tossing and turning?") Not surprisingly, in such conversations no one really listens to anyone else; everybody keeps repeating his or her own grievances. Nothing gets fixed.

Off Beam   Somehow the conversation drifts off track.

Kitchen-sinking   People start out discussing one issue, but somehow their list of complaints rapidly expands. People "drag in everything but the kitchen sink." Intimates become irritated and overwhelmed. The problems seem insoluble.

Yes-butting   We all know people who solicit our help and the moment we begin to offer suggestions they begin a litany: "Yes, but. . . ." I once had a colleague who, at parties, would drag me into an adjoining room to ask for help on his project. I wasn't really interested, but I would work hard out of a sense of duty. Whenever I offered a solution to one of his problems, he would say, cavalierly, "Yes, but that isn't quite what I had in mind." Naturally, I soon wanted to kill him.

The Standoff   It is easy to recognize a standoff. One person says she will quit nagging if he quits drinking; he says her nagging has driven him to drink; he will change if she will. Nothing happens.

Gottman and his colleagues (1976) have offered some commonsense tips for more enjoyable and valuable conversations: Good conversationalists make an effort to get the dialogue going and keep it going, they listen actively, they draw people out, they talk about themselves and ask about the other, they are rewarding and empathic.

Telling Lies

Humans lie. They lie for many reasons: among them, to be polite or to "protect" their partners, friends, or themselves. They seek to win admiration. They wish to avoid embarrassment or censure. They demonstrate their power. They strive to maintain privacy. They wish to manipulate their mates into giving them what they want. They endeavor to preserve the family (Ekman, 1989).

Deception in Love Relationships   Sandra Metts (1989) asked dating, engaged, and married couples to think of the last time they had not been completely truthful with the person to whom they were closest. How did they lie? (Did they shade the truth, forget to mention something, or tell an out-and-out falsehood?) Why did they lie? What did they lie about?

She found that lying took several different forms:

1. *Falsification:* Some confess to telling an out-and-out lie (e.g., "She asked me where I'd been and I told her I was studying") (p. 165). [He had actually been out with the guys.]
2. *Distortion:* Sometimes, liars simply shade truth a bit (e.g., "She kept pressing me about how I felt. I know she wanted me to say I loved her but I didn't feel that much commitment . . . so I said something vague like it's too soon to say I love you, but I know I care very much about you") (p. 165).
3. *Omission:* Sometimes, one neglects to mention some relevant fact (e.g., "When my wife and I were dating, she became very ill and everyone thought she would die. I couldn't see myself walking out on her so I married her even though I didn't love her. . . . I simply could not tell her I married her out of pity—nor will she ever ask") (p. 177).

Metts found that dating or engaged couples (compared to the married) were more likely to falsify information; the married were more likely to omit the truth. Individuals tended to falsify information when they felt they were being "given the third degree." When they were not being questioned, they went in more for "sins of omission."

Why did men and women lie? They cited a variety of reasons.

A. *Lies to protect the partner.*

1. To avoid hurting partner (e.g., "I knew he would be terribly hurt if I told him").
2. Concern for partner due to a current physical or mental state. ("I felt she couldn't take the truth at that time because she was so tired and under so much stress.")
3. Desire to maintain partner's self-esteem. ("She really does want to please me and to tell her she doesn't would make her think less of herself.")
4. Desire to protect partner's relationship with a third party. ("I was kind of intimate with her good friend and I knew that if she found out, she would have ended her relationship.")
5. Uncertainty about partner's attitudes and feelings. ("I didn't know how he felt about me and I didn't want to scare him away.")
6. Teller had been exempted by partner, either through direct comments such as "never tell me if you do X" or because partner has already been caught in a similar deception. ("I was justified because he lied to me about the same thing.")

7. To regulate or constrain partner's self-image when it is more positive than teller believes it should be. ("He thinks he's such a great quarterback so I told him he really wasn't.")

B. *Lies to protect oneself.*

1. To protect or enhance one's own image. ("He thinks I'm the kind of girl who would never do something like that.")
2. To protect the teller's resources or ensure continuation of rewards or services from partner. ("I knew if I told him I did have money, I would never get it back.")
3. Fear of being resented or abused by partner. ("I knew from past experience that if he found out he would make life miserable for me and the children.")
4. Teller is too confused about the truth to know how to express it. ("I didn't know how I felt myself, so how could I ask him to understand?")

C. *Relationship-focused reasons.* Deception was motivated by attempts to maintain harmony and stability in the relationship.

1. To avoid conflict and unpleasant scenes. ("I was afraid it would start a fight.")
2. To avoid relational trauma and potential disengagement. ("I think she would have just broken up with me.")

D. *Issue-focused reasons.* Indications that deception was motivated by the privateness or triviality of the information.

1. The issue is too trivial. ("I never told her about my 'fling' because it wasn't really an affair, only a one-night stand.")
2. The issue is too private. ("It was my mistake and not really any of her business.") (p. 166)

When lies occur in love relationships, Metts finds, most claim they do so to protect their partners. They give five main reasons for their lies: avoiding hurt to their partners (20% of the time), protecting their own images (16%), avoiding relational trauma/termination (16%), avoiding conflict/unpleasant scene (11%), and avoiding stress/abuse from the partners (10%).

Such justifications are often self-serving. One of our clients lies chronically. He will glibly promise eternal fidelity ("It will be easy"). But when we try to pin him down as to exactly what he means by "fidelity," he slips through the net. "Well, it means I won't initiate anything with other women." (The unspoken message is that if women come on to *him* it doesn't count.) "There are lots of ways to be unfaithful. If you break our agreement by making me feel unloved, then of course I'd be free to see others." Last week in marital counseling he was explaining how wonderfully their marriage was going. "We made love twice a day, every day for the last week," he said enthusiastically. His wife's eyes widened. He had been away for eight days on a business trip—without her. She knew and we knew who that someone was with whom things had been going so "wonderfully" well, and it wasn't his wife. He had simply mixed up the many women in his life, unable to tell one body from another! When she asked, with fury, how he could have lied to her, he naturally gave the excuse Metts found so common: "I only lied to protect you. I love you too much to ever hurt you." Given his character, we suspect that the chief reason for his chronic and outrageous prevarication is that he lies to get what he wants: a passionate single life getting it on with a bevy of sexy, willing women, buttressed by a compliant wife waiting at home, on the shelf, just in case he gets tired . . . or old.

Words! Words! I'm so sick of words!
I get words all day through.
Is that all you blighters can do?
Don't talk of stars burning above.
If you're in love, show me!
—A frustrated Eliza Doolittle complaining to a reluctant Freddy in
  My Fair Lady

NONVERBAL COMMUNICATION

Researchers have observed that people can carry on two very different kinds of conversations at one and the same time. We are aware both of what people say and of how they say it. In Henry James's (1904/1966) *The Golden Bowl,* Maggie Verver begins to suspect that her husband, Amerigo, may be in love with her best friend, Charlotte. Maggie is shocked at her own suspicions. Yet? She could never think of asking The Prince if he is having an affair. Instead, she delicately scrutinizes his every expression; watches for the tiniest involuntary emotional expression when she mentions Charlotte's name in passing, observes what he does . . . and does not say.

Facial expressions, direction of gaze, changes in coloring, tones of voice, and bodily postures often tell us exactly—and often much more accurately than the words uttered—what our fellows think about us, others, and the world.

Facial Expression of Emotion

Inner lives are written on our faces. Casual observers have long known that facial expressions are a guide to private emotional states. More than 2500 years ago, actors at the Dionysian Theatre in Greece wore masks, which signaled the characters' deepest feelings to the audience. Charles Darwin (1872/1965) discovered the existence of a universal language of emotion. In all cultures, the various emotions are coupled to certain facial patterns. Recent evidence suggests that (as turns out usually to be the case with Darwin) he was right. Jacob Steiner (1979) found that infants respond to sweet, sour, and bitter tastes with smiles, pursing lips, and disgusted faces in the very first hours of life; observers have no trouble reading their feelings. To date, the emotional expressions identified in infants include those for surprise, happiness, fear, sadness, anger, disgust, and pain (Klinnert, Campos, Sorce, Emde, & Svejda, 1983).

Psychologists have recently uncovered compelling evidence that certain emotions are expressed in much the same way in all cultures. Of course, every culture possesses its own display rules. For example, the Japanese and the Arabs are taught very different rules for emotional expression. Japanese children are taught restraint. They avoid conflict; they know they will humiliate not just themselves but their whole family if they express strong feelings in public. In the Middle East, by contrast, Arabs are taught that if people care about others it is appropriate to express their feelings publicly. Women may cry, scream, or tear their clothes when a loved one dies. Men may consider it "manly" to erupt in anger when they are challenged (Argyle, 1975).

Nonetheless, emotions themselves are expressed in fairly similar ways in all cultures. There *is* a universal language of emotion. For example, Paul Ekman and Wallace Friesen (1971) studied members of the Foré group of the South East Highlands of New Guinea. The Foré had had no chance to learn Western conventions of emotional expression. Would these tribespeople instinctively recognize Western expressions of such basic emotions as happiness, sadness, anger, fear, surprise, disgust, and interest?

The authors found they could. Around the world, brows pulled down and inward, squinting eyelids and pressed lips signal anger; a wrinkled nose signals disgust; and so forth. American college students turn out to be equally good at decoding New Guineans' feelings. Ekman and Friesen (Ekman, 1971) asked the Foré to show how they would look if they were sad, happy, fearful, and down the line. When American college students, who had never seen any New Guineans, were asked to judge what emotion was expressed by the tribespeople, they too were quite accurate. Students were easily able to recognize happiness, anger, disgust, and sadness. They had a bit more trouble with fear and surprise. (Interestingly, these were the very emotions that the Foré had difficulty in discriminating in Westerners.) Subsequent research has provided unmistakable evidence that emotional expression may well be universal and innate. People from a variety of cultures—Brazil, Argentina, Chile, the United States, and Japan—have been found to interpret the same facial expressions in much the same way. [See Ekman (1971) for a summary of this research.]

Other Forms of Nonverbal Communication

There are other equally important forms of nonverbal communication—gaze, voice, and posture. In Michael Argyle's (1975) *Bodily Communication*, he illustrates what is known about these various forms of communication.

If two people look into each other's eyes for more than about six seconds they are either going to kill each other or make love.
—*Anthropologist Iven De Vore*

Gaze   People find it hard to fake instinctive gaze patterns. We find it natural to look lovingly at those we love or like. If we tried to gaze at a stranger in the same way, and for the same length of time, we would cringe in shyness (Exline & Winters, 1965; Rubin, 1970). The drill sergeant finds it natural to glare down at the raw recruit. The recruit, overcome with anxiety and embarrassment, longs to look away (Exline & Long, 1971). When Euro-Americans step into an elevator, their eyes dart around. They turn to face the door. They stare up at the ceiling, up at the gauge signaling the floor being passed, down at the floor, ahead at the door, but not into someone else's face. If by chance their eyes lock into another passenger's, they smile sheepishly. They are careful not to invade another's privacy. Gaze then is one way we convey our feelings for others.

Gestures   We all know the language of gesture. We clasp a friend's shoulder in warm greeting, nod our heads enthusiastically in agreement, wave our hands to get attention, shake our fists in fury, and point out directions. We unconsciously signal our inner turmoil by a whole symphony of scratching (our heads), fiddling with our jewelry, drumming (our fingers), and jiggling (our legs). We indicate our boredom with a yawn. [A desperate mother once explained to her son (an extremely long-winded boy) that he should carefully watch his audience when he launches into one of his soliloquies; when his audience's eyes begin to glaze over, when they commence to yawn and fidget, when they squirm in their seats or go limp and sink in despair to the floor, he should perhaps notice and consider terminating his monologue before they expire altogether.]

Posture   Postures reflect emotions. Scientists find that people agree about the "feelings" of stick figure diagrams (Sarbin & Hardyck, 1953). Our postures reveal how we feel about others. When we like people, we generally directly face them, lean forward (to catch their every word), and get closer to them than usual.

When two friends talk, they usually arrange their bodies in very similar configurations; this is called "postural echo." The precision of the postural echo can be quite remarkable (Hatfield et al., 1992). There is an old Marx Brothers' film, *Monkey Business*, that illustrates this process. Not only do the Marx Brothers tilt, sway, and bend in unison, but eventually their reactions become so interlinked they end up smoking the same cigarette. It is unclear who is inhaling and who is exhaling.

When people are relaxed, their arms and legs are akimbo, they lean backwards, and tilt a bit sideways (Mehrabian, 1972).

Bodily Contact We convey our feelings about one another in the way we touch each other.

The Joy of Depression

Humorist David Rudnitsky (1990), in *The Joy of Depression*, provides a tongue-in-cheek lesson in how to read nonverbal messages. He ends with a test of students' decoding ability.

1. Does the position of his head tell you that this man is:
   a. unhappy   b. lonely   c. a womanizer   d. dead.

Nonverbal Lies

So far, we have focused on spontaneous, honest expressions of emotion. But humans are more complex than that. As we observed earlier, sometimes they try to lie about their feelings. They try to mask their feelings, to smile when they feel miserable, to look calm when they are terrified.

In 1973, when the Watergate scandal was just beginning to heat up, we were at a party given by the National Institutes of Mental Health in Washington, D.C., for psychologists. The party came at the end of a long day of reviewing grant proposals. In the midst of the cocktail party, someone motioned to the host to turn on the TV. It was 6:00 P.M. and Richard Nixon was giving a press conference to discuss the growing scandal. The TV went on; a jovial Richard Nixon read a statement and then answered a few questions. Suddenly a pall was cast on the celebration. Everyone's heart sank, the party fell, and we all bid farewell to one another. Something terrible had happened but we didn't know what—not for 16 years.

In 1989, at meetings of the International Society for Research on Emotions, we finally found out what had happened. John Lanzetta was showing some political films. He was slowing them down so that we could look at them frame by frame. On came Nixon at his 1973 press conference. In Lanzetta's analysis, it became clear why it had so dismayed us. We would see frame after frame of Nixon's jovial face. Suddenly in one frame the face would change. A look suddenly passed over his face, repeating at regular intervals. And that expression was always the same—terror. (A second way we know people are hiding their emotions is to look at the muscles that prevent emotions from leaking through; they sometimes show a slight spasm from the effort of continuously holding back an expression. Now and then, you would see a twitch of those muscles cross Nixon's face.)

2. From her actions, would it seem that this woman is:
   a. a good listener   b. being supportive   c. giving space
   d. about to make a point.

Answers: 1-a; 2-d.

When not aimed at the president, the camera would pan to his wife, Pat, smiling bravely in the audience. The slow motion revealed another emotion crossing *her* face. She was holding back tears. Between Richard Nixon's masked terror and Pat's suppressed grief, one could no longer wonder why we all felt so terrible while watching them perform in 1973. No wonder we all went home.

There are times when we long to read faces and minds. For example, was Supreme Court nominee Clarence Thomas telling the truth when he denied sexually harassing Professor Anita Hill? Can the auto dealer really go no lower on this car? Did TV evangelist Jim Bakker visit prostitutes and raid the PTL treasury? Can the accomplished deceiver remove all clues to the deception? The question is an old one, as a remnant of a papyrus Veda from 900 B.C. describing the behavior of a liar reminds us:

> He does not answer questions, or they are evasive answers; he speaks nonsense, rubs the great toe along the ground, and shivers; his face is discolored; he rubs the roots of the hair with his fingers. (Trovillo, 1939, p. 849)

Modern-day psychologists provide some hints as to how we might interpret these and other gestures.

Sigmund Freud (1905) observed:

> He that has eyes to see and ears to hear may convince himself that no mortal can keep a secret. If his lips are silent, he chatters with his finger-tips; betrayal oozes out of him at every pore. (p. 94)

Unfortunately, a master clinician like Freud may be able to read clues that are invisible to the rest of us.

Parents, whether Freudians or not, try to make their kids believe that they'll never get away with a lie. They stare at their children through skeptical narrowed eyes. The children blush, stammer, and confess. A mother in one of our classes observed that she can still catch her son, now 21, in an untruth. When he was a little boy, it was usually easy. His stories were so fantastic that no one would be fooled. When the little boy would ask his mom how she always caught him, she jokingly replied: "When you lie, your ears turn bright red." Today, she laughed, when he is lying ("Really, mom, I was out all night studying"), he unconsciously and automatically adopts a defensive strategy he developed in his youth: he covers his ears with his hands!

In fact, Ekman has discovered that most of us are *not* very good at detecting lies. We are apt to believe the daring child or the used-car salesman who looks us straight in the eye. In a series of experiments, Ekman attempted to find out exactly how people telegraph that they are lying. In his book *Telling Lies* (1985), he reviewed a myriad of ways that we can make educated guesses about the honesty of others. Here are some of Ekman's conclusions:

1. If people come to believe their own lies, it may be impossible to detect their deceptions. After all, they believe they are telling the truth.
2. When people know they are lying, however, they generally feel some sort of strong emotion—guilt, fear of detection, or even the smugness people feel when they know that they are putting something over on someone.

Liars may try to hide these telltale emotions, but they are likely to "leak" out.

3. The more emotion the lie arouses, the more likely it is to "leak."

4. There are facial clues to deceit. The face often contains two messages— what the liar *wants to reveal* and what he or she *hopes to conceal*. Most people have considerable ability to disguise their feelings. Parents teach their children to control their expressions. ("Don't you give me that high and mighty look!" "Don't look so bored." "Wipe that smile off your face.") These display rules become deeply ingrained habits. In part then, we are generally trained to look like we are supposed to look. Nonetheless, when people try to disguise their emotions, they are likely unintentionally to betray their true feelings; indeed, the truth "oozes out of every pore." If one is to ferret out the truth, the first step is to know what to look for—to ignore "unreliable" indicators (which can easily be faked) and to concentrate on "reliable" clues to emotion (telltale signs that cannot be produced at will, inhibited, or squelched).

One can smile and smile and still be a villain.
                        —William Shakespeare

General Facial Cues to Lies   The facial muscles differ greatly in their ease of control. For example, a smile is often used to disguise negative emotions—fear, anger, distress, disgust. We are greatly practiced at smiling while feeling a wide array of emotions. For that reason, the simple presence or absence of a smile does not provide much information; it is an unreliable indicator. [More detailed analysis is necessary to separate happy smiles from those that hide secret unhappiness. Ekman and his colleagues (1988) found that in spontaneous smiles, the cheeks move up and the muscles around the eyes tighten, making "crows' feet." If the smile is broad enough, the skin around the eyebrow droops down a bit toward the eyes. In false smiles, however, the face reveals traces of the sadness which lurks behind the smile. For example, a slight furrowing of the muscle behind the eyebrows can be seen apart from the supposed expression of pleasure.] Unlike oft-practiced smiles, some indicators are extremely reliable; they only occur when people are sad. For example, only about 10% of people can deliberately pull the corners of their lips downward without moving their chin muscles. Yet people inevitably do this spontaneously when they feel sadness, sorrow, or grief. Thus, when one spots this movement, it is a tip-off that the person is sad. Ekman (1985) offered a compendium of such telltale movements, too many to enumerate here. Here is a sampling of some other facial indicators of emotion.

Dilated Eyes   Eye pupils seem to dilate upon emotional arousal—as we become excited, angry, or afraid. Since no one can directly dilate their pupils voluntarily, others can be certain that when someone's pupils dilate, that person is emotionally aroused. Unfortunately, this clue does not say which emotion one is feeling.

Blushing   When emotionally aroused, the autonomic nervous system produces visible changes in the face: blushing, blanching, and sweating. It is difficult to alter these clues.

"Crooked" Expressions   According to Ekman, one extremely important hint about lying centers on whether or not accompanying facial expressions are symmetrical or asymmetrical. He has written that spontaneous (involuntary) expressions of emotion and faked (voluntary) expressions should involve very different neural pathways. When one is expressing one's honest feelings, facial expressions may be triggered by the lower, primitive areas of the brain (the brain stem and limbic system). When one is consciously trying to "fake it," the cerebral cortex gets involved. Since both the right and the left hemispheres of the brain are guiding the faked emotional expression, the timing is a bit off, and the expression becomes somewhat lopsided. Thus, he argued, true expressions are relatively symmetrical; insincere expressions are not. Hence the importance of symmetry versus asymmetry in detecting lying. When the emotions are displayed slightly more strongly on one side of the face than on the other, it may be an important clue to us that the person is pretending to feel something that he is not feeling—feigned surprise, for example. (In the next section, we see that not all researchers agree with Ekman. Some neuroscientists believe that even spontaneous emotions are processed in different hemispheres of the brain. At the present time, we simply do not have enough information to say who is right or even to understand just why they secure such different results.)

Microexpressions   When a person "puts on" a face, the fake facial expression may be interrupted now and then by a fleeting expression, a "microexpression," that flickers across the face for less than a quarter of a second. These expressions are at distinct odds with the expression that is fixed on the person's face. Moreover, they may provide a fuller picture of the concealed emotion. In ordinary conversation, most people are unaware of these microexpressions. They can only consciously spot the distinct movements if the conversation is filmed, slowed down, and examined. Experienced clinicians, however, may not need slow motion. They have learned to detect micromovements because of their importance in therapy. Thus therapists may sense such messages in normal conversation . . . or when viewing a film at full speed. Herein may lie some of the "art" of the clinician's practice.

Such micromovements can send powerful messages. For example, once, when a colleague dropped by to say hello to Elaine, his body was casually draped over her doorway. He stayed just a minute. Nonetheless, as soon as he left, she was filled with enormous apprehension. She felt she had said the wrong thing, done the wrong thing . . . yet nothing had happened. A day later, this colleague was hospitalized. He had undergone a psychotic episode. Now that your author is a therapist, she has learned to tune into her feelings a bit better. She is now aware that her own "inexplicable" feelings are really valuable clues to the emotions of the other. She reads the emotions of clients in their faces, tones, postures—and in the emotions she experiences herself in their presence. Those we encounter often send us powerful, unspoken yet eloquent messages about their emotional states in these and other subtle ways. [For additional research in this area, see DePaulo, Lanier, and Davis (1983) and DePaulo, Lassiter, and Stone (1982).]

Timing   Timing includes onset (how long it takes a facial expression to appear), how long it lasts, and offset (how long it takes to disappear). All three of these variables can provide signs concerning deception. Ekman observed, for instance, that expressions of long duration, say five seconds or more, are likely to be false.

He also cautioned that lie catchers should never try to rely on *one* clue to deceit. We need the evidence of many facial clues to provide convincing evidence that someone is lying. Furthermore, these clues should be confirmed by cues from the voice, words, or bodily gestures. [For other clues to lying, see Zuckerman, DePaulo, and Rosenthal (1981).]

EMOTIONAL CONTAGION

For more than a decade, we have worked together as therapists. Often, as we talk through the sessions over dinner, we are struck by how easy it is to catch the rhythms of our clients' feelings from moment to moment and, in consequence, how profoundly our mood can shift from hour to hour.

One day, for example, Dick complained irritably at the end of a session: "I really felt out on a limb today. I kept hoping you'd come in and say something, but you just left me hanging there. What was going on?" I was startled. He had been brilliant during the hour. I couldn't think of a thing to add; in fact, I had felt out of my depth and ill-at-ease the whole time. As we replayed the session, we realized that both of us had felt on the spot, anxious, incompetent. The cause of our anxiety soon became clear. We had been so focused on our own responsibilities and feelings that we had missed how anxious was our client. We had been taken in by her calm, cool, cover-up. Later, she admitted that she had been afraid the whole hour that we would ask her about her drug use and also discover that she had returned to her abusive drug-dealing husband.

Generally, it is fairly easy to recognize that you are tracking a client's emotion. You quickly learn to recognize the flash of anger that you feel at clients who are seething with hidden anger at you and the rest of the world. The dead, sleepy feeling you get when talking . . . ever so slowly . . . to a depressed client. Elaine is so prone to the deadening effects of the depressed that she finds it hard to keep even a minimal conversation going with the depressed; she keeps finding herself sinking off into sleep.

We were a bit slower to recognize that we experienced the same emotional contagion in private, personal encounters as well.

Once sensitive to the pervasiveness of contagion, we became fascinated with the topic. How could we have made such self-centered and erroneous attributions of our own feelings for so long? How could we have missed the pervasiveness of primitive emotional contagion? Why hadn't we learned to monitor our own feelings to figure out what others were feeling long ago? How did the process work? Recently, scientists began to explore this process of emotional contagion (Hatfield et al., 1992, 1993). Let us begin by defining "emotional contagion" and discussing how this intriguing process operates. Then we review the evidence from a variety of disciplines that such emotional contagion exists.

Definitions

Emotional contagion is defined as: "the tendency to automatically mimic and synchronize expressions, vocalizations, postures, and movements with those of another person's and, consequently, to converge emotionally" (Hatfield et al., 1992, pp. 153–154).

Recently, Lisa Orimoto and Elaine Hatfield (1992) developed a measure of vulnerability to contagion. The *Emotional Contagion Scale* consists of 15 items designed to assess our susceptibility to catching joy/happiness, love, fear/anxiety, anger, sadness/depression, and emotions in general. Some sample scale items are listed in Table 12.1.

Potentially, individuals might catch others' emotions in several ways. Early researchers proposed that conscious reasoning and analysis accounted for the phenomenon. When you, for instance, listen to people describe their emotional experiences, you might remember times you felt much the same way and shared much the same experiences. Such conscious reveries could spark a similar emotional response (Humphrey, 1922). Other researchers argued that people must learn to track others' emotions (Aronfreed, 1970). We would argue that emotional contagion is a more primitive, automatic process. Usually, the process operates like this:

Proposition 1. In conversation, individuals automatically and continuously mimic and synchronize their movements with the facial expressions, voices, postures, and instrumental behaviors of others.

Proposition 2. Subjective emotional experiences are affected, moment to moment, by feedback from such mimicry.

Proposition 3. As a consequence, people tend to "catch" others' emotions, moment to moment.

This tracking process is so pervasive that it may serve as the basis for understanding others. Thus those who are not tuned into their own feelings may find themselves at a serious social disadvantage.

What is the evidence that primitive emotional contagion occurs by the continuous feedback people receive from interactional mimicry and synchrony? Let us begin by reviewing several facts about the nature of emotion. Then we can review evidence for Propositions 1 to 3.

The Nature of Emotion

Emotional Information May Be Processed Consciously or Nonconsciously   We often have powerful emotional reactions to others, yet are at a loss to explain just *why*. Neuroscientists have found that we are consciously aware of

Table 12.1 THE EMOTIONAL CONTAGION SCALE

This is a scale which measures a variety of feelings and behaviors in various situations. There are no right or wrong answers, so try very hard to be completely honest in your answers. Results are *completely confidential*. Read each question and indicate the answer which best applies to you. Please answer each question very carefully. Thank you.

Use the following key:

4. Always = Always true for me.
3. Often = Often true for me.
2. Rarely = Rarely true for me.
1. Never = Never true for me.

Joy/happiness

1. When someone laughs, I laugh too.
2. People who are positive and energetic make me feel the same way.

Love

1. I feel tender and gentle when I see a mother and child hugging each other affectionately.
*2. When people hug me affectionately, I get upset and I want to back away.

Fear/anxiety

1. Riding with a nervous driver makes me feel nervous.
2. When someone paces back and forth, I feel nervous and anxious.

Anger

1. When people yell at me, I find myself yelling back.
2. When I am around people who are angry, I feel angry myself.
*3. I feel like laughing when I hear people ranting and raving.

Sadness/depression

1. I find myself feeling tired when I talk with someone who is depressed.
2. Being around depressed people makes me feel depressed.
3. I get a lump in my throat listening to a sad story.

General Category

1. I pay attention to what other people are feeling.
2. My moods are dependent on my boyfriend's/girlfriend's moods. When he/she is depressed, I am depressed; when he/she feels excited, I feel excited.
3. I'm very accurate in judging other people's feelings.
4. I'm very sensitive in picking up other people's feelings.
5. My boyfriend/girlfriend and I are so "in-tune" with one another that we know how the other is feeling.

*Scored in the reverse direction.

The higher the score, the more susceptible to emotional contagion a person would be said to be.

only a small bit of the information that our brains process moment to moment (Wilson, 1985). Normally, we must consciously attend only to the most important, unusual, or difficult information. Most of the processing of emotional information probably goes on outside conscious awareness (Gazzaniga, 1985; Ohman, 1988; Papez, 1937). For example, while we are carrying on a rational conversation, we may also be continuously monitoring our partners' emotional reactions to that conversation. We may unconsciously and automatically scan our partners' faces for second-by-second information as to their feelings. Are they feeling happiness, love, anger, sadness, or fear? Lovers may even be able to detect their partners' moods by observing facial muscle movements so minute that they *seem* detectable only in *electromyographic* (EMG) recordings (Cacioppo & Petty, 1983). They may also respond to other types of emotional information. They can listen to actual words or to the volume, rhythm, pitch, and rapidity of speech or to the length of their pauses. They can observe the manner in which people gesture, move their hands, legs, and feet, and the way they stand. They can observe instrumental behaviors.

Given this view of emotion, there is really not much mystery about the observations of therapists and others that, although they are not consciously aware that their clients and others are experiencing joy, sadness, fear, or anger, the sensitive observer "somehow" senses what others are feeling, and reacts to it. Today, emotion researchers assume that the information of which we are consciously aware is only a small portion of the information we possess about ourselves and others. Let us now consider Propositions 1 to 3 in greater detail.

Evidence in Favor of Propositions 1 to 3

When people are free to do as they please, they usually imitate each other.
—Eric Hoffer

People Mimic/Synchronize Their Movements with the Movements of Those Around Them   Once people become sensitized to the existence of mimicry, they are sometimes startled and amused to discover how pervasive such mimicry/synchrony is. One colleague told me that he watched in fascination as one person at dinner reached for the salt and all the others at the table reached for a glass of water, the salt, or a napkin a split second later. One person shifted in his seat in an effort to find a more comfortable position; the others almost immediately mirrored his settling-in. People need not be consciously aware that they are synchronizing their actions with others, of course. Any action that is performed continuously is likely to become automatic. Nevertheless, the ability to be "in tune" with those around us is critically important. It allows us to coordinate emotionally and physically with others. We may not notice when synchrony exists; we certainly notice the second that it is *missing* from an interaction, however.

There is voluminous evidence that people synchronize their facial muscle movements, voices, and postural movements with one another, and thus tend to set up an emotional synchrony.

Historical Background   As early as 1759, the philosopher of political economy Adam Smith observed: "When we see a stroke aimed, and just ready to fall upon the leg or arm of another person, we naturally shrink and draw back on our leg or our own arm" (1759/1966, p. 4). Smith felt that such imitation was "almost a reflex." Gordon Allport (1961) believed that a person automatically "felt oneself into" another's mind and emotions in the process of such imitation. An example of motor mimicry appears in the illustration.

Since the eighteenth century, researchers have collected considerable evidence that people do indeed tend to imitate the facial expressions, postures, voices, and behaviors that they see and hear.

Facial Mimicry   The fact that people's faces mirror the emotional facial expressions of those around them has often been documented. Janet Bavelas and her colleagues (Bavelas, Black, Lemery, & Mullett, 1987) found that people imitate others' expressions of pain, laughter, smiling, affection, embarrassment, discomfort, disgust, and the like.

1. *Psychophysiological research.* Sometimes, facial mimicry is almost instantaneous; people seem to be able to track the most subtle of moment-to-moment changes. Scientists observed that emotional experiences and accompanying facial expressions may change with incredible speed. Ernest Haggard and Kenneth Issacs (1966), for instance, reported that unique facial expressions could appear and disappear within a span of 125 to 200 milliseconds:

Occasionally the expression on the patient's face would change dramatically within three to five frames of film (as from smile to grimace to smile), which is equivalent to a period of from one-eighth to one-fifth of a second. (p. 154)

Social–psychophysiological investigations have found that people's emotional experiences and facial expressions, as measured by electromyographic (EMG) procedures, tend to mimic the changes in emotional expression of those they observe, and that this motor mimicry can occur at levels so subtle that they produce no observable facial expressions (Cacioppo, Tassinary, & Fridlund, 1990). For example, Ulf Dimberg (1982) measured subjects' facial EMG activity as they looked at pictures of happy and angry facial expressions. He found that happy and angry faces evoked different facial EMG response patterns. Specifically, minute muscular actions were found to increase over the *zygomaticus major* muscle region when subjects observed happy facial expressions, whereas minute muscular actions decreased over the *corrugator supercilli* muscle region when they observed angry facial stimuli.

2. *Overt facial expression.* Researchers have also found that almost from birth infants imitate their mother's facial expressions of happiness, sadness, and anger. Mothers mimic their infants' expressions of emotion as well. By adulthood, such imitation is a well-honed skill. Laughing and crying are both infectious (Provine, 1990). Yawning is, too (Provine, 1986). (Probably you feel like yawning as you read this.) Some researchers contend that we are especially likely to mimic the facial expressions of those we care for (Scheflen, 1964).

Vocal Mimicry/Synchrony   There is considerable evidence that people mimic and synchronize their vocal utterances. Communication researchers have long argued that communication is as rhythmic as music, dance, or tennis. Different people prefer to speak at different tempos. As people chat with one another, however, their conversational rhythms begin to come into synchrony. Their lengths of vocalizations, mean pause durations, times between turns, length of talkovers, and the probability of breaking silences become increasingly similar (Cappella & Planalp, 1981; Warner, 1990).

Postural Mimicry/Mirroring   Humans instinctively engage in postural mimicry. Thirty years ago, Albert Scheflen (1964) proposed that people often mirror others' postures. He argued that individuals whose postures are carbon copies or mirror images of each other probably share a common viewpoint. There is evidence that he is correct (LaFrance & Ickes, 1981).

Movement Coordination   Finally, there is evidence that people synchronize their movements with those with whom they are interacting. Frank Bernieri and his colleagues (Bernieri, Reznik, & Rosenthal, 1988) measured three kinds of synchrony in parent–child interactions: (1) *simultaneous movement* (e.g., did a mother begin to turn her head at the precise moment her child lifted an arm off the table?), (2) *tempo similarity,* and (3) *coordination and smoothness* (did the interactants' movements mesh evenly and seamlessly?). They found that mothers showed more synchrony when they were interacting with their own children than when they were interacting with other girls and boys.

Some have wondered what happens if we try, self-consciously, to mimic others. Interestingly enough, researchers find that we are not very good at consciously imitating others. There are simply too many things to reproduce in too short a time. Yet, when we are just relaxed, we are capable of unconsciously coordinating with others in a staggering number of ways almost instantaneously. For example, it took even the lightning fast Muhammad Ali a minimum of 190 milliseconds to spot a light and 40 milliseconds more to respond to the light by throwing a punch. Researchers have found, however, that college students can automatically synchronize their movements within 21 milliseconds (the time of one picture frame) (Condon & Ogston, 1966). Some argue that microsynchrony is mediated by basal brain structures and is either "something you've got or something you don't," that there is no way that one can deliberately "do" it (Davis, 1985, p. 69). Those who try consciously to mirror others are doomed to look phony; their timing is off.

Researchers have speculated that people are most "in tune" with those they like and love. Bernieri (1988, p. 121) observed that "high states of rapport are often associated with descriptive terms such as harmonious, smooth, 'in tune with,' or 'on the same wavelength.' Likewise, states of low rapport are often associated with terms such as awkward, 'out of sync,' or 'not getting it together.'" There is considerable evidence that they are correct (Hatfield et al., 1992, 1993). Scientists generally agree that lovers sometimes telegraph their feelings by their close coordination:

> Perhaps nowhere is the human dance more evident than in love. Not only do lovers or prospective lovers share a rhythm, but they also make more frequent and more lengthy movements simultaneously than do casual acquaintances. Without realizing it, after a while they actually begin to mirror each other's movements. She facing him, leans on her right elbow as he leans on his left. They shift postures at the same time. They reach for their wine glasses, raise them and drink simultaneously, an unthinking toast to their closeness. Rhythms may even betray love at first sight to a careful observer before lovers themselves realize what is happening.
>
> Over the course of an evening, a newly acquainted but smitten couple will begin to synchronize first head and arm movements. Then more body parts will join the mating dance, until the two are dancing as one. Biologist Timothy Perper calls sustained mirror synchrony the "best indicator that exists of mutual involvement."
>
> Mirror synchrony is not exclusive to courtship since friends and established couples display it too, but Perper and other scientists suggest that such exquisite coordination may be an unconscious precondition for further intimacy. (Douglis, 1989, p. 6)

In sum: There is considerable evidence that people mimic and synchronize their movements with the facial expressions, voices, postures, movements, and instrumental behaviors of others. People seem capable of mimicking/synchronizing their movements with startling rapidity, and seem capable of automatically mimicking/synchronizing an astounding number of characteristics. Now let us turn to Proposition 2 and evidence that people's subjective emotional experience is affected, moment to moment, by the feedback from such mimicry.

Emotional Experience and Facial, Vocal, and Postural Feedback

There is considerable evidence too that emotional experience is affected by feedback from facial, vocal, postural, and movement mimicry.

The Facial Feedback Hypothesis   Charles Darwin (1872/1965) argued that emotional experience should be profoundly affected by feedback from the facial muscles.

> The free expression by outward signs of an emotion intensified it. On the other hand, the repression, as far as is possible, of all outward signs softens our emotions. He who gives way to violent gestures will increase his rage; he who does not control the signs of fear will experience fear in a greater degree; and he who remains passive when overwhelmed with grief loses his best chance of recovering elasticity of mind. (p. 365)

William James (1890/1961) proposed that people infer their emotions by sensing their muscular, glandular, and visceral responses. "We feel sorry because we cry, angry because we strike, and afraid because we tremble" (p. 243). Today, almost all theorists agree that emotions are tempered to some extent by facial feedback. In one study, for example, Joan Kellerman and her colleagues (1989) investigated the link between love and feedback from expressions of love. The authors reasoned that "only people in love exchange those long, unbroken, close-up gazes" (p. 145). [We are reminded of the line from Rodgers' and Hammerstein's (1943) musical *Oklahoma!* "Don't sigh and gaze at me . . . people will say we're in love."] To test the notion that love would follow gaze, they asked some men and women to gaze into one another's eyes continuously for two minutes. Then they asked them how romantically they felt about one another. How did experimental subjects' feelings compare to the feelings of couples in the control conditions? (The authors devised three kinds of control conditions: In one, one subject gazed into the other's eyes, but the other looked away; in another, both subjects gazed at one another's hands; in yet another, subjects gazed into one another's eyes—but only in order to count how often the other was blinking!) As predicted, couples who gazed into one another's eyes reported greater feelings of romantic love, attraction, interest, warmth, and respect for one another than did control subjects. In a second experiment, the authors found that subjects' passionate and romantic feelings were most powerfully stimulated if they were required to gaze at one another in a romantic setting—that is, if the room was dimly lit and romantic music played softly in the background.

Some researchers have tested the facial feedback hypothesis, being careful to avoid alerting subjects to the fact that their emotions were being studied. For example, in a classic experiment James Laird (1984) told subjects that he was interested in studying the action of facial muscles. The experimental room contained apparatus designed to convince anyone that complicated multichannel recordings were about to be made of facial muscle activity. Silver cup electrodes were attached to the subjects' faces: between their eyebrows, at the corners of their mouths, and at the corners of their jaws. These electrodes were connected via an impressive tangle of strings and wires to electronic apparatus (which, in fact, served no function at all).

The experimenter then proceeded surreptitiously to arrange the subjects' faces into emotional expressions. He arranged them into either smiles or angry frowns by asking subjects to contract various muscles. In the angry condition, they were told to contract the muscles between the eyebrows (to draw them together and down) and to contract the muscles at the corners of the jaw (i.e., to contract them by clenching their teeth). In the happy condition, men and women were asked to contract the muscles near the corners of their mouth (to draw the corners of their mouths back and up). Laird found that emotional attributions *were* shaped, in part, by changes in the facial musculature. Subjects in the frown condition were angrier than usual while those in the smile condition were happier. The subjects' comments give us some idea of how this process worked. One man said, with a kind of puzzlement:

> When my jaw was clenched and my brows down, I tried not to be angry but it just fit the position. I'm not in any angry mood but I found my thoughts wandering to things that made me angry, which is sort of silly I guess. I knew I was in an experiment and knew I had no reason to feel that way, but I just lost control. (p. 480)

In a variety of studies, then, we find that individuals tend to feel the emotions consistent with the facial expressions they adopt and, conversely, that they have trouble feeling emotions inconsistent with those poses. Furthermore, the link between emotion and facial expression appears to be quite specific. When people produced facial expressions of fear, anger, sadness, or disgust, they were more likely to feel the emotion associated with those specific expressions, but not just any unpleasant emotion; that is, people who make a sad expression feel sad, not angry (Duclos, Laird, Schneider, Sexter, Stern, & Van Lighten, 1989). Of course, emotions are not solely or perhaps even primarily shaped by facial feedback. Nevertheless, to the extent that emotions are influenced by facial feedback, spontaneous facial mimicry should contribute to emotional contagion.

The Vocal Feedback Hypothesis   Scientists have also tested the hypothesis that vocal feedback can influence emotional experience (see Box 12.5).

The Postural Feedback Hypothesis   Nina Bull (1951/1968) observed that when hypnotized subjects were told to experience certain emotions, they automatically adopted appropriate postures. Conversely, when subjects were required to adopt these same postures, they soon came to experience the emotions associated with these postures. When instructed to try to experience emotions incompatible with these postures, they had great difficulty doing so. [Similar results were secured by Duclos et al. (1989) and Riskind and Gotay (1982).]

Dramatic Theorists   Theorists such as Konstantin Stanislavski (Moore, 1960) have observed that actors sometimes catch the emotions of those they portray.

In his autobiography, *The Ragman's Son,* Kirk Douglas (1988) reported that he tended to get confused:

> I was close to getting lost in the character of Van Gogh in "Lust for Life." I felt myself going over the line, into the skin of Van Gogh. Not only did I look like him, I was the same age he had been when he committed suicide. Sometimes I had to stop myself from reaching my hand up and touching my ear to find out if it was actually there. It

Box 12.5 THE VOCAL FEEDBACK HYPOTHESIS

Elaine Hatfield and her students (1991) conducted a series of experiments designed to test the vocal feedback hypothesis. Subjects were men and women from the University of Hawaii. The sample was representative of Hawaii's multiethnic population: Subjects were of Japanese, Chinese, Korean, Filipino, Hawaiian, Pacific Island, Hispanic, Caucasian, black, and mixed ancestry. In both experiments, the experimenters claimed that they were conducting applied social psychological research for the Bell Telephone Company. They were interested in finding out how well various kinds of telephone equipment could transmit complex sound patterns.

In the first experiment, the subjects were asked to read, as realistically as possible, a short typescript of a joyous, loving, sad, or angry telephone conversation. The authors assessed subjects' emotional experience (and the impact that vocal feedback had on subjects' emotional experience) in two ways. First, the subjects were asked to describe their own emotional states. Second, judges rated (surreptitiously recorded) videotapes of subjects' faces as they read the emotional typescripts. The authors found that subjects' emotional experiences and facial expressions of emotion were affected by feedback from the emotional messages they delivered.

In a second experiment, the authors made every effort to hide the fact that they were interested in the subjects' emotions. This time, they asked subjects to reproduce a series of *sounds*, again on the pretext that the telephone company was studying the ability of various kinds of telephone systems to reproduce faithfully the human voice. These sounds had been carefully designed to mimic sounds associated with joy, love, anger, fear, and sadness. As before, subjects were asked to report their own emotional states after reproducing one of the sound patterns. Again, the researchers found evidence that emotions were affected by feedback from their vocal productions.

was a frightening experience. That way lies madness . . . I could never play him again. (Lehmann-Haupt, 1988, p. 10)

Stanislavski (Moore, 1960) speculated as to how this process might work: People's emotional experiences might be stored in an "emotional memory." There they remain as distilled essences of emotion. In this theorist's view:

Emotional memory stores our past experiences; to relive them, actors must execute indispensable, logical physical actions in the given circumstances. There are as many nuances of emotions as there are physical actions. (pp. 52–53)

We thus may relive emotions anytime we engage in a variety of small actions that we once associated with those emotions.

In sum, there is an impressive array of evidence supporting Proposition 2: People's subjective emotional experience does seem to be affected, moment to moment, by the feedback from facial, vocal, postural, and movement mimicry. Let us now consider Proposition 3 and review evidence from a variety of disciplines that people do tend to catch others' emotions.

Evidence That Emotional Contagion Exists

Developmental Research Child psychologists have long been interested in primitive emotional contagion, sympathy, and empathy (Eisenberg & Strayer, 1987). Edward Titchener (1909) argued that people could never *know* what another felt by reasoning. They could only know by *feeling* themselves into the other's feelings: "Not only do I see gravity and modesty and pride and courtesy and stateliness, but I feel or act them in the mind's muscle" (p. 21). Later researchers speculated about how this process might work. Gardner Murphy (1947) speculated that people came to feel as others felt because of *motor mimicry:* "His muscles tighten as he watches the tug of war; his larynx tires and his heels rise as the soprano strains upward" (p. 414).

Child psychologists have collected some evidence that, from the start, both parents and children are powerfully enmeshed; both show evidence of emotional contagion. Researchers have found that infants begin to mimic facial expressions of emotion shortly after birth. Jeanette Haviland and Mary Lelwica (1987) found that 10-week-old infants could and would imitate their mothers' facial expressions of happiness, sadness, and anger. Martin Hoffman (1987) added:

> Infants may experience empathetic distress through the simplest arousal models . . . long before they acquire a sense of others as distinct from the self. Distress cues from the dimly perceived other are confounded with unpleasant feelings empathetically aroused in the self. Consequently, infants may at times act as though what happened to the other happened to themselves. Infants also seem to catch their parents' fears and anxiety. (p. 51)

Hoffman cites as examples the case of a child who buries its face in its mother's lap upon seeing another child fall and cry, or who strikes his doctor in anger when another child is seen receiving an injection.

Parents seem to "catch" the emotions of newborns, as well. Ann Frodi and her colleagues (Frodi, Lamb, Leavitt, Donovan, Neff, & Sherry, 1978) found that parents who were asked to observe a sad–angry newborn reported feeling more "annoyed, irritated, distressed, disturbed, indifferent, and less attentive and less happy" than those who viewed a smiling infant. When parents viewed a sad–angry child, their diastolic blood pressure rose and their skin conductance increased as well. Although mothers were most likely to catch and mimic their infants' positive emotions (interest, enjoyment, and surprise), they also, to some extent, mimicked the infants' negative emotions (pain, sadness, and anger) (Malatesta & Haviland, 1982).

Clinical Research Therapists have long observed that clinicians tend to catch their clients' feelings. Clinicians point out that it is difficult to work with depressed clients; one keeps nodding off. Something about the slow voices of the depressed, their sad facial expressions, or the endless, hopeless details they recite keeps putting one to sleep. It is hard to concentrate and attend long enough to be helpful. For example, Carl Gustav Jung (1968) observed:

> Emotions are contagious. . . . In psychotherapy, even if the doctor is entirely detached from the emotional contents of the patient, the very fact that the patient has emotions

has an effect upon him. And it is a great mistake if the doctor thinks he can lift himself out of it. He cannot do more than become conscious of the fact that he is affected. If he does not see that, he is too aloof and then he talks beside the point. It is even his duty to accept the emotions of the patient and to mirror them. (p. 155)

Clinicians have begun recently to speculate about how the process of "counter-transference" might operate and how such emotional information can be used therapeutically (Tansey & Burke, 1989).

Clinical researchers have also collected considerable evidence as to the impact happy, passionate, loving, manic, depressed, anxious, and angry people make on those around them. In some of these research reports we find clear evidence of contagion. For example, scientists (Howes et al., 1985) investigated how people react to friends who are depressed. They assessed college roommates on the *Beck Depression Inventory* over a three-month period. They found that students who had a mildly depressed roommate became ever more depressed over time.

Sometimes we see clients who underestimate how vulnerable people are to contagion. Some who feel they have failed their parents when they were children resolve to go home for Christmas and make it all up to their parents. They plan a long trip home. Once they get there, things may go well for a day or two. Then the children find their resolve fading. They are swept up into the old family pattern again. They find themselves getting furious and shouting at their parents ("Don't tell me to have a good day. I'll have a good day if I feel like it!"); they find themselves getting depressed, unable to drag themselves out of bed. They leave, feeling that they have done more harm than good, owing their parents even more than before. Vivian Gornick (1987) detailed a typical exchange with her mother. Both began with the best of intentions.

> That space. It begins in the middle of my forehead and ends in the middle of my groin. It is, variously, as wide as my body, as narrow as a slit in a fortress wall. On days when thought flows freely or better yet clarifies with effort, it expands gloriously. On days when anxiety and self-pity crowd in, it shrinks, how fast it shrinks! When the space is wide and I occupy it fully, I taste the air, feel the light. I breathe evenly and slowly. I am peaceful and excited, beyond influence or threat. Nothing can touch me. I'm safe. I'm free. I'm thinking. When I lose the battle to think, the boundaries narrow, the air is polluted, the light clouds over. All is vapor and fog, and I have trouble breathing.
>
> Today is promising, tremendously promising. Wherever I go, whatever I see, whatever my eye or ear touches, the space radiates expansion. I want to think. No, I mean today I really want to think. The desire announced itself with the word "concentration."
>
> I go to meet my mother. I'm flying. Flying! I want to give her some of this shiningness bursting in me, siphon into her my immense happiness at being alive. Just because she is my oldest intimate and at this moment I love everybody, even her.
>
> "Oh, Ma! What a day I've had," I say.
>
> "Tell me," she says. "Do you have the rent this month?"
>
> "Ma, listen . . ." I say.
>
> "That review you wrote for the *Times*," she says. "It's for sure they'll pay you?"
>
> "Ma, stop it. Let me tell you what I've been feeling," I say.
>
> "Why aren't you wearing something warmer?" she cries. "It's nearly winter."
>
> The space inside begins to shimmer. The walls collapse inward. I feel breathless. Swallow slowly, I say to myself, slowly. To my mother I say, "You *do* know how to say

the right thing at the right time. It's remarkable, this gift of yours. It quite takes my breath away."

But she doesn't get it. She doesn't know I'm being ironic. Nor does she know she's wiping me out. She doesn't know I take her anxiety personally, feel annihilated by her depression. How can she know this? She doesn't even know I'm there. Were I to tell her that it's death to me, her not knowing I'm there, she would stare at me out of her eyes crowding up with puzzled desolation, this young girl of seventy-seven, and she would cry angrily, "You don't understand! You have never understood!" (pp. 103–104)

Things seem to go best, in situations such as these, if people recognize how much effort it takes to behave well while resisting getting swept up into a whirlpool of anxiety, anger, or depression. People can usually be on their best behavior an hour or two a day; after that they have to go back to their hotel and rest up. Having recharged themselves, things have a small prayer of going well . . . for another hour or two.

Social Psychological Research   Early sociologists such as Gustav Le Bon (1896) sparked an interest in "group mind" and the "madness" of crowds. Since then, researchers have explored the process of "mass hysteria" in a variety of societies. In the Middle Ages, in the wake of the Black Plague, dancing manias swept through Europe. In Malaysia, entire communities fell prey to contagious depression, in East Africa to hysterical laughter and crying, in the New Guinea Highlands to anger, giddiness, and sexual acting out, and in Singapore to hysterical fear.

Ladd Wheeler (1966) and other social psychologists have found that group members in the Western world seem particularly susceptible to catching the laughter, fear, and panicky behavior of other group members (Kerckhoff & Back, 1968; Schachter & Singer, 1962).

Historical Research   Historians have observed that in many eras, certain emotions, especially fear, grief, and anger, have swept through communities (Rude, 1981). They provide a plethora of modern examples ranging from revolutionary anger among the mobs in France during their Revolution in 1789 (including the contagion called the "Reign of Terror" a few years later) to shared national grief among Americans watching on TV a weekend of mournful activities after President John F. Kennedy was murdered in 1963.

Summing up: We have assembled evidence from a variety of disciplines that the phenomenon of emotional contagion exists. In doing this, we hope to have signaled its importance. Cognition clearly enters into *close relationships* in assorted ways. Recognizing this may help couples to read their mates, parents to read their children, and friends and associates to read one another.

Contagion may also occur in larger *social encounters*. Groups of individuals often appear to catch the emotions of others, whether it is laughter in a movie theater or hatred in a lynch mob. Did Hitler employ contagion in stirring up the crowds with his inflammatory oratory? Do totalitarian regimes or religious revival meetings or antiwar (or prowar) rallies exploit emotional contagion? Can emotions be spread by the mass media? With the expansion and increased power of new communications, should we attend more carefully to the way this phenomenon functions?

CONCLUSION

When a couple begins therapy, the most common first sentence that we hear from the troubled duo sitting before us is: "We're having a communication problem." That sentence has become a catchall for characterizing most relationship woes. As we have seen in this chapter, communication indeed is a complex phenomenon. Men and women talk a different language, cues are transmitted in an extraordinary variety of ways, and the opportunities are endless for misunderstanding one another.

The difficulty of communication, of truly understanding each other, has in fact been a major theme in twentieth-century linguistic philosophy, deconstructionist scholarship, and in all the creative arts, beginning a century ago with the groundbreaking modernist fiction of James Joyce, Marcel Proust, and Franz Kafka. And, of course, the novels of their precursors—Jane Austen, E. M. Forster, Henry James, and many others—were centrally about the same subject.

With the help of the huge outpouring of research on communication, only hinted at in this chapter, therapists can frequently improve communication skills and thereby improve the relationships. Communicating with one's partner is obviously a crucial ingredient in a successful relationship. But our experience, more often than not, is that what is coded as a "communication problem" is nothing of the sort. Would that it were that simple.

More frequently than couples care to admit, they communicate well enough; they just don't like what they're hearing. And soon they don't like the person they are hearing it from. It's a bit like the jealous spouses who just want the "truth" about whether their partners are having an affair. "I can handle your having an affair; I just can't handle the lies." But when the partner confesses, in an act of perfect communication, the volcano erupts with dangerous ferocity.

So, frequently, with "communication problems." Most couplings end because the partners understand each other too well and have fallen out of love and respect. They have realized that they made a wrong choice and that there remains no longer any viable alternative to breaking up. The consequences of decoupling are not only immense for the two individuals, but for friends, family, and, most of all, if there are any, for children. We turn our attention in the next two chapters to that painful phenomenon that accompanies the majority of love relationships in Western culture: breaking up.

Chapter 13

Things Go from Bad to Worse

INTRODUCTION

In *Brideshead Revisited*, Charles Ryder recalled the moment that he realized that neither his marriage nor World War II really mattered anymore:

> Here at the age of thirty-nine I began to be old. I felt stiff and weary in the evenings and reluctant to go out of camp; I developed proprietary claims to certain chairs and newspapers; I regularly drank three glasses of gin before dinner, never more or less, and went to bed immediately after the nine o'clock news. I was always awake and fretful an hour before reveille.
>
> Here my last love died. There was nothing remarkable in the manner of its death. One day, not long before this last day in camp, as I lay awake before revielle. . . .—as

I lay in that dark hour, I was aghast to realize that something within me, long sickening, had quietly died, and felt as a husband might feel, who, in the fourth year of his marriage, suddenly knew that he had no longer any desire, or tenderness, or esteem, for a once-beloved wife; no pleasure in her company, no wish to please, no curiosity about anything she might ever do or say or think, no hope of setting things right, no self-reproach for the disaster. I knew it all, the whole drab compass of marital disillusion; we had been through it together, the army and I, from the first importunate courtship until now, when nothing remained to us except the chill bonds of law and duty and custom. I had played every scene in the domestic tragedy, and had found the early tiffs become more frequent, the tears less affecting, the reconciliations less sweet, till they engendered a mood of aloofness and cool criticism, and the growing conviction that it was not myself but the loved one who was at fault. I caught the false notes in her voice and learned to listen for them apprehensively; I recognized the blank, resentful stare of incomprehension in her eyes, and the selfish, hard set of the corners of her mouth. I learned her, as one must learn a woman who one has kept house with, day in, day out, for three and a half years; I learned her slatternly ways, the routine and mechanism of her charm, her jealousy and self-seeking, and her nervous trick with the fingers when she was lying. She was stripped of all enchantment now and I knew her for an uncongenial stranger to whom I had bound myself indissolubly in a moment of folly. (Waugh, 1945, pp. 5–6)

The disintegration of a relationship possesses, in the popular mind, some of the same magical qualities (although it is twisted, evil magic now) as "falling in love." It just happens and devolves of its own momentum; once begun, nothing can arrest the slide toward "splitting up." But the process of disintegration can be understood as systematically as can the early stages of love, and knowledge of the warning signs can, on occasion, catalyze couples to act before it *is* too late to save the relationship. And if rebuilding it no longer remains a possibility, early action can almost certainly help to make the breakup less painful and traumatic than it would otherwise be.

STAGES IN RELATIONSHIP DISSOLUTION

Steve Duck (1982) has stated that relationships beyond rescue may well go through a predictable series of stages as they begin their inevitable slide toward the end. When things first start to go wrong, men or women enter an *intrapsychic stage* (see Box 13.1) in which they begin to think through the relationship problems. They may spend a lot of time brooding: "How could this have happened?" They may blame themselves. "Is there something wrong with *me*? Do I look for losers?"

At other times, people blame their partners. They go over and over in their minds the transgressions of their mates. They agonize. Should they stay in the relationship or get out? When angry, they decide to leave. Then they soften. They feel guilty. "He isn't that bad," she muses. He thinks of the many tender things she once did. They sift endlessly through the evidence. They think what it would be like if they were alone, dating again. Finally, they may decide: "I can't stand this anymore; I am justified in ending this thing."

Next, comes the *dyadic phase*. Here the dissatisfied commence negotiations with their partners. They present their "cases" to their mates. Sometimes, the revelation of dissatisfaction comes as a complete shock. They can't believe it. Lovers often refuse to see what they don't want to see. Simone de Beauvoir tells about a friend of hers whose capacity for self-deceit was prodigious. She simply refused to face the fact that she had been rejected and said of her erstwhile lover's long silence: "When one wants to break off, one writes to announce the break." Then the letter comes, and having finally received a quite unambiguous letter, de Beauvoir's friend asserts: "When one really wants to break off, one doesn't write" (de Beauvoir, 1952/1974, p. 732).

Sometimes, one lover or spouse may plead with the unhappy other to give them a second chance. They present their side of the case. Often, such conversations shake the dissatisfied person's resolve. The costs of separation and divorce may now loom greater than supposed. Reconciliation, withdrawal, and oscillation are characteristic of this stage.

When the announcement comes, there are times that the partners are relieved to have things out in the open; not infrequently they are both eager to break up. Eventually, one way or another, at least one person may decide "I mean it." With firm resolve, it only takes one for dissolution to occur.

Then comes the *social phase*. Now the couple must face the public and acknowledge that their relationship has disintegrated. Their families, children, friends, and workmates have a chance to say what they think about the breakup.

Box 13.1   **DISSOLVING PERSONAL RELATIONSHIPS**

BREAKDOWN: Dissatisfaction with relationship

↓

Threshold: I can't stand this anymore

↓

Intrapsychic Phase

Personal focus on partner's behavior

Assess adequacy of partner's role performance

Depict and evaluate negative aspects of being in the relationship

Consider costs of withdrawal

Assess positive aspects of alternative relationships

Face "express/repress dilemma"

↓

Threshold: I'd be justified in withdrawing

↓

Dyadic Phase

Face "confrontation/avoidance dilemma"

Confront partner

Negotiate in "Our Relationship Talks"

Attempt repair and reconciliation?

Assess joint costs of withdrawal or reduced intimacy

↓

Threshold: I mean it

↓

Social Phase

Negotiate postdissolution state with partner

Initiate gossip/discussion in social network

Create publicly negotiable face-saving/blame-placing stories and accounts

Consider and face up to implied social network effects, if any

Call in intervention teams?

↓

Threshold: It's now inevitable

↓

Grave Dressing Phase

"Getting over" activity

Retrospection; reformulative postmortem attribution

Public distribution of own version of breakup story

Source: S. W. Duck (ed.), 1982, p. 116. *Personal Relationships 4: Dissolving Personal Relationships.* London and New York: Academic Press. Reproduced by permission of Academic Press.

One or both members of the couple may well begin to tell their stories to selected friends. Usually, men and women try to save face and place blame on their partners for what happened. They try to convince their friends to sanction the dissolution. Their friends may urge them to get out. Those friends may also add fuel to the fire by telling things about the mate that they had never heard or suspected. Or friends and families may pressure the couple to stay in the relationship (Mitchell, 1981; Parks & Eggert, 1991). If the latter appeal fails, couples might decide "it's inevitable" and slip into the next phase.

Eventually, couples enter the *grave dressing phase*. They try to tidy up their accounts; to recover from the breakup. Duck (1982, p. 27) reported:

> Once the main psychological "work" of dissolving a personal relationship is over, the problem remains of what to do with the memories associated with it. The processes here remind me of grave-dressing; the attempt to neaten up the last resting place of the corpse and to erect public statements of its form, contribution, and importance. Much of the activity of getting over a relationship concerns simplification, rationalization and beautification of the course, themes, and outcomes of the relationship when it still flourished. . . . [Furthermore] there is a considerable amount of post mortem attributional activity to be accomplished, in terms of retrospective accounting and analysis for both the relationship and the break.

We note in this chapter that some older research omits what has become the fastest growing category among all love relationships: living together (heterosexual and homosexual). Our own assumption is that the joys and miseries of these couplings are much the same as those found in legal marriages. This even extends to the issue of children; increasing numbers of both heterosexuals and homosexuals are choosing to live together, without legal marriage, *and* to raise children. As the industrialized cultures continue to redefine and open up definitions of "family," we are certain to see a dramatic rise in couplings and in familial patterns, which would, not so long ago, have been seen as perverted or sinful. So as we now go on to consider the breaking-up stages in more detail, we often use the word "marriage" as a shorthand for *all* arrangements, homosexual as well as heterosexual, in which individuals live together and feel committed to one another in ways recognizable as wedlock—even if paperless.

To have known love, how bitter a thing it is.
        —Algernon Charles Swinburne

THE INTRAPSYCHIC STAGE

As we have seen, a variety of grievances can cause men and women to begin questioning whether or not it is "worth it" to stay in their dating or marital relationships. In one study, Leslie Baxter (1986) asked 157 dating couples who had just broken up to write an anonymous essay on "why we broke up." She found that the stories of dating couples fell into nine popular categories:

1. *Desire for autonomy.* Some men (27%) and many women (44%) complained that their dates made them feel trapped. One woman observed:

> He was upset whenever I went out with friends, even if I couldn't have been with him at that time because of his obligations. He even expected me to put him in front of my family—which I could not do. I felt trapped by his possessiveness. (p. 295)

2. *Lack of similarity.* Many men (27%) and women (32%) observed that they did not have similar attitudes, beliefs, values, or interests; this was the cause they gave for their breakups.

3. *Lack of supportiveness.* Many men and women (19% of the men and 33% of the women) complained that their dates did not enhance their self-esteem. One woman complained about her boyfriend in an essay she entitled "John Becomes a Jerk":

> He never seemed to be listening to what I had to say. He was inconsiderate and thoughtless about my feelings. He felt he could do whatever he wanted and I'd still be there. I began to feel like I was a convenience put on earth for his benefit. Well, I finally decided that I was through being hurt by him and I decided I wasn't going to put up with his treatment anymore. (p. 295)

4. *Lack of openness.* A few men (8%) and many women (31%) complained that their dates were neither open, genuine, nor authentic with them.

> I wanted him to talk about his feelings. My boyfriend's refusal to try to explain his feelings frustrated me to tears. I had been dating him for more than a year, and I couldn't understand his emotional withdrawal. My crying and pressuring him for communication annoyed him and probably made him withdraw more, now that I think about it. I oscillated between understanding his probably masculine aversion of feelings and thinking everything was my fault. I finally decided it wasn't me and that I couldn't take any more conversations with myself! (p. 296)

5. *Failure to maintain loyalty/fidelity.* Some men and women (14% and 18%, respectively) "cheat" on their mates or felt cheated on themselves. One man comments:

> I felt tremendous guilt because I was intimate with another person at the same time we were going together. I knew that it was wrong, but I was drawn further and further into the relationship. I couldn't face my girlfriend to tell her, so I just broke it off cold. I don't think I was really in love with my girlfriend, or I wouldn't have done what I did. (p. 296)

6. *Reduction in shared time.* Sometimes men (13%) and women (12%) claimed the problem was that they simply were not able to spend enough time

with one another to keep the relationship going. They lived too far apart or were too busy to keep things going.

7. *Absence of equity.* A few men (5%) and more women (17%) complained that their dating relationships were inequitable. One woman said:

> I felt that I wasn't getting as much energy put back into the relationship as I was putting forth. I was giving without getting, selfish though that sounds. I came to the realization that my idea of a relationship was not one and the same as my boyfriend's idea. I decided that being in this relationship was not benefitting me in any way, so I stopped putting energy into it. (p. 297)

8. *Absence of romance.* Far more men (19%) than women (3%) say they left the relationship because the magic had gone out of it. A man lamented its loss:

> It's really hard to express. All I know is that something was missing—the same old feeling just wasn't there anymore. The magic was gone. Words don't express it very well. (p. 297)

Finally, some men and women gave reasons that didn't fit into any category: "You name it and it was a problem for us" (p. 297).

Heaven has no rage like love to hatred turned.
—William Congreve

THE DYADIC STAGE

Confronting the Partner

After thinking it over, the dissatisfied may finally begin to express their feelings to their partners. Do dating couples generally tell their partners the "real" reason why they want to break up, or do they invent a cover story? When David Knox (1985) asked college students how honest they were about their feelings, 85% said they had given their partners some sort of reason why they wanted out; 15% simply stopped dating their partners without giving any explanation. One woman said: "I told him that I just didn't want to see him again, and didn't give him a reason" (p. 131). Generally, when men and women did give a reason, they were honest about why they wanted to break up (89% of the time). Only occasionally (11% of the time) did they lie about their reasons for wanting out.

In Table 13.1 we contrast such "real reasons" for wanting to break up with the cover story told their partners. Generally, people lied because they didn't want to punish their partners ["I didn't want to hurt him and tell him he was a nerd—it was just easier for me to lie" (p. 131).] Sometimes they faked it because they didn't want trouble ("I didn't want to admit I was in love or already involved with someone else"). Women were slightly more likely to lie about why they were breaking up than were men (55% versus 45%).

Sometimes, when men and women did tell the partners the truth and admit they wanted out, their stunned partners couldn't believe what they were hearing. In *Love Stinks*, humorist Joy Overbeck (1990, p. 107) pondered the reluctance of some women to recognize that their love affair was in shambles:

Stage II RetroLust is marked by the expenditure of enormous amounts of energy in twisting his every noncommittal word or deed into a Sign of Hope. It works like this:

His Behavior	Your Interpretation
Asks you to take him to pick up his car from the shop.	He'll use any excuse to see you.
Comes over to pick up his mail.	He just can't stay away from you.
Goes to Mexico with his girlfriend on your anniversary.	He loves you so much he can't bear to be in the same country with you on this special day.
Calls to find out if the tax guy said you should file as a couple.	He can't wait to get back together.

Usually, however, couples are well aware of the problems in their dating relationships and marriages. They talk, negotiate, and agonize. Sometimes this helps; often it does not.

Table 13.1   CONTRAST BETWEEN THE REAL STORY AND THE COVER STORY

Real Story	Cover Story
I wasn't attracted to him anymore.	I'm going off to school and don't want to be tied down.
I was still involved with my old boyfriend.	I need some time to myself.
I started liking someone else.	Our relationship just won't work.
I liked another girl more.	I don't think we are right for each other.
I liked him as a friend only.	I don't want to get serious.
He was a lousy kisser.	I just want us to be friends.
She was ugly.	I told her it just wouldn't work.
She was boring and we weren't compatible.	Things are confusing and I need some time to think things out.
There wasn't enough sex.	I'm going off to school, so let's date others.
He didn't have enough money.	I'm tired of the games we are playing.
He wasn't ambitious; he was lazy.	You're getting too involved.
He was a jerk.	Things just won't work out.
We had different goals.	We're not going anywhere.
She was lousy in bed.	You're pressuring me.
He was too irresponsible.	It's time for us to disconnect.
We couldn't communicate.	I'm going off to school.
I didn't trust him.	We would both be better off dating others.
I was falling in love and it scared me.	I didn't want to get too committed.

Source: Knox, 1985, p. 132.

Some theorists have attempted to predict whether couples will stay in relationships, determined to work things out, or whether they will give up.

Determinants of Deciding "I Mean It"

Couples stay in relationships for two reasons—because they want to or because they are forced to. Researchers have attempted to spell out just how this process works. George Levinger (1979) proposed that a close relationship's cohesiveness (stability) can be defined as "the total field of forces which act" on the pair to keep them in the marriage (p. 39). There are three kinds of forces that influence cohesiveness:

1. *Attractiveness of the relationship.* Is the relationship more (or less) rewarding than the couple expected? The more rewarding and the less costly the relationship, the more stable it will be. [Berg and McQuinn (1986) and Felmlee et al. (1990) summarized research in favor of this hypothesis.]

2. *Alternative attractions.* Is this relationship more attractive than other relationships or than living alone? The more attractive the alternatives, the more likely the marriage is to dissolve. [Berg and McQuinn (1986) and Simpson (1987) provide evidence in support of this proposition.]

3. *Barriers against leaving the relationship.* These are the "psychological restraining forces" that keep people in marriages. They include religious, legal, economic (i.e., money), and social barriers as well as responsibilities to children. [For evidence on the importance of these variables, see Felmlee et al. (1990).]

Michael Johnson (1982) has concluded that four kinds of barriers keep people penned in unhappy marriages (legal and otherwise). (a) *Irretrievable investments.* Romantic relationships are culturally defined as "failures," as wasted efforts, if they do not last a lifetime. If we were casually dating, the pleasure of the moment would be seen as good enough to justify the date. But Americans (in particular) have such a future and goal orientation, that they consider the time, effort, and money invested in a relationship to be a total loss if it goes nowhere. People may feel they have "given up the best years of their lives." They have sacrificed the lover they should have married, the family they should have raised, the career they should have had . . . and now all for naught.

(b) *Social pressures.* When a couple divorces, their action may shock, disappoint, and inconvenience their families and friends. The couple with whom we play tennis may not know how to deal with us. Our children's lives may be damaged. Johnson studied occasionally dating, regularly dating, exclusively dating, engaged, and married couples. He asked them to list those people whose opinions were important to them. How would they feel if their relationship ended? The more committed couples were, the more they knew those people would disapprove of relationship dissolution. The percentages ranged from 19% (for occasionally dating couples), 50% (regularly dating), 63% (exclusively dating), to 86% (for engaged and married couples).

(c) *Available alternatives.* Men and women differ in how easy they think it would be to find another relationship. Dating couples may know "there are plenty more where that one came from." Women who have several children or who have little money and no career or who are very old may have few alternatives.

(d) *Termination procedures.* When couples are casually dating it may be easy to end a relationship: One person only refrains from calling again. To end a living-together arrangement may require emotional loss, explanations to friends, and the *longeurs* of starting over. To end a marriage may require all of the above plus potential problems with kin, painful legal difficulties, all of the upsets of changing residences, the many terrors surrounding money, and the horrors of custody battles.

Johnson asked men and women who were more or less committed to their relationships what steps they would have to take to end their relationships. A few examples make clear how difficulties increase over time. If students were occasionally dating, only 43% of them said they would have to explain the breakup to their parents; 80% of the married couples knew they would have to engage in lots of such justification. Ten percent of dating couples would have to look for a new place to live, while 92% of the married students would have to move. Only 14% of the occasionally dating would have to make some decisions about splitting up possessions; 98% of married couples would have to split things up. Thirteen percent of the occasionally dating respondents would have to look for a job if they broke up; 54% of the married respondents would have to do so. The married have to worry about filing for divorce, how much alimony or child support they will have to pay or will receive, and who will get custody of the children (though, increasingly, common-law mates must face many of these same dilemmas).

Caryl Rusbult (1987) proposed a similar model to explain who likely will persevere in a relationship as opposed to those most likely to separate or divorce. She argued that the more *satisfied* couples are, the more eager they will be to preserve their relationships; the more they have *invested* in their relationships (in time, money, and effort) and the *more limited* their *alternatives*, the more reluctant they will be to sacrifice everything by leaving.

Recently, Mary Lund (1985) attempted to test the relative importance of the factors that attract people to relationships (love and reward) versus the factors that prevent them from leaving (feelings of commitment and a knowledge that they have invested a great deal in the relationship) in keeping couples together in times of stress. She found that although love and rewards are important, even more important are the commitments couples feel they have made to the relationships and the practical investments they have made in them. Some of these investments are listed in Table 13.2. (Investments are defined as resources put into a relationship that could not be retrieved if it were to end.)

Patterns of Deciding "I Mean It"

The preceding theorizing makes it sound as if behavior during the dyadic phase is logical and orderly. In fact, of course, we all know that the process by which couples decide to call it quits is confusing, painful, and disorderly. Leslie Baxter (1984) interviewed men and women whose romantic affairs had just ended. She found that relationships could come to an end in several different ways.

1. *Was the onset of the problem sudden or gradual?* Did a critical incident spark the crisis (e.g., did he suddenly discover she was having an affair)? Or did the problems simply build up gradually, until the couple finally decided enough is

Table 13.2   INVESTMENTS IN RELATIONSHIPS

1. Spending your free time with your partner rather than doing other things or seeing other people.
2. Continuing the relationship over a period of time.
3. Sharing important personal feelings, problems, and beliefs with your partner.
4. Sharing each other's homes by exchanging keys, keeping belongings at each other's homes, sharing a dwelling, and so on.
5. Sharing material possessions such as sporting equipment, furniture, a car, or a house.
6. Sharing something of sentimental value with your partner such as a pet or a musical instrument.
7. Sharing income and expenses with your partner, such as transportation costs, food costs, or having a joint bank account and debts.
8. Contributing financially to your partner or your relationship in general.
9. Making formal agreements about your relationship such as deciding to go steady, get engaged, or get married.
10. Letting friends know your feelings and plans about your relationship.
11. Integrating your partner into your family.
12. Doing favors for or helping your partner.
13. Restricting your relationship with other potential partners such as not dating or having sex with others.
14. Changing your career plans or other interests to continue your relationship.

Source: Lund, 1985, p. 9.

enough? In *Ship of Fools*, Katherine Anne Porter (1962, p. 144) dramatized an affair that slowly and painfully unraveled:

> During the first month after she began to live with David, she had gone by bus from Mexico City to Taxco, to look at a house there. At the noon of the burning bright day they had slowed down in passing through a small Indian village with the little thick-walled windowless houses sitting along the road, the bare earth swept before each door. The dust was bitter to taste, the heat made her long for sleep in a cool place.
>
> Half a dozen Indians, men and women, were standing together quietly in the bare spot near one of the small houses, and they were watching something very intensely. As the bus rolled by, Jenny saw a man and a woman, some distance from the group, locked in a death battle. They swayed and staggered together in a strange embrace, as if they supported each other; but in the man's raised hand was a long knife, and the woman's breast and stomach were pierced. The blood ran down her body and over her thighs, her skirts were sticking to her legs with her own blood. She was beating him on the head with a jagged stone, and his features were veiled in rivulets of blood. They were silent, and their faces had taken on a saint-like patience in suffering, abstract, purified of rage and hatred in their one holy dedicated purpose to kill each other. Their flesh swayed together and clung, their left arms were wound about each other's bodies as if in love. Their weapons were raised again, but their heads lowered little by little, until the woman's head rested upon his breast and his head was on her shoulder, and holding thus, they both struck again.
>
> It was a mere flash of vision, but in Jenny's memory it lived in an ample eternal day illuminated by a cruel sun, full of the jolly senseless motion of the bus, the deep bright arch of the sky, the flooding violet-blue shadows of the mountains over the

valleys; her thirst; and the gentle peeping of newly hatched chickens in a basket on the knees of the Indian boy beside her. She had not known how frightened she was until the scene began repeating itself in her dream, always with some grotesque variation which she could not understand. But this latest time, she had been among the watchers, as if she were at play, and the two narrow white-clad figures were unreal as small sculptured altar pieces in a country church. Then with horror she saw that their features were changing, had changed entirely—the faces were David's and her own, and there she was looking up into David's blood-streaming face, a bloody stone in her hand, and David's knife was raised against her pierced bleeding breast. . . .

In her relief at waking, and her melancholy in remembering that time when she had been enchanted with David and had believed in their love, she almost wept.

2. *The decision to exit: Who wanted out—one or both of them?* Of course, often it is impossible to tell who "really" wanted out. For example, if Janet is a shrew and refuses to change, who is responsible for the collapse of a dating relationship—Janet or the long-suffering boyfriend, who finally decides he has had enough?

3. When at least one person has decided to exit, he or she faces the task of informing the other person of the decision. She can do this in a variety of ways: *Did she end the relationship by taking direct action?* Did she simply tell her lover she was leaving? Did she explain why she wanted out? *Was she indirect?* Did she lie about her reasons for leaving? For withdrawing? For claiming just to want a "time out"? Saying she "just wanted to be friends" when she knew all along that she wanted out? Did she behave obnoxiously to drive her mate away?

4. *The initial reaction of the other. How long did it take to end things?* Did things end with a bang? Did negotiations go on and on?

5. How ambivalent was the couple about the breakup? *Did the couple attempt to repair their relationship or just give up?* Often, after deciding to breakup, they change their minds. Sometimes they change their minds again and again.

6. *Did the relationship actually end or did the duo get back together in some way or other*, perhaps deciding to be "just friends"?

Baxter (1986) found that relationships could end in a wide variety of ways. However, two trajectories were most typical. Sometimes, love affairs ended with a bang. Vivian Gornick (1987) evoked a long smoldering feud between her mother and her next-door neighbor that ended with a "sudden-death" explosion:

We could purge ourselves of neither fantasy nor rage. Beneath an intact surface each of us smoldered in silence. It was the smoldering that did us in. The quarrel between Nettie and Mama, when it broke out, moved with the speed of brushfire. Released from subterranean heat, it burned so hot, so fast, within seconds it had achieved scorched earth: on this ground nothing would grow again. (pp. 114–115)

Sometimes, however, partners are caught in a tangle of "mutual ambivalence." They decide to break up, separate, realize they love one another, fight, break up, get back together again—on and on in a tortuous cycle. Here one man detailed just such an ambivalant relationship and its eventual termination.

I met a blonde who made a spectacle of herself in a nightclub. . . . She had. . . . gone home with my friend, who had been struck by her curious mixture of innocence and sophistication. He had looked at her and been unsure whether to give her a stick of gum or a bracelet. He didn't know what had struck her about *him;* perhaps it had been his lucky night.

We talked for a while, at the bar, waiting for a table. It was the weather, Gorbachev, what a groovy place this was and how groovy we were to be in it— predictable stuff. Then she slapped my friend's face. I asked why he put up with it. She kissed him lovingly on the mouth. I said I knew why he put up with it. . . .

My friend was fascinated and obsessed. Who could blame him? In the following weeks, he told me stories. Lucy came to dinner with his boss and his wife and charmed them both with stories of her childhood—long summers on the farm and lazy afternoons at the soda fountain, like something from a Norman Rockwell painting, all lies of course. Lucy took him on bonanza shopping expeditions. He bought her clothes; she bought him a $1,200 watch, a rare Fifties Hamilton, shaped like a melted triangle; she told him David Lynch had one just like it.

The anecdotes got crazier. . . .

After a couple of weeks, he was bored, or scared, or both, so he told her it was over. Lucy looked at him furiously and said: "This is not going to be easy. This is going to cost you thousands of dollars." It cost him more than that. She left obscene messages on his machine. She wrote letters with "HANGING TOO GOOD FOR HIM" scrawled in big capitals on the back. Lucy called his boss and asked if he was aware that my friend was a degenerate, drug-taking pervert who liked to fuck her from behind with his thumb stuck up her ass. . . .

This went on and on, until she also got bored, or scared, or both, and she tried another approach. It was sweet-talk on the machine now, and hefty envelopes pushed through his letter box containing photographs of Lucy wearing fancy lingerie, or no clothes at all. They had phone conversations that went on all night. But my friend was determined they weren't getting back together, so one night she swallowed a bottle of pills and was ambulanced to the hospital. One of the hospital staff found his number on a piece of paper in her otherwise empty handbag. He waited in the corridor while she had her stomach pumped. She almost didn't make it.

Discharged from the hospital, Lucy took it for granted that she would be moving into his place, which is precisely what happened, despite his objections. For a while they played happy family. She painted in the day and kept the apartment spotless, and at night, when he came home, cooked huge plates of pasta, imagining that this feast of domesticity would increase her hold on him. He put on weight, but—for him— sexual fascination had turned to loathing; he no longer touched her. Couldn't bear to. By now she was even more bruised and vulnerable, perhaps a little mad, but she hadn't lost that quality of calculation that enabled her to know her impact exactly, something women are better at than men: they know how they affect us, the starting point being that many men react to them in a predictably open-mouthed fashion.

The last time I saw the two of them together was at a party when sex was coming off her like a floodlight. He was the only man in the room whose brains weren't frothing like sherbert. She said to him: "I love you." He said nothing, and when she walked away, said to me: "I tell you, and this is gospel, I sleep with a hammer by the side of the bed in case I wake up in the night and she's coming at me with a kitchen-knife. Sometimes I pray that she will, so I can kill the bitch."

Then I didn't hear from him. I was nervous of getting in touch, which I needn't have been, because the next time I saw him he was grinning like an escapee from a chain gang. Murder had not been committed. He was off the hook, and the only cost was a $1,000 suit. He had come back from work one night to find one of his Armanis painted in garish oils and nailed to the wall. This artwork was her final legacy. A note taped to the coffee jug stated that she had gone back to Tennessee. She wanted to be with her boy. She thought it would be best if they didn't see each other for a while, which was, of course, fine by him.

Within a month they were on the phone again. (Rayner, 1991, pp. 122–124)

There are occasions, for couples who are caught up in an ambivalent relationship and we have been getting nowhere in therapy, when we suggest they talk specifically and practically about separation and divorce. Sometimes, this suggestion hits like a shock of cold water. They become very angry at us for making such a suggestion and set out, with great solidarity, to repair their relationships. At other times, however, our proposal comes to them as an enormous relief. They have tried to make things go for so long, that the realization that it could end fills them with relief and joy.

In any case, the partners may eventually decide that no hope remains. There are those who give up not just on this relationship, but on all relationships. Marilyn French (1978), in *The Women's Room*, wrote about characters who recognized the disparity between what they hoped for in love (the love that will fill all needs) and the reality (that one must surrender, as French sees it, a great deal to capture very little). So they throw in the towel.

> She long ago gave up the hope that she would ever find the grail. You know . . . the love that fills all need, assuages all hurt, excites and stimulates when boredom fails, and is absolute, I mean absolute, that never fails no matter what you are or fail to be. I think we all spend our lives searching for that, and obviously we never find it. . . . So we go on searching, feeling discontent, sensing that the world or what it promised us has failed us, or even worse . . . that we have failed it. And some of us learn, late I'm afraid, that that isn't possible. And we give up the hope. (p. 660)

[For other research on the reasons dating couples leave relationships, the strategies they use to get out, and how effective various strategies seem to be, see Banks, Altendorf, Dayle, Greene, and Cody (1987); Cody (1982); or Wilmot, Carbaugh, and Baxter (1985).]

THE SOCIAL PHASE

There are very few people who are not ashamed of having been in love when they no longer love each other.

—François, Duc de La Rochefoucauld

At some point, couples begin to confide their marital problems and their thoughts about leaving the marriage to a few family members and friends.

Susan Cheever (1984) wrote of her parents' frequent announcements that they planned to divorce.

> I used to imagine my parents' complaints about each other as an operatic scenario, with the porch as the stage set. He would take me behind one column and complain that she had rejected him. She would take me behind another column and complain that he had never understood her. In between, they would go *pssst, pssst, psst* behind their hands to the audience. Two duets. (p. 49)

My parents' marriage had always been characterized by periods of anger and

silence, alternating with times when they seemed to rediscover each other and the possibilities of romantic love. In the early 1970s, as my father drank more and more and my mother developed her private life through a career, her poetry, and new friends, the periods of anger and silence between them increased. In July of 1971 my father was arrested by the state police in Somers, New York, for driving while intoxicated. . . . This . . . seemed a tangible proof of how far he had fallen. Once he had been rich, successful, and loved by thousands of readers. Now he was poor and very sick, a bloated old man with a funny accent trying to talk his way out of a drunk-driving charge at a small-town police station. A lot had happened in five years. He blamed my mother bitterly for withholding her love from him. This, he said, drove him to drink, to other women, to despair. She blamed him for the family's financial situation, for her own lack of freedom, and for a lot of other things.

When we children were at home during these years between 1969 and the mid-1970s, my parents would have dinner together at the long table in front of the downstairs fireplace as they always had, but they could rarely get through the meal without a fight. She would leave the table in tears, or he would get up in a cold, self-righteous rage. His drinking had begun to have remarkable physical effects. His speech slurred and his step was unsteady. Often after he left the table we would hear him stamp and stumble up the stairs and then there would be a series of crashes and thuds as he tried to get down the narrow hall and up the two steps into the bedroom. Both of my parents began to talk a lot about the other people in their lives—people who understood them. They both confided in length and in explicit detail to me, or anyone else who would sit still long enough to listen. Not only did I wish they wouldn't; I began to wish they would get divorced. (pp. 182–183)

Men may have a bit more trouble finding support in the social phase than do women. In one study, Anita Barbee and her colleagues (1990) asked college men and women who they would prefer to talk to about emotional problems (say, a romantic breakup) or practical problems (say, being passed over for a promotion). They found that, ideally, both men and women would *prefer* to talk to someone of their own gender about both sorts of problems. Yet, previous research makes it clear that that is not how men and women *behave*. Women friends stress emotional support, intimate self-disclosure, sensitivity and caring for others' feelings, and helping more than do men (Hays, 1988). Women friends chat about people and relationships; men tend to talk about shared activities and objects. Men disclose more to women friends than men friends! They are more satisfied with their women friends (Burhke & Fuqua, 1987). Not surprisingly, then, both men and women generally end up talking to women about their faltering relationships and to men about the problems they face at work (Eagly & Crowley, 1986).

How can we account for this anomaly? Barbee and her colleagues pointed out that men and women expect a very different reaction from male and female friends should they begin talking about their dating and marital troubles. Potentially, when men and women begin confiding in others, their friends could react in four very different ways. (1) They could offer emotional *support* (say, a hug). (2) They could try to *escape*. (3) They could try to *solve* the problem. (They can offer suggestions and tangible assistance.) (4) They could *dismiss* the other's problems. In this study, Barbee and her colleagues asked men and women how their friends would react if they did, in fact, share their concerns about love and work with them. Men stated matter of factly that if they tried to confide their love problems to men, they would dismiss those issues. They could talk to them about work, however. Women were confident that if they raised love problems with their women friends, they would support them and try to come up with solutions. Women worried that if they tried to raise issues of love or work with their men friends, they would dismiss their concerns or try to escape. No wonder then that both men and women generally end up confiding in women about relationship problems.

Sometimes, when people confide in others, the friends give them wise advice. They send them to therapists, analyze the situations, or recount experiences of their own. Sometimes, friends' advice is not helpful. They may try to say something consoling. We cannot count the number of times that men and women in terrible relationships with unloving mates have been assured by friends that "I'm sure he (she) really loves you deep down. He (she) just doesn't know how to express it." Those platitudes often leave couples perplexed.

In John Updike's (1964) *Rabbit, Run,* Rabbit Angstrom visits his old coach Tothero to tell him he has decided to leave his wife. First Tothero gives him a few off the top of the head suggestions.

"Mr Tothero! Hey Mr Tothero!" His voice sounds flaked and rusty after hours of disuse.

The man turns, looking stranger than Rabbit had expected. He looks like a big tired dwarf. He seems foreshortened: a balding big head and a massively checkered sports coat and then stubby legs in blue trousers that are too long, so the crease buckles and zigzags above the shoes. As he breaks his run, and walks the last strides, Rabbit fears he's made a mistake.

But Tothero says the perfect thing. "Harry," he says, "the great Harry Angstrom." He puts out his hand for Harry to seize and with the other squeezes the boy's arm in a clasp of rigour. It comes back to Rabbit how he always had his hands on you. Tothero just stands there holding on and looking at him, smiling crookedly, the nose bent, one eye wide open and the other heavy-lidded. His face has grown more lopsided with the years. He is not going bald evenly; brushed strands of grey and pale brown streak the top of his skull.

"I need your advice," Rabbit says, and corrects himself. "What I really need is a place to sleep."

Tothero is silent before replying. His great strength is in these silences; he has the disciplinarian's trick of waiting a moment while his words gather weight. At last he asks, "What's happened to your home?"

"Well, it kind of went."

"How do you mean?"

"It was no good. I've run out. I really have."

Another pause. Rabbit narrows his eyes against the sunlight that rebounds off the asphalt. His left ear aches. His teeth on that side feel as if they might start hurting.

"That doesn't sound like very mature behaviour," Tothero says.

"It was sort of a mess as it was."

"What sort of mess?"

"I don't know. My wife's an alcoholic."

"And have you tried to help her?"

"Sure. How?"

"Did you drink with her?"

"No sir, never. I can't stand the stuff, I just don't like the taste." He says this readily, proud to be able to report to his old coach that he has not abused his body.

"Perhaps you should have,' Tothero offers after a moment. 'Perhaps if you had shared this pleasure with her, she could have controlled it."

Rabbit, dazed by the sun, numb through weariness, can't follow his thought.

"It's Janice Springer, isn't it?" Tothero asks.

"Yeah. God she's dumb. She really is." (pp. 35–37)

When those suggestions fail, Tothero suggests they go out drinking themselves and meet a few women.

Often, when couples announce their tentative plans to separate, well-meaning friends seal the doom of the marriage, by finally revealing long withheld gossip to the mates. For the first time, couples learn that others could not stand their partners, knew about secret affairs or shady business dealings.

THE GRAVE DRESSING STAGE

John Harvey and his colleagues (Harvey, Weber, & Orbuch, 1990) noted that people have an irresistible urge to search for meaning in their own lives. They contended: "We may have an account for each 'era' in our relationship lives—just as we may have a set of illustrative photographs" (p. 7). (See Box 13.2.) When one love affair ends, we spend a great deal of time trying to figure out why. "Why didn't he love me? I tried so hard!" "Why is she so stubborn and selfish?" "Why is it so hard to live without her?" "Why did we fight about such petty matters?" Sociologist Robert Weiss (1975, pp. 14–15) described this process:

For months after the end of the marriage, the events leading to its breakdown are likely to occupy the thoughts of the separated husband and wife. Again and again they

Box 13.2 VIVID MEMORIES OF VIVID LOVES GONE BY

John Harvey and his colleagues (Harvey, Flanary, & Morgan, 1986) illustrated how people often have vivid "flashbulb memories" of events that made a deep emotional impact. For example, many people can still recall what they were doing at the moment they heard that President John Kennedy had been shot. Some have speculated that there may be a biological value connected with keeping an exact record of the circumstances surrounding a dramatic event. The researchers told men and women:

> A flashbulb memory occurs when your brain "takes a picture" of an event. You have particularly vivid memories of these events long after they occur. You tend to remember your exact surroundings in exceptional detail. (pp. 364–365)

They asked people to recall their most vivid memories of events in a past relationship. They found that men and women were often still powerfully linked to their old love affairs. About 50% of them still loved their ex-partners; the same percentage thought their partners still loved them. One woman, describing a three-year love affair that ended 10 years ago, observed: "I think of him all the time even after all of these years. It is as if he is always there" (p. 369). Many still dreamed about their ex-partners and wondered how the lives of their former loves had turned out. They still cherished old memories and old photographs.

Most of the vivid memories people had of lost loves dealt with the beginnings, special occasions, beginnings of the end, and the endings of their relationships. Here are some typical memories:

Beginnings

> Met him at a bar when I noticed he had a New York Yankees jacket on and I was interested in finding someone driving to New York (my home). I introduced myself and spent the evening talking to him and exchanging phone numbers.

> The first time we slept together I was living alone in a little house in a tiny town in the middle of nowhere. We stayed in bed for fourteen hours—it was wonderful.

> Our first (almost) sexual encounter, we were at a retreat and in the kitchen, and people kept walking in. It was rather amusing; it was ludicrous.

> I met him at a small party given by our apartment manager. It was like in the movies—our eyes kept meeting across the room as we sat in a circle and got to know each other. When the party was over, we both managed to saunter out the door at the same time. He invited me up to his apartment—I remember sitting in his bean bag chair and listening to the Eagles sing, "The Best of My Love."

Special Occasions (Both Pleasant and Painful)

> First time he told me how he loved me . . . considering he was a married man.

After seven years, he brought home yellow roses. Trips to New Orleans. Five wonderful days of being together, sightseeing, eating out, etc. Time alone in the hotel room.

Some birthday. Father absent, no note, no message. Returned late the next evening with makeup on his shirt. Said he was on a business trip. Very rushed, no time to phone. Emotion: anger, disgust.

Seeing him after relationship ended—very poignant memory of the way he looked.

Being raped by him when he was drunk.

Trip to Colorado the year I became pregnant. Trip was fun and special because we had just found out the news.

Going to the divorce lawyer's office . . . moving out of the apartment.

August 15, 1964, the date we intended to marry.

I dream of her as if we were still together and wake up sad to realize it's not true.

Major breakup on February 14, 1982. I felt destroyed. Hurt badly.

Receiving the "letter" January 21, 1978.

Beginning of the End

Being with my parents and him at a restaurant and watching him leave the table and realizing the relationship was going to end. I can see the clothes he was wearing and the way he walked.

I remember the first time he got really angry with me—it was as if nothing I could say or do would make a difference. I began crying, sobbing, telling him how I felt, but the more upset I got, the more distance he seemed to put between us. I still feel hurt and angry now as I remember that the more out-of-control I felt, the more calm and unconcerned he seemed to be.

I remember waiting up for him to come home to my house after work. I ended up feeling resentment after too many hours spent worrying.

Confrontation with girlfriend and husband. Stated he did not love me . . . that he loved her . . . no sense prolonging our relationship.

Endings

I remember the time I caught him throwing rocks at my car.

He took someone else home in front of me.

He decided to go to graduate school elsewhere. He came to my house to talk and we made love. It was the only time I cried in front of him—as I told him goodbye.

Our final interaction was an angry goodbye in the car when I was moving away. Time seemed to stand still for a long time.

> We were lying in bed at the end of the weekend. We both were
> aware that the end was upon us, but we had waited until the end of
> his visit to talk about things. I remember lying there stiff with the
> sun streaming in the window, telling him what I wanted from a mar-
> riage and how I doubted he was willing to fulfill that expectation. I
> lay there wanting him to say I was wrong, but knowing that he
> wouldn't. He just turned, looked at me sadly, and said "You're
> right." (pp. 267–368)

review what went wrong, justify or regret the actions they took, consider and reconsider their own words and those of their spouse. Endlessly they replay actual scenes
in their minds or create scenes that did not happen but could have, in which they said
different things or took different actions so that the separation was averted or the
spouse was told off once and for all.

Gradually the separated come to terms with the events of their marriage. They
develop an *account*, a history of the marital failure, a story of what their spouse did
and what they did and what happened in consequence. Often the account focuses on
a few significant events that dramatize what went wrong, or on a few themes that ran
through the marriage; in addition it allocates blame among the self, the spouse, and
any third parties who may have entered their lives, and so settles the moral issues of
the separation.

The account is of major psychological importance to the separated, not only
because it settles the issue of who was responsible for what, but also because it imposes
on the confused marital events that preceded the separation a plot structure with a
beginning, middle, and end and so organizes the events into a conceptually manageable unity. Once understood in this way, the events can be dealt with: They can be
seen as outcomes of identifiable causes and, eventually, can be seen as past, over, and
external to the individual's present self. Those who cannot construct accounts sometimes feel that their perplexity keeps them from detaching themselves from the distressing experiences.

Real-life relationships inhabit an extremely confusing and complex world.
Their "true" story lies in shadows, ever-changing, and subject to Rashomon-like
interpretations. But once one comes to an end, individuals usually come up with
a simple "story" to sum it all up. Here follow two typical accounts. In one case a
28-year-old woman analyzes her relationship and concludes, as many women do,
that her boyfriend was immature and could not make a commitment. Have you
ever heard this tale?

I was more mature, in many ways, than Philip was. . . . It was as if I had, in some way,
a stronger sense of who I was. . . . and this was, I think, threatening to him. So he would
push me away and be rejecting. And yet. . . . I always understood. I understood this,
and didn't drag him into long hassles about it; I was pretty tolerant. . . . With Philip,
though, it was the first time . . . I ever became that involved. And yet it didn't work
out. I knew, almost at once, that it wouldn't work. (Scarf, 1980, p. 221)

In the second, the wife analyzes their marriage and concludes that she and her
husband neglected one another.

Who could ever imagine anything like that happening to my marriage? My husband was the squarest, straightest of men—a deacon in the church, a Little League Dad, a Cub Scoutmaster, a non-drinking, crew-cut junior executive. But I let it happen: Our marriage had become nothing but a kind of corporate enterprise without my ever taking time to wonder about it. How it got that way I don't know. It seemed as if we were so busy with the children, the house, and local activities, that we never paid any attention to each other; we never said anything real to each other. As for sex, I was bored by it. I felt I could live nicely forever without it, and tried to avoid it as much as possible. I hardly ever thought about any of this, but when I did, I told myself that every marriage goes through phases of this sort and there was nothing to worry about. I was living in never-never land, refusing to see the truth or do anything about it. (Hunt, 1969, pp. 233–234)

Harvey and his colleagues (1990) found that such "grave dressing" accounts generally have the following characteristics:

1. Accounts often have "all of the components of dramatic presentation such as plot, characters, scenes, lines, on-stage happenings, behind-the-scenes happenings, and so on" (Harvey, Weber, Galvin, Huszti, & Garnick, 1985, p. 192).

2. Couples begin trying to make sense out of their marriage and separation and divorce early on. (Again, "marriage," "separation," and "divorce" are words that can apply to all close relationships in all forms, whether or not a "legal" marriage took place.) They are, however, not often able to settle finally on a story that "makes sense" until months or even years after the breakup or divorce. In the process of storytelling, couples think back and rewrite their histories again and again so that eventually the outcome seems inevitable. Moreover, accounts change as time passes and prior attachments erode. Husbands and wives often end up, of course, with strikingly different accounts of their marriages and divorces (Weiss, 1975). Generally, they seem to end up blaming their mates for what happened.

Why do we construct such accounts? Harvey and his colleagues suggested several reasons why we are motivated to hammer out The Story. First, most of us have a need to understand what has happened so that we can control things the next time. Accounts provide such order and certainty. Consider this account:

I didn't know anything was really wrong. It was like a bomb dropping. Oh, we had been married a lot of years, and I knew we had a couple of problems, but I would say, "I feel sorry for all those people who are married and the marriage gets very dull. We still love each other." And we did, you know, in terms of sex. That is why it was such a bomb falling on me. Now I see it was there all the time, but our way of communicating was so poor that it just never got to me. (Weiss, 1975, p. 28)

We may vow next time to avoid "men who can't commit" or "men who can't talk" or "alcoholics" or "women who had terrible relationships with their fathers" or "clingy women"—if we conclude that we were attracted to "the wrong kind of person," that our affair was "doomed from the start." Events that once seemed impossible now seem understandable, inevitable: "How could I have believed her; it was obvious she was having an affair." Next time things will be different. That conclusion is not available if we decide that "it was just one of those things." That says nothing and furnishes no particular information for adopting different strategies the next time out.

Second, after a breakup, one's self-esteem is fragile, damaged, almost beyond repair. Accounts help people shore up their self-regard. They help to show off their shaky selves in the most flattering light ("It was not my fault. He/she made me do it.") Shortly after a breakup, people often find themselves changing their stories ever so slightly when they recount the saga of their separation and divorce to different audiences. A woman may tell her women friends: "He's one of those men who hate women." Yet, she'll turn around and reassure her mother: "We *both* felt we ought to stop seeing each other for awhile." She may tell a new date yet another story. "I wanted to see what else the world has to offer." The whole account, like an iceberg, remains mainly submerged and private; only the tips are revealed to selected audiences. When storytellers are interested in *ingratiation,* they subtly shade their stories to ensure that others will like them. When they are interested in *self-promotion,* they try to emphasize their competence. In *exemplification,* storytellers seek to project integrity; they may present themselves as honest, disciplined, charitable, or self-abnegating. In *supplication,* actors may attempt to exploit personal weakness or independence (Jones & Pittman, 1982). Not surprisingly, sometimes account makers tell so many versions of the same story that they themselves are unable to recall "the truth."

Third, people tell stories for *emotional release:* to help purge feelings of distress, anger, insecurity, confusion, loneliness, and depression.

Fourth, a life account may be told and retold because it gives people the *strength to go on.* After a death, the bereaved may find hope and solace in telling their stories. For example, a Jewish refugee might discover some meaning in telling the tale of those he lost in the Holocaust:

> But finally, this group [a Living History class] brought out such beautiful memories, not always so beautiful, but still, all the pictures came up. It touched the layers of the kind that it was on those dead people already. It was laying on them like layers, separate layers of earth, and all of a sudden in this class I feel it coming up like lava. . . . It melted away. . . . And then . . . it looked like they were never dead. (Myerhoff, 1982, p. 39)

Finally, humans seek *closure.* They feel ill-at-ease if a story remains unfinished. A definitive account seems to tie up loose ends; it makes the world seem less disorderly, chancy, chaotic, and devoid of meaning. In *Heartburn,* humorist Nora Ephron (1983) provided a witty, sassy, and thinly disguised account of her breakup with journalist Carl Bernstein. Here, her therapist Vera wonders why she always tells funny stories about heartbreaking events:

> Vera said: "Why do you feel you have to turn everything into a story?"
> So I told her why:
> Because if I tell the story, I control the version.
> Because if I tell the story, I can make you laugh, and I would rather have you laugh at me than feel sorry for me.
> Because if I tell the story, it doesn't hurt so much.
> Because if I tell the story, I can get on with it. (pp. 176–177)

A final reason people construct accounts then is to control the past; to enable them to get on with their lives.

CONCLUSION

The deepest problem with these stories may lie in their inaccuracy; the world may be, in fact, largely disorderly, chancy, chaotic, and without a certain purpose. The only certainties are birth and death, and if life is a piece of theater, whoever wrote the last act is not a sentimentalist. Except for those sure of a free trip to paradise, the ending is not happy. What holds for existence most certainly applies to love affairs. The stories we tell ourselves—at the beginnings and after the endings— are too neat, insufficiently complex, and hence not accurate enough; we need to spin tales with a richer texture.

Take, for illustration, the common love tale mentioned earlier in this chapter: "It fell apart because he can't commit; he is incapable of love." Though the story has generally been told by women about men, the scenario is gender-free and many men say the same thing about many women. The injured party often wishes to drag the noncommitting mate into therapy. The unwillingness to risk getting close ranks, for many, as a pathology, curable perhaps by the psychotherapist.

In therapy, fear of intimacy sometimes does signify the existence of an old tape made by bad experiences in one's family or in previous love affairs. With conversations and goodwill, the fears can be overcome. But more often, we see something else: The uncommitted one has no wish to commit. The client wishes to remain "free." Is that pathology or choice?

The fact is that nowhere is it written that the good life requires an intimate, committed love relationship. While such a connection can be soaringly wonderful, it is hard to find and to achieve. Furthermore, deeply fulfilling lives based on valuable work, good friendships, and the passions of mind, body, and feeling add up to a considerable richness. Individuals can choose not to commit for reasons that are not pathological.

In modern cultures, living the "single life" can be done. Apartments filled with labor-saving machines render daily logistics easy. Careers are no longer family enterprises. Friends, fun, sex, avocations, and personal interests are readily available and can be pursued without one being part of a committed relationship. The cultural celebration of personal freedom removes the stigma from being single and leads to the development of capacities not necessarily consistent with the achievement of intimacy.

This does not mean that noncommitment is superior to intimacy and family life. But it may not be true that those who have "marriage" and family life can claim superiority above those who do not. Past traditional, communal cultures practically mandated marriage and family life, but there is no historical evidence to indicate that our forebears were "happier" than we are today. The weight of evidence, in fact, tends the other way.

So the story that he or she can't commit, like other love stories, may, in its order and simplicity, make us feel better. But reality has a harder edge. The search for good *dates* is an easy one; we need to match up on only a few variables. "Does she like Italian movies?" "Does he like to dance?" "Can he enjoy playing with my daughter?" "Does she enjoy hiking?" One "yes" may be good enough to justify the date.

The search for the right *mate* is arduous, requiring patience, luck, and good judgment. It requires matching up on a huge number of variables and it takes only a few differences to derail the relationship. And once having found a compatible mate, relationship skills and the inclination to make the partnership work then come to the fore. In an individualistic culture, with the high expectations we place on relationships for our emotional and sexual fulfillment, and with our insatiable thirst for personal growth, the wonder is not that relationships fall apart. The glory is that some survive (not out of habit and necessity, but out of delight) and that no small number flourish.

While this assessment of love may strike some as downbeat, we wish to state a larger upbeat point. Love may often fall short, but the prospect for generally valuable and happy lives, even in the absence of one central relationship, has never been greater. Nonetheless, the loss of love hurts people deeply, and the desire to begin over and this time find the Right One possesses an intensity in modern life that few other quests can equal. So we bring this book to a close by dealing in the final chapter and epilogue with endings and with new beginnings in the world of love.

Chapter
14

Endings

INTRODUCTION

The odds against finding a fully compatible mate for life are formidable. Of the first 1000 people you see on the street, you might not consider dating more than two or three of them. The likelihood that one of those two or three will wish to date you is not great; they may be involved already or not have much reason in general to socialize with you. When you go out on one of those first dates, only rarely will you both be interested enough to follow it up with a second date. When you finally find someone to begin seeing seriously, even then at least half the time these relationships will have broken up by the end of two years (Hill et al., 1979). And if you marry, you face a 50% probability that you will divorce (Norton & Moorman, 1987). Nearly everyone you know has experienced break-ups in relationships that had begun promisingly, and the topic of endings must be addressed.

The best divorce is the one you get before you get married.
                                                    —Folk saying

There must be 50 ways to leave your lover.   *Hop on the bus, Gus*
Just slip out the back, Jack   *You don't need to discuss much*
Make a new plan, Stan   *Drop off the key, Lee*
You don't need to be coy, Roy   *And get yourself free.*
Just listen to me   *—Paul Simon*

BREAKING UP OF DATING RELATIONSHIPS

A century or more ago, people were generally a bit skeptical about the likely fate of passionate lovers. Charles Dickens (1836/1944), in *The Pickwick Papers*, commented wryly on the "perfect" love affair:

> "Conquests! Thousands. Don Bolaro Fizzgig—Grandee—only daughter—Donna Christina—splendid creature—loved me to distraction—jealous father—high souled daughter—handsome Englishmen—Donna Christina in despair—prussic acid—stomach pump in my portmanteau—operation performed—old Bolaro in ecstasies—consent to our union—join hands and flood of tears—romantic story—very."
>
> "Is the lady in England now, sir?" inquired Mr. Tupman, on whom the description of her charms had produced a powerful impression.
>
> "Dead, sir—dead," said the stranger, applying to his right eye the brief remnant of a very old cambric handkerchief. "Never recovered the stomach pump—undetermined constitution—fell a victim."
>
> "And her father?" inquired the poetic Snodgrass.
>
> "Remorse and misery," replied the stranger. "Sudden disappearance—talk of the whole city—search made everywhere—without success—public fountain in the great square suddenly ceased playing—weeks elapsed—still a stoppage—workmen employed to clear it—water drawn off—father-in-law discovered sticking head first in the main pipe, with a full confession in his right boot—took him out, and the fountain played again, as well as ever."
>
> "Will you allow me to note that little romance down, sir?" said Mr. Snodgrass, deeply affected. (pp. 11–12)

Today, most people are more optimistic about the fate of love, perhaps too optimistic. Charles Hill, Zick Rubin, and Anne Peplau (1979) carefully selected 231 young Boston couples; they wanted to see what happened to love affairs over a two-year period. At the beginning of the study, most couples (60%) saw each other every day. Most (75%) were dating one another exclusively; some (20%) were living together; a few (10%) were engaged. They interviewed these same couples again six months, one year, and two years later. By the end of two years, 45% of the couples had broken up.

Couples had the best chance of staying together if, from the start, they had been in love, had an intimate relationship, and were *equally* committed to one another. (Try as we might, one person cannot will a relationship. It takes two to love.) Couples did best if they were well matched from the start: equally attractive, about the same age, level of intelligence, and with similar educational attainments and aspirations. Opposites may attract for passionate love, but quasi-clones do better for the long run!

Very few of the breakups (7%) were truly mutual. Women were more eager to break up (51% of women and 42% of men). Generally, women first recognized the relationship was in trouble and going nowhere. Women tended to be very sensitive to interpersonal problems; they could easily identify the specific difficulties that led to the breakup. "He wanted a traditional marriage; I didn't." "I was smarter than he was." "Our interests were wildly different." "I wanted to be independent." "I was attracted to another man." Men tended to be less sure what caused the breakup. When they did acknowledge problems, they tended to focus on an external problem ("We lived too far apart; it took an hour to get to her house"). Couples rarely agreed on what caused the breakup or on how gradually (or abruptly) it came about! Women were the ones who generally "wanted out."

Not surprisingly, it is easier to leave someone than to be left. Both men and women felt considerably less depressed, less lonely, freer, happier, and more relieved (but guiltier) when they were the rejecting lover than when they were rejected. In fact, the emotional reactions of the mates tended to be mirror opposites of one another: the happier one person was to get out, the worse the partner felt about the breakup. The authors noted:

> Men were hit harder than women by the breakup. Men tended more than women to report that in the wake of the breakup they felt depressed, lonely, less happy, less free, and less guilty. . . . Some men found it extremely difficult to reconcile themselves to the fact that they were no longer loved and that the relationship was over. . . . Women who are rejected may also react with considerable grief and despair, but they seem less likely to retain the hope that their rejectors "really love them after all." (p. 78)

How often were men and women able to remain friends after the breakup? If the man rejected the woman, it was possible for love to turn into friendship. (Couples remained "just friends" 70% of the time.) If the woman left the man, however, they were usually not able to remain friends. (Couples remained friends only 46% of the time.) In more recent research, Sandra Metts and her colleagues (Metts, Cupach, & Bejlovec, 1989) painted a more optimistic picture of the possibilities of turning love into friendship. They found that if couples were friends before the breakup, treated one another fairly during the relationship, and were open and honest with each other when the time came to break up, their chances of remaining friends were vastly improved.

Phillip Shaver and Cindy Hazan (1988) speculated that childhood experiences may well shape one's passionate choices in adulthood. When we ask what individuals crave in a mate, everyone agrees—everything! Everyone longs for someone who is solid, caring, and generous; wild, defiant, abandoned, and sexy. The dream mate should also be free to spend unlimited time at home. Why not a high-powered, thrilling career? But also be willing to take care of children. The list can go on and on.

The trick, of course, is that no single human can embody all these contradictory characteristics. We must choose, and different kinds of people make different choices. Some opt for fantasy. They may be attracted to mates who pretend to match the current cultural ideal, say, Tom Cruise or Julia Roberts. Others look to love real people. Mature and experienced seekers realize that when they speak honestly about their feelings and confess their vulnerabilities, they may look less ideal than the person who "fakes it." But they can offer something authentic, with better staying power.

As we observed in Chapter 2, Shaver and Hazan (1988) proposed that because romantic love should be conceived as a form of attachment, it follows that the early experiences of children shape their adult choices. Children and adults who are *securely attached* look for love that is pleasurable. They want someone they can trust; a love that can last. Children and adults who are *anxious/ambivalent* expect

love to be more complicated. They are either too clingy, expecting their lovers to disappear at any moment, or they are too fearful of being smothered. Sometimes they are both. They tend to want what they don't have and despise what they do have. Their love affairs are likely to be fleeting. The *avoidant* avoid love. They are afraid to trust; they fear intimacy.

In therapy, we often meet men and women who say they are looking for love, but for some "mysterious" reason can never find anyone. When we investigate their daily encounters, the mystery becomes solvable. They are attracted to those who are great looking, sexy, independent, and *unavailable*. The person who is interested in *them* seems flawed, boring. Philip Roth (1990, p. 127), in a conversation between a college professor and one of his students, created such an anxious/ambivalent woman:

"You fell for the boys who shoot to kill."
"Yes, sex merchants, basically. The libido mob. Couldn't resist them. Didn't know how to flirt with them. Didn't know how to handle them at all. That's something we failed to cover in that seminar. And, of course, I was catnip for the ones who wanted me who I didn't want. What was driving me crazy was that there was always somebody running after me passionately, calling me up on the phone, and coming after me, and swamping me with invitations; you know—drowning me, basically. And at the same time there was the absentee lover, who was gone and not interested, or playing a lot of games with me, and I went a little bit crazy, kind of nuts. It happens. It was all right at the beginning, but the mistake was that it happened over and over and over and I couldn't seem to get out of it. And that's been my nemesis. That's been the whole thing."
"Didn't you have any affairs that weren't fraught—that were pleasant?"
"Sort of."
"What happened to those?"
"I got bored."

Most relationships, then, end before they really begin. Some folks go for relationships that have a chance. Others choose relationships because there is no chance.

A girl must marry for love, and keep on marrying until she finds it.
—Zsa Zsa Gabor

DIVORCE

Many people assume that it is "normal" to have a happy marriage. Almost 90% of Americans choose to marry at least once (Glick, 1989). When Elaine Hatfield was a freshman at Ladywood High School, a Catholic girls' school in Detroit, she was assigned to recite a poem at a public assembly:

St. Catherine, St. Catherine, oh lend me thine aid
And grant that I never will be an old maid
A husband, St. Catherine!
A good one, St. Catherine!
But anyone better than no one, St. Catherine!
Rich, St. Catherine!
Young, St. Catherine!
Soon, St. Catherine!

When spouses are first asked whether they are satisfied with their marriages, most (84%) say yes. However, when pollsters press on, underlying problems begin to emerge. Forty percent admit that they have considered leaving their partners (Gallup Poll, 1989). Philip Roth (1990, pp. 137–138) traced the trajectory of many marriages:

> I used to tell my students that you don't need three men to go through what she [Madame Bovary] does. One will usually fill the bill, as Rodolphe [a passionate impractical lover], then Leon [a "sensible" choice], then Charles Bovary [a profound disappointment]. First the rapture and the passion. All the voluptuous sins of the flesh. In his bondage. Swept away. After the torrid scene up at his chateau, combing your hair with his comb—and so on. Unbearable love with the perfect man who does everything beautifully. Then, with time, the fantastical lover erodes into the workaday lover, the practical lover—becomes a Leon, a rube after all. The tyranny of the actual begins. . . .
>
> A hick. A provincial. Sweet enough, attractive enough, but not exactly a man of valor, sublime in all things and knowing all. A little foolish, you know. A little flawed. A little stupid. Still ardent, sometimes charming, but if the truth be known, in his soul a bit of a clerk. And then, with marriage or without—though marriage will always speed things along—he who was a Rodolphe and has become Leon is transformed into Bovary. He puts on weight. He cleans his teeth with his tongue. He makes gulping sounds when he swallows his soup. He's clumsy, he's ignorant, he's coarse, even his back is irritating to look at. This merely gets on your nerves at first; in the end it drives you nuts. The prince who saved you from your boring existence is now the slob and the core of the boring existence. Dull, dull, dull.

Before the modern era, divorce was virtually forbidden in all societies by law, religion, and custom. Many historians regard the liberalization of divorce laws and attitudes to be one of history's epochal developments. Though mostly a symptom of the expansion of individualism, it also helped forge it in major ways (Stone, 1990).

Yet, even 30 years ago in the non-Catholic United States, divorce remained virtually taboo. Today, almost 50% of marriages will end in divorce (Glick, 1989). Some question whether this represents an advance for humankind, but given the torture of being required to stay in a miserable marriage in an age that supports the idea of personal happiness, a return to repressive divorce statutes would hardly seem a triumph for the human race.

So we live in a society in which divorce occurs commonly. In September 1988, columnist Ellen Goodman described marriage as "a phase women go through." Marriage itself, and the search for the right one, remains robust. Although about half of first marriages fail, about 75% of men and women will later remarry. Approximately half of those remarriages will also fail. Margaret Mead once contended that our society is moving toward "serial monogamy." Couples pair up, break up, and pair up again . . . and again.

Gunhild Hagestad and Michael Smyer (1982) studied the reaction of middle-aged adults to divorce. The 93 couples they interviewed ranged in age from 41 to 61. Typically, they had been married for 25 years. All had at least one child. These 93 displayed striking contrasts in their divorce experiences. Some of them had 20 years in which to prepare marital exits while others had little more than two months. Some of them carefully controlled and planned the marital dissolution—taking things one at a time. Others had a whole complex of changes thrown at them with no warning. The divorces seemed to follow one of the following patterns.

Changes. . . . in the character of a relationship don't announce themselves dramatically; they steal slowly over months, masking themselves behind reconciliations, periods of happiness, new resolves. Like some form of lethal disease, they invite every myth of comforting explanation before they exact the truth.

—John Fowles

1. *Patterns of orderly divorce.* Sixty-six percent of respondents described their divorces as orderly. Most stories detailed long-standing problems. They had struggled (generally for nine or more years!) to keep the marriages together. Finally, they realized that it was not possible. They concluded "enough is enough!"

In the orderly divorces, the estranged had time to make a psychological break prior to the legal divorce. They had had time to dissolve three kinds of bonds:

a. *Attachment to spouse role.* They had time to start thinking of themselves as divorced persons.
b. *Emotional cathexis.* They had time to pull back from investing their emotional energy in the other.
c. *The routines of everyday living.* They had a chance to establish a myriad of new habits and routines. Such orderly divorces were the easiest to bear.

There is hardly any activity, any enterprise, which has started with such tremendous hopes and expectations and which fails so regularly as love.

—Erich Fromm

2. *Patterns of disorderly divorce.* One-third of the respondents reported that they were still attached to the role, person, or shared routines of marriage at the time of their official divorces. Their divorces fell into the following subpatterns.

   a. *Divorced in name only.* A few men and women (3%) still "felt married," were attached to their mates, and were still even living together. They had divorced only in the hope of gaining power over mates who periodically abused them.

   b. *"I wish it hadn't happened."* Many men and women (19%) were still reeling from the shock of an unexpected divorce. Five men, for example, had given their wives an ultimatum: "Come home where you belong, or I'll divorce you," confident that their wives would return. Instead, their wives had called the bluff.

   c. *"I've got you under my skin."* One woman remained emotionally married in the paradoxical sense that she continued to be obsessed with hating her husband despite a long and difficult process of marital separation.

   d. *Married status has its advantage.* Several women (6%) and one man longed for the advantages of marriage; they had, however, no feelings for their spouses and no desire to live with them.

Disorderly divorces were ones in which couples had not had time to disengage psychologically before their divorces occurred. Such hurried dissolutions left a legacy of anger, bitterness, sadness, and despair.

PROBLEMS ASSOCIATED WITH BREAKUPS AND DIVORCE

Paul Bohannan (1970) wrote that divorcing couples, whether they have had orderly or disorderly divorces, face six complex tasks:

   1. The legal divorce.
   2. The emotional divorce.
   3. The economic divorce—they must work out a settlement and divide up the property.
   4. The co-parental divorce—they must make decisions about the custody of the children, visitation rights, and so forth.
   5. The community divorce—they must "divide up" family, friends, and business acquaintances and make new friends and acquaintances
   6. The psychic divorce—they must begin to gain an identity as a single person. (p. 34)

Let us consider how couples go about accomplishing these separate tasks.

The Emotional Aftermath

Happiness is not something you experience, it's something you remember.
                                                    —*Oscar Levant*

Unrequited Love   The tradition of love literature, romantic poetry, and grand opera expresses, almost exclusively, great passion that ended very badly. Today, country music, novels, and films are filled with stories of lovers who loved and lost. Surprisingly, we rarely see reports of people who were loved but failed to love in return.

Recently, Roy Baumeister and Sara Wotman (1991) asked college students to write two stories of unrequited love: to describe a time when they were in love with someone who didn't love them and to describe another time when they were loved but found it impossible to reciprocate that love. They found that the lovers and their beloveds react very differently to unrequited love. Those who are loved suffer the most. At first, their self-esteem may be slightly bolstered by all the adoration they receive from the supplicant. At the same time, they find themselves in an impossible situation. They feel guilty. Whatever they do is wrong. First, it is wrong to reject someone. (It is hard enough to tell someone you are not interested, much less why.) Second, it is worse to lead them on. But, as the supplicant persists, guilt turns to irritation and then to rage. Eventually, the beloved begins to feel trapped and persecuted. What can be motivating him? Why won't she go away? Is he crazy? How can she deceive herself this way? Doesn't he see he's driving me crazy?

For the "broken-hearted" lovers, Glenn Close's experience of "fatal attraction" is, strangely enough, far more pleasant—if one stays alive! It is true that their self-esteem is bruised slightly by being rejected. But, all in all, lovers fare far better than do their prey. At first they are filled with love and hope. They focus entirely on their own needs, wants, and desires; they may even wallow in the drama of their misery (see Box 14.1). They are oblivious and indifferent to what the rejecting person may be going through. They view the beloved with incomprehension. How can X not love Y when Y loves X? They blame X for not reciprocating their love; they feel angry, annoyed, and resentful at X's stubborness. They care little about X's feelings. They feel released from normal moral constraints ("all's fair in love and war"). They remember the infatuation as a bittersweet affair despite the poison of disappointment at the current state of things.

Sometimes, the rejected lover's pursuit of the other turns into harassment (see Box 14.2) (Brenner, 1991). In one study (Jason, Reichler, Easton, Neal, & Wilson, 1984), a majority of college women (56%) reported that they had been romantically harassed. (Researchers haven't investigated how many men are harassed.) Harassment is defined as "the persistent use of psychological or physical abuse in an attempt to begin or continue dating someone else after they have clearly indicated a desire to terminate a relationship" (p. 261).

Romantic harassment includes such behaviors as these: Rejected lovers repeatedly telephone late at night; they ring the bell and run; watch, follow, repeatedly telephone at home or work; besiege with an avalanche of letters; send flowers; jump out of the bushes when the other returns home late at night from a date; insult or physically attack; or threaten to kill. Interestingly enough, when harassers are interviewed, they generally do not think of such activities as harassment! They think they are trying to establish a love relationship.

In attempting to combat male harassment (it can go both ways), women attempt a variety of strategies. Some do nothing. Some try to "be nice" ("Can't we just be friends"?) and reason with the man; some are direct or rude, saying or yelling "leave me alone!" Some change their telephone numbers or move. Some

Box 14.1   WHY ME, GOD: WHY ME?

One woman in Richard Rapson's American history class responded to his book *American Yearnings* in an essay entitled "Why me, God: Why me?" In her story of unrequited love, we see many of these themes.

"Why me, God? Why me! What have I done to deserve such pain?" These are the words I keep repeating over and over to myself. It does not seem fair. What have I done to deserve this excruciating pain that is tearing my heart into millions of pieces? Is it all my fault? Did I expect too much out of life? All I know is that God, it hurts so bad and I am so lonely. I know the hurt will never ever go away.

It all began my freshman year of high school. Every morning at 7:50 I would secretly spy on David. I would be in "my" world, holding his hand as he walked me to my classes while all the jealous girls watched him kiss me good-bye. "God, he was so handsome" I thought to myself, "if only I could have him for my boyfriend." His smile triggered every thrill in my body, he acted macho amongst the girls, he joked and laughed along with the guys, he was just . . . popular!

[They meet, begin to date, and eventually have sexual relations.] We became inseparable, almost as one. I would not want him out of my sight and most of all not talking to any other girl. I felt that David belonged to me. He owed me total commitment because he had taken something from me that he in return could never offer—his virginity. [Eventually, of course, she and David go to college. They meet others. That she concludes was her mistake. They should never have left their small town; never expanded their horizons. They were greedy and now she must pay.]

But you say I am much too young to feel such a pain! At the age of 19 I feel the same pain a person of 50 would feel. Never in my life had I dreamt such pain existed. The hurt is unbearable. It tears up every functioning organ that created life for me. I was 14 years old when the relationship started. Young you say, but the hurt I received when it ended felt as if it could kill off the entire population of the world.

It has been four years since the breakup . . . but at least now I can say I deserve everything that happened to me. I was greedy; I wanted the very best life had to offer. I wanted the most popular, handsomest, and smartest guy in the world and I got him. Was I born in a corrupt society? I will not let myself get involved in another relationship. It is my loss to let-down males that come along that seem right for me. I don't think it is fair that God has created man to fall into the sea of love only to find that sea was so vast. I know I am not the only one who has experienced such a pitiful life, but do we learn from our mistakes to never make that wrong move again or is it that the mistakes we made only make us stronger to face the same torture again? Only God knows that answer for me.

Box 14.2 EROTOMANIA

Diane Schaefer was brilliant, beautiful, funny . . . and relentless. She was used to getting what she wanted. And what she wanted was Dr. Murray Brennan, head of surgery at Memorial Sloan-Kettering. She first met Dr. Murray Brennan, a plump, balding, middle-aged married man, at a medical conference in San Francisco. She became convinced that Brennan secretly loved her and that they had had an affair. For the next eight years, she tracked him, trying to rekindle the flame. She followed him to medical conventions; pushed her way into his cabs. She called his office hundreds of time. She wrote long, tender, and hotly passionate letters to him:

> Such a brilliant, beautiful, funny woman and her needs are so simple . . . all she wants to do is get *The New York Times* each night at 10:30 at the stand on 1st Ave. btwn. 68th & 69th and get into bed with you and read all the wonderful things in the paper to you. (p. 192)

> She warned Susan Brennan, "I'm going to marry your husband" (p. 260). The Brennans threatened to go to the district attorney if Diane Schaefer didn't quit hounding them. Diane was undeterred.

In 1984, the tone of Diane Schaefer's communications began to change. She left threatening messages on Murray Brennan's answering machine:

> I can't live while you are alive on this earth. I am going to kill you! Kill you or kill myself—I am *degraded* by your being alive. Shoot yourself or jump off a building so your spleen ruptures, and you suffer before you die. You're the Antichrist. Oh, I want to see you hooked up to a hospital bed with tubes running out of every orifice. . . . And then, when you're lying in your hospital bed, paralyzed, you can think of me and get aroused in your head—if you have a head left. I would like to see you vomit from chemotherapy. Wait— you'll find out what rape is one day. (p. 262)

> Finally, such threats emboldened the Brennans, who were frightened for themselves and their children, to take action. They filed charges. In 1991, after a continuing series of trials and agreements that Diane Schaefer would seek counseling, the New York prosecutors finally gave up and prosecuted. She was sentenced to two years in prison.

get boyfriends or parents to talk to or threaten the man; some file harassment charges in civil court. Such harassment is painful for women. They experience fear, anxiety, and depression. They suffer from stomachaches and nervous tics. In the short run, nothing works terribly well; lovers refuse to give up.

The best strategy for anyone who wants to get rid of someone who just won't quit seems to be to adopt a "zombie" approach—being polite, brief, and displaying no emotion. This approach means that harassers no longer can get any rewards for calling, writing, following, or threatening. Most harassers find it extremely rewarding if the woman is "nice" and tries to explain her feelings with infinite patience because they get the contact they crave. They experience equal rewards if she gets furious since they are finally getting through to her.

Better to say in a lifeless tone, "I put that in the hands of my lawyer." As a zombie you may be permitted one more polite sentence, such as: "Feel free to talk to him." Eventually, lovers/harassers lose interest in zombies. If there is no emotion off which to bounce, the unrequited passion turns into boredom. Time eventually dims the fervor, and the nightmare comes to an end.

The Breakup of Established Relationships   Robert Weiss (1979) contended that most men and women are likely to experience intense and conflicting emotions after a divorce. They may, on the one hand, feel euphoric and relieved *and,* on the other, feel anxious, depressed, and angry. The newly separated feel a whirlpool of emotions, and their feelings shift with such dizzying rapidity that it is difficult for them to deal with the turbulence. Loving and venomous feelings may rapidly alternate. It can be unsettling to hear someone plead with his or her mate to come back by cataloguing that mate's failings: "You don't know the meaning of love; you are incapable of commitment. You've treated me shamefully; please come back."

Yet, such wild alterations should come as no surprise. Long after love has died, people may remain strongly attached (Weiss, 1979). In adults the symptoms of separation distress are very similar to those displayed by young children who have become attached and then separated from or abandoned by their parents. As one woman observed (of lost love):

> It is like the battered child syndrome. You never find a battered child that does not want to be back with its parents, because they are the only parents it has. I just have very much this feeling. (Weiss, 1979, p. 203)

Earlier, we described Ellen Berscheid's (1983) model of close relationships (see Chapter 2). She defined a close relationship as one in which "the causal interconnections between participants' chains of events are strong, frequent, and diverse" (p. 118). She contended that intimates may or may not feel strong emotion for one another while they are caught up in a love affair or a marriage. Nevertheless, intimates are emotionally invested in close relationships, whether or not they are aware of it. When couples lose their mates, they lose, in part, the ability to run off their well-oiled action sequences. She keeps losing her place in the grocery list. She can't find anything on the shelves. John knew where everything was. She has no one to share "that look" with when their parents begin to argue about Oliver North's role in the Iran–Contra affair. When relationships end, both lives are severely disrupted. The more connected their lives were, the more emotional will be their parting.

Berscheid's propositions have some fascinating implications. For example, as long as they are together, happy couples who have a set routine—either out of dependence or independence—may well feel a sort of tepid affection for one another. (For Berscheid, strong emotion can only arise if our mates surprise us, either by their unexpected kindness, which brings us up short, or by unexpectedly thwarting our actions.) The partners may well have simply taken one another for granted.

It would be incorrect, however, to predict that both types of couples would respond similarly to the loss of their mates. The connection between the independent duo may have been emotionally dead for some time. Even actual death may produce surprisingly little emotion; little change in the remaining life. The couple whose life was tightly linked, however, had a relationship that was very much alive. Under its tranquil surface was an emotional time bomb, ticking. Once separated, the world explodes. Almost every act reminds them of their loss; each event grows difficult, now that they carry on alone.

How couples linked in hostility will react, once they are parted, can be harder to predict. On the one hand, such couples often discover that separation simply brings relief. Separation means the severing of painful and destructive ties. On the other hand, some conflict-ridden couples discover that they have lost more than they expected. While it is easy to focus on things that don't work well in a relationship, it is harder to remember all the things that do—the literally thousands of interconnected action sequences that may run off without a pause. Couples who lose their sense of perspective may discover after separation, divorce, or a spouse's death how much their mates really meant to them.

Most newly separated lovers do gain perspective and experience a mixture of feelings (see Box 14.3).

1. *Love*. At times, the estranged are filled with love for their mates. They think of the early days of their relationships when things went so well.

Box 14.3 LOVE STINKS

With self-mockery, in *Love Stinks*, humorist Joy Overbeck (1990) discussed her thoughts in the aftermath of a breakup:

He's gone. You're alone. You've decided to get separated. Some typical questions and concerns likely to be flitting through your head in this time of emotional turbulence are:

1. Have the police in my area seen that Alfred Hitchcock episode where the woman bludgeons her husband to death with the leg of lamb, serves the murder weapon to the detectives for dinner and gets off?

2. Am I such a vile and repulsive specimen that no man will ever again love me, cherish me, and break my heart?

3. Will I always feel as if my vital organs are being used for a nuclear testing site?

4. If I kill myself, will he be sorry he's treated me so badly?

The answers to these all-important questions are as follows:
1. Yes.
2. Of course not!
3. No.
4. Maybe; but your satisfaction will be short lived.

Source: Overbeck, 1990, p. 45.

2. *Elation.* Some feel surprisingly elated once they have made a decision and have "escaped to freedom." We have seen clients who, after agonizing for years over their decision, are filled with joy the moment they walk into their new apartments. "Whoopee! I'm free!" or "Thank heaven," they shout to the walls. These are people who did their grieving while *in* the relationship; they probably completed that process before they physically separated from their mates. They may luxuriate in getting to watch the TV programs they like for a change, spending their money as they like without a Greek chorus of criticism, disciplining or treating the children as they please, going to sleep when they are tired. They may feel sheepish about feeling so good so soon, but they probably had their share of sorrow before they could experience such pure relief.

3. *Confusion.* There are some ideas we hold so deeply that we would have trouble even labeling them as an idea. We tend to think of them as eternal truths. Many people take it for granted that if they love someone, are kind and generous to another, that person will love them back. After a divorce, they are stunned. "How could she not love me when I loved her so much?" they ask again and again in disbelief. "She'll never find someone who loves her as much as I do." (Outside observers, of course, may be bemused by their confusion; whoever said love was fair.)

"He's so wonderful 25% of the time. Why can't he *always* be that nice?" they ask. They then run through a series of strategies, sometimes going at it for decades—sweetness, persuasion, guilt manipulations, making him jealous, anger, tears—designed to regularize the loving side of their mates. Again, the observers smile ruefully. They know full well that if someone is nice 25% of the time and awful 75% of the time, with five years of continuous work, the 25% could probably move up to being 26.7%. (Insanity, said the ancients, is doing the same thing over and over and expecting it—this time—to come out differently. This time Lucy won't pull away the football when Charlie Brown runs up to kick it.)

Couples may make love in the evening and find themselves telling their divorce lawyer the next afternoon that they have put their love affair back together. Or, they wish to put the divorce on hold until they to go away the next weekend to "say goodbye." They are ashamed at their ambivalence. One man reported:

> I was gone for a week and I came back. . . . And we had the most fantastic weekend, really. It was great, it was fantastic. And then things started up again. The bickering, the whole thing, started up Sunday. (Weiss, 1979, p. 209)

4. *Sadness.* Researchers (Means, 1991) interviewed college students who recently broke up. Almost all the men and women said they were still feeling strong love for their partners. Their relationships had all been exclusive; they were psychologically involving and important. To some extent, both wanted the relationship to continue. Nonetheless, it had failed. Two months after things had fallen apart, over 40% of students in these doomed relationships were still experiencing clinically measurable depression. Scores in the *Beck Depression Inventory* (Beck, 1967) revealed that 2% of them were experiencing "severe depression," 10% were experiencing "moderate to severe depression," 31% were experiencing "mild to moderate depression," and 1% were experiencing "minimal depression."

5. *Guilt.* Couples worry "Maybe I should have tried harder."

6. *Anger and bitterness.* Sometimes when the newly separated think back on their relationship, a flood tide of anger is released. They may have suppressed their own feelings for decades in the interests of harmony. Now they realize how angry they had been for so much of the time. One young woman observed:

> In separating from someone you discover in yourself things that you had never felt before in your life. That's one of the things that really freaks you out. I've always used my mind to keep down anything I didn't like. And now I discover, wow, I can hate! (Weiss, 1979, p. 208)

The dread of loneliness is greater than the fear of bondage, so we get married.
—Cyril Connolly

7. *Loneliness.* Researchers point out that the divorced can suffer from either emotional loneliness (the lack of a special someone to love) or from social loneliness (the lack of friends and acquaintances). Many newly separated and divorced couples suffer from both. Jenny de Jong-Gierveld (1986) interviewed 556 men and women, who ranged in age from 25 to 75. The loneliest were parents without partners (60% of them mentioned feelings of loneliness); 50% of those who lived alone and 13% of those living with somebody admitted to emotional loneliness. In one study, 48% of widows viewed loneliness as the major problem of widowhood (Lopata, 1969). The lonely hunger for love, and in its absence they may also be angry, anxious, bored, or depressed (Perlman & Peplau, 1981).

Three psychologists (Russell, Peplau, & Ferguson, 1978) have developed a loneliness scale (see Box 14.4). How would you answer a sampling of questions from this scale?

8. *Stress.* Newly separated and divorced people have more mental problems than do married couples (Redick & Johnson, 1974). When we look at admissions to psychiatric hospitals, we discover that men with disrupted marriages are nine times as likely as married men to be in trouble. Women with disrupted marriages are three times as likely as married women to be in trouble (Bloom, White, & Asher, 1979).

The newly divorced are also especially vulnerable to disease. Generally, separated and divorced men and women are at greater risk than those who either are married or who never married. The newly divorced are vulnerable to alcoholism, diabetes, heart disease, tuberculosis, and cirrhosis of the liver. The separated and divorced are more likely to die from natural causes, twice as likely to commit suicide, and more likely to be murdered than are the married (Bloom et al., 1979).

Dealing with Loss   It is normal, naturally, to suffer after a breakup or a divorce. Usually, the estranged simply need to be sad for a while before they move to reenter social life. Some, however, suffer so obsessively or so long from a breakup that they decide to take action to deal with their feelings. Clinical psychologists have written a variety of self-help books offering advice on how to deal with the loss of love. Such books make a number of practical suggestions; interestingly enough, almost all of them are based on what scientists have discovered about cognitive–behavioral techniques for dealing with emotions. Behavioral

Box 14.4   EXCERPT FROM
THE UCLA LONELINESS SCALE

For the following questions, you are to circle the choice that best illustrates how often each of the statements would be descriptive of you.

O = (4) I *often* feel this way.
S = (3) I *sometimes* feel this way.
R = (2) I *rarely* feel this way.
N = (1) I *never* feel this way.

1. I am unhappy doing so many things alone.   O   S   R   N

2. I have nobody to talk to.   O   S   R   N

3. I lack companionship.   O   S   R   N

4. I feel as if nobody really understands me.   O   S   R   N

The higher the score, the more lonely people are said to be.

Source: Russell, Peplau, & Ferguson. 1978.

---

therapist Debora Phillips (1978), for instance, in *How to Fall Out of Love* offered the following techniques for getting over a love affair. First, of course, one has to begin by acknowledging the pain of breakup and wallowing in it briefly. But after a while it will be time to move on. She suggested use of three techniques—thought stopping, silent ridicule, and repulsion—to eliminate the pain of the dissolution. Let us now consider each of these strategies in some detail.

1. *Thought stopping.* (This is a technique often used by cognitive–behavioral theorists.) Sometimes, people find it impossible to stop thinking of someone they loved. "Why?" "Why did we break up?" "Why did she leave me?" "Why couldn't it work?" The brain races on and on. The author recommended that each time you find yourself dwelling on your ex-lover, you shout STOP (to force you to quit thinking of the one you love) and try to think of something else that you find extremely pleasant. (She proposed you make up a list of pleasant scenes, places, events, and feelings that do not involve the person you love.) One client's list looked like this:

Aaron's List

1. The sweet, fat crack of the bat as you hit a home run in the World Series. Cheers, rounding the bases, TV contracts.
2. Finding a cool freshwater stream running into a beach in Mendocino, California.

3. Sitting at the kitchen table when you were six and watching your mother make supper.
4. Winning the Olympic marathon and going on, nonstop, to grab a pole, vault and set a new world record at twenty-one-feet even. (When you go over the top you can feel the sun shine on the soles of your bare feet.)
5. Sliding your hand inside the bikini of the innocent MJ. (p. 33)

Each time you think of the person, you shout STOP and switch to thinking about one of the best thoughts from the list. (If shouting is too much for you, you might snap a rubber band around your wrist or clench both of your fists.)

Phillips also proposed you keep a record of how many times a day you think of your former partner. Simply mark a card with the days of the week and place an X beside the day each time you think of that person. It's an excellent way to measure your progress. Here, for example, is the card of one lover:

Wed.   xxxxxxxxxxxxxxxxxxxxxxxxxxxxxxxxxxxxx

Thurs. xxxxxxxxxxxxxxxxxxxxxxxxxxxxxx

Fri.   xxxxxxxxx

Sat.   xxxxxxxxxxxxxxxxxxxxxxxxxxxxxxxxx

Sun.   xxxxxxxxxxxxxxxxxxxxxxxxxxxxxxxxx

Mon.   xxxxxxxxxxxxxxxxxxxxx

Tues.   xxxxxxxxxxxxxxxxx

Wed.   xxxxxxxxxxxxx

Thurs. xxxxxxxxxxxxxxxx

Fri.   xxxxxxx

Sat.   xxxx

If successful in controlling your thoughts, give yourself a reward. Indulge in an expensive dinner at a nice restaurant or get a massage.

2. *Silent ridicule.* (A Pavlovian, classical conditioning technique. Perhaps you have seen such methods used in Stanley Kubrick's classic film, *A Clockwork Orange.* In the aversion therapies, clients are given training whereby an unpleasant stimulus—say, electric shock—becomes linked to another stimulus—say, looking at pictures of the beloved—in an effort to reduce the appeal of the second stimulus. In effect, the therapist tries to induce a phobic reaction.) Sometimes, you have to do more than stop thinking about the other person. Perhaps you see your lost love every day at school or at work. Perhaps you have to discuss the children on the telephone. One way to make such interactions bearable involves inventing a way to ridicule silently your ex-lover. First, you microscopically examine your lover for little foibles or flaws.

Is that person vain, shy, aggressive, submissive, overly frank, slightly deceitful, sloppy, a fuss-budget, careless, overcautious, too thin, over-weight, a health freak, conceited, self-deprecating? Does he pick his nose, teeth, or toes? Does she . . . well, the list of possible human frailties is endless and often grubby. (p. 57)

Then try imagining your lover in an absurd or comic context. An example:

Karl, thirty-year old policeman. He was married and in love with his best friend's wife. The two couples spent weekends and holidays together, and saw each other at least one evening a week. Karl was secretly in love with her but did not want to break up his marriage and lose his best friend. Her smile, he said, made him afraid he was going to make a fool of himself and spoil everything, so he pictured her with no teeth. (p. 58)

3. *Repulsion.* (Another example of a technique based on Pavlovian, classical conditioning.) If all else fails, Phillips suggested that you try to associate physical contact with the one you love with something that is so negative that it's repulsive. Here's how it works. First draw up a short list of the things that are most repulsive to you—the smellier, slimier, and nastier, the better. Some examples: "excrement, sewer flows, flies, vomit, blood, cockroaches, snakes, garbage, manure, and pus. One of the most sickening is 'ooze from a dead rat' " (p. 114). Find a place where you won't be disturbed. Think of a scene in which you are about to have physical contact with the person you loved. Just as you are about to touch, embrace, or kiss that person you see and smell that he or she is covered with ooze or excrement or whatever you find most repulsive. You pull back, not wanting to touch or kiss excrement, and as you turn away, suddenly everything is gone. The air is clear and sweet and you feel fresh and new.

Zev Wanderer and Tracy Cabot (1978), in *Letting Go,* added some more suggestions.

- If you must feel sad, confine it to a special "sob hour" at a particularly inconvenient time each day when you would rather be doing something else. Stand up in an uncomfortable place during that hour.
- (Based on a Pavlovian conditioning technique called flooding. Rehearse the sad scene over and over, not just in the clinic but at home, at work, in the car, at a friend's house, until gradually it loses its power. It no longer has the effect it once had.) Pull out and confront your ex's photos, jewelry, and assorted memorabilia that you had earlier put away. Cry as long and as much as you want. Eventually, you'll get bored.

Lawrence Durrell (1961), in *The Alexandria Quartet,* detailed a lover's reaction at coming upon a photograph of Melissa, someone he had once loved, when he revisited their apartment.

It was a street-photograph and very faded. Melissa and I walked arm in arm talking down Rue Fuad. Her face was half turned away from me, smiling—dividing her attention between what I was saying so earnestly and the lighted shop-windows we passed. It must have been taken, this snapshot, on a winter afternoon around the hour of four. What on earth could I have been telling her with such earnestness? For the life of me I could not recall the time and place; yet there it was, in black and white, as they say. Perhaps the words I was uttering were momentous, significant—or perhaps they were meaningless! I had a pile of books under my arm and was wearing the dirty old mackintosh which I finally gave to Zoltan. It was in need of a dry-clean. My hair, too, seemed to need cutting at the back. Impossible to restore this vanished afternoon to mind! I gazed carefully at the circumstantial detail of the picture like someone bent upon restoring an irremediably faded fresco. Yes, it was winter, at four o'clock. She was wearing her tatty sealskin and carried a handbag which I had not ever seen in her possession. "Sometime in August—*was* it August?" I mentally quoted to myself again.

Turning back to the wretched rack-like bed again I whispered her name softly. With surprise and chagrin I discovered that she had *utterly vanished*. The waters had simply closed over her head. It was as if she had never existed, never inspired in me the pain and pity which (I had always told myself) would live on, transmuted into other forms perhaps—but live triumphantly on forever. I had worn her out *like an old pair of socks,* and the utterness of this disappearance surprised and shocked me. Could "love" simply wear out like this? (pp. 40–41)

Gender Differences in Strategies for Dealing with Loss   Historically, women have been stereotyped as the more emotional gender, especially in their close relationships (Broverman et al., 1972; Sprecher & Hatfield, 1987). In addition, stress researchers contend that men and women may cope with stressful life events in different ways. Men seem to ignore stressful events and to distract themselves from what they are feeling. They may exercise, take drugs, drink, or lose themselves in their work. Women tend to brood about problems. They try to figure out if they were to blame, to sort out exactly what went wrong. They talk to other people to get their ideas. They try to set things right (Ingram, Cruet, Johnson, & Wisnicki, 1988; Nolen-Hoeksema, 1987). These are the stereotypes. Recent research suggests, however, that at least in the area of love, men and women are not so different as they are purported to be (see Box 14.5).

The Divorce Settlement

Men and women are often quite clever and quite ruthless about getting the things they want after a breakup. Sociologists Gerald Marwell and David Schmitt (1967) found that people employed 16 different techniques to get their way. In Table 14.1, using the preceding framework, we have indicated the "tricks" that those who are divorcing often use to get what they think they deserve in a divorce settlement (or far more than they know they deserve).

One often sees in therapy how men generally feel they are entitled to at least half of the money the family has accumulated. Women are sometimes willing to settle for far less than half. One elderly woman felt so betrayed and angry at her husband, who was leaving her for a far younger woman, that she wanted to surrender all ties with him. "I don't want anything of his. If he cares so much about the money, let him keep it." Sometimes women are willing to give everything, hoping to appease the man into coming back or else they feel virtuous and superior by taking possession of the moral highground. Whether for appeasement or self-righteousness, the tactic ranks high in the annals of stupidity. We know from experience that they will feel very differently about their sacrifice a year later. By then, women will have faced the horror of trying to live on too little money. Their friends will have filled them in on things they never knew about their husbands. Fury now mixes with resentment and self-flagellation.

We counsel both men and women to take exactly that to which they are

Box 14.5 GENDER DIFFERENCES IN DEALING WITH LOSS

Lisa Orimoto and her colleagues (Orimoto, Hatfield, Yamakawa, & Denney, 1991) interviewed 237 University of Hawaii students. The researchers asked the subjects how they felt after a recent breakup and how they tried to cope with the situation. The authors found that men's and women's emotional reactions differed surprisingly little. Both were usually devastated by the breakup. They felt a kaleidoscope of emotions—love, anger, and grief—as well as occasional relief that things were finally over.

How did they deal with their feelings and with the practical problems they faced following the breakup? Women were more likely to try to focus on the problem and try to figure out what had happened and whether they could make improvements next time around. In the main, however, both men and women used similar strategies. Both men and women felt that they should have coped better than they actually did.

1. *Women paid attention to the problem.* They were more prone to cry, to talk to their friends, to read self-help books and magazines, and to see therapists in an effort to understanding better the workings of love.

Men and women were equally likely to use the other techniques.

2. *Both men and women sometimes tried to play things down.* They tried to hide their feelings so others wouldn't know what they were going through. They binged. They drank or took drugs (tranquilizers, sleeping pills, marijuana). They went out of their way to avoid bumping into the one they loved. They avoided going to places or doing things that had been parts of their lives together. They stayed in bed.

3. *Both used cognitive techniques to manage their feelings.* They talked to themselves like a dutch uncle. "Who needs him (or her) anyway?" "It's his (her) loss!" "There are lots of good fish in the sea." "I'm lucky to have gotten out of that relationship." Or, "You've learned a valuable lesson."

4. *Both tried to distract themselves from their loss.* They did things to improve their looks or sex appeal (got a haircut, bought clothes, or went on a diet). They kept themselves busy with sports, schoolwork, or career. They engaged in physical activities (they jogged, played basketball, or went swimming).

entitled by law. In most no-fault divorce states that is defined as child support (based on a formula that looks at salaries and a few other variables) plus one-half of any assets the couple has accumulated. If married more than 10 years, that often means one-half of all assets. We remind them that this will buttress them against later feelings of bitterness based on feelings of having been cheated. When the mate later tries to dictate what school the children should attend or what major the college student must select, it may be helpful to have the resources to defend the interests of the children. If clients believe, after one year, that they were awarded too much in the divorce settlement, they can still return the money to their husbands.

Conversely, if someone wants to punish a mate by taking everything, we try

Table 14.1 COMPLIANCE GAINING TECHNIQUES

1. Promise	If you comply, I will reward you. ("I will give you $2000 a month for two years if you trust me. I don't want anything on paper.")
2. Threat	If you do not comply, I will punish you. ("If you cause trouble, I will quit my job; you and the children will starve.")
3. Expertise (positive)	If you comply, you will be rewarded because of "the nature of things." ("If we can agree on a divorce settlement, it will save thousands in legal fees.")
4. Expertise (negative)	If you do not comply, you will be punished because of "the nature of things." ("If you raise these issues in court, the children will never live it down; there will be a public scandal.")
5. Liking	Actor is friendly and helpful to get target in "good frame of mind" so that he will comply with the request. ("You're too good for me. I don't know why I'm attracted to a slut like her; perhaps some day we'll be together again . . . but for now.")
6. Pregiving	Actor rewards target before requesting compliance. ("We've had a wonderful time on this anniversary cruise, right? Now there's something I have to tell you.")
7. Aversive stimulation	Actor continuously punishes target, making cessation contingent on compliance. ("I'm not talking to you or giving you a penny until you agree to give me a divorce.")
8. Debt	You owe me compliance because of past favors. ("I've given you the best years of my life. The least you can do is stay with me until the children are grown.")
9. Moral appeal	You are immoral if you do not comply. ("What God has joined together, let no man put asunder. You'll burn in hell if you leave me.")
10. Self-feeling (positive)	You will feel better about yourself if you comply. ("It may be hard, but you'll respect yourself more if you give me my freedom.")
11. Self-feeling (negative)	You will feel worse about yourself if you do not comply. ("You'll never forgive yourself if you go through with this.")
12. Altercasting (positive)	A person with "good" qualities would comply. ("A truly Christian person would be happy that I'd found someone to love.")
13. Altercasting (negative)	Only a person with "bad" qualities would not comply. ("Only a selfish person would want to hang on to someone who doesn't want them.")
14. Altruism	I need your compliance very badly, so do it for me. ("I can't take it anymore. You have to come home. I may do something drastic if you don't.")
15. Esteem (positive)	People you value will think better of you if you comply. ("I told everyone what a wonderful husband you are. You wouldn't let us down.")
16. Esteem (negative)	People you value will think worse of you if you do not comply. ("My parents will be shocked if we divorce. There's never been a divorce in our family.")

Source: Based on Marwell & Schmitt, 1967, pp. 357–358.

to persuade them such a Pyrrhic victory can produce only everlasting bitterness. More effective than moral persuasion may be the reminder that such strategies very likely never get consummated. We have had clients, who, against our advice, spent over $100,000 a year for three years on high-powered lawyers only to get what we predicted at the beginning: type A visitation (she gets the children during the week; he gets them Wednesday nights and every other weekend), normal child support, and one-half of all their assets. Moral and ethical standards for who "deserves" what after a marriage can be a very sticky business; the highest morality may be to give and receive that which the law, in its flawed wisdom, mandates.

Recently, some experts have proposed divorce mediation as a better way to settle marital disputes. Mediation procedures permit both couples to speak their piece, keep things issue-oriented when feelings get out-of-hand, and promote useful compromises (Knebel & Clay, 1987). If all else fails, however, issues must be settled in court.

In any case, after a divorce, legal precedents do not currently result in equity. Men usually emerge far better off economically than they were before; women and children suffer the losses. For example, Mary Ann Mason (1988) has written:

> The California Divorce Law Research Project, headed by Lenore Weitzman, has carefully analyzed all divorces since 1970 and has produced some startling statistics. No matter what income level they began in, divorced wives and their children experience extreme downward mobility—averaging a 73 percent lessened standard of living one year following the divorce, while ex-husbands improve their standard of living during this same period by a rise of 42 percent. (p. 64)

Some economists (such as Saul Hoffman) and social scientists (such as Gregory Duncan) have taken issue with Weitzman's statistics (Faludi, 1991). According to *their* calculations, women's standard of living declines 30% while men's improves 10 to 15% in the first year after divorce. Within five years, however, things have turned around. The average woman's living standard is actually slightly higher than when she was married.

Nonetheless, in the short run, women and children seem to suffer more economically from a divorce than do men. It is easy to see why this is so. Men generally have reasonably paying full-time careers. After divorce, they usually have no alimony requirements and they pay (when they do) modest child support (the amount equals, on the average, less than one-half of the real costs of raising children). Worse yet, less than 50% keep up with their child support payments (*The New York Times*, 1985). They have only themselves to support.

Women are almost always granted the children; they head 90% of single-parent families. Even if they work full time, at high prestige "men's" jobs, they can expect to earn only about 70 cents for every dollar earned by men (Bureau of Census, 1987). This is true despite the fact that women are generally better educated than the men who hold similar jobs (Degler, 1980). [Women fare worse in America than they do in other industrialized nations. In Italy, women's wages in 1982 were 86% of men's, in Denmark 86%, in France 78%, in Sweden 74%, and in West Germany 73% (Hewlett, 1986).] Many divorced women, however, have not worked full time for years. Many lack marketable skills. Thus they earn far less than their ex-husbands (Clark-Stewart & Bailey, 1989). Skilled or not, if women have young children they naturally find it almost impossible to work full time outside the home. (There is no job more time-consuming and demanding than raising small children.) Furthermore, single mothers must pay for child care out of their meager earnings. The upshot: A stunning 54% of single-parent families in the United States now live below the poverty line (Mason, 1988).

The Impact of Divorce on Children

Marriages have been disrupted throughout history—mostly by death. Children born as late as between 1901 and 1910, for example, were actually more likely to suffer some form of marital disruption before age 18 (due to parental death) than children born in 1951 to 1960. And this comes two centuries after the average life span began to grow well beyond the mid-thirties range.

Today, if present trends continue, about 40% or more of American children will witness the breakup of their parents' marriages before the children reach 18 (Bumpass, 1984). This represents a significant increase over the 1951 to 1960 figures. When couples divorce, parents are filled with guilt; they naturally worry about the tragic effects of the breakup on their children. This father speaks for many:

> We wanted there to be as little disruption as possible for the kids. Because both of the kids were loved very much by both of us and because of our agreement to share custody, I feel they suffered only minimally. . . . Now they don't have to compete with the other parent for attention and they don't have to live with constant quarreling. (Spanier & Castro, 1979, p. 216)

Recently, there has appeared a spate of books arguing that divorce is terrible for children. They point out that children of divorce possess lower self-esteem, more emotional problems, and are more likely to get into serious trouble than are other children. They have lower grades, achieve less educationally and socio-economically over the long term. They are more likely to end up with unstable marriages themselves. Divorce seems to be especially hard on boys (Hetherington, et al., 1982; Scanzoni & Scanzoni, 1988).

Unfortunately, the scientific methodology in some of these studies has often been seriously flawed. Sometimes, researchers compare the children of the happily married (their self-esteem, emotional security, grades, run-ins with the police) with those of divorced parents. Children from happy families are, of course, better off (Reid & Cristafulli, 1990). Sometimes the critics simply ask children what problems the divorce caused them; they do not ask children—in either happy or unhappy marriages—what problems *they* have faced.

The real question that faces most parents who have struggled to achieve a happy marriage and failed—again and again and again—is whether it is better to stay in an unhappy marriage for the sake of the children or to divorce. The answer to this real-life conundrum is not at all self-evident. Is it better to keep a family together at all costs if one of the parents is chronically verbally or physically abusive to the marital partner or to the children? Surely not. A harder one: How about if one parent or both parents are emotionally distant and the marriage is unhappy? What about the workaholic parent? How important is it for children to see a model of a loving couple? Today some 15.8 million children live in single-parent households. How much does it cost children when parents separate? Do kids need two parents or will one loving mother or father provide sufficient emotional anchorage? How critical is the chance for children to remain in their old, familiar neighborhood? To play with their old friends? To have enough food and shelter? To have money for college?

A classic study of the effects of marital discord and divorce on parents and children was conducted by Mavis Hetherington and her colleagues (1982). The team interviewed 72 parents and children from intact families (which varied in how much marital conflict existed) and 72 parents and children from divorced families. The researchers painstakingly assessed family functioning: They gave parents and children a battery of personality tests; interviewed parents, teachers, children and their peers; studied parental diaries; and observed parents' and children's behavior in carefully controlled laboratory settings and at home and in school. They conducted their interviews and observations two months after the divorce, and one year, two years, and six years later. The researchers found that, initially, both parents and children were unsettled by the divorce. Things got worse before they got better. By the second year, parents and children had settled down; their lives had settled into a new order. The authors concluded: "These findings suggest that in the long run it is not a good idea for parents to remain in a conflicted marriage for the sake of the children if the alternative is a stable nonconflicted one-parent household. In the long run, marital discord may be associated with more adverse outcomes for the children than is divorce" (p. 262). Both discord and divorce seemed to take a bigger toll on boys than on girls. Of course, a few divorced couples never quit fighting. Their relationships remained angry, bitter, and conflicted. In such cases, the children continued to suffer from the lingering, or even escalating, conflict (Wallerstein & Kelly, 1980).

One recent study (Cherlin et al., 1991) has addressed this same question (should parents stay in a bad marriage for the sake of the children) and has come up with the same answer (see Box 14.6). Deborah Luepnitz (1979) concluded that it may be far more distressing for a child to live in a conflict-ridden home than to come from a broken one.

Currently, about one in two marriages ends in divorce; 50% of all American children under 18 experience divorce (Weitzman, 1981a). In the 1990s, 50 to 60% of the nation's children will spend some part of their childhood in a single-parent family (Hanson, 1988; Weitzman, 1985). More than 25 to 33% will live in blended families (Bronstein, 1988).

Agreeing on Custody

What about custody? What is best for children—to live with a mother or father who has sole legal and physical custody or to shuttle back and forth between two parents who share legal and physical custody? Or some other formula? Historians remind us that courts changed radically in what they consider to be appropriate (Ahrons & Wallisch, 1987; Folberg, 1984). Under English common law (prior to the middle of the nineteenth century), the father was assumed to be the natural

Box 14.6   TO DIVORCE OR NOT TO DIVORCE: THE EFFECT OF DIVORCE ON CHILDREN

Andrew Cherlin and his colleagues followed 2,279 American and 17,414 British families over a four-year period. They first interviewed parents, teachers, and children when the children were 7 or 11 years old. They gave the children reading and mathematics achievement tests and interviewed their parents and teachers to find out how well they behaved. Were the children depressed? Anxious? Aggressive? They asked other questions. Were the children reluctant to go to school, did they have bad dreams, difficulty sleeping, poor appetite, difficulty concentrating? Were they miserable or tearful, squirmy or fidgety, continually worried, upset by new situations? Did they twitch or have other nervous habits? Did other children bully them? Did they sleepwalk? Were they destructive, irritable? Did they have temper tantrums, fight with other children? Were they disobedient? How well did they behave? Did they have any behavior problems?

During the next four years, 239 of the couples divorced. When the children were age 11 or 16, their parents and current teachers were interviewed once again. They found, according to Chase-Lansdale, that "if a marriage is in trouble, there are effects on the children whether or not the parents divorce" (Brody, 1991, p. A 18). Children usually had the same problems at 7 (before their parents divorced) that they had at 11 (after the divorce).

If these researchers had only studied the children after divorce, they would, naturally, have been inclined to attribute the children's problems not to the differences between growing up in a happy family as opposed to an unhappy one, but—erroneously—to the effects of the divorce itself. Cherlin did not fall into that trap. He concluded that if a marriage is marred by conflict, it is not particularly helpful for parents to stay together for the sake of the children. The children suffer regardless of what parents do. Children from troubled marriages suffer. Boys often become aggressive and defiant. Girls become anxious and depressed. Both boys' and girls' grades begin to fall. They score lower on reading and mathematical achievement tests. They get into trouble with their teachers and the police.

Cherlin went a step farther: In "families wracked by conflict or abuse, the children are probably better off if the parents divorce" (Brody, 1991, p. A 18). But he cautioned against treating divorce too casually.

guardian of children. They were his property. As the Doctrine of the Two Spheres came into vogue during the Victorian era, that began to change. Mothers became full-time caretakers; fathers began to go to work in the city. Judges began to see mothers as "naturally" responsible for their children, especially during their "tender years"—from birth to six or seven years of age. One Idaho court observed that the preference for mothers "needs no argument to support it because it arises out of the very nature and instincts of motherhood; Nature has ordained it" (Weitzman, 1981b, p. 101). Fathers were only granted custody if the mother was obviously unfit. In the 1950s, a new doctrine began to emerge. Some judges began to realize that parental "rights" weren't as important as the best interests of the child. In 1973, the American Bar Association drafted the Uniform Marriage and

Divorce Act, which prescribed that custody decisions should be based on the "best interests of the child doctrine." Whichever parent (mother, father, or both) could take best care of the child should be awarded custody. In the 1970s, more fathers began to seek sole custody. Sometimes they got it. More commonly, courts began to award men and women sole custody but give the noncustodial parent visitation rights that were so ample that it approached joint custody. (Children might be assigned to stay with the noncustodial parent Wednesdays and every other weekend; or allowed to visit the noncustodial parent during the Easter and Christmas holiday season plus perhaps six weeks during summer vacations.) Sometimes, when the parents could get along, the arrangements would be left flexible and vague: providing for "reasonable visitation."

Judith Wallerstein and Joan Berlin Kelly (1980) studied 60 families and 131 children of divorce over a five-year period. They emphasized "the desirability of the child's continuing relationship with both parents during the postdivorce years in an arrangement which enables each parent to be responsible for and genuinely concerned with the well being of the children" (p. 310).

They concluded that parents should have joint *legal* custody; whether one or both parents should share *physical* custody depended on the people involved and their situation.

Today, however, mothers are still generally (90% of the time) granted sole legal and physical custody; fathers are generally granted liberal visitation—they may get to spend every other weekend, half of each holiday period, and four to eight weeks in the summer with their children (Bronstein, 1988). Today, legal scholars have begun to push couples toward joint legal and physical custody. A more egalitarian spirit, the women's movement, the fact that both men and women are often involved in child rearing, and that both are now in the labor force has led family judges and lawyers to encourage many couples to share responsibility for their children.

Sole Custody—Pros and Cons   Sometimes one parent should take sole custody of the children. One parent may be mentally ill, an alcoholic or drug addict, irresponsible, or just plain unwilling to be a parent. Sometimes couples hate one another so much that it is impossible to share custody. We mentioned earlier the client who, in spite of our advice, squandered $100,000 a year for three years in a futile attempt to secure sole custody of her children. Every waking moment with her children she filled them with subtle to blatant indictments of her husband. She was like the Ancient Mariner, plucking strangers' sleeves with a bony hand, telling "Her Story." Finally, the courts took the children away from both parents. Their love of the battle with one another was far stronger than their love for their children. They found a purpose in life in reviling and vilifying each other.

Frequently, it is easier to raise children alone than to try to negotiate the shoals of a difficult marriage (Kohen, Brown, & Feldberg, 1979). Single parents no longer are caught in the middle. They can devise a consistent set of rules and do things their way. One mother observed:

I don't have to be on any schedules. Housework is my own business. I don't have to answer to anyone. I can be more relaxed. No one says, "You god-damn slob, why isn't the floor clean?'' I can spend more time with the children, it's more relaxed. I can make my own time. I'm my own boss. (Kohen et al., 1979, p. 240)

Yet sole parenting is difficult too. Single parents sometimes report an over-powering sense of responsibility. They are short of money. Eighty-five percent of divorced women received no alimony at all. In 1985, although 82% of custodian mothers were awarded child support, only 54% received any; on the average, mothers and children received $200 a month (Ellwood, 1988). When child support is collected, it pays for less than half of the cost of raising a child (Mason, 1988). Single parents may feel trapped. It is hard to date, work, or have much of a social life if you are always with your children. Two mothers stated:

[My major problem was] knowing I had four children on my own to be responsible for—trying to keep us together, raising two boys to be boys. That was hard. (Spanier & Casto, 1979, p. 222)

I hate feeling totally responsible for the kids. They're mine completely. At least when I was married, I could mentally not feel responsible at times. . . . It gets lonely with the kids in bed by 8:00. It's an ambiguous role. [I want to go out but] I don't want the kids to be stuck with a babysitter three or four nights a week. (Spanier & Casto, 1979, p. 223)

Parents without custody (generally this could read ''fathers'') suffer as well. Most noncustodial fathers wish they could have a close relationship with their children. Most men feel guilty about ''deserting'' their children. They miss them and long to see them regularly. They worry about how they will turn out. Even so, visitation may be painful. It is painful to have to deal with an angry ex-mate; to engage in humiliating power struggles. (Wives may think of the children as ''theirs''; they assume the fathers are incompetent; they may schedule their children's lives in ways that make visitation difficult or impossible.) Fathers may hesitate to confront children who resent them or who are bored with them. Fathers may not know how to entertain little strangers over a long weekend. In any case, most fathers visit their children regularly for two years or so and then things begin to fall apart. In the end, most fathers rarely see the children of divorce. In one national sample, it was found that fewer than one-half of divorced fathers had seen their children even once in the preceding 12 months! Fewer than one-sixth of the fathers saw their children once a week. When fathers stopped visiting, they generally stopped writing or calling as well (Furstenberg, 1983). Both parents and children are the losers when visitation ends. Daughters may be left with a deep, lifelong yearning for their fathers. Boys may begin to run wild; their school achievements plummet (Loewen, 1988). Divorce may cause fathers and children to lose touch with one another permanently. In one study, most older fathers (53% of fathers 50 to 79 years of age) reported they ''frequently'' saw their sons and daughters; few divorced fathers (only 11%) saw their adult children as frequently. Normally, fathers never lost contact with their adult children; 33% of divorced fathers did (Uhlenberg, 1991).

Joint Custody—Pros and Cons   Many couples who cannot live together are still able to do a fine job of cooperative parenting. They both love their children and want to be involved in their lives; they are able to communicate and to negotiate differences. They are willing to arrange their lives to accommodate to the children's needs (Elkin, 1984). Constance Ahrons and Lynn Wallisch (1987) searched Wisconsin court records and selected 98 divorced couples with young children for intensive study. They interviewed couples about their lives one, three, and five years after divorce. Eventually, almost all these men and women had remarried, were engaged, or were living with someone. Most divorced couples agreed that they *should* get together now and then to consult about their children's lives. They believed that each parent should be allowed to have a solid, independent relationship with his or her children and that the children should not be drawn into taking sides, being pawns in their parents' battle. How did these beliefs translate into reality?

During the first year after the divorce, parents did reasonably well in living up to their ideals. Most still got together fairly often to consult about their children's lives. One year after divorce, 80% of the couples still got together or talked with some regularity about parenting issues. They consulted with each other about major or even day-to-day decisions, celebrated their children's accomplishments, planned birthday celebrations, attended birthday parties, school plays, and graduations together, worried over their offspring's personal, school, or medical problems, and debated about how they should be raised. Although parents often felt tense when discussing such issues with their ex-spouses, most said they rarely or never argued. Although most of them were well aware that they had basic differences of opinion about child rearing, they were able to stick to the point—making the lives of their children better.

By three years after the divorce, there was less conversation. Now only 9% of parents had a great deal of interaction, 67% had a moderate amount of interaction, and 24% had a low amount of interaction.

If estranged couples can get along and if they live in the same city, most authorities think it best if both parents continue to take an active interest in their children's lives. "Real" parents generally have ties of love to their offspring that a second father or mother in a blended family finds it hard to duplicate. Most parents report a tendency to favor their own biological child over the child that joined their family late in life. Interestingly enough, although most couples are determined to gain sole custody before the divorce, after the divorce many are glad they were granted only joint custody. That gives individuals the chance to be with their children half the time; during the other half they can date, wash their hair, clean the apartment, or get caught up on work.

Though the nation talks sanctimoniously about the sanctity of the family, America could and must do much better to help real parents and children. The United States remains the only one of 75 industrialized nations that does not have a government-sponsored family policy that provides some form of paid maternity benefits, health care for women and children, parental leave, and subsidized child care (Kamerman, 1980a; Silverstein, 1991). Recently, family lawyer and sociologist Mary Ann Mason (1988) proposed that America rethink its national policy regarding families. She suggested that society should provide maternity and pediatric care for families without insurance. It should adopt a caregiver income, which would allow caregivers with infants to stay home to tend their children until the children are old enough to enroll in day care. Parents should be allowed to take a bigger tax deduction for children; preschool education should be subsidized. Child care should be provided for older children so they need not be "latchkey" children.

If couples are divorced, all states should strictly enforce divorce decrees; they should automatically withhold child-support payments from parental income. To Americans many of these protective measures sound revolutionary; to Europeans, who care more about their children (if national action constitutes a guide), such provisions seem necessary. For example, Sweden guarantees intensive prenatal care, total medical coverage for childbirth, and postnatal care for mothers and babies. As a consequence, Sweden can claim the lowest rates of infant mortality in the world with only 10 infant deaths per 1000 (Adams & Winston, 1980). The United States has 18 infant deaths per 1000. Sweden also has a parental leave system. Every family receives a nine-month allowance to help with the expenses generated by a new baby. If both parents are employed, they are also entitled to nine months' leave of absence between them at 90% pay and an additional three months at reduced pay. After the parents return to work they are allowed a maximum of 60 days per year for either one of them to stay home with a sick child. Parents with children under the age of 8 may work a six-hour day rather than the traditional eight, but with a corresponding reduction in pay (Sidell, 1986). America is the only industrialized nation that does not provide paid maternity leaves. The minimum paid leave other industrialized countries grant to caretakers is 12 weeks; most European countries grant caretakers five months leave (Sidell, 1986).

In America, many such proposals abound in a national atmosphere of growing crisis and concern. Perhaps with the end of the Cold War, a few dollars of money formerly aimed at the production of nuclear missiles could be sent the way of children and their struggling parents. A society could possibly derive a few benefits by investing in its children!

Developing a Social Network

Eighty-four percent of the divorced claim that their relatives, friends, and other acquaintances were extremely supportive in the aftermath of their split-up. Nonetheless, most divorcees must do the work to develop a broader social network. Their old "married" friends just don't seem to be enough. One man observed:

> Mostly we had a group of friends in common. We ran around with a group of other married couples. . . . I think most of them knew it was coming. I still see some of them occasionally and we're friendly, but my main social group now is very different. I think it was mostly my idea and my doing to break up with the group. I used to get invitations and such from them but I wanted to end it. I was single and they were all married and I was sort of out of place. (Spanier & Casto, 1979, p. 224)

In Chapter 1, Beginnings, we discussed the strategy that seems to work best for meeting dates and potential mates: Don't seek mates; look for friends. The same advice holds true for the newly separated and divorced. Men and women who are eager to reenter the world should begin—for social as well as intrinsic purposes—by starting to reengage in activities they enjoy. Almost any newspaper has a weekend column listing upcoming activities. People may choose to sign up for the symphony or barbershop chorus, go on a hike with the Sierra Club, join a walking tour of the nearby university or Chinatown neighborhood. They can attend quilting classes, band or rock 'n' roll concerts, gay or lesbian support groups, Mothers Against Drunken Driving; they can volunteer for neighborhood justice centers, join singles groups, Parents Without Partners, career networking groups, sports teams, computer workshops, ethnic associations. Once again, the aim is not to find a lover (that will come in time) but to find a few best friends and a number of acquaintances, folks you can call on the spur of the moment when you want to go to dinner, shopping, a movie, a concert, a walk to the beach or even to Paris. Eventually, dating and the formation of new relationships follow in the wake of participation in new activities and meeting new people.

Starting Over: Remarriage

Most couples eventually remarry. Almost all men remarry shortly after divorce. Whether or not women remarry depends on their age. Lenore Weitzman (1985) wrote:

> If she is under thirty, she has a 75 percent chance of remarrying. But her chances diminish significantly as she grows older: between thirty and forty, the proportion is closer to 50 percent, and if she is forty or older, she has only a 28 percent chance of remarriage. (p. 204)

The average length of time between divorce and remarriage is just under two years (National Center for Health Statistics, 1984).

Relationships can make us smarter. They certainly shape what we look for in the next relationship. Therapists used to be very pessimistic about the chances that couples who were remarrying would succeed the second time around. They thought that people would be drawn, zombielike, to select the same types of mismatched partners again and again.

We do not believe that. When we are young, most of us, when it comes to understanding love relationships, are imbeciles. We look for a cute person with a great body. We are driven by our hormones and the need to impress our friends.

After being kicked around in the quirky world of love, many people become wiser. One researcher (Albrecht, 1979) found that 88% of remarried couples stated that their present marriage was "much better" than the former marriage that had ended in divorce, and that 65% felt that the experience gained in the earlier marriage helped them in adjusting to the present one. We have had many relatives, friends, and clients go from intense suffering in a disastrous first marriage to bliss in a second. They learned from suffering. Now they knew better how to choose. Some of the pessimists about the prospects for second marriages may have done their research when divorces were rarer and perhaps numbered a higher ratio of troubled individuals. Today, in an age of higher marital expectations and simpler divorce laws, divorce hardly ranks as aberrant behavior by maladjusted folks; it has become a commonplace activity carried on by the normal range of human beings.

People, however, do not *always* become wiser with experience. There are some data suggesting that many face bleak prospects in their second marriages. Janet Farrell and Howard Markman (1986), for example, studied couples immediately before their marriages who were about to be married for the first (FM) or second (RM) time. They painted a picture of the couple about to marry for the second time that made the problems they can face emerge with stark clarity.

First, FM couples are more similar—in age, education, and religion—than are the RMs. In one study, Farrell and Markman (1986) interviewed 12 RM and 13 FM couples. First they asked them to fill out the marital preferences questionnare twice—once to indicate their attitudes, values, and beliefs concerning such salient marital issues as finances, sex roles, and children. The second time they were asked to guess their partners' answers. The data revealed that the RMs were at a double disadvantage. They were less similar than the FM couples in their attitudes—but they didn't know it. They were also less accurate than the FMs at knowing where their partners stood.

The authors portrayed a typical, problematic remarriage couple. Their self-esteem has been shattered by their first divorce. They are lonely and perhaps desperate to remarry but know that their options are limited. They are less valuable in the dating market than they once were, particularly in a culture in which age counts as a handicap. Women stand at a further, special disadvantage. Five out of six RM women had custody of their children; only one in 10 fathers did. The RM women had far lower incomes than did the RM men. They were so eager for things to go well that they were afraid to express their real feelings about issues to their mates. "Let it wait." They temporarily chose to sacrifice affective rewards for emotional and financial security. Hence, of course, a time bomb lay waiting to go off.

The problem is compounded by the fact that the RMs are likely to have many problems to work out. They have emotional entanglements, financial obligations, and children from their previous marriages with which to deal. These last two factors are often cited as the two biggest problems in remarriage (Cherlin, 1978; Messinger, 1976). So we find structural difficulties when it comes to remarriage, compensated in some circumstances by the increased knowledge and intelligence of the actors in the play.

In any case, most couples are happy with their remarriages. One study asked couples which was happiest—their first marriage or their current one? They generally agreed that their second marriage was better (Albrecht, 1979). Researchers conclude that "the second marriage usually benefits by comparison to the first. It is as if individuals moved from a dreary, unpleasant job to a better one" (Furstenberg & Spanier, 1984, p. 84).

Remarriages are somewhat more likely to end in divorce than are first marriages. About 49% of first marriages end in divorce. About 61% of men and 54% of women who have remarried will experience redivorce as well (Glick, 1984).

DEATH

We die only once, and for such a long time!
                              —Molière

Grief

The death of a loved one is one of the most traumatic experiences people ever face (Beach et al., 1990).

Since old custodians of culture used to regard death as too "morbid" an interest, it was not until the 1940s that investigators began to study bereavement and grief. Today, of course, things have changed. One journal, *Omega,* is totally devoted to publishing research on death and bereavement. Numerous books on death and dying are published each year. Elisabeth Kübler-Ross's (1969) *On Death and Dying* even hit the best-seller charts. In 1944, an incident became the catalyst for research on the subject. Couples and families gathered in the Coconut Grove, a Boston nightclub, to celebrate. The club was jammed. In the midst of the fun, a fire started and quickly swept through the Grove. At the first smell of fire, people panicked. They rushed to the exits. They found some exit doors locked. The remaining exits were soon jammed with bodies. As frantic men and women pushed and shoved to get through the doors, many fell and were trampled underfoot. Four hundred and ninety-one people lost their lives. The Boston community sat stunned.

Stages of Grief

Shock and Numbness   Psychiatrist Erich Lindemann (1944) set out to study the reactions of bereaved survivors. He detailed the symptomatology of grief. He concluded that grief is a syndrome with distinctive symptoms and a predictable course. [Recently, others have investigated the grieving process. See Solsberry and Krupnick (1984) and Stroebe and Stroebe (1987).] This research showed that, whether or not the loss was anticipated, the most frequent immediate reaction following death is shock, numbness, and a sense of disbelief. Because the reality of the death has not yet penetrated awareness, survivors may appear to be accepting and coping well.

An example: On December 7, 1988, an earthquake rumbled through Leninaka, Armenia. In a matter of hours, 55,000 men, women, and children were dead—buried beneath the rubble. Their family and friends stood stolidly at the scene in 20 degree below zero weather, refusing to leave, waiting for rescue workers. Newspeople asked how they were managing to cope so well when their families had been decimated. One man observed: "Before, if someone died, you were expected to cry. If you didn't, people said 'You have a heart of stone.' Now no one cries. All our hearts have turned to stone."

Despair and a Sense of Loss   Eventually, in the hours or months following the death, numbness turns to an intense feeling of loss and pain. Vivian Gornick (1987) depicted her mother's reaction to her father's sudden death this way:

> My father died at four o'clock in the morning on a day in late November. A telegram was delivered at five-thirty from the hospital where he had lain, terrified, for a week under an oxygen tent they said would save his life but I knew better. He had had three heart seizures in five days. The last one killed him. He was fifty-one years old. My mother was forty-six. My brother was nineteen. I was thirteen. . . .

"Oh," my mother screamed.

"Oh, my God," my mother screamed.

"Oh, my God, help me," my mother screamed.

The tears fell and rose and filled the hallway and ran into the kitchen and down across the living room and pushed against the walls of the two bedrooms and washed us all away. . . .

She was consumed by a sense of loss so primeval she had taken all grief into her. Everyone's grief. That of the wife, the mother, and the daughter. Grief had filled her, and emptied her. She had become a vessel, a conduit, a manifestation. A remarkable fluidity, sensual and demanding, was now hers. She'd be lying on the couch a rag doll, her eyes dull, unseeing, tongue edging out of a half-open mouth, arms hanging slack. Suddenly she'd jerk straight up, body tense and alert, eyes sharp, forehead bathed in sweat, a vein pulsing in her neck. Two minutes later she was thrashing about, groveling against the couch, falling to the floor, skin chalky, eyes squeezed shut, mouth tightly compressed. It went on for hours. For days. For weeks, and for years. (pp. 62–63)

During this phase, searching behaviors—dreams in which the deceased is still alive, seeing the deceased in the street, and other misperceptions, illusions, and hallucinations—are common. When the lost person fails to return, these perceptions diminish and despair sets in. People become sad, moody, guilty, angry, irritable, lonely, anxious, and restless. They have difficulty in concentrating. Offers of comfort and support are often spurned (Averill, 1968). Researchers (Clayton, 1982) find that one-third of all widowers are still sad, crying, and depressed more than a year after their wives' deaths.

Some grieving people express their feelings in a variety of physical symptoms (Solsberry & Krupnick, 1984). They cry easily. Their stomachs are often upset. They may eat too little or too much. One moment they are agitated and restless, the next they can barely move. They can't sleep or they sleep all the time. They lack interest in the outside world and often give up the friends and activities they used to enjoy. They exist in pain. They may begin to eat excessively, drink, or take drugs (Beach et al., 1990). In Box 14.7, Wolfgang and Margaret Stroebe (1987) listed the symptoms of grief.

Investigators find that bereavement increases the likelihood of a host of mental and physical problems (Klerman & Clayton, 1984; Laudenslager & Reite, 1984; Stroebe & Stroebe, 1987; Troupmann & Hatfield, 1987). Bereavement (1) increases a person's vulnerability to mental illness; (2) produces a variety of physical symptoms (including migraines, headaches, facial pain, rashes, indigestion, peptic ulcers, weight gain or loss, heart palpitations, chest pain, asthma, infections, and fatigue); (3) aggravates existing illnesses; (4) causes physical illness; (5) predisposes a person to engage in risky behaviors—such as smoking, drinking, and drug use; and (6) increases the likelihood of death.

For example, C. Murray Parkes (1964) found that of 4486 widowers, 55 years or older, 213 died within the first six months of their mates' deaths. This was 40% above the expected rate. After six months, the rates gradually fell back to normal. The stress of bereavement may elevate the risk of death in several ways. It may lead to depression, and the depressed may then neglect their own health (Satariano & Syme, 1981); or in extreme cases, depression may lead to drug abuse and/or suicide (Schuckit, 1977, Sendbuehler & Goldstein, 1977). The stress may

Box 14.7 GRIEF SYMPTOMS

Symptom	Description
Attitudes toward self, the deceased, and the environment	
Low self-esteem	Feelings of worthlessness, inadequacy, and failure
Self-reproach	Guilt
Hopelessness; helplessness	Thoughts of death and suicide; pessimism about the present and future
Sense of unreality	Feeling of "not being there," as if one is watching events that are happening to someone else
Suspiciousness	Doubting the motives of those who offer help or advice
Interpersonal problems	Rejection of friendship and withdrawal from social functions
Attitudes toward the deceased	Yearning for the deceased; idealization; imitation of his or her behavior; ambivalence; images of the deceased, often very vivid, almost hallucinatory; firm conviction of having seen him or her; preoccupation with the memory of the deceased and the need to talk, sometimes incessantly, about him or her
Emotional reactions	
Depression	
Anxiety	
Guilt	
Anger and hostility	
Inability to feel pleasure	
Loneliness	
Behavioral reactions	
Agitation	Tenseness, restlessness, jitteryness
Fatigue	
Crying	
Cognitive impairment	
Retardation of thought and concentration	
Physiological changes and bodily complaints	
Loss of appetite or overeating	
Sleep disturbances	Insomnia or oversleeping
Energy loss	
Bodily complaints	These include headaches, back pain, cramps, nausea, vomiting, heartburn, blurred vision, tightness in throat, palpitations, tremor, hair loss, and so forth
Duplicating physical complaints of the deceased	
Increase in drug taking	
Susceptibility to illness and disease	

Source: Adapted from Stroebe & Stroebe, 1987, p. 10.

also lead to dysfunctions in neuroendocrine balance and, in turn, a reduction in immunity to disease (Timiras, 1972). For example, the bereaved are at risk for coronary heart disease and cirrhosis of the liver (Jacobs & Ostfeld, 1977).

Resolution   Finally, the bereaved enter the phase of resolution or reorganization. In this final phase, they can recall the deceased without being overwhelmed by sadness and are at last ready to get reinvolved in the world (Bowlby, 1980).

Some grief shows much of love; But much of grief shows still some want of wit.

—Shakespeare

It used to be thought that the grieving process normally lasted a year or two. For example, in Lindemann's study of 101 bereaved persons, he concluded that normal bereavement followed a set pattern: After the initial shock, the bereaved felt intense sadness, withdrew, protested the loss, and then within a year or so resolved their grief.

This turns out to be not quite true. Things *do* get better after a year or so, but if people really meant a great deal to us, we continue to remember them and to regret their injury, suffering, or death throughout our lives. Sadness wells up when we think of what might have been.

In a variation on this theme, Elaine Hatfield and her colleagues (Wikler, Wasow, & Hatfield, 1981) interviewed both social workers and parents of mentally retarded children. Once, clinicians generally assumed that parents' grief would be time-bound, that following the discovery of the child's condition, parents of a mentally retarded child would go through a predictable grieving process: first shock, then despair, guilt, withdrawal, acceptance, and finally "adjustment" (Parks, 1977). But what parents actually reported was that they experienced *chronic sorrow*. Again and again, on special occasions—when the child should have begun walking or talking, when younger brothers or sisters overtook the retarded child in ability, when other children his or her age were going off to the first grade, or beginning to date, or getting ready for their senior proms, or marrying—parents could not help but mourn what might have been. Other observers have noted the same phenomenon (Joyce, 1984; Olshansky, 1962).

Similarly, Darrin Lehman, Camille Wortman, and Allan Williams (1987) found that men and women continue to mourn the death of those they love for many years. They interviewed people who lost a mate or a child in an automobile accident four or more years previously. They found that their thoughts and conversations were still filled with references to those they had lost. They were more likely to be depressed or suffering from other psychiatric symptoms than their peers. They had difficulty functioning socially. Their marriages were shaky (if it was their child who had died) and they were still plagued with financial problems. The bereaved continued to worry over the accident and wonder what might have been done to prevent it. They were unable to accept, resolve, or find any meaning in their loss.

In time, most people recover from their losses. We continue, of course, to retain bittersweet memories of those we loved but lost. Eventually, however, most people form new attachments, develop new coping skills, go back to work, and begin to live again (Solsberry & Krupnick, 1984).

A few do not: Queen Victoria's Prince Albert died when they were 42. She continued to mourn his death for the next 40 years. During their marriage, Queen Victoria had been extremely dependent on Prince Albert; she could not bear even a night of separation. After his death she continued to idealize him. "To have conceived of him as anything short of perfect—perfect in virtue, in wisdom, in beauty, in all the glories and graces of man—would have been an unthinkable blasphemy" (Strachey, 1921/1971, p. 187). She grieved and wore black throughout her life. Her bed had attached to it, at the back and above "Albert's" pillow, a photograph of his head and shoulders as he lay in his coffin, surrounded by a wreath of immortelles. Victoria resented her subjects because, she thought, they failed to admire Albert as much as he deserved.

Who Suffers Grief the Most?

Some researchers have attempted to determine what kinds of people grieve the most and are most "at risk" following the death of a father or mother, husband or wife, or child (see Klerman & Clayton, 1984). Their findings are interesting. They find that it is children and young adults who suffer the most intensely after a death in the family. (Perhaps older people, those over 60, have experienced so much suffering, illness, and death that a new death does not touch them so profoundly.) Men seem to suffer more from the loss of their mates than do women. (Perhaps this is because men generally have far fewer intimate friends than do women and are less likely to possess the social skills needed to make new close friends. Thus men lack the social support they need after a death.) For both men and women, the loss of a child is more upsetting than any other loss, even if the child has grown to be an adult. The bereaved are most "at risk" if they are of low socioeconomic status. (Perhaps it is hard to cope with both change and poverty.)

Therapists have long argued that the "ideal" of mental health is that rare person who possesses capacities for both close intimacy *and* independence; this kind of person also seems to cope best with the death of a mate. Men and women who were unusually dependent on their mates (like Queen Victoria) suffer especially intense grief after the loss of their mates. So do men and women who had a love–hate relationship with their mates before their death. Couples who were ambivalent about their partners before death are plagued by wrenching and conflicting emotions—guilt and anger as well as loneliness and remorse—after the death.

Not surprisingly, people who had poor mental and physical health *before* their loved one's death suffer even more afterward. Alcoholics and drug users, for example, are more likely to descend more deeply into addiction, grow ill, be hospitalized, and commit suicide or die after their mates' deaths than are their peers.

Some deaths are sudden, others are expected. Sudden deaths—deaths due to car accidents, suicide, homicide, or war—are especially shocking. Usually (more than 80% of the time) family members have at least two weeks' warning that a terminally ill person faces imminent death. The evidence suggests that both the kind of death and the suddenness of a death have an impact on how intensely people mourn. Not surprisingly, they have more trouble dealing with a sudden death than one that was anticipated. If family members are warned that death is close, they have a chance to say all the things they wish to say to the dying person, to ask for their forgiveness, to try to make things "right," and to get the family affairs in order. As a consequence, family members who have some warning of an impending death seem to experience less guilt, anger, and confusion and have fewer practical problems than those who are taken by surprise. Of course, family members who have to cope with a lingering illness may confront unusual stresses and strains as well. The survivors may feel guilty that they were not up to the task of dealing with a slow, painful, and interminable illness. Or they may simply be worn out from trying too hard for too long.

Some types of death pose special risks to the survivors. How well one can cope with the death of a family member who is killed in a war seems to depend on how much "sense" the death makes. If it is seen as a heroic act in defense of one's country, it is easier to bear than if it is seen as an absurd and useless sacrifice. If one's mate committed suicide or was murdered, one's grief is likely to be far more intense than if one's mate died a natural death. Paul Theroux (1977), in *The Consul's File*, reminded us of why a murder represents an assault on the family as well as the victim:

> The least dignified thing that can happen to a man is to be murdered. If he dies in his sleep he gets a respectful obituary and perhaps a smiling portrait; it is how we all want to be remembered. But murder is the great exposer: here is the victim in his torn underwear, face down on the floor, unpaid bills on his dresser, a meagre shopping list, some loose change, and worst of all the fact that he is alone. Investigation reveals what he did that day—it all matters—his habits are examined, his behaviour scrutinized, his trunks rifled, and a balance sheet is drawn up at the hospital giving the contents of his stomach. Dying, the last private act we perform, is made public: the murder victim has no secrets. (p. 123)

Finally, if the bereaved can rely on their families and friends to stand by and help them, they are likely to be better able to cope with death. Immediately after a death, parents are the most important source of support for young men and women. Once they begin to recover, friends become important once again. For the old (whose parents are usually gone), friends rank as most important.

Caring for the Bereaved

In a popular book of etiquette published in England in 1929, Lady Troubridge (1929/1979) advised readers how to behave in the face of death:

> One chief rule to remember . . . is that sorrow is sacred and that it is one of the most unforgivable breaches of good behavior to intrude upon it. . . . The members of the bereaved family should be left as much alone in their grief as possible. (p. 55)

The reason the bereaved should be left to themselves, Lady Troubridge contended, was because they were in danger of breaking down and revealing unseemly emotions:

> It is difficult to keep a firm hold over the emotions at such a time and it is therefore wiser to see no one if there is a chance of breaking down. (p. 57)

Today, by contrast, health care professionals have instituted a variety of programs to help the grieving deal with their loss [see Green (1984) for more information on these programs]. Initially, when patients are hospitalized, health care professionals try to make sure that the family and friends of the dying receive adequate updates on the course of the illness. Nurses visit patients each day to furnish them information and find out what kinds of information they want transmitted to their various relatives. The nurses then carry these progress reports to the family. The nurses try to be sympathetic and they are supposed to make it clear that they have time to help. Thus they can help family members deal with the grief, anger, guilt, fear, and confusion they feel when they discover their family member or friend is going to die. Most people want to know in minute detail exactly what is happening to the patient while alive, and what caused the death. The nurses also try to prepare the bereaved for the grief reactions and physical symptoms they may experience in the months to come. The survivors generally are less anxious if forewarned about reactions that would otherwise seem "bizarre." Nurses may help the bereaved notify the next of kin and make burial plans. They may also help survivors make appointments with visiting nurses, homemaker services, public welfare, or other community agencies.

Health care professionals may refer survivors to specialized support groups. A variety of groups, such as Widows to Widows, help people come to terms with their grief and cope with their vastly changed lives (Osterweis, 1984). The principle behind such programs is that recently bereaved persons can be helped most by others who themselves have been through the same things and who have survived. Another widow can serve as a role model as well to help the bereaved gain perspective on their emotions (Silverman & Cooperband, 1975).

Many recently bereaved men and women need nothing more than a friend who possesses the patience to let the sorrowing survivor talk over the loss. Others need reassurance that their reactions are normal—that they are not "going crazy." Friends can also provide a great deal of practical support (picking up flowers from here, a few groceries from there), especially in the first few weeks after the death.

Immediately after the death, many bereaved men and women are tempted to "make a fresh start"—to move to a new city with "no memories," to take another job, to do what they've always wanted to do. Those who do make such precipitous moves often come to regret it. When people are grief stricken, their judgment can be erratic. Plans that seemed a good idea at the time are often found to be wildly impractical later on. Worse yet, such sudden changes may cut men and women off from just that social support they desperately need.

Finally, after a long period of mourning, friends and acquaintances often sense that the bereaved hopes to be given permission to *stop* grieving. They long to be assured that it will not constitute a dishonor to the memory of the deceased if they put the past behind them and begin to invest in new relationships and a new life. Finally, if mourning is especially severe or prolonged, the bereaved may benefit from talking to a psychologist or psychiatrist.

CONCLUSION

Death stands as the ultimate ending to relationships. Before 1750, in nearly all cultures, it was the *only* ending to most marriages and relationships. They were not generally "love" affairs as much as social arrangements. Expectations for emotional, intellectual, and sexual fulfillment were minimal compared to ours today. Divorce was impermissible and most individuals—certainly women—died having had only one relationship. As best as we can tell, the ideas of "relationships" of our forebears bore little resemblance to ours in the late twentieth century.

Today, most people experience the pain of an ended love affair several times. We go through many relationships. And while we focus sometimes on the pathos of lost love and long for the supposed stabilities of the past, it is well to remind ourselves of a couple of ideas. First, humans tend to learn through pain. By the experience of many relationships, the opportunities for gaining wisdom about ourselves, others, and the complexities of love do exist. Without doubt, most moderns are significantly smarter about love, through experience, than our ancestors. And second, more of us *have* loved. The taste of love can be so sweet (or bittersweet) that lost love only deters us from seeking more love for a short while. Fewer lines of poetry are spoken more frequently, almost to the point of cliché, than those composed in 1850, at the height of the Romantic Movement, by Alfred, Lord Tennyson: "'Tis better to have loved and lost / Than never to have loved at all."

Epilogue: Starting Over

Lovers are deeply disappointed when their most recent love affair, which began so promisingly, comes to a sad or bitter end (as, more often than not, love affairs do). Yet they find themselves, after a period of grieving, trying again. This is testimony to the lingering power of the now-somewhat-tarnished Dream of Love. The traditional dream, with its long, honored lineage in love poetry, courtly love, literary romances, and grand opera, tells of *Unrequited Love*. The modern dream is for love happily-ever-after, made most accessible and glamorous in movies, on television, and in the mass media generally. Many measure the success or failure of their very existences by one criterion: Have they found their "forever romance"?

One who simply peruses this volume, let alone the discerning reader, has discovered how many things can send a relationship on the skids; the miracle may be that good relationships can ever survive and prosper. Yet even though disappointment with love abounds and marriages that do *not* end in divorce tend to fall well short of The Dream, an interesting truth remains: Most people claim they have lived happy lives. This may be denial at work or else an example of the remarkable adaptability of the human species.

Both denial and adaptability are undeniable human qualities; but we think additional factors are at work. For one thing, most of us are glad to have experienced the thrill of love at all, even if it turned out to be short-lived or ended badly. Falling in passionate or shaping companionate love allows us to experience a range of intense emotions, sexual excitement, and the joys of intimacy that can rarely be matched in other realms. For another, most persons have felt the sweetness of good friendships and family loyalty and deeply cherish them.

Finally, there are *many* things that make life rich and fulfilling. Besides romance and intimacy, besides friendship and family, we can discover a multitude of wonders in satisfying and challenging work, in intellectual and aesthetic pas-

sions, and in intensely enjoyable physical delights: swimming in the ocean, skiing down a mountain, making love. The person who demands a lasting and enriching love affair as *the* standard for happiness approaches life as though it were a lottery. The odds against attaining a lifetime romance may not be as long as those for winning the lottery, but the odds are not terrifically in favor of achieving that sort of love.

Nonetheless we do try, and the chief reason may not have as much to do with Hollywood as with the fact that we all know some who have achieved the long and happy marriage. When it occurs we see two people who are not alone, who have developed a shared and rich history together, who look happy, and who can grow old together in harmony and intimacy. Perhaps we can count on the fingers of one hand the number of such couples who have truly achieved this sweet state. (We have all also encountered divorce announcements from couples we were certain had achieved the "perfect marriage.") But wonderful relationships do exist and The Dream is not a total chimera.

We hope that some of the ideas contained in this book can help a few people become smarter about love, make better selections of dates and mates, and, when they do, create relationships that can flower. Though many would-be lovers long to have this happen magically and without effort, the odds of the lottery can be significantly reduced when we use our brains. There are many dimensions to the love experience—both positive and negative—that we now can identify and understand. Knowledge, intelligence, and good judgment about love are indeed attainable (though some ignorant folk still regard intelligence as the enemy of love). And while being smart about love guarantees nothing, it does improve our chances for making better relationships (see Erich Fromm's comments on the art of loving in Box E.1).

But in the last analysis, we wish to leave the reader of this book about love,

---

Box E.1   THE ART OF LOVING

This attitude—that nothing is easier than to love—has continued to be the prevalent idea about love in spite of the overwhelming evidence to the contrary. There is hardly any activity, any enterprise, which is started with such tremendous hopes and expectations, and yet, which fails so regularly, as love. If this were the case with any other activity, people would be eager to know the reasons for the failure and to learn how one could do better—or they would give up the activity. Since the latter is impossible in the case of love, there seems to be only one adequate way to overcome the failure of love—to examine the reasons for this failure, and to proceed to study the meaning of love.

The first step to take is to become aware that love is an art, just as living is an art; if we want to learn how to love we must proceed in the same way we have to proceed if we want to learn any other art, say, music, painting, carpentry, or the art of medicine or engineering.

What are the necessary steps in learning any art?

The process of learning an art can be divided conveniently into two parts: one, the mastery of the theory; the other, the mastery of the practice. If I want to learn the art of medicine, I must first know the facts about the human body, and about various diseases. When I have all this theoretical knowledge, I am by no means competent in the art of medicine. I shall become a master in this art only after a great deal of practice, until eventually the results of my theoretical knowledge and the results of my practice are blended into one—my intuition, the essence of the mastery of any art.

But, aside from learning the theory and practice, there is a third factor necessary to becoming a master in any art—the mastery of the art must be a matter of ultimate concern; there must be nothing else in the world more important than the art. This holds true for music, for medicine, for carpentry—and for love. And, maybe, here lies the answer to the question of why people in our culture try so rarely to learn this art, in spite of their obvious failures: In spite of the deep-seated craving for love, almost everything else is considered to be more important than love. Success, prestige, money, power—almost all of our energy is used for the learning of how to achieve these aims, and almost none to learn the art of loving.

Could it be that only those things are considered worthy of being learned with which one can earn money or prestige, and that love, which "only" profits the soul, but is profitless in the modern sense, is a luxury we have no right to spend much energy on? (Fromm, 1956, pp. 4–6)

sex, and intimacy with this paradox: The best way to gain fulfilling relationships lies less through obsession with love than with greater efforts toward building a balanced life based on one's unique biology, history, personality, and individuality. Romantic intimacy can bestow on us one of the glories of being alive. But there are other kinds of intimacy and other glories as well that form parts of the gift of life and that can enhance romance or even replace it when necessary: fruitful work, family, friends, fun, children, healing, creation, Mozart, sunrises, and sunsets.

References

Abelard, P., & Heloise. (1974). *The letters of Abelard and Heloise* (B. Radice, Trans.). New York: Penguin Classics.

Abramson, L. Y., Seligman, M. E. P., & Teasdale, J. E. (1986). Learned helplessness in humans: Critique and reformulation. In J. C. Coyne (Ed.), *Essential papers on depression* (pp. 259–301). New York: New York University Press.

Ackerman, D. (1990). *A natural history of the senses.* New York: Random House.

Adams, C. T., & Winston, K. (1980). *Mothers at work.* New York: Longman.

Ahrons, C. R., & Wallisch, L. S. (1987). The relationship between former spouses. In D. Perlman & S. Duck (Eds.), *Intimate relationships: Development, dynamics and deterioration* (pp. 269–296). London: Sage Publications.

Ainsworth, M. D. S. (1989). Attachments beyond infancy. *American Psychologist, 44,* 709–716.

Ainsworth, M. D. S., Blehar, M. C., Waters, E., & Wall, S. (1978). *Patterns of attachment: A psychological study of the strange situation.* Hillsdale, NJ: Erlbaum.

Albrecht, S. L. (1979). Correlates of marital happiness among the remarried. *Journal of Marriage and the Family, 41,* 857–867.

Alexander, J. (1989). *The other side of the street.* London: FONTANA/Collins.

Alighieri, D. (1964). Beatrice. In I. Schneider (Ed.), *The world of love* (Vol. 1, p. 178). New York: George Braziller.

Allen, W. (1982). *Four films of Woody Allen.* New York: Random House.

Allgeier, E. R. (1981). The influence of androgynous identification on heterosexual relations. *Sex Roles, 7,* 321–330.

Allgeier, E. R., & Byrne, D. (1973). Attraction toward the opposite sex as a determinant of physical proximity. *Journal of Social Psychology, 90,* 213–219.

Allgeier, E. R., & Fogel, A. F. (1978). Coital position and sex roles: Responses to cross-sex behavior in bed. *Journal of Consulting and Clinical Psychology, 46,* 588–589.

Allport, G. W. (1961). *Pattern and growth in personality*. New York: Holt, Rinehart & Winston.

Altman, I. (1973). Reciprocity of interpersonal exchange. *Journal for the Theory of Social Behavior, 3,* 249–261.

Altman, I., & Taylor, D. A. (1973). *Social penetration: The development of interpersonal relationships*. New York: Holt, Rinehart & Winston.

Amir, M. (1971). *Patterns in forcible rape*. Chicago: University of Chicago Press.

Angier, N. (1985, January 28). Sexes: Finding trouble in paradise. *Time, 125,* p. 76.

Angier, N. (1991, January 22). A potent peptide prompts an urge to cuddle. *The New York Times,* pp. B5, 8.

Appian of Alexandria. (1962). The Syrian wars. In *Roman history, xi, cap. x.* (Vol. 2) (H. White, Trans.). Cambridge, MA: Loeb Classical Library.

Arafat, I. S., & Cotton, W. L. (1974). Masturbation practices of males and females. *The Journal of Sex Research, 10,* 293–307.

Arendt, H. (1962). The Graebe memorandum. In Contemporary Civilization Staff of Columbia College, Columbia University (Eds.), *Man in contemporary society* (pp. 1070–1073). New York: Columbia University Press.

Argyle, M. (1967). *The psychology of interpersonal behavior*. Baltimore, MD: Penguin Books.

Argyle, M. (1975). *Bodily communication*. New York: International Universities Press.

Argyle, M. (1987). *The psychology of happiness*. London: Methuen.

Argyle, M., & Dean, J. (1965). Eye-contact, distance and affiliation. *Sociometry, 28,* 289–304.

Argyle, M., Lalljee, M., & Cook, M. (1968). The effects of visibility on interaction in a dyad. *Human Relations, 21,* 3–17.

Arnold, M. (1950). An excitatory theory of emotion. In M. L. Reymert (Ed.), *Feelings and emotions: The Mooseheart symposium* (pp. 11–33). New York: McGraw-Hill.

Aron, A., & Aron, E. N. (1986). *Love and the expansion of self: Understanding attraction and satisfaction*. New York: Hemisphere Publishing.

Aronfreed, J. (1970). The socialization of altruistic and sympathic behavior: Some theoretical and experimental analyses. In J. Macaulay & L. Berkowitz (Eds.), *Altruism and helping behavior* (pp. 103–126). New York: Academic Press.

Aronson, E., Willerman, B., & Floyd, J. (1966). The effect of a pratfall on increasing interpersonal attractiveness. *Psychonomic Science, 4,* 157–158.

Asch, S. E. (1946). Forming impressions of personality. *Journal of Abnormal and Social Psychology, 41,* 258–290.

Astin, A. (1985). *The American freshman: National norms*. Los Angeles: UCLA Graduate School of Education.

Atkinson, J., & Huston, T. L. (1984). Sex role orientation and division of labor early in marriage. *Journal of Personality and Social Psychology, 46,* 330–345.

Atwater, L. (1982). *The extramarital connection: Sex, intimacy, and identity*. New York: Irvington Publishers.

Austin, W., & Hatfield, E. (1974). Reactions to confirmations and disconfirmations of expectancies of equity and inequity. *Journal of Personality and Social Psychology, 30,* 208–216.

Averill, J. R. (1968). Grief: Its nature and significance. *Psychological Bulletin, 70,* 721–748.

Averill, J. R. (1982). *Anger and aggression: An essay on emotion.* New York: Springer-Verlag.

Averill, J. R. (1983). Studies on anger and aggression: Implications for theories of emotions? *American Psychologist, 38,* 1145–1160.

Ayllon, T., & Azrin, N. (1968). *The token economy: A motivational system for therapy and rehabilitation.* New York: Appleton-Century-Crofts.

Ax, A. F. (1953). The physiological differentiation between fear and anger in humans. *Psychosomatic Medicine, 15,* 433–442.

Baez, J. (1990). *And a voice to sing with.* New York: Signet.

Bandura, A. (1982). Self-efficacy mechanism in human agency. *American Psychologist, 37,* 122–147.

Bandura, A. (1983). Psychological mechanisms of aggression. In R. Geen & E. Donnerstein (Eds.), *Aggression: Theoretical and empirical reviews* (Vol. 1, pp. 1–40). New York: Academic Press.

Bandura, A., & Walters, R. H. (1959). *Adolescent aggression.* New York: Ronald Press.

Banks, S. P., Altendorf, D. M., Greene, J. O., & Cody, M. J. (1987). An examination of relationship disengagement: Perceptions, breakup strategies, and outcomes. *Western Journal of Speech Communication, 51,* 19–41.

Banner, L. W. (1983). *American beauty.* Chicago: University of Chicago Press.

Barbach, L. G. (1976). *For yourself: The fulfillment of female sexuality.* Garden City, NY: Anchor Books.

Barbee, A. P., Gulley, M. R., & Cunningham, M. R. (1990). Support seeking in personal relationships. *Journal of Social and Personal Relationships, 7,* 531–540.

Barclay, A. M. (1969). The effect of hostility on physiological and fantasy responses. *Journal of Personality, 37,* 651–667.

Barling, J. (1990). Employment and marital functioning. In F. D. Fincham & T. N. Bradbury (Eds.), *The psychology of marriage: Basic issues and applications* (pp. 201–225). New York: Guilford Press.

Barnett, R. C., & Baruch, G. K. (1987). Social roles, gender and psychological distress. In R. C. Barnett, L. Biener, & G. K. Baruch (Eds.), *Gender and stress* (pp. 122–143). New York: Free Press.

Baron, R. A. (1977). *Human aggression.* New York: Plenum Press.

Bartholomew, K. (1990). Avoidance of intimacy: An attachment perspective. *Journal of Social and Personal Relationships, 7,* 147–178.

Bartholomew, K., & Horowitz, L. M. (1991). Attachment styles among young adults: A test of a four-category model. *Journal of Personality and Social Psychology, 61,* 226–244.

Baucom, D. H., & Adams, A. N. (1987). Assessing communication in marital interaction. In D. D. O'Leary (Ed.), *Assessment of marital discord* (pp. 139–181). Hillsdale, NJ: Erlbaum.

Baumeister, R. F., & Wotman, S. R. (1991). *Unrequited love: On heartbreak, anger, guilt, scriptlessness, and humiliation.* Unpublished manuscript, Case Western Reserve University, Cleveland, OH.

Bavelas, J. B., Black, A., Lemery, C. R., & Mullett, J. (1987). Motor mimicry as primitive empathy. In N. Eisenberg & J. Strayer (Eds.), *Empathy and its development* (pp. 317–338). New York: Cambridge University Press.

Baxter, L. A. (1984). Trajectories of relationship disengagement. *Journal of Social and Personal Relationships, 1,* 29–48.

Baxter, L. A. (1986). Gender differences in the heterosexual relationship rules embedded in break-up accounts. *Journal of Social and Personal Relationships, 3,* 289–306.

Baxter, L. A. (1987). Self-disclosure and relationship development. In V. J. Derlega & J. Berg (Eds.), *Self-disclosure: Theory, research and therapy* (pp. 155–174). New York: Plenum Press.

Baxter, L., & Bullis, C. (1986). Turning points in developing romantic relationships. *Human Communication Research, 12,* 469–493.

Baxter, L. A., & Wilmot, W. (1984). Secret tests: Social strategies for acquiring information about the state of a relationship. *Human Communication Research, 11,* 171–201.

Baxter, L. A., & Wilmot, W. W. (1985). Taboo topics in close relationships. *Journal of Social and Personal Relationships, 2,* 253–269.

Beach, S. R. H., Arias, I., & O'Leary, K. D. (1987). The relationship of marital satisfaction and social support to depressive symptomatology. *Journal of Psychopathology and Behavioral Assessment, 8,* 305–316.

Beach, S. R. H., Jouriles, E. N., & O'Leary, K. D. (1985). Extramarital sex: Impact on depression and commitment in couples seeking marital therapy. *Journal of Sex and Marital Therapy, 11,* 99–108.

Beach, S. R. H., Sandeen, E. E., & O'Leary, K. D. (1990). *Depression in marriage.* New York: Guilford Press.

Beattie, A. (1989). *Picturing Will.* New York: Vintage Books.

Beauvoir, S. de (1952/1974). *The second sex* (H. M. Parshley, Trans.). New York: Vintage Books.

Beauvoir, S. de (1967). *The woman destroyed* (P. O'Brien, Trans.). New York: Putnam Publishing.

Beck, A. (1967). *Depression: Clinical, experimental, and theoretical aspects.* New York: Hoeber.

Beck, A. (1976). *Cognitive therapy in the emotional disorders.* New York: International Universities Press.

Beck, A. T., Emery, G., & Greenburg, R. L. (1985). *Anxiety disorders and phobias: A cognitive perspective.* New York: Basic Books.

Bee, L. S. (1959). *Marriage and family relations.* New York: Harper & Bros.

Beecher, M., & Beecher, W. (1971). *The mark of Cain: An anatomy of jealousy.* New York: Harper & Row.

Bell, A. G. (1884), Upon the formation of a deaf variety of the human race. *National Academy of Sciences Memoirs, 2,* 177–262.

Bell, A. P., & Weinberg, M. S. (1978). *Homosexualities: A study of diversity among men and women.* New York: Simon & Schuster.

Bell, A. P., Weinberg, M. S., & Hammersmith, S. (1981). *Sexual preference: Statistical appendix.* Bloomington: Indiana University Press.

Bell, S. (1902). A preliminary study of the emotion of love between the sexes. *The American Journal of Psychology, 13,* 325–354.

Belle, D., Burr, R., & Cooney, J. (1987). Boys and girls as social support theorists. *Sex Roles, 17,* 657–665.

Bellew-Smith, M., & Korn, J. H. (1986). Merger intimacy status in adult women. *Journal of Personality and Social Psychology, 50,* 1186–1191.

Belsky, J. (1990). Children and marriage. In F. D. Fincham & T. N. Bradbury (Eds.), *The psychology of marriage: Basic issues and applications* (pp. 172–200). New York: Guilford Press.

Belsky, J., & Rovine, M. (1990). Patterns of marital change across the transition to parenthood: Pregnancy to three years postpartum. *Journal of Marriage and the Family, 52,* 5–19.

Bem, S. L., Martyna, W., & Watson, C. (1976). Sex typing and androgyny: Further explorations of the expressive domain. *Journal of Personality and Social Psychology, 34,* 1016–1023.

Benin, M. H., & Nienstedt, B. C. (1985). Happiness in single- and dual-earner families: The effects of marital happiness, job satisfaction, and life cycle. *Journal of Marriage and the Family, 47,* 975–984.

Benson, H. (1975). *The relaxation response.* New York: Morrow.

Berg, J. H., & McQuinn, R. D. (1986). Attraction and exchange in continuing and noncontinuing dating relationships. *Journal of Personality and Social Psychology, 50,* 942–952.

Berkow, J. H. (1989). *Darwin, sex, and status: Biological approaches to mind and culture.* Toronto: University of Toronto Press.

Bernard, J. (1972). *The sex game.* New York: Atheneum.

Bernard, J. (1973). *The future of marriage.* New York: Bantam Books.

Bernieri, F. J. (1988). Coordinated movement and rapport in teacher–student interactions. *Journal of Nonverbal Behavior, 12,* 120–138.

Bernieri, F. J., Reznick, J. S., & Rosenthal, R. (1988). *Journal of Personality and Social Psychology, 54,* 243–253.

Bernstein, L. (1976). Oh, happy we. *Candide* (pp. 50–57). New York: Schirmer Books.

Bernstein, L. (music), & Wilbur, R., LaTouche, J., & Sondheim S. (lyrics). (1976). *Candide.* New York: Schirmer Books.

Berscheid, E. (1983). Emotion. In H. H. Kelley, E. Berscheid, A. Christensen, J. H. Harvey, T. L. Huston, G. Levinger, E. McClintock, L. A. Peplau, & D. R. Peterson (Eds.), *Close relationships* (pp. 110–168). New York: Freeman.

Berscheid, E. (1984). Compatibility, interdependence, and emotion. In W. Ickes (Ed.), *Compatible and incompatible relationships* (pp. 143–162). New York: Springer-Verlag.

Berscheid, E. (1985). Interpersonal attraction. In G. Lindzey & E. Aronson (Eds.), *Handbook of social psychology* (Vol. II, 3rd ed., pp. 413–484). New York: Random House.

Berscheid, E., & Fei, J. (1977). Romantic love and sexual jealousy. In G. Clanton & L. G. Smith (Eds.), *Jealousy* (pp. 101–114). Englewood Cliffs, NJ: Prentice-Hall.

Berscheid, E., Graziano, W., Monson, T., & Dermer, M. (1976). Outcome dependency: Attention, attribution, and attraction. *Journal of Personality and Social Psychology, 34,* 978–989.

Berscheid, E., & Hatfield, E. (1969). *Interpersonal attraction.* Reading, MA: Addison-Wesley.

Berscheid, E., & Hatfield, E. (1978) *Interpersonal attraction* (2nd ed.). Reading, MA: Addison-Wesley.

Berscheid, E., & Peplau, L. A. (1983). The emerging science of relationships. In H. H. Kelley, E. Berscheid, A. Christensen, J. H. Harvey, T. L. Huston, G. Levinger, E. McClintock, L. A. Peplau, & D. R. Peterson (Eds.), *Close relationships* (pp. 1–19). New York: Freeman.

Berzins, J. I., Welling, M. A., & Wetter, R. E. (1978). A new measure of psychological androgyny based on the Personality Research Form. *Journal of Consulting and Clinical Psychology, 46*, 126–138.

Betzig, L. (1989). Causes of conjugal dissolution. *Current Anthropology, 30*, 654–676.

Bing, L. (1991). *Do or die.* New York: HarperCollins.

Birchler, G. R., Weiss, R. L., & Vincent, J. P. (1975). Multimethod analysis of social reinforcement exchange between maritally distressed and nondistressed spouse and stranger dyads. *Journal of Personality and Social Psychology, 31*, 349–360.

Black, C. (1982). *It will never happen to me!* Denver, CO: M. A. C. Press.

Blanchard, D. C., & Blanchard, R. J. (1982). Violence in Hawaii: A preliminary analysis. In A. Goldstein and M. Segal (Eds.), *Global perspectives on aggression* (pp. 159–192). New York: Pergamon Press.

Blatt, C. S., & Blatt, R. C. (1970). An evolutionary theory of social interaction. Unpublished manuscript.

Bloch, S., Orthous, P., & Santibanez-H, G. (1987). Effector patterns of basic emotions: A psychophysiological method for training actors. *Journal of Social and Biological Structures, 10*, 1–19.

Block, J. H., Block, J., & Morrison, J. (1981). Parental agreement–disagreement on child-rearing orientations and gender-related personality correlates in children. *Child Development, 52*, 965–974.

Blood, R. O., & Wolfe, D. M. (1960). *Husbands and wives: The dynamics of married living.* New York: Free Press.

Bloom, B. L., White, S. W., & Asher, S. J. (1979). Marital disruption as a stressful life event. In G. Levinger & O. C. Moles (Eds.), *Divorce and separation* (pp. 184–200). New York: Basic Books.

Blumstein, P., & Schwartz, P. (1983). *American couples.* New York: Morrow.

Bohannan, P. (1970). *Divorce and after.* Garden City, NY: Doubleday.

Bohm, E. (1967). Jealousy. In A. Ellis & A. Abarbanel (Eds.), *Encyclopedia of sexual behavior* (pp. 56–64). New York: Hawthorne Books.

Boszormenyi-Nagy, I., & Spark, G. M. (1973). *Invisible loyalties.* New York: Harper & Row.

Bowlby, J. (1969). *Attachment and loss: Vol. 1. Attachment.* New York: Basic Books.

Bowlby, J. (1973). Affectional bonds: Their nature and origin. In R. Weiss (Ed.), *Loneliness: The experience of emotional and social isolation* (pp. 38–52). Cambridge, MA: MIT Press.

Bowlby, J. (1980). *Attachment and loss: Vol 3. Sadness and depression.* New York: Basic Books.

Bradbury, T. N., & Fincham, F. D. (1990). Attributions in marriage: Review and critique. *Psychological Bulletin, 107*, 3–33.

Braiker H. B., & Kelley, H. H. (1979). Conflict in the development of close relationships. In R. L. Burgess & T. L. Huston (Eds.), *Social exchange in developing relationships* (pp. 136–168). New York: Academic Press.

Brain, P. F. (1980). Diverse action of hormones on aggression in animals and man. In L. Valzelli & I. Morgese (Eds.), *Aggression and violence: A psychobiological and clinical approach* (pp. 99–149). Milan, Italy: Edizioni/Saint Vincent.

Bramel, D., Taub, B., & Blum, B. (1968). An observer's reaction to the suffering of his enemy. *Journal of Personality and Social Psychology, 8,* 384–392.

Brehm, J. W. (1966). *A theory of psychological reactance.* New York: Academic Press.

Brehm, J. W., Gatz, M., Goethals, G., McCrimmon, J., & Ward, L. (1978). Psychological arousal and interpersonal attraction. *JSAS Catalogue of Selected Documents in Psychology, 8,* 63 (ms. #1724).

Brehm, S. S. (1992). *Intimate relationships* (2nd ed.). New York: McGraw-Hill.

Brenner, M. (1991). Erotomania. *Vanity Fair, 54,* 188–195.

Bretschneider, J. G., & McCoy, N. L. (1988). Sexual interest and behavior in healthy 80- to 102-year-olds. *Archives of Sexual Behavior, 17,* 109–130.

Briere, J., & Malamuth, N. M. (1983). Self-reported likelihood of sexually aggressive behavior: Attitudinal versus sexual explanations. *Journal of Research in Personality, 17,* 315–323.

Bringle, R. G., & Boebinger, K. L. G. (1990). Jealousy and the "third" person in the love triangle. *Journal of Social and Personal Relationships, 7,* 119–134.

Bringle, R. G., & Buunk, B. (1986). Examining the causes and consequences of jealousy: Some recent findings and issues. In R. Gilmour & S. Duck (Eds.), *The emerging field of personal relationships* (pp. 225–240). Hillsdale, NJ: Erlbaum.

Brock, T. C., & Buss, A. H. (1962). Dissonance, aggression, and evaluation of pain. *Journal of Abnormal and Social Psychology, 65,* 197–202.

Brody, J. E. (1991, June 7). A new look at children and divorce. *The New York Times National,* p. A18.

Bronstein, P. (1988). Father–child interaction: Implications for gender role socialization. In P. Bronstein & C. P. Cowan (Eds.), *Fatherhood today: Men's changing role in the family* (pp. 107–126). New York: Wiley.

Brontë, E. (1976). *Wuthering heights.* Oxford, England: Clarendon Press.

Brooke, J. (1991, March 29). "Honor" killing of wives is outlawed in Brazil. *The New York Times,* p. B9.

Broome, B. J. (1983). The attraction paradigm revisited: Responses to dissimilar others. *Human Communication Research, 10,* 137–151.

Broverman, I., Vogel, S., Broverman, D., Clarkson, F., & Rosenkrantz, P. (1972). Sex role stereotypes: A current appraisal. *Journal of Social Issues, 28,* 59–78.

Brown, J. J., & Hart, D. H. (1977). Correlates of females' sexual fantasies. *Perceptual and Motor Skills, 45,* 819–825.

Brown, M., & Auerback, A. (1981). Communication patterns in initiation of marital sex. *Medical Aspects of Human Sexuality, 15,* 107–117.

Bryson, J. B. (1977, August). Situational determinants of the expression of jealousy. In H. Sigall (Chair), *Sexual jealousy.* Symposium presented at the meeting of the American Psychological Association, San Francisco, CA.

Bull, N. (1951/1968). The attitude theory of emotion. *Nervous and Mental Disease Monographs, 81.*

Bull, R., & Rumsey, N. (1988). *The social psychology of facial appearance.* New York: Springer-Verlag.

Bumpass, L. (1984). Children and marital disruption: A replication and update. *Demography, 21,* 71.

Bumpass, L. L., & Sweet, J. A. (1989). National estimates of cohabitation. *Demography, 26,* 615–625.

Burgoon, J. K., & Koper, R. J. (1984). Nonverbal and relational communication associated with reticence. *Human Communication Research, 10,* 601–626.

Burhke, R. A., & Fuqua, D. R. (1987). Sex differences in same- and cross-sex friendships. *Sex Roles, 17,* 339–352.

Burleson, B. R. (1982). The development of comforting communication skills in childhood and adolescence. *Child Development, 53,* 1578–1588.

Burton, R. (1621/1927). *The anatomy of melancholy.* London: Longman.

Buss, A. H. (1961). *The psychology of aggression.* New York: Wiley.

Buss, D. M. (1988a). Love acts: The evolutionary biology of love. In R. J. Sternberg & M. L. Barnes (Eds.), *The psychology of love* (pp. 100–118). New Haven: Yale University Press.

Buss, D. M. (1988b). The evolution of human intrasexual competition: Tactics of mate attraction. *Journal of Personality and Social Psychology, 54,* 616–628.

Buss, D. M. (1989). Sex differences in human mate preferences: Evolutionary hypotheses tested in 37 cultures. *Behavioral and Brain Sciences, 12,* 1–49.

Buss, D. M., & Barnes, M. (1986). Preferences in human mate selection. *Journal of Personality and Social Psychology, 50,* 559–570.

Butler, R. N., & Lewis, M. I. (1986). *Love and sex after 40.* New York: Harper & Row.

Buunk, B. (1980). Intieme relaties met derden. *Eeen sociaal psychologische studie.* Alphen aan de Rign: Samson.

Buunk, B. (1982). Anticipated sexual jealousy: Its relationship to self-esteem, dependency, and reciprocity. *Personality and Social Psychology Bulletin, 8,* 310–316.

Buunk, B., & Bringle, R. G. (1987). Jealousy in love relationships. In D. Perlman and S. Duck (Eds.), *Intimate relationships: Development, dynamics, and deterioration* (pp. 123–147). London: Sage Publications.

Buunk, B. P., & Van Yperen, N. W. (1989). Social comparison, equality, and relationship satisfaction: Gender differences over a ten-year period. *Social Justice Research, 3,* 157–180.

Byatt, A. S. (1985). *Still life.* New York: Vintage Books.

Byrne, D. (1971). *The attraction paradigm.* New York: Academic Press.

Byrne, D., Clore, G. L., & Smeaton, G. (1986). The attraction hypothesis: Do similar attitudes affect anything? *Journal of Personality and Social Psychology, 51,* 1167–1170.

Byrne, D., Ervin, C. R., & Lamberth, J. (1970). Continuity between the experimental study of attraction and "real life" computer dating. *Journal of Personality and Social Psychology, 16,* 157–165.

Byrne, D., & Murnen, S. K. (1988). Maintaining loving relationships. In R. J. Sternberg & Michael L. Barnes (Eds.), *The psychology of love* (pp. 293–310). New Haven: Yale University Press.

Byrne, D., Przybyla, D. P. J., & Infantino, A. (1981, April). *The influence of social threat on subsequent romantic attraction.* Paper presented at the meetings of the Eastern Psychological Association, New York.

Cacioppo, J. T., & Petty, R. E. (1983). *Social psychophysiology: A sourcebook*. New York: Guilford Press.

Cacioppo, J. T., Tassinary, L. G., & Fridlund, A. J. (1990). Skeletomotor system. In J. T. Cacioppo & L. G. Tassinary (Eds.), *Principles of psychophysiology: Physical, social, and inferential elements* (pp. 325–384). New York: Cambridge University Press.

Cahn, D. D. (1990). *Intimates in conflict: A communication perspective*. Hillsdale, NJ: Erlbaum.

Caldwell, J. D., Jirikowski, G. F., Greer, E. R., & Pedersen, C. A. (1989). Medial preoptic area oxytocin and female sexual receptivity. *Behavioral Neuroscience, 103,* 655–662.

Caldwell, M. A., & Peplau, L. A. (1982). Sex differences in same-sex friendship. *Sex Roles, 8,* 721–732.

Caldwell, M. A., & Peplau, L. A. (1984). The balance of power in lesbian relationships. *Sex Roles, 10,* 587–599.

Calhoun, K. S. (1991, August 17). *Social, emotional, and cognitive factors in coercive sexual behavior*. Paper presented at meetings of the American Psychological Association, San Francisco, CA.

Califia, P. (1979). Lesbian sexuality. *Journal of Homosexuality, 4,* 255–266.

Cantor, J., Zillman, D., & Bryant, J. (1975). Enhancement of experienced sexual arousal in response to erotic stimuli through misattribution of unrelated residual excitation. *Journal of Personality and Social Psychology, 32,* 69–75.

Capellanus, A. (1174/1941). *The art of courtly love* (J. J. Parry, Trans.). New York: Norton.

Capote, T. (1958). *Breakfast at Tiffany's* (p. 40). New York: Random House.

Cappella, J. N., & Palmer, M. T. (1990). Attitude similarity, relational history, and attraction: The mediating effects of kinesic and vocal behaviors. *Communication Monographs, 57,* 161–183.

Cappella, J. N., & Planalp, S. (1981). Talk and silence sequences in informal conversations III: Interspeaker influence. *Human Communication Research, 7,* 117–132.

Cargan, L. (1991). *Marriages & families*. New York: HarperCollins.

Carlson, J. G., & Hatfield, E. (1992). *Psychology of emotion*. Fort Worth, TX: Harcourt, Brace, Jovanovich.

Carnegie, D. (1936). *How to win friends and influence people*. New York: Simon & Schuster.

Carns, D. E. (1973). Talking about sex: Notes on first coitus and the double sexual standard. *Journal of Marriage and the Family, 35,* 677–688.

Caro, R. A. (1975). *The power broker: Robert Moses and the fall of New York*. New York: Vintage Books/Random House.

Carter, C. S. (1991). Oxytocin and the human sexual response. *Neuroscience and Biobehavioral Reviews, 15.*

Cate, R. M., Henton, J., Koval, J., Christopher, F. S., & Lloyd, S. A. (1982). Premarital abuse: A social psychological perspective. *Journal of Family Issues, 3,* 79–90.

Cate, R. M., Lloyd, S. A., & Long, E. (1988). The role of rewards and fairness in developing premarital relationships. *Journal of Marriage and the Family, 50,* 443–452.

Cavior, N., Miller, K., & Cohen, S. (1975). Physical attractiveness, attitude similarity and length of acquaintance as contributors to interpersonal attraction among adolescents. *Social Behavior and Personality, 3,* 133–141.

Chamberlain, W. (1991). *A view from above*. New York: Random House.

Cheever, S. (1984). *Home before dark*. Boston: Houghton Mifflin.

Cherlin, A. (1978). Remarriage as an incomplete institution. *American Journal of Sociology, 3*, 634–650.

Cherlin, A. J., Furstenberg, F. F., Jr., Chase-Lansdale, L., Kiernan, K. E., Robins, P. K., Morrison, D. R., & Teitler, J. O. (1991, June 7). Longitudinal studies of effects of divorce on children in Great Britain and the United States. *Science, 252*, 1386–1389.

Cherry, C. (1966). *On human communication: A review, a survey, and a criticism* (2nd ed.). Cambridge, MA: MIT Press.

Christensen, A., & Heavey, C. L. (1990). Gender and social structure in the demand/withdraw pattern of marital conflict. *Journal of Personality and Social Psychology, 59*, 73–81.

Christopher, F. S., & Frandsen, M. M. (1990). Strategies of influence in sex and dating. *Journal of Social and Personal Relationships, 7*, 89–105.

Clanton, G., & Smith, L. G. (Eds.) (1987). *Jealousy*. Lanham, MA: University Press of America.

Clark, K. (1969). *Civilisation*. New York: Harper & Row.

Clark, L., & Lewis, D. (1977). *Rape: The price of coercive sexuality*. Toronto: Women's Educational Press.

Clark, M. S. (1984). Record keeping in two types of relationships. *Journal of Personality and Social Psychology, 47*, 549–557.

Clark, M. S., & Mills, J. (1979). Interpersonal attraction in exchange and communal relationships. *Journal of Personality and Social Psychology, 37*, 12–24.

Clark, M. S., Mills, J., & Powell, M. C. (1986). Keeping track of needs in communal and exchange relationships. *Journal of Personality and Social Psychology, 53*, 94–103.

Clark, M. S., Ouellette, R., Powell, M. C., & Milberg, S. (1987). Recipient's mood, relationship type, and helping. *Journal of Personality and Social Psychology, 53*, 94–103.

Clark, M. S., & Reis, H. T. (1988). Interpersonal processes in close relationships. *Annual Review of Psychology, 39*, 609–672.

Clark, M. S., & Waddell, B. (1985). Perceptions of exploitation in communal and exchange relationships. *Journal of Social and Personal Relationships, 2*, 403–418.

Clark, R. D. (1990). The impact of AIDS on gender differences in willingness to engage in casual sex. *Journal of Applied Social Psychology, 20*, 771–782.

Clark, R. D., III, & Hatfield, E. (1989). Gender differences in receptivity to sexual offers. *Journal of Psychology and Human Sexuality, 2*, 39–55.

Clarke, A. C. (1952). An examination of the operation of residential propinquity as a factor in mate selection. *American Sociological Review, 17*, 17–22.

Clark-Stewart, K. A., & Bailey, B. L. (1989). Adjusting to divorce: Why do men have it easier? *Journal of Divorce, 13*, 75–94.

Clayton, P. J. (1982). Bereavement. In E. S. Paykel (Ed.), *Handbook of affective disorders* (pp. 403–415). New York: Guilford Press.

Clegg, F. (1979). Mammalian pheromones—sense or nonsense? In M. Cook & G. Wilson (Eds.), *Love and attraction* (pp. 63–70). New York: Pergamon Press.

Clewlow, C. (1989). *A woman's guide to adultery*. New York: Poseidon Press.

Cody, M. J. (1982). A typology of disengagement strategies and an examination of the role intimacy, reactions to inequity and relational problems play in strategy selection. *Communication Monographs, 49*, 148–170.

Cohen, S. (1976). *Social and personality development in childhood*. New York: Macmillan.

Cohen, S., & Syme, S. L. (1985). Issues in the study and application of social support. In S. Cohen & S. L. Syme (Eds.), *Social support and health* (pp. 2–33). Orlando, FL: Academic Press.

Coleman, E. (1987). Marital and relationship problems among chemically dependent and codependent relationships. Special Issue: Chemical dependency and intimacy dysfunction, *Journal of Chemical Dependency Treatment, 1*, 39–59.

Colwin, L. (1981). *The lone pilgrim: Stories*. New York: Harper & Row.

Condon, W. S., & Ogston, W. D. (1966). Sound film analysis of normal and pathological behavior patterns. *Journal of Nervous Mental Disorders, 143*, 338–347.

Costa, P. T., Jr., & McCrae, R. R. (1988). Personality in adulthood: A six-year longitudinal study of self-reports and spouse ratings on the NEO personality inventory. *Journal of Personality and Social Psychology, 54*, 853–863.

Cowan, C. P., Cowan, P. A., Heming, G., Garrett, E., Coysh, W., Curtis-Boles, H., & Boles, A. J. (1985). Transitions to parenthood: His, hers, and theirs. *Journal of Family Issues, 6*, 435–450.

Cowan, P., & Cowan, C. (1989). Changes in marriage during the transition to parenthood: Must we blame the baby? In G. Michaels & W. Goldberg (Eds.), *The transition to parenthood: Current theory and research* (pp. 114–154). New York: Cambridge University Press.

Coyne, J. C., & Bolger, N. (1990). Doing without social support as an explanatory concept. *Journal of Social and Clinical Psychology, 9*, 148–158.

Cozby, P. C. (1973). Self-disclosure: A literature review. *Psychological Bulletin, 79*, 73–91.

Cruver, D. (1986, August 20). Husbands and housework: It's still an uneven load. *USA Today*, p. 5D.

Cuber, J. F., & Harroff, P. (1965). *Sex and the significant Americans*. Baltimore, MD: Penguin Books.

Cunningham, M. R., Barbee, A. P., & Pike, C. L. (1990). What do women want? Facialmetric assessment of multiple motives in the perception of male facial physical attractiveness. *Journal of Personality and Social Psychology, 59*, 61–72.

Curran, J. (1975). Convergence toward a single sexual standard. *Social Behavior and Personality, 3*, 189–195.

Curtis, R. C., & Miller, K. (1986). Believing another likes or dislikes you: Behaviors making the beliefs come true. *Journal of Personality and Social Psychology, 51*, 284–290.

Cutrona, C. E. (1982). Transition to college: Loneliness and the process of social adjustment. In L. A. Peplau & D. Perlman (Eds.), *Loneliness: A sourcebook of current theory, research, and therapy* (pp. 291–309). New York: Wiley-Interscience.

Dabbs, J. M. (1990). Testosterone, social class, and antisocial behavior in a sample of 4,462 men. *Psychological Science, 1*, 209–211.

Daly, M., Wilson, M., & Weghorst, S. J. (1982). Male sexual jealousy. *Ethnology and Sociobiology, 3*, 11–27.

D'Andrade, R. G. (1966). Sex differences and cultural institutions. In E. Maccoby (Ed.), *The development of sex differences* (pp. 174–204). Stanford, CA: Stanford University Press.

Darnton, R. (1984). *The great cat massacre*. New York: Basic Books.

Dart, R. A. (1953). The predatory transition from ape to man. *International Anthropological and Linguistic Review, 1*(4), 201–213.

Darwin, C. (1871). *The descent of man, and selection in relation to sex*. New York: Appleton and Co.

Darwin, C. (1872/1965) *The expression of the emotions in man and animals*. Chicago: University of Chicago Press.

Davidson, B. (1984). A test of equity theory for marital adjustment. *Social Psychology Quarterly, 47*, 36–42.

Davidson, J. K., & Hoffman, L. E. (1986). Sexual fantasies and sexual satisfaction: An empirical analysis of erotic thought. *The Journal of Sex Research, 22*, 184–205.

Davis, D., Dewitt, J., & Charney, A. (1986). *Limitation on some rules of conversation: When response behavior is expected and condoned*. Unpublished manuscript. Reno: University of Nevada.

Davis, K. E., & Jones, E. E. (1960). Changes in interpersonal perception as a means of reducing cognitive dissonance. *Journal of Abnormal and Social Psychology, 61*, 402–410.

Davis, M. R. (1985). Perceptual and affective reverberation components. In A. B. Goldstein and G. Y. Michaels (Eds.), *Empathy: Development, training, and consequences* (pp. 62–108). Hillsdale, NJ: Erlbaum.

Davitz, J. R. (1969). *The language of emotion*. New York: Academic Press.

Degler, C. (1980). *At odds: Women and the family in America from the revolution to the present*. Oxford, England: Oxford University Press.

de Jong-Gierveld, J. (1986). Loneliness and the degree of intimacy in interpersonal relationships. In R. Gilmour & S. Duck (Eds.), *The emerging field of personal relationships* (pp. 241–249). Hillsdale, NJ: Erlbaum.

DeLamater, J. (1987). Gender differences in sexual scenarios. In K. Kelley (Ed.), *Females, males, and sexuality: Theories and research* (pp. 127–139). Albany, NY: SUNY Press.

DeLamater, J., & MacCorquodale, P. (1979). *Premarital sexuality: Attitudes, relationships, behavior*. Madison: University of Wisconsin Press.

DeLora, J. S., & Warren, C. A. B. (1977). *Understanding sexual interaction*. Boston: Houghton Mifflin.

DeLuca, J. R. (Ed.) (1980, January). *Fourth special report to the U.S. Congress on alcohol and health*. Washington, DC: U.S. Department of Health, Education, and Welfare.

D'Emilio, J., & Freedman, E., (1988). *Intimate matters: A history of sexuality in America*. New York: Harper & Row.

DePaulo, B. M., Lanier, K., & Davis, T. (1983). Detecting the deceit of the motivated liar. *Journal of Personality and Social Psychology, 45*, 1096–1103.

DePaulo, B. M., Lassiter, G. D., & Stone, J. I. (1982). Attentional determinants of success at detecting deception and truth. *Personality and Social Psychology Bulletin, 8*, 273–279.

Derlega, V. J., & Chaikin, A. L. (1975). *Sharing intimacy: What we reveal to others and why*. Englewood Cliffs, NJ: Prentice-Hall.

Derlega, V. J., Winstead, B. A., Wong, P. T. P., & Greenspan, M. (1987). Self-disclosure and relationship development: An attributional analysis. In M. Roloff & G. Miller (Eds.), *Interpersonal processes: New directions in communication research* (Vol. 14, pp. 172–187). Beverly Hills, CA: Sage Publications.

Dermer, M., & Thiel, D. L. (1975). When beauty may fail. *Journal of Personality and Social Psychology, 31,* 1168–1176.

de Rougemont, D. (1940). *Love in the Western world* (M. Belgion, Trans.). New York: Harcourt, Brace & World.

Descartes, R. (1694/1967). The passions of the soul. *The philosophical work of Descartes* (Vols. 1 and 2, pp. 329–427) (E. S. Haldane & G. R. T. Ross, Trans.). Cambridge, England: Cambridge University Press.

Deutsch, M. (1975). Equity, equality, and need: What determines which value will be used as a basis for distributive justice? *Journal of Social Issues, 31,* 137–149.

Deutsch, M. (1980). Fifty years of conflict. In L. Festinger (Ed.), *Four decades of social psychology* (pp. 46–77). New York: Oxford University Press.

Diamond, M. J., & Shapiro, J. L. (1981). *The paradoxes of intimate relating.* (Available from Dr. J. L. Shapiro, King Kalakaua Center for Humanistic Psychology, Honolulu, HI 96821).

Dickens, C. (1836/1944). *The Pickwick papers.* Garden City, NY: Dodd, Mead.

Dickens, C. (1859/1962). *A tale of two cities.* New York: Oxford University Press.

Dienstbier, R. A. (1978). Emotion-attribution theory: Establishing roots and exploring future perspectives. In H. E. Howe & R. A. Dienstbier (Eds.), *Nebraska Symposium on Motivation* (Vol. 26, pp. 237–306). Lincoln: University of Nebraska Press.

Digman, J. M. (1990). Personality structure: Emergence of the five-factor model. *Annual Review of Psychology, 41,* 417–440.

Digman, J. M., & Inouye, J. (1986). Further specification of the five robust factors of personality. *Journal of Personality and Social Psychology, 50,* 116–123.

Dimberg, U. (1982). Facial reactions to facial expressions. *Psychophysiology, 19,* 643–647.

Dindia, K., & Baxter, L. A. (1987). Maintenance and repair strategies in marital relationships. *Journal of Social and Personal Relationships, 4,* 143–158.

Dion, K., Berscheid, E., & Hatfield, E. (1972). What is beautiful is good. *Journal of Personality and Social Psychology, 24,* 285–290.

Dion, K. L., & Dion, K. K. (1988). Romantic love: Individual and cultural perspectives. In R. J. Sternberg & M. L. Barnes (Eds.), *The psychology of love* (pp. 264–289). New Haven: Yale University Press.

Doob, A. N. (1970). Catharsis and aggression: The effect of hurting one's enemy. *Journal of Experimental Research in Personality, 4,* 291–296.

Douglas, K. (1988). *The ragman's son.* New York: Simon & Schuster.

Douglis, C. (1989, April 14). We've got rhythm. *Pacific Sun,* pp. 3–6.

Doyle, Arthur Conan (1891/1974). *Sherlock Holmes: His most famous mysteries.* New York: Grosset & Dunlap.

Drabble, M. (1969). *The waterfall* (p. 52). New York: Alfred A. Knopf.

Drabble, M. (1972). *The needle's eye.* New York: Alfred A. Knopf.

Drabman, R. S., & Thomas, M. H. (1974). Does media violence increase children's tolerance of real-life aggression? *Developmental Psychology, 10,* 418–421.

Driscoll, R., Davis, K. E., & Lipetz, M. E. (1972). Parental interference and romantic love: The Romeo & Juliet effect. *Journal of Personality and Social Psychology, 24,* 1–10.

Duberman, L. (1975). *The reconstructed family.* Chicago: Nelson-Hall.

Duck, S. (1982). A topography of relationship disengagement and dissolution. In S. Duck (Ed.), *Personal relationships: Vol. 4: Dissolving personal relationships* (pp. 1–30). New York: Academic Press.

Duck, S. (1988). *Handbook of personal relationships: Theory, research, and interventions.* New York: Wiley.

Duck, S. (1991). *Personal relationships and social support.* London: Sage Publications.

Duck, S., & Gilmour, R. (Eds.) (1981a). *Personal relationships: Vol. 1: Studying personal relationships.* New York: Academic Press.

Duck, S. & Gilmour, R. (Eds.) (1981b). *Personal relationships: Vol. 2: Developing personal relationships.* New York: Academic Press.

Duck, S., & Gilmour, R. (Eds.) (1981c). *Personal relationships: Vol. 3: Personal relationships in disorder.* New York: Academic Press.

Duclos, S. E., Laird, J. D., Schneider, E., Sexter, M., Stern, L., & Van Lighten, O. (1989). Emotion-specific effects of facial expressions and postures on emotional experience. *Journal of Personality and Social Psychology, 57,* 100–108.

Durrell, L. (1961). *The Alexandria Quartet: Clea.* New York: Dutton.

Dutton, D. (1979) *The arousal–attraction link in the absence of negative reinforcement.* Toronto: Meetings of the Canadian Psychological Association.

Dutton, D., & Aron, A. (1974). Some evidence for heightened sexual attraction under conditions of high anxiety. *Journal of Personality and Social Psychology, 30,* 510–517.

Eagly, A. H., Ashmore, R. D., Makhijani, M. G., & Kennedy, L. C. (1991). *What is beautiful is good, but . . . ; a meta-analytic review of research on the physical attractiveness stereotype.* Unpublished manuscript. West Lafayette, IN: Purdue University.

Eagly, A. H., & Crowley, M. (1986). Gender and helping behavior: A meta-analytic review of the social psychological literature. *Psychological Bulletin, 100,* 283–308.

Ebbessen, E. G., Duncan, B., & Konecni, V. J. (1975). Effects of content of verbal aggression on future verbal aggression: A field experiment. *Journal of Experimental Social Psychology, 11,* 192–204.

Egeland, J. A., Gerhard, D. S., Pauls, D. L., Sussex, J. N., Kidd, K. K., Allen, C. R., Hostetter, A. M., & Housman, D. E. (1987, February 26). Bipolar affective disorders linked to DNA markers on chromosome 11. *Nature, 325,* 783–787.

Ehrmann, W. (1959). *Premarital dating behavior.* New York: Holt, Rinehart & Winston.

Eibl-Eibesfeldt, I. (1971). *Love and hate.* New York: Holt, Rinehart & Winston.

Eisenberg, N., & Strayer, J. (1987). *Empathy and its development.* New York: Cambridge University Press.

Ekman, P. (1971). Universals and cultural differences in facial expressions of emotion. In J. K. Cole (Ed.), *Nebraska Symposium on Motivation* (Vol. 19, pp. 207–282). Lincoln: University of Nebraska Press.

Ekman, P. (1985). *Telling lies.* New York: Berkley Books.

Ekman, P. (1989). *Why kids lie: How parents can encourage truthfulness.* New York: Charles Scribner's Sons.

Ekman, P. (Ed.) (1982). *Emotion in the human face*. London: Cambridge University Press.

Ekman, P., & Friesen, W. V. (1971). Constants across cultures in the face and emotion. *Journal of Personality and Social Psychology, 17,* 124–129.

Ekman, P., Friesen, W. V., & O'Sullivan, M. (1988). Smiles when lying. *Journal of Personality and Social Psychology, 54,* 414–420.

Ekman, P., Levenson, R. W., & Friesen, W. V. (1983, September 16). Autonomic nervous system activity distinguishes among emotions. *Science, 221,* 1208–1210.

Elkin, M. (1984). Joint custody: In the best interest of the family. In J. Folberg (Ed.), *Joint custody and shared parenting* (pp. 11–15). Washington, DC: Bureau of National Affairs.

Ellis, A., & Harper, R. (1961). *Creative marriage.* New York: Lyle Stuart.

Ellis, H. (1937). *On life and sex: Essays of love and virtue.* Garden City, NY: Garden City Publishing.

Ellwood, D. (1988). *Poor support: Poverty in the American family.* New York: Basic Books.

Emde, R. (1983). The prerepresentational self and its affective core. *Psychoanalytic Study of the Child, 38,* 165–192.

Emerson, R. (1962). Power-dependence relations. *American Sociological Review, 27,* 31–41.

Emery, C. F., & Blumenthal, J. A. (1990). Perceived change among participants in an exercise program for older adults. *Gerontologist, 30,* 516–521.

English, H. B., & English, A. C. (1958). *A comprehensive dictionary of psychological and psychoanalytical terms.* New York: David McKay.

Ephron, N. (1983). *Heartburn.* New York: Pocket Books.

Erikson, E. H. (1959). Identity and the life cycle. *Psychological Issues, 1,* Monograph 1.

Erikson, E. (1982). *The life cycle completed: A review.* New York: Norton.

Exline, R. V., & Long, B. (1971). Reported in M. Argyle (1975), *Bodily communication* (pp. 229–249). New York: International Universities Press.

Exline, R. V., & Winters, L. C. (1965). Affective relations and mutual gaze in dyads. In S. Tomkins & C. Izard (Eds.), *Affect, cognition, and personality* (pp. 319–350). New York: Springer.

Falbo, T., & Peplau, L. A. (1980). Power strategies in intimate relationships. *Journal of Personality and Social Psychology, 38,* 618–628.

Faludi, S. (1991). *Backlash.* New York: Crown Publishers.

Farrell, J., & Markman, H. J. (1986). Individual and interpersonal factors in the etiology of marital distress: The example of remarital couples. In R. Gilmour & S. Duck (Eds.), *The emerging field of personal relationships* (pp. 251–263). Hillsdale, NJ: Erlbaum.

Fay, R. E., Turner, C. F., Klassen, A. D., & Gagnon, J. H. (1989). Prevalence and patterns of same-gender sexual contact among men. *Science, 243,* 338–348.

Fei, J., & Berscheid, E. (1977). *Perceived dependency, insecurity, and love in heterosexual relationships: The eternal triangle.* Unpublished manuscript, Minneapolis: University of Minnesota.

Feingold, A. (1988). Matching for attractiveness in romantic partners and same-sex friends: A meta-analysis and theoretical critique. *Psychological Bulletin, 104,* 226–235.

Feingold, A. (1990). Gender differences in effects of physical attractiveness on romantic attraction: A comparison across five research paradigms. *Journal of Personality and Social Psychology, 5,* 981–993.

Felmlee, D., Sprecher, S., & Bassin, E. (1990). The dissolution of intimate relationships: A hazard model. *Social Psychology Quarterly, 53,* 13–30.

Feshbach, N. D., & Feshbach, S. (1981). *Empathy training and the regulation of aggression: Potentialities and stimulations.* Paper presented at the Western Psychological Association meetings, Los Angeles, CA.

Feshbach, S. (1956). The catharsis hypothesis and some consequences of interaction with aggression and neutral play objects. *Journal of Personality, 24,* 449–462.

Festinger, L. (1951). Architecture and group membership. *Journal of Social Issues, 1,* 152–163.

Finkelhor, D., & Yllo, K. (1985). *License to rape.* New York: Holt, Rinehart & Winston.

Finnegan, D. G., & McNally, E. B. (1989). The lonely journey: Lesbians and gay men who are co-dependent. Special Issue: Co-dependency: Issues in treatment and recovery. *Alcoholism Treatment Quarterly, 6,* 121–134.

Fischer, K. W., Shaver, P. R., & Carnochan, P. (1990). How emotions develop and how they organize development. *Cognition and Emotion, 4,* 81–127.

Fisher, A. E. (1955). *The effects of differential early treatment on the social and exploratory behavior of puppies.* Unpublished doctoral dissertation, Pennsylvania State University, University Park.

Fisher, M., & Stricker, G. (Eds.) (1982). *Intimacy.* New York: Plenum Press.

Fishman, P. M. (1978). Interaction: The work women do. *Social Problems, 25,* 397–406.

Fitzgerald, F. S. (1925). *The great Gatsby.* New York: Charles Scribner's Sons.

Fitzgerald, F. S. (1962). *Tender is the night.* New York: Charles Scribner's Sons.

Fitzpatrick, M. A. (1987). Marriage and verbal intimacy. In V. J. Derlega & J. Berg (Eds.), *Self-disclosure: Theory, research, and therapy* (pp. 131–154). New York: Plenum Press.

Fitzpatrick, M. A. (1988). *Between husbands & wives: Communication in marriage.* London: Sage Publications.

Foa, U. G. (1971). Interpersonal and economic resources. *Science, 171,* 345–351.

Foa, U. G., & Foa, E. B. (1974). *Societal structures of the mind.* Springfield, IL: Charles C. Thomas.

Folberg, J. (1984). Custody overview. In J. Folberg (Ed.), *Joint custody and shared parenting* (pp. 3–11). Washington, DC: Bureau of National Affairs.

Folkes, V. (1982). Forming relationships and the matching hypothesis. *Personality and Social Psychology Bulletin, 8,* 631–636.

Folkes, V. S., & Sears, D. O. (1977). Does everybody like a liker? *Journal of Experimental Social Psychology, 13,* 505–519.

Folkman, S., & Lazarus, R. S. (1980). An analysis of coping in a middle-aged community sample. *Journal of Health and Social Behavior, 21,* 219–239.

Ford, C. S., & Beach, F. A. (1951). *Patterns of sexual behavior.* New York: Harper & Row.

Forman, B. (1982). Reported male rape. *Victimology: An International Journal, 7,* 235–236.

Fowles, J. (1969). *The French lieutenant's woman.* Boston: Little, Brown.

Freedman, J. L. (1978). *Happy people: What happiness is, who has it, and why.* New York: Harcourt Brace Jovanovich.

Freedman, J. L. (1984). Effects of television violence on aggressiveness. *Psychological Bulletin, 96,* 227–246.

French, J. R. P., Jr., & Raven, B. (1959). The bases of social power. In D. Cartwright (Ed.), *Studies in social power* (pp. 150–167). Ann Arbor: University of Michigan Press.

French, M. (1978). *The women's room.* New York: Jove Publishers.

Freud, A. (1966). *The ego and the mechanisms of defense* (rev. ed.). New York: International Universities Press.

Freud, S. (1905). Fragment of an analysis of a case of hysteria. In *Sigmund Freud: Collected Papers. Vol. 3. The International Psycho-Analytical Library, No. 9.* (pp. 13–146) (E. Jones, Ed.; A. & J. Strachey, Trans.). New York: Basic Books.

Freud, S. (1917/1959). Mourning and melancholia. In E. Jones (Ed.), *Sigmund Freud: Collected papers. Vol. 4. The International Psycho-analytical Library, No. 10* (pp. 152–170) (J. Riviere, Trans.). New York: Basic Books.

Freud, S. (1922). Certain neurotic mechanisms in jealousy, paranoia, and homosexuality. In E. Jones (Ed.), *Collected papers* (Vol. II, p. 213). London: Hogarth Press.

Freud, S. (1953). Contributions to the psychology of love: A special type of choice of objects made by men. In E. Jones (Ed.), *Collected papers* (Vol. 4, pp. 192–202). London: Hogarth Press.

Friday, N. (1973). *My secret garden.* New York: Pocket Books.

Frodi, A. M., Lamb, M. E., Leavitt, L. A., Donovan, W. L., Neff, C., & Sherry, D. (1978). Fathers' and mothers' responses to the faces and cries of normal and premature infants. *Developmental Psychology, 14,* 490–498.

Fromm, E. (1956). *The art of loving.* New York: Harper & Row.

Frost, D. E., & Stahelski, A. J. (1988). The systemic measurement of French and Raven's bases of social power in workgroups. *Journal of Applied Social Psychology, 18,* 375–389.

Frost, J. H., & Wilmot, W. W. (1978). *Interpersonal conflict.* Dubuque, IA: Wm. C. Brown Group.

Furstenberg, F., Jr. (1983). *Marital disruption and childcare.* Invited talk, Catholic University, Washington, DC.

Furstenberg, F. F., Jr., & Spanier, G. B. (1984). *Recycling the family: Remarriage after divorce.* Beverly Hills, CA: Sage Publications.

Gadlin, H. (1977). Private lives and public order: A critical view of the history of intimate relationships in the United States. In G. Levinger & H. L. Rausch (Eds.), *Perspectives on the meaning of intimacy* (pp. 33–72). Amherst: University of Massachusetts Press.

Gadpaille, W. (1975). *The cycles of sex.* New York: Charles Scribner's Sons.

Gagnon, J. H. (1977). *Human sexualities.* Glenview, IL: Scott, Foresman.

Gallagher, W. (1986, May). The dark affliction of mind and body. *Discover,* pp. 66–76.

Gallant, M. (1957). *My heart is broken.* New York: Penguin Books.

Gallup Poll. (1989). *Marriage satisfaction.* Los Angeles: Los Angeles Times Syndicate.

Galton, F. (1884). Measurement of character. *Fortnightly Review, 42,* 179–185.

Gambrill, E., & Richey, C. (1985). *Taking charge of your social life.* Belmont, CA: Wadsworth Publishing.

Gay, P. (1986). *The bourgeois experience: The tender passion.* New York: Oxford University Press.

Gayford, J. J. (1979). Battered wives. *British Journal of Hospital Medicine, 22,* 496–503.

Gazzaniga, M. S. (1985). *The social brain: Discovering the networks of the mind.* New York: Basic Books.

Gebhard, P. H. (1968). Postmarital coitus among widows and divorcees. In P. Bohannan (Ed.), *Divorce and after* (pp. 81–96). Garden City, NY: Doubleday.

Gerbner, G., Gross, L., Segnorielli, N., & Morgan, M. (1980). Television violence, victimization, and power. *American Behavioral Scientist, 23,* 705–716.

Gibbs, N. (1991, June 3). When is it rape? *Time,* pp. 48–54.

Gilligan, C. (1982). *In a different voice.* Cambridge, MA: Harvard University Press.

Glass, D. C. (1964). Changes in liking as a means of reducing cognitive discrepancies between self-esteem and aggression. *Journal of Personality, 32,* 520–549.

Glauberman, S. (1991, September 17). Miss America: Old ex-beau troubles. *The Honolulu Advertiser,* pp. A1, A4.

Glick, P. C. (1984). Marriage, divorce, and living arrangements: Prospective changes. *Journal of Family Issues, 5,* 7–26.

Glick, P. C. (1989). Remarried families, stepfamilies and stepchildren: A brief demographic profile. *Family Relations, 38,* 24–37.

Goldstein, J. W., & Rosenfeld, H. (1969). Insecurity and preference for persons similar to oneself. *Journal of Personality, 37,* 253–268.

Goldwater, B. C., & Collins, M. L. (1985). Psychologic effects of cardiovascular conditioning: A controlled experiment. *Psychosomatic Medicine, 47,* 174–181.

Goleman, D. (1984, November 20). Psychologists starting to take measure of love. *The New York Times,* p. 20.

Goleman, D. (1985, September 10). Patterns of love charted in studies. *The New York Times,* p. Y13.

Goleman, D. (1986, April 1). Two views of marriage explored: His and hers. *The New York Times,* p. Y19.

Goodman, E. (1991, May 3). Sexual assault's "gray area." *The Honolulu Advertiser,* p. A22.

Goodwin, G. (1942). *The social organization of the western Apache.* Chicago: University of Chicago Press.

Gornick, V. (1987). *Fierce attachments: A memoir.* New York: Touchstone Books.

Gottman, J. M. (1979). *Marital interaction: Experimental investigations.* New York: Academic Press.

Gottman, J., Notarius, C., Gonso, J., & Markman, H. (1976). *A couple's guide to communication.* Champaign, IL: Research Press.

Gould, J. (1951 March 4). Costello TV's first headless star; only his hands entertain audience. *The New York Times,* p. 1.

Gouldsbury, C., & Sheane, H. (1911). *The Great Plateau of Northern Rhodesia.* London: Edward Arnold.

Gove, W. R., Hughes, M., & Style, C. B. (1983). Does marriage have positive effects on the psychological well-being of the individual? *Journal of Health and Social Behavior, 24,* 122–131.

Graham, J. (1991, April). Why women leave you. Do you want the truth? *GQ*, pp. 100–101. London: Condé Nast Publications.

Grauerholz, E. (1987). Balancing the power in dating relationships. *Sex Roles, 17*, 563–570.

Gray-Little, B., & Burks, N. (1983). Power and satisfaction in marriage: A review and critique. *Psychological Bulletin, 93*, 513–538.

Greeley, A. M., Michael, R. T., & Smith, T. W. (1990). A most monogamous people: Americans and their sexual partners. *Society, 27* 36–42.

Green, M. (1984). Roles of health professionals and institutions. In M. Osterweis, F. Solomon, & M. Green (Eds.), *Bereavement: Reactions, consequences, and care* (pp. 215–238). Washington, DC: National Academy Press.

Green, S. K., & Sandos, P. (1983). Perceptions of male and female initiators of relationships. *Sex Roles, 9*, 849–852.

Greenberg, M. (1986). *The birth of a father*. New York: Continuum.

Greenburg, D., & Jacobs, M. (1966). *How to make yourself miserable*. New York: Random House.

Griffith, W. (1970). Environmental effects on interpersonal affective behavior. *Journal of Personality and Social Psychology, 15*, 240–244.

Griffitt, W., & Hatfield, E. (1985). *Human sexual behavior*. Glenview, IL: Scott, Foresman.

Groth, A. N., & Birnbaum, H. J. (1979). *Men who rape: The psychology of the offender*. New York: Plenum Press.

Gruber, K. J., & White, J. W. (1986). Gender differences in the perceptions of self's and others' use of power strategies. *Sex Roles, 15*, 109–118.

Gryl, F. E., Stith, S. M., & Bird, G. W. (1991). Close dating relationships among college students: Differences by use of violence and by gender. *Journal of Social and Personal Relationships, 8*, 243–264.

Guerney, B. G. (1977). *Relationship enhancement*. San Francisco: Jossey-Bass.

Guerrero, L. K., & Andersen, P. A. (1991). The waxing and waning of relational intimacy: Touch as a function of relational stage, gender and touch avoidance. *Journal of Social and Personal Relationships, 8*, 147–165.

Guttentag, M., & Secord, P. F. (1983). *Too many women? The sex ratio question*. Beverly Hills, CA: Sage Publications.

Hagestad, G. O., & Smyer, M. A. (1982). Dissolving long-term relationships: Patterns of divorcing in middle age. In S. Duck (Ed.), *Personal relationships 4: Dissolving personal relationships* (pp. 155–188). London: Academic Press.

Haggard, E. A., & Issacs, F. S. (1966). Micromomentary facial expressions as indicators of ego mechanisms in psychotherapy. In C. A. Gottschalk & A. Averback (Eds.), *Methods of research in psychotherapy* (pp. 154–165). New York: Appleton-Century-Crofts.

Hall, C. (1991, May 15). Ted and Jane, a press agent's dream. *International Herald Tribune*, p. 20.

Hall, J. A. (1978). Gender effects in decoding nonverbal cues. *Psychological Bulletin, 85*, 845–857.

Hamilton, E. (1942). *Mythology*. New York: New American Library of World Literature.

Hamlin, R. L., Buckholdt, D., Bushell, D., Ellis, D., & Ferritor, D. (1969, January). Changing the game from "get the teacher" to "learn." *Trans-action, 6*, 20–31.

Hanson, S. M. H. (1988). Divorced fathers with custody. In P. Bronstein & C. P. Cowan (Eds.), *Fatherhood today: Men's changing role in the family* (pp. 166–194). New York: Wiley.

Hardy, T. (1891). *Tess of the D'Urbervilles.* New York: Viking Penguin.

Hariton, E. B. (1973, March). The sexual fantasies of women. *Psychology Today, 6,* 39–44.

Harlow, H. F. (1973). *Learning to love.* New York: Ballantine.

Harlow, H. F. (1975). Lust, latency and love: Simian secrets of successful sex. *Journal of Sex Research, 11,* 79–90.

Harlow, H. F., Harlow, M. K., & Suomi, S. J. (1971). From thought to therapy: Lessons from a primate laboratory. *American Scientist, 59,* 539–549.

Harvey, J. H., Flanary, R., & Morgan, M. (1986). Vivid memories of vivid loves gone by. *Journal of Social and Personal Relationships, 3,* 359–373.

Harvey, J., Weber, A., Galvin, K., Huszti, H., & Garnick, N. (1985). Attribution in the termination of close relationships: A special focus on the account. In R. Gilmour & S. W. Duck (Eds.), *The emerging field of personal relationships* (pp. 189–201). Hillsdale, NJ: Erlbaum.

Harvey, J. H., Weber, A. L., & Orbuch, T. L. (1990). *Interpersonal accounts: A social psychological perspective.* Cambridge, MA: Basil Blackwell.

Hatfield, E. (1965). The effect of self-esteem on romantic liking. *Journal of Experimental Social Psychology, 1,* 184–197.

Hatfield, E. (1970). The effect of self-esteem on liking for dates of various social desirability. *Journal of Experimental Social Psychology, 6,* 248–253.

Hatfield, E. (1971a). Passionate love. In B. I. Murstein (Ed.), *Theories of attraction and love* (pp. 85–99). New York: Springer Press.

Hatfield, E. (1971b). Studies testing a theory of positive affect. Proposal for National Science Foundation Grant 30822X.

Hatfield, E. (1982a). Passionate love, companionate love, and intimacy. In M. Fisher & G. Stricker (Eds.), *Intimacy* (pp. 267–292). New York: Plenum Press.

Hatfield, E. (1982b). What do women and men want from love and sex? In E. R. Allgeier & N. B. McCormick (Eds.), *Changing boundaries: Gender roles and sexual behavior* (pp. 106–134). Palo Alto, CA: Mayfield.

Hatfield, E. (1984). The dangers of intimacy. In V. Derlaga (Ed.), *Communication, intimacy, and close relationships* (pp. 207–220). New York: Academic Press.

Hatfield, E., Aronson, E., Abrahams, D., & Rottman, L. (1966). The importance of physical attractiveness in dating behavior. *Journal of Personality and Social Psychology, 4,* 508–516.

Hatfield, E., Brinton, C., & Cornelius, J. (1989). Passionate love and anxiety in young adolescents. *Motivation and Emotion, 13,* 271–289.

Hatfield, E., Cacioppo, J., & Rapson, R. L. (1992). Primitive emotional contagion. In M. S. Clark (Ed.), *Review of Personality and Social Psychology, 14,* (pp. xx). Newbury Park, CA: Sage Publications.

Hatfield, E., Cacioppo, J., & Rapson, R. L. (1993). *Emotional contagion.* Cambridge: Cambridge University Press.

Hatfield, E., Costello, J., Schalekamp, M., Denney, C., & Hsee, C. (1991). *The effect of vocal feedback on emotional experience/expression.* Unpublished manuscript. Honolulu: University of Hawaii.

Hatfield, E., Greenberger, D., Pillemer, J., & Lambert, P. (1982). Equity and sexual satisfaction in recently married couples. *Journal of Sex Research, 18,* 18–32.

Hatfield, E., & Rapson, R. L. (1987a). Gender differences in love and intimacy: The fantasy vs. the reality. In W. Ricketts & H. L. Gochros (Eds.), *Intimate relationships: Some social work perspectives on love* (pp. 15–26). New York: Hayworth Press.

Hatfield, E., & Rapson, R. L. (1987b). Passionate love/sexual desire: Can the same paradigm explain both? *Archives of Sexual Behavior, 16,* 259–278.

Hatfield, E., & Rapson, R. (1990a). Emotions: A trinity. In E. A. Bleckman (Ed.), *Emotions and the family: For better or worse* (pp. 11–33). Hillsdale, NJ: Erlbaum.

Hatfield, E., & Rapson, R. L. (1990b). Passionate love in intimate relationships. In B. S. Moore & A. Isen (Eds.), *Affect and social behavior* (pp. 126–152). Cambridge, England: Cambridge University Press.

Hatfield, E., Roberts, D., & Schmidt, L. (1980). The impact of sex and physical attractiveness on an initial social encounter. *Recherches de Psychologie Sociale, 2,* 27–40.

Hatfield, E., Schmitz, E., Cornelius, J. & Rapson, R. L. (1988). Passionate love: How early does it begin? *Journal of Psychology and Human Sexuality, 1,* 35–52.

Hatfield, E., Schmitz, E., Parpart, L., & Weaver, H. B. (1986). *Ethnic and gender differences in emotional experience and expression.* Unpublished manuscript, University of Hawaii, Honolulu.

Hatfield, E., & Sprecher, S. (1986a). Measuring passionate love in intimate relations. *Journal of Adolescence, 9,* 383–410.

Hatfield, E., & Sprecher, S. (1986b). *Mirror, mirror: The importance of looks in everyday life.* Albany, NY: SUNY Press.

Hatfield, E., Sprecher, S., Pillemer, J. T., Greenberger, D., & Wexler, P. (1988). Gender differences in what is desired in the sexual relationship. *Journal of Psychology and Human Sexuality, 1,* 39–52.

Hatfield, E., Pillemer, J., Sprecher, S., Utne, M., & Hay, J. (1984). Equity and intimate relations: Recent research. In W. Ickes (Ed.), *Compatible and incompatible relationships* (pp. 1–27). New York: Springer-Verlag.

Hatfield, E., Pillemer, J., & Walster, G. W. (1979). Equity and extramarital sex. In M. Cook & G. Wilson (Eds.), *Love and attraction: An international conference* (pp. 323–334). Oxford: Pergamon Press.

Hatfield, E., & Walster, G. W. (1963). Effect of expecting to be liked on choice of associates. *Journal of Abnormal and Social Psychology, 67,* 402–404.

Hatfield, E., & Walster, G. W. (1978). *A new look at love.* Lanham, MD: University Press of America.

Hatfield, E., Walster, G. W., & Berscheid, E. (1978). *Equity: Theory and research.* Boston: Allyn & Bacon.

Hatfield, E., Walster, G. W., Piliavin, J., & Schmidt, L. (1973). Playing hard-to-get: Understanding an elusive phenomenon. *Journal of Personality and Social Psychology, 26,* 113–121.

Haviland, J. M., & Lelwica, M. (1987). The induced affect response: 10-week-old infants' responses to three emotion expressions. *Developmental Psychology, 23,* 97–104.

Hays, R. B. (1985). A longitudinal study of friendship development. *Journal of Personality and Social Psychology, 48,* 909–924.

Hays, R. B. (1988). Friendship. In S. W. Duck (Ed.), *Handbook of personal relationships* (pp. 391–408). New York: Wiley.

Hazan, C., & Shaver, P. (1987). Romantic love conceptualized as an attachment process. *Journal of Personality and Social Psychology, 52,* 511–524.

Hazan, C., & Shaver, P. R. (1990). Love and work: An attachment–theoretical perspective. *Journal of Personality and Social Psychology, 59,* 270–280.

Hechinger, F. M. (1990, August 1). Why France outstrips the United States in nurturing its children. *The New York Times,* p. B8.

Heiby, E. M. (1979). Conditions which occasion depression: A review of three behavioral models. *Psychological Reports, 45,* 683–714.

Heider, F. (1980). *The psychology of interpersonal relations.* New York: Wiley.

Heiman, J. R. (1977). A psychophysiological exploration of sexual arousal patterns in females and males. *Psychophysiology, 14,* 266–274.

Helgeson, V. S., Shaver, P., & Dyer, M. (1987). Prototypes of intimacy and distance in same-sex and opposite-sex relationships. *Journal of Social and Personal Relationships, 4,* 195–233.

Helmreich, R., Aronson, E. M., & Lefan, J. (1970). To err is humanizing—sometimes: Effects of self-esteem competence and pratfall on interpersonal attraction. *Journal of Personality and Social Psychology, 16,* 259–264.

Hendrick, C., & Hendrick, S. S. (1988). Lovers wear rose colored glasses. *Journal of Social and Personal Relationships, 5,* 161–183.

Hendrick, C., & Hendrick, S. S. (1989). Research on love: Does it measure up? *Journal of Personality and Social Psychology, 56,* 784–794.

Henley, N. M. (1977). *Body politics: Power, sex, and nonverbal communication.* Englewood Cliffs, NJ: Prentice-Hall.

Henry, O. (Pseud.) (1906/1942). *The gift of the Magi.* Garden City, NY: Doubleday.

Henton, J., Cate, R., Koval, J., Lloyd, S., & Christopher, F. S. (1983). Romance and violence in dating relationships. *Journal of Family Issues, 4,* 467–482.

Hetherington, E. M., Cox, M., & Cox, R. (1982). Effects of divorce on parents and children. In M. E. Lamb (Ed.), *Nontraditional families: Parenting and child development* (pp. 233–288). Hillsdale, NJ: Erlbaum.

Hewlett, S. (1986). *A lesser life.* New York: Morrow.

Hijuelos, O. (1989). *The Mambo Kings play songs of love.* New York: Harper Perennial.

Hill, C. T., Rubin, Z., & Peplau, L. A. (1979). Breakups before marriage: The end of 103 affairs. In G. Levinger & O. C. Moles (Eds.), *Divorce and separation* (pp. 64–82). New York: Basic Books.

Hill, R. (1945). Campus values in mate selection. *Journal of Home Economics, 37,* 554–558.

Hill, R. (1949). *Families under stress.* New York: Harper & Row.

Hill, R. (1965). Generic features of families under stress. In H. J. Parad (Ed.), *Crisis intervention: Selected readings* (pp. 32–52). New York: Family Service Association of America.

Hindy, C. G., Schwarz, J. C., & Brodsky, A. (1989) *If this is love why do I feel so insecure?.* New York: Atlantic Monthly Press.

Hite, S. (1976). *The Hite report: A nationwide study of female sexuality.* New York: Macmillan.

Hite, S. (1981). *The Hite report on male sexuality*. New York: Alfred A. Knopf.

Hite, S. (1987). *Women and love*. New York: Alfred A. Knopf.

Hobfoll, S. E. (1990). Special issue: Social support. *Journal of Social and Personal Relationships, 7*, 435–588.

Hobfoll, S. E., & Stokes, J. P. (1988). The process and mechanics of social support. In S. Duck (Ed.), *Handbook of personal relationships: Theory, research and interventions* (pp. 497–517). New York: Wiley.

Hochschild, A. R. (1983). *The managed heart: Commercialization of human feeling*. Los Angeles: University of California Press.

Hochschild, A. (1989). *The second shift*. New York: Avon Books.

Hodgson, J. W., & Fischer, J. L. (1979). Sex differences in identity and intimacy development. *Journal of Youth and Adolescence, 8*, 37–50.

Hoffer, E. (1954). *The true believer: Thoughts on the nature of mass movements* (p. 7). New York: Harper & Row.

Hoffman, L. W., & Manis, J. D. (1982). The value of children in the United States. In F. I. Nye (Ed.), *Family relationships: Rewards and costs* (pp. 143–170). Beverly Hills, CA: Sage Publications.

Hoffman, M. L. (1987). The contribution of empathy to justice and moral judgement. In N. Eisenberg & J. Strayer (Eds.), *Empathy and its development* (pp. 47–80). New York: Cambridge University Press.

Hokanson, J. E. (1970). Psychophysiological evaluation of the catharsis hypothesis. In E. I. Megaree & J. E. Hokanson (Eds.), *The dynamics of aggression* (pp. 74–86). New York: Harper & Row.

Hokanson, J. E., & Burgess, M. (1962a). The effects of status, type of frustration and aggression on vascular processes. *Journal of Abnormal and Social Psychology, 65*, 232–237.

Hokanson, J. E., & Burgess, M. (1962b). The effects of three types of aggression on vascular processes. *Journal of Abnormal and Social Psychology, 64*, 446–449.

Hokanson, J. E., Burgess, M., & Cohen, M. F. (1963). Effects of displaced aggression on systolic blood pressure. *Journal of Abnormal and Social Psychology, 67*, 214–218.

Hokanson, J. E., & Edelman, R. (1969). Arousal reduction via self-punitive behavior. *Journal of Personality and Social Psychology, 12*, 72–79.

Hokanson, J. E., & Stone, L. (1969). *Intensity of self-punishment as a factor in intropunitive behavior*. Unpublished manuscript, Florida State University, Tallahassee.

Hokanson, J. E., Willers, K. R., & Koropsak, E. (1968). The modification of autonomic responses during aggressive interchange. *Journal of Personality, 36*, 386–404.

Holmes, T. H., & Rahe, R. H. (1967). The social readjustment rating scale. *Journal of Psychosomatic Research, 11*, 213–218.

Holstrom, L. L., & Burgess, A. W. (1980). Sexual behavior of assailants during reported rapes. *Archives of Sexual Behavior, 9*, 427–439.

Hoon, P. W., Wincze, J. P., & Hoon, E. F. (1977). A test of reciprocal inhibition: Are anxiety and sexual arousal in women mutually inhibitory? *Journal of Abnormal Psychology, 86*, 65–74.

Hopkins, J. R. (1977). Sexual behavior in adolescence. *Journal of Social Issues, 33*, 67–85.

Hopson, J., & Rosenfeld, A. (1984). PMS: Puzzling monthly symptoms. *Psychology Today, 18*, 30–35.

Houston, P. (1992). *Cowboys are my weakness.* New York: Norton.

Howard, J. A., Blumstein, P., & Schwartz, P. (1986). Sex, power, and influence tactics in intimate relationships. *Journal of Personality and Social Psychology, 51,* 102–109.

Howard, J. A., Blumstein, P., & Schwartz, P. (1987). Social or evolutionary theories? Some observations on preferences in human mate selection. *Journal of Personality and Social Psychology, 53,* 194–200.

Howes, M. J., Hokanson, J. E., & Lowenstein, D. A. (1985). Induction of depressive affect after prolonged exposure to a mildly depressed individual. *Journal of Personality and Social Psychology, 49,* 1110–1113.

Hudson, J. W., & Henze, L. F. (1969). Campus values in mate selection: A replication. *Journal of Marriage and the Family, 31,* 772–775.

Humphrey, G. (1922). The conditioned reflex and the elementary social reaction. *Journal of Abnormal and Social Psychology, 17,* 113–119.

Hunt, M. (1959). *The natural history of love.* New York: Grove Press.

Hunt, M. (1969). *The affair.* Cleveland: World Publishing.

Hunt, M. (1974). *Sexual behavior in the 1970s.* Chicago: Playboy Press.

Hunt, M., & Hunt, B. (1977). *The divorce experience.* New York: McGraw-Hill.

Huston, T. L. (1973). Ambiguity of acceptance, social desirability and dating choice. *Journal of Experimental Social Psychology, 9,* 32–42.

Huston, T. L. (1983). Power. In H. H. Kelley, E. Berscheid, A. Christensen, J. H. Harvey, T. L. Huston, G. Levinger, E. McClintock, L. A. Peplau, & D. R. Peterson (Eds.), *Close relationships* (pp. 169–219). New York: Freeman.

Huston, T. L., & Burgess, R. L. (1979). Social exchange in developing relationships: An overview. In R. L. Burgess & T. L. Huston (Eds.), *Social exchange in developing relationships* (pp. 3–28). New York: Academic Press.

Hyde, J. S. (1990). *Understanding human sexuality.* New York: McGraw-Hill.

Ingram, R. E., Cruet, D., Johnson, B. R., & Wisnicki, K. S. (1988). Self-focused attention, gender, gender role, and vulnerability to negative affect. *Journal of Personality and Social Psychology, 55,* 967–978.

Istvan, J., & Griffitt, W. (1978). *Emotional arousal and sexual attraction.* Unpublished manuscript, Kansas State University, Manhattan.

Istvan, S., Griffitt, W., & Weidner, G. (1983). Sexual arousal and the polarization of perceived sexual attractiveness. *Basic and Applied Social Psychology, 4,* 307–318.

Ivins, M. (1991). *Molly Ivins can't say that, can she?* New York: Random House.

Izard, C. E. (1977). *Human emotions.* New York: Plenum Press.

Jacobs, L., Berscheid, E., & Hatfield, E. (1971). Self-esteem and attraction. *Journal of Personality and Social Psychology, 17,* 84–91.

Jacobs, S., & Ostfeld, A. (1977). An epidemiological review of the mortality of bereavement. *Psychosomatic Medicine, 39,* 344–357.

James, H. (1904/1966). *The golden bowl.* New York: Penguin Books.

James, W. (1892/1920). Emotions. *Psychology: Briefer course* (pp. 324–338). Cambridge, MA: Harvard University Press.

Jason, L. A., Reichler, A., Easton, J., Neal, A., & Wilson, M. (1984). Female harassment after ending a relationship: A preliminary study. *Alternative Lifestyles, 6,* 259–269.

Jay, K., & Young, A. (1979). *The gay report*. New York: Summit Books.

Jeffares, N. (Ed.) (1984). The second coming. *Poems of W. B. Yeats* (p. 246). London: Macmillan.

Jemmott, J. B., III, & Magloire, K. (1988). Academic stress, social support, and secretory immunoglobulin A. *Journal of Personality and Social Psychology, 55,* 803–810.

Jesser, C. J. (1978). Male responses to direct verbal sexual initiatives of females. *Journal of Sex Research, 14,* 118–128.

Johnson, M. P. (1982). Social and cognitive features of the dissolution of commitment to relationships. In S. Duck (Ed.), *Personal relationships. Vol. 4: Dissolving personal relationships* (pp. 51–74). London: Academic Press.

Johnson, P. (1978). Women and interpersonal power. In I. H. Frieze, J. E. Parsons, P. Johnson, D. Ruble., & G. Zellerman (Eds.), *Women and sex roles: A social psychological perspective* (pp. 301–320). New York: Norton.

Johnson, R. (1973). *Emotional development: Aggression*. A film in the Developmental Psychology Series, F-E115. New York: McGraw-Hill.

Jones, E. E. (1964). *Ingratiation*. New York: Appleton-Century-Crofts.

Jones, E. E., Kanouse, D. E., Kelley, H. H., Nisbett, R. E., Valines, S., & Weiner, B. (Eds.) (1971). *Attribution: Perceiving the causes of behavior*. Morristown, NJ: General Learning Press.

Jones, E. E., & Pittman, T. S. (1982). Toward a general theory of strategic self presentation. In J. Suls (Ed.), *Psychological perspective on the self* (pp. 231–262). Hillsdale, NJ: Erlbaum.

Jones, V. C. (1948). *The Hatfields and the McCoys*. Chapel Hill: University of North Carolina Press.

Jones, W. H., Cavert, C. W., Snider, R. C., & Bruce, T. (1985). Relational stress: An analysis of situations and events associated with loneliness. In S. W. Duck & D. Perlman (Eds.), *Understanding personal relationships research: An interdisciplinary approach* (pp. 221–242). London: Sage Publications.

Jourard, S. M. (1964). *The transparent self*. Princeton, NJ: Van Nostrand.

Jourard, S. M. (1971). *Self-disclosure: An experimental analysis of the transparent self*. New York: Wiley.

Jourard, S. M., & Lasakow, P. (1958). Some factors in self disclosure. *Journal of Abnormal and Social Psychology, 56,* 91–98.

Joyce, C. (1984, November). A time for grieving. *Psychology Today, 18,* 42–46.

Joyce, J. (1934/1961). *Ulysses*. New York: The Modern Library.

Jung, C. G. (1938). *Psychological types* (H. G. Baynes, Trans.). New York: Harcourt, Brace and Co.

Jung, C. G. (1953). Two essays on analytical psychology. In H. Read, M. Fordham, & G. Adler (Eds.), *Collected works* (Vol. 7, pp. 243–292). Princeton, NJ: Princeton University Press.

Jung, C. G. (1968). Lecture five. *Analytical psychology: Its theory and practice* (pp. 151–160). New York: Random House.

Kaats, C., & Davis, K. (1970). The dynamics of sexual behavior of college students. *Journal of Marriage and the Family, 32,* 390–399.

Kama Sutra of Vatsyayana, The. (1963). (R. Burton & F. F. Arbuchnot, Trans.). New York: Putnam.

Kamerman, S. B. (1980a). *Maternity and parental benefits and leaves: An international review* (Impact on Policy Series Monograph No. 1). New York: Columbia University, Center for the Social Sciences.

Kamerman, S. B. (1980b). *Parenting in an unresponsive society.* New York: Free Press.

Kanner, A. D., Coyne, J. C., Schaeffer, C., & Lazarus, R. S. (1981). Comparison of two modes of stress measurement: Daily hassles and uplifts versus major life events. *Journal of Behavioral Medicine, 4,* 1–39.

Kaplan, H. S. (1979). *Disorders of sexual desire.* New York: Simon & Schuster.

Kaplan, J. F., & Anderson, N. H. (1973). Information integration theory and reinforcement theory as approaches to interpersonal attraction. *Journal of Personality and Social Psychology, 28,* 301–312.

Katz, J. M. (1976). How do you love me? Let me count the ways. *Sociological Inquiry, 46,* 17–22.

Kellerman, J., Lewis, J., & Laird, J. D. (1989). Looking and loving: The effects of mutual gaze on feelings of romantic love. *Journal of Research in Personality, 23,* 145–161.

Kelley, H. H. (1979). *Personal relationships: Their structures and processes.* Hillsdale, NJ: Erlbaum.

Kelley, H. H., Berscheid, E., Christensen, A., Harvey, J. H., Huston, T. L., Levinger, G., McClintock, E., Peplau, L. A., & Peterson, D. R. (Eds.) (1983). *Close relationships.* New York: Freeman.

Kelley, H. H., Cunningham, J. D., Grisham, J. A., Lefebvre, L. M., Sink, C. R., & Yablon, G. (1978). Sex differences in comments made during conflict within close heterosexual pairs. *Sex Roles, 4,* 473–491.

Kelley, K., Pilchowicz, E., & Byrne, D. (1981). Responses of males to female-initiated dates. *Bulletin of the Psychonomic Society, 17,* 195–196.

Kelley, K., & Rolker-Dolinsky, B. (1987). The psychosexology of female initiation and dominance. In D. Perlman & S. Duck (Eds.), *Intimate relationships: Development, dynamics, and deterioration* (pp. 63–87). Beverly Hills, CA: Sage Publications.

Kendler, K. S., Heath, A. C., Martin, N. G., & Eaves, L. J. (1987). Symptoms of anxiety and symptoms of depression. *Archives of General Psychiatry, 44,* 451–457.

Kendrick, D. T., & Cialdini, R. B. (1977). Romantic attraction: Misattribution vs. reinforcement explanations. *Journal of Personality and Social Psychology, 35,* 381–391.

Kennedy, R. (1989). *Life choices* (2nd ed.) New York: Holt, Rinehart & Winston.

Kephart, W. M., & Jedlicka, D. (1991). *The family, society, and the individual* (7th ed.). New York: HarperCollins.

Kerckhoff, A. C. (1974). The social context of interpersonal attraction. In T. L. Huston (Ed.), *Foundations of interpersonal attraction* (pp. 61–78). New York: Academic Press.

Kerckhoff, A. C., & Back, K. W. (1968). *The June bug: A study of hysterical contagion.* New York: Appleton-Century-Crofts.

Kern, J. (music), & Hammerstein, O. (lyrics). (1956). I might fall back on you. Selection from *Showboat,* RCA Victor LM 2008.

Kidman, A. (1989). Neurochemical and cognitive aspects of anxiety disorders. *Progress in Neurobiology, 32,* 391–402.

Kilmann, R., & Thomas, K. (1975). Interpersonal conflict-handling behavior as reflections of Jungian personality dimensions. *Psychological Reports, 37,* 971–980.

Kinney, J., & Leaton, G. (1982). *Loosening the grip: A handbook of alcohol information.* St. Louis, MO: C. V. Mosby.

Kinsey, A. C., Pomeroy, W. B., & Martin, C. E. (1948). *Sexual behavior in the human male.* Philadelphia: Saunders.

Kinsey, A. C., Pomeroy, W. B., Martin, C. E., & Gebhard, P. H. (1953). *Sexual behavior in the human female.* Philadelphia: Saunders.

Klerman, G. L., & Clayton, P. (1984). Epidemiological perspectives on the health consequences of bereavement. In M. Osterweis, F. Solomon, & M. Green (Eds.), *Bereavement: Reactions, consequences, and care* (pp. 15–46). Washington, DC: National Academy Press.

Klinger, E. (1977). *Meaning and void: Inner experience and the incentives in people's lives.* Minneapolis: University of Minnesota Press.

Klinnert, M. D., Campos, J. J., Sorce, J. F., Emde, R. N., & Svejda, M. (1983). Emotions as behavior regulators: Social referencing in infancy. In R. Plutchik & H. Kellerman (Eds.), *Emotion: Theory, research, and experience* (Vol. 2, pp. 57–86). New York: Academic Press.

Knapp, M. L., Stafford, L., & Daly, J. A. (1986). Regrettable messages: Things people wish they hadn't said. *Journal of Communication, 36,* 40–58.

Knebel, F., & Clay, G. S. (1987). *Before you sue: How to get justice without going to court.* New York: Morrow.

Knox, D. (1985). Breaking up: The cover story versus the real story. *Free Inquiry in Creative Sociology, 13,* 131–132.

Knox, D., & Wilson, K. (1981). Dating behaviors of university students. *Family Relations, 30,* 255–258.

Kohen, J. A., Brown, C. A., & Feldberg, R. (1979). Divorced mothers: The costs and benefits of female family control. In G. Levinger & O. C. Moles (Eds.), *Divorce and separation* (pp. 228–245). New York: Basic Books.

Kollock, P., Blumstein, P., & Schwartz, P. (1985). Sex and power in interaction: Conversational privileges and duties. *American Sociological Review, 50,* 34–46.

Komarovsky, M. (1967). *Blue-collar marriage.* New York: Random House.

Konecni, V. J. (1984). Methodological issues in human aggression research. In R. M. Kaplan, V. J. Konecni, & R. W. Novaco (Eds.), *Aggression in children and youth* (pp. 1–43). The Hague: Martinus Nijhoff Publishers.

Konner, M. (1982). *The tangled wing: Biological constraints on the human spirit.* New York: Henry Holt.

Koss, M. P., Dinero, T. E., Seibel, C. A., & Cox, S. L. (1988). Stranger and acquaintance rape: Are there differences in the victim's experience? *Psychology of Women Quarterly, 12,* 1–24.

Koss, M. P., & Leonard, K. E. (1984). In N. M. Malamuth & E. Donnerstein (Eds.), *Pornography and sexual aggression* (pp. 213–232). New York: Academic Press.

Kristof, N. D. (1991, July 19). A peek through the keyhole at a new China. *The New York Times,* pp. A1, A7.

Kroll, J. (1987, March 9). The most famous artist. The arts. *Newsweek, 110,* 64–66.

Kübler-Ross, E. (1969). *On death and dying.* New York: Macmillan.

Lacey, J. I., & Lacey, B. C. (1970). Some autonomic–central nervous system interrelationships. In P. Black (Ed.), *Physiological correlates of emotion* (pp. 205–227). New York: Academic Press.

Ladurie, E. L. R. (1979). *Montaillou: The promised land of error*. New York: Vintage Books.

La Fave, W. R., & Scott, A. W. (1972). *Handbook on criminal law*. New York: West.

La France, M., & Ickes, W. (1981). Posture mirroring and interactional involvement: Sex and sex typing effects. *Journal of Nonverbal Behavior, 5,* 139–154.

Laird, J. D. (1984). The real role of facial response in the experience of emotion: A reply to Tourangeau and Ellsworth, and others. *Journal of Personality and Social Psychology, 47,* 909–917.

Lande, J. S., Scarr, S., & Gunzenhauser, N. (Eds.) (1989). *Caring for children: Challenge to America*. Hillsdale, NJ: Erlbaum.

Langlois, J. H., & Roggman, L. A. (1990). Attractive faces are only average. *Psychological Science, 1,* 115–121.

La Plante, M., McCormick, N., & Brannigan, G. (1980). Living the sexual script: College students' views of influence in sexual encounters. *Journal of Sex Research, 16,* 338–355.

Larson, R. (1978). Thirty years of research on the subjective well-being of older Americans. *Journal of Gerontology, 33,* 109–125.

Laudenslager, M. L., & Reite, M. L. (1984). Losses and separations. Immunological consequences and health implications. In P. Shauer (Ed.), *Review of Personality and Social Psychology. Emotions, Relations and Health* (Vol. 5, pp. 285–312). London: Sage Publications.

Lavarkas, P. (1975). Female preferences for male physiques. *Journal of Research in Personality, 9,* 324–334.

LaVee, Y., McCubbin, H. I., & Patterson, J. M. (1985). *Journal of Marriage and the Family, 47,* 811–825.

Lazarus, R. S. (1977). A cognitive analysis of biofeedback control. In G. E. Schwartz & J. Beatty (Eds.), *Biofeedback: Theory and research* (pp. 69–71). New York: Academic Press.

Lazarus, R. S. (1991). *Emotion and adaptation*. New York: Oxford University Press.

Lazarus, R. S., & Folkman, S. (1984). Coping and adaptation. In W. G. Gentry (Ed.), *The handbook of behavioral medicine* (pp. 282–325). New York: Guilford Press.

Leamer, L. (1986). *As time goes by*. New York: Harper & Row.

Leaming, B. (1989). *If this was happiness: A biography of Rita Hayworth*. New York: Viking Penguin.

Leary, M. R., Rogers, P. A., Canfield, R. W., & Coe, C. (1986). Boredom in interpersonal encounters: Antecedents and social implications. *Journal of Personality and Social Psychology, 51,* 968–975.

Le Bon, G. (1896). *The crowd: A study of the popular mind*. London: Ernest Benn Ltd.

Lee, J. A. (1973). *The colors of love: An exploration of the ways of loving*. Don Mills, Ontario: New Press.

Lee, L. (1984). Sequences in separation: A framework for investigating endings of the personal (romantic) relationship. *Journal of Social and Personal Relationships, 1,* 49–74.

Lefcourt, H. M., Martin, R. A., & Saleh, W. E. (1984). Locus of control and social support: Interactive moderators of stress. *Journal of Personality and Social Psychology, 47,* 378–389.

Lehman, D. R., Wortman, C. B., & Williams, A. F. (1987). Long term effects of losing a spouse or child in a motor vehicle crash. *Journal of Personality and Social Psychology, 52,* 218–231.

Lehmann-Haupt, C. (1988, August 4). Books of the times: How an actor found success, and himself. *The New York Times,* p. 2.

LePoire, B. A., & Strzyewski, K. (1992). *Gender differences in the nonverbal expression of jealousy.* Tempe, AZ: University of Arizona.

Lerner, G. (1986). *The creation of patriarchy.* New York: Oxford University Press.

Levenson, R. W., & Gottman, J. M. (1985). Physiological and affective predictors of change in relationship satisfaction. *Journal of Personality and Social Psychology, 49,* 85–94.

Leventhal, G. S., & Bergman, J. T. (1969). Self-depriving behavior as a response to unprofitable inequity. *Journal of Experimental Social Psychology, 5,* 153–171.

Levinger, G. (1979). A social psychological perspective on marital dissolution. In G. Levinger & O. C. Moses (Eds.), *Divorce and separation* (pp. 37–60). New York: Basic Books.

Levinger, G. (1983). Development and change. In H. H. Kelley, E. Berscheid, A. Christensen, J. H. Harvey, T. L. Huston, G. Levinger, E. McClintock, L. A. Peplau, & D. R. Peterson (Eds.), *Close relationships* (pp. 315–359). New York: Freeman.

Levitz-Jones, E. M., & Orlofsky, J. L. (1985). Separation-individuation and intimacy capacity in college women. *Journal of Personality and Social Psychology, 49,* 156–169.

Lewinsohn, P. M. (1986). A behavioral approach to depression. In J. C. Coyne (Ed.), *Essential papers on depression* (pp. 150–180). New York: New York University Press.

Lewinsohn, P. M., Hoberman, H. M., Terri, L., & Hautzinger, M. (1985). An integrative theory of depression. In S. Reiss & R. Bootzin (Eds.), *Theoretical issues in behavior therapy* (pp. 331–359). Orlando, FL: Academic Press.

Lewinsohn, P. M., & Talkington, J. (1979). Studies on the measurement of unpleasant events and relations with depression. *Applied Psychological Measurement, 3,* 83–101.

Lewis, C. S. (1960). *The four loves.* New York: Harcourt, Brace, & World.

Liebowitz, M. R. (1983). *The chemistry of love.* Boston: Little, Brown.

Lindemann, E. (1944). Symptomatology and management of acute grief. *American Journal of Psychiatry, 101,* 141–149.

Lloyd, S. A., & Cate, R. M. (1985). Attributions associated with significant turning points in premarital relationship development and dissolution. *Journal of Social and Personal Relationships, 2,* 419–436.

Lockard, J. S., & Adams, R. M. (1980). Courtship behaviors in public: Different age/sex roles. *Ethology and Sociobiology, 1,* 245–253.

Lodge, D. (1980). *How far can you go?* London: Penguin Books.

Loehlin, J. C. (1989). Partitioning environmental and genetic contributions to behavioral development. *American Psychologist, 44,* 1285–1292.

Loevinger, J. (1976). *Ego development.* San Francisco: Jossey-Bass.

Loewen, J. W. (1988). Visitation fatherhood. In P. Bronstein & C. P. Cowan (Eds.), *Fatherhood today: Men's changing role in the family* (pp. 195–213). New York: Wiley.

Long-Laws, J. (1979). *The second X: Sex role and social role*. New York: Elsevier/North-Holland.

Lopata, H. Z. (1969). Loneliness: Forms and components. *Social Problems, 17,* 248–261.

Lorenz, K. (1965). *Evolution and the modification of behavior*. Chicago: University of Chicago Press.

Los Angeles Times, The. (1992, February 8). Broderick gets maximum term for two killings. pp. A1.

Luepnitz, D. (1979, January). Which aspects of divorce affect children? *The Family Coordinator, 28,* 79–85.

Lund, M. (1985). The development of investment and commitment scales for predicting continuity of personal relationships. *Journal of Social and Personal Relationships, 2,* 3–23.

Lurie, A. (1974). *The war between the Tates*. London: Abacus.

MacDermid, S. M., Huston, T. L., & McHale, S. M. (1990). Changes in marriage associated with the transition to parenthood: Individual differences as a function of sex-role attitudes and changes in the division of household labor. *Journal of Marriage and the Family, 52,* 475–486.

Mace, D., & Mace, V. (1980). *Marriage: East and west*. New York: Dolphin Books.

MacLean, P. D. (1986). Ictal symptoms relating to the nature of affects and their cerebral substrate. In R. Plutchik & H. Kellerman (Eds.), *Emotion, theory, research, and experience. Vol. 3. Biological foundations of emotion* (pp. 61–90). New York: Academic Press.

MacNeil, R. (1989). *Wordstruck*. New York: Penguin Books.

Makepeace, J. M. (1986). Gender differences in courtship violence victimization. *Family Relations: Journal of Applied Family and Child Studies, 35,* 383–388.

Malamuth, N. M. (1984). Aggression against women: Cultural and individual causes. In N. M. Malamuth & E. Donnerstein (Eds.), *Pornography and sexual aggression* (pp. 19–52). New York: Academic Press.

Malatesta, C. Z., & Haviland, J. M. (1982). Learning display rules: The socialization of emotion expression in infancy. *Child Development, 53,* 991–1003.

Mann, T. (1969). *The magic mountain*. New York: Vintage Books.

Maret, E., & Finlay, B. (1984). The distribution of household labor among women in dual-earner families. *Journal of Marriage and the Family, 46,* 357–364.

Markoff, R. A., Ryan, P. R., & Young, T. (1982). Endorphins and mood changes in long-distance running. *Medicine and Science in Sports and Exercise, 14,* 11–15.

Márquez, G. G. (1985). *Love in the time of cholera*. New York: Penguin Books.

Marshall, L. L., & Rose, P. (1987). Gender, stress and violence in the adult relationships of a sample of college students. *Journal of Social and Personal Relationships, 4,* 299–316.

Marwell, G. (1975). Why ascription? Parts of a more or less formal theory of the functions and dysfunctions of sex roles. *American Sociological Review, 40,* 445–455.

Marwell, G., McKinney, K., Sprecher, S., DeLamater, J., & Smith, S. (1982, May). *Legitimizing factors in the initiation of heterosexual relationships*. Paper presented at the First International Conference on Personal Relationships, Madison, WI.

Marwell, G., & Schmitt, D. R. (1967). Dimensions of compliance-gaining behavior: An empirical analysis. *Sociometry, 30,* 350–364.

Maslin, J. (1991, July 17). False goddess: Thinness for women. *The New York Times*, p. B3.

Maslow, A. (1968). *Toward a psychology of being*. Princeton, NJ: Van Nostrand.

Maslow, A. H., & Mintz, N. L. (1956). Effects of esthetic surroundings: I. Initial effects of three esthetic conditions upon perceiving "energy" and "well-being" in faces. *Journal of Psychology, 41,* 247–254.

Mason, K. O., Czajka, J. L., & Arber, S. (1976). Changes in the U.S. women's sex-role attitudes. *American Sociological Review, 41,* 573–596.

Mason, M. A. (1988). *The equality trap.* New York: Simon & Schuster.

Masters, W. H., & Johnson, V. E. (1966). *Human sexual response.* Boston: Little, Brown.

Masters, W. H., & Johnson, V. E. (1970). *Human sexual inadequacy.* Boston: Little, Brown.

Matthews, C., & Clark, R. D., III. (1991). *Marital satisfaction: A validation approach.* Unpublished doctoral dissertation, Florida State University.

Maugham, W. S. (1953). *Of human bondage.* New York: Pocket Books.

Maurois, A. (1953). *Lelia: The life of George Sand* (G. Hopkins, Trans.). London: Alden.

May, J. L., & Hamilton, P. A. (1980). Effects of musically evoked affect on women's interpersonal attraction and perceptual judgments of physical attractiveness of men. *Motivation and Emotion, 4,* 217–228.

Mayer, W. (1983). Alcohol abuse and alcoholism: The psychologist's role in prevention, research, and treatment. *American Psychologist, 38,* 1116–1121.

Mazur, R. (1987). Beyond jealousy and possessiveness. In G. Clanton & L. G. Smith (Eds.), *Jealousy* (pp. 181–189). Lanham, MD: University Press of America.

McAdams, D. P. (1980). A thematic coding scheme for the intimacy motive. *Journal of Research in Personality, 14,* 413–432.

McAdams, D. P. (1982). Intimacy motivation. In A. J. Stewart (Ed.), *Motivation and society* (pp. 133–171). San Francisco: Jossey-Bass.

McAdams, D. P. (1992). *Intimacy: The need to be close.* New York: Doubleday.

McAdams, D. P., & Vaillant, G. E. (1982). Intimacy motivation and psychosocial adjustment: A longitudinal study. *Journal of Personality Assessment, 46,* 586–593.

McCarthy, M. (1942). *The company she keeps.* New York: Simon & Schuster.

McCarthy, M. (1954). *A charmed life.* New York: New American Library.

McCormack, E. (1975, October). Maximum tumescence and repose. *Rolling Stones, 9,* 36–71.

McCormick, N. B. (1977). Gender role and expected social power behavior in sexual decision-making. *Dissertation Abstracts International, 37,* 422-B (University Microfilms No. 77-1646, 151).

McCormick, N. B. (1979). Come-ons and put-offs: Unmarried students' strategies for having and avoiding sexual intercourse. *Psychology of Women Quarterly, 4,* 194–211.

McCormick, N. B., & Jesser, C. J. (1982). The courtship game: Power in the sexual encounter. In E. R. Allegier & N. B. McCormick (Eds.), *Changing boundaries: Gender roles and sexual behavior* (pp. 64–86). Palo Alto, CA: Mayfield.

McCubbin, H. I., Joy, C. B., Cauble, A. E., Comeau, J. K., Patterson, J. M., & Needle, R. H. (1980). Family stress and coping: A decade review. *Journal of Marriage and the Family, 42,* 855–871.

McCubbin, H. I., & Patterson, J. M. (1982). Family adaptation to crisis. In H. I. McCubbin, A. E. Cauble, & J. M. Patterson (Eds.), *Family stress, coping, and social support* (pp. 26–47). Springfield, IL: Charles C. Thomas.

McWhirter, D. P., & Mattison, A. M. (1984). *The male couple: How relationships develop.* Englewood Cliffs, NJ: Prentice-Hall.

Mead, M. (1931). Jealousy: Primitive and civilized. In S. Schmalhausen & V. F. Calverton (Eds.), *Woman's coming of age* (pp. 35–48). New York: Liveright.

Mead, M. (1969). *Sex and temperament in three primitive societies.* New York: Dell Publishing.

Means, J. (1991). Coping with a breakup: Negative mood regulation expectancies and depression following the end of a romantic relationship. *Journal of Personality and Social Psychology, 60,* 327–334.

Meerloo, J. A. M. (1964). *Unobtrusive communication.* Assen, The Netherlands: Roy Van Gorcum.

Mehrabian, A. (1968). Relationship of attitude to seated posture, orientation, and distance. *Journal of Personality and Social Psychology, 10,* 26–30.

Mehrabian, A. (1972). *Nonverbal communication.* Chicago: Aldine-Atherton.

Meichenbaum, D. (1977). *Cognitive-behavior modification: An integrative approach.* New York: Plenum Press.

Meichenbaum, D. (1985). *Stress inoculation training.* Elmsford, NJ: Pergamon Press.

Messinger, L. (1976). Remarriage between divorced people with children from previous marriages: A proposal for preparation for remarriage. *Journal of Marriage and Family Counseling, 38,* 273–281.

Mesulam, M.-M., & Perry, J. (1972). The diagnosis of love-sickness: Experimental psychophysiology without the polygraph. *Psychophysiology, 9,* 546–551.

Metts, S. (1989). An exploratory investigation of deception in close relationships. *Journal of Social and Personal Relationships, 6,* 159–179.

Metts, S., Cupach, W. R., & Bejlovec, R. A. (1989). "I love you too much to ever start liking you": Redefining romantic relationships. *Journal of Social and Personal Relationships, 6,* 259–274.

Michaels, J. W., Acock, A. C., & Edwards, J. N. (1986). Social exchange and equity determinants of relationship commitment. *Journal of Social and Personal Relationships, 3,* 161–175.

Michaels, J. W., Edwards, J. N., & Acock, A. C. (1984). Satisfaction in intimate relationships as a function of inequality, inequity, and outcomes. *Social Psychology Quarterly, 47,* 347–357.

Miell, D., & Duck, S. (1986). Strategies in developing friendships. In V. J. Derlega & V. A. Winstead (Eds.), *Friendship and social interaction* (pp. 129–143). New York: Springer-Verlag.

Milardo, R. M., Johnson, M. P., & Huston, T. L. (1983). Developing close relationships: Changing patterns of interaction between pair members and social networks. *Journal of Personality and Social Psychology, 44,* 964–976.

Miller, H. (1938/1963). *Black spring.* New York: Grove Press.

Miller, H. (1965). *Sexus.* New York: Grove Press.

Miller, L., Berg, J. H., & Archer, R. L. (1983). Openers: Individuals who elicit intimate self-disclosure. *Journal of Personality and Social Psychology, 44,* 1234–1244.

Miller, L. C., & Read, S. J. (1987). Why am I telling you this? Self-disclosure in a goal-based model of personality. In V. Derlega & J. Berg (Eds.), *Self-disclosure: Theory, research, and therapy* (pp. 35–58). New York: Plenum Press.

Miller, R. S., & Lefcourt, H. M. (1982). The assessment of intimacy. *Journal of Personality Assessment, 46,* 514–518.

Millett, K. (1970). *Sexual politics.* Garden City, NY: Doubleday.

Mitchell, A. K. (1981). *Someone to turn to: Experiences of help before divorce.* Aberdeen, Scotland: Aberdeen University Press.

Mitchell, M. (1936). *Gone with the wind.* New York: Macmillan.

Money, J. (1980) *Love and love sickness.* Baltimore, MD: Johns Hopkins University Press.

Montgomery, J. (1982). *Family crisis as process: Persistence and change.* Washington, DC: University Press of America.

Moore, S. (1960). *The Stanislavski system.* New York: Viking Press.

Morris, D. (1971). *Intimate behaviour.* London: Triad/Grafton Books.

Morris, D. (1977). *Manwatching: A field guide to human behavior.* New York: Harry N. Abrams.

Morton, T. L. (1978). Intimacy and reciprocity of exchange: A comparison of spouses and strangers. *Journal of Personality and Social Psychology, 36,* 72–81.

Moyer, K. E. (1968). Kinds of aggression and their physiological basis. *Communications in Behavioral Biology, 2,* 64–87.

Muehlenhard, C. L., & Cook, S. W. (1988). Men's self-reports of unwanted sexual activity. *The Journal of Sex Research, 24,* 58–72.

Muehlenhard, C. L., Goggins, M. F., Jones, J., & Satterfield, A. (1991). Sexual violence and coercion in close relationships. In K. McKinney & S. Sprecher (Eds.), *Sexuality in close relationships* (pp. 155–175). Hillsdale, NJ: Erlbaum.

Muehlenhard, C. L., & Hollabaugh, L. C. (1988). Do women sometimes say no when they mean yes? The prevalence and correlates of women's token resistance to sex. *Journal of Personality and Social Psychology, 54,* 872–879.

Muehlenhard, C. L., Koralewski, M. A., Andrews, S. L., & Burdick, C. (1986). Verbal and nonverbal cues that convey interest in dating: Two studies. *Behavior Therapy, 17,* 404–419.

Muehlenhard, C. L., & McFall, R. M. (1981). Dating initiation from a woman's perspective. *Behavior Therapy, 12,* 682–691.

Muehlenhard, C. L., & McFall, R. M. (1982, December). Assertiveness breeds attempt. *Psychology Today,* p. 75.

Muehlenhard, C. L., & Miller, E. N. (1988). Traditional and nontraditional men's responses to women's dating initiation. *Behavior Modification, 12,* 385–403.

Muehlenhard, C. L., & Scardino, T. J. (1985). What will he think? Men's impressions of women who initiate dates and achieve academically. *Journal of Consulting Psychology, 32,* 560–569.

Murphy, G. (1947). *Personality: A biosocial approach to origins and structure.* New York: Harper.

Murphy, G. E., Simons, A. D., Wetzel, G. D., & Lustman, P. J. (1984). Cognitive therapy and pharmacotherapy. *Archives of General Psychiatry, 41,* 33–41.

Murstein, B. I. (1970). Stimulus-value-role: A theory of marital choice. *Journal of Marriage and the Family, 32,* 465–481.

Murstein, B. I., Cerreto, M., & MacDongald, M. G. (1977). A theory and investigation of the effect of exchange-orientation on marriage and friendship. *Journal of Marriage and Family, 39,* 543–548.

Murstein, B. I., Wadlin, R., & Bond, C. F., Jr. (1987). The revised exchange-orientation scale. *Small Group Behavior, 18,* 212–223.

Myerhoff, B. (1982). Life history among the elderly: Performance visibility, and remembering. In R. Ruby (Ed.), *A crack in the mirror: Reflective perspectives in anthropology* (pp. 1–35). Philadelphia: University of Pennsylvania Press.

Myers, D. (1983). *Social psychology* (2nd ed.). New York: McGraw-Hill.

Myers, I. B. (1962). *Myers–Briggs Type Indicator.* Princeton, NJ: Educational Testing Service.

Napier, A. Y. (1977). *The rejection–intrusion pattern: A central family dynamic.* Unpublished manuscript, School of Family Resources, University of Wisconsin, Madison.

Napier, A. Y., & Whitaker, C. (1978). *The family crucible.* New York: Harper & Row.

National Center for Health Statistics. (1984). *Monthly Vital Statistics Report, 32,* Supplement. Advance report of final marriage statistics, 1981. U.S. Department of Health and Human Services: National Center for Health Statistics.

National Institute of Mental Health. (1992). *Depression: What you need to know.* U.S. Department of Health and Human Services. Public Health Service. Alcohol, Drug Abuse, and Mental Health Administration. Rockville, MD.

Nerem, R. M., Levesque, M. J., & Cornhill, J. F. (1980). Social environment as a factor in diet-induced arteriosclerosis. *Science, 208,* 1475–1476.

Newsweek (1986, June 2). Too late for Prince Charming? pp. 54–61.

Newsweek (1988, December 12). A tale of abuse. p. 59.

New Yorker, The. (1984, July 2). Annals of Law: The insanity defense, pp. 46–48.

New York Times, The. (1985, July 8).

New York Times, The. (1990, March 23). Transcript of March 22 presidential press conference.

New York Times, The. (1991, June 16). Fatherhood: The second round, p. E16.

New York Times, The. (1991, September 20). Marriage gone bad, double slaying and hung jury leave a city divided. Section A, p. A17.

New York Times Book Review, The. (1991, August 11). Bringing home the hate, p. 7.

Nicolson, N. (1973). *Portrait of a marriage.* New York: Bantam Books.

Nielsen Television 81. (1981). Chicago: A. C. Nielsen.

Nolen-Hoeksema, S. (1987). Sex differences in unipolar depression: Evidence and theory. *Psychological Bulletin, 101,* 259–282.

Noller, P. (1982). Couple communication and marital satisfaction. *Australian Journal of Sex, Marriage and Family, 3,* 69–75.

Noller, P. (1987). Nonverbal communication in marriage. In D. Perlman & S. Duck (Eds.), *Intimate relationships: Development, dynamics, and deterioration* (pp. 149–175). London: Sage Publications.

Noller, P., Law, H., & Comrey, A. L. (1987). Cattell, Comrey, and Eysenck personality factors compared: More evidence for the five robust factors? *Journal of Personality and Social Psychology, 53,* 775–782.

Nordheimer, J. (1990, October 18). Stepfathers: The shoes rarely fit. *The New York Times,* p. C8.

Norton, A. J., & Moorman, J. E. (1987). Current trends in marriage and divorce among American women. *Journal of Marriage and the Family, 49,* 3–14.

Norton, R. (1979). *Communicator style: Theory, applications, and measures.* Beverly Hills, CA: Sage Publications.

Norwood, R. (1985). *Women who love too much.* Los Angeles: Jeremy P. Archer.

Notarius, C. I., & Johnson, J. S. (1982). Emotional expression in husbands and wives. *Journal of Marriage and the Family, 44,* 483–489.

Nurnberger, J. I., & Gershorn, E. S. (1982). Genetics. In E. S. Paykel (Ed.), *Handbook of affective disorders* (pp. 126–145). New York: Guilford Press.

Oates, J. C. (1989). Détente. In G. D. Chipps & B. Henderson (Eds.), *Love stories for the time being* (pp. 79–106). Wainscott, NY: Pushcart Press.

O'Brien, J. E. (1972, August). *Interrelationship of conflict and satisfaction in unstable marriages: A methodological analysis.* Paper presented at the annual meeting of the American Sociological Association, New Orleans.

Ohman, A. (1988). Nonconscious control of autonomic responses: A role for Pavlovian conditioning? *Biological Psychology, 27,* 113–135.

O'Leary, K. D., Arias, I., Rosenbaum, A., & Barling, J. (1986). *Premarital physical aggression.* Unpublished manuscript, State University of New York at Stony Brook.

Olshansky, S. (1962, April). Chronic sorrow: A response to having a mentally defective child. *Social Casework, 43,* 190–193.

Olson, D. H. (1972). The powerlessness of family power: Empirical and clinical considerations. In J. H. Masserman (Ed.), *Science and psychoanalysis, Vol. XX: The dynamics of power* (pp. 139–147). New York: Grune & Stratton.

Olson, D. H., McCubbin, H. I., Barnes, H., Larsen, A., Muxen, M., & Wilson, M. (1983). *Families: What makes them work.* Beverly Hills, CA: Sage Publications.

Olson, D. H., & Rabunsky, C. (1972). Validity of four measures of family power. *Journal of Marriage and the Family, 34,* 224–234.

Olson, D. H., & Schaefer, M. T. (1977). *Quest for intimacy.* Unpublished manuscript, University of Minnesota, St. Paul.

Olson, D. H., & Schaefer, M. T. (1981). *PAIR: Personal Assessment of Intimacy in Relationships. Procedure Manual and Item Booklet.* Family Social Science, University of Minnesota, St. Paul, MN 55108.

O'Neill, N., & O'Neill, G. (1972). *Open marriage: A new lifestyle for couples.* New York: M. Evans.

Orimoto, L., & Hatfield, E. (1991). An individual difference measure of emotional contagion. Reported in E. Hatfield, J. Cacioppo, & R. Rapson (1992), *Emotional contagion.* Madison, WI: C. W. Brown.

Orimoto, L., Hatfield, E., Yamakawa, R., & Denney, C. (1991). *Gender differences in emotional reactions and coping strategies following a break-up.* Unpublished manuscript, University of Hawaii, Honolulu.

Orlofsky, J. L., & Ginsburg, S. D. (1981). Intimacy status: Relationship to affect cognition. *Adolescence, 16*, 91–100.

Ornstein, R., & Thompson, R. F. (1984). *The amazing brain.* Boston: Houghton Mifflin.

Osterweis, M. (1984). Bereavement intervention programs. In M. Osterweis, F. Solomon, & M. Green (Eds.), *Bereavement: Reactions, consequences, and care* (pp. 239–282). Washington, DC: National Academy Press.

Overbeck, J. (1990). *Love stinks.* New York: Pocket Books.

Ovris, B. R., Kelley, H. H., & Butler, D. (1976). Attributional conflict in young couples. In J. H. Harvey, W. J. Ickes, & R. E. Kidd (Eds.), *New directions in attribution research* (Vol. 1, pp. 353–386). Hillsdale, NJ: Erlbaum.

Owens, D. J., & Straus, M. A. (1975). The social structure of violence in childhood and approval of violence as an adult. *Aggressive Behavior, 1*, 193–211.

Papez, J. W. (1937). A proposed mechanism of emotion. *Archives of Neurology and Psychiatry, 38*, 725–743.

Parker, D. (1944). *The portable Dorothy Parker.* New York: Viking Press.

Parkes, C. M. (1964). The effects of bereavement on physical and mental health: A study of the records of widows. *British Medical Journal, 2*, 274–279.

Parks, M. R., & Eggert, L. L. (1991). The role of social context in the dynamics of personal relationships. In W. H. Jones & D. Perlman (Eds.), *Advances in Personal Relationships* (Vol. 2, pp. 1–34). London: Jessica Kingsley Publishers.

Parks, R. (1977). Parental reactions to the birth of a handicapped child. *Health Social Work, 2*, 52–66.

Patterson, G. R. (1971). *Families: Applications of social learning to family life.* Champaign, IL: Research Press.

Patterson, G. R., Littman, R. A., & Brecker, W. (1967). Aggression behavior in children: A step toward a theory of aggression. *Monographs of the Society for Research in Child Development, 32*, Serial No. 113.

Patterson, M. L. (1976). An arousal model of interpersonal intimacy. *Psychological Review, 83*, 235–245.

Paul, J., & Paul, M. (1983). *Do I have to give up me to be loved by you?* Minneapolis, MN: Compcare.

Pedersen, C. A., Caldwell, J. D., Jirikowski, G., & Insel, T. R. (1991, May 19–22). *Oxytocin in maternal, sexual and social behaviors.* Paper presented at the meetings of the New York Academy of Sciences, Arlington, VA.

Peele, S. (1975). *Love and addiction.* New York: Taplinger Publishing.

Pennebaker, J. W. (1990). *Opening up: The healing power of confiding in others.* New York: Morrow.

Pennebaker, J. W., & Beale, S. K. (1986). Confronting a traumatic event. *Journal of Abnormal Psychology, 95*, 274–281.

Pepitone, A. (1964). *Attraction & hostility: An experimental analysis of interpersonal and self-evaluation.* New York: Atherton Press.

Peplau, L. A. (1979). Power in dating relationships. In J. Freeman (Ed.), *Women: A feminist perspective* (3rd ed., pp 100–113). Palo Alto, CA: Mayfield.

Peplau, L. A. (1983). Roles and gender. In H. H. Kelley, E. Berscheid, A. Christensen, J. H. Harvey, T. L. Huston, G. Levinger, E. McClintock, L. A. Peplau, & D. R. Peterson (Eds.), *Close relationships* (pp. 220–260). New York: Freeman.

Peplau, L. A., & Amaro, H. (1982). Understanding lesbian relationships. In W. Paul, J. D. Weinrich, J. C. Gonsiorek, & M. E. Hotvedt (Eds.), *Homosexuality: Social, psychological, and biological issues* (pp. 233–247). Beverly Hills, CA: Sage Publications.

Peplau, L. A., & Perlman, D. (1982). *Loneliness*. New York: Wiley-Interscience.

Peplau, L. A., Rubin, Z., & Hill, C. T. (1976). The sexual balance of power. *Psychology Today, 10,* 142–151.

Peplau, L. A., Rubin, Z., & Hill, C. (1977). Sexual intimacy in dating couples. *Journal of Social Issues, 33,* 86–109.

Perlez, J. (1991, July 29). Kenyans do some soul-searching after the rape of 71 girls. *The New York Times,* pp. A1, A4.

Perlman, D., & Fehr, B. (1987). The development of intimate relationships. In D. Perlman & S. Duck (Eds.), *Intimate relationships: Development, dynamics, and deterioration* (pp. 13–42). Beverly Hills, CA: Sage Publications.

Perlman, D., & Peplau, L. A. (1981). Toward a social psychology of loneliness. In S. Duck & R. Gilmour (Eds.), *Personal relationships. 3: Personal relationships in disorder* (pp. 31–56). London: Academic Press.

Perper, T., & Fox, V. S. (1980, April). *Flirtation and pickup patterns in bars.* Paper presented at the meeting of the Eastern Conference on Reproductive Behavior, New York.

Persky, H., Smith, K. D., & Basu, G. K. (1971). Relation of psychologic measures of aggression and hostility to testosterone production in man. *Psychosomatic Medicine, 33,* 265–277.

Peterson, D. R. (1979). Assessing interpersonal relationships by means of interaction records. *Behavioral Assessment, 1,* 221–236.

Peterson, D. R. (1983). Conflict. In H. H. Kelley, E. Berscheid, A. Christensen, J. H. Harvey, T. L. Huston, G. Levinger, E. McClintock, L. A. Peplau, & D. R. Peterson (Eds.), *Close relationships* (pp. 360–396). New York: Freeman.

Pfeiffer, S. M., & Wong, P. T. P. (1989). Multidimensional jealousy. *Journal of Social and Personal Relationships, 6,* 181–196.

Phillips, D. (1978). *How to fall out of love.* New York: Fawcett Popular Library.

Phillips, R. (1988). *Putting asunder: A history of divorce in Western society* (pp. 630–640). Cambridge: Cambridge University Press.

Piercy, M. (1973). *Small changes* (p. 438). New York: Doubleday.

Pike, G. R., & Sillars, A. L. (1985). Reciprocity of marital communication. *Journal of Social and Personal Relations, 2,* 303–324.

Pilisuk, M. (1982). Delivery of social support: The social inoculation. *American Journal of Orthopsychiatry, 52,* 20–36.

Pilisuk, M., & Parks, S. H. (1983). Social support and family stress. In H. I. McCubbin, M. B. Sussman, & J. M. Patterson (Eds.), *Social stress and the family: Advances and developments in family stress theory research* (pp. 137–156). New York: Haworth Press.

Pilkington, C. J., & Richardson, D. R. (1988). Perceptions of risk in intimacy. *Journal of Social and Personal Relationships, 5,* 503–508.

Pillemer, J., & Hatfield, E. (1981). Love and its effect on mental and physical health. In R. Fogel, E. Hatfield, S. Kiesler, & E. Shanas (Eds.), *Aging: Stability and change in the family* (pp. 253–274). New York: Academic Press.

Pillemer, J., & Hatfield, E. (1983). How important is marital fairness over the lifespan? *International Journal of Aging and Human Development, 17,* 89–101.

Pillemer, J., Peterson, R., Utne, M., & Hatfield, E. (1981). Measuring equity in intimate relations. *Applied Psychological Measurement, 5,* 467–480.

Pittman, F. (1989). *Private lies: Infidelity and the betrayal of intimacy.* New York: Norton.

Plante, T. G., & Rodin, J. (1990). Physical fitness and enhanced psychological health. *Current Psychology Research and Reviews, 9,* 3–24.

Pleck, J. H., & Sawyer, J. (Eds.) (1974). *Men and masculinity.* Englewood Cliffs, NJ: Prentice-Hall.

Plutchik, R. (1980). *Emotion: A psychoevolutionary synthesis.* New York: Harper & Row.

Pollak, S., & Gilligan, C. (1982). Images of violence in thematic apperception test stories. *Journal of Personality and Social Psychology, 42,* 159–167.

Porter, K. A. (1962). *Ship of fools.* Boston: Atlantic–Little, Brown.

Potter-Efron, R. T., & Potter-Efron, P. S. (1989). Assessment of co-dependency with individuals from alcoholic and chemically dependent families. *Alcoholism Treatment Quarterly, 6,* 37–57.

Prather, J. E. (1990). "It's just as easy to marry a rich man as a poor one!" Students' accounts of parental messages about marital partners. *Mid-American Review of Sociology, 14,* 151–162.

Prins, K. S., Buunk, B. P., & Van Ypern, N. W. (1991). *Equity, normative disapproval and extramarital relationships.* Paper presented at the International Network on Personal Relationships Conference, Bloomington, IL.

Proust, M. (1956). *Swann in love* (C. K. Scott Moncrieff & T. Kilmartin, Trans.). New York: Modern Library.

Provine, R. R. (1986). Yawning as a stereotyped action pattern and releasing stimulus. *Ethology, 72,* 109–122.

Provine, R. R. (1990, October 28–November 2). *Laughter: Social context, structure, and contagion.* Paper presented at the annual meeting, Society for Neuroscience, St. Louis, MO.

Pruitt, D. G., & Carnevale, P. J. D. (1982). The development of integrative agreements in social conflict. In V. J. Derlega & J. Grzelak (Eds.), *Cooperation and helping behavior* (pp. 152–185). New York: Academic Press.

Quindlen, A. (1990, September 27). Moving pictures. Public and private. *The New York Times,* p. A19.

Rabehl, S. M., Ridge, R. D., & Berscheid, E. (1992). *Love vs. in love.* Unpublished manuscript. University of Minnesota: Minneapolis.

Radloff, L. S. (1975). Sex differences in depression: The effects of occupation and marital status. *Sex Roles, 1,* 249–265.

Rankin, R., & Maneker, J. (1985). The duration of marriage in a divorcing population: The impact of children. *Journal of Marriage and the Family, 47,* 43–52.

Rapoport, J. L. (1989). *The boy who couldn't stop washing: The experience and treatment of obsessive–compulsive disorder.* New York: Dutton.

Rapson, K. E. (1990). *Relationship and achievement stressors: Gender differences in appraisals, coping and outcome.* Unpublished doctoral dissertation, Virginia Consortioum for Professional Psychology, Norfolk.

Rapson, R. L. (1980). *Denials of doubt: An interpretation of American history*. Lanham, MD: University Press of America.

Rapson, R. L. (1988). *American yearnings: Love, money, and endless possibility*. Lanham, MD: University Press of America.

Raush, H. L., Barry, W. A., Hertel, R. K., & Swain, M. A. (1974). *Communication, conflict and marriage*. San Francisco: Jossey-Bass.

Raven, B. H. (1988, August). *French & Raven 30 years later: Power/interaction and interpersonal influence*. Paper presented at the International Congress of Psychology, Sydney, Australia.

Raven, B. H., Centers, R., & Rodrigues, A. (1975). The bases of conjugal power. In R. E. Cromwell & D. H. Olson (Eds.), *Power in families* (pp. 217–232). New York: Wiley.

Rayner, R. (1991). The perfect blonde. *GQ*, pp. 122–125. London, England.

Redbook. (1977, January). New York: The Redbook Publishing Co.

Redick, R. W., & Johnson, C. (1974). Marital status, living arrangements and family characteristics of admissions to state and county mental hospitals and out-patient psychiatric clinics. *United States 1970. Statistical note 100: National Institute of Mental Health*. Washington, DC: U.S. Government Printing Office.

Reid, W. J., & Crisafulli, A. (1990). Marital discord and child behavior problems: A meta-analysis. *Journal of Abnormal Child Psychology, 18*, 105–117.

Reik, T. (1948). *Listening with the third ear*. New York: Farrar, Straus & Giroux.

Reik, T. (1949). *Of love and lust*. New York: Farrar, Straus & Co.

Reik, T. (1972). *A psychologist looks at love*. New York: Holt, Rinehart & Winston.

Reis, H. T. (1987). *Where does social support come from?* Unpublished manuscript, University of Rochester, Rochester, NY.

Reis, H. T., & Shaver, P. (1988). Intimacy as an interpersonal process. In S. Duck (Ed.), *Handbook of personal relationships: Theory, research, and interventions* (pp. 367–389). New York: Wiley.

Reiss, I. L. (1967). *The social context of premarital sexual permissiveness*. New York: Holt, Rinehart & Winston.

Reiss, I. L., Anderson, R. E., & Sponaugle, G. C. (1980). A multivariate model of the determinants of extramarital sexual permissiveness. *Journal of Marriage and the Family, 42*, 395–411.

Reiss, I. L., & Lee, G. R. (1988). *Family systems in America* (4th ed.). New York: Holt, Rinehart & Winston.

Riggio, R. E. (1986). Assessment of basic social skills. *Journal of Personality and Social Psychology, 51*, 649–660.

Riordan, C. A., & Tedeschi, J. T. (1983) Attraction in aversive environments: Some evidence for classical conditioning and negative reinforcement. *Journal of Personality and Social Psychology, 44*, 683–692.

Riportella-Muller, R. (1989). Sexuality in the elderly: A review. In K. McKinney & S. Sprecher (Eds.), *Human sexuality: The societal and interpersonal context* (pp. 210–236). Norwood: NJ: Ablex.

Riskind, J. H., & Gotay, C. C. (1982). Physical posture: Could it have regulatory or feedback effects on motivation and emotion? *Motivation and Emotion, 6*, 273–298.

Roberts, L. J., & Krokoff, L. L. (1990). A time-series analysis of withdrawal, hostility, and displeasure in satisfied and dissatisfied marriages. *Journal of Marriage and the Family, 52,* 95–105.

Rodgers, R., & Hammerstein, O. (1943). *Oklahoma!* New York: Random House.

Rodman, H. (1972). Marital power and the theory of resources in cultural context. *Journal of Comparative Family Studies, 3,* 50–69.

Rollins, B. C., & Cannon, K. L. (1974). Marital satisfaction over the family life cycle: A re-evaluation. *Journal of Marriage and the Family, 36,* 271–283.

Roloff, M. E., & Cloven, D. (1990). The chilling effect in interpersonal relationships: The reluctance to speak one's mind. In D. D. Cahn (Ed.), *Intimates in conflict* (pp. 49–76). Hillsdale, NJ: Erlbaum.

Rook, K. S., & Hammen, C. L. (1977). A cognitive perspective on the experience of sexual arousal. *Journal of Social Issues, 33,* 7–29.

Rook, K. S., & Pietromonaco, P. (1987). Close relationships: Ties that heal or ties that bind? In W. H. Jones & D. Perlman (Eds.), *Advances in Personal Relationships* (Vol. 1, pp. 1–35). Greenwich, CT: JAI Press.

Rosenbaum, M. (1980). A schedule for assessing self-control behaviors: Preliminary findings. *Behavior Therapy, 11,* 109–112.

Rosenbaum, M. E. (1986). The repulsion hypothesis: On the nondevelopment of relationships. *Journal of Personality and Social Psychology, 51,* 1156–1166.

Rosenberg, S., Nelson, C., & Vivekananthan, P. S. (1968). A multidimensional approach to the structure of personality impressions. *Journal of Personality and Social Psychology, 9,* 283–294.

Rosenblum, L. A. (1985, September 18). *Discussant: Passionate love and the nonhuman primate.* Paper presented at the International Academy of Sex Research meetings, Seattle, WA.

Rosenblum, L. A., & Plimpton, L. A. (1981). The infant's effort to cope with separation. In M. Lewis & L. Rosenblum (Eds.), *The uncommon child* (pp. 225–257). New York: Plenum Press.

Rosenfeld, A. H. (1985, June). Depression: Dispelling despair. *Psychology Today,* pp. 29–34.

Rosenthal, E. (1990, June 27). U.S. is by far the leader in homicide. *The New York Times National,* p. A10.

Ross, E. A. (1921). *Principles of sociology.* New York: Century.

Roth, P. (1990). *Deception.* New York: Simon & Schuster.

Roth, P. (1991). *Patrimony: A true story.* New York: Simon & Schuster.

Rounsaville, B. J., Weissman, M. M., Prusoff, B. A., & Herceg-Baron, R. L. (1979a). Marital disputes and treatment outcome in depressed women. *Comprehensive Psychiatry, 20,* 483–490.

Rounsaville, B. J., Weissman, M. M., Prusoff, B. A., & Herceg-Baron, R. L. (1979b). Process of psychotherapy among depressed women with marital disputes. *American Journal of Orthopsychiatry, 49,* 505–510.

Royko, M. (1985, January 25). Sex or bowling: The nation replies. *Honolulu Star Bulletin,* p. B-2.

Rubin, J. (1970). *Do it!* New York: Simon & Schuster.

Rubin, L. B. (1976). *Worlds of pain: Life in the working class family*. New York: Basic Books.

Rubin, L. B. (1986). *Just friends: The role of friendship in our lives*. New York: Harper & Row.

Rubin, Z. (1970). Measurement of romantic love. *Journal of Personality and Social Psychology, 16*, 265–273.

Rubin, Z. (1973). *Liking and loving: An invitation to social psychology*. New York: Holt, Rinehart & Winston.

Rubin, Z., Hill, C. T., Peplau, L. A., & Dunke-Schetter, C. (1980). Self-disclosure in dating couples: Sex roles and the ethic of openness. *Journal of Marriage and the Family, 42*, 305–317.

Rude, G. P. E. (1981). *The crowd in history: A study of popular disturbances in France and England*. London: Lawrence and Wishart.

Rusbult, C. E. (1987). Responses to dissatisfaction in close relationships: The Exit–Voice–Loyalty–Neglect model. In D. Perlman & S. Duck (Eds.), *Intimate relationships: Development, dynamics, and deterioration* (pp. 209–237). London: Sage Publications.

Rusbult, C. E., Verette, J., Whitney, G. A., Slovik, L. F., & Lipkus, I. (1991). Accommodation processes in close relationships: Theory and preliminary empirical evidence. *Journal of Personality and Social Psychology, 60*, 53–78.

Rusbult, C. E., Zembrodt, I., & Iwaniszek, J. (1986). The impact of gender and sex-role orientation on responses to dissatisfaction in close relationships. *Sex Roles, 15*, 1–20.

Russell, D., Peplau, L. A., & Ferguson, M. L. (1978). Developing a measure of loneliness. *Journal of Personality Assessment, 42*, 290–294.

Russell, D. E. H., & Howell, N. (1983). The prevalence of rape in the United States revisited. *Signs, 8*, 688–695.

Safilios-Rothschild, C. (1969). Family sociology or wives' family sociology: A cross-cultural examination of decision-making. *Journal of Marriage and the Family, 31*, 290–301.

Safilios-Rothschild, C. (1976). A macro- and micro-examination of family power and love: An exchange model. *Journal of Marriage and the Family, 38*, 355–362.

Saikaku, I. (1686/1956). *Five women who loved love* (W. T. De Bary, Trans.). Rutland, VT: Charles E. Tuttle.

St. Paul Pioneer Press Dispatch. (1987, April 8). Panel defeats sodomy law repeal. *St. Paul Pioneer Press Dispatch*, p. 3b.

Salovey, P., & Rodin, J. (1985, September). The heart of jealousy. *Psychology Today, 19*, 22–29.

Santrock, J. W., Sitterle, K. A., & Warshak, R. A. (1988). Parent–child relationship in stepfather families. In P. Bronstein & C. P. Cowan (Eds.), *Fatherhood today: Men's changing role in the family* (pp. 144–165). New York: Wiley.

Sarbin, T. R., & Hardyck, C. D. (1953). *Contributions to role-taking theory: Role perception on the basis of postural cues*. Unpublished manuscript, University of California, Berkeley.

Sarton, M. (1982). *Anger*. New York: Norton.

Satariano, W. A., & Syme, S. L. (1981). Life changes and disease in elderly populations: Coping with change. In J. L. McGaugh & S. B. Kiesler (Eds.), *Aging: Biology and behavior* (pp. 311–327). New York: Academic Press.

Saul, S., & Waldman, M. S. (1991, April 14). Kennedy's political hold. *Star-Bulletin & Advertiser*, p. A31.

Scanzoni, J. (1979). Social processes and power in families. In W. R. Burr, R. Hill, F. I. Nye, & I. L. Reiss (Eds.), *Contemporary theories about the family: Research-based theories* (Vol. 1, pp. 295–316). New York: Free Press.

Scanzoni, L. D., & Scanzoni, J. (1988). *Men, women, and change: A sociology of marriage and family* (3rd ed.). New York: McGraw-Hill.

Scarf, M. (1980). *Unfinished business*. New York: Ballantine.

Schachter, S., & Singer, J. (1962). Cognitive, social, and physiological determinants of emotional state. *Psychological Review, 69*, 379–399.

Schaefer, M. T., & Olson, D. H. (1981). Assessing intimacy: The Pair Inventory. *Journal of Marital and Family Therapy, 7*, 47–60.

Scheflen, A. E. (1964). The significance of posture in communication systems. *Psychiatry, 27*, 316–331.

Schmidt, G., & Sigusch, V. (1970). Sex differences in response to psychosexual stimulation by films and slides. *Journal of Sex Research, 6*, 268–283.

Schmidt, C., Sigusch, V., & Schafer, S. (1973). Responses to reading erotic stories: Male–female differences. *Archives of Sexual Behavior, 2*, 181–199.

Schuckit, M. A. (1977). Geriatric alcoholism and drug abuse. *Gerontologist, 17*, 168–174.

Schwarzer, R., & Leppin, A. (1991). Social support and health: A theoretical and empirical overview. *Journal of Social and Personal Relationships, 8*, 99–128.

Sechrest, L. (1965). *Situational sampling and contrived situations in the assessment of behavior*. Unpublished manuscript, Northwestern University, Evanston, IL.

Sechrest, L., & Flores, L., Jr. (1971). The occurrence of a nervous mannerism in two cultures. *Asian Studies, 9* (1), 55–63.

Selye, H. (1978). *The stress of life* (rev. ed.). New York: McGraw-Hill.

Sendbuehler, J. M., & Goldstein, S. (1977). Attempted suicide among the aged. *Journal of the American Geriatric Society, 25*, 245–253.

Shapiro, J. L. (1987). *When men are pregnant: Needs and concerns of expectant fathers*. San Luis Obispo, CA: Impact Publishers.

Sharpsteen, D. J. (1991). The organization of jealousy knowledge: Romantic jealousy as a blended emotion. In P. Salovey (Ed.), *The psychology of jealousy and envy* (pp. 31–51). New York: Guilford Press.

Shaver, P., & Hazan, C. (1988). A biased overview of the study of love. *Journal of Social and Personal Relationships, 5*, 474–501.

Shaver, P. R., Wu, S., & Schwartz, J. C. (1991). Cross-cultural similarities and differences in emotion and its representation: A prototype approach. In M. S. Clark (Ed.), *Review of personality and social psychology* (Vol. 13, pp. 175–212). Beverly Hills, CA: Sage Publications.

Shearer, L. (1986, September 28). Murder is closer than you think. *Parade Magazine*, p. 20. [Summary of the F.B.I.'s, Appendix 5: Probability of Lifetime Murder Victimization, 1984. *Crime in the United States*.]

Sidell, R. (1986). *Women and children last*. New York: Viking Penguin.

Silver, R. L., & Wortman, C. B. (1980). Coping with undesirable life events. In J. Garber & M. E. P. Seligman (Eds.), *Human helplessness* (pp. 279–375). New York: Academic Press.

Silverman, I. (1971, September). Physical attractiveness and courtship. *Sexual Behavior, 1,* 22–25.

Silverman, P. R., & Cooperband, A. (1975). On widowhood: Mutual help and the elderly widow. *Journal of Geriatric Psychiatry, 8,* 9–27.

Silverstein, L. B. (1991). Transforming the debate about child care and maternal employment. *American Psychologist, 46,* 1025–1032.

Simenauer, J., & Carroll, D. (1982). *Singles: The new Americans.* New York: Simon & Schuster.

Simpson, J. A. (1987). The dissolution of romantic relationships: Factors involved in relationship stability and emotional distress. *Journal of Personality and Social Psychology, 53,* 683–692.

Skolnick, A. S. (1992). *The intimate environment.* New York: HarperCollins.

Small, S. A., & Riley, D. (1990). Toward a multidimensional assessment of work spillover into family life. *Journal of Marriage and the Family, 52,* 51–61.

Smalley, S., & Coleman, E. (1987). Treating intimacy dysfunctions in dyadic relationships among chemically dependent and codependent clients. Special Issue: Chemical dependency and intimacy dysfunction. *Journal of Chemical Dependency Treatment, 1,* 229–243.

Smeaton, G., Byrne, D., & Murnen, S. K. (1989). *Journal of Personality and Social Psychology, 56,* 54–59.

Smith, A. (1759/1966). *The theory of moral sentiments.* New York: Augustus M. Kelley.

Smith, J. C., & Hogan, B. (1983). *Criminal law* (5th ed.). London: Butterworths.

Smith, T. M. (1991, August 19). *Developmental aspects of cynical hostility.* Paper presented at the American Psychological Association meetings, San Francisco, CA.

Smith, T. W. (1990). The polls—a report: The sexual revolution? *Public Opinion Quarterly, 54,* 415–435.

Smith, T. W., & Brehm, S. S. (1981). Person perception and the Type A coronary-prone behavior pattern. *Journal of Personality and Social Psychology, 40,* 1137–1149.

Snodgrass, S. E. (1985). Women's intuition: The effect of subordinate role on interpersonal sensitivity. *Journal of Personality and Social Psychology, 49,* 146–155.

Snow, C. P. (1960/1981). *Strangers and brothers.* New York: Scribner.

Snyder, C. R., Higgins, R. L., & Stucky, R. J. (1983). *Excuses: Masquerades in search of grace.* New York: Wiley.

Snyder, M., Berscheid, E., & Glick, P. (1985). Focusing on the exterior and the interior: Two investigations of the initiation of personal relationships. *Journal of Personality and Social Psychology, 48,* 1427–1439.

Snyder, M., Tanke, E. D., & Berscheid, E. (1977). Social perception and interpersonal behavior: On the self-fulfilling nature of social stereotypes. *Journal of Personality and Social Psychology, 35,* 656–666.

Solomon, R. L. (1980). The opponent-process theory of acquired motivation: The costs of pleasure and the benefits of pain. *American Psychologist, 35,* 691–712.

Solomon, R. L., & Corbit, J. D. (1974). An opponent process theory of motivation. I. The temporal dynamics of affect. *Psychological Review, 81,* 119–145.

Solomon, S., & Saxe, L. (1977). What is intelligent, as well as attractive, is good. *Personality and Social Psychology Bulletin, 3,* 670–673.

Solsberry, V., & Krupnick, J. (1984). Adults' reactions to bereavement. In M. Osterweis, F. Solomon, & M. Green (Eds.), *Bereavement: Reactions, consequences, and care* (pp. 47–68). Washington, DC: National Academy Press.

Somerville, B. T. (1894). Notes on some islands of the New Hebrides (IV). Clothing, ornaments, etc. *The Journal of the Anthropological Institute*, p. 368.

Sorensen, R. C. (1973). *Adolescent sexuality in contemporary America.* New York: World Book.

Spanier, G. B., & Castro, R. F. (1979). Adjustment to separation and divorce: A qualitative analysis. In G. Levinger & O. C. Moles (Eds.), *Divorce and separation* (pp. 211–227). New York: Basic Books.

Spielberger, C. D., Gorsuch, R. L., & Lushene, R. E. (1970). *STAI manual for the State-Trait Inventory.* Palo Alto, CA: Consulting Psychologist Press.

Sponaugle, G. C. (1976). *Correlates of attitudes toward extramarital sexual relations.* Paper presented at the 1976 (April) meeting of the Midwest Sociological Society, St. Louis, MO.

Sponaugle, G. C. (1989). Attitudes toward extramarital relations. In K. McKinney & S. Sprecher (Eds.), *Human sexuality: The societal and interpersonal context* (pp. 187–209). Norwood, NJ: Ablex.

Spoto, D. (1983). *The dark side of genius: The life of Alfred Hitchcock.* New York: Random House.

Sprecher, S. (1985). Sex differences in bases of power in dating relationships. *Sex Roles, 12,* 449–462.

Sprecher, S. (1986). The relation between inequity and emotions in close relationships. *Social Psychology Quarterly, 49,* 309–321.

Sprecher, S. (1988). Investment model, equity, and social support determinants of relationship commitment. *Social Psychology Quarterly, 51,* 318–328.

Sprecher, S. (1992). How men and women expect to feel and behave in response to inequity in close relationships. *Social Psychology Quarterly, 55,* 57–69.

Sprecher, S. (1992). Social exchange perspectives to the dissolution of close relationships. In T. L. Orbuch (Ed.), *Close relationship loss: Theoretical approaches* (pp. 47–66). New York: Springer-Verlag.

Sprecher, S., & Felmlee, D. (1991, August). *Effects of parents and friends on the quality and stability of romantic relationships: A three-wave longitudinal investigation.* Paper presented at the American Sociological Association Meetings, Cincinnati, OH.

Sprecher, S., & Hatfield, E. (1982). Self-esteem and romantic attraction: Four experiments. *Recherches de Psychologie Sociale, 4,* 61–81.

Sprecher, S., & Hatfield, E. (1987). *Gender differences in emotional experience and expression in close relationships.* Unpublished manuscript, University of Wisconsin, Madison.

Sprecher, S., & McKinney, K. (1987). Barriers in the initiation of intimate heterosexual relationships and strategies for intervention. In H. Gochros & W. Ricketts (Eds.), *Intimate relationships* (pp. 97–110). New York: Haworth Press.

Sprecher, S., Metts, S., & Hatfield, E. (1990). *Feelings and behaviors in close relationships as a function of gender and relationship involvement.* Paper presented at the 5th International Conference on Personal Relationships, Oxford, England.

Sprecher, S., Hatfield, E., Potapova, E., Levitskaya, A., & Cortese, A. (1992). Saying no when meaning yes and saying yes when meaning no. *Journal of Social and Personal Relationships.*

Sprecher, S., & Schwartz, P. (1992.) Equity and balance in the exchange of contributions in close relationships. In M. J. Lerner & G. Mikula (Eds.), *Entitlement and the affectional bond.* New York: Plenum Press.

Spuhler, J. N. (1968). Assortative mating with respect to physical characteristics. *Eugenics Quarterly, 15,* 128–140.

Staats, A. W., & Heiby, E. M. (1985). Paradigmatic behaviorism's theory of depression: Unified, explanatory, and heuristic. *Theoretical issues in behavior therapy* (pp. 279–330). New York: Academic Press.

Starr, B. D. (1985). Sexuality and aging. *Annual Review of Gerontology & Geriatrics, 5,* 97–126.

Starr, B. D., & Weiner, M. B. (1981). *The Starr–Weiner report on sex and sexuality in the mature years.* Briarcliff Manor, NY: Stein & Day.

Steinbeck, J., IV. (1990, December). Predisposed and stuck with it. *Lear's, 3,* 56–57.

Steinberg, L. (1987). The impact of puberty on family relations. *Developmental Psychology, 23,* 451–460.

Steiner, J. E. (1979). Human facial expressions in response to taste and smell stimulation. *Advances in Child Development and Behavior, 13,* 257–295.

Steinmetz, S. K. (1978). Violence between family members. *Marriage and Family Review, 1*(3), 1–16.

Steinmetz, S. K., & Straus, M. A. (1973). The family as cradle of violence. *Society, 10,* 50–56.

Stephan, W., Berscheid, E., & Hatfield, E. (1971). Sexual arousal and heterosexual perception. *Journal of Personality and Social Psychology, 20,* 93–101.

Sternberg, R. J. (1986), *Construct validation of a triangular theory of love.* Unpublished manuscript, Yale University, New Haven.

Sternberg, R. J. (1988). Triangulating love. In R. J. Sternberg & M. L. Barnes (Eds.), *The psychology of love* (pp. 119–138). New Haven: Yale University Press.

Sternberg, R. J., & Soriano, L. J. (1984). Styles of conflict resolution. *Journal of Personality and Social Psychology, 47,* 115–126.

Stets, J., & Pirog-Good, M. A. (1987). Violence in dating relationships. *Social Psychology Quarterly, 50,* 237–246.

Stone, L. (1977). *The family, sex, and marriage: In England 1500–1800.* New York: Harper & Row.

Stone, L. (1990). *Road to divorce: England 1530–1987.* Oxford, England: Oxford University Press.

Strachey, L. (1921/1971). *Queen Victoria.* Harmondsworth, England: Penguin Books.

Straus, M. A., & Gelles, R. J. (1986). Societal change and change in family violence from 1975 to 1985 as revealed by two national surveys. *Journal of Marriage and the Family, 48,* 465–479.

Straus, M. A., Gelles, R. J., & Steinmetz, S. K. (1980). *Behind closed doors: Violence in the American family.* New York: Anchor/Doubleday.

Stroebe, W., & Stroebe, M. S. (1987). *Bereavement and health: The psychological and physical consequences of partner loss.* New York: Cambridge University Press.

Struckman-Johnson, C. (1988). Forced sex on dates: It happens to men, too. *Journal of Sex Research, 24,* 234–241.

Styron, W. (1990). *Darkness visible: A memoir of madness.* New York: Random House.

Sullivan, H. S. (1947). *Conceptions of modern psychiatry.* Washington, DC: William Alanson White Psychiatric Foundation.

Surra, C. A. (1990). Research and theory on mate selection and premarital relationships in the 1980s. *Journal of Marriage and the Family, 52,* 844–865.

Sykes, G. M., & Matza, D. (1957). Techniques of neutralization: A theory of delinquency. *American Sociological Review, 22,* 664–670.

Symons, D. (1979). *The evolution of human sexuality.* New York: Oxford University Press.

Szinovacz, M. E. (1987). Family power. In M. Sussman & S. Steinmetz (Eds.), *Handbook of marriage and the family* (2nd ed., pp. 651–693). New York: Plenum Press.

Tannen, D. (1986). *That's not what I meant!* New York: Ballantine.

Tannen, D. (1990). *You just don't understand.* New York: Ballantine.

Tansey, M. J., & Burke, W. F. (1989). *Understanding counter-transference: From projective identification to empathy.* Hillsdale, NJ: Analytic Press.

Tavris, C. (1978, February). 40,000 men tell about their sexual behavior, their fantasies, the ideal woman, and their wives. *Redbook Magazine,* pp. 111–113.

Tavris, C. (1989). *Anger: The misunderstood emotion* (rev. ed.). New York: Touchstone Books/Simon & Schuster.

Tavris, C., & Offir, C. (1977). *The longest war: Sex differences in perspective.* New York: Harcourt Brace Jovanovich.

Taylor, C. (1989). *Sources of the self: The making of the modern identity.* Cambridge, MA: Harvard University Press.

Taylor, D. A., Altman, I., & Sorrentino, R. (1969). Interpersonal exchange as a function of rewards and costs and situational factors: Expectancy confirmation–disconfirmation. *Journal of Experimental Social Psychology, 5,* 324–339.

TBR (R. Strout). (1974, May 14). The plot sickens. *Boston Globe,* p. 23.

Tellegen, A., Dykken, D. T., Bouchard, T. J., Jr., Wilcox, K. J., Segal, N. L., & Rich, S. (1988). Personality similarity in twins reared apart and together. *Journal of Personality and Social Psychology, 54,* 1031–1039.

Tennov, D. (1979). *Love and limerence.* New York: Stein & Day.

Tesch, S. A. (1985). The Psychosocial Intimacy Questionnaire: Validational studies and an investigation of sex roles. *Journal of Social and Personal Relationships, 2,* 471–488.

Tesch, S. A., & Whitbourne, S. K. (1982). Intimacy and identity status in young adults. *Journal of Personality and Social Psychology, 43,* 1041–1051.

Theroux, P. (1977). *The consul's file.* New York: Penguin Books.

Thibaut, J. W., & Kelley, H. H. (1959). *The social psychology of groups.* New York: Wiley.

Thomas, M. H. (1982). Physiological arousal, exposure to a relatively lengthy aggressive film, and aggressive behavior. *Journal of Research in Personality, 16,* 72–81.

Thompson, A. P. (1983). Extramarital sex: A review of the research literature. *The Journal of Sex Research, 19,* 1–22.

Time. (1991, April 22). The beauty part, p. 61.

Timiras, P. S. (1972). *Developmental physiology and aging.* New York: Macmillan.

Tinbergen, N. (1951). *The study of instinct.* Oxford, England: Clarendon Press.

Titchener, E. (1909). *Experimental psychology of the thought processes.* New York: Macmillan.

Tolstedt, B. E., & Stokes, J. P. (1984). Self-disclosure, intimacy, and the depenetration process. *Journal of Personality and Social Psychology, 46,* 84–90.

Tolstoy, L. (1889/1985). *The Kreutzer sonata and other stories* (D. McDuff, Trans.). Harmondsworth, England: Penguin Books.

Townsend, J. M. (1989). Mate selection criteria: A pilot study. *Ethology and Sociobiology, 10,* 241–254.

Totenberg, N. (1975, January 20). Obiter dicta from the Watergate press table. *New York, 8* (3), 38–43.

Troubridge, L. (1929/1979). *A book of etiquette.* Kingswood: Cedar Books.

Trovillo, P. V. (1939). A history of lie detection. *Journal of Criminal Law and Criminology, 29,* 848–881.

Tyler, A. (1989). The artificial family. In G. D. Chipps & B. Henderson (Eds.), *Love stories for the time being* (pp. 137–146). Wainscott, NY: Pushcart Press.

Uhlenberg, P. (1991, August 19). *Relationships between older divorced men and their adult children.* Paper presented at the meetings of the American Psychological Association, San Francisco, CA.

U.S. Bureau of the Census (1987a). Money income and poverty studies in families. *Current Population Reports.* Washington, DC: Bureau of the Census.

U.S. Bureau of the Census. (1987b). *Statistical Abstract of the United States: 1987* (107th ed.). Washington, DC: U.S. Government Printing Office.

U.S. Bureau of the Census. (1988). Households, families, marital status, and living arrangements: March 1988 (Advance Report). *Current Population Reports,* Series P-20, No. 432. Washington, DC: U.S. Government Printing Office.

Updike, J. (1964). *Rabbit, run.* London: Penguin Books.

Ustinov, P. (1957). *Romanoff and Juliet: A comedy in three acts.* New York: Dramatists Play Service.

Vance, E. B., & Wagner, N. N. (1976). Written descriptions of orgasm: A study of sex differences. *Archives of Sexual Behavior, 5,* 87–98.

Vanity Fair (1991, December). LaBelle Bette, p. 260.

Van Ypern, N. W., & Buunk, B. P. (1990). A longitudinal study of equity and satisfaction in intimate relationships. *European Journal of Social Psychology, 20,* 287–309.

Van Ypern, N. W., & Buunk, B. P. (1991). Equity theory and exchange and communal orientation from a cross-national perspective. *Journal of Social Psychology, 131,* 5–20.

VerMeuler, M. (1991, June). The nasty girl. *Gentleman's Quarterly,* p. 86.

Veroff, J., Douvan, E., & Kulka, R. A. (1981). *The inner American.* New York: Basic Books.

Viorst, J. (1972). *Yes Married.* New York: Saturday Review Press.

Visher, E. G., & Visher, J. W. (1979). *Stepfamilies: A guide to working with stepparents and stepchildren.* New York: Brunner/Mazel.

Wade, C., & Tavris, C. (1990). *Psychology* (2nd ed.). New York: Harper & Row.

Wallace, I. (1981). *The intimate sex lives of famous people.* New York: Delacorte Press.

Waller, W. W., & Hill, R. (1951). *The family, a dynamic interpretation,* New York: Dryden Press.

Wallerstein, J. S., & Kelly, J. B. (1980). *Surviving the breakup: How children and parents cope with divorce.* New York: Basic Books.

Walsh, D. G., & Hewitt, J. (1985). Giving men the come-on: Effect of eye contact and smiling in a bar environment. *Perceptual and Motor Skills, 61,* 873–874.

Walsh, R. H. (1989). Premarital sex among teenagers and young adults. In K. McKinney & S. Sprecher (Eds.), *Human sexuality: The societal and interpersonal context* (pp. 162–186). Norwood, NJ: Ablex.

Wanderer, Z., & Cabot, T. (1978). *Letting go.* New York: Putnam's Sons.

Ward, G. C. (1989). *A first-class temperament: The emergence of Franklin Roosevelt.* New York: Harper & Row.

Waring, E. M. (1984). The measurement of marital intimacy. *Journal of Marital and Family Therapy, 10,* 185–192.

Warner, R. (1990). *Interaction tempo and evaluation of affect in social interaction: Rhythmic systems versus causal modeling approaches.* Unpublished manuscript, University of New Hampshire, Durham.

Warner, S. (1991, July 28). School teaches Japanese men art of flirting. *The Star-Bulletin & Advertiser,* p. F3.

Washburn, S., & DeVore, I. (1962). The social life of baboons. In C. H. Southwick (Ed.), *Primate social behavior.* Princeton, NJ: Van Nostrand.

Waterman, C. K., Dawson, L. J., & Bologna, M. J. (1989). Sexual coercion in gay male and lesbian relationships: Predictions and implications for support services. *Journal of Sex Research, 26,* 118–124.

Waters, H. F., & Malamud, P. (1975, March 10). Drop that gun, Captain Video. *Newsweek,* pp. 81–82.

Watson, D. L., & Tharp, R. G. (1990). *Self-directed behavior* (6th ed.). Monterey, CA: Brooks-Cole.

Watson, J. B. (1924/1930). *Behaviorism.* Chicago: University of Chicago Press.

Waugh, E. (1945). *Brideshead revisited.* Boston: Little, Brown.

Wegner, D. M., Lane, J. D., & Dimitri, S. (1992). Secret liaisons: The allure of covert relationships. Unpublished manuscript, University of Virginia, Charlottesville.

Weiner, B. (1986). *An attributional theory of emotion and motivation.* New York: Springer-Verlag.

Weiner, M. F. (1980). Healthy and pathological love—psychodynamic views. In K. S. Pope and associates (Eds.), *On love and loving* (pp. 114–132). San Francisco: Jossey-Bass.

Weis, D. L., & Slosnerick, M. (1981). Attitudes toward sexual and nonsexual extramarital involvements among a sample of college students. *Journal of Marriage and the Family, 43,* 349–358.

Weiss, R. S. (1973). *Loneliness: The experience of emotional and social isolation.* Cambridge, MA: MIT Press.

Weiss, R. S. (1975). *Marital separation.* New York: Basic Books.

Weiss, R. S. (1979). The emotional impact of marital separation. In G. Levinger & O. C. Moles (Eds.), *Divorce and separation* (pp. 201–210). New York: Basic Books.

Weissman, M. M. (1987). Advances in psychiatric epidemiology: Rates and risks for major depression. *American Journal of Public Health, 77,* 445–451.

Weitzman, L. J. (1981a). The economics of divorce: Social and economic consequences of property, alimony and child support awards. *UCLA Law Review, 28,* 1181–1268.

Weitzman, L. J. (1981b). *The marriage contract.* New York: Free Press.

Weitzman, L. J. (1985). *The divorce revolution.* New York: Free Press.

Weldon, F. (1974). *Female friends.* New York: St. Martin's Press.

Werner, C., & Parmelee, P. (1979). Similarity of activity preferences among friends: Those who play together stay together. *Social Psychology Quarterly, 42,* 62–66.

Wheeler, L. (1966). Toward a theory of behavioral contagion. *Psychological Review, 73,* 179–192.

Wheeler, L., Reis, H. T., & Nezlek, J. (1983). Loneliness, social interaction, and sex roles. *Journal of Personality and Social Psychology, 45,* 943–953.

White, G. (1980). Physical attractiveness and courtship progress. *Journal of Personality and Social Psychology, 39,* 660–668.

White, G. L., & Devine, K. (in press). Romantic jealousy: Therapists' perception of causes, consequences, and treatment. *Family Relations.*

White, G. L., Fishbein, S., & Rutstein, J. (1981). Passionate love and the misattribution of arousal. *Journal of Personality and Social Psychology, 41,* 56–62.

White, G. L., & Helbick, T. M. (1988). Understanding and treating jealousy. In R. A. Brown & J. R. Field (Eds.), *Treatment of sexual problems in individual and couples therapy* (pp. 245–266). Boston: PMA Publishing.

White, G. L., & Mullen, P. E. (1989). *Jealousy: Theory, research, and clinical strategies.* New York: Guilford Press.

White, K. M., Speisman, J. C., Jackson, D., Bartis, S., & Costos, D. (1986). Intimacy maturity and its correlates in young married couples. *Journal of Personality and Social Psychology, 50,* 152–162.

White, T. H. (1961). *The making of the President 1960.* New York: Atheneum.

Wiggins, J. N. N. (Hirshberg), & Conger, J. C. (1968). Correlates of heterosexual somatic preference. *Journal of Personality and Social Psychology, 10,* 82–90.

Wiggins, J. S., & Holzmuller, A. (1981). Further evidence on androgyny and interpersonal flexibility. *Journal of Research in Personality, 15,* 67–80.

Wikler, L., Wasow, M., & Hatfield, E. (1981). Chronic sorrow revisited: Parent vs. professional depiction of the adjustment of parents of mentally retarded children. *American Journal of Orthopsychiatry, 51,* 63–70.

Wilmot, W. W., Carbaugh, D. A., & Baxter, L. A. (1985). Communicative strategies used to terminate romantic relationships. *Western Journal of Speech Communication, 49,* 204–216.

Wilson, E. O. (1975). *Sociobiology: The new systhesis.* Cambridge, MA: Harvard University Press.

Wilson, T. D. (1985). Strangers to ourselves: The origins and accuracy of beliefs about one's own mental status. In J. N. Harvey & G. Weary (Eds.), *Attribution: Basic issues and applications* (pp. 9–36). New York: Academic Press.

Winter, D. G. (1988). The power motive in women—and men. *Journal of Personality and Social Psychology, 54,* 510–519.

Wolpe, J. (1973/1982). *The practice of behavior therapy* (3rd ed.). New York: Pergamon Press.

Won-Doornick, M. J. (1979). On getting to know you: The association between the stage of a relationship and reciprocity of self-disclosure. *Journal of Experimental Social Psychology, 15,* 229–241.

Woolf, V. (1953). *A writer's diary.* New York: Harcourt, Brace, & World.

Wright, P. H., & Wright, K. D. (1990). Measuring codependents' close relationships: A preliminary study. *Journal of Substance Abuse, 2,* 335–344.

Wright, R. A., & Contrada, R. J. (1986). Dating selectivity and interpersonal attraction: Toward a better understanding of the "elusive phenomenon." *Journal of Social and Personal Relationships, 3,* 131–148.

WuDunn, S. (1991, July 17). Romance, a novel idea, rocks marriages in China. *The New York Times International,* p. A4.

Wyatt, G. E., Peters, S. D., & Guthrie, D. (1988). Kinsey revisited, Part I: Comparisons of the sexual socialization and sexual behavior of white women over 33 years. *Archives of Sexual Behavior, 17,* 201–239.

Yeats, W. B. (1983). *For Anne Gregory, The Poems* (p. 245). New York: Macmillan.

Zilbergeld, B. (1978). *Male sexuality: A guide to sexual fulfillment.* Boston: Little, Brown.

Zillman, D. (1984). *Connections between sex and aggression.* Hillsdale, NJ: Erlbaum.

Zimbardo, P. G. (1977). *Shyness: What it is, what to do about it.* Reading, MA: Addison-Wesley.

Zimmerman, D. H., & West, C. (1975). Sex roles, interruptions and silences in conversation. In B. Thorne & N. Henley (Eds.), *Language and sex: Difference and dominance* (pp. 105–129). Rowley, MA: Newbury House.

Zola, E. (1890/1948). *The human beast* (L. Colman, Trans.). New York: United Book Guild.

Zuckerman, M. (1979). *Sensation seeking: Beyond the optimal level of arousal.* Hillsdale, NJ: Erlbaum.

Zuckerman, M., DePaulo, B. M., & Rosenthal, R. (1981). Verbal and nonverbal communication of deception. *Advances in Experimental Social Psychology, 14,* 1–59.

Zung, W. W. K. (1971). A rating instrument for anxiety disorders. *Psychosomatics, 12,* 371–379.

Credits

TEXT

7 Box 1.1, from "Measuring passionate love in intimate relations" by E. Hatfield and S. Sprecher in *Journal of Adolescence, 9*, pp. 383–410. Copyright © 1986 by the Association for the Psychiatric Study of Adolescents. Reprinted by permission. **9** Box 1.2, "Companionate Love Scale" from *Construct Validation of a Triangular Theory of Love* by Robert J. Sternberg. Reprinted by permission. **10** From "Compatibility, interdependence, and emotion" by Ellen Berscheid in *Compatible and Incompatible Relationships*, edited by W. Ickes, 1984. Reprinted by permission of Springer-Verlag. **27** Box 1.3, From *How to Make Yourself Miserable* by Dan Greenberg and Marcia Jacobs. Copyright © 1986 by Dan Greenberg and Marcia Jacobs. Reprinted by permission of Ballantine Books, a Division of Random House, Inc. **28** Table 1.3, From Verbal and nonverbal cues that convey interest in dating: Two studies" by C.L. Muehlenhard, M.A. Korelewski, S.L. Andrews and C. Burdick in *Behavior Therapy*, 17, 1986. Reprinted by permission. **30** Table 1.4, From "Measuring passionate love in intimate relations" by E. Hatfield and S. Sprecher in *Journal of Adolescence, 9*, p. 133. Copyright © 1986 by the Association for the Psychiatric Study of Adolescents. Reprinted by permission. **38** Box 2.1, R. Ornstein & R.F. Thompson, *The Amazing Brain*. Boston: Houghton Mifflin, 1984, pp. 3–12. **44** Table 2.1, From "Romantic love conceptualized as an attachment process," by C. Hazen and P. Shaver in *Journal of Personality and Social Psychology*, 52. Copyright © 1987 by the American Psychological Association. Reprinted by permission. **47** Box 2.2, From *How to Make Yourself Miserable* by Dan Greenberg and Marcia Jacobs. Copyright © 1986 by Dan Greenberg and Marcia Jacobs. Reprinted by permission of Ballantine Books, a Division of Random House, Inc. **49** "Symptom Recital," copyright 1926, renewed © 1954 by Dorothy Parker, from *The Portable Dorothy Parker* by Dorothy Parker, Introduction by Brendan Gill. Used by permission of Viking Penguin, a division of Penguin Books USA Inc. **71** Box 3.1, From *The French Lieutenant's Woman* by John Fowles. Copyright © 1969 by John Fowles Ltd. By permission of Little, Brown and Company and the author. **83** Table 3.3, Reproduced with permission from Playboy Enterprises, Inc., from *Sexual Behavior in the 1970's* by Morton Hunt. Copyright © 1974 by Morton Hunt. **84** Table 3.4, From *Premarital Sexuality: Attitudes, Relationships, Behavior* by J. DeLamater and P. MacCorquodale, 1979. Reprinted by permission of The University of Wisconsin Press. **87** Table 3.5, From "Written descriptions of orgasm: A study of sex differences" by E.B. Vance and N.N. Wagner in *Archives of Sexual Behavior, 5*, 1976, pp. 87–89. Reprinted by permission of Plenum Publishing Corporation and the author. **88** Table 3.6, Reproduced with permission from Playboy Enterprises, Inc., from *Sexual Behavior in the 1970's* by Morton Hunt. Copyright © 1974 by Morton Hunt. **89** Table 3.7, From "A most monogamous people: Americans and their sexual partners" by A.M. Greeley, R.T. Michael, and T.W. Smith in *Society, 27*, 1990, pp. 36–42. Reprinted by permission of Transaction Publishers. **90** Table 3.9, From "Sexual Fantasies of Women" by E. Barbara Hariton in *Psychology Today*, March 1973. Reprinted with permission from Psychology Today Magazine. Copyright © 1973 Sussex Publishers, Inc. **91** From "Communication patterns in initiation of marital sex" by M. Brown and A. Auerback in *Medical Aspects of Human Sexuality*, Vol. 15, No. 1, January 1981. Reprinted by permission. **94** From "Responses to reading erotic stories: Male-female differences" by G. Schmidt, V. Sigusch, and S. Schafer in *Archives of Sexual Behavior*, 1973, 2. Reprinted by permission of Plenum Publishing Corporation. **118** Lyrics, "I Might Fall Back On You," written by Jerome Kern and Oscar Hammerstein II. Copyright © 1927 PolyGram International Publishing, Inc. Copyright renewed. Used by permission. All rights reserved.**122** From "Ted and Jane: A press agent's dream" by Carla Hall in *The International Herald Tribune*, May 15, 1991. Copyright © 1993, The Washington Post. Reprinted by permission. **126** Box 4.2, "The Exchange Orientation Scale" based on earlier research by Murstein et al., 1977. Reprinted by permission of Sue Sprecher. **136** Box 5.1, From *Pair-Personal Assessment of Intimacy in Relationships* by D.H. Olson and M.T. Schaefer, 1981. Reprinted by permission. **148** Woody Allen, *Four Films of Woody Allen*. New York: Random House, Inc., 1982, pp. 258–59. **150** From *Slip Slidin' Away*, Copyright © 1977 Paul Simon. Reprinted by permission. **151** Table 5.2a, From "Taboo topics in close relationships" by L.A. Baxter and W.W. Wilmot in *Journal of Social and Personal Relationships*, 1985, 2. Reprinted by permission of Sage Publications, Ltd. and the author. **152** Table 5.2b, From "Taboo topics in close relationships" by L.A. Baxter and W.W. Wilmot in *Journal of Social and Personal Relationships*, 1985, 2. Reprinted by permission of Sage Publications, Ltd. and the author. **153** Box 5.3, From "Perceptions of risk in intimacy" by C.J. Pilkington and D.R. Richardson in *Journal of Social and Personal Relationships*, 1988, 5. Reprinted by permission of Sage Publications, Ltd. and the author. **157** Box 5.4, Deborah Tannen, *You Just Don't Understand*. New York: Ballantine, 1990, pp. 49–50, 86. **162** Table 5.3, "The Broderick Commitment Scale" from *Depression in Marriage* by S.R.H. Beach, E.E. Sandeen, and K.D. O'Leary. Reprinted with permission of Guilford Press. **163** From *Cowboys Are My Weakness*, stories by Pam Houston, by permission of W.W. Norton & Company, Inc. Copyright © 1992 by Pam Houston. **169** Table 6.1, From *Body Politics: Power, Sex, and Nonverbal Communication* by Nancy M. Henley. Copyright © 1977 by Simon & Schuster, Inc. Reprinted by permission of Simon & Schuster, Inc. **171** Table 6.2, D. Cartwright, ed., *Studies in Social Power*. Ann Arbor, MI: Institute for Social Research, 1959. **177** Table 6.3, From "Power strategies in intimate relationships" by T. Falbo and L.A. Peplau in *Journal of Personality and Social Psychology*, 38. Copyright © 1980 by the American Psychological Association. Reprinted by permission. **180** Box 6.2, From "Why women leave—Do you want the truth?" by John Graham in *GQ*, April 1991. John Graham © GQ—The Condé Nast Publications Ltd. Reprinted by permission. **185** Table 6.4, From "Strategies of influence in sex and dating" by F.S. Christopher and M.M. Frandsen in *Journal of Social and Personal Relationships*, 7, 1990, pp. 89–105. Reprinted by permission of Sage Publications, Ltd. and the author. **189** From "Sexual assault's 'gray area' " by Ellen Goodman. Copyright © 1991, The Boston Globe Newspaper Co./Washington Post Writers Group. Reprinted by permission. **190** Box 6.3, Excerpts from *A Charmed Life*, Copyright © 1955 and renewed 1983 by Mary McCarthy, reprinted by permission of Harcourt Brace Jovanovich, Inc. **204** From *The Boy Who Couldn't Stop Washing* by Dr. Judith Rapoport. Copyright © 1989 by Judith L. Rapoport, M.D. Used by permission of the publisher, Dutton, an imprint of New American Library, a division of

Index